POTS PANS & PIONEERS II

COUNCILS OF LOUISIANA

CHAPTER # 24

TELEPHONE PIONEERS

OF AMERICA

Published By
Cookbook Publishers, Inc.
P.O. Box 1260
Olathe, Kansas 66061

In Appreciation

Pots, Pans and Pioneers, Book II, comes to life as the handiwork of many. These recipes have been collected from employees and their families, both active and retired, of the Telephone Industry.

I would also like to take this opportunity to express thanks to all who have encouraged, aided and nagged to collect these recipes and without whose efforts this second venture would not have been forthcoming.

A very special thank you to Gladys Domingues and June Harllee who worked many long hours in setting up these recipes in a semblance of order.

Again, thanks to all.

Marilou Bridges

TELEPHONE PIONEERS OF AMERICA
1979 - 1980
LOUISIANA CHAPTER No. 24

EDITOR
Marilou Bridges
Shreveport, La.

PRESIDENT
Claude Roberts
Shreveport, La.

VICE-PRESIDENT
John Lutenbacher
New Orleans, La.

SECRETARY-TREASURER
Ruth Good
New Orleans, La.

PAST PRESIDENT
Max Zimmer
New Orleans, La.

1979 - 1980

COUNCIL	PRESIDENT	LOCATION
Caddo	John Haygood	Shreveport, La.
Calcasieu	E.J. Wales, Jr.	Lake Charles, La.
Capitol	Winn Landry	Baton Rouge, La.
Central	A.T. McKneely	Alexandria, La.
Crescent City	Louis Rehm	New Orleans, La.
Evangeline	William Rowell	Lafayette, La.
Gentilly	Albert Stevens	New Orleans, La.
LeBayou	Armand Kitto	Houma, La.
Magnolia	Patric a Parrish	New Orleans, La.
Metairie	Joycelyn Duchmann	Metairie, La.
Ouachita	W.A. Foreman	Monroe, La.
Ozone	Jeanne O'Keefe	Covington, La.
West Bank	Joseph Ringuette	Gretna, La.
Shreveport Works	Harvey Wilkening	Shreveport, La.
Westmoor	Nelson Guidry	Kenner, La.

COUNCIL	VICE-PRESIDENT	LOCATION
Caddo	E.H. Tooley	Shreveport, La.
Calcasieu	Dallas Sarvaunt	Lake Charles, La.
Capitol	Berlin . ohnson	Baton Rouge, La.
Central	Parsy Basco	Alexandria, La.
Crescent City	Dale Caston	New Orleans, La.
Evangeline	W.G. Domingue	Lafayette, La.
Gentilly	Calvin Callais	New Orleans, La.
LeBayou	Anna Mae Menard	Houma, La.
Magnolia	Dell Rupp	New Orleans, La.
Metairie	P.J. Boogaerts	Metairie, La.
Ouachita	Maxine Fletcher	Monroe, La.
Ozone	Robert Murray	Hammond, La.
West Bank	Willis Boudreaux	Gretna, La.
Shreveport Works	P.J. Cicchetti	Shreveport, La.
Westmoor	Joycelyn Lopez	New Orleans, La.

TABLE OF CONTENTS

1723-79

APPETIZERS, PICKLES
RELISHES

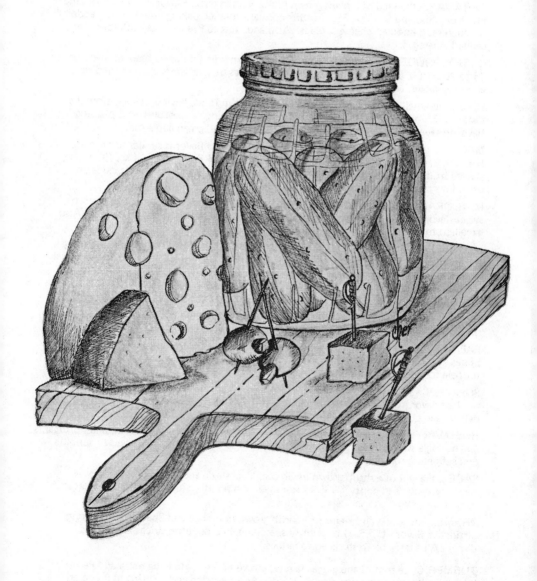

A HANDY SPICE GUIDE
TO MAKE YOU BECOME A SEASONED SEASONER

ALLSPICE....a pea-sized fruit that grows in Mexico, Jamaica, Central and South America. Its delicate flavor resembles a blend of cloves, cinnamon and nutmeg. USES: (Whole) Pickles, meats, boiled fish, gravies. (Ground) Puddings, relishes, fruit preserves, baking.

BASIL....the dried leaves and stems of an herb grown in the United States and North Mediterranean area. Has an aromatic, leafy flavor. USES: For flavoring tomato dishes and tomato paste, turtle soup; also use in cooked peas, squash, snap beans; sprinkle chopped over lamb chops and poultry.

BAY LEAVES....the dried leaves of an evergreen grown in the eastern Mediterranean countries. Has a sweet, herbaceous floral spice note. USES: For pickling, stews, for spicing sauces and soup. Also use with a variety of meats and fish.

CARAWAY....the seed of a plant grown in the Netherlands. Flavor that combines the tastes of Anise and Dill. USES: For the cordial Kummel, baking breads; often added to sauerkraut, noodles, cheese spreads. Also adds zest to French fried potatoes, liver, canned asparagus.

CURRY POWDER....a ground blend of ginger, turmeric, fenugreek seed, as many as 16 to 20 spices. USES: For all Indian curry recipes such as lamb, chicken, and rice, eggs, vegetables, and curry puffs.

DILL....the small, dark seed of the dill plant grown in India, having a clean, aromatic taste. USES: Dill is a predominant seasoning in pickling recipes; also adds pleasing flavor to sauerkraut, potato salad, cooked macaroni, and green apple pie.

MACE....the dried covering around the nutmeg seed. Its flavor is similar to nutmeg, but with a fragrant, delicate difference. USES: (Whole) For pickling, fish, fish sauce, stewed fruit. (Ground) Delicious in baked goods, pastries and doughnuts, adds unusual flavor to chocolate desserts.

MARJORAM....an herb of the mint family, grown in France and Chile. Has a minty-sweet flavor. USES: In beverages, jellies and to flavor soups, stews, fish, sauces. Also excellent to sprinkle on lamb while roasting.

MSG (MONOSODIUM GLUTAMATE)....is a vegetable protein derivative for raising the effectiveness of natural food flavors. USES: Small amounts, adjusted to individual taste, can be added to steaks, roasts, chops, seafoods, stews, soups, chowder, chop suey and cooked vegetables.

OREGANO....the leaf of a safe bush growing in Italy, Greece and Mexico. USES: An excellent flavoring for any tomato dish, especially Pizza, chili con carne, and Italian specialties.

PAPRIKA....a mild, sweet red pepper growing in Spain, Central Europe and the United States. Slightly aromatic and prized for brilliant red color. USES: A colorful garnish for pale foods, and for seasoning Chicken Paprika, Hungarian Goulash, salad dressings.

POPPY....the seed of a flower grown in Holland. Has a rich fragrance and crunchy, nut-like flavor. USES: Excellent as a topping for breads, rolls and cookies. Also delicious in buttered noodles.

ROSEMARY....an herb (like a curved pine needle) grown in France, Spain, and Portugal, and having a sweet, fresh taste. USES: In lamb dishes, in soups, stews and to sprinkle on beef before roasting.

SAGE....the leaf of a shrub grown in Greece, Yugoslavia and Albania. Flavor is camphoraceous and minty. USES: For meat and poultry stuffing, sausages, meat loaf, hamburgers, stews and salads.

THYME....the leaves and stems of a shrub grown in France and Spain. Has a strong, distinctive flavor. USES: For poultry seasoning, in croquettes, fricassees and fish dishes. Also tasty on fresh sliced tomatoes.

TURMERIC....a root of the ginger family, grown in India, Haiti, Jamaica and Peru, having a mild, ginger-pepper flavor. USES: As a flavoring and coloring in prepared mustard and in combination with mustard as a flavoring for meats, dressings, salads.

ARTICHOKE BALLS

1 (15 oz.) can artichoke
  hearts
1 tsp. garlic powder

1 c. Italian bread crumos
3/4 c. grated Italian Parmesan cheese
3/4 c. olive oil

    Wash and drain artichoke hearts. Mix all ingredients together and chill for 1 hour. Shape into balls and roll in Italian cheese. Serve at room temperature.

        Henrietta Victor
        Magnolia Council
        New Orleans, La.

ARTICHOKE BALLS

2 cans artichoke hearts
1/2 can (3 oz. size) Par-
  mesan cheese

1 (8 oz.) bottle olive oil
1 (8 oz.) can Progresso
  bread crumbs
2 1/2 tsp. garlic powder

    Drain hearts, reserving liquid. Combine all ingredients including artichoke liquid, except artichoke hearts. The mixture will appear very wet. Refrigerate until it becomes firm; overnight or several hours. Cut hearts into quarters. Holding a quarter of a heart in the palm of your hand, take a teaspoon of mixture and spoon into artichoke. Press mixture and flatten with fingers. Place on a tray or flat covered container, such as Tupperware cold cut keeper. Refrigerate until ready to serve. If left out of refrigerator, they become soft.

        Mrs. Marie Louise Pizzitola
        Capital Council
        Chalmette, La.

SMOKED BEEF BALL

2 pkg. smoked beef
6 green onions, chopped
1/2 tsp. Accent

2 (8 oz.) pkg. cream cheese
1 Tbsp. Worcestershire
  sauce

    Cut beef in small pieces and reserve 1/4 cup. Mix all ingredients, except reserved beef, and form into a ball.

Roll in the reserved beef and serve with crackers. Excellent for any gathering.　　　　Mrs. Floyd (Barbara) Jessup
Calcasieu Council
Lake Charles, La.

BEER-CHEESE SPREAD

1 lb. Cheddar cheese,
　shredded (at room
　temperature)
1/2 c. beer
2 Tbsp. catsup

Dash of hot pepper sauce
1/2 small onion, grated
　(2 Tbsp.)
1 clove crushed garlic
2 Tbsp. Worcestershire
　sauce

Beat cheese until creamy. Add remaining ingredients and continue beating until light and fluffy. Chill in covered container. Can be stored in refrigerator for up to 2 weeks. Flavor improves with age.　　　June Harllee, Caddo Council
Shreveport, La.

BOLTS AND NUTS

1 box Cheerios
1 box Wheat Chex
1 box Rice Chex
3/4 c. salad oil
2 tsp. red pepper
2 tsp. chili powder
1 Tbsp. Worcestershire
　sauce

1 box Corn Chex
2 boxes thin pretzels
2 c. nuts
3 tsp. Accent
3 tsp. garlic salt
3 Tbsp. Tabasco sauce
1 1/2 sticks oleo

Mix all ingredients thoroughly. Place on cookie sheet and bake at 250° for about 1 hour. Stir every 15 minutes.
　　　　Lorraine McManemin
　　　　Calcasieu Council
　　　　Lake Charles, La.

BOUDIN BALLS

2 lb. cooked boudin
Seasoned bread crumbs

1 or 2 eggs, beaten slightly
Cooking oil

Remove boudin from casing. Form dressing into balls about the size of walnuts. Dip balls in beaten egg, then into bread crumbs. Deep fry balls in cooking oil at about 325° until lightly browned. Drain on paper towels. Serve hot with toothpicks. Makes 20-25. This is a simple and excellent appetizer or an hors d'oeuvre.

Ann Orr, Evangeline Council
New Iberia, La.

BOURBON FRANKS

1 (14 oz.) bottle catsup
1 c. dark brown sugar
1 c. bourbon

4 pkg. (8 oz. each) miniature cocktail franks, or 2 lb. frankfurters, cut in small pieces

Mix all ingredients in large saucepan, except frankfurters. Cover and simmer at least 2 hours, stirring occasionally. Add franks and simmer about 5 minutes.

Cheryl Hageni
Crescent City Council
New Orleans, La.

CAPONATA
(Italian Hors D'Oeuvre)

1/4 lb. black Italian olives, split and seed removed
1 small stalk celery, chopped
1 large can tomatoes, mash pulp and reserve juice
2 cloves garlic, minced

2 eggplants (medium size), peeled and cubed
1 small bottle capers, drained
1/2 c. sugar
1/2 c. apple cider vinegar
Olive oil (I mix olive oil and corn oil, not quite as rich)

Saute eggplants in olive oil, drain. In same oil, saute celery, garlic and tomato pulp. Add eggplant, olives and capers. Dissolve sugar in vinegar, add to mixture, add tomato juice. Cook about 1/2 hour uncovered. Place in hot canning jars and seal. Chill in refrigerator before using. Serve with crackers for cocktails or with an antipasto before dinner. Makes 2 or 3 pints.

Althea Rome Brossett
Capital Council
Baton Rouge, La.

CAPONTINA
(Italian Eggplant Appetizer)

1/2 c. corn oil (do not substitute)
2 medium bell peppers diced
3 stalks celery, cut on slant
1 tsp. salt
1 (16 oz.) can peeled tomatoes
1/4 c. capers (optional)

1 Tbsp. sugar
2 or 3 large onions, diced
2 cloves garlic, crushed
2 medium carrots, diced
1 medium potato, diced
1 medium eggplant, peeled and diced
1/2 c. pitted green olives
1/4 c. wine vinegar

In large skillet, fry in order given. Do not cover skillet. After sauteing onion, add garlic in corn oil until limp. Add bell peppers, carrots, celery and potatoes. Saute until tender, stirring constantly, so that they do not stick. Season with salt. Add eggplant and cook about 7 minutes. Stir frequently with a wooden spoon. Add tomatoes. Cook for 6-7 minutes, stirring frequently. Let mixture rest 10 minutes. When all vegetables are tender, add olives, capers, wine vinegar and sugar. Stir well. Cook another 3 minutes. Cool. Store in refrigerator several hours. Never serve hot. Serve on crackers. Serves about 25 people.

Gayle Palermo
Westmoor Council
Kenner, La.

INSTANT CATSUP

1 (6 oz.) can tomato paste
2 Tbsp. sugar
1 tsp. cinnamon

1/4 tsp. cloves
1/2 "paste can" of sweet pickle juice or other vinegar
1/2 tsp. salt

Put tomato paste in pint jar. Add sugar, cinnamon, salt and cloves. If desired, add garlic or onion salt, or hot sauce. Mix thoroughly. Add the vinegar a little at a time, stirring after each time. If a little too thick, add more vinegar.

Calcasieu Council
Lake Charles, La.

CHEESE APPETIZER

Jalapeno pepper
4 eggs, beaten

1 lb. Cheddar cheese,
grated

Layer 9x12-inch dish with jalapeno pepper slices.
Sprinkle cheese over pepper and pour eggs over all. Bake
at 350° for 30 minutes.　　Rose Nichol, Caddo Council
Shreveport, La.

CHEESE BALL

1/2 bell pepper, chopped
1/2 c. crushed pineapple
1/2 jar chopped pimento
1 tsp. seasoned salt

8 oz. Cheddar cheese
8 oz. cream cheese
2 green onions, chopped
1 c. chopped pecans

Have cheese at room temperature. Combine all ingredients, except pecans, in mixer. Chill. Shape into 2
balls and roll in chopped pecans. Chill until ready to
serve. Yield: 2 balls.　　Melinda Wilson
Caddo Council
Shreveport, La.

CHEESE BALL

1 (8 oz.) pkg. cream
　cheese, softened
1/3 c. minced stuffed
　olives

1 c. parsley flakes
1/4 c. minced black olives
1/2 tsp. Tabasco sauce

Combine cheese, olives and Tabasco sauce. Form into
ball. Roll in parsley flakes.　　Debi Magalian
Central Council
Silver Springs, Md.

CHEESE BALL

8 oz. sharp Cheddar
　cheese, grated
1 Tbsp. chopped pimento
1 tsp. chopped onion

2 tsp. Worcestershire sauce
8 oz. cream cheese
1 tsp. chopped green pepper
1 tsp. lemon juice
Chopped pecans

Mix all ingredients, except nuts. Form into ball and roll in chopped pecans. Chill 24 hours. Serve at room temperature on tray with a variety of crackers. Can be put on bed of parsley with ripe olives or small tomatoes added for decoration.
Helen Patton
Shreveport Works Council
Shreveport, La.

CRUNCHY CHEESE BALL

1 (8 oz.) pkg. cream
   cheese
2 c. ground cooked ham
1 tsp. minced onion
1/4 tsp. hot pepper sauce

1/4 c. Hellmann's mayonnaise
2 Tbsp. chopped parsley
1/4 tsp. dry mustard
1/2 c. chopped peanuts or
   pecans

Beat cream cheese and mayonnaise until smooth. Stir in all ingredients, except nuts. Chill several hours, covered. Form into ball, roll in chopped nuts to coat. Serve with crackers.
Becky Flack, Central Council
Natchitoches, La.

CRUNCHY CHEESE TIDBITS

2 sticks butter, softened
2 c. flour
1/2 tsp. red pepper

2 c. grated sharp cheese
2 c. Rice Krispies

Mix all ingredients well. Roll small balls of dough, about 1/2-inch in diameter, between palms of the hands until smooth. Place on cookie sheet about 1 inch apart. Press lightly with tines of fork for crisscross pattern on each. Bake in preheated 325° oven for 20-25 minutes. Do not brown! Yield: 100 tidbits. These tidbits freeze perfectly.
Mavis W. O'Rourke
Shreveport Works Council
Shreveport, La.

OLIVE AND CHEESE BALLS

1 pkg. pie crust mix
1 1/2 c. grated sharp
  cheese

2 tsp. paprika
1/2 tsp. dry mustard
4 Tbsp. water

Mix and wrap around well drained olives. May prepare and stick in oven when needed. Bake at 375° for 10-12 minutes.

Calcasieu Council
Lake Charles, La.

CHEESE AND CHIPS

Dorito chips

Jalapeno pepper and cheese
  in jar

You may substitute any other favorite cheese. Place chips with about 1/2 teaspoon of spread on each on a cookie sheet, or if using sliced cheese, cut into squares and place 1 square on each Dorito chip. Bake in preheated 350° oven about 5 minutes or until cheese is melted. Let cool a little before serving.

Mollie Porrovecchio, Metairie
Council, New Orleans, La.

CHEESE COOKIES

1 lb. mild Cheddar
  cheese, grated
1 tsp. salt
2 c. nuts, chopped fine

2 1/2 c. sifted flour
1 stick butter or oleo
Dash of red pepper

Let cheese and butter stand at room temperature until soft. Combine all ingredients together and mix by hand. Form into rolls, wrap in waxed paper and refrigerate overnight. Cut in 1/2-inch slices and bake 15 or 20 minutes at 350°. Will keep in refrigerator several days. Yield: About 5 rolls.

Theda S. Thomas, Caddo
Council, Shreveport, La.

RO-TEL CHEESE FONDUE

1 can Ro-Tel tomatoes

1 large pkg. Velveeta
pasteurized cheese spread

Melt cheese and tomatoes in double boiler. When melted, pour into fondue pot. Serve with chips and crackers. An added touch would be to have chunks of French bread ready for dipping.
Sonia A. Hunt, Capital
Council, Baton Rouge, La.

CHEESE PUFFS

2 c. grated natural
sharp Cheddar cheese
1/2 tsp. salt
48 stuffed olives

1/2 c. soft butter
1 c. sifted all-purpose flour
1 tsp. paprika

Blend cheese with butter. Stir in flour, salt, paprika and mix well. Wrap 1 teaspoon of this mixture around each olive, covering it completely. Arrange on a flat pan or baking sheet and freeze firm. Place in plastic bags, tie and return to freezer until needed. To serve, bake 15 minutes at 400°.
Gayle Wilkening, Shreveport
Works Council, Longview, Tx.

PUFFED CHEESE SANDWICHES

1 - 1 1/4 c. grated
cheese
3 Tbsp. top milk or
cream

1/2 tsp. paprika
1 egg
Few grains salt
8 slices bread

Heat oven to 375°. Toast 1 side of bread. Combine remaining ingredients and spread cheese mixture on un-toasted side. Place open face sandwiches under broiler until cheese is puffed up and slightly browned. Serve them very hot. Yield: 8 open faced sandwiches.
Marjorie Rowell, Evangeline
Council, Lafayette, La.

CHEESE ROLL

1 lb. Cheddar cheese
1 lb. sharp cheese
3 cloves minced garlic
   or garlic or onion salt

1 lb. cream cheese
3 tsp. A.1. sauce
Chili powder
1 c. chopped pecans

Grate cheese and mix together. Add A.1. sauce and garlic. Form into 1 large ball, 1 roll or 2 small balls. Roll in chili powder and pecans. Chill or can freeze for later use.

Chris Evans, LeBayou
Council, Houma, La.

CHEESE ROLL

1 lb. Cheddar cheese,
   grated

1 c. pecan meal
1 (8 oz.) pkg. cream cheese

Mix well. Flavor with either garlic, onion or wine. Shape into roll and roll in red pepper, paprika or ground pecans.

Connie Younker
Shreveport Works Council
Shreveport, La.

CHEESE ROLLED LOGS

2 lb. shredded sharp
   Cheddar cheese
1 1/2 tsp. Worcestershire
   sauce
1 tsp. salt

Chili powder
1 large pkg. cream cheese
2 tsp. garlic salt
1 tsp. pepper

Mix all ingredients, except chili powder, with electric mixer. Roll into logs. Lay logs on waxed paper sprinkled heavily with chili powder. Cover logs heavily with chili powder. Wrap each log tightly in foil and chill 1-2 days until firm. Unwrap and cut into slices. Serve on Ritz crackers.

Pat Uhle, West Bank
Council, Gretna, La.

CHEESE STRAWS

4 c. plain flour, sifted
1 lb. sharp Cheddar
   cheese, grated

1 tsp. salt
3 sticks oleo or butter
2 tsp. cayenne pepper

Melt butter. Mix in other ingredients. Put dough in cookie press; use star blade. Place long strips on cookie sheet. Bake about 12 minutes at 375° until brown. Do not overcook.
      Virginia Lowrey, Ouachita Council, Monroe, La.

CHEESE STRAWS

3/4 lb. grated sharp
   cheese
1 1/2 c. flour
1 tsp. salt

1/4 lb. butter or oleo
1 tsp. baking powder
1/2 tsp. red pepper or to
   taste

Cream butter and cheese with hands until smooth, work in dry ingredients until firm dough is made. Roll out and cut into thin strips. Bake on cookie sheet at 375° until light brown. Can run through cookie press with dough if desired.
      Doris Bullion, Central Council, Alexandria, Va.

CHEESE YULE LOG

2 pkg. (8 oz. size) cream
   cheese, softened and
   divided
1 c. (3/4 lb.) ground
   Polish ham
2 tsp. yellow prepared
   mustard
1/4 tsp. ground black
   pepper

2 Tbsp. minced onion
2/3 c. Bleu cheese or Cheddar
   cheese flavored cold pack
   cheese food
1 tsp. chili sauce
1 tsp. soy sauce
1/3 tsp. salt
1/4 c. freeze dried chives

Combine 1 1/2 packages (12 ounces) cream cheese with cheese food. Chill slightly. Combine remaining cream cheese, ham and remainder of ingredients and chill slightly. To assemble, spread cream cheese and cheese mixture on piece of waxed paper into a 9x7-inch rectangle. Cover with ham mixture, chill 30 minutes. Starting from longer edge, roll up tightly, jelly roll fashion, using waxed paper to help shape log. Press chives into outside of log. Place on serving plate, cover and chill at least 2 hours before serving. Accompany cheese log with assorted crackers.

Jeanette English, Caddo
Council, Shreveport, La.

CHILI CHEESE LOG

1 can whipped Roquefort
cream cheese
2 pkg. Old English sliced
cheese
Dash of garlic salt or
powder
Chili powder

1 can Blue cheese
2 pkg. (32 slices) American
cheese
2 cloves garlic, finely
crushed
Dash of Worcestershire
sauce

Have cheese at room temperature. Combine and knead as dough until mixed. Add garlic salt, garlic cloves and Worcestershire sauce. Shape into 5 or 6 long thin logs. Roll in chili powder and refrigerate. May be frozen if desired. Slice thinly and serve on crackers.

Allice (Lucille) Williams
Caddo Council
Shreveport, La.

CRAB BALLS

2 doz. boiled crabs
2 eggs
1 c. flour
2 onions, finely chopped

3 c. bread crumbs
Green onions and bell
pepper, finely chopped
(optional)

Clean crabs. Mix onions and crabmeat, saute until onions are soft. Remove from heat, add eggs, bread crumbs and 1/2 - 3/4 cup of flour. Stir until mixture is thick. More bread crumbs may be added if necessary. Shape into 1-inch balls. Roll in remaining flour and then in bread crumbs. Deep fry until brown. Makes 3-5 dozen.

Christine Moras, Central
Council, Hessmer, La.

DEEDEE'S CRABMEAT HORS D'OEUVRES

1 (7 1/2 oz.) can crab-
  meat, or 1 pkg. frozen
  crabmeat
1 jar Old English Cheddar
  cheese

1/2 tsp. garlic salt
5 or 6 English muffins
1 stick oleo, soft
2 tsp. mayonnaise
Bit of sherry

Cut muffins in half. Blend remaining ingredients and spread on muffins. Cut each half of muffin into eighths. Put on cookie sheet and freeze. When frozen, place in plastic bag in freezer. When ready to use, bake at 450° for 8-10 minutes.

Mildred (Mimi) Kutzelman
Shreveport Works Council
Shreveport, La.

CRABMEAT HENRIETTA

1 lb. picked crabmeat
4 artichoke hearts, cubed
1/2 stick butter
1/4 c. chopped parsley

1 c. canned mushrooms,
  diced
Salt, pepper and cayenne
  pepper

Saute crabmeat, mushrooms and artichoke hearts in butter. Season to taste. Sprinkle with parsley. Serve on toast points.

Henrietta Victor, Magnolia
Council, New Orleans, La.

CREAMED CRABMEAT

1 can crabmeat
1/2 c. mayonnaise
Grated onion to taste

1 c. grated sharp cheese
Worcestershire sauce, lemon
  juice, salt, pepper and
  paprika to taste

Mix ingredients together. Spread on toasted bun or English muffin. Run under broiler until bubbly. Makes 4 servings.

Connie Younker
Shreveport Works Council
Shreveport, La.

CRABMEAT AND MUSHROOM SAUCE FOR FISH

2 eggs, beaten
1 tsp. lemon juice
1/2 c. chopped mush-
   rooms

Paprika, salt and pepper to
   taste
2 sticks butter, melted
1 1/2 c. crabmeat
1/2 c. dry white wine

Add ingredients together and cook in double boiler for 15 minutes until sauce starts to brown. Pour over baked fillet of fish and serve.
          Sandy Daquana, Crescent
          City Council, New Orleans, La.

CRESCENT SURPRISES

1 can refrigerator
   crescent rolls
2 slices American cheese,
   cut in quarters

1 (1 lb.) can asparagus
   spears (cut may be used)
4 slices ham, cut in half

Unfold 8 crescent rolls. Place cheese, ham and 1 asparagus spear on each piece of dough. Roll up and fasten with toothpick if necessary. Bake 20 minutes at 375°. Serves 4.
          Aline Well, Capital Council,
          Baton Rouge, La.

CURRIED OLIVES

1/4 c. chopped onion
2 Tbsp. curry powder
3 Tbsp. lemon juice

1 1/2 c. drained, stuffed
   olives
1/2 c. salad oil

Combine and marinate 2 or 3 days before serving. These keep well.
          Lois Clover, Central Council,
          Jackson, Ms.

DEVILS IN DISGUISE

2 c. all-purpose flour
1 1/2 tsp. red pepper
12 oz. grated sharp
   Cheddar cheese

2 1/2 c. crisp rice cereal
2 sticks softened oleo
3/4 tsp. salt

Blend oleo and flour, add salt, pepper and cheese.

1723-79

Fold in cereal carefully. Form into pecan size balls and flatten with fork tines on ungreased cookie sheet. Bake 12-15 minutes at 350°. Makes 7 dozen.

Zelda R. Anderson, Calcasieu
Council, Lake Charles, La.

BEAU MONDE DIP

2/3 c. sour cream
1 Tbsp. parsley flakes
1 tsp. Beau Monde sea-
  soning

2/3 c. mayonnaise
1 Tbsp. minced onion
1 tsp. dill weed

Mix together 8 hours before using and refrigerate. Serve with vegetables and crackers.
Suggested Vegetables: Cauliflower, carrots, celery, radishes, bell pepper rings, cucumbers.

Billie Longkabel, Ouachita
Council, Monroe, La.

BROCCOLI DIP

1 large can mushrooms
  with stems
1 small chopped onion
1 can cream of mush-
  room soup (not
  golden)

Dash of salt
2 Tbsp. jalapeno pepper
  Cheez Whiz
1 block butter
1 (10 oz.) pkg. frozen
  chopped broccoli
1 (6 oz.) Kraft garlic cheese

Cook broccoli until soft, add salt and drain. Saute onion in butter. Add soup, mushrooms and cheese. Heat over low fire until melted and creamy. Add broccoli. Serve hot.

Barbara E. Wellman
Metairie Council
New Orleans, La.

BROCCOLI DIP

1 pkg. frozen chopped
  broccoli
1 stick oleo
1 small can mushroom
  stems and pieces
1/4 tsp. pepper

1 tsp. Worcestershire sauce
3/4 c. slivered almonds
1/2 c. water
1 can mushroom soup
1 tsp. Accent
1/2 tsp. salt

16

1/4 c. chopped onion   1 roll Kraft garlic cheese

Cook broccoli, drain and set aside. Saute onion in oleo, add soup. Melt cheese in mixture. Add salt, pepper, Accent, Worcestershire sauce and mushrooms. Stir in broccoli. Add almonds. Serve warm with Fritos, tacos or Melba rounds.

Susan Austin, Ouachita
Council, Monroe, La.

LOW-CAL CARROT NIBBLES

1 lb. carrots, pared
1 Tbsp. onion, coarsely
  chopped
1/3 c. vinegar
1/2 tsp. dry mustard
3 cloves garlic, minced

1 Tbsp. pickling spice, tied
  in cheesecloth bag
1 Tbsp. salad oil
1 1/2 tsp. salt
1/3 tsp. pepper
1 onion, sliced and separated
  into rings

Cut carrots into 3-inch long and 1/4-inch square strips. Saute garlic and chopped onion in oil over low heat until soft. Stir in vinegar, salt, mustard, pepper and add spice bag. Bring to a boil. Add carrot strips, cover and simmer for 5 minutes, stirring occasionally. Carrots should remain crisp and crunchy. Discard pickling spice bag. Transfer carrot mixture to shallow dish. Top with layer of onion rings. Cover and refrigerate until needed, basting occasionally. The longer they marinate, the better. Onions are tasty, too. Makes 8-12 servings.

Ann Orr, Evangeline Council,
New Iberia, La.

CHEESE BALL DIP

2 (8 oz.) pkg. cream
  cheese
1 (8 oz.) can crushed
  pineapple, drained
1/2 tsp. chopped onion

1 c. chopped nuts
1 Tbsp. chopped bell
  pepper
1 Tbsp. seasoned salt

Cream cheese, add pineapple gradually. Mix in remainder of ingredients.

Evie Croswell, Caddo
Council, Shreveport, La.

HOT CHEESE DIP

1 can Cheddar cheese
  soup
1 can Ro-Tel tomatoes
  with pepper

Dash of Tabasco sauce or
  red pepper
1/4 lb. Velveeta cheese
Dash of Worcestershire
  sauce

Melt ingredients in top of double boiler. Serve hot with corn or potato chips.

Molly Hoskins, Caddo
Council, Shreveport, La.

CHILI DIP

1 can plain chili
1 lb. sharp cheese,
  cubed
1 Tbsp. Worcestershire
  sauce

1 can tamales, mashed
2 cloves garlic, grated
1 large onion, grated
Dash of Tabasco sauce

Add tamales and chili together in top of double boiler. Add cheese and other ingredients. Stir constantly until cheese is melted. Serve hot, using corn or potato chips for dipping.

Mary R. Jones, Ouachita
Council, Monroe, La.

CHILI CON QUESO DIP

1 can Ro-Tel tomatoes

Velveeta cheese

Cut up tomatoes and cheese. Melt in top of doubler boiler. Serve with chips, Fritos, etc.

Cindy Kendrick, Caddo
Council, Shreveport, La.

CRABMEAT DIP

2 c. crabmeat
1 (8 oz.) pkg. cream
  cheese
1 (3 oz.) pkg. cream
  cheese

1/2 lb. raw shrimp
1 medium onion, chopped
1/4 Tbsp. garlic powder
1/4 tsp. seafood seasoning
Salt and pepper to taste

Saute onion and garlic powder. Add crabmeat and

shrimp, simmer until shrimp are cooked. Add softened cream cheese and remaining ingredients. Cook 10 minutes on low heat. Serve hot with Escort crackers.

Linda Myers, Magnolia
Council, New Orleans, La.

CURRY DIP

1 c. mayonnaise
1 tsp. celery seed
1 tsp. seasoned salt
1 dash Tabasco sauce
   or season to taste
1 heaping tsp. horse-
   radish

1 tsp. black pepper
2 tsp. Durkee sauce
1/2 tsp. Worcestershire
   sauce
1 clove garlic, pressed
   and chopped fine
1 tsp. curry powder

Mix ingredients. This is good appetizer for dipping carrot sticks, cauliflower, cucumbers and radishes.

Pat Mora, LeBayou Council,
Franklin, La.

CURRIED VEGETABLE DIP

1 1/2 c. mayonnaise
1 Tbsp. grated onion
1/2 tsp. salt
Tabasco sauce to taste

2 tsp. curry
1/2 tsp. dry mustard
Black pepper to taste

Mix all ingredients. Cover and refrigerate for 24 hours for flavors to blend.

Mavis W. O'Rourke
Shreveport Works Council
Shreveport, La.

DILL DIP

2 c. sour cream
1 tsp. mayonnaise
1 tsp. seasoning salt

1 tsp. dill weed
1 tsp. garlic salt

Mix ingredients well. Serve chilled with raw vegetables as cauliflower, celery, carrots, radishes, etc. Keep refrigerated.

Henrietta Victor, Magnolia
Council, New Orleans, La.

1723-79

19

GARLIC DIP

1 (3 oz.) pkg. cream
  cheese
3 tsp. chopped pickles
1/4 tsp. Worcestershire
  sauce

2/3 c. mayonnaise
4 stuffed olives, chopped
  fine
2 cloves garlic, pressed or
  minced
Dash of red pepper

Soften cream cheese, add olives, pickles, garlic, red pepper and Worcestershire sauce. Beat well. Beat in mayonnaise until well mixed. Place in tightly closed bowl or jar. Refrigerate. Better if made a day in advance.

Gloria Fontenot, Evangeline
Council, Lafayette, La.

HAMBURGER DIP

1 lb. hamburger
Dash of garlic

1 lb. Velveeta cheese
Dash of salt and pepper

Brown hamburger in skillet, drain. Add seasonings. Slowly add cheese, cut in pieces. Stir until melted. Put in fondue pot and serve with chips. I've had many compliments on this recipe.

Becky Flynn, Central
Council, Alexandria, La.

MEXENE MONTERRY DIP

1 c. sour cream
1 Tbsp. oleo
1 Tbsp. Mexene chili
  powder

1 Tbsp. onion, finely minced
1 tsp. prepared mustard
1/4 tsp. garlic salt
8 drops Tabasco sauce

Combine all ingredients and allow to set at least 30 minutes.

Annie Hawkins, Caddo
Council, Shreveport, La.

MEXICAN DIP FOR FRITOS

1 can enchiladas
1 lb. Velveeta cheese
Fritos

1 can chili without beans
Tabasco sauce to taste

Mix enchiladas, chili and cheese. Heat until cheese

melts. Add Tabasco sauce to taste and continue stirring until red crystals form. This keeps well. Serve only with Fritos. This is yummy for your tummy!

Jean Coon, Caddo Council
Shreveport, La.

ZIPPY ONION DIP

1 c. Hellmann's mayon-
   naise
2 Tbsp. finely chopped
   celery
1 Tbsp. finely chopped
   ripe olives

Tabasco sauce to taste
1/4 c. chopped green onions
1 tsp. Worcestershire sauce
1 small clove garlic, crushed
   or garlic powder

Combine all ingredients, cover and chill 1 hour or longer Serve with raw vegetables and crackers. Makes 1 1/3 cups. Very good.

Raw Vegetables: Cauliflower, celery, cucumbers, bell pepper, yellow squash, turnips.

Margie Clover, Central
Council, Dickinson, Tx.

OYSTER DIP

20 oysters
2 Tbsp. oleo
2 Tbsp. soy sauce
2 Tbsp. Worcestershire
   sauce
2 buds grated garlic

1 1/2 pkg. (8 oz.) cream
   cheese
1/2 medium grated onion
2 tsp. curry powder
20 stuffed olives
2 tsp. salad dressing

Saute oysters in oleo, soy sauce, Worcestershire sauce. Cream until smooth the cream cheese. Add grated onion, grated garlic, curry powder, stuffed olives, salad dressing. Chop the oysters fine, return to the juice. Combine oysters and juice with cream cheese mixture. Cream until mixed well.

Calcasieu Council
Lake Charles, La.

OYSTER DIP

2 pt. oysters, cut up
1 c. chopped green
   onion, celery and
   parsley
Oyster liquid

Salt and pepper
1 stick butter
1 jalapeno pepper, cut up
2 Tbsp. flour
Parmesan cheese

Simmer oysters and some of oyster liquid in saucepan until plump; place in casserole. Saute green onion, celery, parsley and jalapeno pepper in melted oleo until limp. Stir in flour and remainder of oyster liquid. Add water if more liquid is needed. Season with salt and pepper and simmer for a few minutes. Pour this mixture over oysters in casserole. Top with Parmesan cheese. Bake at 350° until hot and bubbly.

Betty Jean Doyle, LeBayou
Council, Houma, La.

MOCK OYSTER DIP

1 stick butter, divided
1 pkg. chopped cooked
   broccoli
1 large can mushrooms
Tabasco sauce to taste

1 can mushroom soup
1 roll garlic cheese
Sliced red pepper
1 tsp. Lea & Perrins
   sauce

Saute onion in 1/2 stick melted oleo. Add soup and cheese roll; melt. Add cooked broccoli and remainder of ingredients. No salt.

Floyd Shumann
Ozone Council
Hammond, La.

Betty Winston
Caddo Council
Shreveport, La.

MOCK OYSTER DIP

1 (4 oz.) can mushroom
   stems and pieces,
   drained
1 roll garlic cheese, cut
   in pieces
1 stick butter or oleo
Salt and pepper to taste

Worcestershire sauce
   (optional)
1 can cream of mushroom
   soup
3 stalks celery, minced
1/2 large onion, minced
2 pkg. frozen chopped
   broccoli

Saute onions, celery and mushrooms about 5 minutes.
Add remaining ingredients and cook until creamy. If very
soupy, add a cornstarch and water mixture.

Elmer E. Harrison
Crescent City Council
New Orleans, La.

OYSTER ROCKEFELLER DIP

1 stick butter
2 bunches green onions,
  chopped
1 box frozen chopped
  spinach, defrosted
Pinch of thyme
1 1/2 Tbsp. Worcester-
  shire sauce
1/2 tsp. sugar
1 oz. pernod or
  Herbsaint

6 doz. oysters, drained
  (save liquid)
1 c. minced celery
1 bunch parsley, chopped
3 cloves garlic, minced
Salt and pepper to taste
2 tsp. lemon juice
1/2 tsp. MSG
6 anchovy fillets, mashed,
  or 2 Tbsp. anchovy paste
Seasoned bread crumbs

Saute celery in butter until limp. Add celery, green
onions, parsley and spinach. Simmer about 15 minutes.
Add all remaining ingredients, except oysters and bread
crumbs. Mix well. Blend mixture, little at a time, in
blender or food processor, using oyster liquid to thin and
make mixture easy to blend. Return mixture to saucepan.
Saute oysters in large skillet until edges curl; cool. Chop
oysters coarsely and add to blended sauce mixture. Heat
4 or 5 minutes. Add seasoned bread crumbs until proper
dipping consistency. Transfer to chafing dish and keep
warm. Serve as a dip with cocktail crackers or chips.
Good!

Ann Orr, Evangeline Council,
New Iberia, La.

OYSTER SPINACH DIP

2 boxes frozen chopped
  spinach
1/2 c. chopped green
  onions
1/2 c. chopped parsley
1/4 c. butter or oleo
1 Tbsp. Worcestershire
  sauce

1 Tbsp. Tabasco sauce
1 Tbsp. horseradish
3 doz. oysters
1 can white crabmeat,
  drained
1 can cream of mushroom
  soup
1 small jar Cheez Whiz

1723-79

Saute greens until done. Meanwhile, bake oysters about 7 minutes at 350° until ends curl (drain). Slice in half. Add remaining ingredients. Serve in chafing dish with chips or Melba toast. Mrs. Brenda Wagnon, Central Council, Pineville, La.

PARTY DIP

2 lb. Velveeta cheese
1 large onion
2 Tbsp. pepper juice

1 qt. mayonnaise
3 jalapeno peppers, chopped
   fine

Grate cheese. Mix all ingredients with mixer or blender. Makes enough dip for a bunch.
Louise Malone, Caddo
Council, Shreveport, La.

QUICKIE BUT GOOD DIP

1 roll jalapena cheese
Fritos

1 can chili with beans

Melt jalapena cheese with can of chili in double boiler. Serve in chafing dish as dip with Fritos on side.
Betty Winston, Caddo
Council, Shreveport, La.

SHRIMP DIP

1 stick oleo or butter
1 bunch green onions,
   chopped
1 (4 oz.) can mushrooms,
   stems and pieces

1/4 c. flour
1 pt. sour cream
1 lb. peeled shrimp
Tabasco sauce, salt and
   pepper

Saute shrimp in small amount of the butter. In another skillet, saute green onions in butter, add flour to make a paste. Add drained mushrooms, stir in shrimp, sour cream and season to taste with Tabasco sauce, salt and pepper. Serve hot with chips, crackers or tortillas.
Nell Corkern, Central
Council, Alexandria, La.

24

SHRIMP DIP

1 (8 oz.) carton sour
   cream

1 (4 1/2 oz.) can shrimp
1 (4 oz.) pkg. cream cheese

    Soften cream cheese. Chop shrimp fine, add to sour cream. Blend ingredients together, using mixer.

Harry Klundt, Crescent City
Council, New Orleans, La.

SHRIMP DIP

1 (5 oz.) can shrimp
1/4 c. chili sauce
1/4 tsp. salt
1 tsp. prepared horse-
   radish

1 c. sour cream
2 tsp. lemon juice
Pepper to taste
1 dash Tabasco sauce

    Mix ingredients together. Refrigerate until ready to serve.

Gayle Cummings, Caddo
Council, Shreveport, La.

SHRIMP DIP

1 (8 oz.) pkg. cream
   cheese
1/2 c. shrimp, chopped
2 Tbsp. sandwich spread

2 Tbsp. mayonnaise
2 Tbsp. minced onions
Tabasco sauce or red
   pepper to taste

    Mix ingredients together and chill until served.

Mrs. J.E. Rutledge, LeBayou
Council, Houma, La.

SHRIMP DIP

1 lb. peeled and de-
   veined, boiled shrimp
1 c. mayonnaise
2 Tbsp. French dress-
   ing
1 large pkg. Philadel-
   phia cream cheese
2 Tbsp. lemon juice

1/2 bell pepper, chopped
   fine
1/2 onion, chopped fine
1 clove garlic, chopped
   fine
2 strips celery, chopped
   fine
1 tsp. black pepper

Mix all of the ingredients together for the Shrimp Dip
and serve.
Calcasieu Council
Lake Charles, La.

SHRIMP DIP

1 can frozen shrimp soup
1 (8 oz.) pkg. cream
  cheese, softened
2 tsp. lemon juice
1/4 tsp. garlic salt
Salt and pepper to taste

3/4 c. shrimp, diced
1/4 tsp. curry powder
1/2 c. stuffed olives,
  chopped
Dash of Tabasco sauce

Thaw soup, mix with shrimp and cheese. Add remaining ingredients. Mix well. Chill 2 hours. Serve with chips or crackers.
Jeannette Purcell
Crescent City Council
New Orleans, La.

SHRIMP-N-DIP

2 cans shrimp, washed,
  drained and chopped
1 stalk celery, chopped

Oil, mayonnaise, salt and
  pepper to taste
2 boiled eggs, chopped
1 green onion, finely chopped

Mix ingredients well and serve on crackers.
Ann Orr, Evangeline
Council, New Iberia, La.

SPINACH DIP

2 c. mayonnaise
1 pkg. chopped spinach,
  boiled and drained

Salt and pepper to taste
1/4 c. chopped parsley
1/4 c. chopped green onions

Whip in blender or mix well by hand. Serve with crispy fresh vegetables of your choice.
Penny Ross, Capital
Council, Baton Rouge, La.

HOT TUNA DIP

2 cans tuna
3 Tbsp. mayonnaise
3 Tbsp. mustard
1/2 bell pepper, chopped
3 stalks celery, chopped
Paprika to taste
Garlic powder to taste

Chopped jalapeno peppers
2 1/2 small jars pimento cheese spread
3 boiled eggs, sliced or chopped
1/2 onion, chopped
Salt, black and red pepper to taste
Chopped dill pickles

Combine and mix the ingredients.

Sonjie Ebarb
Shreveport Works Council
Shreveport, La.

SPICY TUNA DIP

1 regular size can tuna
4 Tbsp. mayonnaise
6 dashes hot sauce
Few drops milk (optional)

1 (8 oz.) pkg. cream cheese
3 big shakes catsup
1 small onion, chopped, or equivalent in shallots

Put all ingredients, except tuna, in blender. Mix well. If too thick, add milk to desired consistency. Add tuna and mix. This is better if chilled overnight. Shrimp Dip can be made by substituting 1 pound cleaned and chopped shrimp for tuna.

Jennifer Ulmer
Crescent City Council
New Orleans, La.

VEGETABLE DIP

1 c. mayonnaise
1 tsp. vinegar
1 tsp. garlic powder

1 tsp. horseradish
1 Tbsp. minced dried onion
1 tsp. curry powder

Stir together. Refrigerate overnight. Keeps 3 weeks in refrigerator.

Mearl S. Byles, Central
Council, Natchitoches, La.

VEGETABLE DIP

1 (8 oz.) pkg. cream
  cheese
1 Tbsp. parsley,
  chopped
1 c. mayonnaise

1 Tbsp. onion, chopped
1 carton sour cream
Pepper to taste
1 tsp. garlic, powdered

Mix ingredients until well blended. Use as a dip for carrots, celery, cauliflower, cucumber, etc.

Sonia A. Hunt, Capital
Council, Baton Rouge, La.

RAW VEGETABLE DIP

1 pt. mayonnaise
3 Tbsp. minced fresh
  parsley
1 1/2 Tbsp. seasoned salt

1 pt. sour cream
3 Tbsp. grated onion
3 Tbsp. dill weed

Blend all ingredients together and chill before serving. Yield: 4 1/2 cups. May be made several days in advance.

Noonie Wilkinson, Capital
Council, Baton Rouge, La.

DIP FOR VEGETABLE TRAY

1 pkg. Lawrey's spaghetti
  sauce mix
1 Tbsp. Lea & Perrins sauce

2 cartons sour cream
1 tsp. garlic powder

Blend all ingredients well. Serve chilled in small bowl with tray of chilled raw vegetables.

Etta Williams, Magnolia
Council, New Orleans, La.

CHICKEN SALAD BALLS

1 c. chopped, cooked
  chicken
2 Tbsp. chopped pimiento
Dash of hot sauce

1 Tbsp. chopped onion
1/2 c. mayonnaise
1 c. chopped pecans

28

Combine all ingredients, mix well and chill for several hours. Shape into small balls; about 2 dozen.

Jeanette Williams, Caddo
Council, Shreveport, La.

HAM STUFFED EGGS

4 hard boiled eggs
1 Tbsp. Dijon mustard
1/4 tsp. Worcestershire
   sauce
Salt and pepper to taste

Cut outs of olives, pimento,
   etc. (optional)
1 oz. boiled ham
2 Tbsp. butter, softened
2 tsp. mayonnaise
1 Tbsp. finely chopped chives

Dice and chop ham. Combine egg yolks and ham, add mustard and butter. Stir to blend. Add remaining ingredients, except cut outs, and blend thoroughly. Place mixture into egg hollow and garnish with cut outs.

Jeanette English, Caddo
Council, Shreveport, La.

ALTHEA'S COCKTAIL MEAT BALLS

2 lb. ground meat
1 tsp. instant minced
   garlic
2 tsp. Tony's creole
   seasoning
4 eggs

1/2 c. bread crumbs
   (regular)
1/2 c. Italian bread
   crumbs
1 tsp. white pepper

Mix ingredients together well. Roll into small balls (approximately 100-120). Brown in iron skillet. Can be made ahead and frozen. Freeze meat balls and sauce separately.

Sauce:

1/4 c. butter
1 onion, finely chopped
1 (10 oz.) can beef gravy
1 Tbsp. lemon juice
1 tsp. cracked pepper

2 cloves garlic, crushed
3/4 c. red wine
1 Tbsp. Worcestershire
   sauce
1 Tbsp. dry mustard
1 tsp. creole seasoning

Saute onions and garlic until wilted, but not brown. Mix

1723-79

in remaining ingredients and bring to a boil. Pour boiling sauce over meat balls, even frozen ones, and bring to a boil again. Simmer at least 30 minutes or so. The longer the better.   Althea Brossett, Capital
                                    Council, Baton Rouge, La.

MEXICAN MEAT BALLS
(Appetizer)

Sauce:

2 (1 lb.) cans tomatoes   2 tsp. salt
1 onion, minced   2 Tbsp. bacon drippings
1 c. water

Combine ingredients in saucepan. Cover and cook slowly while meat balls are being prepared. Cook for about 20 minutes.

Meat Balls:

2 lb. ground meat   1 c. corn meal
2 tsp. salt   3 tsp. chili powder
3/4 c. sauce

Combine and make into small balls. Drop in sauce. Cover and simmer 45 minutes. Makes about 2 dozen appetizers.   Sally Davenport, Central
                                    Council, Alexandria, La.

MARY LESLIE'S MEAT PIES

3 sticks oleo   3 c. flour
3 (8 oz.) pkg. cream   1 iced tea spoon cayenne
   cheese   pepper

Soften oleo and cheese and mix together. Add other ingredients and mix well. Roll out and cut with biscuit cutter.

Filling:

1 1/2 lb. lean ground meat   1 can mushroom soup
1 bell pepper, chopped   3 chopped onions
Salt and cayenne pepper   6 cloves garlic, minced
   to taste   2 eggs

30

Brown meat and add remaining ingredients, except soup and eggs. Cook until done. Add soup and raw eggs, mix well. Cool and chill. Use 1 iced tea spoon stuffing to each biscuit. Fold over biscuit and seal with fork tines. Bake in 350° oven until lightly browned. Pies may be made up in advance, frozen on cookie sheets and stored in freezer bags until needed.   June Harllee, Caddo
                              Council, Shreveport, La.

MOSS BALLS

1 (8 oz.) pkg. cream
  cheese
1/2 lb. sharp Cheddar
  cheese, grated
Minced onion
Dash of Worcestershire
  sauce

1/4 lb. or less crumbled
  Blue cheese
1/2 c. chopped nuts
Parsley, finely cut
Pecans, finely chopped

Combine cheeses and mix well. Add onion, 1/2 cup pecans and Worcestershire sauce. Mix and chill 3-4 hours. Form in balls and chill, roll in finely cut parsley and pecans.   Doris Reeves, Capital
                              Council, Baton Rouge, La.

PARTY HOT SAUSAGE

2 c. dark brown sugar
4 Tbsp. Worcestershire
  sauce
2 c. ketchup
Tabasco sauce to taste

1 c. barbecue sauce with
  onion bits
4 Tbsp. dry mustard
3 pkg. (about 9 links) hot
  sausage, sliced

Mix sugar, barbecue sauce and Worcestershire sauce, ketchup and mustard, adding the Tabasco sauce. Pour over sliced sausage. Cook covered at 350° for 1 hour. Uncover and cook 1/2 hour more. Chill and remove grease. Reheat and serve in chafing dish with toothpicks. May be made ahead and frozen.   Ann Orr, Evangeline
                              Council, New Iberia, La.

PARTY PICKS

1 can luncheon meat
(Spam, Treet, etc.)
1 large red apple

1 (No. 2) can pineapple
chunks, drained
Toothpicks

Cut luncheon meat and apples in 1/2-inch cubes. Alternate meat, apple and pineapple on toothpicks, beginning with luncheon meat. Broil under high flame until brown, about 5 minutes. Turn and broil other side until brown. Serve warm.
Marjorie Rowell, Evangeline Council, Lafayette, La.

PARTY SANDWICHES

1 large pkg. cream cheese
1/2 lb. bacon, fried
crisp
Green olives
Bread

1 c. grated Cheddar cheese
Sweet pickles
1 can ripe olives, chopped
Hot pepper relish to taste

Mix all ingredients, except bread, in blender. Trim bread and spread mixture. Roll jelly roll style and wrap in Saran Wrap. Freeze until shortly before serving. Slice while frozen.
Billie Longkabel, Ouachita Council, Monroe, La.

PARTY TOMATOES

18 cherry tomatoes
1 Tbsp. chives
2 tsp. Worcestershire
sauce
Salt and pepper to taste

1 (8 oz.) pkg. cream cheese, softened
1 small can smoked oysters, drained and chopped

Scoop out pulp from tomatoes. Mix with other ingredients and fill each tomato shell. Garnish with parsley, if desired. Yield: 1 1/2 dozen.
Mae Briley, Central Council, Alexandria, La.

PARTY TREAT

1 c. bacon fat
3 Tbsp. Worcestershire
  sauce
2 tsp. garlic salt or
  powder
1 tsp. onion salt
Chili powder to taste
1 Tbsp. Accent
1 box Wheat Chex
1 box pretzels

1 box Corn Chex
1 1/2 lb. butter, melted
3 Tbsp. Tabasco sauce
1 tsp. savory salt
2 tsp. celery salt
Barbecue season to taste
1/2 tsp. cayenne pepper
1 box Rice Chex
3 c. pecans
Other mixed nuts

Blend liquids and pour over all. Mix thoroughly and bake on cookie sheets for 1 hour at 250°. Stir every 20 minutes.

Selman Kinaul, Ouachita
Council, Monroe, La.

PUFFY ONION CHEESE WEDGES

1 c. (2 medium) onions,
  sliced and separated
  into rings
1 egg, beaten
1 c. shredded Cheddar
  cheese

Poppy seed
1 tsp. oleo or butter
1 can refrigerated flakv
  biscuits
1/2 tsp. salt
1 c. sour cream

Saute onions in butter until transparent. Separate biscuits and press on bottom of 8 or 9-inch pie plate to form crust. Spoon onions over crust. Combine egg, salt, cheese and sour cream. Spread evenly over onions. Sprinkle with poppy seed. Bake at 350° for 30-40 minutes or until filling is set. Cut into wedges to serve. To reheat, cover loosely with foil. Heat at 375° for 15-20 minutes. Makes 6 servings.

Katherine Slover, Caddo
Council, Phoenix, Az.

SARDINE CANAPES

8 slices toast
3 hard boiled eggs
Anchovies

1 tin sardines
Juice of 1 lemon
Dash of Tabasco sauce

Trim toast, cut each into 4 triangle slices. Pound the sardines and eggs to paste. Season with Tabasco sauce and lemon juice. Spread the toast with the mixture. Decorate with a small piece of anchovy.

Robert Carnahan, LeBayou
Council, Houma, La.

SAUSAGE BALLS

1 lb. Jimmy Dean hot
sausage, or your
choice

1 (5 1/2 oz.) pkg. Bisquick
mix
2 c. or more grated cheese

Mix ingredients and roll into balls the size of walnuts. Bake on ungreased cookie sheet for 15 or 20 minutes.

Marie Pamplin
Shreveport Works Council
Shreveport, La.

SAUSAGE CHEESE BALLS

1 lb. good pork sausage
3 c. Bisquick

1 lb. sharp cheese, grated

Mix ingredients together and make small balls about the size of a nickel. Place on cookie sheet and bake at 325° for 15 minutes.

Lorraine McManemin

EASY SAUSAGE BALLS

3 c. biscuit mix
1 lb. hot bulk pork sausage

1 (10 oz.) pkg. grated
sharp Cheddar cheese

Crumble sausage and mix with cheese. Add biscuit mix, 1 cup at a time. Form into 1-inch balls and place on ungreased cookie sheets. May be frozen at this time. Bake in preheated 350°-375° oven about 13-15 minutes or until light brown. If frozen, cooking may take few extra minutes. Serve warm. Makes about 7 dozen.

Gretna Anderson, Central
Council, Alexandria, La.

SAUSAGE ROLLS

2 c. flour
3 tsp. baking powder
2/3 c. milk
1/2 tsp. salt
5 Tbsp. Crisco
1 lb. hot sausage

Mix all ingredients, except sausage, as for biscuits. Divide dough in half. Roll each piece 1/4-inch thick and spread 1/2 of sausage on each piece. Roll jelly roll style. Place in waxed paper and freeze. Will keep indefinitely in freezer. To cook, slice 1/4-inch thick, bake on rack in broiler pan at 400° for 30-35 minutes or until golden brown. Serve immediately. Mild sausage can be used instead of hot, if desired. Yield: 2 rolls. Betty Spear, Ouachita Council, Monroe, La.

SHRIMP BUTTER

1 (8 oz.) pkg. cream
   cheese
2 tsp. horseradish
1 tsp. lemon juice
1 can small shrimp
1/4 c. butter
2 tsp. sugar
2 Tbsp. grated onion

Mix cream cheese, horseradish, lemon juice, butter, sugar and onion together. Fold in shrimp. Form into balls and serve with crackers. Ruth Smolenski Evangeline Council

SHRIMP CANAPES

1 pt. fresh homemade
   mayonnaise
1/2 lb. Cheddar cheese,
   grated
3 doz. Ritz crackers
3 doz. medium shrimp,
   boiled and seasoned
3 doz. slices dill pickles

When ready to serve, place crackers on cookie sheet with round of pickle on top. Place shrimp on top of pickle. Make a sauce mixture of mayonnaise and cheese and place portion on top of shrimp. Cook in 425° oven until sauce bubbles. Makes 36. Calcasieu Council Lake Charles, La.

SHRIMP CHEESE BALL

1 1/2 lb. boiled shrimp, chopped
1/4 tsp. McCormick seafood seasoning
1 c. chopped pecans
1 Tbsp. green onion
1 1/2 Tbsp. parsley
1 Tbsp. mayonnaise
2 pkg. (8 oz. size) cream cheese

Combine and mix all ingredients, except pecans. Place in waxed paper and mold in bowl. Sprinkle pecans on bottom of dish, flip ball over, rounded side up. Sprinkle all over with pecans. Chill.   Cynthia Lewis, Magnolia Council, New Orleans, La.

SHRIMP CHEESE BALL

2 c. tiny shrimp, washed, drained and mashed
1 Tbsp. mayonnaise
3 oz. softened cream cheese
1 tsp. garlic salt

Combine and mix ingredients. Form in ball. Chill.

Sauce:

1/2 c. chili sauce
1 tsp. lemon juice
1 tsp. Worcestershire sauce
1 tsp. horseradish

Mix well. Pour over shrimp ball before serving.
Mary Jones, Ouchita Council, Monroe, La.

SHRIMP MARINADE

2 lb. shrimp, cooked, peeled and deveined
1 Tbsp. minced parsley
1/2 tsp. Worcestershire sauce
1 c. mayonnaise
1 clove minced garlic
Few drops Tabasco sauce

Blend all seasonings with mayonnaise. Add shrimp and refrigerate overnight. Serve with Escort crackers.
Etta Williams, Magnolia Council, New Orleans, La.

SHRIMP MOLD

3 doz. fresh shrimp, boiled in crab boil
1 large pkg. cream cheese
1 small pkg. cream cheese
1 c. cold water
4 env. Knox gelatine (plain)
1 can tomato soup
1 c. mayonnaise
3 ribs of celery, chopped fine
1 bunch green onions, chopped fine (shallots)
Salt, pepper and cayenne pepper to taste

Warm undiluted soup until simmering. Remove from stove. Mix gelatine in cold water. Add packages of cream cheese, mix well with soup. Cheese will be a little lumpy; stir well. Add cleaned cooked shrimp, seasoning, mayonnaise. Mix well and put in Tupperware ring mold. Chill in refrigerator until ready to serve. Serve on Ritz or Encore crackers.
Dorothy Zimmer, Chapter Past President Pioneer Partner, New Orleans, La.

SHRIMP PASTE

1 small can cooked shrimp (small shrimp)
1 (8 oz.) pkg. cream cheese
1 very small onion (grate until juicy)
1 1/2 Tbsp. chili sauce
1 1/2 tsp. horseradish

Rinse and clean shrimp, breaking it into small pieces. Begin mixing softened cream cheese with other ingredients, except the shrimp. Mix well, then add shrimp and continue mixing, leaving the shrimp in small chunky bits. This is not a dip, but it is used as a spread for crackers or potato chips. It should be made several hours ahead of serving time and refrigerated.
Calcasieu Council Lake Charles, La.

SHRIMP REMOULADE

6 Tbsp. olive oil
1 Tbsp. paprika
4 green onions, chopped
4 Tbsp. Mr. Mustard, or creole style mustard
2 Tbsp. vinegar
1/2 tsp. white pepper
1/2 tsp. salt
2 ribs celery, chopped fine
Chopped parsley to taste
1/4 head lettuce, shredded

1723-79

2 lb. cleaned, cold,	2 hard cooked eggs, chopped
boiled shrimp	(keep yolk separate from
	white)

Combine all ingredients, except lettuce, eggs and shrimp. Chill. Place shrimp on plate of shredded lettuce. Pour remoulade over shrimp and garnish with eggs.

June Harllee, Caddo Council, Shreveport, La.

SHRIMP REMOULADE

6 Tbsp. oil	2 Tbsp. vinegar
1 Tbsp. paprika	1/2 tsp. white pepper
1/2 tsp. salt	4 Tbsp. creole mustard
1/2 heart of celery,	1/2 white onion, chopped fine
chopped fine	Chopped parsley

Mix all ingredients well and chill. Serve on cold boiled shrimp.

Esther Kenneys, LeBayou Council, Houma, La.

SALLY'S REMOULADE SAUCE

2 cloves garlic, grated	1 small onion, grated
1 c. mayonnaise	1/2 c. chili sauce
1/2 c. ketchup	1/2 c. Wesson oil
1 tsp. black pepper	1 Tbsp. water
1 tsp. lemon juice	Dash of paprika
Dash of Tabasco sauce	1 Tbsp. Worcestershire
Horseradish to taste	sauce
1 Tbsp. vinegar	1 tsp. mustard

Blend all ingredients together in blender. Serve over shrimp salad.

Mrs. Sim S. Davenport
Central Council
Alexandria, La.

SHRIMP REMOULADE SAUCE

1/2 c. celery (5)	3 Tbsp. brown mustard
4 cloves garlic	1/2 c. green onions (6)
1 Tbsp. paprika	1 tsp. cayenne pepper
1/3 c. vinegar	1/2 c. olive oil

1 tsp. salt   1 Tbsp. horseradish
3 Tbsp. catsup

Put ingredients in blender about 3-5 minutes until mixed. Chill.

Elmer E. Harrison
Crescent City Council
New Orleans, La.

SHRIMP SAUCE

2 1/2 lb. chopped,   1/4 c. sherry wine
  boiled shrimp   2 oz. chopped mushrooms
3 strips raw bacon,   3 small green onions,
  chopped   chopped
2 cloves garlic, minced   1 Tbsp. seafood seasoning
2 c. milk, scalded   1 tsp. parsley flakes
2 drops yellow food   1/2 c. flour
  coloring   1/4 c. lemon juice
1/4 stick butter or oleo

Fry bacon, add green onions and saute until soft, not brown. Add mushrooms. Add garlic. Let cook a few minutes. Add butter, then flour. Reduce heat and saute until light brown. Add milk gradually. Add lemon juice and wine. Add chopped shrimp and seafood seasoning. Mixture will be thick. Cook over low heat for 5 minutes. Freeze or refrigerate until ready to use. Stuffs 100 bite size patty shells or can be used over toast or as sauce for broiled fish. Thin with milk if used as sauce.

Joyce Hattier, Magnolia
Council, New Orleans, La.

SHRIMP SAUCE

3/4 c. chili sauce   1 tsp. Worcestershire sauce
3/4 c. Wesson oil   3/4 c. catsup
1 tsp. black pepper   1/2 tsp. red pepper
1/2 tsp. paprika   1 onion
3 cloves garlic   1 tsp. salt
1 c. mayonnaise

Put all ingredients into blender and set on liquefy for about 2 minutes.

Lorraine McManemin
Calcasieu Council
Lake Charles, La.

HOLLANDAISE SAUCE

4 egg yolks
2 sticks butter

2 Tbsp. lemon juice
1/4 tsp. salt

Beat egg yolks and stir in lemon juice. Cook very slowly in top of double boiler, never allowing the water in the bottom to come to a boil. Melt butter and add gradually, stirring constantly with a wooden spoon. Add salt, season to taste and continue cooking slowly until thickened. Yield: 1 cup.
Robert E. Carnahan, LeBayou Council, Houma, La.

HOLLANDAISE SAUCE

5 egg yolks
Dash of Tabasco sauce
4 sticks butter, melted

1/4 c. tarragon wine vinegar
Salt to taste
1/8 c. tepid water

Combine in a stainless steel mixing bowl the egg yolks, vinegar and Tabasco sauce. Whip until very frothy and while continuing to whip, gradually add melted butter (heated to 200°) in the manner of making mayonnaise. When butter has been blended, season and add water to rectify consistency. Yield: 3 cups.
Robert E. Carnahan, LeBayou Council, Houma, La.

KING'S BROWN SAUCE

3 small white onions,
    minced
1 Winesap apple, grated
    (can use 3 Tbsp. mince-
    meat, blended)
3 oz. Kikkoman soy sauce

2 cloves garlic, crushed
1 (5 oz.) jar Pickapeppa
    sauce (do not substitute)
4 oz. olive oil
Red pepper, black pepper,
    salt

Saute onion and garlic in oil, add remaining ingredients and simmer 30 minutes. Use for crab legs or cook shrimp in sauce. Serve shrimp in brown sauce with toasted hard rolls and garlic butter.
Carol King, Shreveport Works Council, Shreveport, La.

OYSTER COCKTAIL SAUCE

1 c. catsup
3 Tbsp. horseradish

1/4 tsp. hot sauce
1 Tbsp. lemon juice

Combine ingredients and use sauce to make oyster or shrimp cocktails or use with raw oysters on half shell.

John Haygood, Caddo
Council, Shreveport, La.

DILLED PICKLED BEANS

2 lb. fresh green beans
4 sprigs fresh dill
2 Tbsp. coarse salt
4 c. water

4 cloves garlic
1 tsp. red pepper or to taste
4 c. white vinegar

Trim green beans to fit jars, pack standing up in 4 prepared sterilized jars. Add 1 clove garlic, 1 sprig of dill and 1/4 teaspoon red pepper to each jar. Heat salt, water and vinegar to boiling in large saucepan and pour over beans. Seal jars and keep 2 weeks or longer before serving.

June Harllee, Caddo
Council, Shreveport, La.

PICKLED GREEN BEANS

2 lb. fresh green beans
1 1/2 c. water
4 tsp. salt
1 Tbsp. whole black pepper
2 cloves garlic, split

1 3/4 c. white vinegar
3/4 c. sugar
1 Tbsp. mustard seed
1 cinnamon stick (3-inch)
3 medium onions, chopped

Wash, trim and cut beans into 2-inch diagonal pieces. Cook covered in boiling salted water until tender, drain. Combine vinegar, water, sugar and salt in saucepan, add spices and garlic tied in cheesecloth bag. Heat to boiling, add onions and beans to vinegar mixture. Bring to boil, simmer 15 minutes. Continue simmering while filling jars. Fill to within 1/2-inch of top, making sure vinegar solution covers beans. Cap jars and process 5 minutes in boiling water bath. Makes 3 pints.

Ann Orr, Evangeline
Council, Lafayette, La.

PICKLED BEETS

1 c. water
1/3 c. sugar

1/2 c. vinegar
Canned or fresh beets

Bring water, sugar and vinegar to boil. Pour over cooked beets. Let stand for few hours for beets to absorb liquid flavor. Keeps well in refrigerator for several weeks. If canned beets are used, use liquid from the beets and add enough water to make 1 cup. Goes well with cook-outs, fish fries or almost any meal.
Elaine Squyres, Central Council, Alexandria, La.

PINK PICKLED EGGS

6 eggs
1 c. canned beet juice
1 c. cider vinegar
1 garlic clove, crushed

1/2 bay leaf
1/4 tsp. ground allspice
1 tsp. salt
Freshly ground black pepper

Hard boil eggs. Plunge into cold water and shell immediately. Put eggs in quart jar. Combine remaining ingredients, bring to a boil and pour over eggs. Cover, cool and refrigerate overnight or for at least 8 hours.
Calcasieu Council Lake Charles, La.

PICKLED JALAPENOS

Jalapeno peppers
1/4 c. water
1 tsp. salt

1 c. vinegar
1/4 c. olive oil
1 tsp. mixed pickling spice

Wash and pack jalapeno peppers tightly into hot jars. Combine remaining ingredients and bring to boil. Cover peppers with boiling liquid, leaving 1/2-inch head space. Seal jars and process in boiling water bath 10 minutes. Start to count processing time when water returns to boiling.
Betty Barron, Caddo Council, Shreveport, La.

PICKLED OKRA OR CORN

1 tsp. red pepper
1 tsp. mustard seed
2 tsp. salt (not iodized)
1/4 c. water

Okra or corn
1 tsp. dill seed
1 c. white vinegar
3 cloves garlic

Use small okra or corn. (Pick corn when it is 2-3 inches long or no kernels have formed.) Wash well. Soak in ice water 1 hour per pint. Mix together seasonings of pepper, dill seed, salt. Mix together vinegar and water. Pack in sterilized jars. Bring to boil. Put seasoning over okra or corn. Pour vinegar and water mixture into jars. Seal. This takes about 2-3 weeks to pickle properly.

Betty Harmon, Caddo
Council, Shreveport, La.

BREAD AND BUTTER PICKLES

25-30 medium sized
  cucumbers
2 large sweet peppers,
  chopped
5 c. cider vinegar
1 tsp. celery seed
1 tsp. ground cloves

8 large white onions,
  chopped
1/2 c. salt (not iodized)
5 c. sugar
2 Tbsp. mustard seed
1 tsp. turmeric

Wash cucumbers (do not peel) and slice thin as possible. Combine onions, salt, peppers and cucumbers. Let stand 3 hours or overnight in refrigerator. Combine vinegar, sugar and spices in large kettle or pot, bring to boil. Add drained cucumbers, onions and peppers. Heat thoroughly, but do not boil. They will begin to look transparent. Pack into sterilized jars and seal at once. Can be eaten within a week after being canned.

Helen Patton
Shreveport Works Council
Shreveport, La.

BREAD AND BUTTER PICKLES

9 c. thinly sliced
  cucumbers

4 Tbsp. uniodized salt
2 c. thinly sliced onions

Mix ingredients and cover with ice cubes. Let stand 3 hours. Drain off liquid thoroughly.

1723-79

Bring following ingredients to a boil:

2 c. white vinegar
2 c. sugar
2 tsp. mustard seed

1 tsp. turmeric
2 tsp. celery seed
1/8 tsp. ground cloves

Add cucumbers, heat through about 5 minutes. Do not boil. Fill hot jars and seal immediately.

Mearl S. Byles, Central
Council, Natchitoches, La.

BROOKSHIRE'S BREAD AND BUTTER PICKLES

1 gal. cucumbers
2 red peppers
1/2 c. salt

8 onions
2 green peppers
1/2 gal. cracked ice

Part II:

5 c. sugar
1/2 tsp. ground cloves
5 c. vinegar

1 1/2 tsp. turmeric
2 tsp. mustard seed
1 tsp. celery seed

Slice cucumbers, onions and peppers very thin. Place in stone jar. Mix ice and salt. Pack over cucumbers, let stand 3 hours. Drain off water and add Part II. Bring to slow boil. Place in jars and seal.

Gayle Wilkening
Shreveport Works Council
Longview, Tx.

CRISP PICKLE MIX

4 qt. sliced cucumbers,
  or green tomatoes
1 c. green peppers, cut up
1/2 c. salt
1 1/2 tsp. celery seed
3 c. cider vinegar

1 qt. sliced onions
3 c. cauliflower
3 cloves garlic, cut up
2 Tbsp. mustard seed
1 1/2 tsp. turmeric

Combine vegetables and garlic, add salt. Mix well and cover with ice cubes. Let stand about 3 hours, drain. Combine remaining ingredients and pour over vegetables; bring to boil. Put in hot jars and seal. Yield: 8-9 pints.

Virginia Lowrey, Ouachita
Council, Monroe, La.

44

DILL PICKLES

3 heads dill, or 3 tsp.
   dill seed
1 1/2 c. water
Pinch of alum

1 tsp. mustard seed
1 1/2 c. vinegar
1 Tbsp. salt

Mix ingredients. Place cucumbers in jar, whole or sliced lengthwise. Pour mixture in jar until liquid is 1/2 inch from top. Seal. Place jars in container of water and boil for 20 minutes.
                            Mrs. Manuel Duhon
                            Calcasieu Council
                            Lake Charles, La.

RUBY LEE'S PICKLES

16 lb. cucumbers
1/2 box alum
10 lb. sugar

1 gal. vinegar
2 small boxes pickling
   spice

Brine: Put enough salt in water to float an egg.
Cover cucumbers in brine for 14 days. Drain and wash cucumbers and cut. Mix 1/2 box alum in enough water to cover pickles and let set for 24 hours. Drain and rinse pickles and cover with pure cider vinegar for 6 hours. After 6 hours, drain pickles and put a layer of pickles, a layer of sugar, then sprinkle pickling spice on top of sugar. Layer pickles, sugar and spice until all is used. Cover and let syrup finish pickles. Will keep indefinitely!
                            Karen Odom, LeBayou
                            Council, Houma, La.

MARINATED SQUASH

Squash
Romano or Parmesan
   cheese (optional)

Bottled Italian salad
   dressing

Place thinly sliced, washed, raw squash in large jar, packing tightly as possible. Cover with bottled dressing to about 1/2 inch of top of jar. Romano or Parmesan cheese may be added with dressing if desired. Refrigerate for about 2 weeks. The squash will be firm and crunchy.
                            Althea Rome Brossett
                            Capital Council
                            Baton Rouge, La.

B&B RELISH

1 gal. green tomatoes,
  quartered
1/2 gal. bell peppers
  (green and red)
5 c. sugar

Black and red pepper to taste
1/2 gal. diced onions
1 qt. vinegar
1 c. peppers, ground fine
  (red)
1/2 c. salt

Mix all ingredients and cook for 20 minutes. Bottle and seal.

Lois S. Leger, Evangeline
Council, Lafayette, La.

CARROT RELISH

2 c. grated carrots
1 c. sugar

1 lemon with rind, chopped
  (no white membrane)

Combine ingredients and let set for 12 hours. Can be frozen if desired. Great with fish.

June E. Nickels
Shreveport Works Council
Shreveport, La.

CAULIFLOWER RELISH

1 head cauliflower (about
  2 lb.)
1/3 c. white wine vinegar
1 tsp. leaf oregano,
  crumbled
1 (6 oz.) can pitted large
  ripe olives, drained

1/4 tsp. pepper
2/3 c. pure vegetable oil
2 tsp. salt
1/2 tsp. sugar
1 clove garlic, crushed
1 green pepper, seeded and
  cut into 1/2-inch strips

Remove outer leaves and stalks from cauliflower. Trim off any blemishes on flowerets, wash well. Cut head or separate into flowerets. Bring oil, vinegar, salt, oregano, sugar and pepper to a boil in large saucepan. Add cauliflower. Cover, cook over low heat about 10 minutes or until cauliflower is tender; stir occasionally. Discard garlic, add olives and green pepper. Transfer to serving bowl. Cover and chill. Drain before serving. Serves 12.

Betty Harman, Caddo
Council, Shreveport, La.

SPICY CORN RELISH

1 qt. whole canned corn
   or fresh, if you prefer
1 c. chopped celery
1/2 c. sugar
1 Tbsp. salt

1 c. cut up pimiento
1 c. green pepper, chopped
1/2 c. chopped onion
1 pt. vinegar (2 c.)
1 tsp. celery seed

Mix sugar, salt, celery seed and vinegar together and pour over the vegetables and boil 20 minutes. Seal while hot.

June Harllee, Caddo Council, Shreveport, La.

EGGPLANT RELISH

2 eggplants
2 onions, diced
5 cloves garlic, diced
1 (6 oz.) can tomato
   paste
1/2 c. wine vinegar
1 (10 oz.) jar olive
   salad mix

2 bell peppers, diced
2 stalks celery, diced
1 (8 oz.) can tomato sauce
1/2 c. olive oil
1/2 c. sugar
Salt, red and black pepper
   to taste
1/2 tsp. oregano

Peel, dice and boil eggplant until tender. Drain and add remainder of ingredients. Cook 30 minutes. Celery should still be crunchy. Can usual way. After opening, keep refrigerated. Will keep 3-4 weeks in refrigerator. Serve chilled on crackers.

Nancy Smith, Capital Council, Baton Rouge, La.

LEMON RELISH

2 large lemons
6 green onions with tops
1/2 green pepper, seeded
1/4 c. parsley sprigs
1 c. chopped celery

1/2 tsp. dry mustard
1/4 tsp. ground cardamom
1 tsp. salt
1 small hot red pepper
1 Tbsp. sugar

Grate lemons, save the grated peel. Cut away remaining yellow and white. Put lemons, onions, pepper and parsley sprigs through coarse blade. Stir in grated peel. Add celery, mustard, cardamom, salt, chopped red pepper, sugar. Cover and refrigerate overnight.

Calcasieu Council
Lake Charles, La.

PEAR RELISH

2 qt. pears, minced and
  measured
9 large white onions,
  minced
1/2 c. salt
3 tsp. turmeric
4 c. sugar .

9 large red and green
  peppers, minced
2 or more hot peppers
4 Tbsp. dry mustard
1 1/2 qt. white vinegar
8 Tbsp. flour

Combine and mix pears, onions, bell peppers and hot
pepper. Cover with salt and let set 1 hour; squeeze dry.
Combine pulp with mustard, turmeric, sugar and vinegar.
Cook about 30-45 minutes. Be careful, do not let burn.
Make paste of flour and little water. Add to mixture. Cook
another 10-15 minutes. Let cool and place in jars.

Frankie Meeks, Ouachita
Council, Monroe, La.

CHOW-CHOW

1 c. ground white onions
1 qt. ground cabbage
1 oz. salt
2 c. vinegar
1 tsp. dry mustard
1/2 tsp. ginger

1 qt. ground green tomatoes
1 1/2 bell peppers, ground
3/4 lb. sugar
1/4 tsp. turmeric
1 tsp. celery seed
1/2 tsp. ground cloves

Combine onions, tomatoes, cabbage, bell peppers and
salt in large container. Let set for 1 hour. Drain off
excess liquid. Add remaining ingredients and cook for 1/2
hour. Put in jars and seal.   Cecile Gallet, Evangeline
Council, Lafayette, La.

SOUPS, SALADS
VEGETABLES

TO QUICK-FREEZE VEGETABLES

Vegetables for freezing are prepared as for cooking, then blanched (scalded) and packed dry, or with the brine. The dry pack is less trouble and is satisfactory for all vegetables except green peppers.

Blanching vegetables is important because it minimizes loss of flavor and color. To blanch in boiling water, put about one pound of vegetables in a fine-mesh wire basket with a wire cover to hold food under the water and lower into rapidly boiling water, enough to cover food. Cover the kettle and then COUNT THE TIME RECOMMENDED FOR EACH vegetable. After blanching, chill quickly and thoroughly, plunge the vegetables into ice water, or hold under cold running water. When completely chilled, remove and drain, and PACK AT ONCE.

VEGETABLE	HOW PREPARED	BLANCHING
ASPARAGUS	Wash, cut, sort into groups according to thickness of stalk. Blanch, chill, pack.	3 to 4 minutes in boiling water, depending on size.
BEANS, GREEN AND WAX	Wash, stem, slice, cut or leave whole. Blanch, chill, pack.	Cut: 2 minutes in boiling water. Whole: 2 1/2 minutes in boiling water.
BEANS, LIMA	Shell, wash, blanch, chill. Remove white beans, which may be used for cooking. Pack.	1 to 2 minutes in boiling water, depending on size.
CARROTS	Remove tops, wash, scrape. Slice lengthwise or cross-wise as preferred, or leave small carrots whole.	Whole: 4 1/2 minutes in boiling water. Sliced: 3 minutes in boiling water.
CAULIFLOWER	Break heads into flowerets about 1 inch across. Wash, blanch, chill, pack.	3 to 4 minutes in boiling water.
CORN, ON COB	Husk, trim away silk and spots. Wash, blanch, chill, pack.	7 minutes in boiling water for slender ears. 9 for medium, 11 for large.
CORN, KERNELS	Same as corn on cob. After chilling, cut off kernels and pack.	
GREENS Beet, Chard, Kale, Mustard, Spinach, Collards, etc.	Wash, discard bad leaves, tough stems. Blanch, chill, pack.	2 minutes in boiling water.
PEAS	Shell, sort, blanch, chill, pack.	1 to 2 minutes in boiling water, depending on size.
PEPPERS, GREEN	Wash, cut away seeds, slice. Blanch, pack in brine of 1 tsp. salt to 1 c. cold water.	3 minutes in boiling water.

CRAYFISH BISQUE

10 lb. crayfish tails
1 bunch celery
4 cloves garlic
6 bunches green onions
Flour and oil

1 large bunch parsley
5 lb. onions
Salt and pepper to taste
6 loaves toasted French bread
2 gal. boiling water

Take 30 pounds of crayfish, boil and peel tails; this will give you approximately 10 pounds of tails. Save and clean about 300 heads. Grind tails, onions, parsley, garlic, celery, green onions and bread in food grinder. Add eggs, salt and pepper. Mix well. Stuff heads with mixture. Roll heads in flour and fry in deep hot oil until golden brown. Reserve enough stuffing to make 3 large patties. Make patties by rolling in flour and patting flour into mixture several times. Fry slowly until patties are golden brown and a hard crust has formed. Put heads and patties in boiling water. Cook 4 hours or until patties are all broken up, adding more hot water as needed. Serve over hot steamed rice.

Genevieve Whitehead, Capital
Council, Baton Rouge, La.

CRAWFISH BISQUE

Use 1 sack crawfish (about 40 pounds). Scald crawfish in almost boiling water for about 15 minutes. Drain and cool. Peel crawfish and save the fat in a separate bowl. Clean about 200 heads to stuff.

Gravy:

1 c. cooking oil
2 large onions
4 stalks celery
4 cloves garlic
2 1/2 c. ground crawfish
    tails
9 c. hot water
5 tsp. salt

2 c. flour (about)
6 green onions
1/4 medium bell pepper
10 sprigs parsley
1/2 of crawfish fat
2 tsp. red pepper
4 heaping tsp. tomato paste

Grind onions, celery, bell pepper, garlic and parsley. Make roux with oil and flour. Stir constantly until browned. Add ground seasonings. Cook on low fire about 30 minutes. Add tomato paste and crawfish fat. Cook about 30 minutes longer. Add hot water and let cook on low fire. Add ground crawfish tails, add salt and pepper. Cook on high fire about 20 minutes. Add baked crawfish heads. Cook on low fire about 1 hour. More hot water may be added if too thick. Stir carefully. Serve in soup bowls over rice. Delicious.

Stuffing for Heads:

Rest of ground crawfish
   tails
3 stalks celery
1/4 medium bell pepper
4 cloves garlic
10 sprigs parsley
2-3 c. bread crumbs
2 tsp. red pepper

2 large onions
6 green onions
Rest of crawfish fat
1/4 c. cooking oil
2 eggs, beaten
4 tsp. salt
Flour

Grind onions, celery, bell pepper, garlic and parsley. Fry crawfish and ground seasonings in hot cooking oil; cool. Add crawfish fat and eggs. Mix in bread crumbs, salt and pepper. Stuff heads. Dip the stuffed part of head in flour and place on cookie sheet. Bake for 20 minutes in 400° oven.
      Mrs. Wayne Knotts, Capital Council, Brushy, La.

CRAWFISH BISQUE

Use 20 pounds live crawfish, or 3 pounds crawfish tails, 60 cleaned crawfish heads. Pick over the crawfish to remove any dead ones. Purge. Pour boiling water over live crawfish and let stand for about 5 minutes until they turn red. Separate the heads from the tails. If fat is used, remove from each head at this time and place in a separate dish. Select 60 of the largest heads, clean out thoroughly, remove eyes, wash and boil a few minutes. Let stand in water until ready to use. To prepare the bisque:

4 1/2 c. boiling water
1/2 c. minced parsley
1/2 c. onion tops, chopped
1/2 of the cleaned craw-
   fish tails
1/2 c. crawfish fat
   (optional)

3/4 block butter
1/2 c. olive oil or salad oil
1 c. flour
2 large onions, chopped
3 stalks celery, chopped
1 large bell pepper,
   chopped

3 pods garlic, chopped   1 tsp. red pepper
3 tsp. salt

Make a golden brown roux by cooking the oil and flour together, slowly stirring constantly. Add onions, bell pepper and celery. Cook until onions are transparent, stirring frequently. Add crawfish tails and fat. Cook on low heat for about 20 minutes. Stir occasionally. Gradually add the boiling water, salt and pepper. Cook for 20 minutes. Add garlic, onion tops and parsley. Just before serving, add the stuffed and baked crawfish heads. Serve in soup plates with fluffy steamed rice, croutons or garlic bread.

Stuffing for Crawfish Heads:

1/4 c. cooking oil
1/2 c. flour
2 medium onions, chopped
1 large bell pepper,
  chopped
2 tsp. salt
1 tsp. red pepper
1 1/2 c. bread crumbs
1/4 c. minced parsley

1/4 c. green onion tops,
  chopped
3 pods garlic, chopped
3/4 c. water
1/2 block butter
1/2 of the crawfish tails
  (reserved)
1/2 of the fat reserved
  (optional)

Before starting to stuff the heads, remove from water and let drip dry. Have bread crumbs ready. Grind onions, pepper and crawfish tails in a separate dish. Make a golden brown roux by cooking the oil and flour together on low heat, stirring constantly. Add onions and bell pepper and cook until onions are transparent. Add ground crawfish tails and fat. Let simmer for 15 minutes. Add water, salt, pepper, bread crumbs, parsley, garlic and onion tops. Add 1/2 block melted butter if desired. Mix thoroughly. Stuff each head, roll in flour, place in a baking pan side by side with the stuffed side up. Bake 15 minutes in 375° oven. Add to bisque gravy just before serving.   Eugene Cottrell, Caddo
                    Council, Shreveport, La.

SHRIMP BISQUE

1 lb. shrimp, cooked
   and ground
2 Tbsp. chopped celery
3 Tbsp. all-purpose flour
1/4 tsp. paprika
Dash of pepper

2 Tbsp. chopped onion
1/4 c. oleo, melted
1 tsp. salt
4 c. hot milk
Parsley

   Put shrimp through meat grinder. Saute onion and celery in butter until tender. Blend in flour and seasonings. Add milk and cook until thick, stirring constantly. Stir in shrimp and heat through. Sprinkle with chopped parsley in serving bowl. Serves 6-8. Mrs. Larry D. Chambers
Metairie Council
Slidell, La.

CHILI

2 Tbsp. chili powder
2 cans tomato sauce
1 stalk celery, chopped
2 Tbsp. flour
Salt, pepper and garlic
   to taste

1 lb. ground meat
1 large onion, chopped
2 c. water
2 Tbsp. Worcestershire
   sauce

   Brown meat, onion and celery. Add water, tomato sauce, Worcestershire sauce, chili powder, garlic, salt and pepper. Cook about 30 minutes over medium heat. Mix flour with little water and add to chili. Cook until thickened. Mrs. Iona Botzong, Central
Council, Tioga, La.

CHILI

1 Tbsp. cooking oil
1 lb. ground beef
1 large onion
Seasoning or condiments
   according to taste
   (garlic powder, onion
   salt, celery salt, etc.)
1 can tomatoes
1 bottle chili sauce

1 can tomato sauce or
   paste
1 chili stick
2 or 3 cans red beans
2 Tbsp. Mexene chili powder
1/2 tsp. cayenne pepper
1/2 tsp. sugar (optional)
1 can water
Salt and pepper to taste

Brown meat in large skillet. Add onion and seasoning. Cook until beef is separated well. Add tomatoes and sauce. Melt chili stick and add to beef. Add water, sugar, salt and pepper, chili powder and cayenne pepper. Cook slowly for 1 1/2 hours. Add beans, cook 1/2 hour.

Mary Ann Wiebelt
Crescent City Council
New Orleans, La.

CHILI

3 lb. lean diced beef
1 qt. water
3 tsp. salt
5 cloves garlic, finely
  chopped
1 tsp. marjoram
1 Tbsp. sugar
1/4 c. liquid shortening

8 chili pods, or 6 Tbsp.
  chili powder
1 tsp. ground cumin
1 tsp. red pepper
3 Tbsp. paprika
6 Tbsp. corn meal, 3 Tbsp.
  flour and 1 c. water for
  thickening

Heat oil in large pot, add meat and sear over high heat. Stir constantly until meat is gray, but not brown. Add water and cover, cook over low fire for 1 1/2 - 2 hours. Add remaining ingredients, except thickening, and cook at a bubbling simmer 30 minutes. Mix thickening ingredients together, add to chili mixture, cook about 5 minutes, stirring to prevent sticking. More water may be added for desired consistency. If meat is very fat, skim off before adding thickening. For milder flavor, cut chili powder and red pepper in half, but add 2 more tablespoons paprika for color.

Betty Harman, Caddo
Council, Shreveport, La.

CHILI

1 lb. lean ground beef
2 medium onions,
  chopped
1 small can tomato sauce
Salt and pepper

1 stick oleo
2 Tbsp. flour
2 Tbsp. chili powder or mix
2-3 cans water (tomato
  sauce can)

Brown beef in 1/2 of oleo, add flour and brown, stirring. Brown onions in remaining oleo. Mix, add seasonings and tomato sauce. Add water. Cook slowly about 1 1/2 - 2 hours. Add more seasoning or water if desired.

Maxine Fletcher, Ouachita
Council, Monroe, La.

HOMEMADE CHILI

2 1/2 lb. ground meat
6-8 cloves garlic,
  chopped fine
3 cans (15 oz. size)
  tomato sauce
2 tsp. chopped parsley

8 tsp. hot chili powder
3 medium onions, chopped
  fine
1 (16 oz.) can tomatoes
Salt and pepper to taste
1/4 piece bell pepper,
  chopped

Fry meat and onions, drain. Add remaining ingredients and cook over low to medium heat about 1 1/2 hours. Add a little water if needed.
Earline Bergeron
Crescent City Council
New Orleans, La.

MEXICAN STYLE CHILI

2 lb. ground meat
1 clove minced garlic
2 Tbsp. paprika
Salt and cayenne pepper
  to taste

3 cans tomato sauce
1 large grated onion
3 Tbsp. ground cumino
4 Tbsp. chili powder
2 cans water

Fry meat, onion and garlic in large skillet until meat is browned and onion is tender; drain. Add remaining ingredients, mix thoroughly. Cook about 30-40 minutes on low to medium heat until slightly thickened.
Pam Marchese, Metairie
Council, Metairie, La.

QUICK CHILI

1 1/2 lb. ground beef
1 env. Lipton's onion
  soup mix (dry)
1-2 Tbsp. chili powder,
  to taste

2 (1 lb.) cans red kidney
  beans
1/2 c. water
1 (1 lb.) can tomatoes

Brown meat well in large skillet, add soup mix, chili powder, beans, water, tomatoes. Simmer covered for 30-45 minutes.
Calcasieu Council
Lake Charles, La.

TEXAS HOT CHILI

2 large onions, sliced
1 medium or small jalapeno
  pepper, finely chopped
1 tsp. cumin seed
1 1/2 Tbsp. oregano
1 (28 oz.) can whole
  tomatoes
1 Tbsp. chopped parsley
2 cans (15 oz. each) red
  beans
1 (7 1/2 oz.) can tomatoes
  and jalapeno peppers

3 cloves garlic, minced
1 Tbsp. peanut oil
3 lb. boneless chuck roast,
  finely diced
1 (1 1/2 oz.) can chili
  powder
3 1/2 c. water
1 Tbsp. Worcestershire
  sauce
1 (6 oz.) can tomato paste
Salt and pepper to taste

Saute onions, garlic and jalapeno pepper in oil until
tender; set aside. Combine meat, cumin and oregano in
heavy large pot, cook until meat is browned. Add onion
mixture and remaining ingredients. Bring to a boil,
reduce heat and simmer 2-3 hours. Stir occasionally to
prevent sticking. Velma Walker, Central
Council, Alexandria, La.

BROCCOLI CHOWDER

2 lb. fresh broccoli
3 c. milk
2 tsp. salt
1 c. half & half
1/4 c. butter or oleo

2 cans chicken broth
1 c. chopped, cooked ham
1/4 tsp. pepper
2 c. shredded Swiss cheese

Combine broccoli and 1 can chicken broth, cover and
cook until broccoli is crisp-tender, about 7 minutes. Remove broccoli and chop coarsely. Add remaining broth,
milk, ham, salt and pepper to pot, bring to boil over
medium heat, stirring occasionally. Stir in broccoli and
remaining ingredients. Cook over low heat until thoroughly
heated. Do not boil. Yield: 6-8 servings.
Una Mize, Caddo Council,
Shreveport, La.

BROCCOLI SOUP

2 Tbsp. butter
1/4 c. chopped onion
2 c. beef broth
1/2 tsp. salt
1 c. milk

3/4 c. chopped celery with
leaves
1 bunch broccoli (about
1 1/2 lb.), cut in small
pieces
1/4 tsp. pepper

Saute celery and onion in butter until wilted, add broccoli, broth, salt and pepper. Bring to a boil, cover and cook over medium heat until broccoli is tender, about 20 minutes. Puree ingredients in electric blender, food mill or mixer. Stir in milk and reheat. Makes about 1 quart. If too thick, add broth or milk and correct the seasoning.

Rebecca Scott, Caddo
Council, Shreveport, La.

CLAM CHOWDER

1 slice (1-inch thick) salt
pork
1 1/2 pt. fresh clams,
minced
3 qt. water

2 1/2 potatoes, peeled and
diced
1 onion, chopped
2 1/4 tsp. salt

Fry salt pork over medium heat in large Dutch oven until done. Remove pork, reserving drippings in pan. Dice pork. Combine with remaining ingredients in Dutch oven. Bring to a boil, reduce heat, cover and simmer about 2 hours and 15 minutes or until potatoes are tender. Yield: 10-12 servings.

Marjorie B. Harris, Capital
Council, Baton Rouge, La.

CORN CHOWDER

2 oz. salt pork, diced
1 small onion, sliced
1 (No. 2) can corn
(2 1/2 c.)
2 c. diced potatoes
1 1/2 c. fresh or canned
tomatoes

1 Tbsp. sugar
1 tsp. salt
1/2 tsp. pepper
4 c. boiling water
1 c. hot milk
Crackers

Fry salt pork golden brown, add onion and cook without

browning 5 minutes. Add vegetables in layers; sprinkle with sugar and seasonings; add water and cook slowly until potatoes are tender. Remove from heat and slowly stir in milk. Place crackers in hot soup bowls and pour chowder over. Serves 8.   Calcasieu Council
Lake Charles, La.

FISH CHOWDER

1 lb. fillet of fish (catfish or any fresh
   water fish)
4 potatoes, peeled and
   sliced

Salt and pepper
1/4 c. diced salt pork
1 small onion, diced
2 c. milk, scalded

Cook fish slowly in small amount of water until fish flakes when tried with a fork. Remove fish and flake. Cook potatoes in fish water until tender. Fry out salt pork, add onion and cook slowly until lightly browned. Add fish, salt pork and onions to potatoes in fish water. Next, pour milk into onion pan, heat and add to chowder. Season with salt and pepper. Crushed crackers may be added to the chowder. Serves 4.   Calcasieu Council
Lake Charles, La.

FISH CHOWDER

1 c. diced potatoes
1 c. boiling water
3/4 lb. fish fillets, cubed
1/2 tsp. salt
1/8 tsp. pepper

2 Tbsp. chopped fresh
   parsley
3 slices bacon, chopped
1 medium onion, chopped
1 c. milk

Place potatoes in Dutch oven with boiling water, cover and cook 10-15 minutes. Fry bacon until transparent, add onion and cook until onion is soft and bacon is lightly browned. Add bacon, onion, bacon drippings and fish fillets to potatoes. Simmer 10 minutes or until potatoes and fish are done. Stir in milk, salt and pepper. Simmer 5 minutes. Sprinkle with parsley. Yield: 2-3 servings.
Una Miza, Caddo Council,
Shreveport, La.

HAM AND CORN CHOWDER

1/2 c. sliced onion
1 large can cream style
corn
1/2 tsp. salt
Croutons or oyster
crackers

1/2 c. butter or oleo,
melted
1/2 c. half & half
1 c. chopped ham
1/8 tsp. pepper

Saute onion in butter until tender. Add remaining ingredients to pot and cook over low heat until thoroughly heated. Garnish with croutons or crackers. Makes 6-8 servings.
Marilou Bridges, Caddo
Council, Shreveport, La.

GUMBO

3 lb. okra, cut up
1 clove garlic, minced
1 can tomato paste
1 qt. water
2 lb. shrimp, peeled
1 can stewed tomatoes

Hot red pepper and cayenne
pepper to taste
1 onion, chopped
1 bay leaf
2 Tbsp. flour
4 crabs

Combine okra, garlic, tomato paste, stewed tomatoes, onion, bay leaf and water. Cook slowly until done. Brown flour, add enough water to make a roux. Add roux, shrimp, crabs and season to taste. Cook slowly until done.
Colleen Ahrens, Caddo
Council, Shreveport, La.

GUMBO

2 lb. shrimp, crawfish
or chicken
1 stick oleo
1 large onion, chopped
1 stalk celery, chopped
3 qt. water
1 Tbsp. green onions
2 cans tomatoes

2 c. okra, cut up
2 Tbsp. oil
4 Tbsp. flour
1 large bell pepper, chopped
2 cloves garlic
4 Tbsp. Worcestershire
sauce

Fry fresh okra in oil; do not burn. Add oleo and flour. Make roux. Add onion, celery, bell pepper and garlic. Saute until soft. Add water and Worcestershire sauce.

58

Add the tomatoes. Cook for 1-2 hours. Add the meat of your choice. Let simmer for 30 minutes. Serve with rice.

Frankie Meeks, Ouachita
Council, Monroe, La.

CAJUN GUMBO

1 chicken (any size)	3 smoked sausage links
6 eggs	2 1/2 c. peeled shrimp
2 c. oysters	1 1/2 Tbsp. file
1 large onion, chopped	1/2 c. green onions,
1/2 c. chopped parsley	chopped
Salt and pepper to taste	1 qt. water

No cooking oil is needed; chicken fat will melt. Preheat large pot over medium heat for 5 minutes. Add cut up chicken and fry about 10 minutes. Add onion and let chicken and onion brown together. When browned, add green onions and parsley. Let cook about 15 minutes. Don't stir chicken too much. Add sausage, shrimp and oysters. Let cook 10 minutes and add water. Let mixture come to a boil for 15 minutes. Break raw eggs, 1 at a time, in boiling mixture in separate places in your pot. Continue to cook for 10 minutes. Do not stir during this time. Add file. Stir and turn heat off. Add salt and pepper to taste. Serves 10-12.

Mona Reis, Metairie
Council, Metairie, La.

CHICKEN GUMBO

1 large chicken, cut up	4 Tbsp. cooking oil
1 large onion, chopped	2 qt. chicken stock, heated
2 Tbsp. minced parsley	2 Tbsp. chopped green
Thyme, fresh if available	onion
1 lb. smoked sausage or	Salt and pepper to taste
Andouille	1 pt. oysters
1 Tbsp. file powder	1 clove minced garlic

Brown chicken slowly in oil in heavy pot. Remove chicken pieces and saute onion until soft. Return chicken to pot with onions, cover and cook over low heat, about 10 minutes, stirring occasionally to prevent burning. Add heated chicken stock, parsley, green onion and garlic. Season with thyme, salt and pepper. Cook over low heat

1723-79

until chicken is tender. Add sausage and cook for 10 minutes. Add oysters and oyster water, cook for 10 minutes longer. Skim off excess fat. Remove from fire and immediately add file powder, stirring while adding. Serve over steamed rice.　　　　　　　Lois Leger, Evangeline
Council, Lafayette, La.

CHICKEN AND SAUSAGE GUMBO

1/4 c. parsley, chopped
1/4 c. chopped shallots
3 cloves garlic, minced
1/4 c. cooking oil
Salt and cayenne pepper
　　to taste
Sausage

1/4 c. onions, chopped
1/4 c. chopped bell pepper
3 Tbsp. flour
1 1/2 lb. chicken wings or
　　any desired chicken pieces
10 c. water

Cut sausage in thin pieces. Combine oil and flour to make a roux. Stir over low heat until brown. Add parsley, onions, shallots, bell peppers, garlic, sausage and 1 cup water. Bring to a boil, reduce heat and simmer for 3 minutes. Add remaining 9 cups water and bring to a boil. Add chicken, salt and cayenne pepper, bring to a boil. Reduce heat, cover and simmer for about 2 hours. Serve over rice. Makes 6 servings.　　　　Mona F. Reis, Metairie
Council, Metairie, La.

CRAWFISH FILE GUMBO

1 c. shortening
1 c. flour
1 onion, minced
1/4 c. minced parsley
1/4 c. onion tops, minced
3 pods garlic, minced

1/4 c. celery leaves, minced
1 lb. cleaned crawfish
　　tails
8 c. water
1/2 c. crawfish fat
　　(optional)
Seasonings to taste

Make a roux by cooking the shortening and flour together to a golden brown color while stirring constantly. Add onions and cook until soft. Add crawfish fat. Stir constantly while cooking over low heat until shortening floats on top. Add water and seasonings. Simmer over a low heat for 30 minutes. About 1/2 hour before serving, add garlic and crawfish tails and let simmer for 25 minutes longer. Add parsley, green onion tops, celery leaves and simmer 5 minutes longer. Just before serving, add about 3/4 teaspoon file powder, if desired. Serve in soup plates with hot steamed rice and Tabasco sauce, if desired.

Eugene Cottrell, Caddo
Council, Shreveport, La.

FOWL GUMBO

1 large bell pepper, diced	3 stalks green onions, diced
3 celery stalks, diced	1 large can tomatoes
1 can tomato paste	1/8 tsp. garlic salt
1 tsp. red pepper	4 c. okra, cut up
1 chicken	File (gumbo)

Boil fowl until tender. Debone and cut into small pieces. Reserve broth. Add bell pepper, onions, celery, tomatoes, tomato paste, garlic salt, red pepper and okra to broth. Boil until vegetables are tender. Add chicken. Make 3 cups of thick brown gravy and add this to above cooked mixture. Salt to taste. Just prior to serving, add enough file until mixture is slightly ropy. Serve hot on rice or corn bread.

Betty Elenburg, Caddo
Council, Shreveport, La.

MARY'S SEAFOOD GUMBO

5 lb. okra	3 tomatoes, or 1 (No. 2) can
2 large chopped onions	5 lb. deheaded shrimp
1 can frozen crabmeat	6 or more crabs
Salt and pepper to taste	Red hot pepper sauce
Small amount oil or	Garlic, bay leaf and thyme
shortening	(optional)

Use large aluminum pot, not iron. Wash, stem and cut okra into 1/2-inch pieces. Season with salt and pepper. Smother okra in as little oil as possible. When almost done, add onion. Cook onion until tender, add tomatoes. Let simmer, add remaining ingredients and simmer until done. If there is a favorite vegetable of the South, it is surely okra. Gumbo gets its name from the Choctaw Indian word 'Kombo' for any thick soup made with okra.

Mary Weeks, Metairie
Council, Metairie, La.

OKRA-SHRIMP GUMBO

1 can whole tomatoes
1 1/2 heaping cook spoons
  plain flour
4 stalks celery, chopped
3 lb. shrimp, peeled and
  deveined
1/8 c. cooking oil

4 qt. water
Salt and pepper to taste
1 large onion, chopped
1/2 bell pepper, chopped
1/4 c. chopped shallots
1 pt. salty oysters (optional)
2 boxes frozen okra, un-
  thawed

In large pot, make roux of flour and oil, stirring until dark brown. Add vegetables until wilted. Cook okra in separate pot by frying in grease until almost all of rope is gone. Do not prepare ahead. Add shrimp to vegetables, cook until bright pink. Add tomatoes, cook about 5 minutes. Add cooked okra. Simmer for 5 minutes, add water, more or less depending upon consistency you prefer. Season with salt and pepper. Cook about 1 1/2 hours. Add oysters 5 minutes before gumbo is done. Serve with rice.

Jeannett Parr, West Bank
Council, Gretna, La.

OYSTER GUMBO

4 doz. oysters
2 qt. oyster liquid
1 large chopped onion
1 sprig thyme, minced
1 qt. hot water
2 Tbsp. file

2 Tbsp. shortening or butter
2 Tbsp. flour
1 bay leaf, crushed
1 sprig minced parsley
Salt and pepper to taste

Make roux with shortening and flour. When brown, add onion and parsley. Cook until onions are well browned and soft. Add bay leaf, thyme and hot oyster liquid. Add hot water. Simmer about 15 minutes. Add drained oysters and continue to cook 5 minutes more. Remove from heat and gradually stir in file. Serve immediately over cooked rice in soup bowl. Serves 6-8. John E. Haygood, Caddo
Council, Shreveport, La.

SAUSAGE GUMBO

1/2 lb. hot sausage	1 lb. pork links
1 lb. smoked sausage	1 lb. Italian sausage
1 beef round	1 jar oysters
Gumbo file	Garlic
Green peppers	Parsley
1 large onion	Green onions
Celery	Salt and pepper
Flour	Water

Fry sausages, cool and cut into thin slices (pork links each into 3 pieces). Cut beef round into pieces. Fry pieces in large pot until meat is brown and tender, remove meat. Chop all vegetables, add to drippings in pot, saute until light brown. Add flour to make a roux. When roux is golden brown, add water, sausage and meat. Cook until meat and sausages are tender and gumbo thickens. Add oysters. Cook until tender. Add file 1/2 hour before gumbo is finished. Serve over rice. The meat can be placed into deep pie shell and served as pot pie; drain off broth before placing meat in shell.

Betty Stevens, Gentilly
Council, New Orleans, La.

SCHUMANN'S SEAFOOD GUMBO

6 level Tbsp. flour	1/2 c. shortening
6 cloves garlic, chopped	1/2 c. diced onion
1/4 c. chopped bell pepper	1/2 c. chopped celery
3 lb. unpeeled shrimp	3 qt. water, salted
1 (8 oz.) can tomato	1 lb. crabmeat
sauce	1/2 tsp. thyme
1/4 bunch chopped parsley	3 bay leaves
1/2 tsp. Tabasco sauce	1 Tbsp. Worcestershire
2 lb. selected okra	sauce
Salt and pepper to taste	

Boil shrimp in salted water for 5 minutes; save stock. Clean shrimp and set aside. Cut okra into thin rounds and brown in shortening. Do not scorch. In another pan, make a roux with flour and shortening. Add garlic and cook until golden brown. Add onion, bell pepper, celery and parsley. Cook until transparent. Add tomato sauce, simmer 10 minutes. Stir in shrimp stock and blend well. Add thyme and bay leaves, cook 1 hour. Last 20 minutes,

add shrimp, crab, salt, pepper, Tabasco sauce, Worcestershire sauce and okra. Cover pot and allow to simmer gently at least 1 hour.
Floyd Shumann, Ozone Council, Hammond, La.

SHRIMP GUMBO

2 lb. shrimp	2 qt. water
2 Tbsp. oil	1 bay leaf
2 Tbsp. flour	1 tsp. salt
3 c. okra, chopped	3 pods garlic (optional)
Red pepper	2 Tbsp. oil
1 can tomatoes	

Peel shrimp and devein. Make roux of flour and oil. Add shrimp, stirring constantly. Set aside. Smother okra and onions in oil. Add tomatoes when okra is almost cooked. Then add water, bay leaf, garlic, salt and pepper. Add shrimp and roux to this. Cover and cook 30 minutes. If file is used, put it in after it is cooked. Serve over rice.
Calcasieu Council Lake Charles, La.

SHRIMP GUMBO

2 cloves garlic, minced	2 sliced onions
1/2 thinly sliced bell pepper	1/4 c. butter or oleo
2 Tbsp. flour	2 1/2 c. tomatoes (No. 2 can)
1 (No. 2) can okra, drained, or 1 pkg. frozen	1 (6 oz.) can tomato paste
3 beef bouillon cubes	4 tsp. Worcestershire sauce
1/8 tsp. ground cloves	1/2 tsp. chili powder
Pinch of dried basil	1 bay leaf
1 1/2 tsp. salt	1/4 tsp. pepper
3 c. water	1 1/2 lb. cleaned and peeled shrimp

In large heavy pot, saute garlic, onions and green pepper in butter. Stir in flour. Cook over low heat until vegetables are tender. Add remaining ingredients, except shrimp. Simmer 45 minutes. Add shrimp and simmer additional 5 minutes until tender. Serve over rice.
Dorothy Trent, Caddo Council, Shreveport, La.

QUICK SHRIMP GUMBO

2 Tbsp. cooking oil	2 Tbsp. flour
1 c. okra	1 can chicken soup with
1 can chicken gumbo	rice
2 (4 1/2 oz.) cans shrimp	Salt and pepper to taste

Make roux with cooking oil and flour. Brown until dark brown color. Add okra, salt and pepper. Add soup and carefully rinsed shrimp. Simmer until hot. Serve over rice. If more vegetables desired, add chopped bell pepper, minced garlic and green onion blades.

Una Mize, Caddo Council,
Shreveport, La.

TURKEY GUMBO
(Canned soup adds flavor to a quick turkey fix-up.)

2 Tbsp. cornstarch	2 c. cubed, cooked turkey
1 c. water	2 Tbsp. chopped pimiento
1 Tbsp. soy sauce	1 (3 oz.) can (2 1/4 c.)
1 can condensed chicken	chow mein noodles
gumbo soup	

In saucepan, combine cornstarch, water and soy sauce. Add soup. Cook and stir until mixture is thickened and bubbly. Stir in turkey and pimiento. Heat through. Serve over chow mein noodles. Makes 4 servings.

Calcasieu Council
Lake Charles, La.

ARTICHOKE SOUP

3 Tbsp. butter	1 1/2 Tbsp. minced green
1 1/2 Tbsp. flour	onions
4 large cans artichoke	3 1/2 c. chicken stock or
bottoms or hearts	chicken broth in cans
Salt and pepper to taste	3/4 c. half & half
1/4 tsp. minced garlic	2 dashes Lea & Perrins sauce
	2 chicken bouillon cubes

Melt butter over medium heat, allowing it to brown slightly. Add green onions and saute briefly. Stir in flour and cook 2-3 minutes. Heat chicken stock in 2-quart saucepan, add flour-onion mixture, stir constantly. Cook over medium heat until slightly thickened, about 3-5 minutes. Puree 3 cans of artichokes in food processor or blender. Add chicken stock mixture and half & half. Blend thoroughly, about 30 seconds. Season with salt and pepper. Cut up remaining can of artichoke hearts and add to pot. Serve hot.

Joyce Hattier, Magnolia
Council, New Orleans, La.

ARTICHOKE SOUP

3 cans (14 oz. size) artichoke hearts, cut in fourths
2 onions, chopped
2-3 Tbsp. flour with enough cold water to make paste
2 tsp. basil leaves
1/2 tsp. thyme
1/4 c. olive oil

12 chicken bouillon cubes, dissolved in 2 c. hot water
6 cloves garlic, minced
Italian cheese
2 Tbsp. dried parsley
2 tsp. oregano
1/2 stick butter or oleo
Handful of vermicelli
10 c. water

Melt butter and olive oil in large pot together. Saute onions and garlic. Add artichoke hearts and cook. Add water. Add dissolved bouillon and water. Add basil, parsley, oregano and thyme. Cook covered for 1 hour. Add flour paste to boiling mixture, cook 15 minutes. Add vermicelli and cook until tender. Sprinkle Italian cheese on soup in bowls before serving. Serves 6.

Mona F. Reis, Metairie
Council, Metairie, La.

ARTICHOKE SOUP

1 can artichoke hearts, drained
1 can cream of celery soup
Butter or oleo

1 can cream of onion soup
1 onion, chopped
Salt and pepper to taste
1 soup can water

Saute onion in butter or oleo until tender. Add soups and water. Add artichoke hearts, salt and pepper to taste. Simmer on low fire about 1 hour.

Mollie Porrovecchio, Metairie
Council, New Orleans, La.

BEAN SOUP

2 lb. Great Northern
   beans
2 large onions, finely
   chopped
2 cloves chopped
   garlic

2 qt. water (more if
   needed)
1 lb. diced smoked sausage
   (links)
Salt and pepper to taste

Presoak beans for faster cooking. Combine ingredients and cook in heavy pot over low heat until tender, at least 2 hours. Mash with potato masher until beans blend into soup. Best served with warm corn bread. This recipe is perfect for crock-pots and slow cookers if cooking time is extended.
   Cindy Kendrick, Caddo Council, Shreveport, La.

BEAN SOUP

1 large pkg. small dry
   lima beans
1 ham bone, or 4-5 ham
   hocks
Lemon pepper
Oleo

1 bunch green onions,
   chopped
5-6 stalks celery, chopped
   fine
Salt and pepper to taste
Accent, water

Wash and pick lima beans. Cook in pressure cooker until done. Saute onions and celery in oleo until wilted. Place beans, vegetables and ham in large soup kettle with plenty of water. Add salt and pepper. Shake on lemon pepper seasoning and dash or two of Accent. Simmer several hours until thick, stirring occasionally. Very good crock-pot recipe. Serve with Mexican corn bread. Freezes well.
   Mary Ferguson, Caddo Council, Shreveport, La.

PUREED GREEN BEAN SOUP

1 (No. 303) can green
   beans, or 1 pkg.
   frozen green beans
1 beef bouillon cube
Sour cream

1 small onion, sliced
2 c. chicken broth
2 oz. Cheddar cheese,
   grated
Salt, pepper and Worcestershire sauce to taste

Cook beans, onion and broth together, add bouillon cube. Puree in blender while hot, season with salt, pepper and Worcestershire sauce. Divide cheese in bottoms of 4 bouillon cups, add soup and garnish with sour cream.

Mrs. Raymond Sparkman
Crescent City Council
New Orleans, La.

CREAM OF BROCCOLI SOUP

1 (10 oz.) pkg. frozen chopped broccoli
1 Tbsp. finely chopped onion
1/4 c. flour
1 Tbsp. margarine

3 c. vegetable cooking liquid and milk
1 1/2 tsp. salt
Pepper, as desired
1 hard cooked egg, sliced (if desired)

Cook broccoli according to package directions, but omit salt and add onion. Drain, saving cooking liquid. Mix flour with part of milk mixture until smooth. Add remaining liquid to broccoli. Stir in flour mixture, fat and seasoning. Cook over moderate heat, stirring occasionally, until soup is slightly thickened and flavors are blended. Garnish with slices of hard cooked egg, if desired. Serve with croutons. Makes 6 servings.

Calcasieu Council
Lake Charles, La.

CAULIFLOWER SOUP

1 head fresh cauliflower
1/2 c. evaporated milk
1 (12-16 oz.) pkg. American processed cheese

1/2 block butter
1/2 c. milk
1 1/2 caps liquid crab boil
Black pepper

Boil cauliflower in salted water until tender. Drain and place in blender with milk and cream. Chop few seconds until thoroughly mixed. Return to pot and over medium heat, add butter and cheese. When cheese is melted, sprinkle pepper over top of soup to taste. Mix in 1 1/2 capfuls (not cups) crab boil. Serve and enjoy.

Norman Barrios, West Bank
Council, Gretna, La.

CREAM OF CAULIFLOWER SOUP

1 large onion, chopped
1 small cauliflower,
    trimmed and roughly
    chopped
Salt and pepper
2 blades mace

Chopped parsley
1/4 c. butter
2 1/2 c. chicken stock
2 1/2 c. milk
1 bay leaf
1/4 pt. cream

Fry onion in butter until soft. Reserve a few flowerets of cauliflower for garnish. Add remaining cauliflower to onion and continue cooking gently for 5 minutes. Add stock and milk, bring to boil. Season. Add bay leaf and mace. Cover and simmer for 30-40 minutes until tender. Discard bay leaf and mace. Sieve or liquidise the soup and return to pot. Adjust seasoning and add cream. Reheat without boiling and add the reserved flowerets of cauliflower. Sprinkle with parsley and serve with Melba toast. Serves 6.
Ann Gubancsik, Capital
Council, Baton Rouge, La.

CELERY SOUP AND NOODLES

1 (8 oz.) pkg. wide
    noodles
1 can mushroom pieces
Butter

1 can celery soup
Salt and pepper to taste
Milk (optional)

Cook noodles, drain. Add other ingredients. Serves 2 or 3 or use as a side dish.
Marie Mallory, Capital
Council, Waterbury, Ct.

CHICKEN SOUP

Chicken pieces
2 qt. water
2 carrots, diced
2-3 sticks celery, diced
1 pkg. limas
1 pkg. corn
Cayenne pepper

Pepper
Parsley
1 (16 oz.) can tomatoes
Okra, to taste
1 small onion
1 small can tomato paste
2-3 potatoes, diced

1. Cook chicken parts in water. 2. Remove meat from bones. 3. Add vegetables and seasonings; macaroni may be added, if desired. 4. Simmer until done.
Calcasieu Council
Lake Charles, La.

CORN SOUP WITH SHRIMP

1 lb. peeled shrimp
1 can creamed corn
3 large potatoes, cubed
Salt and red pepper to
   taste
2 or 3 Tbsp. shortening

1 can whole kernel corn
1 can whole tomatoes
1 1/2 c. chopped onions
2 or 3 Tbsp. flour
Water

In large black iron skillet, make a roux with flour and oil. Add remaining ingredients with enough water to make the consistency of soup. Cook about 1 hour. Serve with hot garlic bread and tossed salad.

Paula Rutledge, LeBayou
Council, Houma, La.

SHE CRAB SOUP

1 leek, diced
8 ribs celery, diced
2 Tbsp. flour
Pinch of oregano
1 qt. fish stock
1/2 lb. crabmeat
1 tsp. Worcestershire
   sauce
2 egg yolks, beaten

1 onion, diced
1/4 lb. butter
1 tsp. tomato paste
1 qt. chicken broth
4 oz. crab roe
4 Tbsp. sherry
Salt and pepper to taste
1/2 pt. cream

Melt butter in saucepan, add vegetables and simmer until tender. Mix flour, tomato paste and oregano. Stir well, add to vegetables. Stir in chicken broth and fish stock. Boil 30 minutes, stirring occasionally. To this mixture, add crab roe, crabmeat, sherry, Worcestershire sauce, salt and pepper. Cook for 5 minutes only. Remove from heat. Add egg yolks and cream. Serve at once. Makes about 1 gallon.

This is a very old and secretive South Carolina recipe that originated in Charleston, S.C., a city much like that of the history of New Orleans. The recipe has never before been given out from the original family of the restaurant first making this dish. Over the years, other restaurants have come up with a good likeness of it, but not the original. Here is the original.

Peggy Childers
Crescent City Council
New Orleans, La.

OLD-FASHIONED DUCK SOUP

1 large or 2 small ducks,
  cut up
1 large carrot, sliced
1 clove garlic, minced
1/4 tsp. marjoram
1 c. cooked rice

10 c. water
1 large onion, sliced
2 stalks celery with leaves,
  diced
1 tsp. salt
1/4 tsp. thyme

Put duck in large saucepan or Dutch oven. Add water and cook 2 1/2 hours. Remove duck meat from bones and return meat to broth. Add onions, carrot, celery, garlic, salt, thyme and marjoram. Simmer 30 minutes, add rice and simmer 30 minutes more. Makes 6-8 servings.

W. A. Foreman, Ouachita
Council, Monroe, La.

EGG DROP SOUP

1 scallion or onion, cut
  in thin strips
3 c. chicken broth
3 c. water
1 tsp. dry sherry

1 Tbsp. vegetable oil
1 c. pork, cut in thin strips
2 Tbsp. soy sauce
2 eggs, slightly beaten
2 tsp. cornstarch, mixed
  with 2 Tbsp. water

Stir-fry scallion in hot oil until golden brown. Add pork and stir-fry until color changes. Add broth, water, soy sauce and sherry. Bring to a boil and remove from heat. Pour in eggs in steady stream, stirring constantly. Add cornstarch mixture and stir until the soup thickens.

Marilou Bridges, Caddo
Council, Shreveport, La.

FRENCH COUNTRY SOUP

2 lb. beef shanks
2 (8 oz.) cans tomato
  sauce
2 tsp. sugar
1/4 tsp. pepper
1 medium onion, chopped
1 wedge cabbage, 1-inch
  thick, chopped
  (optional)

1 (1 lb.) can cut green
  beans, drained
2 qt. water
2 beef bouillon cubes
1 tsp. salt
2 whole cloves
3 turnips or 1 small rutabaga, pared and diced
1 c. uncooked elbow macaroni

1723-79

In Dutch oven or kettle, combine beef, water, onion, tomato sauce, cabbage, bouillon cubes, sugar, salt, pepper and cloves. Bring to boil, simmer covered for 2 hours. Add turnips, macaroni and beans. Simmer uncovered for 20 or 30 minutes more or until tender. Yield: 6-8 servings.

Mrs. Walter R. Sundquist
Shreveport Works Council
Bossier City, La.

MINESTRONE
(Italian Soup)

2 lb. ground meat
1 1/2 c. chopped celery
1 c. shredded cabbage
1/2 c. chopped green
  pepper
1 bay leaf
1/2 tsp. thyme
4 tsp. salt

1 1/2 c. chopped onion
1 1/2 c. diced carrots
1 (16 oz.) can whole tomatoes
1 c. elbow or shell
  macaroni
1/4 tsp. dried oregano
1/8 tsp. pepper
1 1/2 qt. water

Brown meat, add vegetables and water. Bring to a boil. Add spices and pasta. Reduce heat and simmer for about 30 minutes or until vegetables are tender. Ladle soup into individual soup bowls and garnish with 1/4 cup grated Cheddar cheese per serving. Great with corn bread. Makes 6 servings.

Mona F. Reis, Metairie
Council, Metairie, La.

CREAM OF MUSHROOM SOUP

1 large onion, finely
  chopped
6 Tbsp. butter
1/2 c. flour
Salt and pepper
2 1/2 c. milk
2/3 c. single cream

1 clove garlic, crushed
3 c. button mushrooms
2 1/2 c. chicken stock
Pinch of ground mace
1 or 2 tsp. lemon juice
Fried onion rings to garnish

Fry onion and garlic in butter until soft. Roughly chop half the mushrooms, add to pan and fry gently until soft. Stir in flour, gradually add chicken stock and bring to the boil. Season well, add mace. Cover and simmer for 15-20 minutes. Sieve or liquidise the soup and return to pot. Finely chop remaining mushrooms and add to soup together

with milk. Bring back to boil, then simmer for 10 minutes.
Add lemon juice and cream. Reheat, but do not boil.
Garnish with crispy fried onion rings to serve.

Jackie Gubancsik, Capital
Council, Baton Rouge, La.

FRENCH ONION SOUP

1 lb. onions, thinly	5 Tbsp. butter
sliced	2 1/2 pt. beef stock
1 Tbsp. flour	2 bay leaves
Salt and black pepper	3/4 c. Cheddar cheese,
6 slices French bread	finely grated

Fry onions gently in melted butter until evenly browned
all over, stirring frequently to keep any pieces from burning. Stir in flour, gradually add the beef stock and bring
to boil. Season well and add bay leaves. Cover and simmer about 30 minutes. Remove bay leaves and adjust seasoning if desired. Lay slices of bread on a baking sheet,
cover with grated cheese. Allow cheese to just melt under
a warm grill or broiler. Ladle soup into bowls and serve
with the bread slices floating on top.

Ray Well, Capital Council,
Baton Rouge, La.

CREAM OF ONION SOUP

1/4 c. butter	3 c. onions, finely chopped
2 stalks celery, finely	3 3/4 c. chicken stock
chopped	1 bay leaf
1 blade mace	1/4 c. flour
Salt and pepper to taste	2/3 c. single or double
2/3 c. milk	cream
Fried croutons (garnish)	Chopped fresh mixed herbs
	(garnish)

Fry onions and celery for 5 minutes, without browning, in melted butter. Add chicken stock, mace, bay leaf
and seasoning. Bring to a boil, cover and simmer 45 minutes or until tender. Remove bay leaf and mace. The
soup can now be sieved or liquidised if a smooth soup is
preferred. Blend flour with milk and whisk gradually into
soup. Return to a boil, stirring constantly. Reduce heat
and simmer for 5 minutes. Adjust seasoning. Stir in

cream and reheat before serving. Dip the hot fried croutons into finely chopped mixed herbs and float them on top of soup.

Gekri Gubancsik, Capital
Council, Baton Rouge, La.

OYSTER SOUP

4 doz. oysters and liquid
2 Tbsp. butter
3 c. celery, chopped fine
6 green onions, chopped
   fine
2 c. scalded milk

1 Tbsp. oil
3 Tbsp. flour
1 Tbsp. minced parsley
6 c. boiling water
Black pepper

Heat oil and butter in heavy saucepan. Add flour, stir constantly over low heat until roux is rich brown. Add celery and onions, cook until brown, about 10 minutes. Add oysters and juice and cook slowly for another 10 minutes. Add boiling water slowly and cook for 30 minutes. Pour into scalded milk. Add black pepper and parsley. Serves 8.

John E. Haygood, Caddo
Council, Shreveport, La.

TURNIP SOUP

2 c. turnips, peeled
   and diced
1 Tbsp. butter
1 c. heavy cream

1 qt. beef or chicken stock
2 egg yolks
Salt and pepper

Cook turnips in stock until tender, drain, reserving liquid. Puree turnips in blender. Add stock, little at a time, until all is blended. Return to pot and heat, add butter. Beat egg yolks and cream together, add a little hot soup to egg mixture, then stir egg mixture into soup pot. Season to taste. Heat, but do not boil. Serves 6.

Etta Williams, Magnolia
Council, New Orleans, La.

TURTLE SOUP

1 medium size turtle
1 large onion, chopped
1 bay leaf
1 green pepper, cut up
3 Tbsp. flour
Salt and pepper to taste
1 or 2 hard boiled eggs,
   sliced

6 Tbsp. lard
2 stalks celery, cut up
1 sprig thyme
4 Tbsp. tomato paste
1 qt. hot water
1/2 c. wine
1/2 lemon, sliced

Cut turtle meat in small pieces. Fry in hot lard until brown. Add onion, celery, bay leaf, thyme, green pepper, tomato paste, salt, pepper and flour. Stir until all ingredients are mixed. Add hot water and simmer for 1 - 1 1/2 hours. Remove from fire, add wine. Serve with slices of egg and lemon in each bowl of soup.

John E. Haygood, Caddo
Council, Shreveport, La.

VEGETABLE BEEF SOUP

4-5 qt. water
2 onions, chopped
1 (10 oz.) pkg. frozen
   mixed vegetables
1 c. onion tops
1 can cream style corn
1 can butter beans
Cabbage (optional)
4 small cans tomato
   sauce
1 small can tomato
   paste

Any kind canned vegetables
   desired (optional)
2-3 lb. soup meat
4 large potatoes, chopped
   or diced
2 ribs celery, chopped
1 bell pepper, chopped
1 can lima beans
1 can green beans
2 or 3 tomatoes, chopped
1 large pkg. noodles
Salt and pepper to taste

Combine soup meat, water, tomato sauce and tomato paste. Let boil until meat is tender. Add remainder of ingredients, except noodles. When potatoes are almost tender, add noodles. Cook until tender. Makes 1 large pot of soup.

Mona Reis, Metairie
Council, Houma, La.

VEGETABLE-BURGER SOUP

1/2 lb. ground beef
1 (8 oz.) can tomato
  sauce
1 (10 oz.) pkg. mixed
  vegetables

1 tsp. sugar
1 (1 lb.) can stewed tomatoes
2 c. water
1/2 env. dry onion soup
  mix (1/4 c.)

In Dutch oven or large heavy saucepan, lightly brown ground beef, drain. Stir in remaining ingredients and bring to boil. Reduce heat, cover and simmer 20 minutes. Makes 6-8 servings.
Rebecca Scott, Caddo
Council, Shreveport, La.

BEEF STEW

2 lb. boneless stew or
  chuck, cut in 1-inch
  cubes
1 bay leaf
1 tsp. sugar
1/4 tsp. pepper
4 c. cold water
2-3 small whole onions
  (optional)

1 onion, sliced
1 clove garlic
1 Tbsp. salt
1/2 tsp. paprika
2 tsp. Worcestershire sauce
3-6 carrots, sliced in
  2-inch strips
6 small potatoes
Cooking oil

In large pot or Dutch oven, brown meat well on all sides in small amount of cooking oil. As meat browns, add onion, garlic, bay leaf and other seasonings. Add water. Cover pan and simmer for 1 1/2 hours, stirring occasionally. Remove bay leaf and garlic; discard. Add carrots, potatoes and whole onions. Cook at a little higher temperature for 30-45 minutes longer. Season stew with more salt and pepper if needed. Thicken stew with a flour and cold water mixture. I also add 1 teaspoon seasoned bottled beef extract to the mixture as it enriches and darkens the stew gravy. You can also use less potatoes and serve the cooked stew over rice.
Mrs. Joe Nasello, Central
Council, Alexandria, La.

DISTINCTIVE BEEF STEW

2 Tbsp. salad oil
1 tsp. black pepper
1/4 c. chopped onion
1 1/2 lb. stew meat
1 garlic
1 tsp. salt
1 c. meat broth

2 Tbsp. cornstarch
2 tsp. soy sauce
1/4 c. water
1 (10 oz.) pkg. frozen
  English peas
1 (4 oz.) jar pimento,
  drained and cut

Heat salad oil and pepper in large skillet. Add meat to skillet and brown on all sides, occasionally stirring. Add garlic, salt and meat broth, cover and cook about 1 1/2 hours or until meat is tender. Blend together cornstarch, soy sauce and water, add mixture to skillet, blend well. Add peas and pimento. Cook until thickens. Serve over fluffy rice.

Mrs. Virginia McCullough
Central Council
Alexandria, La.

SWEET-SOUR BEEF STEW

2 lb. chuck steak, cut
  in 1-inch cubes
1/2 c. catsup
1/4 c. brown sugar
1 tsp. salt
Celery, sliced (optional)

1/4 c. cooking oil
1 c. water
1/4 c. vinegar
1 Tbsp. Worcestershire
  sauce
1 large onion, sliced
1 can carrots, drained

Combine all ingredients, except meat and carrots. Simmer about 30 minutes. Brown meat and remove from skillet. Pour simmered sauce into pan drippings of skillet. Place meat in baking dish. Pour sauce over. Bake at 325° for about 30 minutes. Add carrots and bake about 20 minutes longer. Garnish with chopped parsley or sprigs, pimento or make a rice ring of 3 cups cooked rice.

Lois Leger, Evangeline
Council, Lafayette, La.

CRAB STEW

6-12 raw crabs, cleaned
4 cloves garlic, minced
1/2 c. cooking oil
1 bay leaf
1 Tbsp. cayenne pepper
1 c. rice
1/2 bunch parsley, chopped
4 stalks celery, finely chopped
2 large onions, finely chopped
3/4 c. plain flour
1 tsp. salt
8 c. water (about)

To clean crabs, remove shell, gills (dead men) and break in halves or quarters and wash clean. Remove all fat from body and shell and save for later. Heat oil to medium, add flour and make roux, stirring constantly until dark brown. Add onions, stirring constantly for 5 minutes or until onions become clear. Add celery and garlic, saute 1 minute. Add water, 1 cup at a time, stirring well until the consistency you want is reached. Add salt and pepper to taste. Drop in bay leaf. Add remainder of water and bring to boil. Reduce heat immediately. Cover and simmer for 20 minutes or until gravy thickens. Add crabs and simmer for about 15 minutes. Add crab fat and parsley and continue to simmer for 10-15 minutes, or until the crabs are fully cooked, and season gravy. The desired taste appears and matures during the last 10 minutes of cooking. Cook rice according to package directions. Serve stew over rice. Makes 6 servings. A happy rose, such as Tavel, goes beautifully with this stew. E. L. Menant, Crescent City Council, New Orleans, La.

CHUCK WAGON STEW

3 Tbsp. flour
1 - 1 1/2 lb. round steak, trimmed and cut into bite size pieces
1 clove garlic, minced
1 (5 3/4 oz.) can mushroom steak sauce
1/2 tsp. basil, crushed
1/4 tsp. celery salt
2-3 medium potatoes, pared and cubed
Cooking oil or fat
Salt and pepper
1 medium onion, sliced and separated into rings
1 (16 oz.) can tomatoes, cut up
1 Tbsp. Worcestershire sauce
1 tsp. salt
1/4 tsp. pepper
Several dashes of cayenne pepper
1 (10 oz.) pkg. mixed vegetables, frozen in butter sauce, or canned

Combine flour, salt and pepper. Coat meat, reserving
excess flour. Brown meat evenly in hot fat. Add onion and
garlic to meat. Blend reserved flour into tomatoes and their
liquid, stir into meat. Blend in steak sauce, Worcestershire sauce and seasonings. Bring to boil, reduce heat,
cover and simmer for 1 hour, stirring occasionally. Remove vegetables from pouch or can and add to meat mixture,
stir in potatoes. Cover and simmer 1 hour longer, stirring
occasionally. Makes 6 servings.

Dorothy Trent, Caddo
Council, Shreveport, La.

4 HOUR BEEF STEW

1 1/2 lb. cubed stew
  meat
2 onions, quartered
1 small can tomato sauce

4 or 5 carrots, in chunks
2 Tbsp. tapioca
Potatoes

Mix all ingredients, except potatoes, and place in casserole. Cover top with raw potatoes. Cover and bake at
250° for 4 hours.

Connie Younker
Shreveport Works Council
Shreveport, La.

GERMAN STEW

2 Tbsp. salad oil
1 clove garlic, crushed
8 1/2 c. beef broth or
  water
1/2 c. white vinegar
2 tsp. salt
1 1/2 lb. potatoes, peeled
  and cut in large chunks
  (4 c.)

1 c. sliced onion
3 lb. stewing beef, cut in
  1-inch cubes
1 Tbsp. sugar
1 bay leaf
2 c. sliced carrots
1 tsp. dill weed, crushed
1/4 c. water
1 Tbsp. flour

Heat oil in large saucepan. Add onion and garlic, saute
until tender, about 5 minutes. Remove with slotted spoon.
Add beef, saute until browned on all sides. Return onion
to pot. Stir in broth, vinegar, sugar, salt and bay leaf.
Bring to a boil. Reduce heat and simmer covered about
1 1/2 hours until tender. Add potatoes, carrots and dill.
Simmer covered until meat and vegetables are tender, about
20 minutes. Refrigerate overnight. Remove layer of fat.

Simmer, stirring frequently, until heated through. Mix flour and 1/4 cup water. Stir in stew, mix well. Cook and stir about 2 minutes until thickened. Yield: 12 cups.

Ann Orr, Evangeline
Council, New Iberia, La.

LAZY MAN'S STEW

(The meat browns nicely, and the gravy thickens. Wonderful flavor!)

2 lb. chuck stew meat
1 (1 1/2 oz.) pkg. de-
   hydrated onion soup

1 can mushroom soup, un-
   diluted
1 (8 oz.) can sliced mushrooms with juice

Mix all together and put in 4-quart casserole. Cover. Bake 3 hours at 325°. Serve over noodles or fluffy white rice. Yield: 6-8 servings.

Calcasieu Council
Lake Charles, La.

OYSTER STEW

1 pt. oysters
3 Tbsp. margarine or
   butter

1 qt. milk, scalded
Salt and pepper
Paprika

Cover oysters with water. Simmer until the edges curl. Skim all foam off the top. Pour into the scalding (not boiling) milk. Add margarine. Season to taste. Serve with a dash of paprika.

Calcasieu Council
Lake Charles, La.

NO PEEK STEW

2 lb. lean stew meat
1 pkg. onion soup mix

2 cans mushroom soup
1 large bottle ginger ale

Combine all ingredients in covered pan and place in 350° oven for 3 1/2 hours. Do not add any other seasonings and do not open pan while cooking. Recipe can be doubled.

Calcasieu Council
Lake Charles, La.

NO WORK STEW

1 lb. stew meat, bite size
  pieces
1 can mushroom soup
1 can mushrooms
1 tsp. garlic salt
1 pkg. frozen stew vegetables
1/2 tsp. pepper

1 can onion soup
1 can whole tomatoes,
  drained
1 tsp. salt
1 Tbsp. Worcestershire
  sauce

Combine all ingredients. Bake uncovered at 350° for 2 hours.

Mary C. Regan
Crescent City Council
New Orleans, La.

QUICK STEW

1 c. chopped onion
1/4 c. chopped bell
  pepper
1 tsp. Tabasco sauce
2 cans vegetable soup

1 lb. ground meat
1/4 c. chopped celery
Salt to taste
2 soup cans water

Smother or saute meat and vegetables. Add seasonings, soup and water. It's very simple, but good.

Paula Rutledge, LeBayou
Council, Houma, La.

SHRIMP STEW

1 c. flour
1 lb. shelled and
  cleaned shrimp
3 c. hot water
Salt to taste
Red pepper or Tabasco
  sauce to taste

1 c. cooking oil
1 c. chopped onion
1/2 c. bell pepper, chopped
  fine
1/2 c. shallots, chopped fine
1 tsp. garlic powder or
  1 clove minced garlic

Make roux of flour and oil. Brown in iron skillet. Add onion, bell pepper and shallots. Add hot water and simmer on low heat. Add remaining ingredients and cook on low heat until done.

Paula Rutledge, LeBayou
Council, Houma, La.

SPICY APPLE SALAD

2 small pkg. lemon jello
1 can applesauce
1/2 c. red cinnamon
  candies

1 small pkg. cream cheese,
  softened
3 Tbsp. canned milk
2 Tbsp. lemon juice

Place candies in 2 cups water, boil until candies melt. Dissolve jello in boiling water. Add applesauce and lemon juice and 1 cup cold water. Chill until set. Mix cream cheese and milk. Spread on top of jello. Cut into squares. Serves 8-10.
Calcasieu Council
Lake Charles, La.

APPLESAUCE SALAD

1 small pkg. red jello,
  any flavor
2 Tbsp. red hot candies
1 1/2 tsp. lemon flavoring

1 c. boiling water
1 env. Knox gelatine
1 (No. 2) can applesauce

Drop red hots in boiling water and simmer until dissolved. Pour over jello and dissolve. Dissolve Knox gelatine in small amount of cold water and add to jello mixture. Stir in applesauce and lemon extract. Cover and congeal in refrigerator. Serve in squares on lettuce leaf topped with mayonnaise. Very good with ham or turkey in place of cranberry sauce.
Calcasieu Council
Lake Charles, La.

APRICOT DELIGHT SALAD

2 pkg. (3 oz. size)
  apricot jello
2/3 c. water
1 (20 oz.) can crushed
  pineapple, undrained
1 1/2 c. chopped nuts

2/3 c. sugar
2 jars apricot baby food
1 (14 oz.) can condensed
  milk, chilled
1 (8 oz.) pkg. cream
  cheese

Combine jello, sugar and water, bring to a boil and dissolve jello. Remove from heat, stir in fruit; set aside to cool. Combine milk and cream cheese, beat until smooth. Stir in jello mixture, add nuts. Pour into mold or bowl and refrigerate.
Sandra K. Autrey, Metairie
Council, Metairie, La.

ARTICHOKE RICE SALAD

1 (8 oz.) pkg. chicken
   Rice-A-Roni
12 small, stuffed olives,
   sliced, or use black
   olives

1/2 green pepper, chopped
   fine
4 green onions, chopped fine
2 jars (6 oz. size) marinated
   artichokes, including oil

Cook the Rice-A-Roni as directed on package. Add remaining ingredients and toss. May be eaten hot as a vegetable, or chilled and served as a salad. Serves 8.

Ann Orr, Evangeline
Council, New Iberia, La.

BEAN SALAD

1 can whole grain corn,
   drained
1 jar pimentos, drained
   and chopped
1 large onion, chopped
1/4 c. vinegar
Salt and pepper to taste

1 can green beans, drained
1 can Ranch Style beans,
   drained
1 large bell pepper, chopped
1/2 c. sugar
1/4 c. oil

Mix ingredients together and refrigerate at least 24 hours before serving.

Lois S. Leger, Evangeline
Council, Lafayette, La.

FROSTED GREEN BEAN SALAD

2 cans whole small green
   beans, drained
Salt and pepper to taste
2 cooked bacon slices,
   crumbled
2 tsp. prepared mustard

3/4 c. salad oil
6 Tbsp. vinegar
2 medium onions, minced
6 Tbsp. mayonnaise
8 hard boiled eggs,
   chopped

Mix together beans, salad oil, vinegar, onions, salt and pepper. Marinate in refrigerator several hours. Just before serving, add remainder of ingredients. Toss gently. Makes 8 servings.

June E. Nickels
Shreveport Works Council
Shreveport, La.

THREE BEAN SALAD

1 (303) can green beans (cut or whole)
1 (303) can yellow wax beans
1 (303) can red kidney beans, drained and washed

1/2 c. chopped green sweet pepper
1/2 c. chopped onions (red or white)
1/2 c. Wesson oil
1/2 c. vinegar (salad or wine)
3/4 c. sugar

Mix all liquids, add sugar; mix well. Add onions, pepper, then add all beans. Mix in big bowl. Cover airtight. Let set 24 hours, then drain and serve.

Gayle Wilkening
Shreveport Works Council
Longview, Tx.

THREE BEAN SALAD

1 (16 oz.) can cut green beans
1 (16 oz.) can cut yellow wax beans
1 (16 oz.) can red kidney beans

1/4 c. chopped green pepper
1 medium onion, sliced thin
1/2 c. vinegar
1/3 c. cooking oil
1/2 c. sugar
1 tsp. salt
1 tsp. pepper

Drain beans, rinse well and drain again. Add green pepper and sliced onion to beans. Mix other ingredients and add to bean mixture. Mix well and let set overnight in refrigerator.

Calcasieu Council
Lake Charles, La.

3 BEAN SALAD

2 cans French style green beans
1 can LeSueur English peas
1 green pepper, chopped

1 small can chopped pimentos
1 can baby lima beans
1 medium chopped onion
2-3 stalks chopped celery

Drain beans and peas, mix together. Add remaining ingredients and toss.

Sauce:

1 c. vinegar   1 c. sugar
1/2 c. salad oil

Heat vinegar and sugar until dissolved, add oil and mix. Cool, pour over salad. Marinate 24 hours in refrigerator.
                                Emma Lee Wallace, LeBayou
                                Council, DeRidder, La.

FOUR-BEAN SALAD

1 can green beans,   1 can wax beans, drained
  drained and rinsed   and rinsed
1 can kidney beans,   1 can lima beans, drained
  drained and rinsed   and rinsed
1 medium size bell pepper,   1 medium onion, thinly
  thinly sliced   sliced and separated into
3/4 c. sugar   rings
1/2 c. salad oil   1/2 c. vinegar
1/2 tsp. pepper   1/2 tsp. salt
                              1 Tbsp. minced parsley

Combine all beans, pepper and onion. Toss gently. Combine remaining ingredients; heat, stirring constantly, until sugar dissolves. Pour hot mixture over vegetables, cover and chill several hours. Yield: 12 servings.
                                Calcasieu Council
                                Lake Charles, La.

BLUEBERRY SALAD

1 large can blueberries   1 large can pineapple tidbits
2 (3 oz.) pkg. raspberry   1/2 c. chopped nuts
  jello   Cool Whip
2 c. boiling water

Dissolve jello in boiling water. Add pineapple, nuts and blueberries. Refrigerate. When jelled, top with Cool Whip.
                                Una Mize, Caddo Council
                                Shreveport, La.

BLUEBERRY SALAD

2 small pkg. blackberry
  jello
1 (15 oz.) can drained
  blueberries
1 (8 oz.) can drained,
  crushed pineapple

1 (8 oz.) pkg. cream cheese
2 c. boiling water
1/2 c. sugar
1/2 pt. sour cream
1/2 tsp. vanilla
1/2 c. chopped pecans

Dissolve jello in boiling water. Drain blueberries and pineapple. Reserve liquid. Add enough water to liquid to measure 1 cup. Add to jello. Stir in blueberries and pineapple. Pour into 2-quart flat pan and refrigerate until set. Combine other ingredients, except pecans. Spread over jello layer, sprinkle pecans on top. Very sweet and rich. May also be used as dessert.   Susan Austin, Ouachita Council, Monroe, La.

BLUEBERRY SALAD

1 (6 oz.) pkg. black
  cherry jello
1 5/8 c. hot water

1 (13 oz.) can crushed pineapple
1 (16 oz.) can whole blueberries

Mix ingredients together and pour in large sheet pan; let congeal.

Topping:

1 (8 oz.) pkg. cream
  cheese
1/2 c. sugar

1 carton sour cream
3/4 c. chopped nuts

Combine and mix ingredients until fluffy. Spread over jello and let stand several hours until chilled.
Elsie Young, Ouachita
Council, Monroe, La.

BROCCOLI SALAD

2 pkg. (10 oz. size)
  frozen, chopped
  broccoli
1 small pkg. cream cheese
2 Tbsp. lemon juice
1 tsp. pepper
3 Tbsp. Worcestershire
  sauce

2 env. unflavored gelatin
1 c. mayonnaise
1 c. beef consomme
1 1/2 tsp. salt
4 hard boiled eggs, cut
  in small pieces
1 tsp. Tabasco sauce
1 can pimientos

Cook broccoli according to package directions, drain. Mix cream cheese and mayonnaise. Dissolve gelatin in lemon juice. Heat consomme, add gelatin mixture, cool. Mix egg pieces with broccoli, add to consomme. Mix in remaining ingredients. Chill in oiled ring mold. Serves 8.

Mona F. Reis, Metairie
Council, Metairie, La.

CARROT SALAD

3 carrots
2 bell peppers
1 can tomato soup
1 tsp. salt
3/4 c. vinegar
1 tsp. pepper

1 c. mushrooms
2 onions
2/3 c. sugar or Sweet 'N
  Low to taste
1/2 c. oil
1 tsp. dry mustard

Slice and boil carrots until cooked but crisp; drain. Slice mushrooms; drain. Slice onion and bell peppers thin. Combine soup, vinegar, sugar, oil, salt, pepper and mustard; heat. Arrange carrots, mushrooms, onion and bell pepper in bowl. Pour soup mix over vegetables. Chill overnight.

Cecile Gallet, Evangeline
Council, Lafayette, La.

CARROT SALAD

1 c. shredded carrots
1/2 c. chopped celery
1/2 c. chopped apples

1/3 c. seedless raisins
1/4 tsp. salt
1/4 c. mayonnaise

Combine carrots, apples, raisins and mix well. Add the salt and mayonnaise. Chill and serve on a nest of lettuce.

Calcasieu Council
Lake Charles, La.

CARROT SALAD

2 lb. carrots
1 c. chopped shallots
1/4 c. chopped sour
  pickle
3 Tbsp. creole mustard
2 tsp. salt

2 c. chopped celery
1 large chopped bell pepper
Juice of 1 lemon
1/2 c. mayonnaise
1 Tbsp. parsley

Scrape and boil carrots until done, but still firm. Cut up and dice small. Add remaining ingredients. Chill. Make day before for better flavor. Very good substitute for potato salad.
Althea Brossett, Capital
Council, Baton Rouge, La.

CARROT SALAD

2 lb. carrots
1 c. chopped shallots
1/4 c. sour pickle,
  chopped fine
3 Tbsp. creole mustard
2 tsp. salt

2 c. chopped celery
1 large bell pepper, chopped
  fine
Juice of 1 lemon
1/2 c. mayonnaise
1 Tbsp. chopped parsley

Boil carrots until done, but still firm. Peel and cut up when cool enough to handle. I dice my carrots very small. Add remaining ingredients and chill. Serve on lettuce leaf if desired. Sort of potato salad without eggs or mayonnaise. Make early in day before serving or better, day before.
Althea Rome Brossett, Capital
Council, Baton Rouge, La.

COPPER PENNY CARROT SALAD

2 cans sliced carrots
1 sliced bell pepper
1 can tomato soup
1/2 c. sugar
1 tsp. prepared mustard

1 onion, sliced in rings
1 clove garlic, chopped
1/2 c. salad oil
2/3 c. vinegar
Salt and pepper to taste

Drain carrots, pour into large bowl. Add onions and bell pepper into bowl. Combine remaining ingredients, bring to boil. Pour over carrot mixture, mix well and refrigerate. The longer it marinates, the better it is.
Ruth Soileau, Evangeline
Council, Opelousas, La.

CAULIFLOWER SALAD

1 large head cauliflower
3/4 c. Parmesan cheese
1 large onion, sliced and
  chopped
1 head lettuce, broken

9-10 crisp bacon strips,
  crumbled
1/2 c. sugar
1 - 1 1/2 c. mayonnaise

In large bowl, layer in order - cauliflower, bacon, cheese, onion, sugar, lettuce and mayonnaise. Marinate in refrigerator overnight. Toss before serving.

Jesse O. Jackson
Shreveport Works Council
Shreveport, La.

CHEESE SALAD

2 pimentos, chopped fine
3/4 c. seedless raisins
Mayonnaise to moisten

3 c. grated Cheddar cheese
3/4 c. celery, chopped fine

Combine pimentos, raisins, celery and cheese. Add enough mayonnaise to moisten.

Marie Pamplin
Shreveport Works Council
Shreveport, La.

CHEF'S SALAD

4 c. torn salad greens
1/4 lb. each cooked ham,
  chicken or turkey
Pitted black olives

1/4 lb. Swiss cheese, cut up
1 tomato, cut in wedges
4 hard boiled eggs, quartered

Place greens in large bowl. Arrange cheese, ham and chicken on top. Garnish with tomato wedges, eggs and olives. Serve with French Dressing or Sour Cream Dressing. Makes 4 servings.

French Dressing:

1 tsp. salt
1 clove garlic, minced
1/4 c. tarragon vinegar
1/4 tsp. pepper sauce

1/8 tsp. dried leaf tarragon
1 1/4 c. salad oil
2 Tbsp. lemon juice

Mix ingredients together. Yield: 1 1/2 cups.

1723-79

Sour Cream Dressing:

1 c. sour cream
1 Tbsp. vinegar
1/2 tsp. sugar
1/4 tsp. celery salt

2 Tbsp. lemon juice
1/2 tsp. salt
2 Tbsp. ketchup
1/4 tsp. pepper sauce

Combine ingredients and keep refrigerated.

Patricia R. Caraway, Capital
Council, Baton Rouge, La.

CHERRY SALAD

1 (16 oz.) can crushed
pineapple, drained
1 (9 oz.) bowl frozen
whipped topping

1 (15 oz.) can condensed
milk
1 (16 oz.) can cherry pie
filling
1 c. chopped pecans

Combine ingredients in salad bowl. Chill until firm.
Good either as salad or dessert.

Para Lee Nugent Cline (Billy
and Harold Nugent's Mom)
Central Council
Dry Prong, La.

CHERRY SALAD SUPREME

1 (3 oz.) pkg. raspberry
jello
1 (3 oz.) pkg. lemon jello
1/3 c. mayonnaise
1 c. miniature marsh-
mallows
2 c. boiling water

1 (21 oz.) can cherry pie
filling
1 (3 oz.) pkg. cream cheese
1 (8 oz.) can crushed pineapple
1/4 c. finely chopped nuts
1/2 c. whipping cream, or
1 c. Dream Whip

Dissolve raspberry jello in 1 cup boiling water. Stir in
pie filling. Turn into 9x9x2-inch oiled baking dish. Chill
until partially set. Dissolve lemon jello in 1 cup boiling
water. Beat together cream cheese and mayonnaise, gradually add lemon jello. Stir in undrained pineapple. Whip the
whipping cream or use prepared cup of Dream Whip. Fold
into lemon mixture with marshmallows. Spread atop cherry
layer. Sprinkle nuts over top. Chill until set. Cut into
squares to serve.

Tracey Delposen, Ouachita
Council, Monroe, La.

CHICKEN SALAD

4 c. cooked chicken, diced	4 hard boiled eggs, diced
2 Tbsp. lemon juice	2 c. diced celery
1/2 c. mayonnaise	1/2 c. sour cream
	1 1/2 tsp. curry powder

Mix all ingredients together and serve on lettuce leaves.

Mrs. Walter (Ella) Payton
Caddo Council
Shreveport, La.

CHICKEN SALAD

1 chicken	4 ribs celery
6 eggs, hard cooked	Garlic powder
Salt and pepper	Mayonnaise

Boil or bake chicken. Take meat from bones and mince finely. Chop eggs and celery. Combine all ingredients. Sprinkle with garlic powder, salt and pepper. Add mayonnaise to taste and mix and chill.

Ham Salad: Same as above, substituting 3 cans of Underwood deviled ham for chicken.

Shrimp Salad: Same as above, substituting 2 pounds cleaned boiled shrimp.

Tuna Salad: Same as above, substituting 2 cans tuna, water packed or oil.

June Harllee, Caddo
Council, Shreveport, La.

CHICKEN SALAD

1 Tbsp. lemon juice	2 c. diced apples
4 c. finely chopped cooked chicken	1 1/2 c. finely chopped celery
3/4 c. salad dressing	1 c. green grapes, halved
1/4 tsp. pepper	1/2 tsp. salt

Sprinkle lemon juice over apples. Add remaining ingredients, mix lightly. Press mixture into 1 1/2-quart bowl. Chill several hours. Unmold on serving platter. Frost (recipe follows) and garnish as desired.

Frosting:

1 (8 oz.) pkg. cream
  cheese

1/4 c. salad dressing

Combine softened cheese and salad dressing, mixing until well blended.

Mrs. Albert D. Well, Capital Council, Waterbury, Ct.

CHICKEN SALAD

2 chicken breasts
2 thighs
2 wings
1 Tbsp. chopped onion
1 grated boiled egg
Black pepper to taste

Salt, pepper, garlic and
  onion salt
1 Tbsp. sweet pickle relish
1 Tbsp. pimento
1 small chopped dill pickle
Juice of 1/2 lemon
Salad dressing to taste

Boil chicken pieces with salt, pepper, garlic and onion salt until tender. Remove from broth, skin and chop very fine. Add remaining ingredients and mix well.

Jeanette English, Caddo Council, Shreveport, La.

CHICKEN SALAD

3 c. cold chicken
1 1/2 c. diced celery
1 tsp. salt

3 hard boiled eggs
3 sweet pickles, chopped
Mayonnaise

Combine chicken, celery, salt, eggs and pickles. Blend with mayonnaise. Serve on lettuce with slices of egg and olives. Serves 8.

Calcasieu Council
Lake Charles, La.

CHRISTMAS SALAD

1 pkg. lime jello
2 c. pineapple juice
1 (3 oz.) pkg. cream
  cheese
1 c. chopped pecans

1 c. boiling water
12 large marshmallows
1 1/2 Tbsp. salad dressing
1 pkg. lemon jello

Prepare lime jello with boiling water and 1 cup pineapple juice. Pour into square Pyrex dish, 10x10 inches. Refrigerate 3-4 hours until firm. Combine lemon jello, remaining cup of pineapple juice and marshmallows. Heat until melted and dissolved, cool. Add remaining ingredients, mix well. Pour over lime jello and refrigerate.

Cecile Gallet, Evangeline
Council, Lafayette, La.

COKE SALAD

1 can black cherries
1 small can crushed
  pineapple, drained

1 (3 oz.) pkg. cherry jello
1 small (6 oz.) bottle Coke
1/2 c. chopped pecans

Drain cherries. Heat cherry juice and dissolve jello in hot juice. Cool. Add other ingredients and refrigerate.

Delores Bridges
Shreveport Works Council
Shreveport, La.

CONGEALED SALAD

20 marshmallows
1 c. grated Cheddar
  cheese
1/2 pt. whipping cream,
  or Cool Whip
2 c. boiling water

1 pkg. lime jello
1 small can crushed pineapple, drained
1 c. chopped pecans
1 small bottle maraschino
  cherries

Melt marshmallows in water. Add lime jello. Set to soft congeal. Fold in whipped cream or Cool Whip and remainder of ingredients and congeal.

Annie Hawkins, Caddo
Council, Shreveport, La.

COOL SALAD

1 small carton cottage
  cheese, not creamed
1 large can crushed pineapple, drained

1 bowl Cool Whip (largest)
1 c. chopped nuts
1 pkg. lime jello

Mix Cool Whip, cottage cheese, pineapple and nuts together. Sprinkle dry jello over mixture. Toss and refrigerate. Can be served immediately. Strawberries and strawberry jello can be used in place of pineapple and lime jello. Both are good and very colorful, especially at Christmas. Also low calorie. Maxine Fletcher, Ouachita Council, Monroe, La.

CORN SALAD

1 can kernel corn, drained
1 small jar pimentos
1 c. sour cream

1 chopped onion
1 Tbsp. lemon juice

Mix all ingredients together. Refrigerate until ready to serve. Mary Ahrens, Caddo Council, Shreveport, La.

SHOE PEG CORN SALAD

5 stalks celery
1/2 green pepper
1 can shoe peg corn,
   drained
1 tsp. dry mustard
1/4 tsp. horseradish

1 small onion
2 Tbsp. pimento
1/3 c. salad oil
2 Tbsp. vinegar
1 tsp. sugar
White pepper to taste

Chop celery, pepper, onion and pimento. Add corn. Mix remainder of ingredients in separate bowl and beat with fork until fluffy. Pour over corn mixture. Refrigerate at least 1/2 day or better still, let marinate 48 hours.
Althea Brossett, Capital Council, Baton Rouge, La.

COTTAGE CHEESE SALAD

1 (12 oz.) carton small
   curd cottage cheese
1 (11 oz.) can Mandarin
   oranges, drained
1/2 c. chopped nuts

1 (4 1/2 oz.) bowl Cool Whip
1 (20 oz.) can crushed pineapple, drained
1 (3 oz.) pkg. orange jello

Combine cottage cheese and Cool Whip, blend gently. Add fruit and nuts. Add dry jello and mix well. Chill. Serves 6-8. Maxine Bridges, Caddo Council, Shreveport, La.

COTTAGE CHEESE SALAD

1 (6 oz.) pkg. lime jello
5 c. miniature marsh-
  mallows
1 c. chopped pecans
10-12 maraschino
  cherries

2 c. boiling water
1 (15 oz.) can crushed pineapple, drained
1 c. whipping cream,
  whipped
1 (12 oz.) carton small curd
  cottage cheese

Dissolve gelatin in boiling water, add marshmallows, stirring until melted. Stir in pineapple. Chill until thick, but not firm. Add cherries, pecans and cottage cheese, fold in whipped cream. Pour into oiled mold and chill until firm. Makes 8-10 servings.   Mrs. Johnnie B. Cole, Caddo
Council, Shreveport, La.

CRANBERRY SALAD

2 boxes cherry jello
2 c. raw cranberries
1 orange with peel
1 orange without peel

2 medium sized apples
2 c. sugar
1 c. chopped nuts

Fix jello by directions on box. Grind cranberries, apples and oranges. Add sugar and nuts, mix with jello after it congeals.   Calcasieu Council
Lake Charles, La.

CRANBERRY SALAD

1 lb. cranberries, ground
Juice of 2 oranges +
  grated rind
1 1/2 c. miniature marsh-
  mallows

1 qt. pecans, or less
1/2 c. sugar
1 small box strawberry or
  cherry jello

Use orange juice for second cup of water for jello. Combine ingredients and refrigerate.
Gayle Cummings, Caddo
Council, Shreveport, La.

CRANBERRY SALAD

1 lb. pkg. cranberries
1 lb. pkg. small marsh-
   mallows

2 small cans crushed pineapple
1 1/2 c. sugar
1/2 pt. whipping cream

Grind raw cranberries. Add crushed pineapple, sugar, marshmallows and fold in whipped cream. Chill. This salad freezes well. Patricia McManemin, Calcasieu Council, Lake Charles, La.

CRANBERRY SALAD

1 pkg. cranberries
2 oranges and rind
1 1/2 c. hot water

1 1/2 c. sugar
1 (3 oz.) pkg. strawberry or
   raspberry jello

Dissolve jello in water. Peel and cut up oranges. Put through grinder along with cranberries. Add to jello, mix well and refrigerate until set. Katherine Slover, Caddo Council, Phoenix, Az.

CRANBERRY SALAD

1 pt. cranberries
1 apple, unpeeled
1/2 c. chopped nuts

1 c. sugar
1 grated apple, unpeeled
1/4 c. whipped cream

Grind together cranberries, sugar and 1 apple. Refrigerate overnight. Next day, add nuts, whipped cream and 1 grated apple. Mix well. Chill and serve.
Una Mize, Caddo Council
Shreveport, La.

CRANBERRY SALAD

1/2 lb. cranberries
1 c. chopped pecans
1 pkg. cherry jello
1 1/3 c. hot water

1 c. sugar
1 pkg. small marshmallows
Juice and pulp of 1 orange

Put cranberries through coarse food chopper. Dissolve jello in hot water and cool. Add all ingredients together. Pour into mold or bowl and chill. Gay Irwin, Capital Council Baton Rouge, La.

CREAMY CRANBERRY SALAD

1 (8 oz.) can crushed
  pineapple
1/3 c. mayonnaise
2 Tbsp. sugar
1 small can Pet milk

1 (3 oz.) pkg. strawberry
  jello
1/4 tsp. salt
2 Tbsp. vinegar
1 (16 oz.) can whole cranberry sauce

Drain juice from pineapple into measuring cup, add enough water to make 3/4 cup liquid. Heat to boiling and dissolve jello; cool slightly. Combine mayonnaise, salt and vinegar, add to cooled gelatin, stir until smooth. Mix milk, pineapple and cranberry sauce, add to mixture. Pour into oiled 5-cup mold. Chill until firm. Turn on lettuce leaf to serve. Makes 8 servings.   Frances Kennedy, Caddo
                                    Council, Shreveport, La.

CRAWFISH SALAD

1 c. mayonnaise
1/4 c. French dressing
1/4 c. chili sauce
1 tsp. horseradish
1/2 tsp. salt
2 Tbsp. dill pickles,
  chopped

1 c. celery, chopped
1 tsp. Worcestershire sauce
1/2 tsp. Tabasco sauce
3 hard boiled eggs, chopped
1 lb. crawfish tails, boiled
  and cleaned
1 head lettuce

Combine mayonnaise, French dressing, chili sauce, salt, celery, dill pickle, horseradish, Worcestershire sauce, Tabasco sauce. Add eggs and crawfish, mix well. Serve on lettuce.   Eugene Cottrell, Caddo
                                    Council, Shreveport, La.

DATE-AT-THE-WALDORF SALAD

3 c. cubed, unpeeled
  apples
1/4 c. chopped dates
1 c. chopped celery
Salad dressing

2 Tbsp. orange juice
1 tsp. orange rind
1/4 c. chopped walnuts
1 c. miniature marshmallows
Lettuce

Sprinkle orange juice over apples. Add orange rind, dates, nuts, celery, marshmallows and enough salad dressing to moisten. Toss lightly. Serve in lettuce lined bowls.

Garnish with apple slices, if desired, with a cap of salad dressing on top. Serves 6. Katherine Slover, Caddo Council, Phoenix, Az.

DIET SALAD

1 small bowl Cool Whip
1 small can fruit cocktail,
  drained

1 small carton low fat Lite
  Line cottage cheese
1 small pkg. jello, any flavor

Combine and mix ingredients. Refrigerate 1 hour before serving. Emerite L. Hebert, Evangeline Council, Scott, La.

DUM-DUM SALAD

1 large can crushed pine-
  apple, drained
1 can condensed milk

1 can prepared pie filling
  (your choice)
1 medium bowl Cool Whip

Mix all ingredients together and chill.
Yvonne M. Leslie
Crescent City Council
New Orleans, La.

DUMP SALAD

2 small boxes orange jello
2 c. boiling water
1 (No. 2) can crushed
  pineapple, undrained

1 small can frozen orange
  juice
1 can Mandarin oranges,
  undrained

Dissolve jello in boiling water. Pour into flat Pyrex or aluminum pan. Add pineapple, oranges and undiluted orange juice. Stir well and chill until set.
Jean Coon, Caddo Council
Shreveport, La.

FRUIT SALAD

1 can Mandarin oranges
1 large can drained pine-
   apple tidbits
1 c. miniature marsh-
   mallows

1 c. seedless grapes
1 c. flaked coconut
1 c. sour cream
Nuts and cherries, if
   desired

Combine and mix all ingredients together. Chill over-
night.
Gay Irwin, Capital Council,
Baton Rouge, La.

FRUIT SALAD

1 can chunk pineapple
1 pkg. strawberries
1 can peach pie filling

2 cans Mandarin oranges
3 bananas, sliced

Drain pineapple and oranges. Combine with remainder
of ingredients.
Lucille Smith, Ouachita
Council, Monroe, La.

FRUIT SALAD

1 apple
1 orange
1/2 c. grapes
1/2 c. raisins
2 Tbsp. flour
1/2 c. sugar

1/2 c. coconut
2 doz. small marshmallows
1/3 c. chopped pecans
2 bananas, sliced
1 egg
Juice of 1 lemon

Cut apple, orange and grapes into small pieces. Combine with raisins, coconut, marshmallows, pecans and
bananas in large bowl. Make a sauce of flour, sugar, egg
and lemon juice. Cook until thick and pour over salad.
Dorothy Trent, Caddo
Council, Shreveport, La.

FRUIT SALAD

1 can sliced peaches,
   drained
1 can crushed pine-
   apple, undrained
2 bananas, sliced

1 can pears, sliced and
   drained
1/2 c. maraschino cherries
1 pkg. lemon instant pudding
   mix (dry)

1723-79

Combine fruit. Sprinkle the dry instant pudding mix over the fruit. Mix well. Mrs. Johnnie B. Cole, Caddo Council, Shreveport, La.

GLAZED FRUIT SALAD

1 (1 lb. 4 oz.) can pine-
  apple chunks
1 (1 lb. 14 oz.) can fruit
  cocktail
7 or 8 bananas, sliced

2 cans (11 oz. each) Mandarin
  oranges
2 Tbsp. lemon juice
1 (1 lb. 6 oz.) can peach
  pie filling

Drain all canned fruit and combine in large bowl. Add remaining ingredients, mix gently. Cover and chill several hours or overnight. Makes 12 servings.
Maxine Botzong, Central Council, Tioga, La.

MOLDED FRUIT SALAD

1 can fruit salad
Scant dash of salt
1/2 pt. whipping cream

1 pkg. lime jello
1 pkg. cream cheese

Boil fruit salad with salt. Dissolve jello in hot fruit salad. Let mixture begin to set. Mash cream cheese and enough of the whipped cream to make smooth. Fold cream cheese and remainder of whipped cream into gelatin mixture. Mold and congeal. Linda Bagur, Caddo Council, Shreveport, La.

QUICK FRUIT SALAD

1 large can peach pie
  filling
1 can Mandarin oranges,
  drained

1 large can crushed pineapple
1 (10 oz.) pkg. frozen
  strawberries
3 or 4 large bananas
1 c. chopped pecans

Mix all ingredients and chill. Ready to serve in 1 hour. You can use apple pie filling for a change, if desired.
Elsie C. Young, Ouachita Council, Monroe, La.

QUICK FRUIT SALAD

1 (6 oz.) box jello,
  any flavor
1 lb. carton small curd
  cottage cheese

1 (9 oz.) bowl thawed Cool
  Whip
1 small can crushed pine-
  apple, well drained

Mix all ingredients together and serve.

Gayle Wilkening
Shreveport Works Council
Longview, Tx.

STRAWBERRY FRUIT SALAD

1 large box strawberry
  jello
2 small cans crushed
  pineapple, drained
2 medium bananas,
  mashed

1 c. boiling water
1 large box frozen straw-
  berries
1 c. broken walnuts
1 c. sour cream

Dissolve jello in water, add strawberries, add pine-apple and bananas, add nuts and mix. Pour 1/2 of mixture into a long glass Pyrex dish. Refrigerate to set. Spread sour cream on top when set, pour remaining jello (which is at room temperature) over sour cream. Refrigerate until set. Very colorful dish for holidays.

Peggy Childers
Crescent City Council
New Orleans, La.

FRUIT SALAD SAUCE

2 eggs, well beaten
1 (6 1/2 oz.) pkg. minia-
  ture marshmallows

1/4 c. vinegar
1/2 c. sugar
1 can chunk pineapple,
  drained

Cook sugar, eggs and vinegar until thick. Pour over pineapple and marshmallows. Chill overnight in refrigerator. Add fruits (apples, oranges, bananas, etc.) and whipping cream just before serving.

Una Mize, Caddo Council,
Shreveport, La.

HAWAIIAN SALAD

1 1/2 c. small marsh-
   mallows
1/2 c. halved cherries
1 1/2 c. pineapple cubes

1 c. coconut
1 or 2 ripe bananas, sliced
3/4 pt. sour cream

    Mix together and chill. Serves 4-6.
                Mae Briley, Central Council,
                Alexandria, La.

JELLO SALAD

1 c. boiling water
12-18 large marshmallows
1 pkg. orange jello
1/2 c. chopped nuts

1 apple, diced
1 small can crushed pine-
   apple
1 small can evaporated milk

    Melt marshmallows in water, stir in jello and dissolve.
Place pan in cold water. Add apple, pineapple and nuts to
jello mixture. Pour in milk and stir. Pour mixture into
oiled mold and refrigerate until set.
                Linda Teague, Caddo Council,
                Shreveport, La.

JELLO SALAD

1 1/2 small pkg. lime
   jello
1 small can crushed
   pineapple

1 small can evaporated milk
1 c. hot water
1 c. chopped nuts

    Dissolve jello in hot water. Add remainder of ingre-
dients, chill. Double recipe will serve 15 people.
                Gay Irwin, Capital Council,
                Baton Rouge, La.

JELLO AH-LA-POOCH

1 (3 oz.) box lemon jello
2 c. hot water
3 c. finely chopped apple
1/2 c. chopped pecans
   (optional)

1 (3 oz.) box strawberry jello
1 c. pineapple juice
1 can whole cranberry sauce
1 box Lucky Whip
Skim milk

Grind cranberries in food chopper. Dissolve jellos in water. Mix with cranberries, apples and pineapple juice. Let congeal in refrigerator until almost firm; whip. Prepare Lucky Whip with skim milk as directed on box and fold into whipped jello mix. Place in molds and let congeal completely. Nuts may be added if desired. Good with ham, turkey or seafood.   Grace Bell, Ouachita
Council, Monroe, La.

KOOL DELIGHT

1 small pkg. orange jello
1 container Cool Whip
1 can Mandarin oranges

1 container cottage cheese
1 small can crushed pineapple

Combine cottage cheese, jello and drained fruit. Mix well. Blend in Cool Whip. Chill.
Ozella O. Pierce
Crescent City Council
New Orleans, La.

LIME JELLO SALAD

1 pkg. lime jello
1 c. boiling water
1 tsp. sugar
1 (8 oz.) pkg. cream cheese

1/2 c. chopped nuts
1 small can crushed pineapple, drained
1 small bottle 7-Up

Dissolve jello in boiling water, add remaining ingredient, adding 7-Up last. Mix and chill.
Marilou Bridges, Caddo
Council, Shreveport, La.

LIME JELLO SALAD

1 large box lime jello
2 c. hot water
1 large pkg. cream cheese
2 c. cold water

1 small can crushed pineapple
1 c. coconut
1 c. chopped pecans

Dissolve jello in hot water. Add cream cheese, stir until melted. Add cold water. Add pineapple, coconut and pecans. Chill until firm. Calcasieu Council
Lake Charles, La.

LIME JELLO SALAD

1 (16 oz.) carton cottage
  cheese
1 (6 oz.) box lime jello

1 (15 1/4 oz.) can pine-
  apple
1 (10 oz.) carton Cool Whip

Combine cottage cheese and jello, stir. Add pineapple
and Cool Whip, and blend well. Can be served at once or
refrigerated.   Calcasieu Council
                                 Lake Charles, La.

LIME AND CUCUMBER SALAD

1 pkg. lime jello
1 c. hot water
1/2 c. mayonnaise
1/2 c. diced cucumber
1 or 2 green onion, chopped

1 1/2 tsp. vinegar
3/4 tsp. salt
3/4 c. cottage cheese
3 Tbsp. diced green pepper

Dissolve jello in hot water. Cool and add remaining ingredients. Pour into mold and chill.
                                 Connie Younker
                                 Shreveport Works Council
                                 Shreveport, La.

MADELINE'S MEAT SALAD

1 can luncheon meat,
  ground
1 large dill pickle,
  chopped
1/2 c. celery, chopped
  fine

1 Tbsp. chopped pimiento
3 Tbsp. mayonnaise
2 hard boiled eggs, chopped
1 small onion, chopped fine
Salt and pepper to taste

Mix all ingredients. Chill for about 1 hour. Serve on
dry toast. Makes 6-8 servings.
                                 Mona Reis, Metairie Council,
                                 Metairie, La.

MANDARIN DELIGHT SALAD

1 small can Mandarin
  oranges, drained
1 small can pineapple
  chunks, drained

1 c. sour cream
1 small pkg. miniature
  marshmallows
1 c. shredded coconut

Mix all ingredients together well. Chill overnight.
Mary Weeks, Metairie
Council, New Orleans, La.

MEAL IN ONE DISH SALAD

1 large head lettuce
1 can water chestnuts,
  sliced and drained
2 c. grated American
  or Cheddar cheese
2 tsp. sugar

2 large cans boned
  chicken, strained
2 small boxes frozen green
  peas
1 1/2 c. mayonnaise

In large salad bowl, cover entire bottom of bowl with
a lettuce bed. In layers, place chicken, chestnuts, frozen
peas and cheese. Cover with mayonnaise and sprinkle sugar
over top. Refrigerate 1 hour. Great for picnics and out-
ings.
Delores Hirstius, Metairie
Council, Metairie, La.

MEXICAN SALAD

1 head lettuce, cut or
  torn up
1 chopped onion
1 can Ranch Style beans,
  drained
1 (39¢) pkg. Fritos,
  crushed

1 large tomato, cut up or
  sliced
5 oz. grated Longhorn
  cheese
1 bottle Kraft Catalina
  dressing

Mix all ingredients together, except Fritos, in large
bowl. Refrigerate. Toss in Fritos before serving. Makes
12-15 servings.
Dona Stephens, Central
Council, Houston, Tx.

MUSHROOM MACARONI SALAD

1 (6 or 8 oz.) can sliced
  mushrooms
2 Tbsp. prepared mustard
2 Tbsp. chopped parsley
2 tsp. lemon juice
2 c. cold, cooked maca-
  roni

1 tsp. salt
3/4 c. mayonnaise
2 Tbsp. minced onion
1 c. chopped celery
1 tsp. tarragon leaves,
  crumbled
1/2 tsp. black pepper

Combine mayonnaise, mustard, onion, parsley, lemon juice, tarragon leaves, salt and pepper. Mix thoroughly. Drain and slice mushrooms; add celery, macaroni and mushrooms to mixture. Cover and refrigerate 1 or 2 hours before serving, to let flavors mingle. Makes 1 quart.

Mrs. J. B. Coker, Central
Council, Alexandria, La.

MY 24 HOUR SALAD

1 can pineapple chunks
1 (10 oz.) jar mara-
  schino cherries
1 (12 oz.) pkg. miniature
  marshmallows
1 can seedless grapes
2 eggs, beaten
1 Tbsp. lemon juice
1/2 c. juice from fruit

1 can tropical fruit salad
  (Del Monte)
1 large can Mandarin oranges
2 bananas
1 Tbsp. vinegar
2 Tbsp. oleo
1/2 pt. whipping cream,
  whipped

Drain fruit, reserve 1/2 cup juice. Combine eggs, oleo, vinegar and juice. Cook over hot water until thick and smooth; chill. Fold in cream. Combine fruits and marshmallows. Fold in dressing. Chill 24 hours.

Grace Bell, Ouachita Council,
Monroe, La.

GREEN ONION SALAD

1 pkg. lemon jello
1 c. cottage cheese
5-6 green onions,
  chopped

1 c. hot water
1 c. celery, chopped
2/3 c. mayonnaise

Dissolve jello in hot water, cool. Combine all of the

ingredients. Pour into a square dish. Cut into squares to serve.
Jeanette Williams, Caddo Council, Shreveport, La.

ORANGE CONGEALED SALAD

1 small box orange jello
1 small box cottage cheese
1 large Cool Whip

1 small can Mandarin oranges, drained

Mix ingredients together and chill overnight. Save few orange slices for garnish. Keeps several days in refrigerator.
Mildred Pace, Caddo Council, Shreveport, La.

ORANGE JELLO SALAD

1 large pkg. orange jello
1 small can crushed pine-
  apple
2 c. boiling water

1 medium bowl Cool Whip
1/2 c. chopped pecans
1/4 lb. grated American cheese

Prepare jello with 2 cups water. Refrigerate until it begins to jell. Add remaining ingredients and pour in pan, bowl or mold. Refrigerate.
Mary L. Breland, Magnolia Council, New Orleans, La.

ORANGE RICE SALAD

1 can chicken broth
3/4 c. raw regular rice
1 1/2 c. diced, cooked
  chicken or turkey
1 small green pepper,
  cut in 1-inch long
  strips
1/2 tsp. salt

1/4 c. water
1/2 c. mayonnaise
1 c. cut up orange sections
1/2 c. coarsely chopped
  radishes
1 tsp. finely chopped onion
1/2 tsp. grated orange rind
1/8 tsp. mace

Combine broth, water and rice in saucepan. Bring to boil, reduce heat, cover and simmer 25 minutes or until done. Stir occasionally. Add remaining ingredients, chill. Serve on salad greens, garnish with orange slices, if desired. Makes about 4 servings.
Ann Orr, Evangeline Council, New Iberia, La.

ORANGE SHERBET SALAD

2 small pkg. orange jello
1 c. drained pineapple
2 small cans Mandarin
  orange slices, drained

2 c. boiling water
1 pt. orange sherbet
2 sliced bananas

Dissolve jello in boiling water. Add remaining ingredients. Chill.

Ruth Smolenski
Evangeline Council

PEANUT SALAD

1 (10 oz.) bag Spanish
  peanuts, well ground
1 egg, beaten
1/2 stick butter
2 or 3 Tbsp. water

1 Tbsp. flour
1/2 c. sugar
1/2 c. vinegar
4 Tbsp. mustard

Mix flour and sugar. Add remaining ingredients, except peanuts. Bring to boil over medium heat for 1 or 2 minutes. Cool and mix with ground peanuts. Serve on toast, crackers, bread, etc.

Ronda Decuir, Metairie
Council, Metairie, La.

PEAR SALAD

1 (8 oz.) pkg. cream
  cheese, softened
Lettuce leaves

1 can pears
1 small pkg. pecan or walnut pieces

Mix cream cheese with juice of pears to soft creamy consistency. Add nuts. Place 2 pear halves on each lettuce leaf. Top each pear with cream cheese mixture. Nice for spring and summer light meals.

Peggy Childers
Crescent City Council
New Orleans, La.

PEGGY'S SPECIAL SALAD

1 pkg. frozen broccoli
10 small okra pods
2 oz. olive oil
Romaine lettuce
Salt and pepper

1 pkg. frozen cauliflower
Cherry tomatoes
1 oz. white vinegar
Juice of 2 slices lemon
Oregano flakes

Use separate pots. Bring water to boil and drop in broccoli, cauliflower and okra. Let pots come back to a boil or until vegetables look thawed; they should be crisp. Drain thoroughly and cool. Cut tomatoes in half. Place lettuce on bottom of large salad bowl. Put in vegetables with cherry tomatoes on top. Mix olive oil, vinegar, lemon juice, salt and pepper. Add oregano flakes just seconds before putting on salad. Shake well. Toss salad with dressing until saturated. When serving, place one of the lettuce leaves on bottom of individual salad bowl, then put salad into bowl. Serves 4-6. To go with salad, serve Cornish hens, wild rice, acorn squash and for dessert, Irish coffee or ice cream with amaretta. A good autumn dinner.

Peggy Childers
Crescent City Council
New Orleans, La.

PHILADELPHIA CREAM CHEESE SALAD

1 (No. 2) can crushed
  pineapple
1 (8 oz.) pkg. cream
  cheese

1 c. pecans, chopped
  (optional)
1 pkg. lime jello
1 c. celery, chopped
1 c. whipped cream

Add cream cheese to pineapple and heat just enough to melt cheese. Stir constantly. Remove from heat and add jello, celery and nuts. Refrigerate until congealed. Fold in whipping cream.

Marie Pamplin
Shreveport Works Council
Shreveport, La.

PINEAPPLE CHEESE SALAD

1 small pkg. lime gelatin
1 c. hot water
1 small can crushed pine-
   apple

1 c. cottage cheese
1 small bottle green olives,
   quartered
1/2 c. salad dressing

Dissolve gelatin in hot water, chill. When slightly thick, add pineapple, cheese and olives. Mix well. Add salad dressing and mix again. Pour into mold. Chill until firm. Garnish as desired. For variety, add 1 cup or less of Mandarin oranges, grapefruit sections or grapes.

Calcasieu Council
Lake Charles, La.

PINK SALAD

1 carton cottage cheese
1 small pkg. jello (strawberry or cherry)

1 can fruit cocktail
1 small bowl Cool Whip

Mix ingredients and chill.

Cindy Kendrick, Caddo
Council, Shreveport, La.

PINK SALAD

1 can condensed milk
1 large Cool Whip
1 small can Mandarin
   oranges

1 large can cherry pie filling
1 small can crushed pineapple
20 miniature marshmallows
1/2 c. coconut and pecans

Chill and whip milk with beater. Add remaining ingredients and refrigerate until ready to serve.

Donna McPhearson, Central
Council, Natchitoches, La.

PISTACHIO SALAD

1 box pistachio instant
   pudding mix
1/2 c. nuts

1 c. miniature marshmallows
1 small Cool Whip
1 large can crushed pineapple

Mix ingredients; chill.

Margaret Aletha Keenan, Ozone
Council, Bogalusa, La.

PISTACHIO SALAD

1 (9 oz.) bowl Cool Whip
1 small can crushed pine-
apple, drained

1 small carton cottage cheese
1 pkg. pistachio pudding
1 c. marshmallows
1/2 c. nuts

Mix all ingredients together and chill.

Jo Ann Russell, Caddo
Council, Shreveport, La.

POTATO SALAD

1 can mushroom soup
4 c. cubed, cooked
potatoes
1 c. cucumbers, cut in
2-inch long strips
3 chopped hard boiled
eggs
1 1/2 tsp. sugar

1/3 c. French dressing
1 1/2 c. cubed, cooked ham
1/2 c. sliced celery
1/4 c. thinly sliced green
onions
1/8 tsp. pepper
Paprika

Combine ingredients in bowl, chill. Serve on salad
greens. Garnish with paprika and additional egg slices,
if desired. Makes about 7 cups. Makes 4-6 servings.

Ann Orr, Evangeline
Council, New Iberia, La.

DIFFERENT POTATO SALAD

6 potatoes
1 c. chopped onions
1/4 c. vinegar
1/2 c. prepared mustard
Salt and pepper to taste

2 eggs, boiled
1 c. chopped celery (the
heart and tender leaves)
1/2 c. mayonnaise

Boil and chop potatoes. Add onions, celery, salt and
pepper. Separate egg whites and yolks. Chop whites into
potato mixture. Mix yolk with vinegar, mashing yolk to dissolve. Add mustard and mayonnaise, mixing thoroughly. If
too thick, add more vinegar to form sauce and pour over
potato mixture. Serves 6.   Mrs. Willie Watts, LeBayou
Council, Thibodaux, La.

GERMAN POTATO SALAD

5 lb. potatoes
Salt and pepper to taste
8 boiled eggs, chopped
fine
2 stalks celery, chopped
fine

1 medium onion, chopped fine
2 toes garlic, chopped fine
1 lb. bacon, crumbled
2 Tbsp. vinegar
1/4 c. olive oil
1 Tbsp. parsley

Boil potatoes, let cool. Peel, slice thin and chop. Fry bacon, remove from skillet and drain. Keep drippings. Add to potatoes, eggs, onions, celery, garlic and parsley and crumbled bacon. Mix well. Then add vinegar, olive oil and bacon drippings. Mix very well. Serve at room temperature.

Lucille Castillion, Capital
Council, Baton Rouge, La.

HOT POTATO SALAD

8 small potatoes
1 c. mayonnaise (more
if needed)
Bacon bits

1 lb. diced Velveeta cheese
1/2 c. chopped onion
Salt and pepper to taste
Sliced olives

Cook potatoes in skin. Peel and cut up. Add cheese, mayonnaise and season to taste. Place in flat, oblong casserole dish. Top with bacon bits and olives. Cook at 325° uncovered for 1 hour. Serves 6-8.

Candy Nichols, LeBayou
Council, DeRidder, La.

HOT POTATO CHEESE SALAD

6 c. diced cooked
potatoes (3 lb. raw)
1/4 c. pickle relish, well
drained
1 c. plain yogurt
1 env. dehydrated vege-
table broth

1 c. sliced celery
1/4 c. finely chopped onion
1 c. (8 oz.) skim milk
cottage cheese
1/2 c. chicken broth
Salt and pepper to taste
1/3 c. chopped salted peanuts

In a large skillet, combine all ingredients, except peanuts. Heat until bubbly, seasoning mixture to taste with salt and pepper. Serve piping hot, sprinkled with peanuts. Serves 6.

Ann Orr, Evangeline
Council, New Iberia, La.

HOT POTATO-FRANK SALAD

4 medium potatoes, cooked
2 hard boiled eggs,
 chopped
1/4 c. sliced scallions
1/2 c. Wish-Bone Italian
 dressing
1 Tbsp. prepared mustard
6 frankfurters, cooked and
 sliced
1/4 c. pickle relish
1/2 tsp. salt

Peel and slice hot potatoes, add frankfurters, eggs, scallions and relish. Combine Wish-Bone dressing, salt and mustard in small saucepan. Heat, while stirring, until hot. Pour over potato mixture, tossing gently. Serves 6.

Mae Briley, Central Council,
Alexandria, La.

ITALIAN POTATO SALAD

15 large red potatoes
1/2 c. green onions,
 chopped
3 large cloves garlic,
 crushed
1 Tbsp. sugar
4 oz. tarragon vinegar
1 Tbsp. Worcestershire
 sauce
1/2 c. chopped celery
Parsley
1 tsp. salt
1/2 tsp. dry mustard
1 (8 oz.) bottle olive oil

Boil potatoes, peel and cut into 1-inch chunks. Sprinkle with parsley and green onions. Make sauce from rest of ingredients. Pour over potatoes and stir well. Let stand about 4 hours. Stir often. Do not refrigerate.

Betty Stevens, Gentilly
Council, New Orleans, La.

JIFFY POTATO SALAD

1 env. instant mashed
 potatoes, or prepare
 servings for 4
1/4 c. mayonnaise
1/2 tsp. prepared mustard
1/4 c. chopped celery
1 1/2 Tbsp. relish or chopped
 pickles
Salt and pepper to taste

Prepare potatoes according to package directions. Add mayonnaise, mustard, celery, relish, salt and pepper to taste. Chill. Serves 4. Can also be served warm.

Calcasieu Council
Lake Charles, La.

MARILOU'S POTATO SALAD

5 lb. white potatoes
1 small can pimentos,
  cut up
10 or 12 olives, chopped
1 Tbsp. olive juice
Salt and pepper to taste

1 chopped bell pepper
1 onion, chopped
3 or 4 sweet midget pickles
1 Tbsp. pickle juice
Mustard and mayonnaise
Paprika

Boil potatoes in jackets; drain, peel and chop up. Add onion, bell pepper, pickles, juice of olives and pickles. Mix well. Add 1/2 mustard and 1/2 mayonnaise to moisten. Salt and pepper to taste. Mix well. Sprinkle with paprika. Chill. This keeps several days in refrigerator.

Marilou Bridges, Caddo
Council, Shreveport, La.

RICE SALAD

8 slices bacon, cooked
  and crumbled
1 c. celery, diced
1/2 c. mayonnaise
1/4 tsp. salt
1/4 tsp. pepper

3 c. cooked rice
1 c. cooked English peas
1/4 c. diced pimiento
1/4 c. fresh chives, minced,
  or top of green onions
Stuffed olives (optional)

Combine all ingredients, except olives; toss. Garnish with olives if desired. Chill. Makes 6 servings.

Marilou Bridges
Shreveport, La.

RUSTY PELICAN SALAD

Lettuce
Romaine
Escarole
Chickory
Watercress
Bay leaves
Salt

6 mushrooms, sliced fine
2 tomatoes, cut in wedges
2 hard boiled eggs, chopped
  fine
2 Tbsp. chives, chopped fine
1 c. small shrimp, chopped
  fine
Lemon juice

Cut lettuce, romaine, escarole, chickory and watercress into 1-inch pieces for total of 6 cups. Boil shrimp with bay leaves, lemon juice and salt. Mix all ingredients in large wooden bowl and pour Honey Dressing over when ready to serve. This recipe furnished courtesy of "The Rusty Pelican" restaurant, Key Biscayne, Florida.

Rusty Pelican Honey Dressing:

5 oz. mayonnaise
2 oz. vegetable oil
1 pinch fine chopped
   parsley
Juice of 1/2 lemon
1 pinch Accent

2 oz. honey
1 oz. mustard
1 oz. fine chopped small
   onion
1 pinch salt

Mix ingredients and chill. The Dressing can be used up to 7 days if kept in glass container and refrigerated. To be used with green salads of all kinds and as a cold sauce with cold chicken.

Elmer E. Harrison
Crescent City Council
New Orleans, La.

SALMON SALAD

Empty 1 can of salmon in a bowl and shred. To this, add:

1 c. finely cut sweet
   pickle

1 c. finely cut celery
3 diced, hard boiled eggs

Blend with enough salad dressing to hold together and season with salt and pepper. Can be used as a salad or a sandwich spread.

Calcasieu Council
Lake Charles, La.

MARINATED SAUERKRAUT

1 (2 1/2 lb.) jar sauer-
   kraut
1 onion, sliced in rings
1 small jar pimento

3 stalks celery, chopped
1 small bell pepper,
   chopped

Drain and rinse sauerkraut; take out big tough pieces; cut rest into small pieces. Combine with remaining ingredients. Set aside and make up Marinade (recipe follows).

Marinade:

1 1/4 c. sugar
1/3 c. water

1/2 c. vinegar
1/4 c. cooking oil

Combine and boil until sugar dissolves. Cool and pour over kraut mixture. Refrigerate at least 24 hours.

Jean Coon, Caddo Council, Shreveport, La.

SEVEN LAYER SALAD

1 layer shredded lettuce
1 layer chopped bell pepper
1 layer chopped celery
1 large grated Cheddar
cheese

1 layer frozen green peas,
uncooked
1 layer mayonnaise
1 layer crumbled bacon

Make salad by making layers in this order - lettuce, bell pepper, celery, peas, mayonnaise, cheese and bacon. Do not stir. Make day before using. Will keep several days in the refrigerator.

Marjorie Rowell, Evangeline Council, Lafayette, La.

SHRIMP SALAD

2 c. cooked shrimp,
canned or fresh
2 Tbsp. lemon juice
1/4 c. salad oil
1 tsp. salt
1/4 tsp. black pepper

4 green onions, chopped
1 c. pitted black olives,
chopped
2 Tbsp. wine tarragon
vinegar
1 Tbsp. mustard

Combine all ingredients and marinate at least 2 hours. Serve on lettuce leaf.

Marilou Bridges, Caddo Council, Shreveport, La.

SHRIMP SALAD

1 head lettuce
1 small can asparagus
tips, drained
2 boiled eggs

1 small onion, chopped
2 lb. boiled and peeled
shrimp

116

Tear up lettuce in large bowl. Quarter eggs and add to lettuce. Add onion. Add asparagus. Toss lightly. Place shrimp over top. Serve Remoulade Sauce as dressing. Also serve garlic bread with salad.

Mrs. Sim S. Davenport
Central Council
Alexandria, La.

SHRIMP SALAD

2 lb. boiled shrimp,
  cut in pieces
1 head lettuce, torn in
  bite size pieces
3 Tbsp. chopped dill
  pickles

1/2 lb. Cheddar cheese, cut
  up in small pieces
2 tomatoes, cut in pieces
1 tsp. grated onion
1/4 c. chopped sweet pickles
Mayonnaise
Salt and pepper to taste

Mix ingredients together. Add enough mayonnaise to moisten. Chill until ready to serve.

Susan Lachney, Westmoor
Council, Kenner, La.

SHRIMP SALAD

1 head lettuce, cleaned
  and torn in bite size
  pieces
2 cucumbers, cut in sticks
6-10 slices bacon, fried
  and crumbled

2 1/2 c. boiled shrimp,
  peeled
3 tomatoes, cut in wedges
3 boiled eggs, cut in wedges
1 c. sharp Cheddar cheese,
  cubed
1/2 - 1 c. pitted ripe olives

Combine all ingredients in large salad bowl. Pour Special Dressing over salad. Serves 4.

Special Dressing:

1/2 tsp. salt
1/8 tsp. paprika
1/8 tsp. dry mustard
1/3 c. cooking oil
2 tsp. horseradish

1/8 tsp. pepper
1/4 tsp. sugar
2 Tbsp. white vinegar
3 Tbsp. ketchup
1/3 c. heavy cream, whipped

Combine and blend all dressing ingredients thoroughly before pouring over salad.   Mona F. Reis, Metairie
Council, Metairie, La.

SHRIMP MOLD

1/2 c. water
1 (8 oz.) pkg. cream
  cheese
1/2 c. chopped onions
1 Tbsp. chopped parsley
1 c. mayonnaise

1 can tomato soup
2 env. gelatin
1 c. chopped celery
Dash of Worcestershire sauce
1 1/2 c. cleaned, boiled
  shrimp

Put warm water out of faucet in dish. Sprinkle gelatin over water and let cook on fire as low as you can get for 1 hour, stir occasionally until clear. Combine soup and cream cheese, warm until dissolved. Take off fire, add gelatin mix and other ingredients. Pour into mold sprayed with Pam and chill.   Clarabell J. Hosch, Metairie
Council, Metairie, La.

MOLDED SHRIMP SALAD

1 (6 oz.) pkg. cream
  cheese
1 can mushroom soup
1 (10 oz.) pkg. shrimp,
  crabmeat or salmon
1 c. mayonnaise
Tabasco sauce to taste

2 shallots, chopped fine
1 pkg. (1 Tbsp.) Knox
  gelatine
3 Tbsp. cold water
1 c. celery, chopped
Lemon juice to taste
Crab boil

Dissolve gelatine in cold water. Boil shrimp in crab boil about 5 minutes. Heat soup, add cheese and melt. Add gelatine. Remove from fire and mix all ingredients together. Mold and chill.   Maria Daniel, Crescent City
Council, New Orleans, La.

SHRIMP MOUSSE

2 c. peeled shrimp
2 Tbsp. mayonnaise
1/2 bell pepper, chopped
  fine
1 large onion, chopped
  fine

1 Tbsp. lemon juice
2 tsp. Knox gelatine
1/4 tsp. salt
6 oz. cream cheese
2/3 c. sour cream
1 Tbsp. chili sauce

118

| 2 stalks celery, chopped fine | 4 tsp. cold water |
| | Tabasco sauce to taste |

Heat shrimp on low fire until they are tender and red. Chop cooked shrimp, set aside. Heat together the cream cheese, mayonnaise and sour cream in a non-stick pan on low heat. Add all chopped vegetables and seasonings. Add chili sauce. Simmer. Dissolve gelatin in lemon juice and water over a double boiler for 10 minutes. Gradually add gelatine to cheese mixture along with shrimp, Tabasco sauce and salt. Blend well. Pour into a chilled ring mold and refrigerate overnight. Unmold. Garnish with parsley and shrimp. Serve with party crackers. Serves 15.

Jim Bachiem, Metairie
Council, Metairie, La.

SHRIMP-TOMATO SALAD

2 cans (4 1/2 oz. size) shrimp	1/8 tsp. pepper
3/4 c. chopped celery	1/2 c. salad dressing
2 Tbsp. chopped sweet pickle	2 Tbsp. chopped onion
	2 hard boiled eggs, chopped
	6 large, firm tomatoes

Drain shrimp, rinse in cold water, redrain. Reserve 6 shrimp and cut remainder in half. Combine shrimp with all ingredients, except tomatoes. Cut tomatoes almost through into sixths. Spread open and fill with shrimp mixture. Garnish with the reserved shrimp. Celery, carrot sticks and pickle slices may also be used as garnish.

Denise Barteet, Caddo
Council, Shreveport, La.

SNOWBALL SALAD

1/2 pt. whipping cream	1 c. coconut flakes
1 can fruit cocktail, drained	1/2 c. chopped nuts
4 Tbsp. sugar	4 bananas, sliced

Whip cream until very firm. Gently fold fruit cocktail, sugar, nuts, bananas and 1/2 of coconut into whipped cream. Use remaining coconut as topping and refrigerate.

Ruth Soileau, Evangeline
Council, Opelousas, La.

SPINACH SALAD

Fresh spinach
3 hard boiled eggs,
  chopped
American and Swiss
  cheese, cut into chunks

Fresh mushrooms, sliced
5 strips fried bacon,
  broken into bits
Salad croutons

Wash and cut stems off spinach. Gently tear leaves in half. Mix in salad bowl along with fresh mushrooms, boiled eggs and cheese. Sprinkle bacon bits and croutons on top. Make up salad dressing, pour and mix with salad. If you prefer, soak mushrooms in salad dressing before putting on salad for more flavor. Let set about 10 minutes, then serve.

Salad Dressing:

1/4 c. olive oil
1/4 tsp. dry mustard
1 Tbsp. parsley flakes
Salt and pepper

1/4 c. red wine vinegar
1/4 tsp. thyme
1 egg

Mix all ingredients in bowl and beat with rotary beater until mixed thoroughly.
  Trish Albritton, Metairie
  Council, Metairie, La.

SPINACH SALAD

1 pkg. spinach
1 head lettuce, bite size
  pieces
1/2 lb. American or
  Swiss cheese, grated

5 hard boiled eggs, chopped
2 pkg. frozen green peas
1 bunch chopped green
  onions

Wash, dry and stem spinach. In salad bowl, layer in this order - spinach, eggs, lettuce, frozen green peas, green onions and cheese. Do not stir. Pour dressing over and refrigerate.

Salad Dressing:

2 c. mayonnaise
1/2 c. milk

1 Tbsp. honey or sugar
Salt and pepper to taste

Combine ingredients and beat until well mixed. Pour over spinach salad. Do not stir. Chill and serve with bacon chips and croutons.
  Mrs. Heslin Crockett, Capital
  Council, Baton Rouge, La.

SPINACH SALAD

3 lb. fresh spinach
4 eggs, hard boiled

1 1/2 lb. bacon, fried crisp
1 large red onion, chopped

Combine ingredients and toss. Pour dressing over all when ready to serve.

Dressing:

3/4 c. Wesson oil
3/4 c. chili sauce

1 c. sugar
1 Tbsp. soy sauce (optional)

Mix ingredients and use over Spinach Salad.

Mrs. Johnnie B. Cole, Caddo
Council, Shreveport, La.

STRAWBERRY JELLO SALAD

1 large pkg. strawberry
  jello
1 small can crushed pine-
  apple
1/2 pt. sour cream

1/2 c. pecan pieces
  (optional)
2 bananas, mashed
1 (10 oz.) pkg. frozen
  strawberries, thawed

Dissolve jello as directed on package. Cool. Add bananas, pineapple and strawberries. Pour half of this mixture in greased pan or mold. Chill until jelled. Spread sour cream on top, then pour remaining jello over all. Serve on lettuce leaf. Pecans may be added if desired.

Susan Austin, Ouachita
Council, Monroe, La.

STRAWBERRY JELLO SALAD

1 large pkg. strawberry
  jello
1 pkg. frozen straw-
  berries, cut up small

1 c. sour cream
1 (No. 2) can crushed pineapple, drained
2 c. water

Make jello, using 2 cups water. Add partially thawed strawberries and pineapple. Pour half of the mixture into an 8-inch square dish. Let set, spread with sour cream. Top with remaining jello mixture. Let set. Serve on lettuce leaf.

Lynda Fox, Caddo Council
Shreveport, La.

STRAWBERRY SALAD

1 can strawberry pie
  filling
1 (No. 2) can crushed
  pineapple, drained

1 (9 oz.) container Cool Whip
1 can Eagle Brand milk
1 c. chopped pecans

Mix strawberry filling, pineapple and milk together. Chill for 15 minutes. Fold in remaining ingredients.

Linda May, Ouachita
Council, Monroe, La.

TACO SALAD

1 lb. hamburger
1 can chili beans in chili
  sauce
1 large pkg. taco flavored
  Doritos, slightly crushed
Grated cheese

1 chopped onion
1 head lettuce
2 or 3 tomatoes, cut up
1 bottle Wish-Bone Italian
  salad dressing

Brown hamburger meat and onion in skillet, stir in chili beans. In large salad bowl, tear lettuce, add tomatoes and Doritos. Stir in hamburger mixture. Pour dressing over and sprinkle cheese on top. Makes very large salad. Serves 12.

Caine C. Nettles
Crescent City Council
New Orleans, La.

TACO SALAD

1 lb. ground beef,
  browned
1 lb. sharp cheese, grated
1 (15 oz.) can Ranch Style
  beans, drained
1 large head lettuce, torn
  apart

1 can ripe olives, sliced
1 large onion, chopped
2 large tomatoes, chopped
1 pkg. taco flavor Dorito
  chips
1 bottle Catalina salad
  dressing

Combine browned meat, cheese, beans, olives, onions, tomatoes and lettuce. Add Dorito chips and dressing just before serving. Toss gently. Gladys Domingues, Caddo
Council, Shreveport, La.

TACO SALAD

1 lb. ground meat
1 medium onion, chopped
1 heaping tsp. chili powder
1 head lettuce
1 lb. Velveeta cheese

1 medium bell pepper,
  chopped
1 tsp. cumin seed
1 large tomato
1 medium bag Fritos
1 can Ro-Tel tomatoes

Brown meat, bell pepper, onion, chili powder and cumin seed. Drain and set aside. Chop tomato and lettuce, set aside.   On low heat, melt cheese and Ro-Tel tomatoes. Crunch bag of Fritos. Mix all ingredients when ready to serve.   Billie Longkabel, Ouachita
                                Council, Monroe, La.

TOMATO ASPIC

2 c. V-8 juice
2 cloves garlic
1 Tbsp. Lea & Perrins
  sauce
1/2 tsp. coarse ground
  black pepper
5 whole cloves

1 1/2 c. tomato juice
1/2 c. vinegar, cut with
  1/4 c. water
1 tsp. salt
2 Tbsp. sugar
3 Tbsp. gelatin
1/4 c. cold tomato juice

Place all ingredients in saucepan, except gelatin and 1/4 cup cold tomato juice. Bring to boil and boil uncovered for 10 minutes; strain.   Soften gelatin in cold tomato juice. Add hot strained liquid and dissolve. Chill until set. Mold in ring mold and serve with chicken or shrimp salad or make individual molds by using styrofoam egg cartons sprayed with Pam. Serve molded aspic on lettuce or on cucumber rounds.
                                Althea Brossett, Capital
                                Council, Baton Rouge, La.

TOMATO SALAD

1 can tomato soup
1 (6 oz.) pkg. raspberry
  jello
1/2 c. chopped green
  pepper

1 Tbsp. horseradish
2 c. water
1 c. chopped celery
1 c. sliced or diced
  cucumbers

Heat soup and water to boiling. Add to jello and stir.

Chill. Fold in remaining ingredients and pour into large mold. Refrigerate. Serves 12.

Mrs. Charles (Helen) Patton
Shreveport Works Council
Shreveport, La.

VEGETABLE SALAD

1 medium head cauliflower
1 basket cherry or plum
   tomatoes (leave whole)
1 bunch broccoli

1 (16 oz.) bottle Italian salad
   dressing
1 medium can pitted black
   olives, drained

Cut cauliflower and broccoli into flowerets; tender broccoli stems may also be used. Wash and drain all vegetables. Add olives and salad dressing. Marinate in covered bowl in refrigerator overnight. Turn bowl several times to marinate salad well. Add salt when served if desired. This is a colorful salad to serve during holidays.

Dorothy S. Holliday, Central
Council, Alexandria, La.

VEGETABLE SALAD

Lettuce
Tomatoes
1 can black olives
1 can asparagus

1 can mushrooms
1 jar marinated artichokes
1 bottle Italian dressing

Mix all vegetables and chill. When ready to serve, add bottle of Italian dressing.

Cleo Taylor, Ouachita
Council, Monroe, La.

MARINATED VEGETABLE SALAD

1 (10 oz.) pkg. frozen
   green beans
1 (10 oz.) pkg. frozen
   wax beans
1 (17 1/4 oz.) jar garbanzo
   beans, drained
1 c. reconstituted lemon
   juice

1 (15 1/4 oz.) can red kidney
   beans, drained
1 medium onion, sliced and
   separated into rings
1 c. vegetable oil
1 clove garlic, minced
2/3 c. sugar
Pickled beets

In large bowl, combine frozen green and wax beans, thawed. Add red kidney beans, garbanzo beans and onion. Combine lemon juice, vegetable oil, sugar and garlic, mix until sugar dissolves. Pour over vegetables. Cover and chill overnight. Toss and drain. Place in serving dish. Garnish with chilled pickled beets.

Lynn Babin, Westmoor
Council, Kenner, La.

YUM-YUM SALAD

1/2 c. sugar
1 c. crushed pineapple
1 lemon (juice only)
1 1/4 c. grated cheese

1 lemon jello
1 c. hot water
1/2 c. nuts
1/2 c. whipped cream, Cool Whip or Dream Whip

Heat sugar, pineapple and juice. Do not boil. Dissolve jello in hot water and add to pineapple mixture and chill. When it begins to congeal, fold in remaining ingredients. Refrigerate to set.   Melba Balentine, Calcasieu
Council, Tioga, La.

CABBAGE SLAW WITH BOILED DRESSING

1 large head cabbage,
  shredded
1 c. Wesson oil
3/4 c. sugar
1 1/2 tsp. salt

1 large onion, minced
1/2 c. vinegar
1 tsp. celery seed
1 Tbsp. prepared mustard

Mix cabbage and onion together in large bowl. Combine remaining ingredients and bring to a boil. Pour boiling dressing over cabbage mixture, stir together well and store in airtight jar or container for 24 hours in refrigerator before serving. Stays fresh and keeps indefinitely in refrigerator until all used.   Sylvia Campbell, Caddo
Council, Shreveport, La.

HOT CABBAGE SLAW

1/2 head small cabbage
Salt and pepper
Sour cream
Caraway seeds (optional)

1/4 c. water
2 Tbsp. butter
Vinegar

Remove core from cabbage; shred fine. Boil in saucepan with water, butter, salt and pepper for 4-5 minutes or until tender. All water should be gone. Add sour cream to moisten well, 1 tablespoon or more vinegar to taste and caraway seed. Serve immediately. Good hot or delicious served cold next day. Serves 2.

Diane Clover, Central
Council, Sealy, Tx.

COLE SLAW

1 cabbage, shredded
1 c. sugar
2 Tbsp. sugar
1 Tbsp. salt
1 tsp. celery seed

1 large onion, shredded
1 c. vinegar
3/4 c. oil
1 Tbsp. dry mustard

Sprinkle onion over cabbage. Sprinkle 1 cup sugar over onion. Do not stir. Combine remaining ingredients, heat to boiling and pour over the cabbage mixture. Do not stir. Cover quickly and refrigerate for 4 hours or more.

Jeanette English, Caddo
Council, Shreveport, La.

CABBAGE AND PINEAPPLE SLAW

1 c. pineapple tidbits
2 stalks chopped celery

3 c. shredded cabbage
1/2 c. chopped pecans or
    almonds

Pour Dressing over all ingredients and mix well.

Dressing:

Mayonnaise, thinned
    with lemon juice

2 Tbsp. sugar
Dash of salt

Combine ingredients and pour over salad.

Mrs. Tony Corcoran
Crescent City Council
New Orleans, La.

CREAMY SLAW

1 small can evaporated
   milk
1 tsp. salt
1/8 tsp. pepper
4 c. shredded cabbage
1 stalk celery, diced

1/4 c. apple cider vinegar
2 Tbsp. sugar
1/4 tsp. celery seed
1/2 c. mayonnaise
1 carrot, shredded

Stir together milk, vinegar, sugar, salt, celery seed, pepper and mayonnaise. Chill until ready to serve. Combine cabbage, carrot and celery. Chill. To serve, pour dressing mixture over cabbage mixture. Toss to coat well. Serve immediately. Makes 6 servings.

Ann Orr, Evangeline
Council, New Iberia, La.

PINEAPPLE CARROT SLAW

1 small can evaporated
   milk
1/2 c. mayonnaise
Dash of pepper
1 carrot, shredded

1/4 c. apple cider vinegar
1 tsp. salt
4 c. shredded cabbage
1 (15 1/2 oz.) can chunk
   pineapple, drained

Mix milk, vinegar, mayonnaise, salt and pepper together. Pour over cabbage, carrot and pineapple. Toss to coat well. Serve immediately. Makes 4 cups. Easy to make and colorful.

Ann Orr, Evangeline
Council, New Iberia, La.

PONDEROSA COLE SLAW

1 c. mild honey
1/2 c. chopped onion
1 tsp. celery seed
   (optional)
1 c. diced green pepper

1 c. diced celery
1 c. wine vinegar
1 tsp. salt
1 large head cabbage, finely
   chopped (4 c.)

Combine honey, vinegar, onion, salt, celery seed in small saucepan. Bring to boil, reduce heat, simmer 5 minutes; cool. Pour cooled dressing over prepared vegetables; toss lightly. Cover, chill several hours or overnight. Stir several times while chilling. Makes 10-12 servings.

Mrs. Tony Corcoran
Crescent City Council
New Orleans, La.

STAY CRISP GARDEN SLAW

8 c. shredded cabbage	2 shredded carrots
1 green pepper, cut in	1/2 c. chopped onions
strips	1 env. unflavored gelatin
3/4 c. cold water	2 tsp. celery seed
2/3 c. vinegar	1/4 tsp. black pepper
1 1/2 tsp. salt	2/3 c. salad oil

Mix cabbage, carrots, green pepper and onions. Sprinkle with 1/2 cup cold water and chill. Soften gelatin in remaining 1/4 cup cold water. Combine sugar, vinegar, celery seed, salt and pepper in saucepan. Bring to boil. Stir in softened gelatin. Cool until slightly thickened and beat. Gradually beat in salad oil. Drain vegetables, add dressing. Mix until all vegetables are coated.

Billie Williams, Ouachita
Council, Monroe, La.

TUNA FISH SLAW

2 c. flaked tuna	4 c. cabbage, shredded finely
1/4 c. chopped green	1/4 c. lemon juice
onion	1 tsp. seasoned salt
1/2 c. mayonnaise	1/4 tsp. Worcestershire sauce
2 tsp. sugar	1/4 tsp. Tabasco sauce
1 tsp. prepared mustard	

Combine tuna, cabbage and onion. Combine remaining ingredients and mix well. Pour dressing over cabbage mixture and toss. Chill thoroughly. Canned chopped shrimp may be substituted for tuna. Betty Harman, Caddo
Council, Shreveport, La.

BLEU CHEESE DRESSING

3/4 c. sour cream	1/2 tsp. dry mustard
1/2 tsp. black pepper	1/2 tsp. salt
1/3 tsp. garlic powder	1 tsp. Worcestershire sauce
1 1/3 c. mayonnaise	4 oz. Danish Bleu cheese

In mixing bowl, combine sour cream, mustard, black pepper, salt, garlic powder and Worcestershire sauce. Blend 2 minutes at low speed. Add mayonnaise. Blend 1 minute at low speed, then 2 minutes at medium speed. Crumble Bleu cheese into mixture and blend at low speed no longer than 2 minutes. Refrigerate for 24 hours before using. Makes approximately 2 1/2 cups.

Curt Heximer, Crescent City
Council, New Orleans, La.

BLUE CHEESE DRESSING

1 c. sour cream
2 Tbsp. milk
1/4 tsp. salt

1/4 c. crumbled Blue cheese
1 tsp. grated onion
Dash of pepper

Blend all ingredients well. Refrigerate. Makes about 1 1/3 cups.

Calcasieu Council
Lake Charles, La.

BUTTERMILK DRESSING

2 c. buttermilk
1/2 tsp. garlic powder
2 1/4 Tbsp. parsley flakes
1/2 tsp. MSG

2 c. mayonnaise
1 tsp. onion powder
1 3/4 tsp. salt
1/2 tsp. white pepper

Combine all ingredients, mixing well. Chill at least 4 hours. Dressing will keep 2-3 weeks in refrigerator. Recipe can be halved if desired.

Marilou Bridges, Caddo
Council, Shreveport, La.

CELERY SEED - HONEY DRESSING

1/2 c. sugar
1 tsp. salt
1 tsp. paprika
4 Tbsp. vinegar
1 tsp. celery seed

1 tsp. dry mustard
1/3 c. honey
1 Tbsp. lemon juice
1 tsp. grated onion
1 c. salad oil

Mix dry ingredients. Add honey, lemon juice, vinegar and onion. Pour oil slowly into mixture, beating constantly. Serve with fruit salad.

Mavis W. O'Rourke
Shreveport Works Council
Shreveport, La.

CENTURY OLD FRENCH DRESSING

1/2 c. sugar
1/2 c. lemon juice (fresh
or ReaLemon recon-
stituted)
1/2 c. vinegar
1 c. ketchup

1 c. water
1/2 tsp. salt
1/2 tsp. white pepper, or
slightly less black pepper
2 c. salad oil
1 large onion, grated

Boil sugar and water 10 minutes. Add lemon juice and boil 5 minutes longer. Cool. Mix salt, pepper and vinegar. Add oil, ketchup, onion and cool syrup mixture. Beat until thick (mixer). Shake before using.

Della Delposen, Ouachita
Council, Monroe, La.

CREAMY DRESSING

1 c. sour cream
2 Tbsp. white vinegar

2 Tbsp. sugar
1/2 tsp. salt

Mix well and chill. Keeps for weeks. Good on shredded cabbage or sliced cucumbers. Rose Romano, Crescent City
Council, New Orleans, La.

EMERALD ISLE SALAD DRESSING

1 c. mayonnaise
1 hard boiled egg, peeled
and cut in chunks
1/4 c. dairy sour cream

2 tsp. water
1-2 drops liquid hot pepper
sauce

Combine and place in blender. Mix until thoroughly combined. Sylvia Campbell, Caddo
Council, Shreveport, La.

ITALIAN DRESSING

3/4 c. olive oil
2 tsp. fresh chives,
minced
1/8 tsp. black pepper
1/8 tsp. dill seed

1/4 c. wine vinegar
1 tsp. salt
1 tsp. minced parsley
1/8 tsp. red pepper
1 clove garlic, whole

Combine all ingredients in a jar. Cover tightly and shake vigorously. Chill several hours. Remove garlic clove before serving. Serve over green salad. Yield: About 1 cup.   Betty Harman, Caddo
                                   Council, Shreveport, La.

SALAD DRESSING

1 1/2 Tbsp. minced onion   3 Tbsp. yellow mustard
1 1/3 Tbsp. Accent   1 1/3 Tbsp. salt
2/3 c. vinegar   1 tsp. Lea & Perrins sauce
Dash of Tabasco sauce   2 1/3 c. salad oil

Place onion, mustard, Accent, salt and vinegar in mixer. Mix until well blended. Add remaining ingredients and stir in gradually. Mix well and place in 1-quart container. Store in refrigerator.   Cynthia Lewis, Magnolia
                                   Council, New Orleans, La.

SALAD DRESSING

Fry 3 slices of bacon, or use 4 tablespoons bacon grease in skillet, and add:

1/2 c. cream   1/2 tsp. salt
2 1/2 Tbsp. vinegar   Pepper to taste
1 1/2 Tbsp. water   2 egg yolks
1 Tbsp. sugar

Mix all together and cook until thick, pour hot over leaf lettuce.   Calcasieu Council
                                   Lake Charles, La.

ITALIAN SALAD MIX

10 bell peppers, cut up   1 stalk celery with leaves,
1 qt. green stuffed olives   cut up
1 can crushed oregano   2 cloves garlic, minced
1 pt. capers, ground   1 oz. parsley
   (optional)   Cooking oil
Seasoning salt to taste

Cover all ingredients with cooking oil and let stand for

16 days. Spoon over lettuce and tomatoes for each serving. Note: Seasoning salt recipe found in another section of cookbook.
Marjorie Harris, Capital
Council, Baton Rouge, La.

APPLE AND YAM CASSEROLE

1 (21 oz.) can apple
   pie filling
3 Tbsp. butter
Chopped nuts

2 cans (17 oz. each) whole
   sweet potatoes, drained
Nutmeg

Combine apple pie filling and sweet potatoes in buttered casserole. Dot with 3 tablespoons butter. Sprinkle lightly with nutmeg and nuts. Bake in preheated 325° oven for 30 minutes until bubbly.
Lynn Babin, Westmoor
Council, Kenner, La.

ARTICHOKE CASSEROLE

2 cans (14 oz. size)
   artichoke hearts
1 c. water
1 small can Progresso
   Italian bread crumbs

1/2 c. olive oil
6 cloves garlic, minced
Black pepper to taste
1 (3 oz.) jar Romano cheese

Drain hearts, cut into 4 pieces. Add oil and water; mix. Add remaining ingredients; mix well. Spoon in a 2-quart casserole dish. Cover and bake at 400° for 25-30 minutes.
Lillian Fahrenholt, Metairie
Council, Metairie, La.

ARTICHOKE CASSEROLE OR BALLS

3 cans artichoke hearts
3 cans French cut string
   beans
1 c. olive oil

3 c. Italian bread crumbs
1 c. Italian cheese
1 large chopped onion
3-4 cloves chopped garlic

Simmer onions and garlic in oil. Add drained, chopped string beans and drained, chopped artichoke hearts. Simmer 5 or 10 minutes. Add bread crumbs and cheese. Mix well. Place in casserole dish. Sprinkle crumbs on top and

bake at 350° for 20-25 minutes. Mixture can be rolled into balls, then in crumbs. Bake on tray for 15 minutes at 350°.
Pat Uhle, West Bank
Council, Gretna, La.

STUFFED ARTICHOKES

4 whole fresh artichokes
3 1/2 c. seasoned Italian
  bread crumbs

4 cloves garlic, minced
3/4 c. Italian cheese, grated
Olive oil

Cut off stems of artichokes and across 1 inch of top leaves. Remove prickly tip of other leaves by clipping off top. Rinse thoroughly in cold water, drain. Press top, cut side down, firmly to force leaves to open slightly. Pull leaves gently to open far enough to stuff. Combine bread crumbs, garlic and grated cheese, mix thoroughly. Set artichoke, bottom down, and pour stuffing into cavities formed by leaves. Stuff as many leaves as possible. Put about 1/2 of salted water and 1/4 cup olive oil in pot, bring to a gently boil. Place chokes in pan, bottom down, and cover pot tightly. Cook about 20 minutes. The chokes will steam and stuffing will be moistened. Remove cover and dribble olive oil onto stuffing until thoroughly moistened. Recover and continue to cook 20 minutes longer or until bottom leaves pull away easily. Wanda Reis, Caddo Council
Shreveport, La.

STUFFED ARTICHOKES

4 artichokes
1/2 lb. Swiss cheese,
  grated
1/4 lb. Mozzarella cheese,
  grated
1/2 c. celery, chopped
  fine
1/2 c. onion, chopped
  fine

1 lb. crabmeat
4 oz. hot pepper cheese,
  grated
Salt, black and red pepper
1/4 c. bell pepper, chopped
  fine
1/2 c. bread crumbs
1 stick butter
2 eggs, well beaten

Wash artichokes and cut off tips. Boil until tender. Drain. Saute celery, bell pepper and onions in butter. Remove from heat. Add crabmeat and grated cheeses. Add bread crumbs and eggs. Mix well. Clean out heart of

artichokes and stuff with crab mixture. Stuff each leaf.
Wrap in foil and bake at 375° for 35 minutes.

Agnes F. Rodrigue, LeBayou
Council, Houma, La.

STUFFED ARTICHOKES

3 green artichokes
1 1/2 c. grated Italian
  cheese
2 sprigs parsley, chopped
  fine
1/4 tsp. pepper

2 1/2 c. bread crumbs, not
  toasted
1 clove garlic, minced
1/2 tsp. salt
2 Tbsp. olive oil

Prepare artichokes by cutting off stickers on every leaf;
cut off top of artichokes to make a flat top and cut off stems
at bottom of artichokes. Soak artichokes in salt water about
5 minutes, rinse under faucet water flowing continually for
about 1 minute, opening leaves as they are being rinsed. Set
aside to drain. Mix bread crumbs, Italian cheese, parsley,
pepper, salt, garlic and olive oil. Stuff center and all
leaves with stuffing. Set in a pan with 4 cups boiling salted
water. Cover and cook over very low heat for 2 or 3 hours
or until a leaf can be pulled from artichokes very easily.
Serve either hot or cold.   Mrs. Joe Nasello, Central
Council, Alexandria, La.

ARTICHOKE AND GREEN BEAN CASSEROLE

2 cans French style green
  beans, drained
2 c. Progresso bread
  crumbs

2 cans artichoke hearts,
  drained (save water)
3/4 c. olive oil
1/4 c. Parmesan cheese

Cut artichokes in half and combine in casserole dish
with green beans. Mix olive oil and artichoke liquid, fold
into artichokes. Mix cheese and bread crumbs together and
add to casserole. Mix well. Top with more crumbs and bake
at 350° for 20 minutes, or enough to heat thoroughly.

Bonnie Williams, LeBayou
Council, Thibodaux, La.

ARTICHOKE AND SPINACH CASSEROLE

2 cans artichoke hearts
4 Tbsp. butter
8 Tbsp. milk
1 c. grated Cheddar
  cheese

4 pkg. frozen, chopped
  spinach
1 (12 oz.) pkg. cream cheese
Fresh pepper

Put artichoke hearts in casserole. Squeeze thawed spinach and place over the artichokes. Beat cream cheese and butter together until smooth and gradually add milk. Spread over spinach. Sprinkle with good ground of pepper. Top with grated cheese. Can be prepared ahead and re-frigerated up to 24 hours. Bake covered at 350° for 30 minutes, uncover and bake 10 minutes more.

Rosalie Fitzmorris
Crescent City Council
New Orleans, La.

ASPARAGUS

4 Tbsp. melted butter
  or oleo
2 eggs, slightly beaten
2 c. hot milk
2 tsp. grated onion
1/2 tsp. salt

2 (10 oz.) pkg. asparagus
  or cans, cooked and
  drained
1 c. crumbled saltine
  crackers
1/2 tsp. pepper

Line pan with foil. Saute crackers in butter until golden brown. Combine eggs, milk, salt, pepper and onions; mix well. Add asparagus and crackers. Bake in 350° oven for 30 minutes or until knife comes out clean.

Gretna S. Anderson, Central
Council, Alexandria, La.

ASPARAGUS CASSEROLE

2 cans green asparagus
1 1/2 Tbsp. flour
1/3 c. grated cheese
1 tsp. Worcestershire
  sauce
Paprika

1/2 stick oleo
1 c. milk
1 can mushroom soup
Salt and black pepper to
  taste
Corn flake crumbs

Melt oleo, add flour and blend well. Gradually stir in

milk to make a white sauce, blend in soup and grated cheese. Add Worcestershire sauce, salt and pepper to taste. Drain asparagus and arrange in buttered casserole. Pour sauce over top and cover with a thin layer of corn flake crumbs. Sprinkle with paprika. Bake at 375° for 40 minutes. Serves 6-8.

Mrs. Richard D. (Vermelle) Sylvest, Ozone Council, Hammond, La.

ASPARAGUS SUPREME

1/2 c. minced onion
2 Tbsp. flour
1/2 tsp. pepper
1 1/2 lb. fresh cooked, or
  2 (14 oz.) cans, drained
  asparagus spears

2 Tbsp. oleo
1 tsp. salt
1 c. sour cream
1/2 c. grated sharp Cheddar
  cheese
Seasoned bread crumbs

Saute onion in oleo until golden, add flour, salt and pepper. Mix well and cook until blended. Add sour cream, but do not let mixture come to a boil. Place asparagus in shallow baking dish and cover with sour cream mixture. Sprinkle cheese and seasoned bread crumbs over top. Bake uncovered at 350° for 15-20 minutes or until cheese is melted and casserole is thoroughly heated.

Mary Bonner, Caddo Council, Shreveport, La.

BAKED AVOCADO

3 avocados
2-3 Tbsp. asparagus tips
Pimento (optional)

1/2 c. thick white sauce
Crumbled bacon

Peel and cut avocados in half, remove seed and place in baking dish, cut side up. Fill avocado center with white sauce and sprinkle with crumbled bacon. Decorate with pimento if desired. Bake at 350° for about 20 minutes or until hot. Serves 6.

Jeanne O'Keefe, Ozone Council, Covington, La.

BAKED BEANS

1 large can pork and
   beans
3 Tbsp. bar-b-que sauce
1 tsp. Worcestershire
   sauce

4 strips bacon
2 Tbsp. cane syrup
1 tsp. Tabasco sauce
1 medium chopped onion

Fry bacon, crumble and reserve. Mix remaining ingredients together. Bake in oven or simmer on low heat with bacon crumbled over top.
     Paula Rutledge, LeBayou
     Council, Houma, La.

NEW ENGLAND BAKED BEANS

12 slices thick sliced
   bacon, cut into 1-inch
   lengths
3 cans (14-16 oz. each)
   pork and beans with
   tomato sauce or baked
   beans

1/2 c. chopped onion
1/3 c. diced celery
1/3 c. chili sauce, catsup or
   bottled barbecue sauce
2 Tbsp. brown sugar or
   molasses
2 Tbsp. drained pickle relish

Saute bacon over low heat until about 2/3 done. Drain bacon on paper towel. Cook onion and celery in 2 tablespoons bacon drippings slowly until tender. Add remaining ingredients and 1/3 of bacon pieces; mix carefully. Pour into 1 1/2-quart casserole. Sprinkle remaining bacon over top of beans. Cover and bake at 350° about 35-40 minutes or if preferred, on top of range in frying pan for 25-30 minutes. Serve garnished with additional bacon strips or curls. Makes 6-8 servings.
     Mrs. Walter R. Sundquist
     Shreveport Works Council
     Bossier City, La.

BAKED BEANS IN SHERRY WINE

2 cans Heinz vegetarian
   beans
1/2 c. brown sugar
1 large onion, cut in
   large pieces

1/2 small jar mustard
2 slices bacon, cut in pieces
1 c. sherry wine
1/2 c. Karo syrup

Mix all ingredients together. Bake in high oven until

1723-79

hot. Lower oven temperature to very, very low and bake 3 hours. If beans become dry or stick, add more wine.

Mrs. Willie Watts, LeBayou
Council, Thibodaux, La.

BARBECUE BEANS

1 large can pork 'n beans	Few strips of bacon
1/2 c. tomato catsup	1/2 tsp. garlic salt
1 Tbsp. Worcestershire	1/2 c. brown sugar
sauce	1 Tbsp. lemon juice
Dash of Tabasco sauce	1 onion, sliced

Mix all ingredients, except onion and bacon. Place in casserole and top with onion and bacon. Cook at 375° for 1 1/2 hours, or try beans in Dutch oven over the grill.

Betty Harman, Caddo Council,
Shreveport, La.

GOOD BAR-B-Q BEANS

1 can Campbell's bar-b-q	3/4 tsp. dry mustard
beans	2 Tbsp. Log Cabin buttered
1/4 c. sweet pickle relish	syrup
2 pkg. Sugar Twin	

Mix ingredients and cook slowly over low flame in thick skillet until all juice is absorbed.

Grace Bell, Ouachita
Council, Monroe, La.

BEAN CASSEROLE

1 can pork and beans	1 can white lima beans
1 can red beans	1 large onion, chopped fine
1 c. catsup	3 Tbsp. bacon drippings
1 Tbsp. vinegar	3 cloves garlic, chopped
1 tsp. mustard	1 Tbsp. syrup
1/4 c. water	Salt and pepper to taste

Fry onion and garlic in bacon fat until limp. Mix with remaining ingredients. Pour into casserole dish; bake 1 hour at 350°.

Ruth Albin for Martha Starkey
Capital Council
Baton Rouge, La.

138

BEAN AND CHEESE CASSEROLE

1/2 c. chopped onion
2 tsp. chili powder
1 (16 oz.) can pork and
   beans with tomato sauce
2 c. shredded sharp
   Cheddar cheese

1/4 c. diced green pepper
2 Tbsp. butter or oleo
3 c. cooked elbow macaroni
1/2 c. milk
1/2 tsp. salt
Green pepper rings

Cook onion, green pepper and chili powder in butter until tender. In casserole, combine onion mixture with beans, macaroni, cheese, milk and salt. Bake at 400° for 30 minutes or until hot. Garnish with green pepper rings. Makes 4 servings.   Andy Gubanesik, Capital
Council, Baton Rouge, La.

DELICIOUS BEAN CASSEROLE

4 strips bacon
1/2 tsp. black pepper
2 Tbsp. Worcestershire
   sauce
1/2 c. whiskey

1 c. chopped onion
2 cans (28 oz. size) pork
   and beans
1 c. shredded sharp
   Cheddar cheese

Fry bacon until crisp. Drain on paper towels. Saute onions and black pepper for 5 minutes in bacon drippings. Place onion mixture into 2 1/2-quart casserole. Add beans, Worcestershire sauce and whiskey. Mix well, cover top of beans with cheese and crumbled bacon. Bake at 350° for 1 hour or until bubbly.   Barbara H. Harris, Central
Council, Bunkie, La.

GREEN BEAN CASSEROLE

2 cans (16 oz. each)
   French style green
   beans, drained

1 can mushroom soup
1 (3 1/2 oz.) can French
   fried onion rings

Mix beans and soup in ungreased 1-quart casserole. Bake uncovered at 350° for 35 minutes. Sprinkle onion rings over top and return to oven for 5-10 minutes or until rings are heated through.   Lillian Fahrenholt, Metairie
Council, Metairie, La.

GREEN BEAN CASSEROLE

2 pkg. frozen French style
  green beans, thawed
1 can mushroom soup
8 oz. grated Velveeta
  cheese

1 c. sliced water chestnuts
1 can bean sprouts, drained
1 medium onion, chopped
1 can French fried onion rings
Salt to taste

Mix all ingredients together, except onion rings. Pour into casserole and bake at 400° for 30 minutes. Top with onion rings and bake additional 10 minutes.

Betty Jackson
Shreveport Works Council
Shreveport, La.

PENNSYLVANIA DUTCH GREEN BEANS

3 slices bacon, diced
2 tsp. cornstarch
1/4 tsp. dry mustard
1 Tbsp. firmly packed
  brown sugar

1 small onion, sliced
1/4 tsp. salt
1 (16 oz.) can cut green beans
1 Tbsp. vinegar
1 hard boiled egg, chopped

Cook bacon until crisp, remove from skillet. Add onion to 1 tablespoon bacon drippings, cook until tender. Blend in cornstarch, salt and mustard. Drain beans, reserving 1/2 cup liquid. Stir in reserved bean liquid. Cook, stirring constantly until thickened and translucent. Blend in sugar and vinegar. Add beans. Heat through. Top with crumbled bacon and chopped egg. Serves 4.

Molly Hoskins, Caddo Council,
Shreveport, La.

SNAPPY GREEN BEANS

1/2 lb. hot sausage,
  cut thin
2 cans (1 lb. each) cut
  green beans
2 shallots, cut thin

1/2 tsp. parsley
1/2 tsp. thyme
1 tsp. oil or shortening
Salt to taste

Fry sausage in oil until slightly browned. Add shallots. Cook 1 minute longer. Add liquid from string beans, thyme, salt and parsley. Cook until sausage is very tender. Add green beans and cook 5 minutes longer. Fresh green beans may be used if desired. Boil beans until tender. Use water from boiled beans and prepare as for canned beans.

Barbara P. Woodworth
Crescent City Council
New Orleans, La.

SWEET AND SOUR GREEN BEANS

3 strips bacon
1 can water chestnuts, sliced
2 tsp. cornstarch
1/4 tsp. salt
1 Tbsp. brown sugar

1 small onion, sliced
1 (16 oz.) can French style string beans
1/4 tsp. dry mustard
1 Tbsp. vinegar
3 Tbsp. chopped pimento

In a skillet, fry bacon until crisp. Remove, drain and crumble. Add onion and chestnuts to bacon drippings and saute until onion is golden, stirring frequently. Drain beans, reserving 1/2 cup liquid. Combine bean liquid, cornstarch, salt, mustard, brown sugar, vinegar. Add to skillet. Cook, stirring constantly, until mixture thickens. Add green beans and pimento, heat through. Serve garnished with crumbled bacon. Makes 4 servings of 1 cup each.

Rebecca Scott, Caddo
Council, Shreveport, La.

GREEN BEANS IN TOMATO SAUCE

1 large onion, chopped fine
1 (8 oz.) can tomato sauce

4 strips bacon
2 cans cut green beans
Salt and pepper to taste

Cut bacon into 1/2-inch strips, fry until almost crisp, drain, leaving just enough to saute onion until almost clear, while bacon finishes cooking. Add beans, tomato sauce, salt, pepper and enough bean juice to cover beans. Cover and cook slowly for about 1/2 hour. Remove cover and simmer until sauce becomes thick.

Note: More or less of each ingredient may be used to suit the individual's taste. Louise Malone, Caddo
Council, Shreveport, La.

LOUISIANA BEANS AND RICE

1/2 lb. pork sausage
1 (1 lb.) can tomatoes
1 c. uncooked regular
   rice
1 c. chopped celery

2 c. water
1 (1 lb.) can kidney beans,
   undrained
1 (1 1/2 oz.) env. seasoning
   mix for Sloppy Joes

Brown sausage in large skillet; do not drain. Add remaining ingredients. Stir until well mixed. Cover and simmer 30 minutes, stirring occasionally, until rice is tender. Makes 4-6 servings.

Mavis W. O'Rourke
Shreveport Works Council
Shreveport, La.

LUAU BEANS

1 c. cubed luncheon
   meat
1/8 tsp. ground ginger
1 (16 oz.) can pork and
   beans with tomato sauce
2 tsp. soy sauce

1/2 c. cucumber, cut in
   2-inch strips
2 Tbsp. butter or oleo
1/2 c. drained pineapple
   chunks
1/4 c. diagonally sliced
   green onions

In saucepan, brown meat and cook cucumber with ginger in butter. Add beans, pineapple, soy sauce and onions. Heat, stir occasionally. Makes 4 servings.

Andy Gubanesik, Capital
Council, Baton Rouge, La.

RED BEANS

1 lb. dry red kidney
   beans, washed
2 lb. smoked Frye sausage
2 c. water
2 Tbsp. sausage drippings

1 onion, cut up
1 bay leaf
Flour
Salt and pepper
Crushed red pepper to taste

Place beans in large pot. Cover with water, add onion and bay leaf. Cook about 2 hours, adding more water if needed. Slice and fry sausage. Reserve 2 tablespoons of drippings. Add sausage to beans. Add enough flour to drippings to make gravy. Add 2 cups water to gravy. Stir

gravy into red beans. Add seasoning. Cook for additional 45 minutes or until tender.   Colleen Ahrens, Caddo
Council, Shreveport, La.

NEW ORLEANS RED BEANS

1 lb. red beans
1 small piece green pepper
1 large chopped onion
1 large slice pickle pork,
   cubed
Pinch of thyme

1 large clove garlic, minced
1 bay leaf
1 rib chopped celery
1 large ham hock
4 qt. water

Bring water to boil in large pot with beans. Add all ingredients. Boil for 1/2 hour. Reduce heat to simmer, continue to cook for 3 hours or until tender. Any other dry beans may be used for this recipe.

Theresa Ficarra, Capital
Council, New Orleans, La.

SWEET RED BEANS NEW ORLEANS STYLE

1 lb. red beans
3 ribs celery, chopped
3 cloves garlic, minced
1 stick butter
5 Tbsp. catsup
2 Tbsp. dehydrated
   parsley
Salt and pepper to taste

2 medium onions, chopped
1/2 bell pepper, chopped
1 lb. pickle meat, or
   1/2 lb. salt meat, cubed
5 large carrots, peeled and
   cut in half
4 qt. water (approx.)

Soak beans overnight. Cook in large pot with water until beans start to soften. Saute onions, celery, bell pepper, garlic, cubed pickle meat and parsley. Add to beans. Add carrots, butter and catsup. Cook on low heat for another hour or until tender. Serve with white rice. Serves 12.   Dorothy Zimmer, Chapter
Past President Pioneer
Partner, New Orleans, La.

ELDRED'S PINTO BEANS

5 lb. pinto beans
1 lb. cut up bacon
Water

1 lb. hamburger meat
Salt and black pepper to
taste

Prepare pinto beans and place in large pot about size of 5-gallon can. Build up a good camp fire. Add hamburger meat, bacon and lots of black pepper and salt to your taste. Boil all day on live coals with plenty of smoke.

Eldred T. Smith, Central
Council, Corpus Christi, Tx.

DEVILED BEETS

3 Tbsp. melted butter
  or oleo
1 Tbsp. prepared mustard
1 tsp. Worcestershire
  sauce

2 tsp. vinegar
1 Tbsp. honey
1/2 tsp. paprika
4 c. hot sliced beets

Combine butter, mustard, vinegar, honey, Worcestershire sauce and paprika. Bring to boiling point. Pour over hot, well drained beets. Stir gently to mix and serve immediately.

Molly Hoskins, Caddo
Council, Shreveport, La.

SPICY ORANGE BEETS

1/4 c. sugar
1 (1 lb.) can sliced
  beets, drained

1/2 c. apple cider vinegar
2 bay leaves
1/2 c. orange juice

Simmer sugar, vinegar and bay leaves in saucepan for 5 minutes. Stir in orange juice and pour over beets. Cover, chill overnight to blend flavors. Makes about 2 cups. Two cups sliced fresh beets may be substituted.

Ann Orr, Evangeline
Council, New Iberia, La.

BROCCOLI CASSEROLE

4 pkg. frozen broccoli
1 c. chopped onions
1 stick garlic cheese
Bread crumbs

1 stick butter
1 c. cream of mushroom
  soup
Almonds

Cook broccoli according to directions, drain and place in bottom of casserole or baking dish. Saute onions in melted butter until soft. Add cheese and mushroom soup. Cook until cheese is melted. Pour soup mixture over broccoli. Sprinkle with bread crumbs and top with sliced or slivered almonds. Bake at 350° for 30 minutes.

Marjorie W. Rowell
Evangeline Council
Lafayette, La.

BROCCOLI CASSEROLE

2 pkg. frozen, chopped,
  cooked broccoli
1 can cream of mush-
  room soup
1 small jar Cheez Whiz

1 or 2 cans chopped water
  chestnuts
2-4 c. cooked rice
1 can cream of chicken soup

Combine and mix all ingredients, heat in 350° oven until hot and bubbly. Very good.

Juanita Ridings, Ouachita
Council, Monroe,La.

BROCCOLI CASSEROLE

1 can mushroom soup
2 pkg. broccoli, chopped
  or whole

1 can Cheddar cheese soup
Bread crumbs

Combine soups and heat together until well blended. Drop broccoli in pot of boiling water, remove when water returns to a boil and drain. Place broccoli in large casserole dish, pour soup mixture over broccoli and sprinkle with bread crumbs. Casserole can stay this way until 15 minutes before serving. Cover and bake at 350° for about 15 minutes, or until heated thoroughly. Decrease recipe if desired, by cutting ingredients in half.

Peggy Childers, Crescent City
Council, New Orleans, La.

BROCCOLI CASSEROLE

2 pkg. frozen, chopped
  broccoli
1 c. mayonnaise
1/2 c. buttered crumbs

2 eggs
1 can mushroom soup
1 medium onion, chopped
Grated cheese

Cook broccoli according to package directions, drain. Beat eggs and soup together. Stir in mayonnaise and onion. Add broccoli. Pour into a greased casserole dish and top with buttered crumbs and grated cheese. Cover with foil and bake 30-40 minutes at 350°. When prepared in advance, sprinkle on crumbs just before heating to avoid a soggy topping   Mildred Henderson, Ouachita Council, Monroe, La.

BROCCOLI CORN BAKE

1 (10 oz.) pkg. chopped,
  thawed broccoli
1 2/3 c. Pepperidge Farm
  herb seasoned stuffing
  mix
1 Tbsp. instant minced
  onion

1 (16 oz.) can cream corn
1 egg, beaten
2 Tbsp. melted butter or oleo
1/2 tsp. salt
Dash of pepper
1/2 stick oleo

Combine broccoli, 2/3 cup stuffing mix, corn, egg, 2 tablespoons butter, onion, salt and pepper. Place in 1 1/2-quart casserole dish. Mix 1 cup stuffing mix and 1/2 stick oleo together and sprinkle over top. Bake at 350° for 45 minutes. Serves 6.   Jan Prestridge, Capital Council, Baton Rouge, La.

BROCCOLI ITALIAN STYLE

1 pkg. frozen broccoli
1/2 tsp. salt
2 Tbsp. olive oil

1/2 c. water
1/4 tsp. garlic powder
1/2 c. Italian flavored bread
  crumbs

Cook broccoli in salted water for 8-10 minutes. Stir in garlic powder and olive oil. Add bread crumbs. Serve hot.
    Terri DiFusco, Capital Council, Naugatuck, Ct.

BROCCOLI RICE CASSEROLE

1 can cream of mush-
   room soup
1/4 c. chopped onion
1 small jar Cheez Whiz

2 Tbsp. oleo
1 pkg. frozen, chopped
   broccoli, thawed
3 c. cooked rice

Brown onions in oleo. Add soup, broccoli, rice and Cheez Whiz. Remove from heat and pour into casserole. Bake covered in 350° oven for 30 minutes. Can be frozen or refrigerated before baking. Betty Spear, Ouachita
                     Council, Monroe, La.

BROCCOLI AND RICE CASSEROLE

2 pkg. chopped broccoli
   or 1 bunch fresh
   broccoli
1 stick oleo
1 c. cooked rice
Paprika
1/2 can cream of chicken
   soup

1 onion, chopped
1/2 c. celery, chopped
1 c. chopped mushrooms
1 small jar Cheez
   Whiz
1/2 can cream of mush-
   room soup

Saute onion, celery and mushrooms in oleo until soft. Set aside. Heat soups and Cheez Whiz. Add rice and broccoli to vegetables. Add soup mixture. Sprinkle with paprika. Bake at 350° for 25 minutes.
                     Judy Lawrence, Calcasieu
                     Council, Lake Charles, La.

BROCCOLI AND RICE

1 stick butter or oleo
1 pkg. frozen, chopped
   broccoli
1 c. grated cheese
Salt and pepper to taste

1 chopped onion
1 can cream of chicken soup
1 1/2 c. cooked rice
Bread crumbs
Tabasco sauce

Saute onions in butter until clear. Cook broccoli according to directions, drain. Mix broccoli with soup and cheese, add onions, stir in rice. Season and mix well. Put into greased casserole and top with bread crumbs. Bake at 350° for 45 minutes. Casserole can be made ahead and frozen.
                     Bettye Lee, Shreveport Works
                     Council, Shreveport, La.

BROCCOLI SUPREME

4 c. broccoli
2 sticks (or less) butter
   or oleo
2 c. water chestnuts, sliced

1 c. pecans, chopped coarse
1 env. Lipton onion soup mix
Bread crumbs

Cook broccoli crisp and drain. Melt butter, add soup mix. Stir until well blended. Add pecans and water chestnuts to broccoli. Add butter mixture. Pour into casserole and top with bread crumbs. Bake in 350° oven until hot and crumbs are brown. Do not overcook. Serves 8-10.

Mrs. Raymond Sparkman
Crescent City Council
New Orleans, La.

SUPREME BROCCOLI

2 (10 oz.) pkg. frozen
   broccoli spears
1/4 c. melted butter
1/2 c. cracker crumbs,
   buttered

1/2 c. chopped onion
2 Tbsp. all-purpose flour
1/2 c. water
1 (8 oz.) jar Kraft Cheez Whiz
3 eggs, beaten

Cook broccoli, drain. Saute onion in butter until tender, blend in flour. Stir in water, cook until smooth and thick. Remove from heat. Add eggs and cheese, stir until cheese melts. Add broccoli. Spoon into greased 2 quart casserole dish. Sprinkle with bread crumbs and bake 30-40 minutes at 350°.

Jan Prestridge, Capital
Council, Baton Rouge, La.

CABBAGE AU GRATIN

1 good sized head of
   cabbage
Oleo

1 c. grated American cheese
1/2 c. bread crumbs
Salt and pepper

Wash cabbage, cut into quarters and steam until tender. Drain. Cut slices off quarters and lay in greased baking dish. Sprinkle with salt, pepper, grated cheese and top with bread crumbs. Dot with butter. Larger amounts can be made by repeating layers. Bake at 400° until crumbs are browned.

Marie Louise Pizzitola, Capital
Council, Chalmette, La.

BAKED CABBAGE

1 head cabbage (approx.
   2 1/2 lb.)
2 Tbsp. flour
1/8 tsp. pepper
1 c. hot milk
1 c. water

2 tsp. salt
2 Tbsp. sugar
3 Tbsp. butter or oleo
1 c. grated Cheddar cheese
Butter

Discard outer leaves of cabbage, wash cabbage and cut into 8 wedges. Pour water in large skillet. Bring to a boil. Add 1 teaspoon salt and cabbage. Cover and cook over medium heat for 10 minutes, drain and arrange cabbage in buttered 12x18-inch shallow baking dish. Sprinkle with mixture of flour, sugar, 1 teaspoon salt and the pepper. Dot with butter. Pour hot milk over cabbage and top with grated cheese. Bake uncovered in preheated 350° oven for 35 minutes. Makes 8 servings.

Gay Turner, Caddo Council,
Shreveport, La.

BAKED RED CABBAGE WITH APPLES

1 small head red cabbage
2 cooking apples, pared
   and sliced
2 Tbsp. sugar
1/3 c. red wine
3/4 Tbsp. flour

1/2 c. seedless grapes
1 small chopped onion
3/4 tsp. salt
3/4 Tbsp. butter
Small amount of vinegar

Shred cabbage, cook covered in small amount of boiling salted water for 8-10 minutes. Add small amount of vinegar to preserve color. Drain, reserving 1 cup liquid. Place layer of cabbage in buttered baking dish. Combine grapes, apples, onion, sugar and salt. Arrange in alternate layers with cabbage, making top layer cabbage. Add cabbage liquid and wine. Dot with butter. Cover and bake at 375° for 1 hour. Shake flour over top, mix lightly with fork and bake 15 minutes longer. Serves 6.

Rebecca Scott Bockmon
Caddo Council
Shreveport, La.

CABBAGE CASSEROLE

2 1/2 - 3 lb. cabbage
2 medium onions, minced
1/2 lb. sharp Cheddar
  cheese, grated
Dash of Tabasco sauce

1 stick butter
1 sweet pepper, minced
1 c. plain bread crumbs
1/2 pt. half and half
Salt to taste

Shred cabbage fine. Cook in boiling salted water until tender, drain. Saute onions and peppers in butter. Mix cheese and bread crumbs. Add onions, peppers and 3/4 of cheese mixture to cabbage. Stir together. Spoon in 8x4-inch square baking dish. Pour cream over mixture. Do not stir. Sprinkle with remaining cheese-bread crumb mixture. Bake in 350° oven until heated through and topping is golden brown.
          Pam Marchese, Metairie
          Council, Metairie, La.

CHINESE STYLE CABBAGE

1 Tbsp. salad oil
1/2 c. thin, diagonal
  sliced celery
1/3 c. chopped onion
Dash of pepper
1/2 tsp. salt

1 1/2 c. finely shredded
  cabbage
1/2 medium green pepper,
  cut into thin strips
1 1/2 tsp. soy sauce
  (optional)

Heat oil in small skillet, add vegetables and mix. Cover tightly and cook over low heat, stirring occasionally, until tender-crisp, about 3-5 minutes. Sprinkle with salt and pepper. Add soy sauce if desired just before serving. Makes 2 servings.
          Rebecca Scott, Caddo
          Council, Shreveport, La.

CHOUX GLORIEUX
(Glorious Cabbage)

1 medium head cabbage
1 onion, chopped
1/2 lb. American cheese
Salt and red pepper to taste

3/4 stick butter
1 can mushroom soup
Bread crumbs

Boil cabbage and cut into small pieces. Wilt onion in butter over low flame. Add soup and stir; add cheese, stir until melted. Put in cabbage, salt, pepper and enough

bread crumbs until it becomes correct consistency for casserole. Place in casserole dish and bake in 350° oven until hot and bubbly.
Mary C. Regan
Crescent City Council
New Orleans, La.

SKILLET CABBAGE

2 c. diced celery
2 large fresh tomatoes,
  chopped
1 large bell pepper,
  in strips
1/4 c. bacon drippings

2 large onions, sliced
4 c. cabbage, coarsely
  shredded
2 tsp. sugar
Salt and pepper to taste

In large skillet, heat bacon drippings, add chopped vegetables. Season with sugar, salt and pepper. Cover and cook over medium heat 5 minutes. Vegetables should be crisp-tender. Serves 4-6. Ann Orr, Evangeline Council, New Iberia, La.

CABBAGE STROGANOFF

1 large cabbage, slivered
2 Tbsp. butter
1 Tbsp. vinegar
1 inch water in pan

1 tsp. salt
1 Tbsp. sugar
1 c. sour cream

Boil slivered cabbage in salted water, tightly covered, for 5 minutes; drain. Butter sides and bottom of casserole. Place hot cabbage in casserole, add butter and toss. Add sugar, vinegar and sour cream. Toss well. This is for those who do not like cabbage. Jean Coon, Caddo Council Shreveport, La.

CANDIED CARROTS

2 lb. carrots
1/2 c. Mrs. Butterworth's
  syrup

2 Tbsp. oleo
Boiling water

Wash, peel and cut carrots diagonally into 1-inch slices. Place in 2-quart saucepan. Add boiling water to measure 1 inch. Cover and simmer 20 minutes until tender, drain.

Add oleo and toss until carrots are well coated. Add syrup, heat and roll carrots in syrup until evenly glazed. Cook over medium heat until well glazed. Watch carefully to prevent scorching. Jeanette English, Caddo Council, Shreveport, La.

CARROT CASSEROLE

2 medium size cans of carrot strips or carrot rings, plus juice of 1 can carrots

1 can French fried onion rings
1 small jar Bac-Os
Small amount of butter or oleo

Mix carrots, onion rings and Bac-Os in casserole. Dot with butter. Bake at 350° until hot.

Gayle Palermo, Westmoor Council, Kenner, La.

CARROT COINS

2 Tbsp. tender carrots
1/2 c. salad oil
1 c. sugar
1 onion, sliced thin rings
1 tsp. prepared mustard
1/4 tsp. black pepper

1 c. tomato juice
3/4 c. apple cider vinegar
1 green pepper, sliced thin rings
1 tsp. Worcestershire sauce
3/4 tsp. salt

Scrape carrots, slice like coins. Boil 10 minutes, until crispy. Combine remaining ingredients and add carrots. Refrigerate 24 hours. Remove carrots from marinade before serving. Serves 8-10.

Mrs. Raymond Sparkman Crescent City Council New Orleans, La.

CARROTS SUPREME

2 (No. 2) cans carrots
1 bell pepper, chopped
1/4 c. corn oil
1/4 c. brown sugar

1 can tomato soup
1 onion, chopped
1/4 c. vinegar
2 Tbsp. granulated sugar

Bring carrots to a boil; drain. Add tomato soup. Add other ingredients. Marinate 24 hours in refrigerator.

Rose M. Malone, Central Council, Alexandria, La.

COPPER PENNIES

2 large cans diced carrots
1 green pepper, sliced

1 medium onion, sliced
1 stick celery, chopped

Mix ingredients, add Sauce.

Sauce:

1/2 c. salad oil
1 can tomato soup
1 tsp. Worcestershire
   sauce

1 tsp. mustard
1 c. sugar
1 tsp. salt and pepper
3/4 c. white vinegar

Mix sauce and heat a few minutes. Pour over carrot mixture. Place in refrigerator 24 hours, stirring occasionally.
       Sadie Foil, Ozone Council,
       Bogalusa, La.

COPPER PENNIES

1 can tomato soup
1 c. vinegar
1 tsp. brown sugar
1 Tbsp. Worcestershire
   sauce
Carrots

1/4 c. oil
1/2 c. finely chopped green
   peppers
1 tsp. mustard
1/2 c. chopped onion

Cook carrots, thin rounds. Mix with mixture. Marinate overnight.
       Margaret Aletha Keenan
       Ozone Council, Bogalusa, La.

COPPER PENNIES

2 c. sliced round
   cooked carrots
1 can tomato soup
Salt, black and lemon
   pepper to taste

1 bell pepper
1 large or 2 small white
   onions
1/2 c. cooking oil
Dash of Tabasco sauce
Dash of Worcestershire sauce

Slice peppers and onions into thin slices and separate onions into rings. Mix all ingredients together and store in refrigerator. Keeps indefinitely.
       Katherine Slover, Caddo
       Council, Phoenix, Az.

MARINATED CARROTS

1 pkg. carrots
1/4 c. peanut oil
1/2 tsp. mustard seed
1 Tbsp. oregano
Salt to taste
Pinch of red pepper

2 chopped green onions
1/4 c. vinegar
1/2 tsp. prepared mustard
1/2 stalk celery, chopped
Dash of hot sauce
1/4 tsp. garlic juice

Scrape, peel carrots and cut into strips. Mix remaining ingredients. Marinate carrots in mixture 2 or 3 days, stirring daily.

Mavis W. O'Rourke
Shreveport Works Council
Shreveport, La.

MARINATED CARROTS

3 jars whole small
  carrots
1 purple onion, sliced
1 can tomato sauce
1 Tbsp. Worcestershire
  sauce

1 c. white vinegar
Salt and pepper to taste
1 jar pimientos
1/4 c. sugar or Sugar
  Twin
Beets (optional)

Combine ingredients. Refrigerate. Will keep 2 weeks in refrigerator.

Mary Ahrens, Caddo
Council, Shreveport, La.

FAR EAST CELERY

4 c. celery, sliced in
  1-inch pieces
1 can cream of chicken
  soup
1/4 tsp. salt
1/4 c. slivered almonds

1 (8 oz.) can water chestnuts, drained and sliced
1/4 c. chopped pimento
1/2 c. chow mein noodles
2 Tbsp. melted butter or
  oleo

Cook celery in small amount of boiling, salted water until tender, 6-8 minutes; drain. Combine celery, soup, water chestnuts and salt. Mix well and pour mixture into lightly greased 1 1/2-quart casserole. Combine noodles, almonds and butter, toss lightly and sprinkle over top of casserole. Bake at 350° for 30 minutes. Makes 6 servings.

Denise Barteet, Caddo
Council, Shreveport, La.

SWEET AND SOUR CARROTS

1 lb. carrots, sliced
   diagonally 3/4-inch
   long
1 (8 oz.) can pineapple
   chunks, undrained
1/2 tsp. salt

1 medium bell pepper, cut
   into 1-inch squares
1/3 c. sugar
1 Tbsp. cornstarch
2 Tbsp. vinegar
2 tsp. soy sauce

Cook carrots, covered in small amount of salted water for 15 minutes. Add green pepper, cover and cook additional 3 minutes. Drain and set aside. Drain pineapple and reserve juice; add water to make 1/3 cup liquid. Combine sugar, cornstarch, salt, pineapple liquid, vinegar and soy sauce, cook and stir until bubbly. Pour over vegetables and pineapple, mix thoroughly and heat through.

Mrs. Tony Corcoran
Crescent City Council
New Orleans, La.

CELERY CASSEROLE

2 c. sliced celery
1/2 c. bread crumbs
Hot sauce to taste

1 can cheese soup
1/2 c. Cheddar cheese,
   grated

Cook celery in boiling salty water about 10 minutes, drain. Stir in soup and hot sauce. Pour into casserole dish. Top with bread crumbs and cheese. Bake at 350° about 25-30 minutes.

Marilou Bridges, Caddo
Council, Shreveport, La.

BAKED CORN

1 can kernel corn,
   drained
2 eggs

1 can cream style corn
1 Tbsp. flour
1/2 stick butter or oleo

Combine ingredients and bake in 350° oven for 1 hour.

Sylvia Campbell, Caddo
Council, Shreveport, La.

CREAM CORN CASSEROLE

1 (8 1/2 oz.) can cream
  corn
1/4 c. flour

1 egg
Salt and pepper to taste
Butter or oleo

Mix egg, corn, flour, salt and pepper. Pour into well buttered baking dish. Dot with oleo or butter. Bake 1/2 hour at 400°. Serves 3.   Gretna Anderson, Central
Council, Alexandria, La.

CORN CASSEROLE

1/4 chopped green pepper
2 tsp. chopped pimento
2 Tbsp. oleo or butter
1 (No. 2) can cream style
  corn

1 (3 oz.) can French fried
  onion rings
1 egg, slightly beaten
Salt and pepper to taste
1 Tbsp. milk or cream

Saute pepper in oleo until soft, add pimento. When heated, blend in corn, milk, egg and seasonings. Crush 2/3 of onion rings and add to corn mixture. Pour into 1 1/2-quart casserole. Bake at 350° for about 30 minutes or until firm. Sprinkle with remaining onion rings and return to oven for about 5 more minutes. Serves 4.
    Mrs. Richard D. (Vermelle)
Sylvest, Ozone Council,
Hammond, La.

CORN CASSEROLE

1 (No. 2) can cream style
  corn
1 c. grated Cheddar
  cheese
1 tsp. salt
1/8 tsp. pepper
1/4 c. chopped onion

3 eggs, beaten
1 c. milk
6 Tbsp. butter
1/8 tsp. paprika
1/2 c. chopped celery
1/4 c. chopped green pepper
1 c. cracker crumbs

Combine and mix all ingredients. Bake uncovered in casserole at 350° for 50 minutes. Can be mixed the day before and then baked.   Helen Patton
Shreveport Works Council
Shreveport, La.

CORN FRITTERS

1 (16 oz.) can whole
  kernel corn, drained
1/4 c. milk
2 eggs

1 c. flour
3/4 tsp. salt
1 tsp. baking powder

Mix ingredients; heat salad oil to 400° in electric skillet. Drop batter by tablespoonfuls into hot fat. Fry until browned. Turn once.
    Mearl S. Byles, Central
    Council, Natchitoches, La.

CORN PIE

4 eggs
2 Tbsp. butter

6 ears corn
Salt and pepper to taste

Cut the corn from cob and scrape all juice. Beat eggs lightly. Mix eggs, corn butter, salt and pepper. Bake in moderate oven for 1 hour; if shallow pan, only 1/2 hour. Has appearance of baked custard.
    Catherine (Chadwick) McCraw
    Caddo Council
    Shreveport, La.

CORN PUDDING

1 can cream style corn
8 crackers, crumbled
3 Tbsp. oleo

1 egg
1/2 c. evaporated milk
Salt and pepper

Combine ingredients. Pour into casserole dish. Bake about 45 minutes at 350° or until thick.
    Mary Ahrens, Caddo Council,
    Shreveport, La.

MY RADAR CORN PUDDING

6 c. corn
2 eggs
1 tsp. seasoning salt
1 tsp. pepper
2 pkg. Sugar Twin

1 c. evaporated milk
1 Tbsp. onion flakes
1 tsp. salt
2/3 stick oleo
Enough water to make juicy

Combine and mix ingredients. Pour into buttered Pyrex casserole dish. Bake in radar 20-25 minutes, turning and stirring every 5 minutes until done. Freezes well.

Grace Bell, Ouachita
Council, Monroe, La.

MAQUE CHOUX

12 ears corn
1 medium onion, finely
  chopped
1/2 medium green pepper,
  chopped
1/4 - 1/2 tsp. sugar

2 Tbsp. butter or oleo,
  melted
2 Tbsp. tomatoes and green
  chilies
Salt and pepper to taste

Cut corn from cob, scraping cob to remove pulp. Combine corn and remaining ingredients in heavy saucepan. Cook over low heat 20-30 minutes or until corn is tender, stir frequently. Serves 6-8. Betty Harman, Caddo Council, Shreveport, La.

SPANISH CORN CASSEROLE

1 can cream style corn
3 eggs, beaten
1 green pepper, finely
  chopped
1/2 lb. grated cheese

1 can tomatoes
2 tsp. flour
2 Tbsp. chopped onion
1 tsp. sugar
Salt and pepper to taste

Mix all ingredients. Pour into greased casserole. Bake at 350° for 45-50 minutes. Mary Anne Andrews, Ouachita Council, Monroe, La.

CORN SOUFFLE

2 cans cream corn
1 c. corn bread mix
2 tsp. garlic salt
Grated cheese

4 eggs, beaten
1 c. Wesson oil
1 small jar pimentos

Combine and mix corn, eggs, oil, garlic salt, pimentos, corn bread mix. Pour into casserole; bake at 325° for 45-50 minutes. Sprinkle grated cheese over casserole just before corn gets done. Sandra K. Autrey, Metairie Council, Metairie, La.

158

CORN-ZUCCHINI CASSEROLE

1 medium onion, chopped
3 Tbsp. butter or oleo
1 (8 oz.) can whole kernel
  corn, drained
Salt and pepper to taste

1 green pepper, chopped
6 small zucchini, sliced thin
1 (16 oz.) can tomatoes
1/2 c. Parmesan cheese,
  grated

Saute onion and pepper in butter until golden in color. Add sliced zucchini and simmer until tender. Add tomatoes and drained corn, heat. Add salt and pepper. Pour in casserole and top with cheese. Place under broiler to brown lightly.   Mrs. Johnnie B. Cole, Caddo Council, Shreveport, La.

STUFFED BAKED CUCUMBERS

3 whole cucumbers,
  sliced lengthwise
1 small onion, chopped
  fine
Salt and pepper to taste

1 c. dark bread crumbs
2 Tbsp. oleo
Parmesan cheese
Paprika

Remove cucumber meat with melon scooper or teaspoon, leaving a nice shell. I use another peeled cucumber to have a little more cucumber meat. Chop cucumber fine, add remaining ingredients, except cheese and paprika. Mix well and fill shells, rounding slightly. Sprinkle cheese and paprika on top. I like the fresh ground black pepper on this also. Place in baking dish so they sit well and bake at 350° for 1 hour. Serves 6.   Lou Teixeira, LeBayou Council, Thibodaux, La.

BAKED CUSHAW

6 c. cushaw pulp
1 egg, beaten
Sugar to taste
1 c. pecans, finely chopped

1 stick butter or oleo
1 Tbsp. flour
2 tsp. vanilla

Cut unpeeled cushaw in large pieces and boil in small amount of water until soft. Cool and spoon pulp out of hull. Mash, add egg, flour and sugar. Mix well. Stir in butter and vanilla. Pour into greased Pyrex casserole.

Top casserole with pecans and bake for 1 hour, or more, until bottom begins to brown. June Harllee, Caddo Council, Shreveport, La.

EGGPLANT CASSEROLE

2 medium size eggplants
3 Tbsp. onion soup mix
Garlic powder
Onion flakes
1 Tbsp. or more oleo
Seasoned pepper

Crushed potato chips, Ritz crackers and white crackers (about 3 c.)
1/3 c. grated cheese
3 beaten eggs
Salt to taste

Slice eggplants and soak in salt water about 5 minutes. Drain and rinse. Boil until tender, drain. Add oleo and mash. Add onion soup mix, generous amount of garlic powder, onion flakes, grated cheese, eggs, salt and seasoned pepper to about 2 1/4 cups of the cracker mixture, reserving 3/4 cup for later use. Add mashed eggplant to mixture. The mixture should be about the consistency of soft turkey dressing. If necessary, add a little sweet milk. Pour into a well greased casserole. Grate more cheese on top and cover with the reserved crumb mixture. Bake at 350° for 45 minutes or until tests done. This can be cooked in small loaf pan and frozen for future use for small families.
Verle Oliphant, Caddo Council, Shreveport, La.

EGGPLANT CASSEROLE

1 eggplant
1 c. Pepperidge Farm herb dressing bread
1 can mushroom soup

1/2 c. chopped onion
1/3 c. milk
1 egg

Peel and dice eggplant, cook in salt water; drain. Mix all ingredients and place in buttered casserole dish.

Topping:

1/2 c. stuffing bread
1/2 c. grated cheese

2 Tbsp. melted butter

Mix ingredients and sprinkle over casserole. Bake at 350° until hot and bubbly. Betty Jackson
Shreveport Works Council
Shreveport, La.

EGGPLANT FRITTERS

1 eggplant
1/8 tsp. pepper
1/2 c. cream or evap-
  orated milk
1/2 tsp. salt
3 eggs, beaten
Flour

Boil eggplant, unpeeled, until soft. Cut in half and scoop out pulp. Mash well. Cool. Stir in salt and pepper. Add eggs and mix well. Add cream and sift in enough flour to make a rather stiff batter. Drop by spoonfuls in hot deep fat (350°). Cook until brown. Drain on paper towels. Serves 6.   Katherine Slover, Caddo
                                         Council, Phoenix, Az.

EGGPLANT ORIENTAL

2 green bell peppers
3 Tbsp. cooking oil
3 tsp. salt
2 eggplants
6 ripe tomatoes
1 tsp. paprika

Seed and cut peppers into small pieces. Pare and cut eggplants into small pieces. Cook peppers and eggplants in the fat until slightly brown, add tomatoes and seasonings. Continue cooking until eggplant is done. Serve very hot.   Mearl S. Byles, Central
                                         Council, Natchitoches, La.

OUT OF THIS WORLD EGGPLANT

1 medium eggplant, peeled
  and cubed
Salt and pepper to taste
3/4 c. corn bread crumbs
Buttered crumbs
2 eggs, beaten
1 small onion, chopped
1/4 c. milk
3 Tbsp. butter, melted
Grated Cheddar cheese
  (optional)

Boil eggplant until tender, drain and mash. Add eggs, onion, salt, pepper, milk, corn bread crumbs, butter and cheese. Mix well, pour into buttered casserole. Sprinkle top with buttered crumbs. Bake at 350° for 25-30 minutes.
                                         Ray Ducharme, Caddo
                                         Council, Shreveport, La.

EGGPLANT PARMESAN

1 1/2 lb. eggplant (2-3 small), cut in 1/2-inch slices
1/4 c. butter or oleo
1 tsp. basil, crushed
1/3 c. all-purpose flour
Salt to taste
1 (15 oz.) can tomato sauce
1 1/2 c. (6 oz.) shredded Mozzarella cheese
1/2 c. grated Parmesan cheese

Sprinkle both sides of eggplant lightly with salt and spread them out in one layer on board or platter for about 20 minutes. Pat eggplant dry with paper towels. Dip each slice in flour, shake off excess. Melt butter over low fire in heavy skillet. Brown eggplant slices, few at a time. Transfer to paper towels when browned. Combine tomato sauce and basil. Pour 1/2 cup tomato sauce into buttered 1 1/2-quart shallow baking dish. Spread layer of eggplant slices over sauce. Sprinkle on layer of Mozzarella cheese and Parmesan cheese. Repeat layers. Cover with foil and bake in preheated 350° oven for 20 minutes; uncover, bake 5 minutes.

Mrs. Jeannine Prattini, Capital Council, Chalmette, La.

SCALLOPED EGGPLANT

1 medium eggplant
3 Tbsp. butter, melted
1/2 c. milk
1 medium onion, chopped
3/4 c. soft bread crumbs
Salt and pepper to taste

Pare and dice eggplant. Parboil and drain. Saute onion in 1 tablespoon butter until soft, add to eggplant. Place eggplant mixture in casserole with alternate layers of bread crumbs and remaining butter. Season to taste, pour milk over casserole. Bake at 375° for 30 minutes.

Mrs. Johnnie B. Cole, Caddo Council, Shreveport, La.

SPANISH EGGPLANT

1 medium eggplant, peeled and cut into 1/2-inch slices
1/4 c. bacon drippings
1 1/2 tsp. salt
2 Tbsp. sugar
1/2 c. dry bread crumbs
1/2 c. chopped onion
1/2 c. chopped green pepper
1 (1 lb.) can whole tomatoes, cut into quarters
1/2 c. grated Parmesan cheese

162

Combine eggplant, onion, green pepper and bacon drippings; mix well. Let stand 10 minutes. Stir in tomatoes, salt and sugar. Place in saucepan, cover and cook 5-10 minutes over low heat. Spoon mixture into greased, shallow casserole. Sprinkle with bread crumbs and cheese. Bake at 350° for 20 minutes. Makes 6-8 servings.

Ann Orr, Evangeline
Council, New Iberia, La.

EGGPLANT SUPREME

1 large eggplant
2 ribs celery, chopped
1/2 stick oleo or butter
1 c. sharp cheese, grated
Cracker crumbs

1 small bell pepper, chopped
1 large onion, chopped
1 tsp. Worcestershire sauce
1 c. ripe olives, chopped
Hot sauce to taste

Cut up peeled eggplant and steam in a little water on low heat until tender. Saute onion, bell pepper and celery in oleo. Add drained eggplant. Add Worcestershire sauce and hot sauce, mix well. Add cheese and olives. Pour in casserole dish and top with cracker crumbs. Bake 30 minutes in 375° oven.

Bertile Sanchez, Capital
Council, Baton Rouge, La.

CONFETTI GRITS SOUFFLE

2 c. milk
1 tsp. salt
1/2 tsp. sugar
3 eggs, separated
1 Tbsp. chopped pimento

1/2 c. grits
1/2 tsp. baking powder
2 Tbsp. melted butter
1 Tbsp. chopped green
  pepper

Scald milk, add grits. Cook until thick. Add salt, baking powder, sugar, butter, peppers and pimento (put peppers in boiling water 1 minute). Beat egg yolks and add to mixture. Beat egg whites to soft peaks and fold into mixture. Pour into 1 1/2 - 2-quart buttered casserole and bake uncovered at 375° for 25-30 minutes.

Connie Younker
Shreveport Works Council
Shreveport, La.

GLORIOUS CHEESE GRITS

1 c. grits
2/3 c. milk
1/2 c. Cheddar, shredded
Bacon curls or bits

1/4 lb. butter
3 eggs, beaten
1 roll Kraft's bacon and
   cheese, sliced

Cook grits according to package instructions. While hot, add butter and bacon-cheese slices, stirring until melted. Add milk to beaten eggs, mix into grits mixture. Turn into greased 2-quart casserole dish and top with shredded cheese. Bake in 350° oven for 45 minutes. Garnish with bacon curls. Serves 8. "Nobody turns up their nose at these grits."
   Katherine Slover, Caddo Council, Phoenix, Az.

HOMINY CASSEROLE

2 cans hominy (yellow)
Cheddar cheese

1 can mushroom soup

Place 1 can hominy in casserole dish. Pour 1/2 of soup over top. Layer cheese slices over hominy and soup mixture. Repeat layers with remainder of ingredients and bake in 325° oven until hot and bubbly.
   Eloise H. Stacy, Caddo Council, Shreveport, La.

MARINATED MIRLITON

1 doz. (12) mirlitons
10 Tbsp. apple cider
   vinegar
1/2 tsp. powdered thyme
2 Tbsp. salt

1 c. corn oil
1/2 tsp. powdered oregano
1/2 tsp. chopped red pepper
Powdered garlic and garlic
   cloves to taste

Peel and remove seed from mirlitons and cut into bite size pieces. In large pot of boiling water, place mirlitons and cook for no more than 3 minutes. Drain and cool. Make up marinade and pour over mirlitons.
   Floyd Shumann, Ozone Council, Hammond, La.

STUFFED MIRLITON

3 mirlitons
1 lb. ground meat or
  1/2 lb. ham
Salt and pepper to taste
1 c. cooked rice

1 large onion
Chopped bell pepper, green
  onions and parsley
Bread crumbs
Cooking oil

Boil mirlitons until tender, cut and scoop out insides leaving shell to stuff. Add cooking oil in skillet, add onions and cook until tender. Add mirliton pulp, cook until tender. Add onions, parsley, bell pepper, salt, pepper and cooked rice. Fill shells and sprinkle bread crumbs on top. Bake 30 minutes at 350°.

Leigh Hargis, LeBayou
Council, Lockport, La.

ANNE'S GOLDEN FRIED MUSHROOMS

Fresh whole mushrooms
1/2 c. milk
Cooking oil

2 eggs, beaten
Flour, salt and pepper

Wash and dry mushrooms. Make batter of beaten eggs and milk. Mix flour, salt and pepper in paper bag. Dip mushrooms in egg batter, then shake in the bag containing salt and pepper. Fry in deep fat until golden brown. Serve immediately.

Carolyn Palmer, Capital
Council, Baton Rouge, La.

STUFFED MUSHROOMS

1 box fresh mushrooms
  (remove stems and
  mince them)
1 small bunch shallots,
  cut up
1 shake hot pepper
  flakes

4 Tbsp. butter or oleo
3 Tbsp. flour
3/4 c. milk
1 dash Worcestershire sauce
Salt and pepper to taste
1/2 lb. crabmeat (approx.
  5 fresh crabs)

Saute shallots and mushroom stems in butter. Remove from heat and stir in flour. Add milk, using more or less to create medium white sauce consistency. Add salt, pepper flakes and Worcestershire sauce. Simmer, adding crabmeat,

until hot. Stuff mushroom caps and place in a 350° oven
for 15-20 minutes.   Mae Naccari, Crescent City
                                 Council, New Orleans, La.

STUFFED MUSHROOMS

25 large mushrooms   1 1/2 tsp. chopped shallots
1 stick butter   2 tsp. minced onions
1 1/2 tsp. chopped parsley   3 Tbsp. grated Parmesan
1/2 c. Italian bread   cheese
  crumbs   1/3 c. white wine
Garlic powder to taste   Salt and pepper to taste

Wash mushrooms. Remove stems and chop stems fine.
Saute stems, onions, parsley, shallots in 1/2 stick melted
butter, add cheese, 1/4 cup bread crumbs and wine. Simmer
about 10-15 minutes. Grease casserole. Sprinkle remaining
bread crumbs and chunks of remaining butter in bottom.
Stuff each mushroom cap with mixture and place in casserole. Sprinkle additional bread crumbs on top. Bake in 350°
oven for 10-20 minutes.   Evelyn Sinnigson, Capital
                                Council, Baton Rouge, La.

GREEN PEAS AND MUSHROOMS

1 (10 oz.) pkg. frozen   1 1/2 lb. fresh mushrooms,
  green peas   washed and sliced
1/4 c. chopped onion   Salt and pepper to taste
1/2 pt. heavy cream

Thaw peas in large skillet. Combine mushrooms, onion
and heavy cream. Cook over medium heat until mushrooms
begin to release juices. Add peas, cook over medium heat,
stirring frequently, until liquid reduces to shiny sauce.
Stir in salt and pepper to taste.
                                Lynn Babin, Westmoor
                                Council, Kenner, La.

BAKED ONIONS

12 medium onions
1 (3 3/4 oz.) pkg. potato chips
1/2 c. milk
1/2 lb. Wisconsin mild cheese
2 cans cream of mushroom soup
1/8 tsp. red pepper

In 9x13-inch buttered dish, layer alternate layers of thinly sliced onions, crushed potato chips and grated cheese. Pour soup and milk over top of mixture. It will cook through. Sprinkle red pepper over top and bake at 350° for 1 hour.

Jan Prestridge, Capital
Council, Baton Rouge, La.

STUFFED JALAPENO PEPPERS

15 medium sized pickled jalapeno peppers
2 Tbsp. mayonnaise
1 (4 oz.) can sardines
2 eggs, boiled and shelled

Slice peppers in half lengthwise, remove seeds and rinse in cold water. Thoroughly mix eggs and sardines, blend in mayonnaise to create a pastry mixture. Fill pepper halves with sardine mixture, round off slightly. Place on party tray and chill before serving.

Charley McGrew, Caddo
Council, Shreveport, La.

MISSION INN POTATOES

6 medium potatoes (2 lb.), peeled and sliced 1/4-inch thick
1 tsp. salt
1 lb. Cheddar cheese, shredded
1 egg, lightly beaten
Paprika
1 medium onion, sliced
1 clove garlic, chopped
1 tsp. instant flavored bouillon
1 (4 oz.) can green chiles, seeded and cut into strips
1 c. water
1 (8 oz.) carton sour cream

Bring water to boil in saucepan. Add potatoes, onion, garlic, salt and bouillon. Return to boil, stirring. Lower heat, cook covered 10-12 minutes or until potatoes are almost tender. Pour half the potatoes and liquid into shallow 2-quart casserole or 13x9-inch pan. Cover with half the cheese and half the chiles. Top with remaining potato

mixture and all but 2 tablespoons of the remaining cheese.
Bake in 350° oven for 20 minutes. Remove from oven.
Make mixture of sour cream and egg, spread over potatoes.
Arrange remaining chiles and cheese on sour cream layer.
Sprinkle with paprika. Bake 10 minutes more. Let stand
15 minutes before serving. Makes 6 servings.

Ann Orr, Evangeline
Council, New Iberia, La.

PAPA'S MEXICANA

1/2 c. boiling water
2 c. Ranchera Sauce
Salt and pepper to taste

3 large potatoes
3 Tbsp. shortening

Cut the potatoes into thin slices. Fry them in shortening to a light brown texture. Add Ranchera Sauce, salt, pepper and boiling water. Lower the fire and simmer for 15 minutes. Serves 6.

Ranchera Sauce:

2 c. fresh chopped
tomatoes
1/4 c. chopped hot
green peppers

1/4 c. chopped onions
2 Tbsp. shortening
Salt and pepper to taste

Saute onions and peppers in shortening. When onions are translucent, add the tomatoes and seasoning and simmer over a low fire for 5 minutes. Betty Harman, Caddo
Council, Shreveport, La.

POMMES SOUFFLES

2 lb. Idaho potatoes
or 1 potato per person
1 deep-fat fryer at very
hot temperature

1 deep-fat fryer at moderate
temperature
Salt to taste

Peel potatoes and cut into long narrow slices, 1/8-inch thick. Put slices in wire basket and wash with cold water to remove excess starch. Dry. Place potato slices, few at a time, in frying basket in moderately hot fat. When edges begin to puff slightly, transfer them to very hot fat and cook until fully puffed and golden brown. Drain on absorbent paper, sprinkle with salt and serve at once. Serves 6.

Robert E. Carnahan, LeBayou
Council, Houma, La.

POTATOES AU GRATIN

Potatoes
Salt and pepper to taste
1/2 can water

1 can cheese soup
1 stick oleo

Slice enough potatoes to fill a 2-quart casserole dish. Potatoes are sliced cottage style (round). Cut up butter over potatoes, add soup and water; mix. Cover and bake at 350° for 1 hour. Uncover, add salt and pepper and stir. Bake additional 30 minutes or until done.

Marilou Bridges, Caddo
Council, Shreveport, La.

BRABANT POTATOES

3 lb. Idaho potatoes
4 cloves garlic, chopped
Salt to taste

1 stick butter
2 tsp. chopped parsley
Shortening

Peel and wash potatoes. Cut into small cubes, rinse in cold water and drain. Fry in deep fat until golden brown and set aside. Saute garlic in butter, add potatoes and parsley. Mix well and season to taste. Serves 8.

Robert E. Carnahan, LeBayou
Council, Houma, La.

POTATO CASSEROLE

6 large potatoes
1 c. milk
1 stick butter

2 c. sour cream
2 c. grated cheese
2/3 c. onions, including tops

Boil potatoes in skins. Chill until very cold. Shred on grater. Melt butter in double boiler. Add cheese gradually. Mix sour cream and milk, add to cheese mixture. Add onions, mix well. Add to shredded potatoes. Bake in casserole at 350° for 45 minutes. Sprinkle with grated cheese for last 5 minutes of baking. Linda Teague, Caddo
Council, Bossier City, La.

POTATO CASSEROLE

2 lb. frozen hash brown
  potatoes, at room
  temperature
1 can cream of chicken
  soup

1/2 c. butter, melted
Salt and pepper to taste
1 pt. sour cream
2 c. grated cheese
1/2 c. onion, chopped fine

Pour 1/2 cup melted butter over potatoes. Mix all ingredients together and place in casserole. Sprinkle on topping and bake at 350° for 45 minutes.

Topping:

1/4 c. butter

2 c. crackers, bread or
  corn flake crumbs

Combine and sprinkle over top of casserole.
Carlotta Thomas, Ouachita
Council, Monroe, La.

POTATO CASSEROLE

1 lb. potatoes
1 tsp. salt
1/2 stick butter or oleo
4 oz. jar pimentos,
  chopped

1/2 lb. cheese, grated
1/4 tsp. pepper
2 Tbsp. flour
1 c. milk
1 Tbsp. parsley flakes

Cook potatoes in jackets until tender. Cool, dice potatoes. Add pimento and cheese. Place in casserole. Season with salt and pepper. Melt butter, add flour and blend until smooth. Add milk gradually, stir constantly. Cook until thick. Pour over casserole and sprinkle with parsley flakes. Cook in 400° oven for 30 minutes.
Mrs. Eddie (Vera) Howie
Ouachita Council
Monroe, La.

POTATO CASSEROLE

2 pkg. (12 oz. size)
  frozen grated hash
  brown potatoes, thawed
1/2 stick butter

1 (8 oz.) carton sour cream
1/4 c. chopped green onion
1 can cream of chicken soup
1 c. grated cheese

Combine potatoes, onion, butter, sour cream and soup.
Pour into large shallow baking dish. Bake at 350° for 45
minutes. Top with cheese a few minutes before removing
from oven. Marilou Bridges, Caddo
Council, Shreveport, La.

EASY POTATOES

1 large pkg. frozen
   hash brown potatoes
   (with or without onion),
   or frozen French fries
Oleo

1 can cream of chicken soup
1 soup can water or half
   water and half milk
Cheese (optional)

Defrost potatoes enough to handle. Mix soup and water
together. Grease bottom and sides of casserole dish with
oleo. Put layer of potatoes, pour half of soup mixture over
potatoes. Repeat layers. Dot with butter or oleo. Bake
30 minutes in 350° oven. Add cheese to top if desired, let
melt and serve. Jean Stanley, Crescent City
Council, New Orleans, La.

HASH BROWN POTATOES

3 c. raw diced potatoes
1/2 tsp. salt
3 Tbsp. fat

1 medium onion, chopped
1/8 tsp. pepper

Mix potatoes, onion, salt and pepper. Heat fat in
skillet. Spread potato mixture in skillet, flatten with broad
spatula. Saute over low heat until bottom is brown. Turn
whole cake in one piece if possible, or two halves. Brown
again. Serve hot. Mrs. Johnnie B. Cole, Caddo
Council, Shreveport, La.

POTATOES AND MUSHROOMS

3 Tbsp. butter or oleo
1/2 lb. mushrooms, cut in
   small pieces
1 tsp. salt
Dash of Louisiana red
   hot pepper sauce
1 tsp. dried dill weed

1 small onion, minced
1 lb. potatoes, cooked,
   peeled and sliced thinly
Dash of pepper
1/2 c. sour cream, at room
   temperature

Melt butter in large skillet. Saute onion and mushrooms until tender. Add potatoes, salt, pepper and pepper sauce. Cook over medium heat, stirring carefully with pancake turner, about 5 minutes or until potatoes are heated. Stir in sour cream. Sprinkle with dill. Serve immediately.

June Harllee, Caddo
Council, Shreveport, La.

PIZZA POTATOES

4 large potatoes
4 green onions, sliced
1/4 tsp. oregano
2 medium tomatoes, sliced
Parmesan cheese

8 oz. shredded Mozzarella, Jack or Cheddar cheese
1/4 tsp. basil
1/2 lb. precooked Italian or Polish sausage, sliced 1/2-inch thick

Bake potatoes in 450° oven until tender, 50 or 60 minutes. In small bowl, toss cheese with onion, oregano and basil. Slice potatoes in half lengthwise, place cut side up in baking dish. Sprinkle with half the cheese mixture. Top with tomatoes and sausage, add remaining cheese mixture. Bake at 450° for 8-10 minutes until golden brown. Serve sprinkled with grated Parmesan cheese, if desired. Makes 4 main dish servings.

Ann Orr, Evangeline
Council, New Iberia, La.

SCALLOPED POTATOES

4 c. peeled potatoes, thinly sliced
3/4 tsp. salt
2 Tbsp. butter or oleo
1 1/2 Tbsp. flour

1/4 c. onion, thinly sliced
1 can chicken broth
1/8 tsp. black pepper
1/2 c. bell pepper, diced
2 Tbsp. diced pimiento

Boil potatoes, onion, salt and pepper in chicken broth 10 minutes. Saute bell pepper in skillet 5 minutes, stir in flour until well blended. Stir peppers and pimiento into potatoes, mix well and pour into lightly greased 2-quart casserole. Bake in preheated oven for 35-45 minutes or until lightly browned. Makes 6 servings.

Marion Carter, Central
Council, Bunkie, La.

KATHY'S SPANKED POTATOES

Large Idaho potatoes
Dash of Accent
2 slices bacon per potato,
   fried and crumbled

1/2 stick butter or oleo
1/2 lb. grated Cheddar
   cheese
Salt and pepper to taste
Green onions, chopped fine

Bake large Idaho potatoes until shells are set. If using microwave, bake until done, transfer to regular oven until shells are hard. While hot, split down middle, scoop out potato, place in large container. Add remaining ingredients and mix well. Lightly fill shells, piling high. Return to oven to melt cheese. Can be done ahead. Place in casserole and cover with plastic wrap. At serving time, reheat in oven or microwave.
Kathy Ferguson Bauer
(Bill and Mary Lou's
daughter), Caddo Council,
Shreveport, La.

SWEET POTATO CASSEROLE

4 c. cooked and mashed
   sweet potatoes
4 eggs
1/2 tsp. nutmeg
2 c. evaporated milk

1 c. butter, melted
2 c. sugar
1/2 tsp. cinnamon
1/2 tsp. cloves (ground)
1 c. shredded coconut

Combine potatoes, butter and sugar. Whip in eggs, add spices, milk and part of coconut, saving some to sprinkle on top. Mix well, pour into baking dish, sprinkle with coconut. Bake at 375° for 35 minutes. Yield: 10 servings.
Jean Coon, Caddo Council,
Shreveport, La.

SWEET POTATO CASSEROLE

3 c. sweet potatoes
1/2 tsp. salt
2 eggs, beaten
1/2 tsp. lemon

1/2 c. sugar
1/2 c. butter or oleo
1/2 tsp. vanilla
1/3 c. sweet milk

Mix ingredients and place in greased 13x9x2-inch pan.

Topping:

1/3 c. butter   1/2 c. brown sugar
1/4 c. flour   1 c. chopped nuts

Mix ingredients, sprinkle over top and bake in 350°
oven about 25 minutes.   Selman Kinaul, Ouachita
                                Council, Monroe, La.

SWEET POTATO CASSEROLE

3 c. cooked, mashed   1 c. sugar
   sweet potatoes   1/2 c. oleo, melted
2 eggs, beaten   1 tsp. vanilla
1/3 c. milk

Mix ingredients and place in large buttered shallow
baking dish. Sprinkle with Topping. Bake at 350° for 25
minutes.

Topping:

1 c. light brown sugar   1/2 c. flour
1/3 c. oleo, softened   1 c. chopped nuts

Mix oleo with flour and sugar, using pastry blender or
fingers. Add nuts, mix and top casserole.
                                Louise Malone, Caddo
                                Council, Shreveport, La.

CANDIED SWEET POTATOES

4 sweet potatoes   1/2 c. brown sugar
Marshmallows

Boil sweet potatoes until done, cut up or mash. Add
brown sugar. Place in casserole and cover with marshmallows. Bake in 350° oven until marshmallows are melted
and brown.   Mary Ahrens, Caddo Council,
                    Shreveport, La.

174

PARTY SWEET POTATOES

8 medium size fresh
  sweet potatoes
1 large can whole berry
  cranberry sauce

1/2 c. corn oil oleo
1/2 c. brown sugar
1/2 c. chopped pecans
1/2 c. orange marmalade

Bake sweet potatoes for 1 hour at 400°. Peel and slice potatoes in half lengthwise when cool. Place in Pam sprayed casserole. Heat oleo and sugar, drizzle over potatoes. Heat cranberry sauce and marmalade, pour over potatoes. Sprinkle with pecans. Bake at 350° until bubbly.

Ann Orr, Evangeline
Council, New Iberia, La.

SWEET POTATO SOUFFLE

3 c. mashed sweet
  potatoes
1/2 stick oleo
1/2 c. milk

2 eggs
1/2 tsp. salt
1 c. sugar
1 tsp. vanilla

Mix ingredients in blender and pour into casserole.

Topping:

1/3 c. brown sugar
1 c. chopped nuts

1/3 c. flour
1/2 stick oleo

Mix and spread over potatoes. Bake at 350° for 35 minutes.

Mearl S. Byles, Central
Council, Natchitoches, La.

BAKED RICE

2 cans onion soup
2 c. raw rice

1 1/3 c. water
1 block butter

Mix ingredients and pour into 2 1/2-quart covered casserole dish. Bake at 350° for 45 minutes.
  Note: Bits of mushrooms, cooked pieces of sausage, pork chops or shrimp may be added to make a main dish.

Pat Uhle, West Bank
Council, Gretna, La.

BEKI'S FRIED RICE

2 - 2 1/2 c. cooked rice (cook day before without salt)
1/2 c. chopped bell pepper
1/2 c. chopped fresh mushrooms
1/2 c. chopped white onion
1/2 c. chopped green onion
1 can water chestnuts, sliced
2 eggs, beaten
Soy sauce
1/2 lb. fried bacon (reserve bacon grease)

Saute bell pepper, white onion and mushrooms in bacon grease. Stir in eggs, add part of rice and some soy sauce. Add crumbled bacon, remainder of rice and more soy sauce. Add water chestnuts and green onions. Use very light hand in folding rice in. Corn oil may be substituted for bacon grease; and chicken, pork or beef leftovers for bacon.

Beki Lawrence, Capital
Council, Baton Rouge, La.

RICE CORN CASSEROLE

1 (5 oz.) pkg. yellow rice mix
1 can cream of celery soup
1 stick oleo
1 can Mexicorn
1 c. sharp grated cheese

Cook rice according to directions, omitting butter. When done, add oleo, soup and corn. Mix and place in 1 1/2 - 2-quart casserole. Cover with cheese. Bake at 350° until heated through.

Eloise H. Stacy, Caddo
Council, Shreveport, La.

RICE DISH

2 cut up fryers, or 10-12 pork chops
2 pkg. Lipton onion soup mix
Grated cheese
2 c. rice, uncooked
2 cans celery soup
4 c. water
Salt and pepper to taste

Mix rice, water, soup, onion mix, salt and pepper to taste. Place chicken or pork chops on mixture. Sprinkle grated cheese on top. Cover and bake at 350° for 50 minutes; uncover and bake additional 10 minutes.

Gail Cummings, Caddo
Council, Shreveport, La.

DRY RICE

2 c. rice
1 jar sliced mushrooms

2 cans onion soup
1 stick oleo

Mix rice, oleo and mushrooms with 1 can of soup. Place in casserole dish and bake at 300° until all moisture is gone. Add second can of soup, mix in and cook until rice is done.
Aline Well, Capital Council, Baton Rouge, La.

GREEN RICE

2 c. Minute Rice, or
    4 c. cooked rice (brown
    rice preferable)
1 large onion, chopped
    fine
2 c. shredded sharp
    cheese
2 cans mushrooms, whole
    or pieces, drained

2 c. chopped parsley
2 eggs
1 small can milk
2/3 c. Wesson oil
2 cans mushroom soup
1 1/2 tsp. salt
Pepper to taste
Few shakes of Tabasco sauce

Cook rice. Add enough of drained mushroom juice to milk to make 1 cup. Beat eggs and oil together. Combine ingredients. Place in casserole. Bake at 350° for 45 minutes to 1 hour. May be made without mushrooms or with only 1 can; chop if using whole buttons. Use brown rice if available.
Janie Cox, Central Council, Alexandria, La.

RICE AND MUSHROOMS

1/2 c. uncooked rice
1 can consomme soup

1 small can mushrooms
1/4 stick butter or oleo

Mix ingredients and place in casserole. Cover and cook in 350° oven for 45 minutes.
Annie Hawkins, Caddo Council, Shreveport, La.

NANCY'S RICE

1 c. rice
1 can onion soup
1 can mushroom soup
  (optional)

1 can beef bouillon soup
1/2 stick oleo or butter
1/2 c. sliced almonds
  (optional)

Rub bottom and sides of casserole dish with butter. Put rice and soup in dish, cut up butter and drop in. Bake uncovered in 350° oven for 45 minutes. This dish will hold and may be increased in equal amounts. Great for bar-b-que, parties and large crowds. An easy winner!

Jean Stanley, Crescent City
Council, New Orleans, La.

NEW ORLEANS STYLE RICE

1 c. rice
1 small can chopped
  mushrooms

1 can beef bouillon
1 can onion soup
1 stick butter or oleo

Combine ingredients in casserole dish in any order. Bake for 45 minutes at 375°. The mushrooms always come out on top.

Mearl S. Byles, Central
Council, Natchitoches, La.

OLD ENGLISH RICE

1 c. rice
1 can cream of celery
  soup, or cream of
  mushroom soup
1 bunch green onions,
  chopped

1 c. water
1 can beef consomme
2 medium onions, chopped
1 stick oleo
1 clove garlic, minced

Heat soups together. Add rice to water and cook until water is consumed. Rice will not be done. Saute onions and garlic in oleo. Combine vegetables, oleo, rice and soups. Pour into large casserole. Cover and bake at 350° for 1 hour.

Lynda Fox, Caddo Council,
Shreveport, La.

OVEN RICE DISH

1 c. rice
1/2 onion, chopped
1/4 lb. butter

2 c. beef broth
1 can mushrooms and juice
Almond slivers

Mix ingredients together. Bake in uncovered dish at 350° for 1 hour.

Mary C. Regan
Crescent City Council

RICE PILAF

1 1/2 sticks oleo
1/4 tsp. oregano
1 jar mushrooms
1 can water

1 chopped onion
1 can pitted ripe olives
3 cans beef consomme
12 oz. (1 5/8 c.) uncooked
   rice

Melt butter, stir in onion and oregano. Add olives, mushrooms and rice. Stir in consomme and water. Cover and simmer until done.

Cindy Kendrick, Caddo
Council, Shreveport, La.

RICE PILAF

1 c. rice, washed
1 can beef consomme
1 can mushrooms, un-
   drained

1 can chicken consomme or
   broth
1 stick butter or oleo,
   melted

Combine ingredients and put in covered casserole. Bake 1 hour at 350°.

Dot Anderson, Ozone
Council, Covington, La.

RUTABAGA POTATO FLUFF

4 large white potatoes,
   cubed
1 large rutabaga
   (turnip), cubed

1 tsp. black pepper
3 Tbsp. melted butter
7 Tbsp. butter, divided

Boil potatoes and rutabaga separately in salted water until tender. Drain. Combine potatoes, 3 tablespoons butter and black pepper. Mash. Combine rutabaga and

4 tablespoons butter. Mash. Mix potatoes and rutabaga
together and spoon into 3-quart greased casserole. Pour
3 tablespoons melted butter over mixture and bake at 350°
for 10-15 minutes. Serves 6-8.

Mae Briley, Central Council,
Alexandria, La.

SPINACH A LA ARTICHOKE

1 can artichoke bottoms,
  drained and rinsed
1/2 c. sour cream
2 Tbsp. butter or oleo
2 Tbsp. Italian cheese
Salt to taste

1 (10 oz.) pkg. frozen,
  chopped spinach
1 small onion, chopped fine
Dash of cayenne pepper
Salad Supreme
Extra Italian cheese

Cook spinach according to directions on package, drain.
Cook onions in butter until soft. Remove from heat, add
cheese, spinach, salt, cayenne pepper and sour cream. Mix
well. Place as a mound on top of artichoke bottoms. Sprinkle with extra Italian cheese and Salad Supreme. Set in
square pan with 1 inch water to keep from sticking. Bake at
350° for 20 minutes.

Joyce Hattier, Magnolia
Council, New Orleans, La.

SPINACH ARTICHOKE CASSEROLE

1 stick butter or oleo
2 (10 oz.) pkg. frozen,
  chopped spinach
1/2 c. onions, finely
  chopped

1 large can artichoke hearts
1 pt. sour cream
1/2 c. Parmesan cheeese
Salt and pepper to taste

Cook spinach as directed on box and drain. Saute
onion in butter. Mix together, add hearts and sour cream.
Stir Parmesan into casserole and sprinkle some on top. Bake
in 350° oven for 20 or 30 minutes.

Mamie Fanta, Caddo Council,
Shreveport, La.

SPINACH BALLS

1 (10 oz.) box frozen, chopped spinach
3/4 c. onion, chopped fine
1/4 c. oleo, melted
1/3 tsp. thyme
1 tsp. garlic salt
2 c. herb bread and stuffing mix
3 egg yolks, beaten
1/2 c. grated Parmesan cheese
1 tsp. MSG
1 can Cheddar cheese soup

Cook spinach according to directions, drain and blot with paper towel. Mix in all other ingredients, except cheese soup. Refrigerate 3 hours or overnight. Form into balls. Place in greased baking dish and bake at 350° for 30 minutes. Serve hot with heated undiluted cheese soup poured over balls as sauce. May be made day before or frozen and reheated if desired.

Gail Cummings, Caddo
Council, Shreveport, La.

BAKED SPINACH TIMBALES

2 pkg. frozen, chopped spinach, cooked
1/4 c. grated Parmesan cheese
1/4 c. melted butter
Pinch of thyme
Tomato slices
2 eggs, beaten
1/4 c. seasoned bread crumbs
1/4 c. chopped green onion
2 cloves garlic, minced
Salt and pepper to taste

Mix all ingredients thoroughly, except tomato slices. Make individual molds in demitasse coffee cups. Turn out and place on thick, seasoned tomato slices in shallow baking pan. Bake at 350° in preheated oven about 20 minutes. May be served as is or with a little Hollandaise drizzled over the top.

Ann Orr, Evangeline
Council, New Iberia, La.

SPINACH CASSEROLE

2 pkg. frozen, chopped spinach, cooked
1 large pkg. cream cheese
1/2 can water chestnuts
1/2 stick butter or oleo
1 tall can hearts of artichokes
Italian bread crumbs

Drain artichokes, spinach and chestnuts. Slice

chestnuts, cut artichokes into halves and place in bottom of flat casserole. Melt cheese and oleo. Add spinach, chestnuts and mix. Pour mixture over artichokes and top with Italian bread crumbs. Bake at 350° for 15 minutes or heated through. Serves 6.   Richard P. Mohr
Crescent City Council
New Orleans, La.

SPINACH CASSEROLE

1 box frozen cut spinach,
  thawed
Tabasco sauce to taste

1 Kraft onion dip
1 c. seasoned bread crumbs

Cook spinach according to directions. Drain, squeezing all water out. Mix with onion dip and 1/2 cup of bread crumbs. Pour into buttered casserole. Top with remaining bread crumbs. Bake at 350° for 30-45 minutes. Season with Tabasco sauce to taste.   Lois Milldrum, Central
Council, Alexandria, La.

SPINACH CASSEROLE

2 boxes frozen, chopped
  spinach
1/2 stick butter or oleo

1 (8 oz.) pkg. cream cheese
Salt, pepper and garlic
  powder to taste
1 can artichokes

Cook and drain spinach. Melt butter and cream cheese in double boiler. Drain and cut up artichokes, dump in cheese mixture. Season spinach with salt, pepper and garlic powder and place in casserole. Pour and stir in cheese mixutes. Press down in casserole dish. Bake in 325° oven until bubbly. Bread crumbs or French fried onions may be sprinkled on top if desired. Serves 4.
Eloise H. Stacy, Caddo
Council, Shreveport, La.

SPINACH CASSEROLE

4 pkg. chopped spinach,
  frozen
1 (8 oz.) pkg. cream
  cheese
Dash of salt

1 can water chestnuts,
  shredded
1/4 stick butter
Dash of nutmeg
Dash of red pepper

182

Heat, drain and mash spinach. Add all other ingredients. Put in casserole and bake in 350° oven about 30
minutes.   Calcasieu Council
                                            Lake Charles, La.

SPINACH   CASSEROLE

2 pkg. frozen, chopped   1 carton sour cream
   spinach   1 pkg. dry onion soup
Juice of 1/2 lemon   Dash of seasoning salt
Dash of Tabasco sauce   Dash of Worcestershire
Dash of nutmeg   sauce

   Cook spinach according to directions, drain. Add remaining ingredients to spinach and mix. Put in casserole
and sprinkle with nutmeg. Bake at 350° until hot and
bubbly.   Mary McDow, Caddo
                                            Council, Shreveport, La.

CREAMED   SPINACH   CASSEROLE

2 boxes frozen, chopped   1 stick butter or oleo
   spinach   1 (8 oz.) pkg. cream cheese
1 small can artichoke   1 small can Italian bread
   hearts, drained and   crumbs
   mashed

   Cook and drain spinach according to directions and
place in casserole. Melt butter in saucepan, add cream
cheese, heat until cheese and butter are mixed. Add to
spinach and stir. Add 3/4 of bread crumbs, artichoke
hearts and mix well. Top with remaining bread crumbs.
Bake at 325° for 25 minutes.   James J. Ferraro
                                Crescent City Countil
                                New Orleans,La.

SPINACH 'N CREAM

1 can drained spinach   Evaporated milk
2 or 3 slices American   1 pat butter
   cheese

   Pour evaporated milk to cover bottom of small frying
pan. Add cheese. Heat on medium flame. Stir to combine

1723-79   183

cheese with milk. Cheese melts almost immediately. Add
spinach and butter. Finish heating on low flame. Ready to
serve when spinach is warm. This makes a super quick
vegetable dish and a nice variation from the usual spinach
and hard boiled egg way. Large can of spinach serves 4;
small can serves 2.   B. Berry, Metairie Council,
                                       Metairie, La.

SPINACH MADELINE

2 onions, chopped   1 stick butter or oleo
1 roll jalapeno cheese   1 small can Pet milk
1/4 tsp. black pepper   1/4 tsp. celery salt
1/4 tsp. salt   Dash of Worcestershire sauce
1/2 c. spinach water   2 boxes frozen spinach
   from spinach   Bread crumbs

   Boil spinach, drain and reserve 1/2 cup water. Saute
onions in butter. Add cheese, milk and spinach water. Stir
until cheese melts. Add seasonings. Add spinach to mixture. Pour into casserole, top with bread crumbs and bake
in 350° oven until thoroughly heated.
                                 Leigh Hargis, LeBayou
                                 Council, Lockport, La.

SPINACH MADELINE

2 boxes frozen spinach   1/2 stick butter or oleo
2 Tbsp. flour   Salt and pepper to taste
1 medium onion, chopped   1/2 c. evaporated milk
1/2 c. spinach liquid   3/4 tsp. garlic salt
1 (6 oz.) roll jalapeno   1 Tbsp. Worcestershire
   pepper cheese   sauce
Bread crumbs   Dash of Tabasco sauce

   Cook spinach and drain, reserving part of liquid. Melt
butter, add onions and flour, stir until smooth. Add milk,
mix well. Add rest of seasonings and 1/2 of cheese, cut
in small pieces. Stir until cheese is melted. Combine all
ingredients, except bread crumbs and remaining cheese, in
casserole. Top with crumbs and remainder of cheese. Bake
at 350° for 20-25 minutes.   Madlyn Lavergne
                                 Crescent City Council
                                 New Orleans, La.

SPINACH PARMESAN

4 pkg. (10 oz. each)
  frozen, chopped
  spinach
1/3 c. chopped onion
1/4 c. melted butter

1/2 c. grated Parmesan
  and Romano cheese
1/3 c. heavy cream
1/2 tsp. salt

Cook and drain spinach. Add remaining ingredients. Mix and turn into 9x5-inch loaf pan or square baking dish. Bake in preheated 350° oven for 10-15 minutes or until heated through. Garnish with lemon twist. Makes 8 servings.
                              Lynn Babin, Westmoor
                              Council, Kenner, La.

ZUCCHINI SPINACH BAKE

2 cloves garlic, peeled
2 (10 oz.) pkg. fresh
  spinach, washed and
  trimmed
3/4 lb. zucchini, diced
  (about 2 c.)
1 Tbsp. dried basil leaves
1/8 tsp. pepper

2 Tbsp. + 1 tsp. olive or
  vegetable oil
3/4 tsp. salt
2/3 c. chopped onion
5 eggs
1/2 c. Parmesan cheese
1/4 c. plain bread crumbs

Flatten 1 clove garlic with side of knife. In a large heavy saucepan or Dutch oven, warm 1 teaspoon oil, add spinach and flattened garlic cloves, cover and cook 12-15 minutes, stirring 4 or 5 times until leaves are just wilted. Drain, discard garlic and wipe out pot. Heat pot over moderate heat with 1 1/2 tablespoons oil. Chop remaining garlic clove and mash smooth with 1/4 teaspoon salt. Add to pot with zucchini, onion and basil. Cook just until onion is soft. Mix in spinach. Grease 13 1/2 x 8 3/4-inch baking dish. Beat eggs lightly with remaining 1/2 teaspoon salt and the pepper. Pour eggs over mixture and tilt dish to distribute egg. Sprinkle with cheese and crumbs. Bake about 12 minutes at 350° or until egg is set. Cut into rectangles. Serves 6.
                              Rebecca Scott Bockmon
                              Caddo Council
                              Shreveport, La.

SQUASH CASSEROLE

1 (20 oz.) pkg. frozen
   crookneck squash or
   5-6 fresh squash
1 1/2 c. grated Cheddar
   cheese
Salt and pepper to taste

1 small onion, chopped
1/2 c. cracker crumbs
1 egg
Butter
French fried onion rings
   (optional)

Boil squash in small amount of salted water until tender. Drain. Saute onion in small amount of butter. Add onions, cracker crumbs, egg and about half the cheese to drained squash. Mix well and pour into buttered casserole dish. Top with remaining cheese. Sprinkle crumbled French fried onion rings over cheese if desired. Bake at 350° for 20-25 minutes.

Mollie Hoskins, Caddo
Council, Shreveport, La.

SQUASH CASSEROLE

1 lb. fresh squash
1 c. chopped shallots or
   onions
1/4 c. mushrooms
1/2 c. quick oats
1 egg, beaten
Salt and pepper to taste

1 tsp. salt
1/2 c. chopped celery
1/4 c. pimento
3/4 c. milk
2 hard cooked eggs, chopped
Ritz crackers, crumbled

Cover squash with water, cook until tender. Drain and set aside. Saute celery, shallots, mushrooms and pimento. Add to squash. Add remaining ingredients, except cracker crumbs and place mixture in buttered casserole. Bake at 400° for 15 minutes. Remove from oven, cover with Ritz cracker crumbs and bake additional 15 minutes.

Louise Malone, Caddo
Council, Shreveport, La.

SQUASH CASSEROLE

3 lb. squash
3-4 carrots
1 small jar pimento
1 can cream of chicken
   soup

1 large onion
1 pkg. plain Pepperidge
   Farm corn bread stuffing
1 stick oleo
Salt and pepper

Dice squash, carrots and onions. Boil until tender and drain. Add pimento to oleo and cream of chicken soup. Season with salt and pepper. Cover bottom of baking dish with part of stuffing mix. Layer squash mixture over stuffing and top with remainder of stuffing mix. Bake at 350° until lightly brown.

Mary C. Regan
Crescent City Council
New Orleans, La.

SQUASH CASSEROLE

4 c. cooked squash
6 slices American cheese

1 can cream of mushroom
 soup
3 chopped shallots

Place in casserole dish in layers - squash, 1/2 can soup, 3 slices cheese and 1/2 of shallots. Repeat layers. Bake at 350° for 25-30 minutes.

Carolyn Plavidal
Crescent City Council
New Orleans, La.

CHEESE SQUASH

2 lb. summer squash
1 medium onion, chopped
1 c. Cheddar cheese,
 grated
1 Tbsp. sugar

2 eggs, beaten
3 Tbsp. melted butter
1 tsp. ground sage
Paprika
Salt and pepper

Cook squash in small amount of boiling salted water until tender. Combine all ingredients, except 1/2 of cheese and paprika. Pour into buttered casserole and place remaining cheese over top and sprinkle with paprika. Bake at 350° for 25 minutes. Sage is the surprise in this combination.

Gayle Wilkening
Shreveport Works Council
Longview, Tx.

HONEY-SPICE ACORN SQUASH

3 medium acorn squash
1/4 c. butter or mar-
  garine, melted
1/4 tsp. cinnamon

1/2 tsp. salt
1/4 tsp. ginger
1/3 c. honey

Preheat oven to 375°. Scrub squash, cut in half lengthwise. Remove seeds and stringy fibers. Arrange, cut side down, in shallow baking pan. Surround with 1/2 inch hot water. Bake 30 minutes. Combine remaining ingredients. Pour off excess liquid from baking pan. Turn squash cut side up. Pour sauce into cavities and bake 15 minutes, basting now and then with sauce. Makes 6 servings.

Calcasieu Council
Lake Charles, La.

JALAPENO SQUASH

2 lb. fresh squash, or
  2 (10 oz.) pkg. frozen
1 roll jalapeno cheese,
  cut up

8 slices bacon
1 large onion, cut in rings
Bread crumbs

Boil squash, drain. Fry bacon and crumble. Brown onion rings in bacon drippings. Layer 1/2 of squash, bacon, onions and cheese in 9x9-inch casserole dish. Repeat layers. Top with bread crumbs. Bake at 325° for 40 minutes. Serves 10.

Jan Prestridge, Capital
Council, Baton Rouge, La.

SQUASH FRITTERS

Raw squash
1 - 1 1/2 tsp. salt
1/2 tsp. baking powder
1 Tbsp. sugar

1 medium onion, chopped fine
2 eggs, beaten
1/2 c. flour

Grate raw squash to make 3 cups. Add salt and onion to squash. Let stand for 1 hour or more. Using a large strainer, squeeze a small amount of mixture through at a time, removing as much liquid as possible. Add remaining ingredients; if not thick enough to hold together, add more flour. Drop by heaping tablespoonfuls, well apart, in hot oil and spread each fritter so it is about 3 or 4 inches in

diameter. Fry until golden brown on both sides. Drain
on paper towels. Keep warm and serve immediately.

Delores Jones, Central
Council, Robstown, Tx.

ACORN SQUASH

1 acorn squash   1/2 c. oleo
2 spoons brown sugar   Cinnamon
Brandy (optional)

Cut squash in half and clean. Turn halves upside
down in pan of water and steam 20 minutes or until soft.
Remove from water. Place melted oleo with brandy, if
desired, in each half. Sprinkle with brown sugar, 1 spoonful per half, and pinch of cinnamon each. Place in 350°
oven upright for about 10 minutes. Serve with Cornish
hens, wild rice,special salad and for dessert, ice cream with
amaretta or Irish coffee. This is a great autumn dinner that
has a gourmet flavor.   Peggy M. Childers
                             Crescent City Council
                             New Orleans, La.

MOTHER'S STUFFED TOMATOES

6 tomatoes   1 large onion
4 stalks celery   1 tsp. chopped parsley
1/2 lb. ham   Dash of garlic powder
1/2 c. bread crumbs   Butter or oil

Remove stem portion of tomatoes. Scoop out insides of
tomatoes and set aside. Grind to chop celery, onion and
ham. Simmer celery and onion in small amount of butter
or oil until tender, but not brown. Chop or mash the soft
tomato centers which have been reserved. Add these
tomato centers together with the ham and dash of garlic
powder to mixture in skillet. Continue to simmer until most
of liquid is reduced. Add parsley and most of the bread
crumbs, reserving a small amount for topping. Stuff hot
mixture into tomato shells. Mixture will mound up over
top of shell. Sprinkle reserved bread crumbs over the
stuffed tomatoes and place tomatoes together, touching each
other, in a baking dish. Put a dot of butter on top of each
and bake for about 30 minutes at 350°, or until skins are

tender and tops are brown. This is a special side dish that is especially nice with chicken or pork.

Enola Fee, Crescent City
Council, New Orleans, La.

VEGETABLES AU GRATIN

1 (10 oz.) pkg. frozen
  green peas
2 1/4 c. water
2 Tbsp. oleo or butter
1 (2 oz.) can mushroom
  stems and pieces,
  drained

1 pkg. Betty Crocker au
  gratin potatoes
2/3 c. milk
1 (2 oz.) jar sliced pimiento,
  drained
1/2 tsp. salt

Rinse frozen peas under running cold water to separate, drain. Heat all ingredients to boiling in 10-inch skillet, stirring frequently. Reduce heat, cover and simmer, stirring occasionally, until potatoes are tender, about 30 minutes. Makes 6 servings.

Ann Orr, Evangeline
Council, New Iberia, La.

VEGETABLE CASSEROLE

1 stick butter
1 can water chestnuts
6 slices bread, crumbled
1 c. grated sharp or
  Cheddar cheese

1 (No. 2) can English peas,
  drained
1 can mushroom soup
1 (No. 2) can asparagus
  spears, drained and whole

Melt butter, stir in crumbled bread. Let set. Place in greased casserole in layers the peas, then asparagus and last sliced chestnuts. Pour soup over layers. Cover with grated cheese and top with buttered crumbs. Bake at 350° for 30 minutes. For variations, add pimentos, mushrooms and a layer of boned chicken.

Bettye Lee, Shreveport Works
Council, Shreveport, La.

VEGETABLE CASSEROLE

2 cans Veg-All
1/2 c. chopped onion
1 c. chopped celery
1 stick oleo, melted

1 can corn niblets
1 c. grated cheese
3/4 c mayonnaise
Cracker crumbs

Drain vegetables and mix with onion, celery, cheese and mayonnaise. Top with heavy layer of cracker crumbs and spoon oleo over all. Bake at 350° for 20-30 minutes.

Margaret Aletha Keenan
Ozone Council
Bogalusa, La.

FRIED VEGETABLE ROUND-UP

6 pods okra, medium size	2 small Irish potatoes
1 small bell pepper	1/2 c. chopped onion
1/4 c. chopped celery	1 small clove garlic
1/2 tsp. salt	Corn meal
	Cooking oil

Chop all vegetables very fine. Roll in corn meal and fry in oil until brown.

Mrs. Iona Botzong, Central
Council, Tioga, La.

MIXED VEGETABLE CASSEROLE

2 cans Veg-All, drained	1 can kernel corn, drained
1 c. chopped celery	1 c. chopped onion
1 c. grated cheese	3/4 c. mayonnaise
1 stick oleo, melted	Ritz crackers, crushed

Combine vegetables, cheese and mayonnaise. Place in casserole. Top with Ritz crackers and drizzle oleo over all. Bake at 350° for 30 minutes.

Mildred Lee, Central
Council, Pineville, La.

YAMS

2 cans (30 oz.) yams	1/4 tsp. salt
1/4 c. oleo	1/4 tsp. cinnamon
2 eggs	1 tsp. vanilla
1/2 c. sugar	1/4 tsp. nutmeg

Drain yams. Mix all ingredients together with mixer. Spoon into casserole dish. Sprinkle topping over casserole. Bake at 350° for 30 minutes.

Topping:

1/4 c. oleo, melted
3/4 c. brown sugar

3 Tbsp. flour
1/2 c. chopped pecans

Combine and mix ingredients.

Pam W. McCoy, Central
Council, Bunkie, La.

ZUCCHINI STUFFING CASSEROLE

4 medium zucchini, sliced
  1/2-inch thick
1/2 c. chopped onion
1 can cream of chicken
  soup

6 Tbsp. butter
3/4 c. shredded carrot
2 1/4 c. herbed stuffing
  cubes
1/2 c. sour cream

Cook zucchini in boiling salted water until tender, drain.
In saucepan, melt 4 tablespoons butter. Add carrot and
onion, saute. Remove from heat, stir in soup, sour cream
and 1 1/2 cups stuffing mix. Fold in zucchini gently.
Spoon into 1 1/2-quart casserole. Toss remaining cubes with
2 tablespoons butter and sprinkle on casserole. Bake at
350° for 30-40 minutes. Makes 6-8 servings.

Betty Jackson
Shreveport Works Council
Shreveport, La.

MEAT, SEAFOOD
POULTRY

HANDY CHART OF KITCHEN MATH WITH METRIC

KITCHEN MATH WITH METRIC TABLES

Measure	Equivalent	Metric (ML)
1 Tbsp.	3 tsp.	14.8 milliliters
2 Tbsp.	1 oz.	29.6 milliliters
1 jigger	1½ oz.	44.4 milliliters
¼ cup	4 Tbsp.	59.2 milliliters
1/3 cup	5 Tbsp. plus 1 tsp.	78.9 milliliters
½ cup	8 Tbsp.	118.4 milliliters
1 cup	16 Tbsp.	236.8 milliliters
1 pint	2 cups	473.6 milliliters
1 quart	4 cups	947.2 milliliters
1 liter	4 cups plus 3½ Tbsp.	1,000.0 milliliters
1 oz. (dry)	2 Tbsp.	28.35 grams
1 pound	16 oz.	453.59 grams
2.21 pounds	35.3 oz.	1.00 kilogram

THE APPROXIMATE CONVERSON FACTORS FOR UNITS OF VOLUME

To Convert from	To	Multiply by
teaspoons (tsp.)	milliliters (ml)	5
tablespoons (Tbsp.)	milliliters (ml)	15
fluid ounces (fl. oz.)	milliliters (ml)	30
cups (c)	liters (l)	0.24
pints (pt)	liters (l)	0.47
quarts (qt)	liters (l)	0.95
gallons (gal)	liters (l)	3.8
cubic feet (ft^3)	cubic meters (m^3)	0.03
cubic yards (yd^3)	cubic meters (m^3)	0.76
milliliters (ml)	fluid ounces (fl oz)	0.03
liters (l)	pints (pt)	2.1
liters (l)	quarts (qt)	1.06
liters (l)	gallons (gal)	0.26
cubic meters (m^3)	cubic feet (ft^3)	35
cubic meters (m^3)	cubic yards (yd^3)	1.3

DEEP-FAT FRYING TEMPERATURES WITHOUT A THERMOMETER

A 1-inch cube of white bread will turn golden brown:

345° to 355°	65 seconds
355° to 365°	60 seconds
365° to 375°	50 seconds
375° to 385°	40 seconds
385° to 395°	20 seconds

TABLE OF PROPORTIONS

Gelatin (unflavored) - 1 Tbsp. thickens 2 cups liquid

Salt

Soups & Sauces	1 tsp. to 1 qt. sauce
Dough	1 tsp. to 4 cups flour
Cereals	1 tsp. to 2 cups liquid
Meat	1 tsp. to 1 lb. meat
Vegetables	½ tsp. using 1 qt. water

SIMPLIFIED MEASURES

dash = less than 1/8 teaspoon

3 tsp. = 1 Tbsp.
16 Tbsp. = 1 cup
1 cup = ½ pt.
2 cups = 1 pt.

2 pt. (4 c.) = 1 qt.
4 qt. (liquid) = 1 gal.
8 qt. (solid) = 1 peck
4 pecks = 1 bushel
16 oz. = 1 lb.

If you want to measure part-cups by the tablespoon, remember:

4 Tbsp. = ¼ cup
5 1/3 Tbsp. = 1/3 cup
8 Tbsp. = ½ cup

10 2/3 Tbsp. = 2/3 cup
12 Tbsp. = ¾ cup
14 Tbsp. = 7/8 cup

CONTENTS OF CANS

Of the different sizes of cans used by commercial canners, the most common are:

Size	Average Contents
8-oz.	1 cup
picnic	1¼ cups
No. 300	1¾ cups
No. 1 tall	2 cups
No. 303	2 cups
No. 2	2½ cups
No. 2½	3½ cups
No. 3	4 cups
No. 10	12 to 13 cups

BEEF BRISKET

1 (4-5 lb.) beef brisket   1 bottle Pic-A-Pepper sauce
Salt

Salt brisket lightly. Place in heavy pot or casserole. Pour bottle of Pic-A-Pepper sauce over brisket. Cover and cook about 5 hours at 250°.   Verna Blankenship, Ouachita
Council, Monroe, La.

BARBECUED BRISKET

1 beef brisket, any size   1/2 small bottle liquid smoke
1 1/2 c. barbecue sauce   Salt and pepper
   or Woody's cooking sauce

Rub salt and pepper into each side. Pour liquid smoke over each side of brisket. Wrap completely and place in large cooking pan. Bake in 200° oven for 4 hours. Slow cooking is what makes it so tender. Unwrap foil and drain. Pour on barbecue sauce, over and under brisket. Return wrapped brisket to oven for 45 minutes. When serving, cut slices across the grain.   Marilou Bridges, Caddo
Council, Shreveport, La.

WEBSTER'S NORTH CAROLINA BARBECUED RIBS

Sauce:

1 c. water   1 c. vinegar
12 tsp. powdered mustard   6 tsp. salt
3 tsp. black pepper   1 tsp. garlic powder
1 tsp. chili powder   1 tsp. ground cumin

This is enough sauce for 9 pounds of ribs (for 6 persons) allowing 1 1/2 pounds of pork ribs per person.
Adjust the fire to a "five-second" temperature; that is, you should be able to hold your hand where the meat will be for 5 seconds.
Cooking Time: Skinny ribs - 50 minutes; average ribs - 60 minutes; meaty ribs - 70 minutes. Every 2-3 minutes, stir the sauce to keep it from settling, baste the

ribs and turn them. The sauce should run out 4-6 minutes before the end of the cooking time so the last turn on each side will be "dry." Check the temperature frequently and keep it as even as possible for the entire cooking time. A covered grill is desirable for temperature control and also improves the flavor by smoking the meat as the cooking proceeds. The success of this recipe depends on slow cooking at a moderate temperature, with frequent basting. Grease flare-ups should be suppressed with water to avoid charring.

In some parts of North Carolina, a liquid resembling water is used for refreshment, fueling cars and other purposes. Do not accidentally use it for suppressing the fire unless you want to finish your meal in Georgia.

Gaylord Brunson, Central
Council, Alexandria, La.

BEEF CURRY

1/2 c. chopped onion
2 Tbsp. oleo
1 Tbsp. curry powder
1 1/2 c. cubed, cooked
   roast beef

1 green pepper, cut in strips
1 can beef gravy
1/2 tsp. salt
Pepper to taste

Saute onion and pepper in oleo. Stir in curry powder, gravy, salt and roast beef. Cover and simmer 10-15 minutes, stirring occasionally. Serve over rice or noodles.

Marilou Bridges, Caddo
Council, Shreveport, La.

BEEF PATTIES WITH ONIONS

2 large onions, sliced
Salt to taste
Pepper to taste
1/3 c. fine dry bread
   crumbs
1 Tbsp. prepared mustard

1 Tbsp. oleo
1/2 tsp. sugar
1 lb. ground beef
1/3 c. ice water
1/4 c. hot water

Saute onions in oleo until golden. Add salt, pepper and sugar. Cook until onions are tender. Remove and set aside. Mix beef, bread crumbs, ice water, mustard, salt and pepper to taste. Form into 4 patties. Brown patties on both sides. Drain. Add hot water and onions, simmer until patties are done. Makes 4 servings.   Marilou Bridges, Caddo
Council, Shreveport, La.

194

BEEF SHORTRIBS

2 1/2 - 3 lb. shortribs
1/2 c. water
1 clove garlic, minced
1 c. catsup
1/2 c. vinegar
2 Tbsp. prepared mustard

2 tsp. salt
1/2 c. chopped onion
1 (6 oz.) can tomato paste
3/4 c. firmly packed brown
  sugar

Brown ribs on all sides in large skillet or Dutch oven. Cover and cook over low heat 1 hour, drain. Combine remaining ingredients and pour over ribs. Cover tightly and cook over low heat 1 1/2 hours or until meat is tender. Yield: 4-6 servings.   Mrs. Johnnie B. Cole, Caddo
                                Council, Shreveport, La.

SAVORY SHORT RIBS

3 lb. beef short ribs
2 medium onions, sliced
1 Tbsp. packed brown
  sugar
1/4 tsp. pepper
1 (10 oz.) pkg. frozen
  lima beans

1 1/2 c. water
2 Tbsp. vinegar and lemon
  juice
2 tsp. salt
2 bay leaves
1/4 tsp. ground ginger
4 medium carrots, cut in
  3 x 1/2-inch strips

Trim excess fat from ribs. Brown in skillet and drain off excess grease. Add water, onions, vinegar, salt, pepper and bay leaves. Heat to boiling, reduce heat, cover and simmer for 1 hour. Add frozen beans, carrots, brown sugar and ginger. Heat to boiling, reduce heat and simmer until vegetables are tender, 45 minutes. Remove vegetables and ribs. Make gravy.

Gravy:

1 1/2 c. beef broth
3 Tbsp. flour

1/3 c. water

Mix ingredients and cook until smooth and thick.
                                Tami Landreneau, Capital
                                Council, Baton Rouge, La.

BEEF OR VENISON HASH

2 Tbsp. bacon fat
1 large chopped onion
3 c. cooked, chopped
  beef or venison roast
2 medium potatoes, cut
  in about 16 pieces each

2 Tbsp. flour
1 clove garlic, minced
3 c. beef broth from roast
1/4 Tbsp. seasoned salt and
  black pepper
1/2 Tbsp. chili powder

Brown onion and potatoes in bacon fat. Add flour and brown. Add broth and other ingredients. Let simmer until tender.
Maxine Fletcher, Ouachita Council, Monroe, La.

STUFFED BEEF LOG

2 lb. ground beef
1/2 c. finely chopped
  onion
1/2 c. milk
2 tsp. salt

1/2 c. quick cooking oats,
  uncooked
1 egg, beaten
1/8 tsp. pepper

Combine ingredients, mix well. Shape into a 16x10-inch rectangle on foil or waxed paper.

Filling:

1/2 lb. mild bulk sausage
1 egg, beaten
1/4 c. finely chopped
  onion

1 c. bread crumbs
1 medium potato, peeled and
  grated
1/2 tsp. salt

Combine ingredients, spread evenly over beef mixture. Roll jelly roll fashion, beginning at short side, lifting paper or foil to help roll. Place seam side down on a shallow baking pan. Bake at 300° for 1 hour and 30 minutes. Makes 10-12 servings.
Ann Orr, Evangeline Council, New Iberia, La.

BEEF STROGANOFF

1 c. minced onion
1/4 tsp. minced garlic
1/2 c. butter
2 lb. ground beef

4 tsp. salt
1/2 tsp. pepper
1 can mushroom soup
4 Tbsp. flour
2 c. sour cream

Cook onions and garlic in butter over medium heat, add meat and brown. Add flour, salt, pepper and mushroom soup. Cook 5 minutes, then simmer uncovered for 10 minutes. Stir in sour cream. Heat through and serve with noodles.

Calcasieu Council
Lake Charles, La.

BEEF STROGANOFF

Marinade:

1/4 tsp. Tony's creole seasoning	1/2 tsp. broiled steak seasoning
1/2 tsp. Accent	1/2 c. Worcestershire sauce
1/4 tsp. garlic powder	1/2 c. soy sauce

Mix ingredients and marinate meat cubes overnight.

3 lb. sirloin tip roast, cubed	1 large onion, chopped
1 large bell pepper, chopped (optional)	3 stalks celery, chopped
1 can mushroom soup	1 can cream of chicken soup
2 small jars sliced mushrooms	1 1/4 c. sour cream
1 1/2 Tbsp. flour	Butter
	1 1/2 soup cans water
	Bacon fat
	Salt and pepper to taste

Saute onions, peppers and celery in small amount of butter. Remove meat from marinade and brown in bacon fat. Remove meat and set aside. Make roux of flour and remaining bacon fat. Add soups and water, stir and add mushrooms, meat and season to taste. Add sour cream and simmer 20 minutes. Serve over rice or noodles.

Jan Prestridge, Capital
Council, Baton Rouge, La.

RIBBON BOLOGNA WEDGES

1 (15 oz.) jar cream cheese with olive and pimento	12 slices bologna
	1/4 c. finely chopped pecans
Sliced stuffed olives	Colored toothpicks

Soften cream cheese at room temperature. Spread each slice bologna with cream cheese, sprinkle with pecans.

1723-79

Make 2 stacks with 6 slices of bologna in each. Cover with plastic wrap. Chill well. Cut in 16 wedges, each stack. Garnish with sliced olive and insert colored toothpick.

Mae Briley, Central Council,
Alexandria, La.

BREADED CUTLETS

1 egg	2 Tbsp. Dijon style mustard
1 Tbsp. water	4-6 slices (1/4-inch thick)
2 tsp. minced chives	cooked turkey, chicken,
1/4 c. flour	roast beef or pork roast
1 c. soft bread crumbs	(about 1 lb.)
Lemon wedges (optional)	Cooking oil

Beat egg, mustard, water and chives together. Dredge meat slices in flour, dip in egg mixture, coat with crumbs. Fry meat slices in 1/4 inch hot cooking oil in skillet until golden on both sides, turning once. Add more oil, if needed. Serve with lemon wedges. Makes 4-6 servings.

Marilou Bridges, Caddo
Council, Shreveport, La.

CHILI MAC

1 1/2 lb. ground meat	1 small onion, chopped fine
Salt and pepper to taste	1 tsp. Worcestershire sauce
1 Tbsp. chili powder	2 (1 lb.) cans tomatoes
1 small pkg. tiny shell	Grated Cheddar cheese
macaroni	

Brown meat and onion in skillet. Drain off grease and add salt, pepper, Worcestershire sauce and chili powder. Mix in tomatoes and simmer 5-10 minutes or until tomatoes cook down. Cook macaroni according to package directions. Drain and combine with meat mixture. Place in casserole dish and sprinkle with grated cheese. Place in warm oven until cheese melts.

Delores Bridges
Shreveport Works Council
Shreveport, La.

CHINESE CHOP SUEY

2 or 3 lb. fresh pork
  roast
1 can bean sprouts
1 can bamboo sprouts
Pimento, chopped
4 Tbsp. Worcestershire
  and soy sauce

1 large onion, sliced
5 or 6 stalks celery, cut up
1 can water chestnuts,
  sliced
1 can mushrooms, stems
  and pieces
Water
Salt and pepper to taste

Slice and cut pork into strips. Sear on both sides. Saute onions and celery in drippings. Add meat, cover with water, add salt and pepper. Add soy and Worcestershire sauce. Cover and cook slowly for several hours. Before serving, add remaining ingredients and heat thoroughly. Serve over chow mein noodles or hot cooked rice.

Catherine (Chadwick) McCraw
Caddo Council
Shreveport, La.

CHOP SUEY

1 1/2 - 2 lb. round steak
3-5 stalks celery
2 cans chicken broth
Soy sauce
Salt and pepper to taste
Bacon drippings or cook-
  ing oil

1 1/2 - 2 lb. pork chops
1 large onion
1-2 cans bean sprouts
1-2 cloves garlic, minced
Small amount of flour
Hot boiled rice
Crackers

Cube and brown steak and chops. Sprinkle with flour while browning. Saute chopped celery, onions and garlic in small amount of bacon drippings or cooking oil. Add to meat and mix. Pour chicken broth over and simmer 30-40 minutes, stirring occasionally. Just before serving, mix in bean sprouts and soy sauce to taste. Serve over hot cooked rice and crackers. Marilou Bridges, Caddo
Council, Shreveport, La.

CHOP SUEY

2 c. boiling water
1/3 c. flour
3 c. chopped celery
3 bouillon cubes
1 c. sliced onions
3 Tbsp. oleo or butter

3 Tbsp. soy sauce
1 (4 oz.) can mushrooms,
    undrained
1 can bamboo shoots
1 lb. diced pork or veal
1 can bean sprouts

Pour boiling water over bouillon cubes and soy sauce, stir until smooth. Saute meat until brown, add flour and stir until blended. Remove from heat, stir in bouillon stock, add mushrooms, onions, celery, bean sprouts and bamboo shoots. Cover and simmer 30 minutes, stirring occasionally. Serve over hot rice.

Louise Malone, Caddo
Council, Shreveport, La.

CALVES' EARS

4 calves' ears
Chopped ham and mush-
    rooms

Chopped onion
Butter
Beef stock

Clean calves' ears and blanch in boiling, salted water. Stuff with chopped ham and mushrooms, tying securely to hold stuffing inside. Saute slowly in butter with chopped onion, cover with beef stock and cook slowly for several hours, until tender. Remove ties and serve. Serves 4.

Laura and Bill Baptist, Ozone
Council, Hammond, La.

CARAMEL BACON

Bacon

Honey

Place strips of bacon on cookie sheet with sides. Pour honey over bacon or dip bacon in honey. Be sure honey covers both sides of bacon. Place in 350° oven. When it starts to cook, turn over. Bacon will be as crisp and done as if cooked in skillet. Has a bacon caramel taste.

Peggy Childers
Crescent City Council
New Orleans, La.

GERMAN STYLE CORNED BEEF AND CABBAGE

1 large cabbage, cut in
  6 pieces
2 cloves garlic
2 ribs celery, cut in 4
4 large carrots, cut in
  half

5 small whole onions
6 medium size white potatoes
2 Tbsp. parsley
2 lb. piece of corned beef,
  marinated
Salt and pepper to taste

Preboil corned beef in marinated stock. Use same stock to boil cabbage, onions, garlic, parsley, celery and carrots. Cook for 1/2 hour in small amount of water. Add potatoes. Cover and cook on medium fire until potatoes and carrots are soft. Add salt and pepper to taste.

Maximillian (Max) Zimmer
La. Chapter Past President
New Orleans, La.

CORN DOGS

1 c. flour
2 Tbsp. sugar
1 1/2 tsp. baking powder
1 beaten egg

1 tsp. salt
2/3 c. corn meal
3/4 c. milk
1 lb. franks

Sift together flour, sugar, baking powder and salt. Stir in corn meal. Cut in shortening until mixture looks like fine crumbs. Combine egg and milk, add to corn meal mixture. Stir until well blended. Insert wooden skewer into each frank. Spread each evenly with batter, fry in deep fat at 375° until brown.

Calcasieu Council
Lake Charles, La.

CORN MEAL SCRAPPLE

2 large onions, chopped
1/2 Tbsp. shortening
1 c. corn meal
1 small can mushrooms

1/2 Tbsp. butter
2 lb. ground round steak
1 large can tomatoes
Salt and pepper to taste

Brown onions in fat, add meat. Add corn meal, tomatoes, mushrooms, salt and pepper. Cook for 2 hours in skillet over slow fire. Serves 6-8.

Una W. Mize, Caddo
Council, Shreveport, La.

DILLA DELIGHT

6 fat armadillos
5 sassafras roots
5 tender buckeye balls

2 c. poke salad leaves
2 Tbsp. dandelion seeds

Take nice fat armadillos and wash until clean. Remove meat from shell. Clean shell thoroughly and let drip dry. Mix ingredients and add dilla meat to mixture. Cook 3 hours under very slow fire. Stuff mixture in dilla shell and serve hot as dilla meat has a distinctive odor when cool.

Editor's Note: Some of these ingredients may be dangerous to your health; so don't try recipe. It's a joke, folks!

Buddy Bonner, Caddo
Council, Shreveport, La.

CHINESE AMERICAN EGG ROLLS

2 1/2 c. celery, shredded
2 c. chicken, cooked and
  shredded
1/2 c. chopped water
  chestnuts
1 Tbsp. dry sherry
1/2 tsp. sugar
1/2 tsp. black pepper
1 Tbsp. cornstarch, dis-
  solved in 2 Tbsp.
  chicken stock or water
Cayenne pepper to taste

1/2 lb. lean ground pork
1 c. bamboo shoots, chopped
  or shredded
1/3 c. mushrooms, partially
  drained
2 tsp. salt
1/2 tsp. monosodium glutamate
2 Tbsp. peanut oil
1 medium garlic clove, minced
1 or more Tbsp. Worcestershire sauce

Place celery in boiling water 1 minute, drain and press out all water. Saute pork in oil for 3 minutes, add all ingredients, except cornstarch, cayenne pepper, garlic and Worcestershire sauce. Stir. Saute for 5 minutes. Add cornstarch mixture. Stir until slightly thickened. Remove from fire, add cayenne pepper, garlic, Worcestershire sauce to taste. Cool. Divide mixture into 15 equal portions. Place cooled mixture diagonally on egg roll skins. (Buy these frozen or fresh at grocery store.) Lift lower triangular flap over filling, tuck the point under it. Bring left and right corners toward the center and roll, sealing edges with beaten egg. Deep fry at 325° until golden brown.

Edwina Snyder, Capital
Council, Baton Rouge, La.

ELEPHANT STEW

1 elephant
Salt and pepper

Brown gravy
2 rabbits (optional)

Cut elephant into bite sized pieces. Cover with brown gravy. Cook over low heat about 4 weeks. This will serve 4,200 people. If more are expected, the 2 rabbits may be added, but do this only if necessary, as most people do not like to find hare in their stew.

Buddy Bonner, Caddo
Council, Shreveport, La.

"FRANK" DINNER

1 bunch carrots, cleaned
   and cut
1 c. chicken broth
1 small onion, chopped
Salt
1 bay leaf

4 small potatoes, pared and
   halved
1 small head cabbage,
   quartered
8 frankfurters

Parboil potatoes and carrots for 10 minutes. In large skillet, put the broth, bay leaf and parboiled vegetables. Cover and cook over medium heat 5 minutes. Arrange the cabbage in the skillet, cover and cook another 5 minutes. Sprinkle vegetables with salt. Add frankfurters and simmer 5-10 minutes longer or until vegetables are tender. Serve from skillet, spooning broth over vegetables. Makes 4 servings.

Calcasieu Council
Lake Charles, La.

FROMAGE DE TETE SANS LE TETE
(Hog Head Cheese without the Head, or Coon-Ass By-Pass)

1 fresh pork shoulder
   (6 lb.)
3 bunches green onions,
   chopped
1 1/2 tsp. salt
2 hot peppers (medium
   size), chopped (cayenne
   pepper can be substi-
   tuted)

6 pigs feet
1 large onion, unchopped
2 Tbsp. Kitchen Bouquet
   or black coffee
1 large bunch parsley,
   chopped
8 c. water (approx.)
2 bay leaves

Cut meat into chunks, leaving bones in. Place in large boiling pot and cover well with water. Add salt, pepper, whole onion, 1 bunch green onions and bay leaves. Bring to boil and cook until meat falls from bone. Remove from fire, take meat from pot, cool. Strain liquid and discard all solid contents. Return liquid to pot, chop meat finely; do not grind. Return to liquid in pot. Bring back to hard boil, add remainder of onions, parsley and Kitchen Bouquet. Remove from heat immediately. Adjust seasonings to taste (always better slightly hot to taste). Set aside and cool until can be handled safely. Pour into molds (small bread pans, bowls, cups, etc.). Let stand in molds until room temperature. Place in refrigerator until set. Serve with crackers. Beer is the beverage for hogs head cheese, but if wine is preferred, try a Beaujalais at room temperature.

E. L. Menant, Crescent City
Council, New Orleans, La.

GRAVY ITALIAN SUPREME

1 small beef roast	1 medium onion, chopped
8 links Italian sausage	4 large cans Progresso
3 Tbsp. cooking oil	tomato paste
1/4 tsp. oregano	3 cloves garlic, minced
2 Tbsp. Italian cheese	1 tsp. sugar
Salt and pepper to taste	2 qt. water

In large Dutch oven, brown roast in cooking oil, set aside. Brown sausage lightly, set aside. Saute onion until tender in drippings, add tomato paste and cook, stirring about 30 minutes. Add remainder of ingredients, roast and sausage. Cover and cook on medium heat while making meat balls.

Meat Balls:

1 1/2 lb. ground lean meat	1 1/2 c. Italian bread crumbs
	3 cloves garlic, minced
1 small bunch shallots, cut fine	2 Tbsp. Italian cheese
	2 Tbsp. catsup
1/3 bunch parsley, chopped	2 Tbsp. milk
	Salt and pepper to taste

Mix ingredients well together. Shape into balls. In large baking dish, roast meat balls in oven until brown and solid; drain. Add meat balls to gravy. Cook for 1 1/2 - 2

204

hours with lid cracked on pot for thickness. Stir so it does not stick. Serve over spaghetti. Also makes a very good poor boy sandwich. Serves a bunch.

Lois V. Verdon, Metairie
Council, Horshon, La.

GLAZED HAM BALLS

1 lb. ground cooked ham
3/4 c. soft bread crumbs
3/4 c. unsweetened pineapple juice
2 Tbsp. cornstarch

1/2 lb. ground beef
1/2 c. milk
1/2 c. maple or maple flavored syrup
Hot cooked rice

Combine ham, ground beef, bread crumbs and milk. Mix well. Shape into eighteen 1 1/2-inch meat balls. Place in 8x8x2-inch baking dish. Bake uncovered at 350° for 20 minutes. Combine pineapple juice, syrup and cornstarch in small saucepan. Cook and stir until thickened and bubbly. Pour over meat balls. Bake 20 minutes longer. Serve over rice. Makes 6 servings. To use as party food on a buffet, make balls in miniature size, serve in sauce and use toothpicks for serving.

Mrs. Jeannine M. Prattini
Capital Council
Chalmette, La.

HAM N' CHEESE MELTAWAY SANDWICHES

1 lb. chipped ham
1 onion, minced
1/2 c. mayonnaise
1 doz. hot dog buns

6 hard boiled eggs
1/2 c. chili sauce
Cheese

Mix all ingredients, except cheese and buns, in large container. Fill hot dog buns with mixture. Add strip of cheese to each bun. Wrap each bun in foil. Heat in 425° oven to warm thoroughly and melt cheese. These sandwiches can be frozen. Allow approximately 20 minutes in oven when taken from freezer. Pat Pryor, West Bank
Council, Gretna, La.

HAM WITH CHERRY SAUCE

1 large canned ham
1 Tbsp. prepared mustard
2 Tbsp. dry white wine
1/2 c. light raisins

1 (10 oz.) jar apple jelly
1/3 c. pineapple juice
1 (1 lb. 5 oz.) can cherry
  pie filling

Heat ham according to time schedule on can. Half hour before end of cooking time, remove from oven and score fat in diamonds. Combine jelly, mustard, pineapple juice and white wine. Cook and stir to boiling, reduce heat and simmer for 3 minutes. Pour 1/3 of glaze over ham and return ham to oven for remaining 30 minutes of cooking. Spoon glaze over ham every 10 minutes. Heat pie filling and raisins to boiling, stir occasionally. Remove ham to platter, add glaze from ham pot to cherry sauce. Bring to boil. Spoon some over ham. Pass remainder. Makes 3 cups sauce.

Vera Trosclaw, Central
Council, Lecompte, La.

HAM AND EGG SOUFFLE

4-6 eggs
1 (7 1/2 oz.) can ham,
  flaked (do not drain)

1/4 c. water
1 c. grated cheese
Chives

Beat eggs with water, add other ingredients. Stir and pour into greased hot skillet. Immediately reduce heat as low as possible. Cook approximately 5 minutes or until almost set without stirring. Move to preheated broiler until lightly browned on top. Serve immediately.

Gladys Domingues, Caddo
Council, Shreveport, La.

HAM, OKRA AND TOMATOES

1 lb. fresh sliced okra
  or frozen
1 chopped onion
2 Tbsp. cooking oil

3 or 4 tomatoes, cut up
1 lb. diced ham
1 tsp. salt
1/2 tsp. pepper

Heat cooking oil, add okra and smother down. Add onions and tomatoes, simmer 10 minutes. Add remaining ingredients and continue to simmer for about 30 minutes. Serves 4.

Victoria Hirstius, Metairie
Council, Metairie, La.

HAM PINWHEELS

Sliced ham
Pickles

Old English process cheese
spread

Spread ham with cheese. Roll around a pickle and slice. Place each slice on Ritz cracker, Melba toast or on bread that has been cut with biscuit cutter. Olives can be substituted for pickles if desired.

Jeanette English, Caddo
Council, Shreveport, La.

POLYNESIAN HAM BAKE

1 (5 lb.) canned ham
Whole cloves
2 medium bananas, cut
　in 2-inch pieces
3 Tbsp. cream cheese,
　softened

1/2 c. pineapple preserves
1 (29 oz.) can peach halves,
　drained
1 can cream of chicken soup
1/2 c. water
1 Tbsp. toasted shredded
　coconut

In shallow roasting pan, bake ham at 325° for 1 hour. Drain off fat. Score. Spread with 1/4 cup pineapple preserves. Stud with cloves. Bake 15 minutes. Spread peaches and bananas with 2 tablespoons of preserves and arrange around ham. Bake 15 minutes more. Remove ham and fruit to warm serving platter. On top of stove, in same roasting pan, combine 1 tablespoon fat drippings from ham, soup, water, cream cheese, coconut and remaining preserves. Heat, stirring to loosen browned bits. Serve with ham. Makes 6-8 servings.

Ann Orr, Evangeline
Council, New Iberia, La.

FRIED RICE

1 c. cooked rice
3 or 4 eggs
Soy sauce (small bottle)
1 can bean sprouts
Salt and pepper

4 or 5 slices bacon
4 cut up green onions
Salt and pepper to taste
2 or 3 lb. shrimp, pork,
　chicken or beef, pre-
　cooked

Cook rice day before, store spread on plate in the

refrigerator. If chicken, beef or pork are used, cook rice in their stock. Brown bacon until crisp, then break into pieces. Scramble eggs in bacon drippings until very dry. Salt and pepper to taste. Add bacon bits, green onions, bean sprouts, rice and meat, cut in small pieces. Stir, sprinkle with soy sauce until brown. Heat on top of stove for 20 minutes at low temperature. Serves 4-6 people.

Tommie McHenry, Caddo
Council, Bossier City, La.

FRIED RICE WITH BACON

4 c. cold, cooked rice
1/2 tsp. sugar
1 Tbsp. soy sauce
1/2 lb. bacon, fried
   crisp and broken into
   small pieces

3 Tbsp. vegetable oil
1 tsp. salt
3 eggs, cooked and
   scrambled very soft
2 scallions, chopped

Stir-fry rice in hot oil for 1 minute. Add sugar, salt and soy sauce. Stir until heated through. Add eggs, scallions and bacon. Stir to mix and serve.

Marilou Bridges, Caddo
Council, Shreveport, La.

PORK FRIED RICE

4 pork chops or steaks
1/2 medium chopped onion
2 1/4 c. water
4 Tbsp. soy sauce

1/2 medium chopped bell
   pepper
1 1/2 c. long grain rice
4 Tbsp. oil

Brown pork in oil. Chop in bite size pieces. Add onion and bell pepper to oil. Stir, add rice and let fry until light golden brown.

Jan Prestridge, Capital
Council, Baton Rouge, La.

JENNY'S CREOLE HAMBURGERS

1 lb. ground meat
1/2 onion, chopped
1/2 bell pepper, chopped
1 can chicken gumbo

1/2 can water
2 Tbsp. catsup
1 Tbsp. prepared mustard

Scramble meat and brown with onions and bell peppers, drain. Add remaining ingredients. Simmer until thickened. Serve on large hamburger buns.

Marie Pamplin
Shreveport Works Council
Shreveport, La.

HAMBURGER GRAVY

1 lb. ground beef
1 small onion, chopped
3 c. water
1 clove garlic, minced
4 Tbsp. flour
2 Tbsp. oil

Brown ground beef, onions and garlic, drain and set aside. Make roux of flour and oil, brown. Add water, simmer 15 minutes. Add ground beef, simmer 30 minutes. Add more water if necessary. Gravy should be thick. Serve over mashed potatoes.

Susan Lachney, Westmoor
Council, Kenner, La.

HAMBURGER HASH

1 lb. ground beef
1 medium onion, chopped
1/2 tsp. black pepper
2 c. water
1/2 tsp. salt
3 medium potatoes, peeled
and cut into pieces

Saute ground beef, onion, salt and pepper in skillet until beef is slightly brown. Add potatoes and water. Cook until potatoes are tender. Serve immediately.

Maxine Fletcher, Ouachita
Council, Monroe, La.

HAMBURGER-PANCAKE ROLL-UPS

Hamburger Mixture:

1 lb. ground beef
2 Tbsp. instant, minced
onion (or frozen, or
real, or whatever!)
2 Tbsp. Bisquick (or flour)
1/3 c. catsup
1 Tbsp. prepared mustard
1/2 tsp. salt
1/4 tsp. pepper
1 c. sour cream

Brown meat, then add rest of ingredients. Simmer 5-10

minutes. Make pancake recipe, except add 1/3 cup more milk. Bake each pancake about 6 inches in diameter. Spoon some hamburger mixture on each pancake. Roll and place folded side down in baking dish. Cover with some grated Cheddar cheese. Heat in 350° oven for about 10 minutes.

Calcasieu Council
Lake Charles, La.

HAMBURGER PIE

1 chopped onion	2 lb. ground beef
Salt and pepper to taste	Cooking fat or oil
1 1/2 c. green beans	1 1/2 c. corn
2 medium potatoes, diced	1 (11 oz.) can tomato soup
	Canned biscuits or mashed potatoes

Saute onion in oil. Add beef and seasonings and brown. Add beans, corn, potatoes and soup. Mix well and spoon into casserole. Bake at 350° for 1 hour. Top with canned biscuits or mashed potatoes last 15 minutes of baking.

Louise Malone, Caddo
Council, Shreveport, La.

HAMBURGER SURPRISE

2 lb. ground beef	Italian bread crumbs
1 tsp. minced onion	Cooked chicken, cooked
Salt and pepper to taste	bacon, pork n' beans or
1 egg	cheese

Mix beef, onion, salt, pepper and egg. Add enough bread crumbs to make meat stiff. Form into 8 patties. In the middle of 4 patties, place pieces of chicken, bacon, cheese, etc. Place the remaining patties on top and seal edges. Bake uncovered at 375° until done.

Susan Lachney, Westmoor
Council, Kenner, La.

210

HAMBURGER STROGANOFF

1/4 c. butter or oleo
1/2 c. minced onion
1 lb. ground beef
Garlic salt to taste
1 c. sour cream

2 Tbsp. flour
2 tsp. (or less) salt
1/4 tsp. pepper
1 can cream of chicken or
   cream of mushroom soup

Melt butter in heavy skillet. Add onion and cook slowly
until soft. Add ground beef and garlic salt. Stir until
lightly browned. Stir in flour, salt and pepper. Add
soup and simmer 10 minutes. Stir in sour cream. Heat and
sprinkle with minced parsley, chives or dill. Serve on top
of noodles or rice.
Calcasieu Council
Lake Charles, La.

HAWAIIAN RICE

1 lb. lean ground beef
1 c. chopped celery
1/2 c. chopped onions
1 (2 oz.) can button
   mushrooms, drained

2 (10 1/2 oz.) cans beef
   consomme
1 c. rice
1 tsp. salt
Dash of black pepper

Brown ground beef, add celery, onions and mushrooms.
Cook 10 minutes or until tender. Add consomme and bring
to boil. Add rice and bring to boil. Turn fire down to
low and cover. Cook 25-30 minutes or until rice is done.
Calcasieu Council
Lake Charles, La.

KIELBASA SAUSAGE WITH RED CABBAGE

1/4 c. light brown sugar,
   firmly packed
1 clove garlic, crushed
1/8 tsp. ground cloves
3 medium cooking apples,
   pared, cored and
   sliced
2 lb. red cabbage head,
   shredded

1 Tbsp. grated orange peel
1 1/2 tsp. salt
1/2 tsp. pepper
3 medium onions, sliced
1 large red pepper, cut in
   thin strips
1/4 c. wine vinegar
1/2 c. orange juice
1 ring (2 lb.) kielbasa

Combine brown sugar, orange peel, garlic, salt, nutmeg, pepper and cloves in small bowl. In Dutch oven,

arrange in layers, half of cabbage, half of onions and half of apples. Sprinkle with half of brown sugar mixture. Top with half of pepper strips. Repeat layers. Pour orange juice and vinegar over top. Bake covered for 1 hour in preheated 350° oven. Make 1/4-inch slashes at 2-inch intervals in kielbasa. Place in Dutch oven, pressing down to partially cover the sausage with pan juices. Bake covered for 30 minutes longer.

Rebecca Scott Bockmon, Caddo
Council, Shreveport, La.

LASAGNE

3 Tbsp. oil
1 (6 oz.) can tomato
  paste
1 lb. hamburger meat
2 tsp. salt
1 small container of small
  curd cottage cheese
  (optional)
1/2 lb. grated Parmesan
  cheese

1 large onion, chopped
1 tsp. parsley
1 tsp. sugar
2 c. chopped tomatoes, or
  mashed
1/2 lb. Mozzarella cheese,
  grated
1 small pkg. or 1/2 large pkg
  lasagne noodles

Cook onion and hamburger in oil. Add tomatoes, parsley, sugar, salt, tomato paste on low heat 8-10 minutes. Cook noodles and drain. Place some sauce in bottom of baking dish, layer noodles, layer of each cheese. Repeat layers until all ingredients are used up. Bake at 350° for 30 minutes. Top with additional cheese.

Louise Malone, Caddo
Council, Shreveport, La.

LASAGNE

1 1/2 pt. cottage cheese
1 (8 oz.) pkg. wide
  lasagne noodles
1 pkg. Italian spaghetti
  mix
Chopped onion
1 large can tomato sauce

1 lb. Mozzarella cheese,
  grated
1 lb. Cheddar cheese, grated
2 lb. ground meat
Olive oil
Parmesan cheese
1 small can tomato sauce

Saute onion in olive oil to taste. Add meat and brown, drain excess grease. Add spaghetti mix and tomato sauce. Simmer until meat is done. Cook noodles, drain and cool in

212

cold water. Do not add salt and pepper. Put layer of noodles in casserole, layer with meat sauce and layer of cheese mixture (Mozzarella, Cheddar and cottage). Sprinkle with Parmesan. Repeat layers and sprinkle with Parmesan. Bake in 350° oven until cheese is melted.

Jeanette English, Caddo
Council, Shreveport, La.

LIVER LOUISIANNE

6 slices bacon, diced
1/4 c. flour
1 1/2 tsp. salt
1/3 c. diced green pepper
1/8 tsp. cayenne pepper
1/8 tsp. garlic salt

2 lb. beef liver, sliced
1/2-inch thick
1 large onion, sliced
1 (16 oz.) can tomatoes
1/4 tsp. chili powder
Cooked rice

Cook bacon in frying pan until crisp, remove. Combine flour and salt. Dredge liver in flour mixture and brown lightly on each side in bacon drippings. Pour off remaining drippings. Add onion, green pepper, tomatoes, cayenne pepper, chili powder and garlic salt. Cover tightly and simmer 20 minutes. Thicken gravy if desired. Sprinkle bacon over top. Serve liver and sauce over hot cooked rice. Serves 6-8.

Rebecca Scott, Caddo
Council, Shreveport, La.

SAUTEED LIVER

1 apple, peeled
1 medium onion, sliced
   and rings separated
Salt and pepper to taste
Flour

1 Tbsp. wine vinegar
2 Tbsp. oil
1/2 beef or pork liver
   (fresh, not frozen)

Saute onion in oil. Cut apple in half, then in slices, add to onion. Cut liver in strips, dust with flour and add to mixture. Add vinegar, salt and pepper to taste. Continue cooking over medium heat, stirring constantly until onions are brown and liver is done.

Marilou Bridges, Caddo
Council, Shreveport, La.

LOVE BIRDS FOR TWO

1 can Mandarin oranges,
   drained (reserve syrup)
2/3 c. instant rice
2 Cornish hens (1 lb.
   each)
1 c. orange juice

2 env. onion soup mix
Water
2 Tbsp. finely chopped
   walnuts
2 tsp. cornstarch

Chop enough Mandarin oranges to equal 1/3 cup. Reserve remainder for garnish. Combine syrup with enough water to equal 2/3 cup. Bring syrup and water mixture to boil, add 1 envelope soup mix and rice. Remove from heat. Let stand covered for 5 minutes, add chopped oranges and walnuts. Stuff hens with rice mixture, use toothpicks to close openings. Place hens in shallow baking pan and bake 30 minutes in preheated 375° oven. Combine remaining soup mix, cornstarch and orange juice. Bring to a boil, then simmer, stirring constantly, until slightly thickened, about 1 minute. Brush glaze on hens, continue baking, basting frequently with glaze 30 minutes or until hens are tender. Garnish with reserved Mandarin oranges. Makes 2 servings.

Marjorie B. Harris, Capital
Council, Baton Rouge, La.

MANICOTTI WITH MEAT FILLING

12 manicotti shells
3 Tbsp. butter or oleo
1/3 c. minced onion
1 clove garlic, minced
1/3 c. sherry wine
   (optional)
1/3 - 1/2 c. bread crumbs
4 c. spaghetti sauce

1/2 lb. ground pork
1 1/2 lb. ground beef
1/3 c. minced celery
1/3 c. Parmesan cheese
5 1/2 tsp. salt, divided
4 qt. water
1 tsp. pepper

Bring 4 quarts water to boil, add 4 teaspoons salt. Gradually add 6 manicotti so that water continues to boil. Cook uncovered 3 minutes, drain without rinsing. Repeat for remaining manicotti. Melt butter in large frying pan. Add pork and beef, cook until lightly browned. Add onion, celery and garlic. Cover and cook 10-15 minutes until celery is tender. Remove from heat. Stir in cheese, sherry, pepper, bread crumbs and remaining 1 1/2 teaspoons salt. Fill manicotti shells with mixture, using press, knife or small teaspoon. Heat up spaghetti sauce. Pour half in bottom of baking dish and top with filled manicotti, side by side, in a single layer. Top with remaining sauce, completely covering manicotti. Cover with foil tightly. Bake in preheated 400° oven for 45 minutes. Uncover, sprinkle with Parmesan cheese and bake 5 minutes longer. Serves 6.

Jeanette English, Caddo
Council, Shreveport, La.

MEAT BALLS

2 lb. ground meat in which small amount of ground pork has been added (ground all together)
1 Tbsp. mustard

2 stalks ground celery
2 c. chopped bell pepper
1/2 c. chopped pecans
2 c. dry bread crumbs
2 Tbsp. chopped parsley
Seasoned salt

Blend all ingredients well. Shape into small or large meat balls as desired. Use either in sauce or fried.

Emerite L. Hebert
Evangeline Council
Scott, La.

APPLESAUCE MEAT BALLS

1 lb. ground beef
3/4 c. applesauce
Chopped onion

1 tsp. salt
1/2 c. crushed corn flakes

Mix all well. Make into 8 balls. Cover with:

3/4 c. catsup

3/4 c. water

Bake 1 hour at 375°.

Calcasieu Council
Lake Charles, La.

APPLESAUCE MEAT BALLS

2 lb. ground beef
1 c. soft bread crumbs
Salt and pepper to taste
2 Tbsp. shortening
1 bell pepper, minced
1 carrot, thinly sliced

1 c. applesauce
2 eggs
Flour
1 stalk celery, thinly sliced
1 small onion, thinly sliced
2 c. tomato juice

Mix beef, applesauce and bread crumbs. Add eggs. Season with salt and pepper. Form mixture into small balls, roll in flour and brown in shortening. Place meat balls in casserole. Add vegetables and tomato juice to drippings in pan. Season with salt and pepper. Bring to a boil and pour over meat balls. Cover and bake in 350° oven about 40 minutes. Gravy can be thickened with a little flour if desired before serving. Freezes well. Marilou Bridges, Caddo
Council, Shreveport, La.

FAST MEAT BALLS AND SPAGHETTI

2 lb. ground meat
3 Tbsp. instant minced
    onions
3 eggs
1 qt. Ragu spaghetti
    and mushroom sauce
Grated Romano cheese

1 Tbsp. instant minced garlic
2 Tbsp. parsley flakes
3 slices bread or 1/4 loaf
    stale French bread
Salt and pepper to taste
Cooked hot spaghetti

Soak bread slices or French bread in water, squeeze out excess water. Mix ground meat, onions, garlic, parsley, eggs, bread, salt and pepper. Roll in medium size balls. Fry in small saucepan until brown. Place in large pot, add Ragu sauce and small amount of water. Cook on medium heat for 30 minutes. Cook spaghetti while meat balls are cooking. Top meat balls and spaghetti with grated Romano cheese and serve. Thirty-minute meal.
Dorothy Zimmer, La. Past
President Pioneer Partner
New Orleans, La.

FAVORITE SWEDISH MEAT BALLS

4 eggs, slightly beaten
2 c. milk
1 c. dry bread crumbs
1 c. minced onions
1/4 c. butter
3 c. beef stock
1 tsp. dill weed
Salt

1/4 tsp. nutmeg
1/4 tsp. allspice (optional)
1/4 tsp. cardamon (optional)
2 1/2 lb. ground beef
1/4 c. flour
1 c. light cream
Pepper to taste

Mix eggs, milk and crumbs together, let stand. Cook onions in 2 tablespoons butter in skillet until tender.

216

Remove onions with a slotted spoon and add to crumb mixture. Add 3 teaspoons salt, spices and beef, mix thoroughly. Chill for 1 hour to blend flavors, shape into 1-inch balls. Melt remaining butter in the skillet and brown meat balls on low heat, turning carefully so meat balls hold shape. Place in Dutch oven when browned, add flour to drippings in skillet and make a roux. Cook until flour browns. Add beef broth and cook, stirring until smooth and thickened. Add cream, salt to taste, pepper and dill weed. Strain over meat balls and simmer covered over low heat for 30 minutes. May be baked if desired at 325° for 30 minutes. Serves 10-12.   Rebecca Scott Bockmon, Caddo
Council, Shreveport, La.

HOT TAMALE MEAT BALLS

1 lb. ground beef
1 lb. ground pork
4 cloves garlic, chopped
2 large (No. 303) cans
   tomatoes

1 1/2 c. corn meal
1/2 c. flour
2 Tbsp. chili powder
3/4 c. tomato juice
Salt and pepper to taste

Regrind meat. Mix meats, corn meal, flour, garlic, salt, juice and pepper. Form into approximately 200 small balls. Mix tomatoes, chili powder, salt and pepper to taste. Bring to boil. Add meat balls, lower heat and simmer for 2 hours.
Patricia R. Caraway, Capital
Council, Baton Rouge, La.

ITALIAN MEAT BALLS AND GRAVY OR SAUCE

Gravy:

1 (18 oz.) can Italian
   tomato paste, or 1
   (12 oz.) can and 1
   (6 oz.) can
1 small stalk celery and
   celery leaves, coarsely
   chopped
3 qt. water

3 pods garlic, coarsely
   chopped
1 small onion, coarsely
   chopped
2 or 3 Tbsp. sugar
1 tsp. basil leaves
Olive oil or cooking oil
Salt and pepper

Heat a small amount of olive oil in large Dutch oven. Add chopped garlic, onion and celery. Cook over low heat. Add sugar, stir until sugar dissolves and cook until tender.

Do not brown. Add tomato paste, rinsing the cans with water to get all of tomato paste. Add salt and pepper. Add water, cover and cook over <u>low</u> heat at least 3 hours. Also, any type of meat can be used if desired; steak, pork chops, Italian sausage, ground beef and even hard boiled eggs. Add basil about 15 or 20 minutes before sauce is done. Mix and serve sauce with cooked spaghetti. To cook spaghetti, bring large pot of water to a rolling boil. Add 3 or 4 tablespoons salt. Lower heat and add spaghetti. Cook 30 minutes, stirring often.

Meat Balls:

1 lb. ground round or
   lean chuck
2 or 3 pods garlic, finely
   chopped
Small amount finely chopped
   bell pepper (optional)
1 tsp. parsley flakes or
   fresh parsley
6 eggs

1/4 c. finely chopped onion
1/4 c. finely chopped celery
   and leaves
1/4 c. grated Italian Romano
   cheese
3/4 c. bread crumbs
1 tsp. basil leaves
Salt and pepper to taste

Mix all ingredients, add eggs, mix well. Mixture should be moist. Add salt and pepper. Shape into meat balls and fry in large skillet with about 1 inch olive oil or cooking oil in bottom. Fry meat balls lightly brown, drain and add to the sauce when it is about half cooked and finish cooking together. One meat ball should be fried first to see if meat balls are seasoned enough before adding to sauce. These recipes were handed down to me by aunts who were wonderful "Italian Cooks."   Mrs. Joe Nasello, Central
Council, Alexandria, La.

KIKKOMAN MADHATTER MEAT BALLS

1 lb. ground beef
1/4 c. uncooked long
   grain rice
2 slices bread, torn in
   pieces

1 small onion, chopped fine
1 egg
5 Tbsp. Kikkoman soy sauce
1 can tomato soup
1 c. water

Combine and mix beef, onion, rice, egg, bread and 4 tablespoons soy sauce. Shape into meat balls. In large frying pan, blend soup, water and 1 tablespoon soy sauce.

Arrange meat balls, side by side, in soup mixture. Cover and simmer 1 hour or until rice is cooked.

Rebecca Thames, Caddo
Council, Shreveport, La.

MEAT BALL STEW

1 lb. ground beef
1/4 c. chopped onion
1 tsp. salt
2 c. V-8 juice
1/8 tsp. basil leaves, crushed
2 Tbsp. flour
1/4 c. bread crumbs
1 egg, beaten
2 Tbsp. shortening
1 c. thinly sliced carrots
1 (16 oz.) can small whole potatoes, drained
Pepper, if desired

Mix beef, bread crumbs, onion, egg and salt. Shape into 16 meat balls and brown in shortening, drain. Add 1 1/2 cups V-8 juice, carrots, salt, pepper and basil. Cover and cook 15 minutes, stirring occasionally. Add potatoes and cook 5 minutes or until done. Blend remaining juice into flour until smooth and slowly stir into stew until thickened.

Lynda Fox, Caddo Council,
Shreveport, La.

SWEDISH MEAT BALLS

2 lb. ground meat
1 egg
1 tsp. black pepper
2 tsp. salt
1 pack dry onion soup mix
1/2 c. bread crumbs
1 tsp. red pepper

Combine above ingredients and shape into small meat balls. Fry or bake in 400° oven about 10 minutes or drop raw meat balls into sauce to cook.

Sauce:

2 bottles (14 oz. size) catsup
1 tsp. oregano
1 tsp. black pepper
1 (10 oz.) can applesauce
1 tsp. red pepper
1 tsp. salt

Cook over medium heat, stirring occasionally, about 30 minutes.

Donna Leger, Evangeline
Council, Lafayette, La.

SWEDISH MEAT BALLS

1 1/4 lb. ground chuck
1 medium onion, chopped
1/4 lb. ground pork
1/2 c. evaporated milk
1/3 tsp. ginger

1/2 pkg. cracker crumbs
1/2 tsp. salt and pepper
Dash of nutmeg
2 eggs
1/2 bell pepper, chopped

Combine all ingredients to form meat balls. Brown in fat, set aside until sauce is ready.

Sauce:

1/2 onion, chopped
1 can mushroom soup
1/4 c. barbecue sauce

1/2 can tomato sauce
1 Tbsp. Worcestershire
sauce

To make sauce, begin with a small roux. Add tomato sauce, Worcestershire sauce, salt and pepper. Add soup, prepared to can directions. Add remaining ingredients and simmer for 45 minutes. Add meat balls to sauce and bake at 375° for 45 minutes.　　　　Sonia A. Hunt, Capital
Council, Baton Rouge, La.

TANGY SWEET MEAT BALLS

1 lb. ground beef
2 c. soft bread crumbs
1/2 c. finely chopped onion
2 tsp. salt
1 (10 oz.) jar apricot
preserves

1 lb. ground pork
2 eggs, slightly beaten
1 Tbsp. minced parsley
2 Tbsp. oleo
1/2 c. barbecue sauce

Combine beef, pork, bread crumbs, eggs, onion, parsley and salt. Mix well and shape into 1-inch balls. Brown in oleo, drain on paper towels. Place meat balls in 13x9x2-inch baking dish. Combine preserves and barbecue sauce. Pour over meat balls. Bake at 350° for 30 minutes. Yield: 5 dozen.　　　　Jeanette English, Caddo
Council, Shreveport, La.

PARTY MEAT BALLS

1 (12 oz.) bottle chili
   sauce
1/4 c. water
2 Tbsp. chopped parsley
1 tsp. prepared mustard

1 (18 oz.) jar grape jelly
1 1/2 lb. ground chuck
1/4 tsp. pepper
2 tsp. chili powder
1 clove garlic, minced

Combine jelly, water and chili sauce in saucepan. Heat, stirring until well blended. Combine remaining ingredients, mix well and form into small balls. Place in sauce. Simmer over low heat 30 minutes or until done. Serve with toothpicks. Makes about 3 dozen meat balls.

Marilou Bridges, Caddo
Council, Shreveport, La.

MEAT LOAF

2 lb. ground beef
1 tall can (13 oz.) evap-
   orated milk
2 Tbsp. Worcestershire
   sauce

1 c. bread crumbs
1/2 c. finely chopped onion
1/2 c. catsup or chili sauce
2 tsp. salt
1/2 tsp. pepper

Mix all ingredients together. Shape into loaf in center of 13x9x2-inch baking pan. Bake at 350° about 1 hour and 15 minutes or until well browned. Allow meat loaf to stand 10 minutes for easier slicing. Makes 8 servings.

Ann Orr, Evangeline
Council, Lafayette, La.

MEAT LOAF

2 lb. ground beef
1 1/2 c. bread crumbs
1 tsp. Accent
1 pkg. onion soup mix
2 strips bacon

2 eggs
3/4 c. catsup
1/2 c. warm water
1 (8 oz.) can tomato sauce

Mix beef, eggs, bread crumbs, catsup, Accent, warm water and soup mix. Shape into loaf and place in shallow baking dish. Lay bacon over loaf and pour tomato sauce over all. Bake at 350° for 1 hour. Do not use any salt in meat loaf.

Marilou Bridges, Caddo
Council, Shreveport, La.

MEAT LOAF

1 c. Pet milk
3/4 c. oatmeal
Salt and pepper to taste

1 1/2 lb. ground beef
3 Tbsp. chopped onion

Combine and mix ingredients. Bake 1 hour at 350°.

Sauce:

1 c. catsup
3 Tbsp. sugar
3 Tbsp. onion
Salt and pepper to taste

1/4 c. vinegar
1/2 c. water
3 Tbsp. Worcestershire
  sauce

Combine ingredients, pour over meat loaf and cook with it, or heat and serve on side. Gay Irwin, Capital Council, Baton Rouge, La.

MEAT LOAF BARBECUE STYLE

1 1/2 lb. ground beef
1 c. fresh bread crumbs
1 onion, finely chopped

1 1/2 tsp. salt
1/4 tsp. pepper
2 cans Hunt's tomato sauce
1 egg

Mix together all but 1/2 cup tomato sauce. Form into a loaf and put in 7x10-inch pan. Combine remaining tomato sauce and:

1/2 c. water
3 Tbsp. vinegar
3 Tbsp. brown sugar

2 Tbsp. prepared mustard
2 Tbsp. Worcestershire
  sauce

Pour over loaf. Bake at 350° for 1 hour and 15 minutes. Baste occasionally. Makes 4-6 servings.
Calcasieu Council
Lake Charles, La.

MEAT AND CHEESE LOAF

1 egg
3/4 c. diced process
  American cheese
1 tsp. salt
1/2 tsp. celery salt
1 c. evaporated milk

1 lb. ground beef
1/3 c. chopped onion
1/4 c. chopped green pepper
1/4 tsp. pepper
1/4 tsp. paprika
1/2 c. fine dry bread crumbs

Beat egg with a fork in medium size mixing bowl. Add remaining ingredients. Stir gently until thoroughly mixed. Pack lightly by spoonfuls into a greased 5x9-inch loaf pan. Bake at 350° for 55-60 minutes.

Betty Jackson
Shreveport Works Council
Shreveport, La.

DELICIOUS MEAT LOAF

2 lb. ground round steak
1 1/2 c. bread crumbs
1 tsp. Accent
1 pkg. Lipton's onion soup
  mix

2 eggs
3/4 c. catsup
1/2 c. warm water
1 (8 oz.) can tomato sauce
3 strips bacon

Mix all ingredients, except bacon and tomato sauce. Put in loaf pan. Cover with bacon strips. Pour tomato sauce over all. Bake at 350° for 1 hour or until done.

Ruby Allen, Shreveport Works
Council, Shreveport, La.

ED'S MEAT LOAF

1 1/2 lb. ground beef
1 small onion, diced
1 c. crushed cereal flakes
1 large can sweet potatoes

2 tsp. salt
1/4 tsp. pepper
2 eggs, slightly beaten
1/2 c. diced celery

Combine ingredients, except potatoes, and mix thoroughly. Mold out loaf in pan. Place sweet potatoes around loaf, reserving juice. Punch holes in top of loaf with fork or toothpick and pour juice from sweet potatoes over loaf. Bake in 350° oven for 1 1/2 hours.

Beverly Lumm, Caddo
Council, Shreveport, La.

FANTASTIC MEAT LOAF

3 lb. ground meat
1/2 c. chopped green onion
Salt and pepper to taste
1 pkg. shredded Cheddar
    cheese
1 c. chopped onion
Bread crumbs
1 can cream of mushroom
    soup

Mix ground meat, chopped onions, bread crumbs, salt and pepper together. Shape into loaf and bake in pan until just about done. Sprinkle cheese over loaf and pour mushroom soup over top. Continue to bake at about 350° until meat is done and cheese is melted.

Pete Duplechin, LeBayou
Council, Houma, La.

ITALIAN MEAT LOAF

2 lb. lean ground meat
2 c. bread crumbs
1 pack pepperoni, sliced
8 oz. shredded Mozzar-
    ella cheese
2 eggs
1 small can tomato sauce
Salt, pepper and oregano
    to taste

Combine and mix together the beef, seasonings, eggs, bread crumbs and 1/2 can tomato sauce. Pat meat mixture into 16x10-inch rectangle on waxed paper. Arrange pepperoni slices on meat rectangle. Sprinkle cheese over. Roll up meat jelly roll fashion, seal ends by pressing meat together. Place seam down in shallow pan, sprayed with Pam. Bake at 350° for 1 hour. Top with remaining tomato sauce. Continue baking for 10 minutes or until done.

Bernadette Babin, LeBayou
Council, Houma, La.

JUICY MEAT LOAF

1 1/2 lb. ground lean
    beef
1 small onion, minced
1 clove garlic, minced
    (optional)
2 c. bread crumbs, soaked
    in milk
2 eggs, beaten
Salt and pepper to taste

Combine ingredients and shape in loaf. Place in a greased baking pan. Pour sauce over loaf and bake at 350° about 2 hours, basting frequently. Serves 6.

224

Sauce:

1 c. tomatoes

1/2 c. sliced onion

1 Tbsp. oleo or butter

1 c. water

Combine ingredients and pour over meat loaf.

Mrs. J. B. Coker, Central
Council, Alexandria, La.

MIMI'S MEAT LOAF

1 lb. ground lean beef
1 tsp. Worcestershire
   sauce
1/2 c. chili sauce
1 onion, chopped

1 egg
1 tsp. salt
1/4 tsp. pepper
11 saltine crackers, crushed
2 or 3 strips bacon

Mix all ingredients, except bacon and 3 of the saltine crackers. Pack meat loaf mixture into greased loaf pan. Sprinkle the reserved crackers over top and lay bacon strips over that. Bake 1 hour at 350°. Serve hot or cold. Makes 6 servings.

Mildred (Mimi) Kutzelman
Shreveport Works Council
Shreveport, La.

POLISH MEAT LOAF

2 lb. ground meat
1/2 c. bread crumbs
1 (8 oz.) can sauerkraut,
   drained
Caraway seed

1 egg
1 pkg. onion soup mix
1/4 c. evaporated milk
Black pepper

Combine bread crumbs, milk, egg, onion soup mix and 1/2 of sauerkraut with the ground meat. Shape mixture into a loaf pan. Bake at 350° for 1 hour and 15 minutes. During last 15 minutes of baking, spread the remaining sauerkraut on top of meat loaf and sprinkle with caraway seeds and black pepper.

Mrs. Stanley Tempalski
Ouachita Council
Monroe, La.

MEAT LOAF SURPRISE

1 lb. ground meat
2 onions, chopped
1/2 c. seasoned bread
   crumbs

1/2 lb. bulk hot sausage
2 cloves minced garlic
2 medium eggs
Salt and pepper to taste

Combine and mix all ingredients thoroughly. Take half of mixture and mold into loaf pan, leaving a hollow spot in center. Make certain at least 1 inch of meat mixture around hollow on all sides. Fill hollow area with any filling you desire, such as grated cheese, hard cooked egg, mushrooms, red gravy, etc. Mold remaining meat mixture over top, being certain to close seams well so filling won't escape. Bake at 350° for 1 1/2 - 2 hours. Let set 10-15 minutes before serving.

Wanda T. Reis
Crescent City Council
New Orleans, La.

DAMOND FAVORITE MEAT PATTIES

1 lb. ground beef
1/4 c. plain bread crumbs
1 egg
1/4 c. bell pepper, finely
   chopped
2 cloves garlic, minced
Salt and pepper to taste

1 lb. whole shrimp, peeled
   and deveined
2 slices bread, moistened
1/4 c. onion, finely chopped
1/4 c. parsley, finely chopped
1/2 c. cooking oil
1 c. all-purpose flour

Mix all ingredients, except oil and flour. Mix well. Shape into medium size meat patties. Coat each patty with flour. Render any excess flour. Heat oil in deep skillet, brown patties on both sides.

Gravy:

1/2 c. all-purpose flour
   (including that
   rendered from patties)
1 can tomatoes, chopped
3 cloves garlic, minced
1/2 tsp. oregano

1/2 c. cooking oil (including
   drippings from patties)
1/4 c. chopped onion
1/4 c. bell pepper
3 c. hot water
1/4 c. Parmesan cheese
   (optional)

In the same skillet used for browning patties, add flour and additional oil to make 1/2 cup. Brown under medium

heat, stirring constantly. Add seasonings and cook until tender; do not brown. Add tomatoes, hot water, salt, pepper and oregano. Cook under medium heat for 15 minutes. Add meat patties. Let simmer under low heat for 1 hour. Excellent with either spaghetti or rice or garlic bread. Serves 6.　　　　　　Mary Ann J. Francois
　　　　　　　　　　　　　　　　Metairie Council
　　　　　　　　　　　　　　　　New Orleans, La.

MEXICAN MEAT

1 round steak, cubed
Comino (cumin) seasoning
1 large green pepper, chopped
1 large onion, chopped

Salt and pepper to taste
1/2 c. flour
1 c. water
1 (8 oz.) can tomato sauce

Season meat with salt and pepper. Pour in comino seasoning. Cover all of meat with this seasoning; you can't get too much. Roll in flour. Cover bottom of skillet with shortening or oil and brown meat. Add green peppers and onion. Cook until soft. Add tomato sauce and water. Cover and simmer for about 1 hour.　C. Pierce, LeBayou Council
　　　　　　　　　　　　　　　Morgan City, La.

MOUSSAKA

4 medium eggplants (1 lb. each) and salt
3 medium onions, chopped
1/2 c. dry red wine
1/4 tsp. coarse black pepper
2 eggs, slightly beaten
1/2 c. soft bread crumbs
2 cans (1 lb. 1 oz. each) plum tomatoes, drained
Dash of nutmeg

2 lb. lean beef
1/2 c. oleo
2 tsp. salt
1 tsp. oregano
1 c. grated sharp Cheddar cheese
Vegetable oil
6 Tbsp. flour
3 c. milk
Salt and pepper to taste
4 egg yolks, lightly beaten

Peel eggplant, cut crosswise in 1/4-inch slices. Sprinkle lightly with salt, arrange in stacks, place heavy plate on top. Let stand to drain. Cook beef and onion in 2 tablespoons butter until browned. Add wine, 2 teaspoons salt, coarse black pepper and oregano. Simmer until liquid is absorbed. Stir in 2 beaten eggs, 3/4 cup grated cheese and 1/4 cup bread crumbs. Brown eggplant slices on both sides quickly in vegetable oil. Sprinkle remaining crumbs in bottom of a greased large casserole or baking dish. Fill with alternate layers of eggplant, meat mixture and tomatoes, ending with eggplant. Melt remaining butter, blend in flour, add milk slowly, stirring constantly. Season to taste with salt, pepper and nutmeg. Pour a little hot milk mixture on egg yolks, return to remaining hot milk mixture. Cook about 2 minutes over low heat, stirring until thickened. Pour sauce into casserole. Sprinkle with remaining cheese. Bake at 350° for 45-60 minutes or until top is golden brown and eggplant is tender. Makes 10-12 servings.

Ray Ducharme, Caddo
Council, Shreveport, La.

MUSCATROLLE

1 lb. ground beef
3 large chopped onions
1/2 can tomato sauce
1 lb. Cheddar cheese,
   shredded
1 stick butter or oleo

1 (4 oz.) can mushrooms
1 can tomato soup
1 (8 oz.) pkg. shell macaroni
1 can pimentos
Water if needed

Slowly fry onions in butter, not too brown. Cook meat in dry skillet until crumbly. Mix all other ingredients, except cheese and macaroni, with meat and onions. Cook over low heat until well blended. Add a little water if necessary. Cook and drain macaroni. Add macaroni to meat mixture and simmer. Add cheese to meat and simmer until cheese is melted. Long, slow cooking of meat mixture brings out flavor.

Rebecca Thames, Caddo
Council, Shreveport, La.

PORCUPINE BALLS

1 lb. ground meat
1/4 c. chopped onion
1 can cream of mush-
   room soup

1/2 c. long grain rice
Salt and pepper to taste
1 soup can water
Cooking oil

Mix meat, rice, onion, salt and pepper into small balls. Brown fast in hot cooking oil. Remove from heat and drain skillet. Mix soup and water together, place in skillet or saucepan. Drop meat balls in mixture and simmer about 30 minutes.

Marie Pamplin
Shreveport Works Council
Shreveport, La.

STUFFED PEPPERS

8 medium to large bell
  peppers
Water
1/4 c. butter
4 green onions, chopped
4 stalks celery, chopped
3 lb. shrimp, beef, ham,
  veal or pork sausage
Bread crumbs
3/4 c. milk
5 slices raw bacon, cut
  in thirds

5 slices bacon, fried,
  drained and crumbled
1 large onion, chopped
1 large clove garlic, minced
4 bell pepper tops, chopped
1 c. Pepperidge Farm cubed
  croutons, soaked in water
2 eggs
2 Tbsp. parsley, chopped
4 dashes Worcestershire
  sauce
Salt and pepper to taste

Cut tops off peppers and reserve. Wash, clean and deseed peppers. Steam peppers in large covered pot with small amount of water until color has changed to dull green. Drain and set aside. Saute onions, celery, garlic and pepper tops in butter. Add the selection of meat and cook until thoroughly browned (with the exception of shrimp). If too much liquid, remove with large spoon. Add bread crumbs and croutons to make mixture thicken. Add crumbled fried bacon and parsley. Season to taste with salt, pepper and Worcestershire sauce. Spoon mixture into peppers, mounding. On top of each pepper, make an 'X' with raw bacon strips and fasten with toothpick. Place stuffed peppers in a casserole or pan with a small amount of water in the bottom. Bake at 350° for about 40 minutes. Serves 8.

Floyd Shumann, Ozone
Council, Hammond, La.

STUFFED PEPPERS

6 green peppers
2 c. cooked chicken,
  diced
2 Tbsp. frozen chopped
  chives

3 c. cooked rice
1 can mushroom soup
1 c. Cheddar cheese,
  grated

Slice tops from peppers and remove seeds. Drop peppers into boiling water for 5 minutes, drain. Combine remaining ingredients and spoon into peppers. Place peppers into a shallow casserole. Add 1/2 inch water to casserole to keep peppers from sticking. Bake in preheated 375° oven for 30-35 minutes or until peppers are tender.

Annie Hawkins, Caddo
Council, Shreveport, La.

PORCUPINE BALLS

1 pkg. beef Rice-A-Roni
1 lb. ground meat
2 1/4 c. hot water

1 egg, beaten
Cooking oil
1 beef seasoning packet from Rice-A-Roni

Mix ground meat, Rice-A-Roni, egg. Shape into small balls and fry quickly in hot cooking oil. Make sauce of beef seasoning packet and hot water. Drop in meat balls and simmer on low heat for 30 minutes. Sue Auld, Shreveport Works
Council, Shreveport, La.

PORCUPINES

1 lb. ground meat
1 tsp. salt
2 Tbsp. Worcestershire
    sauce
1 bell pepper, sliced
1 c. water

1/2 c. uncooked rice
1/4 tsp. pepper
1 onion, sliced
2 cans (8 oz. size) tomato
    sauce

Combine meat, rice, salt, pepper, Worcestershire sauce and 1/2 can tomato sauce. Form into meat ball size. Place in baking dish. Top with onion and bell pepper slices. Pour remainder of tomato sauce and 1 cup water over top. Cover. Bake at 350° for 1 - 1 1/4 hours until rice is cooked.

Virginia Jenkins, West Bank
Council, Gretna, La.

PORCUPINE BALLS

1 lb. ground meat
1/4 c. chopped onions
Salt and pepper to taste
1 can mushroom soup

1/2 c. white long grain
    rice, uncooked
Cooking oil
1 soup can water

Mix ground meat, onions, rice, salt, pepper together. Shape into small balls. Brown in hot oil quickly. Mix soup and water in saucepan. Drop in browned meat balls; simmer on low heat for 30 minutes.　　Sue Auld, Shreveport Works
Council, Shreveport, La.

BAKED PORK CHOPS

6 pork chops
1/2 c. milk
1 c. corn flake crumbs

1 egg
Salt and pepper to taste

Season pork chops. Beat egg and milk together. Dip pork chops in egg mixture, then into corn flake crumbs. Place in casserole. Bake at 350° for 40-45 minutes. Turn pork chops once halfway through cooking period.
Marilou Bridges, Caddo
Council, Shreveport, La.

CORN STUFFED PORK CHOPS

1 medium onion, chopped
1/4 c. chopped bell
　pepper
2 Tbsp. butter
1 c. herb seasoned stuff-
　ing mix
Salt and pepper to taste

2 cloves chopped garlic
1 stalk chopped celery
1 c. whole kernel corn,
　drained
1/4 tsp. poultry seasoning
　or thyme
4 thick boneless pork chops

Slit pockets in chops. Cook onions and pepper in butter. Mix corn, crumbs and seasonings in bowl, pour onion mixture over and mix lightly. Stuff chops. Place in shallow pan. Bake 1 hour at 350°.
Jan Prestridge, Capital
Council, Baton Rouge, La.

CREOLE PORK CHOPS

4 loin pork chops
1 c. raw rice
2 medium chopped bell
　peppers

Salt and pepper to taste
2 medium chopped onions
3 c. boiling water
1/4 c. catsup

Season chops with salt and pepper, place in large

skillet. Cover with rice, peppers and onions. Combine water and catsup, pour over chops. Bring to boil. Lower heat, cover and simmer 1 hour or until rice is tender.

Betty Harman, Caddo
Council, Shreveport, La.

PORK CHOP DELIGHT

4 pork chops
Salt and pepper to taste
6 carrots, halved length-
  wise

4 medium potatoes, peeled
  and halved
1 can celery soup
2/3 c. milk

Brown pork chops in skillet. Place vegetables around chops. Blend soup and milk, pour over chops and vegetables. Bring to boil, reduce heat and simmer 45 minutes, or until vegetables are tender and chops are done. Serves 4.

Vera Trosclair, Central
Council, Lecompte, La.

PORK CHOPS AND GRAVY

Pork chops
Salt and pepper

1 can mushroom soup
1 soup can milk

Season chops and cook over medium heat until browned and almost done. Add remaining ingredients and simmer uncovered for about 30 minutes. Serve with chopped spinach, broccoli or boiled potatoes.

Marie Mallory, Capital
Council, Waterbury, Ct.

GLORIFIED PORK CHOPS

3 Tbsp. oil
1 large onion, chopped
2 stalks celery, chopped
1 can celery soup
1 soup can water

4 pork chops
1 large bell pepper, chopped
1 can mushroom soup
1 jar sliced mushrooms

Brown chops in oil. Remove, add onions, pepper and celery; saute until just wilted. Add soups and water. Return chops to skillet. Add mushrooms, stir and mix well. Simmer about 30 minutes. Serve over noodles or rice.

Jan Prestridge, Capital
Council, Baton Rouge, La.

ITALIAN STYLE PORK CHOPS

6 center cut pork chops
1 egg, well beaten
3/4 c. Italian bread
  crumbs
1 can tomato sauce

1/2 c. all-purpose flour
1/4 c. water
1/4 c. olive oil
6 slices Mozzarella cheese

Remove bones from pork chops and flatten to 1/4-inch thickness with meat mallet. Dredge chops in flour. Combine egg and water, dip each chop in egg mixture, then coat well in bread crumbs. Brown chops on both sides in olive oil and place in baking dish. Spoon half of tomato sauce over chops. Place slice of cheese on each chop. Spoon remaining tomato sauce over cheese. Bake at 325° for 45 minutes, or until done. Makes 6 servings.

Una Miz, Caddo Council,
Shreveport, La.

ORANGE CHOPS AND RICE TANGO

4-6 pork chops, 1/2-inch
  thick
1/4 tsp. black pepper
1 medium onion, thinly
  sliced
1 c. orange juice
2 Tbsp. brown sugar

3 env. instant chicken broth
1/4 tsp. ginger
2 c. water
1/4 c. catsup
2 tsp. dry mustard
1 c. uncooked rice
1/2 tsp. salt

Season pork chops with 1 envelope chicken broth, black pepper and ginger. Brown chops on both sides in large skillet. Remove chops and drain. Stir in onion and saute lightly. Stir in water, orange juice, catsup, brown sugar, dry mustard, salt and remaining 2 envelopes chicken broth. Bring to a boil. Stir in rice, place chops on top. Cover, lower heat and simmer 30 minutes. Serves 4-6; 1 chop per serving with 1/2 - 2/3 cup rice each.

Rebecca Scott, Caddo
Council, Shreveport, La.

SPANISH STYLE PORK CHOPS

6 pork chops
2 large bell peppers,
  sliced
2 Tbsp. cornstarch
1 tsp. crushed basil
1 tsp. sugar

2 large onions, sliced
1 tsp. salt
1 (16 oz.) can tomatoes
1/2 tsp. Beau Monde seasoning
1 tsp. water

Trim fat from 1 chop. Rub fat over bottom of skillet on medium heat. Discard fat. Brown chops on both sides. Add onions, green peppers, tomatoes and liquid, basil, Beau Monde seasoning, salt and sugar. Boil, reduce heat to low, cover and simmer 45 minutes. Remove chops to serving dish. Blend cornstarch and water in cup until smooth, gradually stir into liquid and cook until thickened, about 2-3 minutes.

Ronda Decuir, Metairie
Council, Metairie, La.

STUFFED PORK CHOPS

8 thin pork chops
3/4 c. tomato juice
3 c. soft bread crumbs
1/4 tsp. poultry seasoning
2 Tbsp. onion, minced

Salt and pepper to taste
2 Tbsp. butter or oleo, melted
1 tsp. salt
1/4 c. celery, diced
2 Tbsp. parsley, chopped

Season chops with salt and pepper. Combine 1/4 of tomato juice with remaining ingredients. Place chops together with stuffing between, sandwich style, in greased baking dish. Add remaining tomato juice. Bake at 350° for 1 hour or until tender.

Jeanette Williams, Caddo
Council, Shreveport, La.

PORK CHOPS IN WINE

1 large onion, sliced
1 1/2 tsp. salt
6 loin pork chops, 1/2 -
  3/4-inch thick
1/2 tsp. dry mustard

3 Tbsp. chopped parsley
1/2 stick oleo, softened
1 c. dry white wine
3 Tbsp. salad oil
1/8 tsp. pepper

Saute onion in hot oil in large skillet, drain on paper towels and set aside. Reserve drippings. Combine butter, mustard, salt and pepper. Stir to make a paste, spread on

both sides of chops. Brown chops on both sides in reserved
drippings, drain. Return onions to skillet, add wine,
cover and simmer 1 hour or until chops are done. Sprinkle
with chopped parsley before serving.

Mearl S. Byles, Central
Council, Natchitoches, La.

PORKAGHETTI PLATTER

3 pork blade steaks,
  cut 1/2-inch thick
1/8 tsp. pepper
1 (15 oz.) jar tomato
  sauce
1 Tbsp. instant minced
  onion
1/2 tsp. rosemary
2 c. sliced mushrooms
1 (7 oz.) pkg. spaghetti

1/4 c. flour
1 tsp. salt
3 Tbsp. lard or drippings
2/3 c. water
1/2 tsp. oregano
1/8 tsp. garlic powder
1/2 c. halved, stuffed
  green olives
Grated Romano cheese

Cut pork steaks into strips, 1/4-inch thick and 2-3-
inches long. Combine flour, salt and pepper; dredge pork,
reserve excess flour. Brown strips in lard or drippings,
drain. Sprinkle with reserved flour. Add tomato sauce,
water, onion, oregano, rosemary and garlic powder. Stir
to combine. Cover tightly and simmer 45 minutes or until
meat is tender. Stir in mushrooms and olives, continue to
cook covered for 15 minutes. Cook spaghetti according to
directions, drain and arrange on platter. Serve meat and
sauce with spaghetti. Sprinkle with Romano cheese. Makes
6-8 servings.   Bertile A. Sanchez, Capital
                        Council, Baton Rouge, La.

PERFECT PORK ROAST

1 pork roast
1 env. au jus gravy
Turnips, carrots and
  potatoes

2 cloves garlic
Flour, salt and pepper
Mushrooms (optional)

Stuff garlic into roast. Pat flour, salt, pepper on roast,
coating well all over. Place roast in pan and bake for 1 hour
at 425°. Mix up au jus gravy according to directions, pour
over roast. Arrange peeled and prepared vegetables around
roast and bake additional 1 1/2 - 2 hours.

Rose Romano, Crescent City
Council, New Orleans, La.

SWEET AND SOUR PORK

2 lb. boneless pork
1 egg, beaten
2 Tbsp. flour
1 tsp. salt
1/2 tsp. pepper
3/4 c. salad oil
1 clove garlic, crushed
3 green peppers, cut in
   1-inch strips

1 (20 oz.) can pineapple
   chunks, undrained
3 Tbsp. cornstarch
1/2 c. sugar
1/2 c. chicken broth
1/2 c. vinegar
2 tsp. soy sauce
Hot cooked rice

Trim fat from pork and cut meat into 1-inch cubes. Combine egg, flour, salt and pepper, mix well. Pour mixture over pork cubes, coating well. Heat oil and garlic in heavy skillet over medium heat, add pork and cook until each piece is golden brown on all sides. Drain off pan drippings, reserving 1 tablespoon drippings. Add green pepper, 1 tablespoon reserved drippings and undrained pineapple to pork in skillet. Simmer over low heat 5 minutes. Combine cornstarch and sugar, stir in chicken broth, vinegar and soy sauce. Add to skillet. Cook over low heat, stirring constantly, until sauce is smooth and thickened. Serve over rice. Serves 6-8.

Pam Marchese, Metairie
Council, Metairie, La.

PIEROGI FILLINGS

Recipe for Pierogi can be found in the Bread Section of this cookbook. The following are different types of fillings that may be used, or use filling of your choice.

Cheese:

1 c. cottage cheese
1 egg, beaten
3 Tbsp. currants

1 tsp. melted butter
3 Tbsp. sugar
1/4 tsp. cinnamon

Cream cheese with melted butter. Add other ingredients and mix well. Fill Pierogi. Serve with melted butter and sour cream.

Mushrooms:

1 c. chopped mushrooms   Salt and pepper
1 onion, chopped fine   2 egg yolks
Butter

Saute onion in butter. Add mushrooms. Season. Remove from fire, add egg yolks and stir well. Cool and fill Pierogi. Serve with chopped onion browned in butter.

Mushroom and Meat:

1/2 c. cooked beef   1 onion, chopped fine
1/2 c. chopped mushrooms   Butter
Salt and pepper   2 Tbsp. sour cream

Run cooked meat through meat grinder. Fry onion in butter until transparent, add mushrooms and meat. Season to taste. Add sour cream and cool before using.

Prunes:

1 c. cooked prunes   1 tsp. sugar
1 tsp. lemon juice

Soak prunes overnight. Cook with sugar and lemon juice. Cool, remove stones and fill Pierogi. Serve with bread crumbs browned in melted butter.

Mrs. Stanley Tempalski
Ouachita Council
Monroe, La.

PIGS IN BLANKETS

1 pkg. frankfurters   1 can biscuits
10 pieces of bacon   5 slices of cheese

Take each frank, wrap 1/2 slice cheese around it. Take 1 piece bacon and wrap over the frank and cheese. Wrap 1 biscuit around frank. Continue until ingredients are used up. Place on cookie sheet and bake at 450° until golden brown. Serve hot.

Betty Elenbury, Caddo
Council, Shreveport, La.

RAVIOLI OR PIEROGI

Basic Dough:

1 lb. sifted flour	1 tsp. salt
3-4 eggs	Small amount of water

Meat Filling:

1/2 lb. finely chopped beef, pork or chicken	1 well beaten egg
2 Tbsp. chopped parsley	Pepper, salt and nutmeg to taste

Sift flour and salt together, put on a large board or smooth surface. Make a depression in center. Beat eggs well and pour them in, adding about 1 tablespoon water. With a spoon, gradually mix flour into the liquid. When about half of flour has been mixed, start kneading with the hands until all ingredients are well mixed. Continue kneading, pulling dough out to make elastic, until dough is smooth, about 10 minutes. Let stand 30 minutes. Divide dough into 3 or 4 pieces. Roll out each piece very thin. Cut in rounds or squares as desired. Put filling on each piece, fold over, press edges together completely. Drop ravioli in large saucepan of boiling salted water for 4 or 5 minutes. Cook gently. When they come to top of water, they are done. Remove, drain and keep warm on well buttered dish. Serve with melted butter and grated cheese or with meat and tomato sauce.
Theda S. Thomas, Caddo
Council, Shreveport, La.

BARBECUED POT ROAST

1 (4-5 lb.) chuck roast	2 Tbsp. cooking oil
2 medium onions, sliced	2 cloves garlic, minced
1/2 c. catsup	1/2 c. water
1/4 c. wine vinegar	2 Tbsp. Worcestershire sauce
1 tsp. rosemary leaves	
Potatoes (optional)	1 tsp. salt

Brown roast on all sides in hot oil in large roaster, add onions and garlic. Combine remaining ingredients and pour over roast. Bake at 350° for about 2 hours. Small peeled potatoes can be placed around roast at this time if desired. Return to oven and continue to cook additional hour or until roast is tender.
Jeanette Williams, Caddo
Council, Shreveport, La.

238

CALIFORNIA POT ROAST

4-5 lb. chuck or rump
  roast
1/4 tsp. pepper
1 (8 oz.) can tomato
  sauce
3 medium onions, thinly
  sliced
2 Tbsp. brown sugar
1/4 c. lemon juice

3 Tbsp. oil
2 tsp. salt
1/2 c. water
1 Tbsp. Worcestershire
  sauce
2 cloves garlic, minced
1/2 tsp. dry mustard
1/4 c. vinegar
1/4 c. ketchup

Brown roast well on both sides in oil in heavy pan or Dutch oven. Add salt, pepper, water, onions, tomato sauce and garlic. Cover tightly and simmer over low heat about 1 1/2 hours. Combine brown sugar, mustard, lemon juice, vinegar, ketchup and Worcestershire sauce. Pour over meat. Cover and continue cooking about 1 1/2 hours or until meat is fork tender. Remove meat to warm platter. Make gravy. Skim off fat. Measure broth. Add water to make 3 cups. Pour into cooking pan. Mix 6 tablespoons flour with 1/2 cup water to make smooth paste, stir into broth. Return to heat and cook over low heat, stirring constantly, until gravy bubbles all over. Cook and stir about 5 minutes longer. Serve roast cut in thin slices with gravy, or shred meat and mix with gravy to serve on buns. Makes 8-10 servings.   Marjorie Rowell, Evangeline
                               Council, Lafayette, La.

QUICHE LORRAINE

4 green onions, chopped,
  tops and all
Small amount of oil
1 c. diced, cooked ham
  or bacon
3 Tbsp. butter
1/2 tsp salt
2 c. Swiss and Monterey
  Jack cheese, grated
3 Tbsp. grated Cheddar
  cheese

1/2 green pepper, chopped
4 or 5 large fresh mush-
  rooms, sliced
1 (9 inch) pie crust, precooked about 10 minutes
3 Tbsp. flour
2 c. milk
4 beaten eggs
Dash of nutmeg

Green onions, green pepper and mushrooms are optional. If used, saute in small amount of oil and set aside. Melt butter, add flour and salt. When smooth, add milk all at once. Cook and stir until thickened and bubbly. Add vegetables and meat. Pour hot mixture into beaten eggs, stirring constantly. Add grated Swiss and Monterey cheese and mix. Pour into pastry shell and sprinkle nutmeg over top. Bake at 350° for about 20 minutes or until firm. Sprinkle Cheddar cheese over top and return to oven for 10 or 15 minutes. Let set about 5 minutes before cutting.

Mrs. Tony Corcoran
Crescent City Council
New Orleans, La.

QUICHE PEGGY

5-6 slices bacon
8-10 shallots, finely
  chopped
3 eggs
1/2 c. milk (skim is O.K.)
1/4 tsp. freshly ground
  pepper
1 1/2 c. (6 oz.) grated sharp
  Cheddar cheese
1 c. half & half
1/2 tsp. salt
1/2 tsp. dry mustard
1 pie shell (9 inch)
Dash of cayenne pepper

Cook bacon crisp, drain and crumble into bottom of pie shell, reserving 2 slices for top. Sprinkle grated cheese over bacon. Saute shallots in bacon drippings, drain and sprinkle on cheese (for spicier flavor, do not saute shallots). Beat eggs, half & half, milk, salt, pepper, cayenne pepper and dry mustard together. Pour into pie shell. Crumble reserved bacon and sprinkle over top. Bake at 350° for 45 minutes. Serves 6-8. Cut in pie shape or for a party, cut in finger slices that will serve 16.

Peggy Childers
Crescent City Council
New Orleans, La.

RED RICE

1/2 large onion, chopped
1/2 stick butter
1 lb. regular white rice
1 (46 oz.) can tomato
  juice, or 2 cans regular
  stewed tomatoes
Pepper to taste
Dash of celery salt
2 slices ham, chopped, or
  odds and bits of leftover
  ham in pieces
1 Tbsp. sugar
2 tsp. salt
Dash of garlic salt (optional)
Dash of Worcestershire sauce

240

If canned tomatoes are used instead of tomato juice, add cups of water as equal to cups of rice in 1 pound of rice, or just slightly less water; say, 1/2 cup less. Saute onions in butter for 5 minutes. Add other ingredients and mix thoroughly. Transfer to pot if cooking on top of stove or casserole dish if to be baked in oven. Cook 45 minutes to 1 hour on top of stove or bake at 375° on bottom rack of oven for 1 hour. Remove cover, stir 1 time from bottom. Recover and move to higher rack in oven. Bake another hour. Serves 6.

Peggy Childers
Crescent City Council
New Orleans, La.

ROAST BEEF DIABLO

1 (4-5 lb.) chuck roast
1/4 c. onion, finely
  chopped
2 tsp. salt
1/4 c. chili sauce
1 Tbsp. sugar
1 Tbsp. Worcestershire
  sauce

3 Tbsp. vegetable oil
1/2 c. beef broth, divided
1/4 tsp. pepper
2 Tbsp. all-purpose flour
2 Tbsp. prepared mustard
1 Tbsp. vinegar
1/4 c. water

Brown roast on all sides in hot oil in large Dutch oven or roasting pan. Pour off all but 1 tablespoon drippings. Add onion, 1/4 cup broth, salt and pepper. Simmer 2 1/2 hours or until meat is tender. Combine flour, sugar, chili sauce, mustard, Worcestershire sauce and vinegar. Stir in water and pour over roast. Simmer about 30 minutes or until tender. Remove roast and stir in remaining beef broth. Simmer about 5 minutes, strain and serve with roast. Makes 8 servings.

Marilou Bridges, Caddo
Council, Shreveport, La.

INDIAN POT ROAST

3-4 lb. pot roast
2 cloves garlic
Flour
12 whole peppercorns
1 bay leaf, crumbled
1/2 c. good rum or dry
  red wine
4 Tbsp. butter
Salt

1 large onion, sliced
12 whole allspice
1 Tbsp. grated horseradish
1/2 c. water
1 recipe dumplings (optional)
Small whole carrots or
  larger carrots, quartered
  (optional)

1723-79

Use this recipe for either regular meat or venison. Mash garlic and saute in butter. Salt meat and flour. Brown well on all sides in butter. Lay meat on bed of thin sliced onion in large Dutch oven. Add the butter, spices and seasonings. Pour rum or wine over meat. A good pot roast will supply most of its own juices, but pour the water over to make an ample supply of gravy. Cover tightly and simmer for 3-4 hours, either in oven or on stove. If carrots are wanted, add last 1/2 hour of cooking. Add dumplings last 12 minutes of cooking. When roast is done, remove to a hot round platter and surround with dumplings and carrots. Stir gravy until smooth. Pour over roast. If fresh dill is available, cut it over dish with lavish hand. Serves 6-8.

Laura and Bill Baptist, Ozone
Council, Hammond, La.

ROAST WITH SOUR CREAM GRAVY

1 (2-3 lb.) boneless
  chuck roast
1/2 c. water
3 medium carrots, cut
  in 2-inch pieces
1 (8 oz.) carton sour cream

2 Tbsp. cooking oil
3 medium potatoes, peeled
  and quartered
3 medium onions, quartered
1 Tbsp. flour

Brown roast on all sides in hot oil in large roasting pan or Dutch oven. Add water. Cover and simmer about 2 1/2 to 3 hours. Add vegetables. Cover and simmer 30 minutes or until vegetables are tender. Remove roast and vegetables to serving dish. Drain off all but 2 tablespoons drippings, sift flour into drippings. Make roux, stirring constantly. Add water to drained off drippings to make 1 cup. Stir into flour and cook, stirring constantly, until smooth and slightly thickened. Add sour cream and cook, stirring constantly, on low heat until heated. Serve gravy with roast.

Marilou Bridges, Caddo
Council, Shreveport, La.

SALAMI

5 lb. hamburger meat
5 tsp. hickory smoked
  salt
2 1/2 tsp. whole mustard
  seed
1/2 tsp. garlic salt

2 1/2 Tbsp. Morton's Tender-
  Quick salt (no substitution)
2 1/2 tsp. black pepper
2 Tbsp. McCormick's peppercorns (whole)

Mix all ingredients well. Refrigerate for 24 hours; mix 5 times during the 24 hours. Divide into 3 equal parts. Shape into rolls. Place on broiler rack with drip pan. Bake at 150° for 8 hours. Will keep 3-4 weeks in refrigerator, or can be frozen.

Mrs. Tony Corcoran
Crescent City Council
New Orleans, La.

SAUSAGE JAMBALAYA

1 lb. sausage or cubed
  beef
3 Tbsp. bacon drippings
  (if beef used)
3 Tbsp. flour
2 medium onions
2 tsp. salt

1 bunch green onions,
  chopped
2 Tbsp. chopped parsley
2 cloves garlic
2 1/2 c. water
2 c. rice
3/4 tsp. red pepper

Brown meat in bacon drippings, remove and add flour. Use a heavy skillet and brown flour to a dark roux. Add onions, parsley and garlic. Cook until soft, then add water and rice, salt, pepper and browned meat. Bring to a boil, lower heat to lowest point and cook about 1 hour, covered tightly. When rice is done, remove lid and let cook for a few minutes until rice dries a little.

Calcasieu Council
Lake Charles, La.

SAUSAGE JAMBALAYA

1 lb. smoked sausage,
  cut into 1/2-inch slices
1/2 c. chopped green
  onion
1 (28 oz.) can tomatoes
1/4 tsp. pepper
1 1/2 c. water

1 lb. ground beef
1 medium bell pepper,
  chopped
5 cloves minced garlic
1/2 tsp. salt
1 c. uncooked raw rice

Cook sausage in skillet until browned, remove from skillet and discard drippings. Combine beef, green pepper, onion and garlic. Cook until beef is browned. Add tomatoes, salt, pepper and sausage. Cover, simmer 20 minutes. Add rice and water, cover and cook additional 25 minutes or until rice is tender. Yield: 4-6 servings.

Marilou Bridges, Caddo
Council, Shreveport, La.

SMOKED SAUSAGE JAMBALAYA

3 links smoked sausage
1/2 chopped bell pepper
1 1/2 c. rice
2 tsp. tomato paste

1 chopped onion
1 can mushroom steak sauce
1 1/2 c. water

Slice sausage, add small amount of water, allow to boil and fry down. Add onion and bell pepper, fry with sausage. Add mushroom sauce, tomato sauce and small amount of water. Simmer about 1 hour. Wash rice, add to mixture along with 1 1/2 cups water. Cook slowly; do not stir too often. Cook until rice is done and filled with flavor. Serves 4.

Marion Carter, Central
Council, Bunkie, La.

POTATO SAUSAGE

5 lb. ground pork shoulder
5 lb. ground raw potatoes
4 Tbsp. salt
1 Tbsp. garlic salt

5 lb. ground beef round
2-3 large onions, ground or
  chopped fine
2 Tbsp. black pepper

Combine ingredients and mix well. Stuff in casings. Makes about 17 pounds. Freeze in 1 or 2 pound packages. When ready to cook, place sausage in skillet in water to cover. Cook slowly until water is all cooked down and sausage browns in own juice. Takes about 1 hour. Serves plenty.

Lou Teixeira, LeBayou
Council, Thibodaux, La.

SAUSAGE ROLLS

1 lb. short pastry (make
  as for pie crust using
  less shortening)

1-2 lb. pork or beef
  sausage meat

Roll out pastry into 12x12-inch circle, nice and thin. Cut strips approximately 2 inches wide the length of circle. Roll meat until small roll for about 1 teaspoon sausage is filled. Each roll will look like small jelly roll, yielding about 2 dozen rolls. Bake 3/4 hours in 375° oven. Delicious served piping hot or cold as party snacks.

Calcasieu Council
Lake Charles, La.

SUMMER SAUSAGE

2 lb. hamburger or
  ground chuck
2 tsp. Morton's Tender-
  Quick salt
1/4 tsp. mustard seed

1 c. water
1 tsp. liquid smoke
1/4 tsp. garlic powder
1/4 tsp. onion salt
1/4 tsp. ground black
  pepper

Mix well and form into 3 rolls, about 1 1/2 x 8 inches. Wrap in foil, shiny side in towards meat. Refrigerate for 24 hours. Poke holes in bottom of each roll with fork. Place in broiler pan on rack with 1/2 inch of water in bottom of pan. Bake for 90 minutes at 325°. Keeps in refrigerator like cold cuts.   June E. Nickels
                                   Shreveport Works Council
                                   Shreveport, La.

SUMMER SAUSAGE

2 lb. ground beef
1/4 tsp. coarse pepper
2 Tbsp. curing salt
1/4 tsp. garlic salt

1 Tbsp. liquid smoke
1/4 tsp. mustard seed
1/4 tsp. onion salt

Mix all ingredients well. Form into 2 rolls and wrap tightly in foil. Refrigerate 24 hours. Bake over broiler pan with water at 350° for 1 1/2 hours. Remove from foil after baking. Good served hot or cold.
                                   Evelyn Bledsoe, Ouachita
                                   Council, Monroe, La.

QUICK SAUERBRATEN

1 (10 3/4 oz.) can beef
  gravy
1/2 c. cider vinegar
3 Tbsp. sugar
10 whole cloves

1 c. water
1/3 c. finely crushed
  gingersnaps (about 6)
8 thin slices cooked beef
  pot roast

Combine gravy, water, vinegar, gingersnaps, sugar and cloves in large skillet. Bring to boil, stirring. Simmer and stir about 5 minutes or until thickened and smooth. Add

beef slices. Cook until meat is hot, basting with sauce.
Serve with mashed potatoes. Makes 4 servings.

Calcasieu Council
Lake Charles, La.

SHORT CUT SUPPER

1 lb. hamburger
1 pkg. shell macaroni
Onions, sliced

1 small can tomato sauce
Red pepper seasoning

Cook macaroni in water until done, drain. Fry hamburger and onions until done. Add ingredients together and heat.

Colleen Ahrens, Caddo
Council, Shreveport, La.

SPAGHETTI ALLA CARBONARA
(Spaghetti with Eggs and Bacon from Italy)

1 lb. spaghetti
5 eggs, beaten
1/2 tsp. oregano
Salt and pepper to taste

8 slices bacon, cut in small
  pieces
1/2 tsp. marjoram
Parmesan cheese, grated

Cook spaghetti in boiling salted water, drain well. Have bacon crisp and hot. Mix pepper, salt, marjoram and oregano in beaten eggs. Add to hot spaghetti, stir well. Add both bacon and hot bacon drippings to spaghetti mixture. Mix and serve immediately. Have plenty of grated Parmesan cheese to sprinkle on top. Serve with a crisp green salad and end with fresh fruit for a perfect meal.

Theda S. Thomas, Caddo
Council, Shreveport, La.

ITALIAN SPAGHETTI

1 lb. ground steak
3 cloves garlic, minced
1 heaping tsp. comino
2 eggs
Parsley and paprika

1/2 lb. ground pork
2 medium onions, chopped
1 c. bread crumbs
Salt and pepper

Mix and work until fluffy. Wet hands and roll into small balls.

Sauce:

2 medium onions,
  chopped
2 Tbsp. olive oil
1 large can tomatoes
1 tsp. comino

3 cloves garlic, chopped
1 can Italian tomato paste
Salt and pepper
1 can water to each can
  tomatoes and tomato paste

Brown garlic in olive oil. Add tomato paste and tomatoes. Add onions, comino, salt, pepper and water. Cook 30 minutes. Strain. When sauce begins to boil again, add meat balls, 1 at a time. Turn fire very low. Cook about 1 hour. Serve over spaghetti.   Verle Oliphant, Caddo
                                    Council, Shreveport, La.

SPAGHETTI WITH MEAT

1 lb. ground beef
1 tsp. garlic powder
4 bouillon cubes
1 can tomato paste
1 pkg. spaghetti

4 Tbsp. chili powder
1/2 c. onion
2 small cans tomato sauce
1 c. water

Fry ground meat, chili powder and onion together until done. Add water, garlic powder and bouillon cubes. Simmer 15 minutes. Add tomato sauce and paste. Simmer 15 minutes. Add more water if needed to thin sauce. Cook spaghetti according to directions, drain and either add cooked spaghetti to sauce or pour sauce over spaghetti.
                                    Christine Moras, Central
                                    Council, Hessmer, La.

SPINACH QUICHE

2 Tbsp. Parmesan cheese
1/4 c. butter
Dash of salt and pepper
4 eggs
1 c. chopped ham
1 pie shell (9 or 10 inch)

3 Tbsp. onion
3 Tbsp. flour
1 c. half & half
1 pkg. creamed spinach
1 c. Swiss cheese

Pat Parmesan cheese on bottom of pie shell. Melt butter and add to remaining ingredients. Mix well and pour into pastry shell. Bake at 375° about 25-35 minutes or until knife inserted comes out clean. Serve hot.
                                    Ann Orr, Evangeline
                                    Council, New Iberia, La.

TOP OF STOVE SPARERIBS

3 lb. spareribs or pork
   chops
3/4 c. water
2 Tbsp. vinegar
2 onions, sliced
1 tsp. chili powder
1/4 tsp. cayenne pepper

3/4 c. catsup
2 Tbsp. brown sugar
2 Tbsp. Worcestershire
   sauce
1 tsp. paprika
1/2 tsp. black pepper
1 Tbsp. oil

Season meat, brown in oil. Add sliced onions. Mix other ingredients. Cover and let simmer about 3 hours, or until tender.

Mrs. Jim (Verline) Bernard
Evangeline Council
Lafayette, La.

SQUIRREL SAUCE PIQUANTE

2 squirrels
1/2 c. medium chopped
   bell pepper
1 can tomato sauce
Cooking oil

3 medium onions, chopped
1 Tbsp. flour
Water
Black pepper, red pepper
   and salt

Rub squirrels with salt, black and red pepper. Put oil in heavy iron pot 1/4 inch deep. Brown squirrels on all sides and remove from pot. Lower fire to medium heat and saute onions, bell pepper and flour in remaining oil until brown. Place squirrels back in pot, add enough water to cover meat. Add tomato sauce. Cover and simmer on low fire 1 1/2 - 2 hours until tender.

Ruth Albin for Martha Starkey
Capital Council
Baton Rouge, La.

STEAK A LA CARLA

1 round steak or beef
   stew meat, cubed
Sliced bell peppers
Small amount oil or
   shortening

1 pkg. meat marinade
1 can mushrooms, drained
Sliced onions
Fresh tomatoes
Salt and pepper to taste

Prepare marinade as directed. Marinate meat 15 minutes or longer. Brown meat in small amount of oil. Add marinade sauce and simmer. When meat is tender, add mushrooms, bell peppers and onions. Cook about 2 minutes. Add fresh quartered tomatoes and continue cooking only until tomatoes are heated. Salt and pepper to taste.

Carolyn Palmer, Capital
Council, Baton Rouge, La.

OVEN BARBECUED STEAK

1 c. catsup
1/2 c. water
1/4 c. wine vinegar
1/4 c. chopped onion
1/4 c. chopped green
  pepper
1/4 tsp. black pepper

2 lb. chuck steak, cut
  1/2-inch thick
1 1/2 Tbsp. Worcestershire
  sauce
1 Tbsp. prepared mustard
2 Tbsp. brown sugar
1 Tbsp. garlic salt

Combine all ingredients, except steak, salt and pepper in saucepan. Bring to a boil, then simmer for 5 minutes over low heat. Keep sauce hot. Cut steak into serving size pieces, season generously with garlic, salt and pepper. Place pieces in casserole or baking dish. Pour hot sauce over steak. Bake in 325° oven for about 1 1/2 hours or until fork tender. Garnish with bell pepper rings if desired. Makes 4-5 servings.

Lois Leger, Evangeline
Council, Lafayette, La.

CHUCK STEAK IN FOIL

1 (2 lb.) pkg. chuck
  steak
1 can mushroom soup

1 env. onion soup mix
Parsley and crabapples
  for garnish

Place chuck steak in center of large sheet of heavy duty foil. Sprinkle soup mix evenly over steak. Spread mushroom soup over top. Wrap foil and seal well. Place foil package in shallow pan and bake in preheated 375° oven for 1 1/2 hours. Remove from foil and carefully spoon gravy over meat in platter. Garnish with sprigs of parsley and crabapples. Serves 4-6.

Lois S. Leger, Evangeline
Council, Lafayette, La.

CROCK-POT SMOTHERED STEAK

1 1/2 lb. chuck or round
   steak, cut in strips
1/4 tsp. pepper
1 or 2 green peppers,
   sliced
1 (1 lb.) can tomatoes
3 Tbsp. soy sauce

1/3 c. flour
1 tsp. salt
1 large onion, sliced
1 (4 oz.) can mushrooms,
   drained
1 (10 oz.) pkg. frozen green
   beans, French style

Put steak strips, flour, salt and pepper in crock-pot. Stir well to coat steak. Add remaining ingredients. Cover and cook on low 8 hours (high for 4 hours). Serve with rice.

Mrs. Stanley Tempalski
Ouachita Council
Monroe, La.

BEN'S STEAK MILIEU

Sirloin steak, 1-inch thick
Ginger powder
Water chestnuts
Whole black pepper

Garlic powder
Soy sauce
Small amount of cooking oil

Beat whole black pepper into steak. Cut into cubes, 1x1 inch. Sprinkle garlic powder on steak cubes. Sprinkle on ginger lightly. Do opposite side. Fry in small amount of cooking oil. Add chestnuts and soy sauce to taste. Fry on high heat in an iron skillet.

Carolyn Palmer, Capital
Council, Baton Rouge, La.

ONION CHUCK STEAK

2 1/2 - 3 lb. boneless
   chuck steak, trimmed

1 (3 oz.) can sliced mushrooms, drained
1 env. onion soup mix

Place steak on heavy duty foil, large enough to fold over. Sprinkle both sides of steak with onion mix. Top with mushrooms. Wrap foil, sealing edges with double fold. Place seam side up about 5 inches from hot coals. Grill 1 hour until tender. Can also be baked in 350° oven until tender.

Gretna Anderson, Central
Council, Alexandria, La.

PEPPER STEAK

1 1/2 lb. round or sirloin
   steak, 3/4 - 1 inch thick
2 medium bell peppers,
   3/4 inch strips
1 tsp. garlic salt
Pepper to taste
1 Tbsp. cornstarch
2 Tbsp. soy sauce
Hot cooked rice

Oil or oleo
1 medium onion, cut in
   3/4-inch slices
1 c. beer
1 tsp. ginger
1 tsp. salt
2 Tbsp. sugar
2 medium tomatoes, cut in
   eighths

Trim excess fat from meat and cut into 2 x 1/4-inch strips. Heat oil in large skillet. Brown meat in oil about 5 minutes. Add onion and green pepper. Stir in beer, garlic, ginger, salt and pepper. Heat to boiling. Reduce heat, cover and simmer 15 minutes for round steak; 5-8 minutes for sirloin. Blend cornstarch, sugar and soy sauce, stir into meat mixture. Cook, stirring constantly, until mixture thickens and boils. Boil and stir 1 minute. Place tomatoes on meat mixture, cover and cook over low heat about 3 minutes or until tomatoes are heated through. Serve over hot cooked rice. Serves 4-5.

Rebecca Scott, Caddo
Council, Shreveport, La.

PEPPER STEAK

2 lb. round steak, cut
   in strips
1/4 c. soy sauce
1/2 tsp. garlic
2 bell peppers, cut in
   strips

1 c. beef bouillon
   (2 cubes)
1/2 tsp. ginger
2 Tbsp. oil
3 Tbsp. cornstarch
1 1/4 c. water

Combine meat strips, bouillon, soy sauce, ginger and garlic in bowl and marinate 3 hours in refrigerator. Drain meat, reserving 1/2 cup marinade. In large skillet, brown meat in oil, add reserved marinade and 1 cup water. Cover and simmer about 45 minutes. Add pepper strips. Cook 15 minutes more. Tomatoes may also be added with peppers if desired. Blend cornstarch and 1/4 cup water together and gradually stir into meat mixture. Serve over rice.

Jan Prestridge, Capital
Council, Baton Rouge, La.

CHINESE PEPPER STEAK

1 1/2 lb. flank or
  sirloin sandwich
  steak (thin)
1/2 c. water
1/2 tsp. ground ginger
4 Tbsp. soy sauce

2 c. green pepper, 1/2-inch
  strips
5 Tbsp. oil
1/3 c. chopped onions
2 Tbsp. cornstarch

Cut meat in thin strips 3 inches long. In large skillet, add 2 tablespoon oil and pepper. Stir and fry 1 minute. Cover skillet and simmer 1 minute. Remove cover and stir. Add onion and ginger, saute. Push vegetables to one side, add meat and additional oil until no pink shows. Toss vegetables with meat. Blend cornstarch, water and soy sauce and add to meat. Cook over low heat 2 or 3 minutes. If too thick, add more water. Serve over cooked rice. Serves 4.

Arneta Carnahan, LeBayou
Council, Houma, La.

POOR MAN'S STEAK

3 lb. ground beef
2 eggs
1 1/2 tsp. garlic salt
Salt and pepper

1 c. crushed cracker crumbs
1/4 c. milk
1/4 c. Worcestershire sauce

Combine and mix ingredients well. Divide into 8 parts. Form in shape of T-Bone steak. Place on greased grill over hot coals and cook on each side about 15 minutes.

Mrs. Johnnie B. Cole, Caddo
Council, Shreveport, La.

SHERRIED ROUND STEAK

1 1/2 lb. tenderized
  round steak
1 small can mushrooms
1 can cream of mush-
  room soup

2 large onions, sliced and
  separated into rings
1 1/2 Tbsp. cooking oil
1/2 c. sherry
1 1/2 tsp. garlic salt

Cut steak into thin strips and brown in oil. Add onions and cook until tender. Mix soup, sherry, liquid from mushrooms and garlic salt. Pour over steak. Add mushrooms. Cover and simmer 1 hour or until steak is tender, or cover and bake at 350° until done. Serve over rice. Sometimes I add 1/2 cup sour cream to soup mixture before pouring over steak. Marilou Bridges, Caddo Council, Shreveport, La.

STEAK AND SAUCE

1 (15 1/2 oz.) can Chef
 Boy-Ar-Dee's spaghetti
 sauce with meat
2 lb. round steak, cut
 in serving pieces
1 tsp. salt
3 Tbsp. cider vinegar
1/4 c. finely chopped onion
2 tsp. Worcestershire sauce
1/4 c. water
Flour

Combine spaghetti sauce, vinegar, onion, salt and Worcestershire sauce. Bring to a boil. Reduce heat and simmer 10 minutes. Cool and pour over steak. Marinate steak overnight in refrigerator. Rake off marinade and save. Roll steak in flour, fry until browned on both sides. Put meat back in sauce, add water. Bake in covered casserole about 30 minutes at 350°. Dianne Crocker, Central Council, Alexandria, La.

SWISS STEAK

2 lb. round steak
2 Tbsp. shortening
1 c. celery, cut up
1 c. or 1 can tomato soup
Flour, salt and pepper
1 onion, diced
1 green pepper, diced
1/4 c. water

Cut meat into serving pieces, roll in flour, salt and pepper. Sear meat in hot cooking oil until golden brown on both sides. Add remainder of ingredients and cook slowly over low heat until done. Adrienne Delery, Ouachita Council, Monroe, La.

SWISS BLISS

2 lb. chuck steak
1 pkg. onion soup mix
1 (4 oz.) can sliced,
 drained mushrooms
1 Tbsp. chopped parsley
1 (16 oz.) can tomatoes
1 Tbsp. steak sauce
1/2 c. chopped green pepper
1 Tbsp. cornstarch

Cut steak in serving pieces and place in casserole. Drain tomatoes, reserving juice, and arrange over steak. Sprinkle soup mix, mushroom and green peppers over tomatoes. Combine reserved tomato juice with remaining ingredients and pour over contents of casserole. Cover and bake in 350° oven for 2 hours or until meat is tender.

Katherine Slover, Caddo
Council, Phoenix, Az.

SPICY SWISS STEAK

2 lb. chuck steak, 1 1/2 inches thick	Salt and pepper
	1/2 c. flour
2 Tbsp. drippings or fat	2 tsp. salt
1/4 tsp. pepper	1 can tomatoes
2 medium onions, sliced	1 stalk celery, diced
1 bay leaf	2 tsp. Worcestershire sauce

Pound flour into steak with meat pounder or edge of saucer. Brown slowly in hot fat in heavy skillet. Sprinkle with salt and pepper, add remaining ingredients. Cover and cook over low heat or in 325° oven for 2 hours or until meat is tender. Add small amount of water during cooking if necessary. Serve steak with tomato gravy poured over it. For a thicker gravy, mix 2 tablespoons flour and 1/4 cup water. Stir into sauce, over low heat, until gravy becomes smooth and thickened. Season to taste with salt and pepper. You may also vary the Swiss Steak by different seasonings, such as thyme, basil, marjoram, garlic, Worcestershire sauce, chili powder, dry mustard, onion and bay leaf. Instead of tomatoes, use tomato paste, sauce or puree.

Mrs. Albert D. Well, Capital
Council, Waterbury, Ct.

HOT TAMALES

Cooking oil	3 lb. ground meat (not too lean)
2 small onions, chopped	
4 cloves garlic, minced	Salt and pepper
1 can tomatoes and green chili (Old El Paso brand)	1 can beef broth (bouillon)
	3 pkg. McCormick chili mix
1 - 1 1/2 cans water	4 Tbsp. chili powder, divided
2 c. corn meal (Pioneer corn bread mix)	Corn husks, or similar paper

254

Mix 1/4 cup cooking oil, ground meat, onion, garlic, salt and pepper. Simmer until meat is done. Mix tomatoes, water, bouillon, chili mix and 3 tablespoons chili powder. Cook about 1 hour. Strain. Mix corn meal, 1 tablespoon chili powder, a little oil, more salt and pepper and add to meat mixture. Put about 1 tablespoon meat mixture on corn husk, roll and fold ends over. Pour gravy over tamales and simmer 45 minutes.

Phil Manson, Crescent City
Council, New Orleans, La.

ONE STEP TAMALE PIE

1 lb. ground beef
2 cloves garlic, minced
1 c. milk
1 (12 oz.) can whole
  kernel corn
Few dashes bottled hot
  pepper sauce
2 - 2 1/2 tsp. chili
  powder

1 c. chopped onion
2 cans (8 oz. size) tomato
  sauce
2 slightly beaten eggs
1/2 c. sliced pitted ripe
  olives
3/4 c. yellow corn meal
2 tsp. salt

In large skillet, cook ground beef, onion, garlic until meat is browned and onion is tender. Stir in remaining ingredients. Turn into 12 x 7 1/2 x 2-inch baking dish. Bake at 350° for 45 minutes or until knife inserted comes out clean. Cut into squares to serve. Serves 8.

Rebecca Thames, Caddo
Council, Shreveport, La.

BOILED FRESH BEEF TONGUE

1 tongue
3 cloves garlic
Salt and pepper to taste

1 carrot, sliced
6 peppercorns
3 stalks celery with leaves
1 onion studded with 3 cloves

Put washed tongue in deep pot and cover with cold water. Add other ingredients and boil until tender, which may take several hours, depending on the size of the tongue. Cool in the water, skin and slice. Serve either warm or cold. Save water tongue was boiled in; use to cook red beans or green split peas.　　June Harllee, Caddo
Council, Shreveport, La.

BOILED BEEF TONGUE

1 beef tongue
1 carrot, chopped
6 peppercorns
Salt and pepper

1 large onion, chopped
3 ribs celery, chopped
3 garlic cloves, chopped

Cover tongue with water and bring to a rapid boil; skim. Add chopped vegetables and lower heat. Boil gently uncovered, adding boiling water if necessary. Add salt and pepper to taste after tongue has boiled about 1 1/2 hours. Continue cooking until tender, about 2-3 hours, depending on size of tongue. Cool tongue in water it was cooked in. Skin and trim tongue while still warm. Serve hot with a raisin sauce, cold sliced in sandwiches, or julienne for chef's salad.

June Harllee, Caddo
Council, Shreveport, La.

TUFOLI

Tufoli Noodles
1/4 tsp. salt

Cook tufoli noodles in boiling salted water with oil added for 15 minutes or until tender but firm. Wash with cold water and drain. Separate and spread out so the noodles will not stick together.

Sauce:

1 c. chopped onions
2 cloves garlic
1 can tomato sauce (small)
Salt and pepper to taste
1/2 tsp. basil
3 c. hot water

1 1/2 tsp. olive oil
2 cans tomato paste (small)
1 stem parsley
1/2 tsp. sugar
1/2 tsp. oregano

Saute onions and garlic in olive oil until golden. Add tomato sauce, continue stirring until ropy. Add tomato paste and hot water. Add remaining ingredients and cook for 1 hour.

Harriet E. Barton, Capital
Council, Baton Rouge, La.

TURKEY HEAD CHEESE

2 c. chopped green onions
6 c. water
2 c. pan drippings from
  turkey
1/2 tsp. oregano
1/4 tsp. sage
1 tsp. garlic powder
2 c. chopped celery,
  stalks and top

1/2 c. chopped parsley
5 env. Knox unflavored
  gelatine
1 tsp. red pepper
1 tsp. black pepper
1/4 tsp. thyme
2 c. chopped white onions
2 c. chopped leftover turkey
2 cubes chicken bouillon

Combine all ingredients, except the unflavored gelatine, in a large pot. Simmer for 2 hours, adding water as needed to maintain original liquid level. Remove from heat and skim off all grease possible, reheat to boiling and add gelatine, dissolving thoroughly. Remove from heat and pour mixture into suitable molds, then chill until it forms a firm gel. Turkey head cheese keeps in the refrigerator 5-6 days covered and is served sliced on crackers, or as a salad on lettuce leaves. Any extra mixture may be frozen and used at a later date as a gravy base. As many people prefer a more spicy head cheese, taste mixture before adding gelatine and act accordingly. Harry Lever, Caddo Council, Shreveport, La.

VEAL ROLLS

6 veal cutlets
1/2 lb. bacon, minced
1 Tbsp. parsley, chopped
1 Tbsp. chopped green
  onion
4 Tbsp. butter
3/4 c. chicken broth
1/3 c. chopped onion
1 bay leaf
2 Tbsp. cold water

3/4 lb. lean pork, minced or
  ground
Pinch each basil, tarragon,
  thyme and rosemary
2 cloves minced garlic
3/4 c. dry white wine
1/3 c. chopped bell pepper
2 sprigs parsley, chopped
1 Tbsp. cornstarch
Pinch of thyme

Pound cutlets until about 1/4-inch thick. Mix pork, bacon, basil, tarragon, thyme, rosemary, 1 tablespoon parsley, green onion and garlic together. Divide into 6 portions and spread over cutlets to within 1/2 inch of the sides. Fold sides in and roll up cutlets. Secure with toothpicks or string. Brown veal rolls in butter over medium heat, turning frequently. Add wine, chicken broth, bell pepper,

onion, 2 sprigs parsley, bay leaf and pinch of thyme.
Bring to a boil, reduce heat, cover and simmer about 30 minutes or until meat is tender. Transfer to serving dish and remove toothpicks or strings. Drain remaining liquid and return to pan. Bring to a boil. Add cornstarch mixed with cold water. Cook until desired consistency is reached. Pour hot sauce over veal rolls and serve.

Ann Orr, Evangeline
Council, Lafayette, La.

VEAL PAPRIKA

1 lb. boneless veal, cut into 1-inch cubes	1 tsp. salt
1 Tbsp. bacon fat or shortening	1/4 tsp. pepper
1 large Spanish onion, sliced	1 Tbsp. paprika
1 can beef bouillon	1 c. sour cream
	1 Tbsp. flour
	8 oz. noodles (any shape), cooked

Brown meat well. Add onion, stir and cook until onion is lightly browned. Add beef bouillon diluted with 1 can of water. Add salt, pepper and paprika. Cover, cook slowly on surface heat or in 350° oven about 1 hour or until veal is tender. Combine sour cream and flour and stir into broth around veal. Cook to thicken. Serve on hot noodles.
Serves 4.

Calcasieu Council
Lake Charles, La.

VEAL SCALLOPINI

1 1/2 lb. veal cutlets, cut thin	1 1/4 c. flour
1/4 c. cooking oil	Salt and pepper to taste
1/2 c. Marsala or sherry	Oregano, parsley, garlic salt
1 small can sliced mushrooms	1/4 c. beef stock or water
	Butter

Dust veal slices with seasoned flour. Brown slices in hot oil on both sides. Add wine and beef stock. Cover and simmer until veal is tender, about 10-12 minutes. Saute drained mushrooms, seasoned with oregano, parsley and garlic salt in butter. Add to cutlets before serving. Serve with hot buttered noodles.

Marie Leo, Capital Council,
Waterbury, Ct.

258

VEAL SCALLOPINI

2 lb. veal cutlets
   (4 oz. each)
Flour
1 c. sliced mushrooms
1 can consomme
1 Tbsp. Italian seasoning
1/4 c. sherry

3 Tbsp. butter
3 Tbsp. olive oil
1/2 c. finely chopped onion
   tops
1/2 tsp. celery salt
1/2 c. olives, sliced
Tenderizer

Sprinkle meat with tenderizer, flour, salt and pepper. Brown in butter and oil. Add mushrooms, onion tops, consomme and seasonings. Cover and simmer about 35-40 minutes, stirring occasionally. If mixture becomes too thick, add water. Add sherry and olives, stir and simmer for another 10 minutes. Serve with egg noodles.

Floyd Schumann, Ozone
Council, Hammond, La.

VENISON OVER COALS

6 venison steaks
1/2 c. wine vinegar
2 cloves garlic, minced
1 bay leaf, crushed
1 can mushrooms

1 1/2 c. dry red wine
3/4 c. olive oil
1 Tbsp. minced onion
Salt and lemon pepper

Combine and mix all ingredients, except venison and mushrooms. Add steaks to this marinade for 6 hours in refrigerator; 8 hours if frozen. Grill steaks over very hot coals for about 4 minutes per side for medium-rare meat, or longer if you prefer meat cooked more. Or, place steaks under the broiler. Baste several times. Heat mushrooms in butter as steak topping. Serve immediately with green vegetables and/or baked potatoes. Serves 4-6.

Pat Brown, Ouachita
Council, Monroe, La.

VENISON ROAST WITH SAUCE

1 can tomato sauce
Salt and pepper to taste
2 Tbsp. vinegar
1 venison roast

2 Tbsp. sugar
1 small onion, finely chopped
Worcestershire sauce to taste
Sliced bacon

Combine tomato sauce, salt, pepper, onion, vinegar, sugar and Worcestershire sauce. Place the venison on large sheet of heavy foil in baking dish and cover roast with sliced bacon. Pour tomato mixture over roast, fold and seal the foil. Bake at 300° for 3 hours or until tender.

Rebecca Scott, Caddo
Council, Shreveport, La.

VIRGINIA'S LITTLE PRONTOS

1 c. pancake mix   3/4 c. milk
Frankfurters

Make up batter with pancake mix and milk. Cut wieners in 1-inch size. Cut in slanting position instead of straight across. Dip each wiener in batter and fry in deep hot fat until golden brown.

Marie Pamplin
Shreveport Works Council
Shreveport, La.

BARBECUED WIENERS

1 pkg. wieners   2 medium onions, chopped
1 bell pepper, chopped   1 can tomato sauce
3 Tbsp. brown sugar   3 Tbsp. prepared mustard
Red pepper to taste   Salt to taste

Saute onions and bell pepper, stir in tomato sauce, sugar, mustard, red pepper and salt. Split wieners in half, not cutting all the way through. Add to sauce mixture. Cook on top of stove or in 425° oven about 25 minutes.

Calcasieu Council
Lake Charles, La.

WIENERS AND SAUERKRAUT

1 pkg. frankfurters   1/2 c. green pepper, chopped
2 Tbsp. oil   1 can tomatoes
1/2 c. sliced onion   1/2 tsp. salt
1/2 c. chopped celery   1/2 can (2 1/2 oz.) Old El
1 can sauerkraut, drained   Paso brand tomatoes and
1 tsp. oregano   jalapeno peppers, or to
                                       taste

Brown wieners in oil. Add remaining ingredients and cook until vegetables are tender.   Mrs. Leona Botzong Smith
Central Council
Corpus Christi, Tx.

ALMOND CHICKEN WITH SNOW PEAS

1 whole chicken breast	2 Tbsp. oil
1/4 c. sliced almonds	1 c. diagonally sliced celery,
1/2 c. chopped onions	1/4-inch thick
1 pkg. frozen snow peas	1 slice fresh ginger root
1 clove crushed garlic	2 tsp. cornstarch
1/4 tsp. sugar and salt	1/2 c. chicken broth
Soy sauce	Cooked rice

Boil chicken until done, skin and cut into bite size pieces. Reserve 1/2 cup broth. Heat 1 tablespoon oil in wok, stir-fry almonds until lightly brown, drain on paper towels. Stir-fry onion and celery 1-2 minutes, remove to small bowl. Stir-fry snow peas 1-2 minutes, add to onion mixture. Heat remaining oil, add ginger root and garlic, fry until brown and discard. Add chicken, fry 3-4 minutes. Add vegetables, blend in cornstarch, sugar, salt, broth and soy sauce. Stir into chicken and cook until thick. Serve over rice.   Rose Nichols, Caddo
Council, Shreveport, La.

APPLE CHICKEN

1/2 small onion, sliced	1/2 tsp. cumin
2 chicken breasts	1/2 c. apple juice
1 Tbsp. oil	1/2 c. water
2 tsp. lemon juice	Flour
Salt and pepper	

Saute onion in oil. Salt, pepper and flour chicken, add to onion and brown quickly. Add cumin and stir. Add water and juices. Cover, reduce heat and simmer 30 minutes. Serve with some of the sauce and onion over chicken.
Marilou Bridges, Caddo
Council, Shreveport, La.

CHICKEN A LA KING

2/3 c. oleo, melted	2/3 c. flour
2 c. chicken broth	2 c. milk
1 tsp. salt	1/4 tsp. pepper
2 tsp. minced onion	1/2 c. diced bell pepper
1 cooked fryer, boned	2 diced pimientos
1 can mushroom soup	

Add flour to melted oleo and stir over low heat. Add broth and milk all at once. Cook and stir until thickened. Add remaining ingredients and heat. Serve on toast, rice or patty shells.

Gayle Wilkening
Shreveport Works Council
Longview, Tx.

Mary Bonner
Caddo Council
Shreveport, La.

BAKED CHICKEN

4 chicken breasts	Salt and pepper
1 stick oleo, melted	Paprika
Ritz crackers, crushed	

Remove skin from chicken. Salt, pepper and sprinkle with paprika. Dip each piece in melted oleo and roll in crushed crackers. Place in pan, cover with foil and bake at 350° for 1 hour. Remove foil and bake additional 15 minutes.

Marilou Bridges, Caddo
Council, Shreveport, La.

ITALIAN BAKED CHICKEN

1 fryer, cut up	1 c. Italian bread crumbs
1/2 c. Italian cheese	1/4 c. olive oil
2 eggs, well beaten	Butter or oleo

Combine bread crumbs and cheese in 1 bowl. Combine eggs and olive oil in another bowl. Dip chicken pieces in egg mixture, lift quickly to coat with crumb and cheese mixture. Arrange chicken in lightly greased pan and dot each piece with butter. Bake at 375° for about 1 hour or until tests done. Stuffed artichoke lovers will like this dish; tastes like it.

Lois Verdon, Metairie
Council, Harahan, La.

BAKED CHICKEN WITH MUSHROOMS

2 fryers, cut in quarters
1 c. chopped onion
1 clove minced garlic
1 c. olive oil
1 c. dry sherry

1 c. chopped celery
1 c. chopped green peppers
1/2 c. butter or oleo
1 medium can mushrooms
Salt, red and black pepper

Rub chicken quarters with salt, red and black pepper. Place in roasting pan. Cover with chopped onions, celery, green pepper and garlic. Cut up butter over chicken and pour olive oil over top. Bake covered in 375° oven for 1 hour. Add mushrooms and wine. Continue baking uncovered for 15 minutes or until well browned.

John E. Haygood, Caddo
Council, Shreveport, La.

CREAMY ONION BAKED CHICKEN

1 (3 lb.) fryer, cut up
1/2 stick oleo, melted
1 can chicken mushroom
  soup
2 c. (1 lb. can) drained
  whole onions
1/2 soup can water

1/2 c. flour
2/3 c. evaporated milk
1 c. (4 oz.) grated American
  cheese
1/4 lb. sliced mushrooms
  (optional)
Dash of paprika
Salt and pepper

Lightly salt and pepper chicken. Lightly coat with flour. Arrange chicken pieces in single layer with skins down in melted oleo in 13x9x2 inch pan. Bake uncovered in 425° oven for 30 minutes. Turn chicken over and continue to bake for about 15-20 minutes longer. Remove from oven. Drain. Combine remaining ingredients, except paprika and bring to light boil. Pour over chicken. Sprinkle with paprika and cover with foil. Return to oven and bake 15-20 minutes. Serve with rice.

Jeanette English, Caddo
Council, Shreveport, La.

TAVERN STYLE BAKED CHICKEN

1 (3-5 lb.) chicken
1 tsp. salt
2 cans (3 oz. size)
  mushrooms
1/2 c. butter
1 tsp. salt
1/2 c. grated American
  cheese

1 medium onion
Water
1 c. evaporated milk
1/2 c. flour
Pepper to taste
1/4 tsp. oregano
1/2 tsp. turmeric
3 c. cooked rice

Cook chicken with onion and 1 teaspoon salt in water. Remove chicken when tender, debone and sliver. Save broth. Measure mushroom liquid. Add enough chicken broth to make 3 cups in all. Add milk, set aside. Melt butter, blend flour, 1 teaspoon salt, pepper and turmeric, add to butter. Add broth mixture. Cook over low heat, stirring constantly until thickened. Add oregano and 1/4 cup cheese. Stir until cheese melts. Add mushrooms. Spread rice in bottom of greased shallow casserole. Top with slivered chicken. Pour sauce over all. Sprinkle with remaining cheese. Bake at 350° for 30 minutes or until brown.

Connie Younker
Shreveport Works Council
Shreveport, La.

CHICKEN AU PAPILLOTE

1 can Pet milk
1 pkg. dried onion soup
4 or more pieces of
  chicken

1 c. rice
2 c. water
1 Tbsp. paprika

Cook rice as you normally do. Place in double layer of foil. Pour Pet milk over it and sprinkle dried onion soup over that. Place chicken on top. Repeat with rice, milk and soup. Season. Wrap tightly and bake at 350° for about 1 hour. Eat!

Calcasieu Council
Lake Charles, La.

BARBECUED CHICKEN

1 c. salad oil
1/4 c. lemon juice
1/8 tsp. Tabasco sauce
4 tsp. prepared mustard
2 Tbsp. brown sugar

2 tsp. salt
1/8 tsp. pepper
1 clove garlic
Fryers (2 1/2 - 3 lb.), cut
   into pieces for serving

1. Make barbecue sauce by combining salad oil, lemon juice, Tabasco sauce, mustard, sugar, salt and pepper. Blender may be used. Add garlic, cut into halves. Let stand several hours. Remove garlic and shake before using. 2. Let chicken stand in sauce overnight. 3. Remove chicken from sauce and arrange in shallow baking pan. May be done outside on grill. 4. Bake in preheated oven. During baking, brush chicken with sauce 2 or 3 times (temperature - 350°; time - 1 1/2 hours).

Note: Thyme, marjoram or rosemary may be added to sauce, if desired.
Calcasieu Council
Lake Charles, La.

RUSSIAN STYLE BARBECUED CHICKEN

1 fryer
1/2 pkg. dry onion soup
   mix
1/2 c. water

Salt and pepper to taste
1 (8 oz.) jar apricot preserves
1/2 bottle Russian dressing

Cut fryer into quarters. Spread in Corning Ware dish. Salt and pepper to taste. Sprinkle onion soup mix over chicken. Dab the apricot preserves over the chicken by spoonfuls. Cover with Russian dressing and pour water over top. Cover and bake for 2 hours at 300°.
Sally Davenport, Central
Council, Alexandria, La.

CHICKEN BEER BAKE

3 chicken breasts, split
   in half
Salt and pepper to taste
3 tsp. soy sauce
1 (3 oz.) can sliced
   mushrooms, drained

4-5 Tbsp. flour
Cooking oil
2 cans cream of chicken
   soup
3 Tbsp. slivered almonds
1/2 can beer

Coat chicken with flour, season with salt and pepper and brown lightly in oil on both sides. Place browned chicken breasts in Dutch oven or casserole. Mix together soup, soy sauce, 2 tablespoons almonds, mushrooms and beer. Pour over chicken. Bake in preheated 350° oven uncovered for 1 hour. Sprinkle remaining tablespoon of almonds over chicken when ready to serve. To complete your meal, serve fried rice and juicy cling peaches warmed in the oven. Serves 6.   Fae Wells, Central Council,
Alexandria, La.

CHICKEN BONNE FEMME

6 medium potatoes, peeled   3 broilers (chicken), split
  and sliced   in half
Butter   Salt and pepper
3 large onions, sliced   6 strips bacon

Grease chicken with butter, then salt and pepper. Bake skin side up at 300° for 1 hour or until tender. Fry bacon in large heavy skillet. When bacon is crisp, remove and add potatoes and onions to hot bacon fat. Lift and turn constantly over fairly high heat, adding salt and pepper. Cook until well browned. Remove chicken from oven. Lift 1 piece of chicken at a time and in its place, put 1/6 of the potato-onion mixture sprinkled with crushed bacon. Lay chicken on top of this. Continue until potato mixture is used up. Cook until chicken is done. Serve with sliced tomatoes, cheese and melon for dessert. Bonne Femme is French for good woman and the name seems to be associated with this dish because of its rather hearty stick to the ribs quality.
Lois E. Leger, Evangeline
Council, Lafayette, La.

BRAZILIAN APRICOT CHICKEN

1 chicken, cut up   1 small can apricots
1/2 c. ketchup   Salt and pepper
Garlic salt (optional)

Wash chicken pieces, salt and pepper well. Place in casserole dish. Pour ketchup over chicken. Arrange halves of apricots over chicken and pour apricot juice over all. Cover and bake at 350° for about 45 minutes or until done.
Peggy Childers, Crescent City
Council, New Orleans, La.

266

ROLLED CHICKEN BREASTS

6 chicken breasts
2 Tbsp. parsley flakes
1/4 tsp. red cayenne
   pepper
1/4 tsp. pepper
1/2 c. melted butter

1 c. Parmesan cheese
1/4 tsp. garlic powder
1/2 tsp. salt
2 c. corn flake crumbs
2 c. chicken broth

Debone chicken, saving bones and skin for broth. Mix cheese, parsley flakes, garlic powder, peppers and salt together. Dip chicken in melted butter, roll in cheese mixture and then in corn flake crumbs. Fold in tight roll and fasten with toothpick. Place in casserole dish. Spoon broth over chicken. Bake uncovered at 350° for 1 hour. Baste with broth several times while cooking.

Broth:

Chicken bones and skin
2 chopped celery stalks

1 small onion, chopped
Salt and pepper to taste

Combine all ingredients and cover with water. Simmer for 2 hours and strain. Pour in jar. May be made up days ahead and stored in freezer. Thaw before using.

Pat Brown, Ouachita
Council, Monroe,La.

CHICKEN BREASTS IN SOUR CREAM

1 lb. chipped dried
   beef, chopped fine
5 slices bacon
2 c. mushroom soup

5 chicken breasts, boned,
   skinned and split
1 (8 oz.) carton sour cream
Parmesan cheese

Place chipped beef in bottom of casserole dish. Wrap chicken in bacon and arrange on beef. Mix soup and sour cream. Pour over chicken. Cover and bake at 275° for 2 1/2 - 3 hours. Serve the gravy over chicken. Sprinkle top with cheese. Serve with wild rice. Serves 5.

Jan Prestridge, Capital
Council, Baton Rouge, La.

STUFFED CHICKEN BREASTS

3 chicken breasts
1 Tbsp. finely chopped
  celery
2 Tbsp. butter or oleo
1 tsp. salt
1/4 c. melted butter or
  oleo
3 slices bacon
1 Tbsp. lemon juice

1/3 c. finely chopped mushrooms
1 Tbsp. chopped onion
1/4 c. blanched slivered
  almonds
1/8 tsp. pepper
3/4 c. crushed potato chips
Paprika
Toasted slivered almonds

Pat washed chicken breasts dry. Slit each piece of chicken lengthwise. Saute mushrooms, celery, onions in 2 tablespoons butter until tender. Remove from heat and stir in blanched almonds, lemon juice, salt and pepper. Fill each breast with stuffing, then roll in melted butter. Coat each piece of chicken with generous portion of potato chips. Place slice of bacon over each slit, sprinkle with paprika. Place in a greased shallow baking dish and bake at 350° for 1 hour or until fork tender. Sprinkle with toasted slivered almonds before serving.

Dorothy LaRocca
Crescent City Council
New Orleans, La.

BREAST OF CHICKEN IN WHITE WINE

4 chicken breasts
1 3/4 c. white wine
  (divided)
1/2 tsp. salt

1/2 lb. fresh mushrooms
1/2 tsp. tarragon
1 Tbsp. flour
2 Tbsp. butter

Saute chicken in butter in heavy skillet. Add mushrooms, saute 1 minute. Add tarragon, salt and 3/4 cup wine. Reduce heat and simmer until tender. Stir flour into remaining wine until blended well. Stir into chicken mixture and cook until thickened. Serve over hot, fluffy or saffron rice.

Evelyn Bledsoe, Ouachita
Council, Monroe, La.

CHICKEN CACCIATORE

2 1/2 lb. frying chicken,
   cut up
3 Tbsp. shortening
Dash of pepper
1/2 c. sliced onion
1/2 c. chopped celery
1 clove garlic, minced

1 c. catsup
1 c. water
2 Tbsp. chopped parsley
1 bay leaf
1/2 tsp. salt
2 Tbsp. red wine

Brown chicken in shortening. Sprinkle with pepper. Remove chicken from skillet. Saute onion and next 2 ingredients in skillet until lightly browned. Stir in catsup and remaining ingredients. Add chicken and simmer uncovered for 30-40 minutes or until chicken is tender and sauce is desired consistency.

Calcasieu Council
Lake Charles, La.

CALIFORNIA CHICKEN

2 lb. chicken pieces
1 can golden mushroom
   soup
2 Tbsp. frozen concen-
   trated orange juice

2 Tbsp. shortening
1/4 c. chopped onion
1/2 tsp. ground ginger
Avocado slices
Orange slices

Brown chicken in shortening, drain. Add soup, onion, orange juice and ginger. Cover, cook over low heat 45 minutes or until tender. Stir occasionally. Uncover, cook to desired consistency. Garnish with avocado and orange slices to serve. Makes 4 servings.

Ann Orr, Evangeline
Council, New Iberia, La.

CASHEW CHICKEN

1 lb. cubed raw chicken
2 Tbsp. dry sherry
2 Tbsp. water
1/4 tsp. ginger
1 c. small fresh broccoli
   sprigs
1/2 c. raw cashew nuts
1/4 c. soy sauce

1 Tbsp. cornstarch
1/2 tsp. salt
1/2 c. chopped onion
1/2 c. oil, divided
1 c. dried Chinese mush-
   rooms
1 c. water chestnuts,
   sliced

Combine cornstarch, sherry, salt, water, onion and ginger. Dredge chicken cubes in mixture. Reconstitute mushrooms in water, drain and saute in 1/4 cup oil. Remove from pan. Quickly saute cashews until golden brown. Remove from pan. Saute broccoli until tender but crisp, adding more oil if necessary. Remove from pan. Pour remaining oil in pan and saute chicken until tender and golden. Add mushrooms, broccoli, cashews, soy sauce and water chestnuts. Heat thoroughly. Serves 4.

Rebecca Scott, Caddo
Council, Shreveport, La.

CHICKEN CHOW MEIN

2 lb. boneless skinned
   chicken breasts
3 c. celery, sliced
   diagonally
1/4 c. soy sauce
1 chicken bouillon cube
1 (4 oz.) can sliced mushrooms, sliced
2 c. chow mein noodles

2 Tbsp. oleo
2 Tbsp. corn oil
1 c. chopped onion
1 1/2 c. water, divided
1/2 tsp. sugar
2 cans (1 lb. each) bean
   sprouts, undrained
3 Tbsp. cornstarch
4 c. hot cooked rice

Cut chicken into bite size pieces. Heat oil and oleo in heavy kettle. Brown chicken slightly, drain. Stir in celery, onion, 1 cup water, soy sauce, sugar and bouillon cube. Bring to a boil. Cover and simmer about 10 minutes until vegetables are tender crisp. Add bean sprouts and mushrooms. Combine cornstarch and remaining 1/2 cup water. Stir into mixture. Cook, stirring until thickened and boiling. Serve with or over rice and chow mein noodles; 400 calories per serving.

Mavis W. O'Rourke
Shreveport Works Council
Shreveport, La.

CHICKEN CLEMENCEAU

1 (1 1/2 lb.) spring
   chicken
1 stick butter
1 small can green peas
1 sprig minced parsley

2 medium potatoes, diced
   and fried
6 mushrooms, diced
1 clove minced garlic

Cut chicken into 8 pieces. Saute slowly in butter until

well browned. Cook until done. Add remaining ingredients and saute 5-10 minutes longer. Serves 2-4.

Lois Leger, Evangeline
Council, Lafayette, La.

CHICKEN WITH COGNAC SOUFFLE

3 Tbsp. butter
3 Tbsp. flour
1 c. chicken broth
1 c. cooked, chopped
  chicken
Salt and pepper to taste
Juice of 1/2 lemon

3 egg yolks
4 egg whites
1/8 tsp. cream of tartar
2 Tbsp. cognac
Dash of cayenne pepper
Pinch of nutmeg
1/2 tsp. rosemary

Preheat oven to 400°. Melt butter and add flour. Add chicken broth, gradually, stirring with wire whisk to form a thick smooth sauce. Remove pan from heat, add egg yolks, 1 at a time. Add remaining ingredients, except egg whites, pinch of salt and cream of tartar. Beat egg whites with pinch of salt and cream of tartar until stiff. Fold the chicken mixture into egg whites and fill a 4-cup souffle dish. Place souffle dish in oven, immediately reduce heat to 375° and bake 25 minutes. Serve with the following Sauce. Makes 4-6 servings.

Sauce:

1 Tbsp. butter
1 Tbsp. flour
1 c. chicken stock or
  broth

1 egg yolk (optional)
1-2 Tbsp. whipping cream
  (optional)

Melt butter in small saucepan. Remove from heat, add flour, stir with wire whip. Add chicken stock gradually, stirring constantly over moderate heat. If richer sauce is desired, combine egg yolk and cream. Add about 3 tablespoons of the hot mixture into egg and cream and stir together. Return to remaining hot sauce. Do not boil after egg yolk mixture has been added.

Peggy Childers
Crescent City Council
New Orleans, La.

CHICKEN CORDON BLEU

4 large chicken breasts,
   split, boned and
   skinned
4 slices Swiss cheese or
   Gruyere cheese, halved
1/2 c. all-purpose flour
Melted butter or oleo
1/2 c. Parmesan cheese
   (optional)
Salt and pepper to taste
4 thin slices boiled ham,
   halved
1 egg
2 or 3 Tbsp. water
1/2 c. seasoned bread
   crumbs
Hot cooking oil

Place each half of chicken breast on waxed paper, carefully flatten chicken by using a meat mallet or rolling pin. Sprinkle chicken with salt and pepper. Place 1/2 slice of ham and cheese on each half of chicken breast, tuck in sides and roll up jelly roll fashion. Secure with small metal meat picks or toothpicks or tie securely. Combine egg and water, beat well. Combine bread crumbs, flour and 1/2 cup Parmesan cheese (if desired; I've tried with and without, both are great). Dip each piece of chicken in egg, then coat with bread crumb mixture. Brown in mixture of butter and oil. (Reserve pan drippings for use in Creamy Sauce.) Serve with Creamy Sauce.

Creamy Sauce:

2 Tbsp. all-purpose flour
3/4 c. chicken broth
1/2 c. chopped mushrooms
   (optional)
Reserved pan drippings
1/4 c. dry white wine

Blend flour into pan drippings, cook over low heat until bubbly. Gradually blend in broth and wine, cook, stirring constantly, until smooth and thickened. For variety, add 1/2 cup chopped mushrooms. Pour over chicken and bake in 350° oven for 20 minutes. Serves 8.

Yvonne K. D'Angelo, Metairie
Council, New Orleans, La.

CHICKEN CORDON BLEU

6 whole chicken breasts,
   boned and skinned
1 (6 oz.) pkg. sliced,
   cooked ham
6 Tbsp. oleo
1 chicken bouillon cube
4 c. hot cooked rice
3 Tbsp. flour
1 tsp. paprika
1 c. water

1 (8 oz.) pkg. Swiss   1 c. heavy or whipping
  cheese   cream
1 Tbsp. cornstarch

Spread chicken breasts flat, fold cheese and ham slices
to fit on top. Fold breast over filling and fasten edges together with toothpicks. Mix flour and paprika and coat
chicken. Melt oleo in skillet and brown chicken on all
sides. Add water and bouillon cube, heat to boiling, reduce
heat, cover and simmer 30 minutes or until tender. Blend
cream and cornstarch until smooth, gradually stir into
drippings in skillet after chicken is removed. Cook, stirring constantly, until sauce is thickened. Arrange chicken
breasts on platter, remove toothpicks. Pour sauce over
chicken and rice.   Mary Bonner, Caddo
                              Council, Shreveport, La.

CHINESE BROWN CHICKEN

1 clove garlic, chopped   1 Tbsp. coarsely chopped
1 Tbsp. chopped green   ginger root
  onion   1 fryer, cut up in about
1 c. peanut oil   1 1/2-inch pieces, includ-
3 Tbsp. soy sauce   ing bones
1 tsp. sugar   2 Tbsp. white wine
Chicken stock   Salt, pepper and cornstarch

Fry garlic, ginger root and green onion in peanut oil
about 30 seconds over high heat. Remove and discard.
Season chicken with salt and pepper, sprinkle lightly with
cornstarch. Cook chicken in oil until lightly browned. Add
soy sauce, sugar and wine. Add chicken stock to barely
cover chicken. Cover pot and cook over medium heat until
stock is almost gone and thick brown gravy remains.
Serve with rice and Chinese vegetables.
                              Ann Orr, Evangeline
                              Council, New Iberia, La.

CURRIED CHICKEN

4-6 chicken breasts   2 (10 oz.) pkg. frozen
2 c. grated American   broccoli, cut in bite
  cheese slices   size pieces
2 cans cream of chicken   3/4 c. mayonnaise
  soup   1 c. evaporated milk

2 tsp. lemon juice
1 tsp. curry powder

1 1/2 c. buttered bread
    crumbs

Boil chicken, debone and cut into small bite size pieces. Partially cook broccoli, drain and place in bottom of Corning Ware dish. Layer chicken over broccoli. Combine soup, mayonnaise, milk, lemon juice, curry powder and cheese with electric mixer; mix well. Pour over chicken and broccoli. Top with bread crumbs. Cook at 350° for 25-30 minutes.

> Debi Magalian, Central
> Council, Silver Spring, Md.

EASY CHICKEN CREOLE

1 c. onion, chopped
1 clove garlic, crushed
2 Tbsp. flour
2 1/4 c. chicken broth
1/4 tsp. sugar
Black pepper to taste

1 medium green pepper, diced
3 Tbsp. oil
1 (6 oz.) can tomato paste
1/2 tsp. salt
1/4 tsp. hot pepper sauce
2 c. cubed cooked chicken

Saute onion, green pepper and garlic in oil until tender, stirring occasionally. Add flour, stir just until flour starts to brown. Stir in tomato paste, broth, salt, sugar and pepper sauce. Cook and stir until mixture comes to boil and thickens. Stir in chicken and black pepper. Simmer uncovered 5 minutes or until chicken is heated through. Serve over hot cooked rice. Makes 4 servings.

> Metairie Council
> Metairie, La.

DEBI'S CROCK-POT CHICKEN

3-4 chicken breasts
2 cans mushroom soup
1 env. Lipton onion
    soup mix
Pinch of oregano

Salt and pepper
3/4 c. white wine
1 can mushrooms
Pinch of tarragon
1 (8 oz.) carton sour cream

Salt and pepper chicken, place in crock-pot. Mix together soup, white wine, onion soup mix, spices and mushrooms. Pour over chicken. Cook on high for 1/2 hour, reduce to low and cook 8-10 hours. About 1 hour before finishing, add sour cream. Serve over cooked egg noodles.

> Debi Magalian, Central
> Council, Silver Springs, Md.

DIRTY RICE

2 lb. chicken giblets
1 lb. chicken livers
2 stalks celery, chopped
1/2 stick oleo
1/2 c. green onions, chopped

1 large onion, chopped
1 large bell pepper, chopped
1 lb. long grain rice
1 c. stock
Parsley to taste

Boil giblets until tender; drain and chop giblets well. Save stock. Boil rice until 1/2 done, place in strainer and rinse with cold water. Saute livers, celery, onion and bell pepper in oleo until tender. Add giblets, mix well. Add rice, 1 cup of stock, green onion and parsley. Use fork to lift ingredients and mix. Do not stir. Place in about 400° oven for 20 minutes. Marjorie B. Harris, Capital Council, Baton Rouge, La.

EASY CHICKEN AND DUMPLINGS

4 chicken breasts or pieces of your choice
Few drops yellow food color

1 stick oleo
1 can chicken broth (optional)
Salt and pepper
20 small flour tortillas

Put chicken in large pot filled about 3/4 full of water. Cook until tender. Remove chicken and debone, or if you prefer, may leave chicken without deboning. Add remaining ingredients, except tortillas, back in boiling broth water. Take shears and cut the flour tortillas in strips and drop in boiling broth (do not use corn tortillas). Cook about 20 minutes or so until done. These dumplings look and taste as good as regular dumplings. This makes a large quantity, so can be halved if you desire. Marilou Bridges, Caddo Council, Shreveport, La.

CHICKEN EGG FOO YONG

6 eggs
1 c. cooked chicken, cubed or diced
1/2 c. sliced mushrooms
2 tsp. soy sauce
2 Tbsp. vegetable oil

1/2 tsp. salt
1/2 c. chopped onions
1/2 c. chopped celery
2 scallions, minced
1 tsp. dry sherry

Beat eggs, add salt, stir, then add all ingredients, except oil. Heat small frying pan or wok and add vegetable oil. Pour about 3 tablespoons of egg mixture into pan and fry until bottom is light brown. Turn and brown other side. Remove from pan and keep warm while making the remaining omelets. Serve with extra soy sauce. Makes 6-8 omelets.

Marilou Bridges, Caddo
Council, Shreveport, La.

CHICKEN ENCHILADAS

4 chicken breasts or
  1 fryer, cooked and
  chopped in bite size
  pieces
1 can mushroom soup
Chili peppers to taste,
  seeded and chopped

1 can tomato soup
1 can cream of chicken soup
1 c. chicken broth
1 doz. corn tortillas, cut
  in bite size pieces
Brick or American cheese,
  grated

Combine all ingredients, except cheese. Mix and place half in casserole. Cover with cheese. Repeat layers. Bake 1 hour at 350°. This freezes well and is enough to make 2 casseroles.

Velma Carruth, Capital
Council, Baton Rouge, La.

CHICKEN ENCHILADAS

3-4 c. cooked chicken
  breasts, cut in chunks
1/2 c. onion
1 doz. tortillas, broken
  in small pieces

2 cans cream of chicken soup
1 (6 oz.) can evaporated milk
1 can green chili peppers
8 oz. Swiss cheese, grated

Combine and mix chicken, soup, milk, onion and chili peppers. In casserole dish, place a layer of tortillas, layer of chicken mixture and layer of cheese. Repeat layers, ending with cheese on top. Bake at 350° until hot and cheese is melted. Serves 6-8.

Patricia Edmonson, Caddo
Council, Shreveport, La.

CHICKEN EN COCOTTE

1 (4-5 lb.) roasting
  chicken
1 can cream of chicken
  soup
1 soup can water (more
  if needed)

1 tsp. paprika
12 small potatoes, halved
1 lb. small onions
6 medium carrots
1 1/2 tsp. salt
2 Tbsp. parsley for garnish

Wash chicken, tie legs and fold neck under. Pour soup and water over chicken. Cover and bake in preheated 375° oven for 45 minutes. Place remaining ingredients, except parsley, in the liquid around chicken. Recover and cook until tender, for 1 hour or so. Baste vegetables with pan liquid. Remove cover, cut strings on the chicken and bake for 15 minutes to brown. Baste occasionally.

Adrienne Delery, Ouachita
Council, Monroe, La.

CHICKEN FRICASSEE

3 1/2 lb. chicken, cut up
5 Tbsp. flour
1/2 c. chopped celery
1/2 c. chopped parsley
1/2 tsp. dried thyme

3 Tbsp. salad oil
1 large onion, chopped
3 c. hot water
1 bay leaf, crumbled
Salt, pepper

Salt and pepper chicken. Brown slowly in oil over medium heat. Remove pieces of chicken when browned, stir in flour until smooth. Cook about 15 minutes, stirring constantly until a rich brown roux. Lower heat, add onion and celery. Cover and simmer about 10 minutes. Stir often. Gradually stir in water. Add parsley, bay leaf, thyme, chicken pieces, salt and pepper to taste. Cover and simmer about 40 minutes. Serves 6 or more.

John E. Haygood, Caddo
Council, Shreveport, La.

CHICKEN GLACE

3 or 4 lb. fryer or hen
3 Tbsp. flour
4 pkg. unflavored gelatin
1/4 c. green onion tops,
  chopped

3 Tbsp. oil
Salt and red pepper to taste
1 c. chopped celery
1/4 c. chopped onion
1/4 c. chopped parsley

Boil chicken until tender. Remove broth and cool. Skin, debone and chop chicken. Make dark roux of oil and flour. Add salt and red pepper. Mix chicken and vegetables with roux, cook until tender. Mix gelatin as directed on box, add to chicken mixture. Add 2 cups chicken broth, onion and parsley. Mix well and pour into mold. Chill.

Ernestine Briley, Central
Council, New Iberia, La.

ITALIAN CHICKEN

2 cut up chickens
1 1/2 Tbsp. oregano
1/4 tsp. rosemary
Paprika
1 1/2 c. white sauterne
  wine

6-8 cloves garlic, washed
  but not peeled, crushed
  with back of knife
Lemon juice
Salt and pepper
1/2 c. olive oil

Marinate chicken pieces overnight in salt, pepper and lemon juice. Saute oregano, garlic and rosemary in olive oil until heated. Add chicken and paprika. Fry in olive oil mixture until cooked. Add wine and continue to cook on low heat for additional 20-25 minutes. Serve hot.

Joyce Hattier, Magnolia
Council, New Orleans, La.

JAPANESE STYLE CHICKEN AND NOODLES

1 medium size chicken
4 carrots, sliced
2 onions, sliced
3 bell peppers, sliced
Soy sauce to taste
Small amount of oil

1 head cabbage
Green onions, sliced, to taste
4 pkg. Ramen noodles (can
  be found in Oriental foods
  in grocery)

Boil chicken, debone and save broth. Place cabbage, bell peppers and carrots in water until tender and water cooks out. In small amount of oil, cook onions and green onions until tender. Add vegetables and soy sauce and cook additional 15 minutes. Reheat chicken broth to boiling, add noodles and cook until tender; drain. Mix noodles, noodle seasoning, boned chicken and vegetables. Add more soy sauce to taste.

Gertrude Juneau
Crescent City Council
New Orleans, La.

278

KATIE'S CHICKEN DELIGHT

6 large broiler fryer
  thighs
6 large broiler fryer
  drumsticks
1/2 c. grated Parmesan
  cheese
Salt and pepper to taste

4 eggs, beaten
3 c. Italian seasoned
  bread crumbs
4 large white potatoes,
  peeled, split lengthwise
2 c. liquid shortening
Heavy duty aluminum foil

Wash chicken in salted water for 10 minutes. Rinse with clear water and drain. Remove skin, if desired. Dip chicken into beaten eggs. Press into seasoned bread crumb-cheese mixture, coating well on both sides. Alternating potatoes and chicken, place side by side in large 16x10x2-inch open roasting pan. Pour liquid shortening over chicken and potatoes. Cover with foil. Bake at 350° for 45 minutes. Remove foil. Turn chicken and potatoes and bake for an additional 45 minutes. Remove pan from oven immediately. Remove chicken and potatoes from oil, placing on a large serving platter. Makes 6 servings.

Catherine Lena Gelder
Magnolia Council
New Orleans, La.

LEMON CHICKEN

1/3 c. flour
1 tsp. paprika
1 (2 1/2 - 3 lb.) frying
  chicken, cut up
1/4 c. sliced green onions
1 1/2 tsp. grated lemon
  peel
Chopped parsley

1 tsp. salt
1 chicken bouillon cube
3 Tbsp. lemon juice
3 Tbsp. Crisco
2 Tbsp. brown sugar
3/4 c. boiling water
Hot cooked rice

Combine flour, salt and paprika in plastic bag. Brush chicken with lemon juice. Add 2 or 3 pieces of chicken at a time to bag and shake well. Brown chicken in hot Crisco. Dissolve bouillon cube in boiling water and pour over chicken. Stir in onion, sugar, lemon peel and any remaining lemon juice. Cover, reduce heat and cook chicken over low heat, about 40-45 minutes, or until tender. Sprinkle with parsley and serve with hot fluffy rice.

Doris Reeves, Capital
Council, Baton Rouge, La.

LE POULE A LA VIN BLANC

4 small chicken thighs
1 Tbsp. flour
1 small can shrimp,
  chopped
1 cooking spoon white
  wine

1 cube bouillon
1 small can mushrooms,
  chopped and undrained
1 1/2 c. water, divided
Cooking oil

In skillet, place enough oil to cover bottom, fry chicken pieces until brown. Drain skillet and pour in 3/4 cup water, scrape skillet and add bouillon cube. Let simmer until cube is melted. Add shrimp, mushrooms and juice. Mix flour with remaining water, add and stir well. Add wine and chicken pieces. Cover and cook until tender.

Harry Klundt, Crescent City
Council, New Orleans, La.

BROWN IN BAG CHICKEN LIVERS

1 lb. chicken livers
1 regular size Brown-In-
  Bag

1 stick oleo, cut up
1 Tbsp. flour

Place flour in bag and shake. Put chicken livers and oleo in bag. Tie and place bag in shallow pan. Cook at 350° for 45 minutes. About half way through cooking period, shake pan to evenly coat livers with oleo. Continue to cook additional time. Makes own gravy. Calves liver can also be prepared same way. Add onion to calves liver if desired.

Una Mize, Caddo Council,
Shreveport, La.

HARRELL'S CHICKEN LIVERS SUPREME

1 lb. chicken livers
1/4 lb. chopped onions
1/4 c. red wine
Butter

1/4 lb. sliced mushrooms
2 cloves minced garlic
1 tsp. cornstarch

Fry chicken livers in butter, remove from pan. Fry mushrooms in butter drippings, remove from pan. Fry onions and garlic in remainder of butter drippings. Remove from pan. Heat wine in pan, add cornstarch. Mix well, add

all of the cooked ingredients, heat and thicken. Serve with rice or on French bread.　　　Bill Harrell, Jr., Capital
Council, Baton Rouge, La.

MICROWAVE CHICKEN AND DRIED BEEF

3 whole chicken breasts, halved
1 (2 1/2 oz.) jar dried beef, cut into pieces

1 can cream of mushroom soup
1/2 c. sour cream
1 Tbsp. dried parsley flakes

Place chicken breasts, skin side down and thick edges toward outside, in 2-quart glass baking dish. Cover with plastic wrap. Microwave on high 10 minutes, drain. Combine remaining ingredients. Turn chicken over and pour on sauce. Recover with wrap. Microwave on roast for 15-16 minutes or until chicken is fork tender. Let stand covered for 5 minutes before serving. Makes 6 servings.
　　　Denise Barteet, Caddo
Council, Shreveport, La.

CHICKEN WITH MUSHROOMS
(Moo Goo Gai Pan)

4 chicken breast halves, boned, skinned and cut into 1/2-inch cubes
2 scallions, cut into 1/2-inch slices
1 Tbsp. vegetable oil
12 snow pea pods, strings removed
6 water chestnuts, sliced
1/2 c. chicken broth
1/2 tsp. salt

1/4 c. dry white wine
1/2 tsp. salt
1/2 c. celery, cut into 1/2-inch slices
1/4 lb. mushrooms, sliced into "T" shapes
1 Tbsp. cornstarch in 2 Tbsp. cold water
Whole blanched almonds (optional)

Combine chicken with wine and 1/2 teaspoon salt, set aside. Stir-fry scallions and celery in oil for about 1 minute, set aside. Stir-fry pea pods 2 minutes, set aside. Stir-fry mushrooms and water chestnuts 1-2 minutes, set aside. Stir-fry chicken and wine for 2 or 3 minutes or until chicken is done. Combine chicken and vegetables in pan or wok. Stir together broth, cornstarch mixture and other 1/2 teaspoon salt. Add slowly to the chicken and vegetables. Heat until thickened and clear. Serve over rice and sprinkle with almonds, if desired. Serves 4.

Connie Younker
Shreveport Works Council
Shreveport, La.

OVEN FRIED CHICKEN

1 fryer, cut up
1 tsp. salt
1/4 tsp. garlic salt
1/2 c. (1 stick) oleo

1/3 c. flour
1 tsp. paprika
1/8 tsp. black pepper

Wash chicken, drain and pat dry. Mix together flour, salt, paprika, garlic salt, pepper. Roll chicken in mixture. Melt butter in baking dish. Place pieces with skin down in melted butter. Bake at 400° for 45 minutes, or until done.

Calcasieu Council
Lake Charles, La.

CHICKEN PAPRIKAS

1 onion, chopped
1 Tbsp. paprika
2 Tbsp. salt
1 1/2 c. water

4 Tbsp. shortening
1 tsp. black pepper
4-5 lb. chicken, disjointed
1 pt. sour cream

Brown onion in shortening, add seasoning and chicken, brown 10 minutes. Add water, cover and let simmer slowly until tender. Remove chicken, add sour cream to drippings in pan and mix well. Add dumplings, arrange chicken on top. Heat through and serve.

Dumplings:

3 eggs, beaten
1 Tbsp. salt

3 c. flour
1/2 c. water

Mix all ingredients together and beat with a spoon. Drop batter by teaspoonfuls into boiling salted water. Cook about 10 minutes, drain, rinse with cold water. Drain well, add to paprikas.

Sheila Stroupe, Metairie
Council, Metairie, La.

PEACHY CHICKEN

Chicken pieces
1 strip bacon
Onion salt

1 can peach halves
Celery salt

Fry bacon in deep skillet; reserve. Season chicken with celery and onion salt. Brown in bacon drippings. Add peaches and syrup. Simmer chicken until very tender and liquid is reduced. Transfer to serving dish and garnish golden brown peach halves with crumbled bacon. I serve this with wild rice and it's always a big hit.

Enola Fee, Crescent City
Council, New Orleans, La.

CHICKEN POT PIE

3 c. plain flour
1 1/3 c. shortening
Ice water

3 tsp. baking powder
Dash of salt
1 egg, beaten

Cut shortening in flour and salt, add egg, then enough ice water to make texture of pie dough. Roll out 2 crusts; enough for top and bottom.

Filling:

1 hen
2 c. celery
4 boiled eggs
Salt and pepper to taste

1 block oleo
3 c. onions
4 Tbsp. flour
Chicken broth

Boil chicken covered with water, add salt, pepper, onions and celery. Boil until tender. Remove and debone. In another pot, add block of butter or oleo. Melt, stir in flour, then some of the chicken broth, stirring to make smooth. Cut eggs into 8 pieces each and add to mixture. Add deboned chicken. Mix well and pour into bottom crust. Cover with top crust. Bake in top shelf of oven at 375° until light brown and crusts are done.

Genevieve Whitehead, Capital
Council, Baton Rouge, La.

CHICKEN RATATOUILLE

1/4 c. Mazola corn oil
1 large onion, thinly
  sliced
1/2 lb. mushrooms,
  thinly sliced
2 small zucchini squash,
  unpeeled, thinly sliced
1 medium green pepper,
  seeded and cut in
  1-inch pieces

2 whole broiler-fryer chicken
  breasts, skinned, boned
  and cut in 1-inch pieces
1 small eggplant, peeled and
  cut into 1-inch cubes
1 (16 oz.) can tomato wedges
2 Tbsp. garlic salt
1 tsp. dried parsley
1/2 tsp. black pepper
1 tsp. Accent flavor or MSG

Heat corn oil in large fry pan. Add chicken and saute about 2 minutes on each side. Add zucchini, eggplant, onion, green pepper and mushrooms. Cook, stirring occasionally, about 15 minutes or until tender-crisp. Add tomatoes, stirring carefully. Add garlic salt, Accent, basil, parsley and pepper. Simmer about 5 minutes, or until fork can be inserted in chicken with ease. Serves 4.

Rebecca Scott Bockmon, Caddo
Council, Shreveport, La.

CHICKEN RAVIOLI

1 chicken
1 c. chopped celery
1 stick oleo, divided
1 can cream of mush-
  room soup

1 c. onions, chopped
1 c. chopped bell pepper
1 small pkg. egg noodles
Cheese slices

Boil chicken in water until tender, remove and debone. Reserve broth. Place onion, celery and bell pepper in skillet with 1/2 stick oleo and 1 cup chicken broth. Simmer until tender. Add mushroom soup. Cook noodles and 1/2 stick oleo in remaining chicken broth. Drain and mix all ingredients together except cheese. Place in casserole dish and top with cheese slices. Bake in 400° oven until hot and cheese melts.

Mary R. Quimby, Ouachita
Council, Monroe, La.

CHICKEN RAVIOLI OR WHATEVER

1 large fat fryer or
   tender hen, not too fat
1 large onion, chopped
1 jar pimientos, chopped

1 large pkg. egg noodles
1 bell pepper, chopped
1 c. celery, chopped
1/2 lb. grated cheese

Boil chicken until tender. Remove and debone. Skim some of fat from broth, place in pan. Saute onion, bell pepper, celery and pimiento in this fat. Add egg noodles to broth left in pot and cook until tender, drain. Add vegetable mixture and chicken to noodles, mix well. Place in casserole and cover with cheese. Place in oven and bake until cheese melts and casserole is heated through. Serve hot. This can be prepared and frozen. Keeps well.

Maxine Fletcher, Ouachita
Council, Monroe, La.

CHICKEN ROCHAMBEAU

2 chickens (2 1/2 lb.)
1 1/2 sticks butter
1 tsp. garlic, minced
2 c. chicken stock
1 Tbsp. Worcestershire
   sauce
Dash of cayenne pepper
4 Holland rusks

Seasoned flour
1 c. green onion, minced
2 Tbsp. flour
1/2 c. chopped mushrooms
1/2 tsp. salt
1/2 c. burgundy
1/2 lb. sliced, boiled ham
1/2 c. bearnaise sauce

Disjoint and bone chicken, using neck, skin and bones to make stock. Dredge chicken in seasoned flour and saute in butter until golden brown and tender. Keep warm in covered dish. Saute onions and garlic in remaining butter drippings. Add flour and brown well. Blend in chicken stock and mushrooms, simmer 15 minutes. Add Worcestershire sauce, salt, wine and cayenne pepper and heat through. Arrange Holland rusks on platter, cover with ham slices. Pour chicken sauce over ham, arrange chicken pieces on sauce and cover with bearnaise sauce. Serves 4.

Lois Leger, Evangeline
Council, Lafayette, La.

SAUCE PIQUANTE

4-5 lb. chicken
1 c. chopped celery
1 c. chopped bell pepper
1 small can tomato paste
1 tsp. sugar
5 c. water
2 cans crabmeat
3 cans shrimp, drained

2 c. chopped onion
4 cloves garlic, finely
  chopped
1 can Ro-Tel tomatoes
Salt and red pepper to taste
1 small can mushrooms
  (optional)
Onion tops and parsley
  (optional)

Saute chicken until meat comes off the bone, remove from pot and debone. Add onion, celery, 4 cloves garlic and bell pepper to drippings in pot and saute in chicken fat until clear. Add deboned chicken, tomatoes, tomato paste, salt, red pepper and sugar; simmer 5-10 minutes. Add 4 cloves garlic, onion tops, mushrooms and parsley. Add water; more water may be necessary, add according to desired thickness. Cook, slow heat, for 3-4 hours. Approximately 20 minutes before serving, add crabmeat and shrimp. Season to taste and serve over rice.   Bill Baptist, Ozone Council,
                                   Hammond, La.

SAUCE PIQUANTE

4-5 lb. chicken, turtle,
  rabbit or shrimp
1 large can whole tomatoes
1 (8 oz.) can tomato paste
2 c. chopped celery
1 (4 oz.) can mushrooms
1/2 c. onion tops and
  parsley, chopped
Salt, Tabasco sauce and
  black pepper

1 c. cooking oil
1 large can tomato juice
2 cans (8 oz. size) tomato
  sauce
2 c. chopped onions
4 cloves garlic, chopped
  finely
7 c. water
1 tsp. sugar
1 c. chopped bell pepper

Cook meat in oil over low fire until tender and done. Remove meat and set aside. Add onions, celery and bell peppers to oil. Cook slowly until wilted. Add tomato juice, whole tomatoes, tomato sauce, tomato paste and 5 cups water. Cook over medium fire until oil floats above tomatoes. Add meat, mushrooms, sugar and garlic. Season to taste with salt, black pepper and Tabasco sauce, leaning heavily on Tabasco sauce to give pep. Add remaining 2 cups water.

Cook about 1/2 hour on medium fire until well done. Add parsley and onion tops a few minutes before sauce is done. Serves 12.

Randal Malbrough
Crescent City Council
New Orleans, La.

SAUCE PIQUANTE

4-5 lb. chicken, turtle
  or shrimp
1 large can whole tomatoes
1 (6 oz.) can tomato paste
2 c. chopped celery
1 (4 oz.) can mushrooms
1/2 c. green onion tops
  and parsley
1 c. chopped bell pepper

1 c. cooking oil
1 large can tomto juice
2 cans (8 oz. size) tomato
  sauce
2 c. chopped onions
4 cloves garlic, minced
7 c. water
1 tsp. sugar
Salt, red and black pepper
  to taste

Cook meat in oil over low fire until tender. Remove and set aside. Add onions, celery and bell pepper to oil. Saute until soft. Add tomatoes, juice, sauce and paste. Add about 5 cups water. Cook on medium heat until oil floats above tomatoes. Add meat, mushrooms, sugar and garlic. Season to taste with salt and pepper, leaning heavy on red pepper. Add remaining water. Cook about 1/2 hour on medium heat or until done. Add parsley and onion tops about 5 minutes before sauce is done. Serves 12.

Pam Marchese, Metairie
Council, Metairie, La.

CHICKEN WITH SAUSAGE SAUCE

2 Tbsp. sherry
1/4 lb. pecans
1 small white onion,
  chopped
1/4 lb. pork sausage
2 tsp. water

8 whole chicken breasts
1 Tbsp. flour
2 c. chicken stock
1 Tbsp. Kitchen Bouquet
Salt and pepper

Salt and pepper chicken breasts. Bake in uncovered pan in 1 cup chicken stock at 350° for 15 minutes. Cover pan and steam about 25 minutes. Cook sausage in frying pan. Remove sausage meat, brown onions in sausage grease. Put cooked sausage, onion and remaining stock into blender and blend. Stir in Kitchen Bouquet and flour. Add pecans and sherry. Pour over cooked chicken. Makes 8 servings.

Lois Leger, Evangeline
Council, Lafayette, La.

CHICKEN AND SPAGHETTI

2 fryers
1 c. celery
1/2 c. pimiento
1 (10 oz.) pkg. spaghetti

1 c. bell pepper
1 c. onions
2 cans mushroom soup
3 1/2 c. grated Cheddar
cheese

Boil fryers. Bone and cut up in small pieces. Save 1 quart of broth; strain. Add cut up bell pepper, onion and celery to strained broth. Cook until done. Add pimiento, soup and spaghetti. Cook in broth until done. Spread 1 layer of spaghetti in bottom of casserole, next a layer of cheese and a layer of chicken. Repeat layers until mixture is used up. Bake at 350° about 25 minutes.

Gayle Wilkening
Shreveport Works Council
Longview, Tx.

CHICKEN SPAGHETTI

1 (3 lb.) broiler-fryer,
cut up
1 tsp. oregano
1 tsp. salt
1 (4 oz.) can mushrooms
Grated Parmesan cheese
1 medium onion, chopped

1 medium garlic, crushed
1 (15 oz.) can tomato sauce
4 oz. spaghetti
3/4 c. water
1/4 tsp. hot pepper sauce
2 Tbsp. oil

In Dutch oven, brown chicken in oil. Add onion and garlic, saute. Stir in water, tomato sauce, mushrooms, oregano, salt and pepper sauce. Cover and bake at 350° for 30 minutes. Stir in spaghetti. Cover and bake 30 minutes longer or until tender, stirring occasionally. Serve with Parmesan cheese.

Microwave: Cook onion and garlic in oil in 3-quart round casserole 5 minutes until tender. Add unbrowned chicken, using only 3/4 cup water. Cover, cook 15 minutes, stir in spaghetti and cook 15 minutes or until tender.

Della Delposen, Ouachita
Council, Monroe, La.

CHICKEN SPAGHETTI

1 chicken
3/4 c. bell pepper, chopped
2 qt. chicken broth
1 pkg. spaghetti
3/4 c. chopped celery
2 cubes chicken bouillon
1 lb. Velveeta cheese with
  peppers

Boil chicken in water. Remove and debone. Add chicken cubes to broth; should be 2 quarts broth. Cook spaghetti in broth. Add remaining ingredients.

Gail Cummings, Caddo
Council, Shreveport, La.

CHICKEN AND SPAGHETTI

1 large hen
1 c. diced celery
1 large chopped onion
Garlic
1 lb. grated cheese
2 (No. 2) cans tomatoes
2 medium chopped bell
  peppers
1 large can diced mushrooms
1 pkg. spaghetti

Cook hen in water until tender. Remove and debone. Skim fat from broth to use in sauce. Combine fat, tomatoes, celery, bell peppers, onion, mushrooms and garlic. Simmer about 3 hours, adding broth if needed. Cook spaghetti in chicken broth, drain. Layer spaghetti, chicken, sauce and cheese. Put last layer of cheese on just before serving.

Vickie Hidalgo, Capital
Council, Baton Rouge, La.

CHICKEN SPAGHETTI

1 large hen
4 green peppers, chopped
2 c. chopped celery
1 can mushrooms
Salt and pepper to taste
4 large onions, chopped
1 large can pimentos
1 (7 or 8 oz.) pkg. spaghetti
1 lb. grated American cheese

Cook hen until tender in plenty of water. Remove and debone. Simmer celery, onions and green peppers in chicken stock until tender. Cook spaghetti in remainder of chicken stock and salt and pepper to taste. Dice chicken, mushrooms and pimento, add to vegetables and spaghetti.

Add grated cheese to spaghetti while still warm. Reheat for 30 minutes at 320°. Will serve 15.

Molly Haskins, Caddo
Council, Shreveport, La.

CHICKEN AND SPAGHETTI

1 fryer
Garlic salt, pepper
1 pkg. spaghetti
Green chiles or jalapeno
   Cheez Whiz (optional)

Chopped onion
Chopped bell pepper
Chopped celery
1/2 lb. Velveeta cheese and
   pimiento

Boil fryer with garlic salt, pepper, onion, bell pepper and celery. Remove from broth when done and debone. Add spaghetti to broth and cook until nearly all broth is absorbed. Add chicken pieces, Velveeta cheese and about 1/2 can or jar jalapeno Cheez Whiz, if desired.

Jeanette English, Caddo
Council, Shreveport, La.

CHICKEN SPECTACULAR

3 c. cooked chicken
1 can cream of celery
   soup
1 medium (4 oz.) jar
   sliced pimientos
2 c. French style green
   beans, drained

1 pkg. Uncle Ben's combination wild and white rice,
   cooked
1 medium onion, chopped
1 c. Hellmann's mayonnaise
1 can water chestnuts, diced
Salt and pepper to taste

Mix all ingredients. Pour into 2 1/2 or 3-quart casserole. Bake 25-30 minutes at 350°. Serves 16. Freezes well, but do not cook prior to freezing.

Lela Bonner
Ouachita Council
Bastrop, La.

Aline Well
Capital Council
Baton Rouge, La.

Twila "Pete" Dysart
Ouachita Council
Monroe, La.

SPICY CHICKEN ORIENTAL

1 (16 oz.) can Chinese
   vegetables, drained
1 pkg. chicken breasts
   (about 2)
1 tsp. onion flakes

3/4 oz. Fritos corn chips,
   crushed
1/2 c. chicken broth
1 (16 oz.) can cut green
   beans, drained

290

1 (6 oz.) roll Kraft   1 tsp. celery salt
   jalapeno cheese spread

Boil chicken with onion flakes and celery salt until tender. Cool, skin, debone and cut chicken into bite size pieces. Reserve 1/2 cup chicken broth. Mix vegetables, green beans and chicken. Pour into greased casserole. Slice jalapeno roll over casserole mixture. Pour chicken broth over mixture. Sprinkle with crushed Fritos. Bake at 350° about 25 minutes. Makes 5 servings.

Estelle Banker, Capital
Council, Baton Rouge, La.

CHICKEN SUPREME

2 cut up fryers   2 c. raw rice
Salt and pepper to taste   2 cans onion soup
1 stick oleo, melted   1 c. water

Place rice in bottom of roaster. Dip or roll each piece of chicken in melted oleo until well coated, place chicken on top of rice. Add soups and water in skillet with remaining oleo. Bring to a boil and pour over chicken and rice. Bake covered in 300° oven for 45 minutes.

Rebecca Thames, Caddo
Council, Shreveport, La.

TARRAGON SMOKED CHICKEN

3 chickens   3 Tbsp. lemon juice
Garlic salt   Peanut oil
3 tsp. dried tarragon   Seasoned pepper

Rub chicken well with peanut oil. Combine 1 tablespoon lemon juice with 1 teaspoon tarragon and rub into cavity of each chicken. Sprinkle outside with garlic salt and seasoned pepper. Smoke 4-6 hours on lower rack of smoker.

Mearl S. Byles, Central
Council, Natchitoches, La.

CHICKEN TETRAZZINI

1 pkg. vermicelli or
  spaghetti
1 medium can mushrooms,
  stems and pieces,
  chopped fine
1 bunch green onions with
  tops, chopped fine
2 Tbsp. butter or oleo
1 pt. half & half
1/2 tsp. garlic powder

2 c. boned chicken, or
  3 cans boned chicken
1 medium green pepper,
  chopped fine
1 can mushroom soup
1 small can or jar pimiento,
  chopped or mashed fine
1 c. grated sharp cheese
1/2 tsp. salt

Saute onions and green pepers in butter while spaghetti is cooking. Add remaining ingredients, except cheese, to onion mixture, cook on low heat until well blended. Place cooked, drained spaghetti in 3-quart casserole. Pour mixture over top. Cover and bake at 350° for 1 hour. Ten minutes before removing from oven, uncover and sprinkle with grated cheese. Bake uncovered remaining 10 minutes.

Louise Malone, Caddo Council,
Shreveport, La.

CHICKEN TETRAZZINI

1 large fryer
1 medium onion, chopped
1/2 c. chopped celery
1/2 c. chopped bell pepper
1 can cream of mush-
  room soup

1 small jar chopped pimiento
3/4 lb. Velveeta cheese
8 oz. pkg. spaghetti or
  egg noodles
Salt and pepper to taste

Cut up and boil fryer until tender. Remove from broth and remove chicken from bone. Add celery, onion and bell pepper to broth, cook until tender. Then add soup, pimiento, cut up chicken, cheese and cooked spaghetti. Heat slowly until cheese is melted.

Calcasieu Council
Lake Charles, La.

CORNISH HENS AND GRAVY

1 bunch parsley
1/2 c. water
1 c. whipping cream
Salt and pepper

2 Cornish hens
2 pats butter or oleo
1/2 stick oleo or butter

Rub salt and pepper inside and out on Cornish hens. Place 1 pat of butter in each. Divide parsley in half and stuff in cavity of each hen. This is your tenderizer. Brown in 1/2 stick oleo over medium heat in heavy Dutch oven. Turn fire to low. Add water and cover. Cook 45 minutes. Remove hens and add whipping cream to remaining liquid. Stir until thickened. The parsley can be removed for separate vegetable dish if desired. The hens are very tender and delicious served with this special gravy.

Marilou Bridges, Caddo
Council, Shreveport, La.

CORNISH HENS AND WILD RICE

4 Cornish hens
2 bunches shallots,
  chopped
Slivered almonds
Salt and pepper
Fresh parsley

Apricot brandy
Mushrooms
Oleo
Wild rice or wild and long
  grain

Clean hens; salt and pepper outside and cavity. Saute shallots in oleo. Chop giblets and parsley, saute all in oleo until soft. Bring rice to a boil, add sauteed ingredients. Add mushrooms. Let cook until rice is soft and dry. Add almonds. Stuff cavity of hens with this mixture. Tie legs together. Melt more oleo and add apricot brandy, put plenty on outside of hens. Place hens on rack of oven pan with at least 1 inch of water in bottom to steam up. Bake at 350° about 45 minutes until golden brown. You may continue adding melted oleo and brandy. Above can be prepared in advance for dinner guests and when they arrive, start baking. Serve with acorn squash and Peggy's Special Salad for a gourmet autumn dinner.

Peggy M. Childers
Crescent City Council
New Orleans, La.

ORANGE ROAST DUCK

Ducks
Salt, pepper, sage
Brandy or white wine
Olive oil

Fresh whole oranges
Frozen orange juice concentrate

Rub ducks inside and out with olive oil and equal parts of salt, pepper and sage. Place 1/4 orange in cavity of each duck. Place ducks in uncovered pan in preheated 450° oven for 1/2 hour. Mix frozen orange juice concentrate with enough brandy or white wine to make slightly less concentrated. Baste ducks with orange mixture at end of 1/2 hour cooking time. Cover ducks, lower heat to 350°. Baste with orange mixture every 10 minutes. Cook about 1/2 - 1 hour, depending on how you want ducks cooked. Test breast of duck with fork for doneness desired.

Ed Kimble, Crescent City
Council, New Orleans, La.

ROAST GOOSE

1 wild goose
Salt and pepper
3/4 c. chopped onion
1/4 c. sugar
1/4 tsp. sage
12 c. dry bread crumbs
Bacon fat

1 can beef broth
2 c. chopped apple
1/2 c. chopped celery
2 Tbsp. butter
1/8 tsp. nutmeg
Dash of cinnamon

Wash goose, pat dry. Sprinkle with salt and pepper. Combine beef broth, apple, onion, celery, sugar, butter, sage, nutmeg and cinnamon. Simmer over low fire 10 minutes. Pour mixture slowly over bread crumbs, mixing well. Spoon stuffing lightly into goose cavity, close opening with skewers. Place goose breast up on rack in roasting pan. Cover breast with cheesecloth soaked in bacon fat. Roast at 325° for 20-25 minutes per pound or until tender, basting frequently with pan drippings. Remove cheesecloth and skewers, let stand 10 minutes before carving.

W. A. Foreman, Ouachita
Council, Monroe, La.

PARTRIDGE IN MUSHROOM SAUCE

1 c. all-purpose flour
1 tsp. pepper
3/4 c. vegetable oil
3-4 partridges, cut up

1 tsp. salt
1/2 c. milk
1 can golden mushroom soup
1 c. water

Combine flour, salt and pepper. Dip partridge pieces into milk, then roll in flour mixture. Brown pieces in oil. Place browned partridge pieces in 13x9-inch buttered baking dish. Combine soup and water. Pour over partridge. Cover and bake at 350° for 1 hour or until tender, basting once or twice with mushroom sauce. Makes 4-6 servings.

W. A. Foreman, Ouachita
Council, Monroe, La.

SAUSAGE AND CHICKEN JAMBALAYA

4 chicken breasts
1 bell pepper
2 cans beef consomme
2 Tbsp. butter or oleo

1 c. rice
1 onion
1 lb. pkg. hot sausage

Saute sliced pepper, onion and hot sausage in butter 5 minutes. In 9x13-inch pan, mix consomme and rice. Add sausage mixture. Place chicken breasts on top and cover with foil. Bake at 350° for 1 hour, uncover and bake additional 30 minutes. Serves 4. Mona Williams, Capital
Council, Baton Rouge, La.

ORIENTAL TURKEY

1 (4 lb.) turkey breast
1 can golden mushroom
  soup
1 Tbsp. soy sauce
1/8 tsp. ground ginger
1 (16 oz.) can Chinese
  vegetables, drained

2 Tbsp. shortening
2 Tbsp. dry sherry
1 large clove garlic, minced
1 (10 oz.) pkg. frozen
  broccoli spears, partially
  thawed and cut into 1-inch
  pieces

Brown turkey in shortening in large heavy pan; drain. Arrange turkey, breast side down. Add soup, sherry, soy sauce, garlic and ginger. Cover, cook over low heat 1 hour. Turn turkey breast up. Add broccoli and Chinese vegetables, cook 30 minutes more or until done. Stir occasionally.

Remove turkey and vegetables to warm serving platter.
Thicken sauce if desired. Makes 4-6 servings, or more.

Ann Orr, Evangeline
Council, New Iberia, La.

TURKEY POULET

4 c. cut up turkey (left-
over baked turkey)
1 can mushrooms, stems
and pieces, drained
4 Tbsp. oleo
1 1/2 c. grated yellow
cheese
2 Tbsp. chopped green
onion tops (optional)

2 cans cream of mushroom
soup
1 or 2 cans drained asparagus
spears
4 Tbsp. white wine
12 slices cooked bacon,
crumbled
2 Tbsp. chopped parsley
1/2 c. chopped celery

Saute celery, parsley and onion in butter on low fire,
covered, until soft, not brown. Add soup and mushrooms.
When soup is well heated, add 1/2 cup cheese, stir until
melted. Add wine. Place turkey in large or 8 small individual
casserole dishes. Cover with bacon and asparagus. Pour
soup mixture on top. Sprinkle with remaining cheese. Place
under broiler until cheese melts and is slightly brown.
Makes 6-8 servings. Green salad and rolls make a complete
meal. Leftover baked chicken can also be substituted.

Isabelle Stenger, Capital
Council, Baton Rouge, La.

CRABMEAT AU GRATIN

1 stalk celery, chopped
fine
1 lb. oleo
1 large can evaporated
milk
1 tsp. salt
1/4 tsp. black pepper

1 medium onion, chopped fine
1/2 c. flour
2 egg yolks
1/2 tsp. red pepper
1 lb. lump crabmeat
1/4 lb. grated American
cheese

Saute onions and celery in oleo until melted. Blend
flour in with this mixture. Pour in milk gradually, stirring
constantly. Add egg yolks, salt and peppers. Cook 5 minutes. Put crabmeat in bowl suitable for mixing and pour the
cooked sauce over crabmeat. Mix well and transfer to

lightly greased casserole and sprinkle with grated cheese.
Bake at 350° for 10-15 minutes or until light brown.

Doris Reeves, Capital
Council, Baton Rouge, La.

Mary Bonner, Caddo
Council, Shreveport, La.

CRAB AU GRATIN

1/2 lb. crabmeat
1 small onion, finely
chopped
1 1/4 c. milk
1/2 tsp. mustard
2 tsp. lemon juice
1/2 c. Cheddar cheese,
finely grated

3 Tbsp. butter
1/4 c. flour
Salt and pepper
Dash of Worcestershire sauce
1/2 c. fresh bread crumbs
Paprika
Parsley sprigs
Slices of lemon

Flake the crabmeat. If using fresh crab, remove all
meat, brown and white, from shells and claws. Melt butter
and fry onion until soft. Stir in flour and cook 1 minute.
Add milk and bring to a boil. Stir in salt, pepper, mustard,
Worcestershire sauce and lemon juice, simmer for 2 minutes.
Add crabmeat and heat thoroughly. Spoon into 4-6 small
flameproof dishes or scallop shells. Mix bread crumbs with
cheese and a good shake of paprika. Spoon over crab mixture. Place under broiler or grill until topping is well
browned. Garnish with parsley sprigs and lemon slices.
Serves 4-6.

Trina Gubancsik, Capital
Council, Baton Rouge, La.

CRABMEAT AU GRATIN

2 lb. crabmeat
1/2 c. mushrooms
1 c. milk
Grated American cheese

1/2 stick butter
1 c. light cream
4 Tbsp. flour
Salt and pepper to taste

Melt butter, add flour. Add milk and cream, cook until
thick. Add cheese, crabmeat, mushrooms, salt and pepper
to taste. Pour in casserole dish, sprinkle cheese on top.
Bake 15 minutes at 350°.

Leigh Hargis, LeBayou
Council, Lockport, La.

CRABMEAT AU GRATIN

1 lb. fresh or canned
  crabmeat
1 stick butter
1 pt. breakfast cream
2 ribs celery, chopped
3 Tbsp. white wine

1 bunch green onions,
  chopped (shallots)
2 Tbsp. flour
1/2 lb. Swiss cheese, grated
Salt, pepper and cayenne
  pepper to taste

Saute onions and celery in butter until soft. Add flour, blend. Add crabmeat and cheese, blend. Add breakfast cream. Simmer on top of stove until mixture becomes creamy, about 10 minutes. Remove from heat, add wine, salt, pepper and cayenne pepper. Keep warm in chafing dish and serve on Encore crackers.

Dorothy Zimmer, Chapter Past
President Pioneer Partner
New Orleans, La.

CRABMEAT AU GRATIN

1 stalk celery, chopped fine
1 c. onion, chopped fine
2 cloves garlic, chopped
  fine
2 c. whole milk
1 tsp. salt
1/4 tsp. black pepper
1 lb. white or lump crab-
  meat

1/2 stick butter
1/2 small bell pepper,
  chopped fine
1/4 c. all-purpose flour
2 egg yolks, well beaten
1/2 tsp. red pepper
1/4 c. grated Cheddar
  cheese

Saute vegetables in butter until well done, but not brown. Blend flour well into mixture. Pour in milk gradually and stirring constantly. Add egg yolks, salt, red and black peppers and cook for 5 minutes. Add crabmeat to sauce, blend well and transfer into a lightly greased casserole dish. Sprinkle top with cheese and bake in 375° oven for 15 or 20 minutes or until light brown. Serves 4-6.

Sandy Lemoine, Capital
Council, Baton Rouge, La.

CRABMEAT AU GRATIN

1 lb. crabmeat
1 stalk celery, chopped
2 green onions, chopped
1 can cream of mushroom
  soup
1/2 c. white wine

8 Tbsp. butter
2 onions, chopped
2 Tbsp. parsley
1 can mushroom pieces
1 c. grated American
  cheese

Saute onion and celery in butter until soft. Add crabmeat, soup and mushrooms. Blend well, add remaining ingredients. Mix and pour into casserole dish. Bake at 350° until hot and bubbly.   Dolly Daly, Crescent City
                                Council, New Orleans, La.

BAKED AVOCADOS WITH CRAB

2 Tbsp. butter
4-5 oz. crabmeat
1-3 Tbsp. cream
Paprika
1/4 c. finely grated
  Cheddar cheese

1 small onion, finely
  chopped
3 Tbsp. fresh bread crumbs
Salt and pepper to taste
2 ripe avocados
Parsley sprigs to garnish

Melt butter in pan and fry onion until soft. Add crabmeat and cook gently 3-4 minutes, stirring frequently. Stir in bread crumbs, cream, salt, pepper and paprika. Halve avocados and remove stones. Place halves in baking dish. Spoon crab mixture into avocados. Sprinkle with cheese. Bake at 350°-400° for 15-20 minutes. Serve hot, garnished with parsley.   Karen Gubancsik, Capital
                                Council, Baton Rouge, La.

CRAB AND SHRIMP AU GRATIN

4 Tbsp. all-purpose flour
1/2 tsp. pepper
1/3 c. process cheese
  spread
1 c. Cheddar cheese,
  shredded

1/2 tsp. salt
2 c. milk
1/8 tsp. hot sauce
1/4 lb. crabmeat
1/2 lb. cooked shrimp
Cooked rice

Combine flour, salt, pepper and 1 cup milk. Stir until smooth. Combine cheese spread and remaining milk in top of double boiler, cook over hot water until cheese melts.

Add flour mixture and hot sauce to cheese mixture, stir until smooth. Add shrimp and crabmeat. Pour into a greased 1 1/2-quart casserole and top with shredded cheese. Bake at 350° for 20 minutes. Serve over rice. Serves 4.

Mrs. Larry D. Chambers
Metairie Council, Slidell, La.

MARINATED CRABS

2 doz. boiled crabs
2 stalks celery, chopped
1/2 large bell pepper, chopped
3 or 4 dashes wine vinegar
3 dashes Worcestershire sauce
1 1/2 tsp. pepper

6 green onions, chopped
8 cloves garlic, minced
2 1/2 c. olive oil
3 tsp. Pick-A-Pepper sauce
1 1/2 tsp. salt
1/4 tsp. seafood seasoning
1/4 c. white sauterne wine

Crack and clean claws, reserve meat. Put cleaned crabs and claw meat into large Tupperware bowl. Add all ingredients, shake well. Marinate at least 3 days or as long as a week in refrigerator. Shake well each day to blend. Serve in bowls 4-6 pieces each. Serve with hot garlic bread or Italian bread. Pick and eat crabs with fingers and dip bread into sauce and eat chopped seasonings.

Joyce Hattier, Magnolia
Council, New Orleans, La.

CRABMEAT QUICHE

1 unbaked pie shell
2 c. half & half
2 c. grated Swiss cheese
Salt and pepper to taste

1 lb. crabmeat
4 eggs
1/2 tsp. red pepper
2 large onions, minced

Place crabmeat over bottom of pie shell, sprinkle onion and then cheese on top. Beat eggs with salt and cream. Pour egg mixture over all. Bake in preheated 425° oven for 5 minutes. Reduce heat to 350° and cook until firm. Foil can be placed over crust to prevent burning. Slice and serve with sweet type of salad, such as pineapple.

Etta Williams, Magnolia
Council, New Orleans, La.

CRAB AND RICE

3 Tbsp. olive oil
1 medium rib celery,
  chopped fine
1 (7 1/2 oz.) can tendon
  free king crab
1 lb. can tomatoes, un-
  drained
1 1/2 c. water
1/4 tsp. pepper
1 tsp. ground coriander

1 medium size onion, chopped
  fine
1 small green pepper,
  chopped fine
1 clove garlic, minced
1/2 c. converted rice
1 tsp. salt
1/2 tsp. dried crushed
  oregano

Saute onion, celery and green pepper in hot oil gently until wilted or glazed. Add drained crab liquid. Add remaining ingredients, except crabmeat, and mix well. Bring to gentle boil, then simmer, covered, until rice is tender and most of liquid is absorbed, approximately 20 minutes. Break up crabmeat and stir in, remove from heat, covered, about 5 minutes to warm the crab. Nice served in wide soup bowls. Serves 3 or 4.   Mrs. Iuka Goetz, Capital Council, New Orleans, La.

CRAB SOUFFLE WITH GREEN PEPPERS

3 Tbsp. butter
4 Tbsp. flour
1 1/4 c. milk or chicken
  stock
Salt and pepper to taste
1 c. cleaned crabmeat
1 Tbsp. sherry

6 egg yolks
8 egg whites
1/8 tsp. cream of tartar
Pinch of salt
1/2 green pepper, chopped
1/4 c. finely grated Par-
  mesan cheese

Simmer green pepper 10 minutes, drain and immediately add cold water to pan. This keeps pepper green and fresh. Melt butter, add flour, add milk or chicken stock gradually. Remove pan from heat and add egg yolks, 1 at a time. Add drained peppers, crabmeat and sherry to sauce. Add salt and pepper to taste. Beat egg whites with pinch of salt and cream of tartar until stiff. Fold the sauce into egg whites and fill the prepared 6-cup souffle dish. Dust surface of unbaked souffle with Parmesan cheese. Place in preheated 400° oven, reduce heat to 375° immediately and bake for 25 minutes. Serve with Mornay Sauce (recipe follows). A tossed salad and crusty bread will complete the meal.

Mornay Sauce:

1 Tbsp. butter
1 Tbsp. flour
1 Tbsp. grated Parmesan
   cheese
Salt and pepper to taste

1 c. milk
3 Tbsp. grated Swiss or
   Gruyere cheese
1/2 tsp. prepared mustard
   (Dijon type)

Melt butter in saucepan. Remove from heat. Add flour, stirring with wire whisk. Return to moderate heat. Add milk gradually, stirring constantly until sauce is thickened. Add remaining ingredients, salt and pepper to taste.

Peggy Childers
Crescent City Council
New Orleans, La.

CRAB STUFFING

1 lb. crabmeat, fresh or
   frozen
1/3 c. chopped celery
1/3 c. melted fat
2 c. bread cubes
3 eggs, beaten

1/2 c. chopped onion
1/3 c. chopped green pepper
2 cloves garlic, finely chopped
1 Tbsp. chopped parsley
1/2 tsp. pepper
2 tsp. salt

Drain crabmeat. Cook onion, celery, green pepper and garlic in fat until tender. Combine bread cubes, eggs, parsley, salt, pepper, cooked vegetables and crabmeat. Mix well. Fill crab shells with mixture, bake at 350° for about 30 minutes. This can be used as a casserole.

Calcasieu Council
Lake Charles, La.

STUFFED EGGPLANT WITH CRABMEAT

1 c. mixed onions and
   celery, minced
1 egg
1 c. crabmeat
Butter

2 Tbsp. oil
1 c. cracker crumbs
2 eggplants
Lemon juice
Salt and pepper

Saute and brown onions and celery with 1 tablespoon oil for a few minutes, add cracker crumbs and brown more. Boil eggplant until tender, remove pulp from skin, chop and add to onions and celery. Add beaten egg, remaining oil

and season with salt and pepper. Mix well and place back in eggplant shell. Bake at 350° for 1/2 hour. Sprinkle crabmeat with lemon juice. Saute in butter. Spread crab-meat over stuffed eggplant shells and bake for additional 15 minutes.
Mrs. Ray Ducharme, Caddo Council, Shreveport, La.

BOILED CRAWFISH

2 large onions, sliced
12 lemons, sliced
1 clove garlic, chopped
2 bottles (4 oz. size) Zatarain's liquid crab boil

2 boxes salt (26 oz. size)
1 (6 oz.) bottle hot sauce (additional bottle may be added if desired)
10 gal. water
40-50 lb. live crawfish

Mix all ingredients, except crawfish, with water in large tub or pot. Boil for 10-15 minutes to extract the flavors. Add prepared live crawfish. Bring to a boil, cover and cook 15 minutes, stirring occasionally. Turn heat off and let crawfish stand in water for about 10 minutes; sample and let stand longer if more seasoning is desired. When properly seasoned, remove crawfish from water. To make a complete meal, try adding about 5 pounds of small red potatoes and/or several ears of sweet corn immediately before adding crawfish to boiling water.
Eugene Cottrell, Caddo Council, Shreveport, La.

CRAWFISH ETOUFFEE

2 lb. crawfish tails
1/4 c. oil
1 c. chopped onions
2 Tbsp. crawfish fat or more
2 tsp. cornstarch
1/4 c. parsley

1/4 lb. oleo
1/2 c. chopped celery
4 cloves garlic, chopped fine
2 c. cold water
1/4 c. chopped onion tops
Salt, pepper and cayenne pepper to taste

Season crawfish and set aside. Melt oleo, add season-ing, stirring constantly. Add crawfish and 1 1/2 cups water. Bring to boil, lower heat and cook slowly 30 min-utes, stirring occasionally. Dissolve cornstarch in remaining

1/2 cup water. Add to mixture. Add onion tops and parsley. Cook for additional 10 minutes. Serves 4.

Donna Leger, Evangeline
Council, Lafayette, La.

CRAWFISH ETOUFFEE

6 Tbsp. butter
2 c. onions, chopped
2 medium cloves garlic,
  minced (1/2 tsp.)
2 Tbsp. green pepper,
  chopped
2 Tbsp. minced parsley
  (1 tsp. dehydrated)
1/4 c. celery, chopped

2 Tbsp. green onion tops,
  chopped fine
1 lb. or 2 1/2 c. crawfish
  meat
1/4 c. crawfish fat (optional)
1 1/4 tsp. salt
1/4 tsp. black pepper
1/4 tsp. red pepper

Melt butter in iron skillet or heavy pot. Saute onions, garlic, green pepper and celery until onions are clear. Add 1/8 cup water and simmer covered until vegetables are tender, about 15 minutes. Add crawfish fat and cook covered for 15 minutes on very low heat. Stir occasionally. Add tails and other seasonings. Cook 15 minutes. Add green onion tops and parsley and cook 5 minutes for seasoning to blend. Serve with hot steamed rice. Makes 4-5 servings.

Eugene Cottrell, Caddo
Council, Shreveport, La.

CRAYFISH ETOUFFEE

1 lb. crayfish tails,
  cleaned
Crayfish fat
1 onion, chopped fine
2 cloves garlic, minced
Chopped parsley
1 stick oleo

1/2 Tbsp. flour
1 Tbsp. bell pepper, chopped
  fine
Green onion tops, chopped
  fine
Salt, red and black pepper
  to taste

Melt oleo in skillet, add flour and stir until blended. Add onion, bell pepper and garlic. Cook until tender. Add crayfish fat and cook about 15 minutes, stirring occasionally. Add crayfish tails, cover and simmer 20 minutes. Add seasonings, green onions and parsley. Cook over low heat until seasonings blend. Serve over rice.

Lydia M. Gremillian, Central
Council, Pineville, La.

FRIED CRAWFISH TAILS

1 lb. crawfish tail meat
1 1/2 c. plain flour
Red pepper sauce
Cooking oil

1/2 lemon
1 1/2 tsp. baking powder
3 tsp. creole seasoning

Place meat in pan and sprinkle lightly with Louisiana hot sauce or any mild red pepper sauce. Stir and repeat twice more. Do not saturate. Squeeze lemon on meat. Season with creole seasoning. Mix flour and baking powder and coat meat. Place meat in a sifter and shake off excess flour. Fry in hot oil at 385° in large fryer for 1 1/2 - 2 minutes until done, or 3-4 minutes in smaller fryer.

Eugene Cottrell, Caddo
Council, Shreveport, La.

CRAWFISH JAMBALAYA

3 lb. crawfish tails
2 sticks butter
2 Tbsp. flour
6 onions, minced
Crawfish fat

Chopped onion tops
Salt, black and red pepper
    to taste
3 c. cooked rice
Chopped parsley

Make roux of butter and flour. Brown a little bit. Add onions and simmer until soft. Add fat from crawfish, simmer a few minutes. Add tails, parsley, onion tops and seasonings. Cook for 15 minutes. When ready to serve, add cooked rice.

John E. Haygood, Caddo
Council, Shreveport, La.

CRAWFISH JAMBALAYA

1 lb. or 2 1/2 c. craw-
    fish tails
1 1/4 c. rice, uncooked
    (long grain)
1 Tbsp. flour
2 Tbsp. salad oil
1 c. onion, chopped fine
1/2 c. parsley (2 tsp.
    dehydrated)

1/2 c. green onion tops,
    chopped fine
1/2 c. celery, chopped
1/2 c. bell pepper, chopped
1/4 c. crawfish fat (optional)
1 1/2 c. water
2 1/2 tsp. salt
1/2 tsp. black pepper
1/4 tsp. red pepper

Brown flour in oil to a golden brown. Add onions. Stir

constantly until onions are almost cooked. Add 1 1/2 cups cold water and simmer for 1/2 hour. Add crawfish tails and fat. Cook until crawfish turns pink. Add about 2 cups of water and bring to a boil. When water is rapidly boiling, add remainder of ingredients. Stir to blend and cook on low heat covered for about 1/2 hour or until rice is tender. Five minutes before serving, use a 2-prong fork and fluff up jambalaya so that rice will have a tendency to fall apart. Makes 4-5 servings.　　　　　　　Eugene Cottrell, Caddo
Council, Shreveport, La.

PREPARING CRAWFISH FOR PEELING OR BOILING

1. Cover crawfish with water, gently stir and pour water off. 2. Cover crawfish with water and add 1 (26 ounce) box of salt. 3. Stir gently, let crawfish stand in the water for about 5 minutes to purge. Drain. 4. Pour boiling water over purged crawfish to kill them. Let crawfish remain in this water about 5 minutes or until they turn red. Remove from water and allow to cool. 5. Separate tail from the body. Peel tail to remove the meat. Devein by removing the fleshy strip along the outside curvature. 6. Crawfish fat is obtained by removing the 2 yellow pockets inside the head. Slightly open head and remove fat with a small spoon. Place in separate container. The fat can be used as required in crawfish recipe.　　　　　　　Eugene Cottrell, Caddo
Council, Shreveport, La.

EGG ROLLS

6 oz. lean pork, ham or roast pork	4 oz. shrimp, shredded
1/2 oz. shredded onion	1/2 lb. cabbage or bean sprouts
Cooking oil	20 egg roll skins
3 tsp. cornstarch	1 1/4 tsp. salt
1/2 c. soup stock	2 1/2 tsp. cold water
1 tsp. flour	1 1/2 tsp. soy sauce

Cut pork into strips. Marinate in 1/2 teaspoon soy sauce and 1 teaspoon cornstarch. Marinate shrimp in 1/4 teaspoon salt and 1 teaspoon cornstarch. Shred cabbage into string shapes about 1 1/2 inches long. Heat 5 teaspoons oil in frying pan, stir-fry pork about 1/2 minute. Drain and set aside. Fry shrimp in same oil until done, remove to bowl with pork. Add cabbage, stir-fry 1 minute.

Add remaining soy sauce, remaining salt and soup stock. Cover with lid and cook about 2 minutes. Add pork, shrimp and onions, stir-fry another 1/2 minute over high heat. Make paste of remaining cornstarch and 1 teaspoon water. Stir in mixture until thickened. Remove from heat. Place 2 teaspoons filling on each egg roll skin about 1 inch from edge that is toward you. Roll once or twice, then fold right side toward center, then left side toward center. Continue rolling into tight roll. Make up paste with flour and remaining water. Stick outer edge of skin to roll with paste. Place with this side face down to hold tightly and keep shape. Fry in deep hot fat about 3 minutes or until golden, about 10 at a time. Shiko Barron
New Orleans, La.

CHINESE EGG ROLLS

1 lb. pork, thin and
  chopped raw
1 can bean sprouts,
  rinsed
1/2 c. bamboo shoots,
  chopped
6 thin slices ginger root,
  chopped
1 Tbsp. soy sauce

1/2 lb. shrimp, chopped raw
16 whole green onions,
  chopped
16 water chestnuts, chopped
1 tsp. salt
1 Tbsp. sherry
1 pkg. egg roll sheets
  (approx. 22-24)
Cooking oil

Heat oil, add pork, stir-fry 1/2 - 2 minutes, until meat is white. Add shrimp, stir-fry 45 seconds. Remove meat and rechop. Add green onions, bamboo shoots, chestnuts and ginger to pot, stir-fry 1 - 1 1/2 minutes. Add bean sprouts, stir-fry 45 seconds. Return meat, add salt, soy sauce and sherry. Heat through. Remove and place mixture in colander to cool. Separate egg roll papers, 1 at a time, placing 1 heaping tablespoon of mixture near center of paper. Fold in ends like a diaper, then roll. Seal ends by dipping fingers in cold water and pressing against ends. Fry for 4-5 minutes in deep fat. Yield: Approximately 23 egg rolls. Betty Stevens, Gentilly
Council, New Orleans, La.

BARBECUED FISH

1 - 1 1/2 lb. fresh
   fish fillets
1/2 c. catsup
1 tsp. prepared horse-
   radish
Salt to taste

Juice of 1 lemon
1 Tbsp. parsley flakes
1 small onion, chopped fine
1 rib celery, chopped fine
Lemon pepper seasoning

Salt and lemon pepper fish fillets to taste. Place fillets in buttered baking dish. Combine remaining ingredients and pour over fish. Bake at 350° for 35 minutes or until fish flakes when pierced with a fork. Makes 4-6 servings.

Mona Reis, Metairie
Council, Metairie, La.

BASS WITH LOW CAL. STUFFING

3 lb. dressed bass
1 1/2 tsp. salt
2 Tbsp. melted fat or oil

Low Cal. Stuffing
Lemon wedges

Thaw frozen fish, clean, wash and dry. Sprinkle inside and out with salt. Stuff fish loosely. Close opening with toothpicks. Place on a greased pan, brush with fat. Bake at 350° for 40-60 minutes or until fish flakes when tested with fork. Wrap in foil to bake.

Low Cal. Stuffing:

3/4 c. chopped onion
1 1/2 Tbsp. oleo, melted
2 1/4 c. chopped, peeled
   apple
2 Tbsp. lemon juice

1/2 tsp. salt
1/3 c. chopped parsley
1/3 c. chopped celery
1/8 tsp. thyme

Cook onion in oleo until tender. Combine all ingredients and mix thoroughly. Makes approximately 3 cups stuffing.

Mearl S. Byles, Central
Council, Natchitoches, La.

CATFISH BARRIOS

6 mushrooms
1 small onion
4 stalks celery
1 block butter
2 lb. catfish

Salt
Pepper
Parsley flakes
1 Tbsp. flour
1 c. white cooking wine

Slice mushrooms, onions and celery paper thin. Place butter in deep frying pan and melt. Add mushrooms, onions and celery. Cook on low fire until tender. Add flour and wine to make gravy. Add salt and pepper to taste. When gravy begins to bubble, add fish which has been salted and peppered. Cook until fish is firm. Serve with French bread and beer.
Norman Barrios, West Bank
Council, Gretna, La.

FRIED CROSS LAKE CATFISH

2 catfish (8 oz. each)
Salt
Milani dill sauce

Yellow corn meal
White corn meal
Hot fat

Dip fish in Milani dill sauce and roll in mixture of salt, white and yellow corn meal. Refrigerate for several hours to set. Drop in 350° hot fat and cook 10-12 minutes or until fish floats. Serve with tartar sauce, sliced onions and hush puppies.
Mrs. Johnnie B. Cole, Caddo
Council, Shreveport, La.

FISH FILLETS

1 lb. fish fillets
3 Tbsp. vegetable oil
1 onion, chopped
3 Tbsp. parsley
1/2 tsp. basil or oregano

2 medium tomatoes, cut, or
  1 (8 oz.) can stewed
  tomatoes
1/2 c. water or tomato juice
1/2 tsp. salt
Dash of pepper

Thaw fish enough to separate. Heat oil and cook onion and parsley until golden. Add all but fish and cook until tomatoes are done. Add fish. Cover and cook about 10 minutes or until fish are done. Makes 4 servings.
Calcasieu Council
Lake Charles, La.

CHILE STUFFED FILLET OF SOLE

1 small chopped onion
1 c. fresh bread crumbs
1 egg, lightly beaten
Salt and pepper to taste
1 can Cheddar cheese soup

2 Tbsp. butter or oleo
1 (4 oz.) can Ortega diced green chiles
6 fillets of sole (approx. 2 lb.)

Saute onions in butter. Combine bread crumbs, chiles and sauteed onions in bowl. Stir in egg, salt and pepper. Spread some of this mixture evenly over each fillet, roll fillet and fasten with a toothpick. Set, seam side down, in a well greased 6x9 inch pan. Bake uncovered in preheated 350° oven for 15 minutes. Drain excess liquid. Spoon undiluted soup over fillets and continue baking for 15 minutes or until fish flakes. Serve hot. Makes 6 servings.

Denise Barteet, Caddo
Council, Shreveport, La.

SIMMERED OR POACHED FISH

4 large half slices of halibut steak, 1-inch thick
2 Tbsp. vinegar

1 Tbsp. peppercorns
6 bay leaves
1 Tbsp. salt
4 qt. water

In large pot, add water and all seasonings. Bring to a slow boil. Add halibut steaks and cook just under boil for 25-30 minutes. Serve with boiled parsley buttered potatoes. Serves 4. Any leftover fish and potatoes may be used to make "fish hash" with cream sauce; mustard and pepper as seasoning for the sauce.

June E. Nickels
Shreveport Works Council
Shreveport, La.

BEST FISH FRY BATTER

Salt and pepper
3-4 tsp. mustard
Fish (bream, bass, etc.)

Louisiana red hot sauce
Salt and pepper
Corn meal

Salt and pepper fish. Mix red hot sauce and mustard all over fish. Let set 30 minutes or more. Shake in corn meal well. Fry in deep hot fat. This amount per fish. This is good even on old fish that were frozen. Mary La Combe, Central

Council, Alexandria, La.

BROILED FLOUNDER

4 flounder (3/4 - 1 lb.)
  with heads removed
1 clove garlic, minced
Dash of Worcestershire
  sauce
3 Tbsp. chopped parsley
Dash of salt, paprika and
  black pepper

Juice of 3 lemons
4 Tbsp. finely chopped
  green onions
1/4 lb. butter
Marinade of lemon juice,
  Louisiana hot sauce and
  monosodium glutamate

Marinate the fish 2-3 hours in marinade. Score flounder fairly deep at 1 - 1 1/2 inch intervals on the diagonal in a cross hatched pattern. Salt and pepper fish. Set oven on broil. Make basting sauce of melted butter, lemon juice, onions, garlic, parsley, Worcestershire sauce, salt, paprika and pepper. Broil fish, basting with sauce for 20-30 minutes, depending on size. Keep skin side up and serve fish skin side up.
    Ann Orr, Evangeline
    Council, New Iberia, La.

STUFFED FLOUNDER

1 c. minced onion
1 1/2 c. minced celery
1/5 bunch chopped parsley
2 Tbsp. flour
1 c. dry white wine
1/2 c. lump crabmeat
Salt and pepper to taste
18 peeled, boiled shrimp

1/2 c. minced shallots
3 cloves minced garlic
1/2 lb. oleo
1 c. milk
1/2 c. chopped boiled shrimp
2 1/2 c. bread crumbs
6 flounders

Saute onion, shallots, celery, garlic and parsley in oleo. Add flour and blend well. Gradually stir in milk and wine, cooking until thickened. Add chopped shrimp and crabmeat and thicken further with bread crumbs. Season to taste. Split each flounder and fill with this dressing. Top each with 3 whole shrimp. Place under broiler about 20 minutes or until fish is cooked through. Serves 6.
    Floyd Shumann, Ozone
    Council, Hammond, La.

STUFFED FLOUNDER

Clean flounder and split lengthwise. Make stuffing:

1/4 c. chopped onion
1/4 c. chopped celery
4 oz. shrimp

4 oz. crab
3/4 c. bread crumbs
1 beaten egg

Blend all ingredients and fill slits in flounder. Cook in buttered baking dish 30 or 40 minutes in 350° oven.

Calcasieu Council
Lake Charles, La.

BAKED STUFFED FLOUNDER

1/2 c. chopped celery
1 clove minced garlic
1 stick butter
1/2 lb. boiled, chopped
  shrimp
1/2 lb. crabmeat
1 egg, slightly beaten
4 medium flounders

1/2 c. chopped green onions,
  tops included
1 c. Progresso's seasoned
  bread crumbs
2 Tbsp. parsley
Salt, black and cayenne
  pepper

Saute celery, onions and garlic in 1/2 stick melted butter. Add bread crumbs, shrimp, crabmeat and parsley. Mix well. Season to taste with salt, pepper and cayenne pepper. Split thick side of each flounder, lengthwise and crosswise, and loosen meat from bone of fish to form a pocket for stuffing. Brush well with additional melted butter, salt and pepper. Stuff pocket with dressing. Melt remaining 1/2 stick butter in shallow baking pan. Place fish in pan. Cover and bake at 375° for about 30 minutes. Remove cover and bake additional 5 minutes.

Pam Marchese, Metairie
Council, Metairie, La.

LOBSTER SAVANNAH

2 lobsters (2 lb.)
1/2 c. diced green pepper
1 tsp. paprika
2 Tbsp. grated cheese
6 Tbsp. butter
Salt to taste

1/2 c. sliced mushrooms
1/2 c. sherry
2 Tbsp. diced pimiento
1 c. milk
4 Tbsp. flour

Put live lobsters in boiling salted water, cover and boil 25 minutes. Remove and cool. Cut off legs and claws. Hold lobster with top side up and use kitchen shears to cut an oval opening in top of shell from base of head to tail. Remove all meat from body and claws, then cube. Melt butter, add flour. Cook only 5 minutes, add heated milk. Cook mushrooms and green peppers in butter until tender. Add sherry. Paprika and salt to taste. Cook only 5 minutes. Add flour-milk mixture slowly. Add lobster cubes and pimiento to mixture. Place back in lobster shells and top with cheese. Bake at 375° for 15 minutes. Serves 2. This recipe is over 100 years old. It's from South Carolina low country cooking.

Peggy Childers
Crescent City Council
New Orleans, La.

LOBSTER OR SHRIMP THERMIDOR

3/4 lb. cooked, peeled, cleaned shrimp or seafood of your choice
1 tsp. chopped onion
1/4 c. all-purpose flour
1/2 tsp. dry mustard
1/2 c. grated Parmesan cheese

1 (4 oz.) can mushrooms, stems and pieces, drained
1/4 c. melted butter or oleo
1 tsp. Worcestershire sauce
1/4 tsp. salt
2 c. milk
Paprika
Dash of cayenne pepper

Cut large shrimp in half. Saute mushrooms in butter or oleo for 5 minutes. Blend in flour and seasonings. Add milk gradually and cook until thick, stirring constantly. Add shrimp, top with cheese. Serve hot over pieces of dry toast.

Patricia R. Caraway, Capital
Council, Baton Rouge, La.

BAKED OYSTERS ON HALF SHELL

2 doz. oysters on half shell
1 c. milk
1/2 c. Cheddar cheese
1/2 Tbsp. celery flakes
1/3 c. white wine
1/2 c. Parmesan cheese
Dash of Worcestershire sauce

2 Tbsp. cornstarch
2 Tbsp. butter
1/8 tsp. nutmeg
1/4 c. chopped parsley
1/2 Tbsp. garlic powder
1 (4 1/2 oz.) can chopped shrimp
1 egg

Do not rinse oysters; clean shells and return oysters. Set in 400° oven for about 7-10 minutes. Melt butter, add cornstarch and milk. Stir until thick. Add nutmeg, parsley flakes, celery, garlic, Cheddar cheese and egg. Cook about 2 minutes. Add wine, shrimp and dash of Worcestershire sauce. Let stand. When oysters are removed from oven, put 1 tablespoon of the sauce over each oyster with a sprinkle of Parmesan cheese. Return to oven for 10 more minutes.

Nemsie Lindsey, Crescent City
Council, New Orleans, La.

CREOLE OYSTERS AND POULE D'EAU GUMBO

2 1/2 c. cooking oil
1 doz. poule d'eau (small ducks) with gizzards, thoroughly cleaned, salted and peppered
1 bunch parsley, chopped
4 medium chopped onions
1/2 c. chopped bell pepper
2 Tbsp. chopped jalapeno pepper
1 Tbsp. Worcestershire sauce

1 1/2 c. flour
2 lb. smoked sausage or andouille (1/2-inch slices)
2 pt. oysters and juice
1 1/2 stalks chopped celery
2 bunches chopped green onions
1 clove garlic, chopped
1 1/2 Tbsp. yellow mustard
Salt and pepper
2 gal. water

Bring oil to boil. Add flour. Lower oil to light simmer. Brown flour to a dark brown by stirring often (make roux). Add all chopped vegetables except garlic and jalapeno peppers. Saute vegetables until very soft. Add poule d'eau, gizzards and garlic. Raise heat to light bubbling. Saute, stirring occasionally for 20 minutes. Add water, Worcestershire sauce, yellow mustard and jalapeno peppers. Bring to boil, lower to medium boil, add salt and pepper to taste. Cook for 30 minutes. Add smoked sausage. Continue cooking until meat is tender. Skim all excess grease, add oysters. Bring back to simmer and cook 15 minutes. Skim foam when comes to a boil. If desired, 1 or 2 pounds chicken gizzards can be added for extra meat at same time as other gizzards. Variations of this dish can be made by substituting wild duck or chicken for meat items.

J. C. Austin, LeBayou
Council, Gray, La.

OYSTER DRESSING

3 jars oysters	2 bunches shallots
5 onions	1 head garlic
2 bell peppers	Garlic powder
1 can Italian bread crumbs	Grated Italian cheese
2 ends of bread, wet	Butter

Drain oysters, reserve liquid. Chop oysters, vegetables and bread. Fry in Dutch oven, stir, adding oyster water as it fries. Add cheese and 1/2 can of bread crumbs, little at a time. Cook and stir for 45 minutes. Place in casserole. Sprinkle remaining bread crumbs on top. Add several pats of butter. Bake at 350° for 45 minutes.

Patti Regep, Metairie
Council, River Ridge, La.

OYSTER FRITTERS

1 c. pancake mix	1 tsp. baking powder
1 pt. oysters with juice	1 egg
2 Tbsp. onion, finely chopped	Salt and pepper to taste
	1/4 c. cooking oil

Combine pancake mix, oysters, onion, baking powder, egg, salt and pepper. Drop by tablespoonfuls into hot oil. Brown on both sides. Drain on paper towels. Makes about 20 fritters.

Marjorie B. Harris, Capital
Council, Baton Rouge, La.

OYSTER PATTIES

1 stick butter or oleo	1 large onion, chopped
8 cloves garlic, chopped	3/4 c. parsley, chopped
3 Tbsp. flour	2 bunches shallots; chopped
1/2 tsp. salt	1/4 tsp. pepper
1/4 tsp. oregano	2 doz. medium patty shells
	5 doz. oysters

Saute onions, shallots, garlic in butter until golden brown. Add flour and brown. Chop oysters; reserve liquid. Add oysters, parsley and oregano, simmer 15-20 minutes. Add salt and pepper. If mixture is too thick, add oyster water for desired consistency. Fill patty shells and bake at 325° about 15 minutes. Georgia Ford, Crescent City
Council, New Orleans, La.

OYSTER PATTIES

8 doz. small oysters or
   6 doz. regular
1 or 2 little strands fresh
   thyme
Wesson oil

1 bunch fresh shallots
1/2 bunch fresh parsley
6-8 cloves garlic
2 doz. baked patty shells
Plain flour

Chop shallots, parsley, garlic and thyme fine. Cut oysters in 2 or 3 pieces each; save oyster water. Saute vegetables in hot oil on low-medium flame until soft. Add flour gradually to make roux. Don't brown, just gray. Add liquid from oysters and make creamy. Add oysters and cook on low about 15-20 minutes. Pour into shells and bake at 450° for 5 minutes.   Lee Campos, Crescent City
Council, New Orleans, La.

OYSTER PATTIES

1 small bunch green
   onions, finely chopped
2 Tbsp. chopped parsley
1 small onion, grated or
   finely chopped
4 doz. small patty shells

2 Tbsp. butter or oleo
1 can mushroom soup
1 Tbsp. flour
1/4 tsp. lemon juice
Black and red pepper to taste
4 doz. oysters, cut in half if
   small, diced if large

Saute green onions in oleo until tender. Blend in flour until smooth. Add onions, mushroom soup, black and red pepper, parsley, oysters and lemon juice. Simmer 10 minutes. Spoon into patty shells. When ready to serve, bake at 250°-300° for 15 minutes. These freeze well and can be frozen on cookie sheet; then place in plastic bag for easy storage. Yield: 4 dozen.   Henrietta Victor, Magnolia
Council, New Orleans, La.

OYSTER PATTIES

1 stick oleo
1/2 - 1 c. chopped green
   onions
1-2 cans mushroom soup
Salt and pepper to taste
Hot sauce to taste

1 large chopped onion
4-6 cloves garlic, minced
2-3 doz. oysters, chopped,
   and oyster water
Patty shells
Water

Melt butter in pan, add onion, green onions and garlic. Cook until vegetables are transparent. Add water to pan (almost full), cook until water is cooked out. Add oysters and oyster water, cook until liquid is again cooked out. Cool. Add mushroom soup, salt, pepper and hot sauce. Blend well. Fill patty shells and bake at 350° until done.

Etta Williams, Magnolia
Council, New Orleans, La.

OYSTERS IN PATTY SHELLS

8 large patty shells, frozen or homemade
1 stick butter
1 bunch shallots, chopped fine

4 doz. medium oysters
1 qt. oyster liquid
7 Tbsp. flour
1 large onion, chopped fine
3 Tbsp. parsley, chopped fine

Saute onion in butter until soft. Add shallots and parsley. Cook until soft, not brown. Add flour and stir well. Add oyster liquid gradually until mixture is very thick. You may not need all the liquid. Add oysters, cook about 15 minutes. Salt to taste, if needed. Put mixture into shells. Place shells on cookie sheet and bake for 30 minutes at 370°.

John E. Haygood, Caddo
Council, Shreveport, La.

OYSTER PIE

4 doz. oysters, including oyster water
2 cloves garlic, chopped
1 bunch green onions, finely chopped
2 Tbsp. chopped celery
1 tsp. cayenne pepper

1 c. cooked, chopped chicken or turkey (leftovers are best)
1/2 c. plain flour
1/3 c. cooking oil
1/2 tsp. salt
9-inch double pie crust

Make roux of flour and oil until dark brown. Add green onions, saute 3 minutes only, stirring constantly. All at once, add oysters, oyster water and chicken. Bring to medium boil, cook until ingredients thicken heavily, about 15 minutes. Add salt and pepper to taste. Pour into bottom crust and cover with top crust. Slit top crust to prevent blistering. Bake at 425° until crust is golden brown. Serve hot or at room temperature. Most people

1723-79

prefer at room temperature. A young, white burgundy, such as Pouilly-Fousse, goes well with this dish.

Mrs. John A. Menant
Crescent City Council
New Orleans, La.

OYSTER POULETTE

3 doz. oysters
2 Tbsp. flour
3/4 c. oyster liquid
1 c. cream
2 Tbsp. lemon juice
Dash of red pepper
4 egg yolks

2 Tbsp. butter
2 green onions, chopped
1 Tbsp. chopped parsley
1/2 c. dry white wine
Salt to taste
Buttered bread crumbs

Make roux of butter and flour, stir until smooth and light brown. Add onions and cook for a few minutes. Drain oysters and add 3/4 cup oyster liquid. Simmer for 10 minutes. Beat egg yolks with cream. Add seasonings and egg yolk mixture. Add oysters and parsley. Continue to cook for 3 minutes. Add lemon juice and wine. Place in individual casseroles. Top with bread crumbs. Bake at 350° until hot and bubbly. Makes 6 servings. John E. Haygood, Caddo Council, Shreveport, La.

OYSTERS ON SKEWERS

1 doz. oysters
12 cherry tomatoes
1 Tbsp. melted butter

2 Tbsp. grated Parmesan
  cheese
12 mushroom caps
Salt and pepper to taste

Wash oysters and roll in Parmesan cheese. Put oysters, tomatoes and mushroom caps on a skewer. Brush tomatoes and mushrooms with butter. Season with salt and pepper. Place skewers on foil covered cookie sheet in broiler for 3 minutes. Turn once and leave for 3 more minutes. Do not let tomato skins burn. Serve immediately.

Peggy Childers
Crescent City Council
New Orleans, La.

SMOKED OYSTER LOAF

2 pkg. (8 oz. size)
  cream cheese,
  softened
2 Tbsp. Worcestershire
  sauce
2 Tbsp. mayonnaise
  (approx.)

1 large clove garlic,
  crushed
1 small onion, grated
1/4 tsp. seasoned salt
2 cans chopped, smoked
  oysters
Chopped walnuts or pecans

Combine cheese, garlic, onion, salt and Worcestershire sauce with enough mayonnaise to hold together. Chill for 1 hour or firm enough to handle. Spread on waxed paper. Spread oysters evenly over cream cheese mixture and roll up, jelly roll style. Roll in nuts and chill 24 hours to season. Serve with crackers.

Mavis W. O'Rourke
Shreveport Works Council
Shreveport, La.

OYSTER SPAGHETTI

3 doz. fresh oysters,
  drained
5 cloves garlic, minced
1 can mushroom soup
Salt and pepper to taste

1 Tbsp. olive oil
1 Tbsp. butter
1 1/2 tsp. parsley
1 small can Pet milk
2 Tbsp. dry white wine,
  divided

Simmer olive oil, butter, parsley and garlic together. Mix soup, milk and 1 tablespoon wine together. If mixture is too thin, add little flour. Combine all ingredients and cook about 15 minutes. Add remainder of white wine, salt and pepper while cooking. Serve over cooked thin spaghetti.

Peggy Foret, Crescent City
Council, New Orleans, La.

POMPANO EN PAPILLOTE

3 c. boiling salted water
1 sprig thyme
2 Tbsp. butter, melted
1 onion, sliced
1 c. cooked shrimp,
  chopped
1/2 c. mushroom pieces
2 egg yolks, beaten

1 lemon, sliced
1 bay leaf
6 pompano fillets
3 Tbsp. flour
1 1/2 c. fish stock
1/2 c. crabmeat
1/4 tsp. salt
Parchment paper

1723-79

Combine water, lemon slices, bay leaf, thyme and fillets in large saucepan. Simmer for 15 minutes. Remove fillets, open flat and place each on individual sheets of parchment paper. Add flour and onion to melted butter in small saucepan and brown lightly. Add fish stock. Cook until sauce thickens, about 5-6 minutes. Pour sauce over fish fillets. Fold parchment paper to form a case around each fillet. Bake at 400° for 10 minutes. Split and fold back each parchment casement to serve. Serves 6. John E. Haygood, Caddo Council, Shreveport, La.

SALMON CAKES

3 c. salmon
2 c. soft bread crumbs
2 well beaten eggs
1 Tbsp. chopped onion

1 Tbsp. chopped parsley
2 Tbsp. butter
Salt and pepper to taste
2 tsp. baking powder

Mix thoroughly. Chill. Shape and fry in deep fat.
Calcasieu Council
Lake Charles, La.

ESCALLOPED SALMON

1 (1 lb.) can salmon
1 c. bread or cracker
  crumbs
Salt and pepper to taste

3 Tbsp. butter
3 Tbsp. flour
2 1/2 c. milk

Drain salmon; reserve juice. Melt butter, add flour, stirring until smooth. Add milk, stir until thickened, add salmon liquor. Season to taste. Flake salmon, add to sauce and place in greased baking dish. Sprinkle with bread crumbs. Bake at 350° for about 20 minutes.
Mrs. Leona Botzong Smith
Central Council
Corpus Christi, Tx.

SALMON LOAF

1 can pink salmon
1 Tbsp. finely chopped
  onion
1/4 tsp. black pepper and
  parsley

1 egg
1 c. bread crumbs
1/2 tsp. salt
1 c. milk

320

Drain liquid from salmon and reserve. Remove large bones and skin. Break up salmon with fork, add remaining ingredients, using enough of salmon liquid and milk to moisten. Shape into well greased baking dish and bake about 30 minutes at 375°. One pound of ground meat may be substituted for salmon and baked about 1 hour.

Mary Armand, Central
Council, Cottonport, La.

SHRIMP AU GRATIN

1 1/2 c. cooked, cleaned shrimp
2/3 c. grated American cheese

1 c. thick white sauce
1 Tbsp. chopped parsley
1/2 c. buttered bread crumbs

Alternate layers of shrimp, white sauce and 1/2 of the cheese in greased deep baking dish. Sprinkle top with remaining cheese and parsley, then with buttered crumbs. Bake at 400° for 20 minutes or until crumbs are brown.

Jan Prestridge, Capital
Council, Shreveport, La.

SHRIMP AU GRATIN

1 1/2 c. shrimp
1 c. thin white sauce
1/2 c. buttered bread crumbs

2/3 c. American cheese, grated
1 Tbsp. parsley, finely chopped

Alternate layers of cleaned, cooked shrimp, white sauce and 1/2 cup of the cheese in greased baking dish. Sprinkle with parsley and remaining cheese. Sprinkle buttered bread crumbs over top. Bake at 400° for 20 minutes or until crumbs are brown. Serves 4.

Sandy Lemoine, Capital
Council, Baton Rouge, La.

SHRIMP AU GRATIN

2 Tbsp. butter or oleo
1 c. milk
Dash of Tabasco sauce
1 c. sharp cheese, grated
Buttered bread crumbs

3 Tbsp. flour
1 tsp. Lea & Perrins sauce
1 green onion, chopped fine
2 c. shrimp, boiled, peeled, deveined
Salt and pepper to taste

Make white sauce of butter, flour and milk. Add seasonings, cheese and shrimp. Place in casserole or ramekins. Cover with buttered bread crumbs. Bake at 325° about 30 minutes or until hot and bubbly. Serves 4-5.

Eloise Beckham, Crescent City
Council, New Orleans, La.

BAKED BUTTERED SHRIMP

5 lb. shrimp, medium-large
1/4 c. Worcestershire
   sauce
Salt and pepper
Chili powder

5 cloves garlic, pressed, or
   garlic powder
1 lb. butter
2 lemons

Place washed, unpeeled and well drained shrimp in single layer in large baking pan. Sprinkle generously with salt and pepper. Sprinkle sparingly with chili powder. In saucepan, melt butter. Add Worcestershire sauce and garlic. Remove from heat. Cut lemons in half and squeeze juice into butter sauce. Slice lemon pieces and rind left and place on top of shrimp. Spoon butter sauce over all the shrimp. Bake in preheated 500° oven for 20 minutes. Peel shrimp as you eat and serve with hot French bread for sopping gravy.

Marjorie B. Harris, Capital
Council, Baton Rouge, La.

SHRIMP BALLS

3 lb. shrimp, partially
   cooked (save stock for
   shrimp sauce)
1 large onion, chopped fine
1 bunch green onions,
   minced
1 Tbsp. Lea & Perrins
   sauce

1 c. bread crumbs
2 eggs
6 cloves garlic, crushed
1/4 c. celery, chopped fine
1/2 c. shrimp stock
Salt and pepper to taste
Dash of red pepper

Grind shrimp, onions and garlic in food chopper. Place in mixing bowl, add remaining ingredients. Mix well with hands. Shape into small balls, then roll in flour and oil. Fry balls until light brown. Put into shrimp balls sauce last 45 minutes of cooking.

Schumann's Seafood Sauce:

6 level Tbsp. flour	1/2 c. shortening
6 cloves garlic, chopped	1/2 c. diced onion
1/4 c. chopped bell pepper	1/2 c. chopped celery
	3 qt. water (shrimp stock)
1 (8 oz.) can tomato sauce	1/4 bunch chopped parsley
1 lb. crabmeat	1/2 tsp. Tabasco sauce
1/2 tsp. thyme	1 Tbsp. Lea & Perrins sauce
3 bay leaves	Salt and pepper to taste

Make a roux with flour and shortening. Add garlic and cook until golden brown. Add onion, bell pepper, celery and parsley. Cook until transparent. Add tomato sauce, simmer 10 minutes. Stir in stock and blend well. Add thyme, bay leaves; cook 1 hour. Add crab, salt, pepper, Tabasco sauce and Lea & Perrins sauce. Cover pot and allow to simmer gently at least 45 minutes.

Floyd Shumann, Ozone
Council, Hammond, La.

SHRIMP BATTER

1 beaten egg	1 c. cold water
3/4 c. flour	1/3 c. corn meal
1/2 tsp. salt	3 Tbsp. melted shortening

Combine ingredients and dip seasoned shrimp in batter. Fry until brown.

Calcasieu Council
Lake Charles, La.

BAR-B-Q SHRIMP

2-4 lb. jumbo shrimp with heads	1/2 oz. black pepper
	1 Tbsp. cayenne pepper
1 Tbsp. Tabasco sauce	1 Tbsp. Lea & Perrins sauce
4 sticks butter or oleo	Juice of 4 lemons

Soak shrimp in salt water for 5 minutes before cooking. Melt butter and add other ingredients. Lay shrimp in shallow pan and pour sauce over them. Bake at 350° for 45 minutes.

Mary Alice Mistretta, Metairie
Council, Metairie, La.

BROILED SHRIMP WITH GARLIC BUTTER

2 lb. large fresh shrimp in their shells, or defrosted frozen shrimp
8 Tbsp. butter (1/4 lb. stick)
1/2 c. olive oil
1 Tbsp. lemon juice
Lemon quarters
1 Tbsp. finely chopped garlic
1 tsp. salt
Freshly ground black pepper
4 Tbsp. finely chopped fresh parsley, preferably flat leaf Italian type
1/4 c. finely chopped shallots or scallions

Shell shrimp, taking care not to remove last small segment of shell or the tail. With small, sharp knife, slit each shrimp down the back and lift out black or white intestinal vein. Wash shrimp quickly under cold running water and pat dry with paper towels. Preheat broiler to its highest temperature. In shallow flameproof baking dish or pan just large enough to hold the shrimp in one layer, melt butter over low heat, taking care not to let it brown. Stir in 1/2 cup olive oil, lemon juice, shallots, garlic, salt and a few grindings of pepper. Add shrimp and turn them in the butter and oil until they glisten on all sides. Broil 3-4 inches from heat for 5 minutes, then turn over and broil for 5-10 minutes longer, or until lightly browned and firm to the touch. Take care not to overcook. With tongs, transfer shrimp to heated serving platter, pour sauce from the pan over them and sprinkle with chopped parsley. Garnish with lemon quarters and serve. Serves 6.

Calcasieu Council
Lake Charles, La.

CANLIS SHRIMP

2 lb. large shrimp, shelled
1 oz. butter
1 oz. olive oil
1/4 tsp. fresh ground black pepper
1/4 tsp. salt
2 oz. dry vermouth
Juice of 2 lemons
1 small whole garlic clove, crushed

Into large skillet, place olive oil. When simmering, add shrimp; allow to cook until golden brown. Reduce heat; add butter, garlic, salt, pepper. When you think you have too much salt, add more. This is one dish you cannot oversalt. When well blended, raise heat to very hot. Add lemon juice and dry vermouth and cook for about 1 minute, constantly stirring. Serve as appetizer or entree.

Calcasieu Council
Lake Charles, La.

SHRIMP CANTONESE

12 oz. peeled raw shrimp, halved lengthwise
2 c. diagonally sliced celery
1 (15 oz.) can fancy mixed Chinese vegetables
1 1/4 c. chicken broth
2 Tbsp. butter or vegetable oil
2 c. sliced onions
8 oz. fresh spinach
1/4 tsp. pepper
1/4 c. soy sauce
2 Tbsp. cornstarch

Saute shrimp in butter for 1 minute or until shrimp turn pink, using a large skillet. Add celery and onions. Cook, stirring 2 minutes. Add spinach and Chinese vegetables, which have been rinsed and drained. Cover and cook 1 minute. Blend pepper, soy sauce, chicken broth and cornstarch. Stir into shrimp-vegetable mixture. Cook, stirring until sauce is clear and thickened, about 2 minutes. Serve over rice. Serves 6.   Rebecca Scott, Caddo Council, Shreveport, La.

SHRIMP CRAB ROLLS

3/4 c. chopped raw shrimp
3/4 c. cooked crabmeat
1 egg
2 slices dry bread
Dash of cayenne pepper
1/4 c. chopped celery
1/4 c. chopped onion
1/4 c. chopped bell pepper
1 tsp. Worcestershire sauce
Salt and pepper to taste

Mix all ingredients together. Pick up small handful and squeeze into 2 1/2-inch roll. Mix about 1 cup corn meal with 1/2 cup pancake mix. Coat shrimp patty in corn meal and fry in deep fat.   Calcasieu Council Lake Charles, La.

SHRIMP AND CRAB SPAGHETTI

2 lb. peeled shrimp
2 medium onions, chopped
2 Tbsp. vegetable oil
1 can tomato paste
1 tsp. basil
1/2 tsp. salt
1 stick butter
1 doz. crabs, cooked or raw
1 clove garlic, minced
2 cans tomato sauce
1 Tbsp. chili powder
1/2 tsp. sugar
1/4 tsp. pepper
1 pkg. spaghetti

Brown onions and garlic in hot oil. Add remaining

ingredients, except shrimp, crabs and spaghetti. Bring to boil and simmer 30 minutes, stirring constantly. Remove outer shell and legs from crabs, leaving meat in bottom part; break in half. Add shrimp and crabs to sauce, simmer additional 30 minutes. Add uncooked spaghetti to sauce, stir constantly until done or pour sauce over cooked spaghetti. Serves 4 people.

Christine Moras, Central
Council, Hessmer, La.

SEAFOOD SPAGHETTI

1 pt. oysters	1 c. chopped celery
2 1/2 lb. fresh shrimp	1 c. chopped onions
1 c. cooking oil	1 c. chopped bell peppers
1 clove garlic, minced	2 small cans tomato sauce
1 small can tomato paste	1 can whole tomatoes
1/2 c. catsup	Green onion tops, chopped
Salt, black and red	Cooked spaghetti
pepper to taste	

Boil shrimp, peel and save water. Mix oil in heavy pot with celery, onions, bell peppers, garlic, tomato sauce, tomato paste, whole tomatoes and catsup. Cook about 40 minutes or until oil separates. Skim. Add 2 quarts shrimp water, shrimp, oysters and liquid, green onion tops and parsley. Simmer 30 minutes. Serve over hot cooked spaghetti tossed in butter. Serves 8-10.

John E. Haygood, Caddo
Council, Shreveport, La.

SHRIMP CREOLE

2 1/2 lb. raw shrimp	2 Tbsp. butter
1/2 c. chopped onions	2 Tbsp. chopped green pepper
1 clove minced garlic	1 (8 oz.) can tomato sauce
1 Tbsp. flour	1/2 can water
2 Tbsp. chopped parsley	1/8 tsp. pepper or Tabasco
1/8 tsp. thyme	sauce
1 tsp. salt	1/4 tsp. black pepper

Peel, devein and wash shrimp. Melt butter in large skillet over medium heat. Add onion and green pepper. Saute until soft, about 6 minutes. Stir in garlic. Remove from heat, blend in flour until smooth. Add tomato sauce and simmer for 5 minutes. Gradually add water, stirring to blend. Add shrimp and remaining ingredients. Cover and simmer about 40 minutes. Serve over hot cooked rice.

John E. Haygood, Caddo
Council, Shreveport, La.

SHRIMP CREOLE

1 c. flour
1 c. oil
2 c. chopped celery
2 bay leaves
1 large can tomatoes
3 tsp. salt
1/2 tsp. black pepper
2 Tbsp. chopped onion
   tops

1/2 c. chopped bell pepper
2 cloves garlic, minced
3 lb. raw shrimp, cleaned
   and deveined
2 small cans tomato paste
1/4 tsp. red pepper
2 Tbsp. chopped parsley
1 tsp. Worcestershire sauce
6 c. water

Make roux of flour and oil. Brown over low heat, stirring constantly. Add seasonings, onions, celery, bell pepper and garlic. Cook until soft. Add tomatoes and paste, mix well and cook about 5 minutes. Add water. Let simmer 1 1/2 hours. Add shrimp, cook about 20 minutes. Add onion tops and parsley. Serve over rice. Serves about 8 generous portions.

Mrs. Sim S. Davenport
Central Council
Alexandria, La.

BAYOU SHRIMP CREOLE

1 c. salad oil
1 stalk pascal celery,
   diced
5 c. onions, sliced
1 c. chili sauce
1 tsp. curry powder
3 large bay leaves
2 pkg. frozen okra,
   sliced (optional)
2 (No. 303) cans tomatoes

3 large green peppers,
   sliced
1 stalk pascal celery leaves,
   chopped
1 tsp. thyme
Salt, red and black pepper
   to taste
1/2 c. parsley, chopped
5 lb. shrimp, cooked, shelled
   and deveined

Heat oil in large frying pan. Add green peppers, celery, celery leaves and onions. Cook over low heat, stirring until vegetables are slightly softened. Add remaining ingredients except shrimp. Cover and simmer for 1 hour, stirring occasionally. Refrigerate for 24 hours. Add shrimp 1 hour before serving; heat thoroughly. Yield: 16-18 servings.

Allice (Lucille) Williams, Caddo
Council, Shreveport, La.

CHICKEN OR SHRIMP CREOLE

1 chicken	5 c. water
1 tsp. salt	1/2 - 1 lb. sausage
1/4 tsp. pepper	1 bell pepper, chopped
1 can tomatoes	1 can Ro-Tel tomatoes
1 chopped onion	1/3 c. flour

Cook chicken in water with salt and pepper. Remove and debone. Reserve broth. Slice sausage in 1/4-inch circles and cook until brown. Remove from skillet. Saute pepper and onion in drippings for 5 minutes, add flour and make roux. Gradually stir in broth. Add Ro-Tel tomatoes, tomatoes and sausage. Simmer 30 minutes. Add chicken. If using shrimp, use 2 cans shrimp and canned chicken broth.

Bertie Smith, Central
Council, Ball, La.

SKILLET SHRIMP CREOLE

1 (1 lb.) can peeled tomatoes	1 tsp. sugar
	1/8 tsp. pepper
1/2 c. celery	1/2 tsp. salt
1/4 c. diced green peppers	1 bay leaf
1/4 c. onion	1 sprig parsley
3 Tbsp. butter	1/4 tsp. Worcestershire sauce
3/4 lb. shrimp, cleaned and split	1 1/3 c. Minute Rice

Drain tomatoes, measuring liquid. Add water to liquid to make 1 1/3 cups. Saute celery, green pepper and onion in butter until lightly browned. Add shrimp, cook until shrimp turns pink. Add liquid, tomatoes, sugar, salt, pepper, bay leaf, parsley, Worcestershire sauce. Cover and let simmer 3 minutes. Stir in Minute Rice. Cover and simmer an additional 5 minutes. Remove bay leaf and parsley before serving. Makes 6 servings.

Calcasieu Council
Lake Charles, La.

SHRIMP CURRY

Sauce:

3 Tbsp. butter
1 1/2 c. chopped apple
3-4 tsp. curry powder
1 tsp. salt
1/4 tsp. ginger
2 Tbsp. lime juice
2 tsp. grated lime peel

1 1/2 c. chopped onion
1 clove garlic, crushed
1/4 c. unsifted all-purpose
flour
1/4 tsp. pepper
2 (10 1/2 oz.) cans chicken
broth

Heat butter in large skillet, saute chopped onion, chopped apple, garlic and curry powder until onion is tender, about 5 minutes. Remove from heat, blend in flour, 1 teaspoon salt, the ground ginger and pepper. Gradually stir in chicken broth, lime juice and grated lime peel. Bring to boiling, stirring constantly. Reduce heat and simmer uncovered for 20 minutes, stirring occasionally.

Shrimp:

3 lb. raw shrimp, shelled
and deveined (18-20
per lb.)
1 lemon, sliced
1/3 c. chopped chutney

1 Tbsp. salt
1 onion, peeled and sliced
8 whole black peppercorns
2 c. raw regular white rice

In large saucepan, combine 1 1/2 quarts water, 1 tablespoon salt, the sliced onion, sliced lemon and whole black peppercorns. Bring to boiling and add the cleaned shrimp. Return to boiling, reduce heat and simmer shrimp uncovered 5-10 minutes or when they are tender. Drain shrimp, discarding cooking liquid. Add shrimp to curry sauce, stir in chopped chutney, heat gently just to boiling. Cook rice as specified. Serve the Shrimp Curry hot with Curry Accompaniments and fluffy white rice. Makes 6-8 servings.

Curry Accompaniments: Chopped chutney (a must); chopped green peppers; chopped green onions; diced tomatoes; chopped watermelon rind; salted peanuts; shredded coconut; chopped cucumber; raisins. About 4 of the above make a good combination. I recommend the chopped chutney, chopped watermelon rind, diced tomato and shredded coconut.

L. R. McGill, Westmoor
Council, New Orleans La

SCRAMBLED EGGS WITH SHRIMP

1/2 lb. raw shrimp
2 Tbsp. diced onion
4 eggs
1/2 qt. boiling water

3 Tbsp. butter
1 Tbsp. white wine
Salt and pepper to taste

Cook shrimp for 3 minutes in boiling water, cool and peel. Saute onion in melted butter until tender. Add wine and shrimp, simmer for 2 minutes. Add beaten eggs to skillet and stir in with other ingredients. Cook on low heat until done to personal preference. Salt and pepper after removing from skillet. Serves 4. Serve with strawberries in half a cantaloupe, grits with bacon bits, corn muffins and toasted rolls. A traditional low country breakfast.

Peggy Childers, Crescent City
Council, New Orleans, La.

QUICK SHRIMP ETOUFFEE

1 lb. shrimp, cleaned and
  deveined
1 small can tomatoes
4 cloves minced garlic

1/2 c. butter or oleo
1/2 c. finely chopped parsley
1 Tbsp. all-purpose flour
Salt and pepper to taste

Blend tomatoes including liquid until fine. In skillet, make roux of flour and butter. Add garlic and continue browning until tender. Add tomatoes, shrimp, salt and pepper. Simmer for 15-20 minutes. Add chopped parsley before removing from heat. Serve over hot fluffy rice. Serves 2-4.

Mary Ann J. Francois
Metairie Council
New Orleans, La.

FRENCH FRIED SHRIMP

1 c. flour
1 tsp. sugar
1 tsp. salt
1 egg

1 c. ice water
1 Tbsp. shortening, melted,
  or cooking oil
2 lb. large shrimp

Combine ingredients, except shrimp. Beat well. Peel raw shrimp, leaving last section and tail section. Cut slit down center back and remove sand line. Dry shrimp and dip

330

into batter. Fry in deep hot fat until golden brown. Drain on paper towels. Serve hot with tartar sauce.

John Haygood, Caddo
Council, Shreveport, La.

SCHULTZ'S FRIED SHRIMP

3 doz. peeled shrimp	1 c. flour
1/3 c. corn meal	Pinch of baking powder
1 egg with 2 Tbsp. water	Salt and pepper to taste

Season shrimp with salt and pepper. Combine egg and water; season with salt and pepper. Dip shrimp in egg batter. Roll in dry mixture; fry in deep hot fat for 3 minutes. Drain on paper towels.

Leona Schultz, Capital
Council, Baton Rouge, La.

ITALIAN SEASONED SHRIMP

2 lb. large raw unpeeled shrimp	2 sticks melted butter or oleo
1/4 c. olive oil	Dash of Tabasco sauce
1 Tbsp. rosemary	2 Tbsp. Worcestershire sauce
1/2 tsp. oregano	1/2 tsp. thyme
2 bay leaves, crumbled	1/2 tsp. basil
1/2 lemon, squeezed	1/8 tsp. crushed red pepper
3 cloves garlic, sliced	1/4 c. white wine
1 tsp. Accent	1 tsp. sugar
2 large bell peppers, quartered	2 large onions, quartered
Salt to taste	2 ribs celery, cut into chunks
Lots of black pepper	

Melt butter in saucepan and remove from heat. Combine all ingredients, except shrimp and black pepper. Pour sauce mixture into shallow baking pan. Place shrimp over sauce and cover with black pepper. Mix well and refrigerate for several hours or overnight. Stir occasionally to allow shrimp to be well coated with marinade. Preheat oven to 425° and cook shrimp uncovered for about 25 minutes or until shells are loosened around shrimp. Stir twice while cooking, remove from oven and serve with hot French bread. Serves 4-6.

Mona F. Reis, Metairie
Council, Metairie, La.

SHRIMP LOAF

1 lb. raw shrimp, shelled
6 slices bacon, fried crisp
  and crumbled
1/3 c. bread crumbs
1 bell pepper, chopped fine
2 ribs celery, chopped fine

1 link pork sausage
1/2 c. flour
1 1/2 c. cooked rice
Parsley (as much as you
  think)
Salt, pepper, Accent to taste

Grind shrimp and pork sausage together. Add remaining ingredients to mixture. Mix well, form into a loaf. Bake at 350° for 15 minutes or until brown. Serves 5.

Mona Reis, Metairie Council,
Metairie, La.

SHRIMP MANALE

3 lb. large shrimp, washed
  and deheaded
1/2 tsp. Lea & Perrins
  sauce
1/2 tsp. cayenne pepper
1 tsp. thyme
2 tsp. celery salt

1 1/2 sticks oleo
1 tsp. salt
1 1/2 tsp. pepper
2 tsp. garlic puree
2 tsp. rosemary
1 tsp. olive oil

Melt oleo, add all ingredients except shrimp. Place shrimp in Pyrex pan. When oleo mixture is cool, pour over shrimp. Marinate in refrigerator 6 hours. Bake at 450° for 20-30 minutes. Taste test periodically until done. Serve with hot French bread.

Buddy and Betty Stelz
Metairie Council, Metairie, La.

MARINATED SHRIMP

5 qt. water
1 stalk celery, cut in
  1-inch slices
2 tsp. pepper, divided
1 Tbsp. salt
1 large onion, sliced and
  separated into rings
Lettuce leaves

1/4 c. chopped onion
1/2 c. lemon juice
1 1/2 c. apple cider vinegar
1 c. sugar
1 tsp. paprika
1 (38 oz.) bottle salad oil
5 lb. unpeeled jumbo shrimp

Combine water, celery, onion, lemon juice and 1/2 teaspoon pepper in Dutch oven; bring to boil. Add shrimp and return to boil. Cook for 5 minutes; drain shrimp and cool. Shell and devein shrimp. Combine shrimp and remaining ingredients, except lettuce, in airtight plastic container. Refrigerate 1 week, shaking container twice each day. Drain shrimp, discarding marinade. Serve shrimp and onion rings in lettuce lined bowl. Serves 15-18.

Betty Harman, Caddo
Council, Shreveport, La.

SHRIMP WITH MUSHROOMS AND CELERY

1 lb. shrimp, cleaned
  and peeled
3 Tbsp. white wine
1 slice fresh ginger root
2 c. celery, sliced
  diagonally into 1/2-inch
  slices
1 Tbsp. cornstarch

1 tsp. salt
2 Tbsp. vegetable oil
1/4 lb. mushrooms, sliced
  into "T" shapes
1 scallion, sliced in 1/2-inch
  slices
1/2 c. cold chicken broth

Combine shrimp, salt and white wine. Marinate in refrigerator for 30 minutes. Heat oil in wok or pan and brown ginger to flavor the oil. Remove and discard ginger. Stir-fry mushrooms 1-2 minutes; set aside. Stir-fry celery and scallions 1-2 minutes until color brightens; set aside. Stir-fry shrimp and marinate 2 minutes or until shrimp turn pink. Return vegetables to shrimp. Combine cornstarch and broth and add to mixture. Heat until sauce boils. Serve at once with rice.   Connie Younker, Shreveport
Works Council, Shreveport, La.

SHRIMP AND MUSHROOMS IN WINE

1/2 c. green onion,
  chopped
3 cloves garlic, minced
3/4 lb. fresh mush-
  rooms, sliced
1 lb. peeled shrimp

1/2 c. parsley, chopped
1 1/2 sticks butter
1/2 c. seasoned bread
  crumbs
1/2 c. port wine (do not
  substitute)

Saute onion, parsley, garlic in butter. Add mushrooms; saute for a few minutes. Add shrimp, saute on medium heat 5-6 minutes. Add bread crumbs; mix thoroughly. Add wine and heat until well heated throughout. Serve either as appetizer or first course.   Ann Orr, Evangeline
Council, New Iberia, La.

1723-79

TAHITIAN SKILLET SHRIMP

1 (1 lb. 4 oz.) can pine-
  apple chunks
1 medium green pepper,
  chunked
1/2 c. chopped green
  onions
3 Tbsp. soy sauce
1/8 tsp. ginger

2 Tbsp. oil
1 c. diagonally cut celery
1 lb. cooked shrimp, fresh
  or frozen
2 Tbsp. cornstarch
1 tsp. garlic salt
1 c. cherry tomatoes, halved

Drain pineapple, reserving all syrup. Heat oil in heavy skillet. Saute celery and green pepper until they turn bright green. Add shrimp, tossing with vegetables until heated through. Add pineapple chunks and green onions. Combine reserved pineapple syrup, soy sauce, cornstarch, ginger and garlic salt. Stir into shrimp mixture until thickened. Add tomatoes and serve. Makes 4 servings.

Rebecca Scott Bockmon, Caddo
Council, Shreveport, La.

SHRIMP QUICHE

1 (8 oz.) can crescent
  rolls
1-2 Tbsp. Parmesan
  cheese
2 c. Monterey Jack cheese,
  cubed

2 eggs, slightly beaten
Salt and pepper to taste
2 (4 1/2 oz.) cans shrimp or
  crabmeat
2 tsp. chopped green onion
  or parsley

Place 5 dinner rolls in pie pan. Press out in pan to form thin crust. Combine remaining ingredients, pour into crust. Roll out remaining rolls, cut into strips, twist for lattice and place on top. Bake 50-60 minutes at 325°.

Note: For Ham Quiche, substitute 2 cups Swiss cheese and 1 (8 or 9 ounce) can ham for shrimp and Monterey Jack cheese.

Lisa Jackson, Crescent City
Council, New Orleans, La.

SHRIMP AND RICE DRESSING

1 Tbsp. salad oil
1 Tbsp. onion
3 c. cooked rice
3/4 c. shrimp
1 1/2 c. water

3/4 c. oysters
1 Tbsp. celery
1 Tbsp. flour
2 Tbsp. parsley and onion
  tops

Make a roux with oil and flour. Add seasonings and water. Boil 5-10 minutes. Add remaining ingredients and steam for 15 minutes.
Mildred Hale, Ouachita Council, Monroe, La.

DIRTY RICE WITH SHRIMP

1/2 lb. rice
1/8 c. shortening
1 bunch green onions, chopped fine
1 lb. pkg. shrimp, chopped
Butter

1 lb. red onions, chopped
2 cloves garlic, chopped fine
1/4 pod red pepper, chopped
1/6 bunch parsley, chopped fine
Water

Cook rice until almost done. Saute onions in shortening, add shrimp and cook until brown. Add garlic, green onions, parsley, salt, red pepper and water. Pour over rice. When water is absorbed, place in large baking dish and dot with butter. Brown at 350° about 15 minutes.
Genevieve Whitehead, Capital Council, Baton Rouge, La.

SHRIMP SAUTE

8 jumbo shrimp
1/2 stick butter or oleo
1/3 c. dry white wine
Salt, pepper, fresh lemon juice to taste

1 green pepper, finely chopped
1/3 c. heavy cream
Flour

Peel and devein shrimp. Lightly flour shrimp and saute in melted butter for 4 or 5 minutes. Add onion and continue to cook additional minute. Remove shrimp, add wine and cook down until pan juice is thick. Add cream and return shrimp to pan. Add salt, pepper, lemon juice to taste. Cook 1 or 2 minutes. Place under broiler for 1 or 2 minutes. Serve at once with broccoli and broiled tomato, if desired. Serves 1 generously.
June Harllee, Caddo Council, Shreveport, La.

SHRIMP STEW

1 large chopped onion
4 stalks chopped celery
1/2 c. minced shallots
1/2 c. Del Monte sauce
1/4 c. cooking oil
1 qt. water or more

1/2 sweet pepper, chopped
1/4 c. minced parsley
2 or 3 lb. cleaned shrimp
2 heaping cookspoons flour
Salt and pepper to taste

Make a roux by browning flour in oil until dark brown. Add in vegetables. Cook 5 minutes. Add shrimp. Cook until bright pink. Add Del Monte sauce, stir in well. Add 1 quart water and season to taste. Cook about 1 - 1 1/2 hours, adding water whenever necessary. Cook down until brown gravy is creamy. Serve over hot cooked rice.

Jeannett Parr, West Bank
Council, Gretna, La.

STUFFED SHRIMP

1 lb. fresh large shrimp,
  peeled and deveined
Black pepper to taste
2 eggs
3/4 c. chopped celery
Salt to taste
1/2 c. green onion tops,
  chopped fine
1/2 c. bread crumbs
Cayenne pepper to taste

1/2 lb. crabmeat
1/2 lb. boiled shrimp, peeled
1/2 c. chopped onion
1/4 c. chopped bell pepper
1/4 lb. oleo, or 1/2 c. cooking
  oil
1/2 c. fresh parsley, chopped
  fine
2 stale hamburger buns
All-purpose flour

Cook onions and 1/2 cup chopped celery in oil or oleo in heavy pot, uncovered. Season to taste with salt, black and cayenne pepper. Cook slowly until onions are wilted. Grind up boiled shrimp and crabmeat in food chopper. Mix with onion mixture and cook 15 minutes over medium heat uncovered. Add buns which have been soaked in eggs; mix well. Add bell pepper, remainder of celery, green onion tops, parsley and bread crumbs; mix well. Split each fresh large shrimp lengthwise almost to the end and flatten out. Stuff centers of split shrimp with mixture, holding each shrimp in the hand and squeezing it together to form a croquette. Roll in flour, then in batter. Fry quickly for 5 minutes in deep hot fat (375°). Drain.

Shrimp Batter:

2 eggs, beaten
Salt to taste

1/2 c. evaporated milk
Bread crumbs

Combine eggs, milk and salt. Roll floured, stuffed shrimp in mixture and then roll in bread crumbs. Fry.

Genevieve Whitehead, Capital
Council, Baton Rouge, La.

SHRIMP THERMIDOR

1 1/2 lb. shrimp
1 c. chopped celery
8 oz. sliced mushrooms
4 Tbsp. flour
Parmesan cheese
Cheddar cheese, grated
1 pkg. crab boil

1/4 c. chopped onion
1/2 c. chopped bell pepper
1 stick oleo
2 c. milk (one 13 oz. can Pet
   milk and 1/2 c. water)
8-10 baked Pepperidge Farm
   patty shells

Boil shrimp in salted water with crab boil; drain, clean and set aside. Melt oleo and saute bell pepper, onion, celery and mushrooms until vegetables are wilted. Sprinkle flour over mixture and stir well. Add milk slowly, stirring constantly. Cook until thickened. Add shrimp. Pour into greased casserole. Sprinkle Parmesan cheese and then Cheddar cheese over casserole. Bake at 350° about 20 minutes. Spoon into patty shells. Yield: 8-10 shells.

Susan Austin, Ouachita
Council, Monroe, La.

BAKED RED SNAPPER ITALIAN STYLE

3 lb. fish, red snapper,
   or bass
1 clove finely chopped
   garlic
Salt and pepper to taste
Italian cheese
1 small can tomatoes

1 1/2 c. bread crumbs
1/4 c. grated Italian cheese
Mint leaves
1 Tbsp. oil
Onion slices
3 lemon slices

Mix bread crumbs, grated cheese and 3 finely chopped mint leaves (optional); stuff fish, close and fasten with toothpick. Grease baking pan with tablespoon of oil and place fish in it, slit fish on upturned side and in each slit, place 1 small piece cheese, 1 small slice of onion and 1 mint leaf. Pour tomatoes over fish and arrange 3 thin slices of lemon on top. Bake at 350° for 1 hour, basting regularly. Cover last 15 minutes of cooking.

Mrs. Joe Nasello, Central
Council, Alexandria, La.

KING'S RED SNAPPER SHREVE

1 pt. French olive oil
3 bunches parsley
  (approx. 6 oz.)
1 lemon (fresh juice only)
1 small can Contadina
  tomato paste
10-15 lb. red snapper
  fillets

5 bunches (5-6) green onions
1 bottle Cross and Blackwell
  chow-chow (do not substitute)
2 1/2 small cans water
Salt and pepper to taste
Flour, salt, pepper and dill
Cooking oil

Chop parsley and onions coarsely. Saute in small amount of oil. Remove from fire, add chow-chow, tomato paste, lemon juice, water, oil, salt and pepper to taste. Can be refrigerated several weeks. Dip fillets in mixture of flour, salt, pepper and dill; shake. Saute 3-5 minutes. Put in baking dish and bake at 350° for 20-25 minutes. Cover with sauce.

Carl King, Shreveport Works
Council, Shreveport, La.

TROUT AMANDINE

6 filets of trout
1/3 c. flour
1/4 c. butter

3/4 c. milk
Salt and pepper
1/2 c. almonds, chopped

Dip trout in milk. Season with salt and pepper, roll in flour. Cook trout in butter until evenly browned on both sides. Remove fish and saute chopped almonds in drippings. Sprinkle over fish. Serves 6.

John E. Haygood, Caddo
Council, Shreveport, La.

BAKED TROUT

1 filet per person
1 clove garlic, crushed
2 Tbsp. lemon juice
Celery flakes or chopped
   celery to taste

1/2 small onion, chopped
Salt and pepper to taste
1 Tbsp. Worcestershire
   sauce
Dash of Tabasco sauce

Spray foil with Pam. Arrange fish and seasonings on it. Close foil tightly. Bake in preheated oven for 30 minutes. Open foil and broil for a few minutes.

Doris Reeves, Capital
Council, Baton Rouge, La.

TROUT MEUNIERRE ALMONDE

4 fillets of trout (4 oz.
   each)
6 Tbsp. butter, divided
1 Tbsp. Lea & Perrins
   sauce

1/2 Tbsp. flour
2 Tbsp. fresh lemon juice
1/2 c. slivered almonds
Salt, flour, parsley, lemon
   wedges

Sprinkle fish with salt and dredge in flour. Melt 2 tablespoons butter in large skillet. Add trout, saute over moderate heat until golden, about 2 minutes each side. Remove to platter and sprinkle with almonds. Keep warm. In small skillet, melt remaining butter. Add lemon juice and Worcestershire sauce. Simmer until thoroughly heated, about 2 minutes. Pour over fish. Garnish with lemon wedges and parsley if desired. Yield: 2-4 portions. Fillets of sole or flounder may be substituted for trout.

Virgie R. Judge
Crescent City Council
New Orleans, La.

TUNA AU GRATIN

1 (9 oz.) can tuna
1/2 c. cottage cheese
5 slices bread, cubed
2 Tbsp. butter
3 Tbsp. flour

1 tsp. paprika
1 1/2 c. milk
1/2 c. shredded Cheddar
   cheese
2 Tbsp. melted butter

Preheat oven to 350°. Combine tuna, cottage cheese and half the bread crumbs. Spread tuna mixture in bottom

1723-79

of casserole. In saucepan, combine butter, flour and paprika to a smooth paste. Gradually heat and add milk, stirring until thick. Add cheese, stir until melted. Pour sauce over tuna. Top with remaining bread crumbs. Pour melted butter over bread crumbs. Bake 25-30 minutes at 350°.

Calcasieu Council
Lake Charles, La.

BAKED TUNA STUFFED POTATOES

8 large baking potatoes
2 Tbsp. oleo
2 (7 oz.) cans tuna,
  drained
1 Tbsp. grated onion
1 Tbsp. chopped parsley

1 can Cheddar cheese soup
1/4 tsp. paprika
2 drops Tabasco sauce
1/4 tsp. salt
4 slices processed American
  cheese, halved

Wash potatoes and rub skins all over with oleo. Prick with fork. Bake on oven rack in preheated 400° oven for 1 1/2 hours or until tender. Combine tuna, onion, parsley, soup, paprika, Tabasco sauce and salt. Toss with fork to break up tuna and blend well. Remove 1-inch slice from top of each potato. Scoop out inside of potatoes, leaving shell. Add potatoes to tuna mixture, tossing to mix well. Spoon lightly into potato shells, mounding high. Top each with 1/2 slice cheese. Return to oven until cheese melts. Serves 8.

Rebecca Scott Bockmon, Caddo
Council, Shreveport, La.

TUNA FISH LOAVES

3 cans tuna
3 eggs
Salt and pepper to taste
3 c. cooking oil

5 lb. potatoes
1 1/2 c. milk
2 c. plain flour

Peel and boil potatoes until done; drain, mash and add tuna. Mix well and roll into small loaves. Make a batter with eggs and milk. Season to taste. Place flour on board or in a bowl. Dip small loaves in egg mixture, roll in flour and deep fry until brown. Makes about 2 dozen or more, depending on size you make.

Mona Reis, Metairie Council
Metairie, La.

340

ECONOMY TUNA PATTIES

1 large can tuna, un-
   drained

3 eggs
20-25 crackers, crushed
White corn meal

Place tuna, including oil, in large bowl. Mash thoroughly with fork. Add eggs and beat into tuna. Stir in
crackers and add more crackers if not stiff enough to form
patties. Dampen hands, form into patties and turn over
in corn meal. Fry in corn oil or vegetable shortening until
brown.
                                   Mrs. Leona Smith, Central
                                   Council, Corpus Christi, Tx.

TUNA WIGGLE

1 (13 oz.) can evap-
   orated milk
1 large can tuna fish

1 (13 oz.) water
1 (16 oz.) can peas
10 oz. whole milk

Mix ingredients and heat over low flame until hot.
Thicken to desired consistency with flour and water.
Serve over egg noodles or saltine crackers.
                                   Sharon Bell, Capital Council,
                                   Waterbury, Ct.

SWEET 'N SOUR TUNA

2 Tbsp. cooking oil
1 1/4 lb. can pineapple
   chunks
2 Tbsp. cornstarch
1 Tbsp. soy sauce
3 c. cooked rice

2 c. diced green peppers
1 c. chicken bouillon
2 Tbsp. cider vinegar
1/2 c. sugar
2 (7 oz.) cans water packed
   tuna

Saute bell pepper in oil until soft. Add pineapple with
its juice and 3/4 cup chicken bouillon Bring to boil. Dissolve cornstarch in remaining bouillon and add to boiling
sauce. Add vinegar, soy sauce and sugar. Simmer until it
thickens and clears. Drain tuna and fold into sauce. Serve
over hot cooked rice. Serves 6.
                                   Rebecca Scott, Caddo
                                   Council, Shreveport, La.

BREAD, ROLLS
PASTRY

COOKING SUGGESTIONS

To toast coconut for cakes, put in pie pan and place in moderate oven. Stir often from edges, to brown evenly.

* * * * *

Flour should be sifted once before measuring. Fill the cup without packing.

* * * * *

Do not grease the sides of cake pans, grease only the bottoms.

* * * * *

When beating egg whites do not tap beater on bowl of egg whites. The jarring of beater will cause the whites to lose a great deal of their fluffiness. The beater should be tapped on the hand to clear off the whites.

* * * * *

Rub the bottom of the soup cup with a sliced whole garlic to accent the flavor of Navy Bean Soup.

* * * * *

Eggs should be at least three days old before using in cakes.

* * * * *

SLOW OVEN . . . . 250 to 325 degrees
MODERATE OVEN. . . . 350 to 375 degrees
HOT OVEN . . . . 400 to 450 degrees
VERY HOT OVEN . . . . 450 to 500 degrees

* * * * *

When making cake icing or candy consisting of milk or cream and sugar, add one teaspoon of ordinary table syrup for each cup of sugar used. Boil in the usual way. Your finished product will be much smoother and not so apt to become sugary.

PRESERVED CHILDREN

Take 1 large field, half a dozen children, 2 or 3 small dogs, a pinch of brook and some pebbles. Mix the children and dogs well together; put them on the field, stirring constantly. Pour the brook over the pebbles; sprinkle the field with flowers; spread over all a deep blue sky and bake in the sun. When brown, set away to cool in the bathtub.

BISCUITS

2 c. flour
1 tsp. baking powder
  (level)

1/4 tsp. salt
3-4 Tbsp. shortening
2/3 - 3/4 c. milk

Mix, cut and bake at 350° until brown.

Ozone Council, Hammond, La.

BISCUITS

3 c. flour
2 1/2 tsp. sugar
3/4 tsp. cream of tartar
1 c. milk
1 tsp. butter extract

4 1/2 tsp. baking powder
3/4 tsp. salt
3/4 c. shortening
1 egg (optional)

Measure flour into 2-quart bowl. Sprinkle in baking powder, sugar, salt and cream of tartar. Toss lightly with fork. Cut in shortening with pastry blender until mixture is coarse with particles size of peas. Make a well in center of mixture, pour in half the milk. Mix gently with fork. Add egg with remaining milk. Mix lightly with fork. Turn out on lightly floured countertop. Roll or pat out to thickness of 1/2 - 3/4 inch. Cut with lightly floured cutter, about 2 inches in diameter. Place on cookie sheet. Bake at 400° for 12-15 minutes or until lightly browned. Makes about 2 dozen biscuits.

Lynn Babin, Westmoor Council, Kenner, La.

ANGEL BISCUITS

4 c. flour
3 tsp. baking powder
1 tsp. salt
1 pkg. dry yeast
2 c. buttermilk

1/4 c. sugar
1 tsp. soda
1/2 c. shortening
2 tsp. warm water

Sift flour, sugar, baking powder, soda and salt together. Cut in shortening. Soften yeast in water, stir until dissolved. Mix with buttermilk and combine with dry ingredients. Roll out to 1/4-inch thick and cut biscuits.

1723-79

Place in cold oven. Biscuits will rise while oven heats.
Cook at 400° for 15 minutes. These biscuits may be made up
and frozen for future use.   Evelyn Bledsoe, Ouachita
Council, Monroe, La.

ANGEL FLAKE BISCUITS

5 c. flour
3 tsp. baking powder
1 tsp. salt
1 pkg. dry yeast
2 c. buttermilk

1/4 c. sugar
1 tsp. soda
1 c. shortening
2 Tbsp. warm water
Butter or oil

Sift dry ingredients together. Cut in shortening. Dissolve yeast in warm water. Add with buttermilk to dry mixture. Mix well. Turn out on floured board, adding more flour if needed. Roll to 1/4-inch thickness. Spread half of dough with butter or oil. Fold over and spread top with butter or oil. Cut out with biscuit cutter. Bake at 400° about 15 minutes. Extra dough may be kept in refrigerator until needed.   Bob Spivey, Shreveport Works
Council, Shreveport, La.

BUTTER BISCUITS

2 c. sifted flour
1/2 tsp. cream of tartar
4 tsp. baking powder
1 1/2 tsp. Adam's butter
flavoring

1/2 tsp. salt
2 tsp. sugar
1/2 c. shortening
2/3 c. milk

Sift together flour, salt, cream of tartar, sugar and baking powder. Cut in shortening until mixture resembles coarse crumbs. Add flavoring and milk. Stir until dough follows fork around bowl. Turn out on lightly floured surface and knead gently for 1/2 minute. Pat or roll 1/2-inch thick. Cut with biscuit cutter. Bake on ungreased cookie sheet at 450° for 10-12 minutes. Makes 16 medium biscuits.
Orange Biscuits: Add 2 teaspoons orange flavoring along with milk.   Jeanette English, Caddo
Council, Shreveport, La.

BUTTERMILK BISCUITS

2 c. sifted flour
1/2 tsp. salt
5 Tbsp. shortening
Oleo

3 tsp. baking powder
1/4 tsp. soda
1 c. buttermilk

Sift flour, baking powder, salt and soda together. Cut in shortening until mixture has coarse crumbs. Add buttermilk all at once. Stir until dough stays together. Knead well for 1 minute on floured bread board. Pat out dough 3/4-inch thick. Cut in rounds. Place on cookie sheet with a bit of oleo on each. Bake at 450° for 12-15 minutes. Makes 2 dozen.   Molly Hoskins, Caddo
                                       Council, Shreveport, La.

CHEESE BISCUITS

1/4 lb. sharp cheese
1/4 lb. butter or mar-
   garine

1 1/4 c. flour
Pinch of salt

Grate cheese and cream with butter. Add flour, salt and sugar; chill. Make into tiny biscuits, put 1/2 pecan on top of each (optional). Bake at 400° for 10 minutes. Reduce heat to 350° for 10 minutes.
                                       Calcasieu Council
                                       Lake Charles, La.

DROP BISCUITS

2/3 c. unsifted flour
1/4 tsp. salt
1/2 c. milk

1 tsp. baking powder
2 Tbsp. shortening

Mix flour, baking powder and salt. Mix in shortening with fork until crumbly. Stir in milk. Mix enough to wet the dry ingredients. Drop dough from tablespoon onto a greased baking pan. Bake at 450° for 10-12 minutes until lightly browned. Makes about 4 biscuits.
                                       June Harllee, Caddo
                                       Council, Shreveport,La.

IDA'S BISCUITS

2 c. flour
1/2 tsp. soda
3/4 - 1 c. buttermilk

3/4 tsp. salt
1/3 c. Crisco

Cut shortening into dry ingredients. Stir in buttermilk until dough holds together. Turn over on floured board. Pinch off a piece of dough and shape into biscuit. Put into hot greased skillet. Bake at 500° for about 10 minutes. When tops are slightly brown, transfer to broiler until evenly browned.   Ida Guy, Caddo Council,
                                              Shreveport, La.

MAMA'S EASY SOURDOUGH BISCUITS

4 1/2 c. self-rising flour
2 c. buttermilk
2/3 c. cooking oil

2 pkg. yeast
2 Tbsp. sugar
1 tsp. soda

Mix all ingredients. Keep tightly covered in refrigerator. Take out as needed and knead with a little extra flour and bake.   Carolyn Palmer, Capital
                                    Council, Baton Rouge, La.

MAYONNAISE BISCUITS

1 c. self-rising flour
1/2 c. milk

2 Tbsp. mayonnaise

Mix mayonnaise and flour well. Add milk. Drop in greased muffin tins. Bake at 450° about 10 minutes or until lightly browned.   Dot Anderson, Ozone
                                    Council, Covington, La.

MILE-HIGH BISCUITS (Frozen)

3 c. flour
1/4 c. sugar
3/4 tsp. salt
1 egg, beaten

1/2 tsp. cream of tartar
4 tsp. baking powder
1/2 c. shortening
1 1/2 c. milk

Combine dry ingredients in mixing bowl, cut in shortening until mixture resembles coarse crumbs. Add egg and

milk all at once; mix until dough forms a ball. Turn dough out on lightly floured surface and knead 10-12 times. Roll out to 3/4-inch thickness, cut with floured 2 1/2-inch biscuit cutter. Place on ungreased cookie sheet and freeze. Place frozen biscuits in plastic bag in freezer. Bake frozen biscuits on greased baking sheet at 475° for 12-15 minutes when ready to use.　　　　Jeanette English, Caddo
　　　　　　　　　　　　　　Council, Shreveport, La.

SOURDOUGH STARTER

1 env. active dry yeast　　　　2 c. warm water
　　　　　　　　　　　　　　2 c. all-purpose flour

Mix ingredients together in 1 1/2-quart glass or earthenware container. Cover with cheesecloth. This keeps bugs out, but lets airborn wild yeasts make contact. Leave in warm room 48 hours. Stir 2-3 times. It will ferment, bubble and acquire slightly sour smell. Makes 3 cups. To use, stir then pour off as much of this starter as recipe requires. Then add equal parts of flour and water; say, 2 cups each to remaining starter in the pot. Stir and let stand a few hours, uncovered, until it bubbles again, then cover and refrigerate. By replenishing the starter with flour and water, you can keep it going continuously. Never add anything other than flour and water to starter pot.
　　　　　　　　　　　　　　Connie Younker, Shreveport
　　　　　　　　　　　　　　Works Council, Shreveport, La.

SOURDOUGH BISCUITS

1 pkg. yeast　　　　　　　　1 c. warm water
2 c. buttermilk　　　　　　　3/4 c. corn oil
1/4 c. sugar　　　　　　　　5 c. flour
4 tsp. baking powder　　　　1 1/2 tsp. salt
1/4 tsp. soda

Dissolve yeast in water. Add buttermilk, corn oil and sugar. Mix well. Sift flour, baking powder, salt and soda together and add to mixture. Work up dough and place in tight fitted covered bowl. Refrigerate. Pinch off what you need on floured board and roll out as you would biscuits. Return unused portion to refrigerator. This will keep as long as a week.　　　　Mildred Pace, Caddo
　　　　　　　　　　　　　　Council, Shreveport, La.

SWEET POTATO BISCUITS

1 egg, slightly beaten
1/4 - 1/2 c. sugar
2 c. self-rising flour
  or less

1 c. cooked, mashed sweet
  potatoes
2 Tbsp. butter, softened
3 Tbsp. shortening

Combine all ingredients in bowl, except flour; mix well. Stir in enough flour to make a soft dough. Dough will be softer than regular dough. Turn out on floured surface, knead lightly a few times. Roll to 1/4-inch thickness, cut with 2-inch biscuit cutter. Place on ungreased baking sheet and bake at 350° about 15 minutes. Makes 17 biscuits. Use only 1/4 cup sugar if potatoes are naturally sweet and juicy.

Rebecca Scott, Caddo
Council, Shreveport, La.

YEAST BISCUITS

6 c. self-rising flour
1 1/2 tsp. soda
2 c. buttermilk
2 pkg. dry yeast

1/2 c. sugar
1/2 c. oil
1 c. warm water

Dissolve yeast in warm water. Combine all ingredients, mix well and refrigerate. Better if made night before. When ready to cook, roll out, cut and bake as usual for biscuits.

Sandra K. Autrey, Metairie
Council, Metairie, La.

ALICE'S GRANDMA KAZANOWSKI'S BREAD

1 pkg. dry yeast
1/2 c. warm milk
1 c. milk, room temperature
1 tsp. salt
Sprinkle of mace

1 Tbsp. sugar + 1/2 c. sugar
1/4 c. melted butter
3 eggs
2 tsp. grated orange peel
6 1/2 c. flour

Combine yeast, 1 tablespoon sugar and 1/2 cup warm milk; let yeast dissolve. Add remainder of ingredients, little at a time, until well mixed. Knead. Let rise until doubled. Place dough in 2 loaf pans, let rise until doubled in bulk again. Bake about 40 minutes at 375°.

Adrienne Dezendorf, Central
Council, Alexandria, La.

APPLE BREAD

2 eggs
2 c. flour
1 tsp. soda
2 Tbsp. buttermilk
1/2 c. chopped pecans

1 c. chopped apples
1/2 c. cooking oil
1 c. sugar
1/2 tsp. salt
1 tsp. vanilla

Mix ingredients well. Place in greased loaf pan, bake at 350° for 1 hour or until done. Una Mize, Caddo Council, Shreveport, La.

APRICOT NUT BREAD

1 (16 oz.) can apricot
  halves
1/3 c. shortening
1 3/4 c. all-purpose flour
1/2 tsp. soda

1/2 c. sugar
2 eggs
1 tsp. baking powder
1/2 tsp. salt
1/2 c. chopped walnuts

Drain apricots, reserving juice. Press apricots through sieve. Add enough reserved syrup or juice to make 1 cup; set aside. Cream sugar and shortening together until fluffy. Add eggs, 1 at a time, beating well after each addition. Combine dry ingredients and add to creamed mixture. Add apricots. Stir just until all ingredients are moistened. Stir in walnuts. Spoon batter into well greased loaf pan. Bake at 350° for 50 minutes or until bread tests done. Remove from pan and cool. Yield: 1 loaf.

Marilou Bridges, Caddo
Council, Shreveport, La.

QUICK APPLE BREAD

1/2 c. shortening
1 c. sugar
1/4 tsp. salt
1 tsp. vanilla
2 eggs
2 Tbsp. milk

1 c. chopped apples, un-
  peeled
1/4 c. chopped nuts
2 c. sifted flour
2 tsp. baking powder
1/4 tsp. cinnamon

Cream shortening, sugar, salt, vanilla until light and fluffy. Add eggs and beat well. Add milk, apples and nuts, beat. Stir in flour, baking powder, cinnamon. Blend. Pour into greased loaf pan. Bake at 350° for about 50 minutes.

Calcasieu Council
Lake Charles, La.

BANANA BREAD

1 tsp. baking soda
1/2 c. shortening
2 eggs
Pinch of salt

2 bananas
1 c. sugar
1 1/2 c. flour
1/2 c. nuts

Mix soda and bananas together. Combine shortening, sugar, eggs, flour, salt. Mix all ingredients together with nuts. Pour into greased and floured loaf pan and bake at 350° about 1 hour or until done.

Ann Aslinger, Gentilly
Council, Meraux, La.

BANANA BREAD

1 1/4 c. sugar
1/2 c. oil
1 1/2 c. bananas
2 c. flour

2 1/2 tsp. baking powder
2 eggs
1 tsp. vanilla

Mix ingredients together thoroughly. Pour batter into greased and floured loaf pan or pan of your choice. Bake at 350° for 30-45 minutes until golden brown.

Cher White, Capital Council,
Waterbury, Ct.

BANANA BREAD

1/2 c. butter or oleo
1 tsp. soda
1 c. sugar
2 c. plain sifted flour

2 eggs, beaten
3 large bananas, mashed
1/2 tsp. salt
3/4 c. chopped pecans or
    walnuts

Mix in this order: Oleo, eggs, soda, bananas, sugar, flour, salt and nuts. Bake in greased and floured loaf pan at 350° for 1 hour.

Odie Reynolds, Ouachita
Council, Tallulah, La.

BEER BREAD

3 1/2 c. self-rising flour
1 Tbsp. sugar

1 (10 oz.) can beer, any kind

Mix all ingredients together. Shape into greased loaf pan. Bake at 350° for about 30-35 minutes or until golden brown.
Jo Ann Everhardt, Gentilly Council, Meraux, La.

BILL BARKER'S BEER BREAD

3 c. self-rising flour
2 Tbsp. sugar

12 oz. beer, room temperature

Stir flour and sugar together, add beer and stir 25 strokes. Place in buttered bread pan and bake in preheated 350° oven for 1 - 1 1/4 hours. Cool and wrap in foil or plastic bag overnight. This bread has a heavy crust. Variations include the addition of fresh or dried onion, garlic salt, ground oysters, yogurt for a sourdough flavor and egg for texture.
Claudine Chisley, Ouachita Council, Monroe, La.

BRAN BREAD

2 c. All-Bran cereal
2 c. sour milk
1 c. raisins
2 Tbsp. molasses

2 c. flour
1 c. sugar
2 tsp. soda
1/2 tsp. salt

Mix milk, bran, raisins and molasses, add dry ingredients. Pour into three No. 303 cans with waxed paper in bottom. Fill cans 2/3 full. Bake in slow oven for 1 - 1 1/2 hours. To serve, slice and spread with cream cheese which has been softened and chopped nuts added to it.
Calcasieu Council
Lake Charles, La.

BUTTERNUT RAISIN BREAD

3 1/2 c. unbleached flour
1 c. raisins
2 c. sugar
1 1/2 c. cooked, mashed
  butternut squash
1 1/2 tsp. ground nutmeg
1 tsp. ground mace

2 tsp. soda
1 c. vegetable oil
4 eggs
1/2 c. honey
1 c. water
1 1/2 tsp. ground cinnamon
1 1/2 tsp. salt

Combine flour, soda and raisins. Stir well and set aside. Combine oil, sugar and eggs, beat well. Stir in squash, honey, water, spices and salt. Add flour mixture. Stir just until all ingredients are moistened. Pour batter into 3 greased 9x5 inch loaf pans. Bake at 350° for 1 hour. Cool. Makes 3 loaves. Batter may be baked in 3 greased 1-pound coffee cans. Bake at 350° for 1 hour and 20 minutes.

Ann Orr, Evangeline
Council, New Iberia, La.

CHERRY NUT BREAD

2 c. instant blending flour
1 tsp. soda
1 tsp. salt
1/2 c. liquid shortening
3/4 c. sugar

2 eggs
1 c. buttermilk
1 tsp. vanilla
Chopped nuts
Cherries

Grease four No. 303 cans. In large mixer bowl, combine all ingredients, except nuts and cherries. Spoon into cans and bake at 325° for 60 minutes. Cool 10 minutes, remove from pans.

Calcasieu Council
Lake Charles, La.

CORN BREAD

3/4 c. corn meal
1 egg
1 tsp. salt
3 tsp. baking powder

1 1/4 c. flour
1/4 c. sugar
3/4 c. milk
1/4 c. Crisco

Mix ingredients. Place in greased pan or skillet. Bake at 400° about 20 minutes or until done.

Cecile Gallet, Evangeline
Council, Lafayette, La.

CORN BREAD

2 c. corn meal
1/4 tsp. soda
2 tsp. baking powder
1 tsp. salt

2 eggs, beaten
2 c. sour milk
2 Tbsp. melted fat

Sift together dry ingredients. Add eggs to milk and stir into dry ingredients. Add melted fat. Pour into greased pan about 8 inches square and bake at 425° (hot oven) for 20-30 minutes. Makes 8 servings.

Calcasieu Council
Lake Charles, La.

CORN BREAD

1 c. uncooked cream of
    wheat
2 Tbsp. sugar
1/2 tsp. salt
1 egg

1 c. sifted flour
4 tsp. baking powder
1 c. milk, sweet or butter-
    milk

Mix ingredients, stir gently and do not overbeat. Pour into greased pan and bake at 425° until golden brown.

Mrs. Vernie McAlister
Crescent City Council
Chalmette, La.

BUTTERMILK CORN BREAD

2 c. corn meal
2 tsp. baking powder
1/2 tsp. soda
2 c. buttermilk

2/3 c. all-purpose flour
1 tsp. salt
2 eggs, beaten

Combine dry ingredients, add eggs and buttermilk, mixing well. Pour batter in large greased cast iron skillet. Bake at 400° for 20-25 minutes or until browned. Cut into wedges. I don't use this skillet for anything but corn bread and I never wash it, just wipe out well. After a few times you will find the corn bread will fall out of pan easily and intact.

Marilou Bridges, Caddo
Council, Shreveport, La.

DELL'S FRIED CORN BREAD

1 1/2 c. plain yellow
  corn meal
2 tsp. baking powder
1 small onion, chopped
  fine

1/2 c. flour
1 Tbsp. sugar
1 egg
1 c. cream style corn

Mix ingredients and drop by spoonfuls in deep hot fat. If mixture seems too dry or too stiff, add more corn.

Marie Pamplin, Shreveport
Works Council, Shreveport, La.

JALAPENO BREAD

2 c. corn bread mix
3 Tbsp. Crisco oil
1 c. chopped onions
4 jalapeno peppers,
  chopped

1 can cream corn
1/4 lb. sharp cheese, grated
2 eggs
3/4 c. milk

Mix all ingredients and bake at 425° for 40-45 minutes.

Doris B. Reeves, Capital
Council, Baton Rouge, La.

JALAPENO CORN BREAD

2 c. corn meal mix
1 tsp. sugar
1 c. grated Hoop cheese
1 egg
1 jalapeno pepper, chopped

4 Tbsp. flour
1/2 tsp. baking soda
1/2 c. McCormick bacon bits
1/2 c. buttermilk
1 can creamed corn

Mix corn meal, flour, sugar, cheese, bacon bits and chopped jalapeno pepper together. Add soda to buttermilk, stir until smooth and add to corn meal mixture. Add corn and egg, mix thoroughly and pour into pan sprayed with Pam. Bake at 350° for 1 hour.

Estelle Banker, Capital
Council, Baton Rouge, La.

354

JALAPENO CORN BREAD

1 c. buttermilk
2 eggs
1/4 tsp. soda
1 tsp. garlic salt
1 medium onion, chopped
2 Tbsp. melted bacon
  fat

1 c. yellow corn meal
1 tsp. baking powder
1 tsp. salt
1/2 c. grated cheese
1 c. cream style corn
2 small or 1 large jalapeno
  pepper, chopped

Mix ingredients and place in ovenproof pan. Bake at 350° until done or until tester comes out clean.

Verle Oliphant, Caddo
Council, Shreveport, La.

MEXICAN CORN BREAD

1 1/2 c. corn meal
3 tsp. baking powder
2 eggs
2 green peppers, chopped
1 can cream style corn

1 tsp. salt
1 c. sour cream
2/3 c. Wesson oil
2 jalapeno peppers, chopped
1 c. grated cheese

Combine and mix all ingredients, except cheese. Pour into greased skillet and bake 1 hour at 350°. Add cheese last 30 minutes of baking.

Mildred Burton, Ouachita
Council, Monroe, La.

MEXICAN CORN BREAD

1 1/2 c. corn meal
3 tsp. baking powder
2 jalapeno peppers,
  chopped
1 c. cream style corn
1 c. sour cream

3 eggs
1 tsp. salt
1 Tbsp. chopped bell pepper
1/2 c. cooking oil
1 c. grated cheese

Mix all ingredients and bake at 350° for 40-45 minutes.

Evelyn Bledsoe, Ouachita
Council, Monroe, La.

MEXICAN CORN BREAD

1 c. yellow corn meal
3/4 tsp. salt
2 eggs
1 (16 oz.) can cream
　style corn
1/2 lb. Cheddar cheese,
　grated
Chopped bell pepper

1 c. milk
1/4 c. bacon fat
1/2 tsp. soda
1/2 - 3/4 lb. ground beef
Chopped onions
3-4 chopped jalapeno peppers,
　to taste

Mix corn bread, milk, salt, bacon fat, eggs, soda and cream. Pour 1/2 of batter in 9x9 inch dish. Brown ground meat, drain and spread over corn meal mixture. Sprinkle with layer each of onions, bell peppers and jalapeno peppers. Top with remaining corn meal mixture. Bake at 350° for 45 to 50 minutes until golden brown. Jan Prestridge, Capital
Council, Baton Rouge, La.

MEXICAN CORN BREAD

1 c. yellow corn meal
1 c. milk
1/2 tsp. baking soda
1/2 c. cooking oil
1 large onion, finely
　chopped
1/2 lb. grated mild cheese

2 eggs, well beaten
1 can cream style corn
3/4 tsp. salt
1 lb. ground beef
3 chili cortidors (peppers),
　chopped fine (2 if large)

Combine corn meal, milk, eggs, corn, baking soda, salt and oil; mix and set aside. Saute beef and drain. Grease large iron skillet and heat. Sprinkle a very thin layer of corn meal in bottom of skillet and brown lightly. Pour in half of meal batter, sprinkle with grated cheese, then a layer with the meat. Top with the chopped onion and chili peppers. Pour remaining batter on top. Bake 1 hour at 350° or until golden brown. Can be used as main dish with salad or is delicious served with barbeque. Yield: Serves 4 generously as a main dish. Mrs. Richard D. (Vermelle)
Sylvest, Ozone Council,
Hammond, La.

MEXICAN CORN BREAD

1 1/2 c. corn meal
2 eggs
1/2 tsp. soda
1 lb. ground meat
1 lb. mild Cheddar
   cheese, grated

1 c. sweet milk
3/4 tsp. salt
1 large can cream style corn
1 large onion, chopped
2 jalapeno peppers,
   chopped (more if desired)

Combine and mix corn meal, eggs, soda, sweet milk, salt and corn together to make batter. Saute ground meat, drain, add onion and peppers. Prepare skillet or pan for corn bread by greasing and sprinkling with meal and let brown. Pour half of batter into skillet. Sprinkle beef mixture over batter and cover with grated cheese. Pour remainder of batter over top. Bake at 350° for 45 minutes or until done.

Maxine Fletcher, Ouachita
Council, Monroe, La.

MOLASSES CORN BREAD

2 c. Bisquick baking mix
1/2 c. corn meal
1 tsp. baking powder
1/2 c. dark molasses

1/2 c. whole wheat flour
1/3 c. sugar
1 1/4 c. water
1 egg

Mix all ingredients until thoroughly moistened. Pour into greased loaf pan, 9x5x3 inches. Bake in preheated 350° oven about 50-60 minutes or until tester comes out dry. Serve with Orange Butter (recipe in book).

Marie Pamplin, Shreveport
Works Council, Shreveport, La.

HOT CRAB BREAD

1 (7 1/2 oz.) can crab-
   meat, flaked
1/3 c. mayonnaise
1/3 c. dairy sour cream
2 Tbsp. chopped parsley
2 tsp. lemon juice

2 Tbsp. butter
1 loaf French or Italian
   bread (about 15 inches
   long)
1/4 tsp. garlic salt
1/4 lb. sliced Swiss cheese

Combine crabmeat, mayonnaise, sour cream, parsley, lemon juice and garlic salt. Chill. Slice bread in half lengthwise, arrange on baking sheet. Spread cut sides with butter. Top with cheese slices, trimmed to fit bread. Cover cheese with crab mixture. Bake at 350° until lightly browned, 25 minutes. Cut across to serve.

Calcasieu Council
Lake Charles, La.

DILL BREAD

2 pkg. yeast
1/2 c. warm water
2 Tbsp. butter
2 tsp. salt
2 Tbsp. instant minced
   onion
2 eggs

2 c. cottage cheese, cream
   style
4 Tbsp. sugar
1/2 tsp. soda
2 Tbsp. dill seed
4 1/2 - 5 c. flour

Heat cottage cheese to lukewarm. Soften yeast in warm water, let stand 10 minutes. Combine cottage cheese, butter, sugar, salt, soda, onion and dill seed. Add eggs and yeast mixture. Beat well; add flour gradually; beat well after each addition. Cover and let rise until double in size, about 1 to 1 1/2 hours. Punch down, turn into 2 well greased coffee cans. Let rise until double in size. Bake at 350° for 35-45 minutes. Cool 5 minutes, turn on rack. Brush with butter and sprinkle with salt.

Glenda Cox, Caddo
Council, Shreveport, La.

FRENCH BREAD

1 3/4 c. milk
3 tsp. sugar
3 pkg. yeast
7-8 c. unsifted all-
   purpose flour
2 Tbsp. water

3 Tbsp. butter or oleo
1 Tbsp. salt
1 1/4 c. warm water
2 Tbsp. corn meal
1 egg

Heat milk, butter, 2 teaspoons sugar and salt in saucepan until tiny bubbles form around edge. Butter does not need to melt. Cool to lukewarm. In large mixing bowl, dissolve yeast and 1 teaspoon sugar in warm water. Add cooled milk mixture. Stir in 2-3 cups flour and mix at medium speed about 2 minutes. With wooden spoon, stir in enough flour to form a stiff dough. Turn onto a lightly floured surface and knead about 8-10 minutes, adding more flour as needed until smooth and elastic. Shape dough into a ball

and place in large greased bowl, turning to grease top. Cover and set in warm place, free from drafts, until double in bulk, about 1 1/2 hours. Punch dough down. Knead lightly for a minute or two. Divide in quarters. Shape each into oblong loaves about 12 inches long. Grease 2 large cookie sheets and sprinkle with corn meal. Place dough on sheets 3 inches apart. Cover and let rise in warm place, free from drafts, until doubled in bulk, about 1 hour. Brush with egg and water mixture. Make slashes with razor blade or sharp knife on top. Bake in preheated 425° oven for 20-25 minutes until loaves sound hollow when tapped with fingers. Cool completely on wire racks. Makes 4 loaves; about sixteen 1-inch slices per loaf; about 100 calories per slice.   Denise Barteet, Caddo
                                       Council, Shreveport, La.

CHEESE FRENCH BREAD

1/2 c. mayonnaise
1 c. ripe olives, chopped
2 cloves garlic, chopped
1 large loaf French bread

1/2 c. oleo, softened
2 c. grated Mozzarella
   cheese
6 green onions, chopped

Cream oleo and mayonnaise, add other ingredients and spread on bread. Bake at 350° for 15-20 minutes until cheese melts. Good with meat balls and spaghetti or spaghetti sauce.   Billie Williams, Ouachita
                                       Council, Monroe, La.

SAN FRANCISCO SOURDOUGH FRENCH BREAD

1 pkg. active dry yeast
2 Tbsp. sugar
5 c. all-purpose flour

1 c. warm water
1 1/2 c. sourdough starter
2 tsp. salt

In large mixing bowl, sprinkle yeast over warm water, let dissolve 5 minutes. Stir in sugar, starter and gradually add 4 cups of the flour mixed with salt. Cover bowl with damp cloth, let rise 1 - 1 1/2 hours in a warm place. Turn dough onto floured board, work in remaining flour until dough is no longer sticky. Knead until satiny, about 5 minutes. Shape dough into 1 large round or 2 long oval loaves. Set on cookie sheet sprinkled with rice flour or corn meal. Let rise again in warm place for 1 - 1 1/2 hours. Put shallow pan of water in lower shelf of oven; preheat to 400°.

Make diagonal slashes in bread, preferably with razor blade so dough does not fall. Bake 40-50 minutes or until crust is medium dark brown. Set on rack to cool.

Connie Younker, Shreveport
Works Council, Shreveport, La.

FRESH BREAD

1 c. milk	3 Tbsp. sugar
2 tsp. salt	4 Tbsp. butter
1 c. warm water	1 pkg. dry yeast
5 1/2 c. sifted flour	

Scald milk in pot, adding sugar, salt and butter. Cool. In a large bowl, add yeast to warm water. Stir in milk mixture. Add 3 cups flour, beat vigorously until well blended and dough is soft. Place on a floured board, knead until smooth. Shape into a ball. Place in a bowl, cover with cheesecloth. Let stand until dough is twice its size. Divide dough evenly. Place each half into a greased bread pan, cover, let stand for 1 hour. Bake at 400° for 30 minutes. Use a toothpick to test for doneness. Remove from pan. Invert loaves on a wire rack. Let stand for 10 minutes before slicing.

Calcasieu Council
Lake Charles, La.

FRUIT NUT BREAD

2 1/4 c. sifted flour	2 tsp. baking powder
1 tsp. salt	3/4 c. sugar
1/2 c. coarsely chopped pecans	1 c. diced, candied, mixed fruit
2 eggs, beaten	1 c. dairy eggnog
1/4 c. butter, melted	

Sift flour, baking powder, salt and sugar together. Add pecans and fruit. Mix until well blended. Combine eggs, eggnog and butter, add to dry ingredients, mixing until ingredients are moistened. Pour into greased and floured 9x5x3-inch loaf pan. Bake at 350° until done. Cool about 1 hour before removing from pan. Frost with powdered sugar icing with rum flavoring and decorate with glace cherries if desired.

Louise Malone, Caddo
Council, Shreveport, La.

GARLIC BREAD

1 large loaf soft French
  bread
2 Tbsp. garlic powder

1 stick butter
2 Tbsp. parsley flakes
1 tsp. paprika

Melt butter in saucepan. Add garlic powder and parsley flakes. Stir contantly for 10 minutes on low heat. Remove, cover and let set 10 minutes. Add paprika and mix well. Slice bread in 1-inch slices. Spread butter mix on all slices. Place on cookie sheet and brown under broiler. Serve hot.

Willie S. Gains, West Bank
Council, Gretna, La.

HARVEST BREAD

3 c. sugar
4 eggs
1 (16 oz.) can frozen
  orange juice, thawed
2 tsp. soda
2 tsp. nutmeg
1/2 tsp. ground cloves

1 c. oil
2 c. sweet potatoes, cooked
3 1/2 c. flour
1 1/2 tsp. salt
2 tsp. cinnamon
1/2 tsp. allspice
1 c. chopped pecans

Cream sugar and oil, beat in eggs. Add potatoes and orange juice. Sift dry ingredients and add to mixture. Stir in nuts. Bake in four 1-pound well greased coffee cans filled about 1/2 full for 45 minutes at 350°.

Mildred Henderson, Ouachita
Council, Monroe, La.

INDIAN FRY BREAD

3 c. flour
Lukewarm water
1/4 c. instant non-fat
  dry milk

1/2 tsp. salt
1 tsp. baking powder
Hot fat

Combine flour, salt, baking powder and dry milk in large bowl, add enough water to make a soft dough. Pinch off piece about size of egg, shape and pat flat and punch a small hole in middle, stretch as thin as possible. Drop into hot fat in heavy iron skillet, fry to light brown on one side, turn with tongs. It will puff up and hole in middle helps quick cooking. Drain on paper towels and serve with honey, jelly or powdered sugar if desired.

Katherine Slover, Caddo
Council, Phoenix, Az.

IRISH OATMEAL BREAD

3 c. sifted all-purpose
  flour
1 1/2 tsp. baking powder
1 Tbsp. butter or oleo,
melted

1 1/4 c. quick rolled oats
1 1/2 tsp. salt
1 egg
1 1/2 c. milk *Buttermilk*
1/4 c. honey

Mix flour, oats, baking powder and salt in large bowl. Beat egg with honey and milk to beat well. Pour into oat mixture until dry ingredients are just moistened. Batter will not be smooth. Spread batter in pan. Bake in greased loaf pan in preheated 350° oven for 1 1/4 hours or until crusty and tests done. Turn out to cool. While still warm, brush top with melted butter. This is delicious toasted and spread with butter or honey. Yield: 1 loaf. Marilou Bridges, Caddo
Council, Shreveport, La.

IRISH SODA BREAD

2 c. unsifted all-purpose
  flour
1 tsp. baking soda
3 Tbsp. butter or oleo,
  softened
1 c. buttermilk

2 Tbsp. sugar
1 tsp. baking powder
1/2 tsp. salt
1/2 c. seedless raisins
1 Tbsp. butter or oleo, melted

Sift flour, sugar, baking soda, baking powder and salt into a large bowl. Cut in softened butter with pastry blender or fork until mixture looks like fine crumbs. Add raisins and buttermilk. Mix with a fork until ingredients are moistened. Turn out on lightly floured board and knead about 1 minute until smooth. Shape into a ball. Place on lightly greased small cookie sheet. Flatten into a 7-inch circle about 1 1/2 inches thick. Press a large floured knife into center of the loaf halfway through to bottom. Repeat at right angles to divide loaf into quarters. Bake in preheated 375° oven for 30-40 minutes or until top is golden and loaf sounds hollow when tapped. Remove to wire rack to cool. Brush top with melted butter. Later, dust top with flour.

Makes 1 loaf. For whole wheat Irish soda bread, use 1 cup all-purpose flour and 2 cups whole wheat flour. Proceed as for white soda bread recipe. June Harllee, Caddo Council, Shreveport, La.

LEMON BREAD

3/4 c. butter or oleo,
   softened
2 1/4 c. all-purpose flour
1/4 tsp. soda
Grated rind of 1 lemon
Juice of 2 lemons

1 1/2 c. sugar
3 eggs
1/4 tsp. salt
1/4 c. buttermilk
3/4 c. chopped pecans
3/4 c. powdered sugar

Combine butter and sugar, creaming until light and fluffy. Add eggs, beating well. Combine dry ingredients. Add buttermilk and dry ingredients alternately to creamed mixture, stir just until all ingredients are moistened. Stir in lemon rind and pecans. Spoon batter into a greased and floured loaf pan. Bake at 325° for 1 hour and 15 minutes. Cool 15 minutes and remove from pan. Combine lemon juice and powdered sugar, stir well. Punch holes in top of warm bread with toothpick, pour glaze over loaf. Cool.
Calcasieu Council
Lake Charles, La.

NUT BREAD

2 eggs
2 c. flour
1 Tbsp. salt

1 c. sugar
4 Tbsp. baking powder
1 c. nutmeats

Mix sugar and eggs, mix all ingredients together. Spoon or pour batter into two greased and floured loaf pans. Let rise 30-40 minutes. Bake at 350° until done.
Ozone Council, Hammond, La.

ONION BREAD

1 pkg. dry yeast
3 c. all-purpose flour,
   divided
2 tsp. salt, divided
2 tsp. paprika

2 tsp. sugar
2 Tbsp. oleo
1 c. warm water
1/2 c. chopped onions

Dissolve yeast in warm water. Add 1 teaspoon salt, sugar and 2 cups flour. Stir to blend, then beat well. Stir in 1/2 cup additional flour. Sprinkle about 1/4 cup flour on pastry board. Turn dough out, knead 5-7 minutes until smooth, adding remaining flour as needed. Shape into smooth ball. Place in greased bowl, cover and let rise about 1 hour. Punch down, divide in halves, cover and let rise 5 minutes. Place dough into 2 greased 9-inch layer cake pans. Brush tops with oleo and sprinkle evenly with onions. Push onions down into dough. Let rise about 45 minutes or until doubled. Sprinkle each loaf with 1/2 teaspoon salt and dust generously with paprika. Bake at 450° for 20-25 minutes.

Mearl S. Byles, Central
Council, Natchitoches, La.

RYE BREAD

1 pkg. dry yeast
2 c. hot water
2 tsp. salt
1/4 c. molasses

1/4 c. light syrup
5 c. white flour
2 1/2 c. rye flour
2 Tbsp. lard

Soak yeast in 1/2 cup warm water. Put rest of water into a bowl. Add syrup, molasses, salt and lard. Add rye flour and 2 cups white flour; now cool to lukewarm. Beat well, add yeast, beat. Add rest of flour and mix until all flour is used.

Calcasieu Council
Lake Charles, La.

STRAWBERRY BREAD

3 c. all-purpose flour
1 tsp. salt
2 c. sugar
1 1/4 c. vegetable oil
1 1/4 c. chopped pecans

1 tsp. baking soda
1 Tbsp. cinnamon
4 eggs, beaten
2 c. thawed, sliced, frozen strawberries

Combine dry ingredients. Add eggs, oil, strawberries and pecans. Stir just until all ingredients are moistened. Spoon batter into well greased loaf pans. Bake at 350° for 60-70 minutes or until bread tests done. Cool in pan 5 minutes. Remove to wire rack to cool. Makes 2 loaves.

Calcasieu Council
Lake Charles, La.

SWEET POTATO BREAD

3 c. sugar
2 c. mashed sweet
  potatoes
1 tsp. nutmeg
1 1/2 tsp. salt
2/3 c. fresh orange juice
1 c. white raisins

1 c. Wesson oil
4 eggs
2 tsp. soda
1 tsp. cinnamon
3 1/2 c. sifted flour
1 c. chopped dates
2 c. pecans, cut fine

Put all ingredients in bowl and mix well. Add raisins, dates and nuts last. Bake 1 hour at 350° in 4 well greased and floured 1-pound coffee cans. Small loaf pans may also be used if preferred, but coffee cans enable you to slice easily.
Verle Oliphant, Caddo Council, Shreveport, La.

COFFEE CAN SWEET POTATO BREAD

3 1/2 c. flour
3 c. sugar
1 tsp. cinnamon
2 c. baked, mashed
  sweet potatoes
4 eggs
1 c. chopped pecans

1 tsp. salt
2 tsp. soda
1 tsp. nutmeg
1 c. cooking oil
2/3 c. water
1 c. raisins, lightly floured

Sift flour, sugar, salt, soda, cinnamon and nutmeg together; add potatoes, oil and water. Add eggs, 1 at a time, beating after each addition. Stir in pecans and raisins. Grease and flour four 1-pound coffee cans. Fill 1/2 full. Bake at 350° for 1 hour.
Marilou Bridges, Caddo Council, Shreveport, La.

SUMMER FRUIT BREAD

1 (8 oz.) pkg. cream
  cheese
1 1/2 c. sugar
4 eggs
1 1/2 tsp. baking powder
1/2 c. chopped nuts

1 c. oleo
1 1/2 tsp. vanilla
2 1/2 c. flour
1 (17 oz.) can fruit cocktail,
  undrained

Blend cream cheese, oleo, sugar and vanilla. Add eggs,

beating well after each addition. Gradually add flour and baking powder. Fold in fruit and nuts. Pour batter into greased and floured loaf pans and bake at 350° until done.

Cindy Tippett, Caddo
Council, Shreveport, La.

WHOLE WHEAT RAISIN BREAD

2 c. milk
3/4 c. water
1/2 c. sugar
1 tsp. cinnamon
2 pkg. active dry yeast
1 c. rolled oats
Melted butter

1/4 c. cooking oil
3 3/4 c. flour
3 tsp. salt
1/2 tsp. nutmeg
4 c. whole wheat flour
1 c. raisins

Heat milk, water and oil together until very warm (from 120°-130°). In large bowl, combine warm liquid, 2 cups regular flour, sugar, salt, cinnamon, nutmeg and yeast. Beat 4 minutes at medium speed. By hand, stir in whole wheat flour, oats, raisins and remaining flour. On well floured surface, knead dough until smooth and elastic, about 5 minutes. Place in greased bowl, cover and let rise 20-30 minutes in warm place. Grease 2 loaf pans, 9x5 inches or 8x4 inches. Punch down dough, divide and shape into 2 loaves. Place in greased pans. Brush with melted butter. Cover, let rise until light and doubled in warm place, 30-45 minutes. Preheat oven to 375°; or 350° for glass. Bake 40-45 minutes until deep golden brown and loaf sounds hollow when tapped. If loaf becomes too brown, cover with foil last 10 minutes. Remove from pan at once when taken from oven. After baking, brush with butter and sprinkle with sugar.

Rebecca Scott Bockmon, Caddo
Council, Shreveport, La.

WHEAT GERM ZUCCHINI BREAD

3 eggs, beaten
1 c. cooking oil
3 tsp. maple flavoring
2 tsp. soda
1/2 tsp. baking powder
1/2 c. regular wheat germ
1 c. chopped walnuts

1 c. granulated sugar
1 c. brown sugar
2 c. grated, peeled zucchini
    (about 1 large or 2 small)
2 tsp. salt
2 1/2 c. unsifted flour
1/3 c. sesame seed

Beat together eggs, granulated sugar and brown sugar, oil and maple flavoring until foamy and thick. Stir in zucchini. Add soda, baking powder, salt, wheat germ and flour. Mix well. Add nuts. Spoon batter into 2 greased and floured loaf pans. Sprinkle tops with sesame seed. Bake in preheated 350° oven about 1 hour or until tester comes out clean. Cool 10 minutes before removing from pans.   Denise Barteet, Caddo
                                                              Council, Shreveport, La.

YEAST BREAD

1 1/2 c. milk	1/2 stick oleo
3 Tbsp. sugar	1 Tbsp. salt
2 pkg. dry yeast	1/2 c. warm water
1 tsp. sugar	6 c. sifted flour

Combine milk, 3 tablespoons sugar, oleo and salt. Place in saucepan and scald. Dissolve yeast in warm water with 1 teaspoon sugar. Beat eggs in mixer bowl, add milk mixture. When lukewarm, add yeast and 4 cups flour, 1 cup at a time. Remove from mixer, stir in 1 cup flour. Place remaining cup of flour on pastry board. Knead dough until elastic (may require more flour). Place in large greased bowl, cover and set in warm place to rise at least 1 hour. Punch down, shape in loaves. Cover, let rise 1 more hour. Bake in greased loaf pan at 375° for 20-25 minutes or until golden brown.   Mearl S. Byles, Central
                                                    Council, Natchitoches, La.

CAJUN COUCHE COUCHE

1/4 c. oil	2 c. corn meal
1 1/2 tsp. salt	1 tsp. baking powder
3/4 c. milk	3/4 c. water

Heat oil in heavy iron pot. Mix dry ingredients, add milk and water; batter will be soft. Pour batter into hot oil, let crust form on bottom before stirring. Reduce to low heat and stir occasionally until cooked, about 15 minutes. Serve in bowl with milk and sugar as a cereal.
                                              J. Rodney Tassin, Central
                                                  Council, Alexandria, La.

CORN MEAL MUSH

Yellow meal   Salt to taste
Boiling water

Mix salt with meal and slowly pour meal into boiling water until mixture begins to thicken. When corn mush is thick, pour in dish and chill until well set. Slice to fry or bake.
Marie Pamplin, Shreveport
Works Council, Shreveport, La.

DRESSING

1 large potato, grated   6 stalks celery, chopped
1 large onion, chopped   1 pkg. corn bread mix, baked
2/3 - 3/4 loaf bread,   1 lb. sausage, bulk
  minus crust   2 Tbsp. poultry seasoning
2 eggs   Pepper to taste
1 tsp. salt   1 can chicken or turkey
1/2 - 1 c. milk   broth

Crumble breads up, add enough milk to moisten. Add remaining ingredients and saute until onion and celery are tender. Place in big casserole. Bake at 350° for 1-2 hours.
Mary Anne Andrews, Ouachita
Council, Monroe, La.

CORN BREAD DRESSING

1 box Ballard corn bread   4 slices bacon
  mix   2 c. chopped onion
1/2 c. celery, chopped fine   1/2 c. green pepper, chopped
1 c. green onion tops   fine
1 c. parsley, chopped fine   1 stick butter or oleo
1/2 lb. ground veal   1/2 lb. ground pork
1/2 lb. ground liver   1 can mushroom soup
Salt and pepper to taste   1 soup can water

Fry bacon until well done. Add onions, celery and green pepper; cook until tender. Add veal, pork and liver. Cook 1 hour on low flame. Add soup and water, stir well, add green onions and parsley. Season to taste. Bake corn bread as directed on package, crumble and add to mixture. Stir well and serve hot. Serves 6.
Lois Leger, Evangeline
Council, Lafayette, La.

EGGPLANT DRESSING

1 large eggplant
2 onions, chopped
1/2 c. chopped celery
3 c. cracker or bread
   crumbs
1 tsp. black pepper

1 lb. pork sausage, hot or
  or regular
1 chopped bell pepper
2 eggs
1 tsp. salt
Milk

Peel eggplant and cut into small pieces. Cook in boiling salted water until tender, drain and set aside. Saute sausage, onions, celery and pepper until done. Add eggplant to sausage. Soak cracker crumbs in milk to soften. Add crumbs and eggs to mixture. Bake in shallow pan for about 25 minutes or until brown at 350°. If hot sausage is used, omit black pepper. Mrs. Iona Botzong, Central Council, Tioga, La.

GROUND MEAT DRESSING

3 lb. ground meat
Salt, pepper and garlic
  powder to taste
1/2 - 1 bag Sunrise stuffing mix (bread crumbs)
4-5 cloves chopped garlic
Parsley

1 pt. oysters
1 chopped onion
4-5 chopped green onions
2-3 stalks chopped celery
Gizzard, heart and liver
  from chicken or turkey
Pecans

Brown meat, gizzards, heart and liver. Add seasonings and vegetables and cook until onions are soft. Mix Sunrise dressing according to directions on package. Add oysters and pecans and cook 2 or 3 minutes. Cool before stuffing turkey. Serves 20. Cheryl Bossenmeyer
Crescent City Council
New Orleans, La.

OVEN DRESSING

1 c. rice
1 c. chopped celery
1 c. green onions
1/2 c. bell peppers

1 can mushroom soup
1 can chicken noodle soup
Salt and pepper to taste

Calcasieu Council
Lake Charles, La.

GRANDMOTHER'S OYSTER DRESSING

1 lb. dressing meat (mix-
   ture of giblets and
   ground beef)
1/2 c. onion tops
1/2 medium bell pepper,
   chopped (optional)

1 medium onion, chopped
3 cloves garlic, minced
1/2 c. parsley
Salt and pepper to taste
1 can oysters
1 qt. untoasted bread crumbs

Cook dressing mix, onions, garlic and bell pepper to which salt and pepper have been added. (Remember, canned oysters are usually in salty juice.) Cook for about 1 hour. Add onion tops and parsley. Make sure you have enough liquid to make dressing moist. If you have extra gravy from your meat dish, this adds extra flavor. Pour in oysters and stir in bread crumbs. (I make my own bread crumbs in blender from frozen stale bread.) Serve hot. This is used in place of rice dressing and goes well with poultry, beef and pork.

Beverly Foret, Evangeline
Council, Opelousas, La.

POTATO DRESSING

1 lb. hot sausage
2 lb. mild sausage
4 cloves minced garlic
3 qt. water

2 large chopped onions
1 1/2 lb. instant potatoes
1 1/2 Tbsp. salt

Brown sausage well and remove drippings. Saute onions and garlic in small amount of drippings. Heat water to boiling, add salt and remove from heat. Add potatoes, allow to moisten. Add sausage, onions and garlic to potatoes and mix well. Makes 16 servings.

Mrs. Thelma Brunet
Crescent City Council
New Orleans, La.

RICE DRESSING

Giblets from 1 turkey or
   3 hens
3 c. cooked rice
3 large cloves chopped
   garlic
Bacon drippings
Salt and pepper to taste

1 1/2 c. chopped onions
1 large chopped bell pepper
2 c. chopped celery
1/2 c. chopped green onion
1 c. hot water
1 small pod pepper

Boil giblets in salted water until tender, remove, grind and replace in broth. Saute onion, garlic and bell pepper in small amount of bacon drippings. Do not brown. Add 1 cup hot water and cook slowly. Add salt, black pepper and pod of pepper. Add ground giblets and broth, simmer down until mushy. Add rice. Mearl S. Byles, Central Council, Natchitoches, La.

RICE DRESSING

3 cloves garlic, chopped
1/2 bell pepper, chopped
1/2 c. chopped parsley
1 pkg. chicken gizzards
2 lb. ground meat
2 doz. oysters (optional)
4 c. liquid (strained oyster juice and make up the difference in water)

1 large chopped onion
1/2 c. chopped celery
1/2 c. chopped shallots
1 pkg. chicken livers
1 lb. pkg. pork sausage
2 c. uncooked short grain rice
Salt and pepper

Chop all seasonings; grind or blend gizzards and livers. Set aside. Cut oysters in half or smaller depending on size. Cook ground pork, gizzards and livers until brown in large heavy pot, stirring often. Add seasonings and simmer 30 minutes. Add uncooked washed rice. Cook about 10 minutes. Add oysters, liquid, salt and pepper to taste. Mix well, cook on medium heat until liquid is almost absorbed; stir often. Cover and put on low fire. Cook until rice is done and all liquid is absorbed. Stir often to prevent sticking. If rice is not done, but liquid is gone, add 1/4 cup more water, cover and cook about 10 minutes more. Mollie Porrovecchio, Metairie Council, New Orleans, La.

CHERRY'S RICE AND MEAT DRESSING

1 lb. ground meat
1 can cream of chicken soup
1 chopped bell pepper

1 c. raw rice
1 can onion soup
Salt, red and black pepper to taste

Add all ingredients and mix well. Place in oblong dish, seal tightly with foil and bake 1 hour and 15 minutes at 350°. Jan Prestridge, Capital Council, Baton Rouge, La.

DIRTY RICE DRESSING

1 1/2 c. uncooked rice
1 can mushroom soup or
  chicken soup
Salt, pepper and Kitchen
  Bouquet to taste

1 lb. ground meat
1 can onion soup
1 c. chopped celery, onion,
  bell pepper and garlic
  (mixed)

Mix all ingredients and place in baking dish. Cover tightly with foil. Bake at 350° about 1 1/2 hours or more.

Mrs. Drew Holloway, Central
Council, Alexandria, La.

QUICK AND EASY RICE DRESSING CASSEROLE

1 lb. ground meat
1 can cream of mush-
  room soup
1 soup can water
1 stalk celery, diced
2 cloves garlic, chopped
1/2 c. green onions,
  chopped

1 c. raw rice
1 can onion soup
1/4 tsp. red pepper
1/4 bell pepper, diced
1/4 c. dried parsley
Salt and pepper to taste
1 Tbsp. Crisco

Brown ground meat in Crisco. Add celery and bell pepper, cook until tender. Add remaining ingredients and stir until mixture begins to boil. Remove from heat, pour in greased 2-quart casserole. Bake at 350° for 1 hour.

Note: Casserole must be tightly covered; foil paper is probably the best.

Jeanette English, Caddo
Council, Shreveport, La.

SAUSAGE AND RICE DRESSING

1 lb. bulk pork sausage
2 c. long grain brown
  rice, uncooked
1 (8 oz.) can sliced
  mushrooms
1 tsp. salt

1 large onion, minced
2 cans beef broth
1 c. California sauterne wine
1/2 tsp. marjoram
3/4 c. sliced almonds

Brown sausage, breaking it up with fork. Remove sausage and drain off all but 1/4 cup of the fat. Add onion and rice to pan and saute until onion is transparent. Add broth, undrained mushrooms, wine, salt, marjoram and the sausage. Heat to boiling. Turn into large baking dish. Cover and bake at 350° for 1 hour or until rice is tender and liquid is absorbed. Sprinkle with almonds and return to oven for 5 minutes. Serves 6-8.

Dorothy V. Holmes
Crescent City Council
New Orleans, La.

PORK NECK BONE DRESSING

2 lb. pork neck bones
1 Tbsp. sage
1/2 rib celery, minced
1 Tbsp. salt
Meat broth

2 pans corn bread
1 1/2 c. green onions, chopped
1 tsp. black pepper
6 boiled eggs, chopped

Boil neck bones until tender, remove meat from bones. Add crumbled up corn bread and remaining ingredients to mixture, including enough broth from cooked meat to moisten. Freeze until needed. Heat in oven when ready to serve.

Alline Albin for Martha
Starkey, Capital Council
Baton Rouge, La.

VICK'S RICE DRESSING

5 lb. long grain white rice
3 lb. ground chuck
2 lb. chopped bell peppers
3 lb. chopped dry onions
2 bunches chopped green onions, including tops

1/4 c. salt
2 lb. pork sausage (Bryan's or Virginia Reel)
1 small chopped celery stalk
Cayenne pepper to taste
Black pepper to taste
Salt to taste

Combine rice, 1/4 cup salt and water. Prepare as usual. Do not overcook; set aside. Combine beef, pork and dry onions, simmer in large heavy pot until grey, not brown. Add balance of vegetables and seasonings. Simmer at least an hour; do not rush. Mix with rice just before serving. Do not add water as the dressing will become mushy. Serves 25 people.

Normand Vicknair, Central
Council, Alexandria, La.

DUMPLINGS

3 c. plain flour
1 c. boiling water
Salt to taste

1 c. Crisco shortening
2 eggs

Make hole in flour. Place Crisco in hole. Pour boiling water over Crisco to melt. Add eggs and salt. Mix well, divide into 2 parts. Wrap in waxed paper and refrigerate overnight. When ready to make dumplings, roll out, cut and drop into hot boiling broth in which a few drops of yellow food coloring has been added for a nice rich color.

Marie Pamplin, Shreveport
Works Council, Shreveport, La.

CORN MEAL DUMPLINGS

1/2 c. flour
1/2 tsp. salt
1/2 c. milk
1/2 c. yellow corn meal

1 tsp. baking powder
1 egg, beaten
1 Tbsp. oil
1/2 tsp. poultry seasoning

Mix flour, baking powder and salt together and set aside. Mix egg and milk, add oil. Mix all ingredients together. Drop by teaspoonfuls into hot boiling chicken broth or boiling turnip green juice. They stand alone and do not stick together. Cook approximately 6-8 minutes.

Marie Pamplin, Shreveport
Works Council, Shreveport, La.

DUMPLINGS

2 c. flour
1/2 tsp. salt

4 tsp. baking powder
1 scant c. milk

Sift dry ingredients together and add milk gradually. Drop by spoonful into gravy and cook with pot roast or stew during last 12 minutes of cooking.

Laura and Bill Baptist, Ozone
Council, Hammond, La.

YELLOW DUMPLINGS

1 egg, beaten
3 c. flour
Few drops yellow food
    coloring

1 c. sweet milk
1 c. chicken broth
2 Tbsp. baking powder
1/2 tsp. salt

Mix ingredients and drop by iced tea spoon into barely simmering broth. Cover and do not stir for 15 minutes. Place dumplings around chicken and pour over remaining thickened broth. Serves 6-8. Calcasieu Council
Lake Charles, La.

EGG NOODLES

6 eggs
1/2 tsp. baking powder
5 c. flour

1/2 c. milk
1 tsp. salt

Beat eggs and milk together slightly. Add remaining ingredients. Knead until dough is not sticky; add more flour if needed. Roll dough out on a floured surface about 1/16-inch thin. Let dry about 2 hours, turn and let other side dry same amount of time. Cut dough into long sections and cut noodles about 1/4-inch thick. Dry noodles about 2 more hours. Noodles can be frozen until needed.
Clara Fitzgerald, Shreveport
Works Council, Shreveport, La.

HOT CROSS BUNS

1 pkg. active dry yeast
1/3 c. sugar
3/4 tsp. cinnamon
1 c. milk
1/4 c. diced citron
    (optional)

4 c. all-purpose flour
1/2 tsp. salt
1/4 tsp. nutmeg
1/4 c. butter
1/2 c. currants
2 eggs

Combine yeast, 1 cup flour, sugar, salt, cinnamon and nutmeg in mixing bowl. Heat milk and butter to about 125°. Pour over dry ingredients and beat until smooth. Beat in eggs, 1 at a time. Gradually add remaining flour, beating with a heavy duty mixer or wooden spoon. Mix in currants and citron. Turn out on floured board and knead until smooth and satiny. Place in a greased bowl and butter top lightly. Cover and let rise in warm place until almost doubled in size. Turn dough out on a floured board and knead lightly. Cut off pieces, about size of golf balls. Roll between palms of your hands. Place on a lightly greased baking sheet. Cover and let rise until almost doubled in size. With razor blade or sharp knife, cut a cross in the surface of each bun. Bake in 375° oven for 15-20 minutes, or until golden brown. Let cool on cake rack.

Lemon Glaze:

1 c. powdered sugar	1 tsp. grated lemon peel
1 1/2 tsp. milk	

Blend ingredients together and drizzle over buns in a cross design. Makes about 2 dozen.

Denise Barteet, Caddo
Council, Shreveport, La.

BACON MUFFINS

12 slices bacon	1 c. self-rising flour
1 c. self-rising corn meal	1/4 c. sugar
1 c. milk	2 eggs, well beaten

Cook bacon until crisp; drain and crumble, reserving 1/4 cup bacon drippings. Combine flour, corn meal and sugar. Add eggs, milk and bacon drippings, stir until moistened. Stir in crumbled bacon. Spoon batter into greased muffin pans and bake at 425° for 20-25 minutes. Makes 12 muffins.

Marilou Bridges, Caddo
Council, Shreveport, La.

BANANA MUFFINS

2 c. biscuit mix	3 Tbsp. sugar
1 egg	3/4 c. milk
2 Tbsp. melted butter	1 c. sliced bananas

Combine biscuit mix, egg, sugar, milk and butter, mix until well blended. Fold in bananas. Place batter in greased muffin tins and sprinkle with Topping. Bake at 375° for 20-25 minutes.

376

Topping:

2 tsp. cinnamon
4 Tbsp. sugar

2 Tbsp. biscuit mix
2 Tbsp. butter

Mix ingredients until crumbly and sprinkle over muffin batter before baking.　　　　Mary H. Armand, Central
Council, Cottonport, La.

BRAN MUFFINS

1 egg
1 c. milk
1 c. sifted flour
1/2 tsp. salt

3 Tbsp. vegetable oil
1 1/2 c. bran cereal
2 1/2 tsp. baking powder
1/4 c. packed light brown
　　sugar

Beat together the egg, milk and oil. Stir in cereal; let stand 5 minutes. Sift flour, baking powder and salt together. Blend in sugar. Add bran mixture, stirring just until combined. Do not overmix. Fill greased muffin pan cups 2/3 full. Bake in preheated 400° oven for 18-20 minutes, or until done. Makes 12. Rebecca Scott, Caddo
Council, Shreveport, La.

BREAKFAST MUFFINS

1/3 c. shortening
1/2 c. sugar
1 egg
1 1/2 c. flour
1 1/2 tsp. baking powder
1/2 tsp. salt

1/4 tsp. nutmeg
1/2 c. milk
1/2 c. sugar
1 tsp. cinnamon
1/2 c. melted margarine

Heat oven to 350°. Mix shortening, sugar and egg. Stir in flour, baking powder, salt and nutmeg alternately with milk. Fill muffin tins 2/3 full. Bake 20-25 minutes. Mix sugar and cinnamon. After baking, roll in melted margarine, then in cinnamon-sugar.
Calcasieu Council
Lake Charles, La.

CORN BREAD MUFFINS

1 c. yellow corn meal	1 c. flour
2 Tbsp. sugar	1/4 c. shortening
4 tsp. baking powder	1/2 tsp. salt
1 c. milk	1 egg

Blend all ingredients about 20 seconds. Beat vigorously 1 minute. Pour into greased muffin tins. Bake in pre-heated 425° oven about 20-25 minutes. Makes 12 muffins.

Mavis W. O'Rourke, Shreveport
Works Council, Shreveport, La.

CORNSTICKS OR CORN MUFFINS

1 c. yellow corn meal	1/2 tsp. salt
1/2 tsp. baking soda	1/2 pt. sour cream
2 eggs, well beaten	

Combine ingredients and mix well. Spoon into well greased cornstick pans or paper lined muffin cups. Bake in preheated 350° oven for 30 minutes or until golden brown. Serve hot with butter and favorite jams, jellies or preserves. Makes 14 sticks or twelve 2 1/2-inch muffins or twenty-four 1-inch muffins.

Lynn Babin, Westmoor
Council, Kenner, La.

GRANNY'S BLUEBERRY MUFFINS

1 c. blueberries, drained	2 c. flour + 1/2 tsp.
3 tsp. baking powder	1/2 tsp. salt
1/2 c. shortening (no substitute)	1 c. milk
	1 egg, well beaten

Sprinkle berries with 1/2 teaspoon flour, set aside. Sift dry ingredients and cut in shortening. Add milk and beaten egg. Fold in floured berries quickly; careful not to mash them. Bake in hot greased muffin pans for 20 minutes at 350° or until done. Yield: 12-15 muffins.

Cindy Tippett, Caddo
Council, Shreveport, La.

KENTUCKY BLUEBERRY MUFFINS

1/2 c. butter or oleo
1 c. sour cream
1 c. self-rising white
  corn meal mix
1 c. flour
Powdered sugar
  (optional)

1/2 c. sugar
2 eggs
1/4 tsp. soda
1 tsp. vanilla
1/4 c. chopped nuts
3/4 c. fresh or frozen
  blueberries

Cream butter and sugar until light and fluffy. Blend in sour cream, eggs and vanilla. Combine dry ingredients and add to mixture; blend well. Stir in blueberries and nuts. Fill 14-16 greased and paper lined medium sized muffin cups, 3/4 full. Bake in preheated 375° oven for 25-30 minutes. Remove from muffin cups, sprinkle with powdered sugar if desired. Rebecca Scott Bockmon, Caddo Council, Shreveport, La.

ORANGE BLOSSOM MUFFINS

1 egg, slightly beaten
1/2 c. orange juice
2 c. packaged biscuit mix
1/2 c. chopped nuts
1 1/2 Tbsp. flour
1 Tbsp. butter

1/2 c. sugar, divided
2 Tbsp. cooking oil
1/2 c. orange marmalade
1/2 tsp. cinnamon
1/4 tsp. nutmeg

Combine egg, 1/4 cup sugar, orange juice and oil; add biscuit mix and beat vigorously for 30 seconds. Stir in marmalade and nuts. Grease muffin tins and fill 2/3 full. Combine sugar, flour, cinnamon and nutmeg; cut in butter until mixture is crumbly. Sprinkle over batter. Bake at 400° for 20-25 minutes. Yield: 1 dozen. These are delightfully different and very easy to make.
Cindy Tippett, Caddo Council, Shreveport, La.

BAKED PANCAKES

2 Tbsp. sugar
1 c. flour
1 c. milk
1/8 tsp. salt
1/8 tsp. vanilla

6 eggs
Lemon juice
Powdered sugar
1 stick butter

1723-79

Combine flour, sugar, milk, salt and vanilla in mixing bowl, using mixer; beat until well blended. Add the eggs, 1 at a time, beating continuously. Divide butter into 3 parts and put 1 piece in each of 3 pie plates. Place pie plates in preheated 400° oven. When butter has melted, pour batter into each plate and cook 10 minutes. Quickly remove from oven and sprinkle lemon juice on top of each pancake. Return to oven and continue to cook 5 minutes longer. Sprinkle powdered sugar on top and serve immediately with jelly or preserves. Makes 4-6 servings. Very rich.

Jeanette English, Caddo
Council, Shreveport, La.

CRISP WAFFLES OR PANCAKES

1 1/2 c. self-rising flour
1 egg
1 1/2 c. milk
2 tsp. sugar
3 Tbsp. shortening, melted

Make a thin batter that will pour easily and evenly over waffle iron or griddle. For extra crisp waffles, add 2 more tablespoons shortening to batter. Makes 12-15 (5-inch) pancakes or 8 waffles.

J. Rodney Tassin, Central
Council, Alexandria, La.

GOOD MORNING PANCAKES

4 Tbsp. cooking oil
1 c. milk
2 Tbsp. sugar
3 Tbsp. baking powder
1 egg
1 c. flour
1/4 tsp. salt

Combine oil, egg and milk. Add sifted dry ingredients and beat until smooth. Pour by tablespoon and bake on hot griddle or in electric skillet.

Faye Killen, Central Council,
Pineville, La.

POTATO PANCAKES

1/4 c. milk
3 c. diced raw potatoes
3 Tbsp. flour
1/4 tsp. baking powder
2 eggs
1 small onion, quartered
1 tsp. salt

Put all ingredients in blender container in this order: Milk, eggs, potatoes, onion, flour, salt and baking powder. Cover and run on high speed just until all potatoes go through blades, about 10 seconds. Do not overblend or potatoes will be liquefied. Pour small amounts onto a hot, greased griddle or fry pan. Fry until brown on both sides, turning once. Makes 18 pancakes.

Ann Orr, Evangeline
Council, New Iberia, La.

PIEROGI

2 eggs
1/2 c. water

2 c. flour
1/2 tsp. salt

Mound flour on kneading board and make hole in center. Drop eggs into hole and cut into flour with knife. Add salt and water and knead until firm. Let rest for 10 minutes covered with warm bowl. Divide dough into halves and roll thin. Cut circles with large biscuit cutter. Place a small spoonful of filling a little to one side on each round of dough. Moisten edge with water, fold over and press edges together firmly. Be sure they are well sealed. Drop into boiling salted water. Cook gently for 3-5 minutes. Lift out of water with perforated spoon. Dough has a tendency to dry out; a dry dough will not seal completely. We suggest rolling out a large circle of dough, placing small mounds of filling far enough apart to allow for cutting and folding the dough over the mounds of filling. Then cut with small biscuit cutter and seal firmly. Never crowd or pile Pierogi in the boiling water. The uncooked will stick and the cooked will lose shape and lightness.

Mrs. Stanley Tempalski
Ouachita Council, Monroe, La.

PIEROGI

2 c. plain flour
1/4 tsp. salt
1 egg

1 Tbsp. oil or 1 Tbsp. sour
cream
1/2 c. warm potato water

Combine ingredients and make up dough. Keep covered with cloth 10 minutes and let rest. Roll out, cut with biscuit cutter. Place a teaspoon or so of Filling on each one. Fold over and seal completely with fingers dipped in water. Drop in pot of boiling salted water and cook about 10 minutes, stirring with wooden spoon. Do not overcrowd in pot.

Potato Filling:

6 potatoes, cut up
1 onion, cut up

3 slices American cheese, grated
Salt and pepper to taste

Saute onion. Boil and strain potatoes. Combine all ingredients; mash and mix.
Josephine Tempalski
Ouachita Council, Monroe, La.

THICK CRUST PIZZA

2 1/2 c. milk
1/2 c. oleo
5 1/2 c. all-purpose flour
1/2 c. yellow corn meal

3 Tbsp. sugar
1 pkg. dry yeast
1 tsp. salt
2 eggs, beaten

Place milk and butter in saucepan, heat to scalding, stirring occasionally. Remove from heat and cool to 115°. Mix flour, corn meal, sugar, yeast and salt together in bowl. Stir in milk mixture and eggs. Add enough additional flour to make dough easy to handle. Turn dough to slightly floured board. Knead about 10-15 minutes until smooth and elastic. Place dough in greased bowl, cover and let rise in warm place until double in bulk, about 1 - 1 1/2 hours. Punch down dough. Let rise additional hour. Grease bottoms of pizza pans, sprinkle with corn meal. Roll dough on floured surface into circle 16 inches in diameter. Transfer to pans. Cook dough at 400° about 15 minutes or until light brown on top and bottom. Add sauce (I use Ragu), cheese (Mozzarella, Cheddar or Jack), any other desired ingredients (ground meat, bacon, sausage, onions, peppers). Cook until cheese is melted, about 5-10 minutes. Dough can be frozen at any point in recipe for later use. Makes four 14-inch pizza crusts.
Betty Barron, Caddo
Council, Shreveport, La.

HUSH PUPPIES

1/2 c. sifted flour
1 onion, minced
1 egg
1 tsp. sugar

1 c. corn meal
1 1/2 tsp. baking powder
1 tsp. salt
Milk

Mix all ingredients with just enough milk to moisten dough to a stiff consistency, but soft enough to spoon. Dip with tablespoon and drop into deep hot fat. Cook until golden brown. Makes about 18 pups; double recipe if more needed.
John E. Haygood, Caddo Council, Shreveport, La.

HUSH PUPPIES

2 2/3 c. cold water
1 large onion, chopped fine
1 1/2 c. yellow corn meal
1 tsp. baking powder

3 Tbsp. butter or oleo
1/4 c. parsley flakes
2 2/3 Tbsp. plain flour
1 tsp. salt

Add butter to water and bring to a boil. Add onion and parsley flakes to boiling water. Sift together corn meal, flour, baking powder and salt. Stir this into the boiling water mixture and cook 5 minutes. Stir well. Spread on large cookie sheet and cool. Roll into small balls and freeze on a cookie sheet. Fry in deep fat. Makes 20.
Eloise H. Stacy, Caddo Council, Shreveport, La.

HUSH PUPPIES

1 c. plain flour
4 tsp. baking powder
1 egg
1/2 c. milk

1 c. corn meal
1/2 tsp. salt
1 small onion, grated
3 Tbsp. cooking oil

Mix all ingredients well. Dip clean tablespoon in hot oil first, then in mix and drop in hot oil to cook. These are better if deep fried.
Mrs. Tony Corcoran
Crescent City Council
New Orleans, La.

HUSH PUPPIES

1 1/2 c. corn meal	1/2 c. flour
3/4 c. milk	1 egg, beaten
1/2 tsp. salt	2 tsp. baking powder
1 Tbsp. sugar	1 small onion, chopped fine

Mix dry ingredients. Add onion. Add egg and milk; stir. Fry at 360° in deep fat. Hush puppies will turn themselves over and brown on both sides.

Maxine Fletcher, Ouachita
Council, Monroe, La.

HUSH PUPPIES

3 c. corn meal	1 Tbsp. sugar
1 Tbsp. baking powder	1 1/4 c. sweet milk
1 c. chopped onion	1 c. flour
3/4 Tbsp. salt	1/2 c. buttermilk
1 egg	1 jalapeno pepper, chopped

Mix together and cook in deep hot cooking oil until golden brown.

Mearl S. Byles, Central
Council, Natchitoches, La.

HUSH PUPPIES

2 c. self-rising flour	2 c. self-rising meal
1 medium onion, chopped	1 tsp. sugar
1 c. sweet milk	2 c. buttermilk
3 eggs	1 small beer

Mix all ingredients. Shape into balls or small rolls with hands. Drop in deep hot fat and cook until golden brown. Drain on paper towels.

Mildred Henderson, Ouachita
Council, Monroe, La.

MAMA'S SOUTHERN HUSH PUPPIES

1 c. creamed style corn	1 1/2 c. flour
1 c. corn meal	1 egg
Chopped green onion	1/4 small chopped bell
1 Tbsp. beer	pepper
1 tsp. salt	2 tsp. baking powder

Mix ingredients until you have a good, thick consistency, adding more corn meal or flour if needed. Drop by tablespoon into deep hot fat until golden brown; drain.

Adrienne Dezendorf, Central
Council, Alexandria, La.

SMITH'S HUSH PUPPIES

2 c. white corn meal
1/4 tsp. garlic powder
Boiling water

1/2 tsp. salt
1/2 c. onion, chopped fine

Mix corn meal, salt and garlic powder. Scald with boiling water. Add onion to mixture. Pinch off small amount and roll between palms of hand. Continue until mixture is used up. Fry in deep fat, along with fish.

Mrs. Johnnie B. Cole, Caddo
Council, Shreveport, La.

TORTILLAS

To each cup of flour used, add:
1/2 tsp. salt
1 Tbsp. Crisco

1 tsp. baking powder

Add warm water until mixture is elastic and pliable, about like pie dough. Let stand 10 minutes before cooking. Divide dough into small balls. Roll each ball out until quite thin. Fry on dry grill with no fat. Flip over. Fry on both sides until done. Place between a towel to keep warm and moist.

Calcasieu Council
Lake Charles, La.

BARBARA'S DINNER DELIGHTS

2 c. self-rising flour
1 c. milk

3 Tbsp. mayonnaise

Sift flour, then measure. Mix all ingredients with spoon and put into greased muffin tin. Bake at 425° for 10-15 minutes. Makes 12 muffins.

Barbara P. Woodworth
Crescent City Council
New Orleans, La.

BLINTZ BUBBLE RING

2 (3 oz.) pkg. cream
  cheese
1 c. sugar
2 tsp. cinnamon

2 pkg. (10 biscuits each)
  refrigerator biscuits
6 Tbsp. butter, melted
1/4 c. chopped pecans

Cut cream cheese into 20 pieces; roll into balls. Roll out each biscuit in 3-inch circle. Combine sugar and cinnamon. Place 1 cheese ball and 1 teaspoon cinnamon mixture in each biscuit circle. Pinch dough to seal. Pour half of melted butter into bottom of 8 or 10-inch ring mold or Bundt pan. Sprinkle the nuts and half of the remaining cinnamon mixture into pan. Place the rolls close together around bottom of pan, seam sides up. Sprinkle rest of butter and cinnamon mixture over top. Bake at 375° for about 20 minutes until browned. Cool 5 minutes and invert on serving platter. Serve warm. Can be refrigerated and reheated in foil.

Lynn Babin, Westmoor
Council, Kenner, La.

BASIC SWEET DOUGH

1 lb. granulated sugar
1 1/4 oz. salt
1/2 can (14 1/2 oz. size)
  evaporated milk
1/3 lb. yeast

1 lb. shortening
8 eggs, beaten
3/4 qt. water
Vanilla
4 lb. sifted flour

Combine sugar, shortening and salt. Mix thoroughly. Add beaten eggs. Mix milk and water, scald; cool to 80°. Add yeast and vanilla, stir until well mixed. Add to egg mixture. Add flour, mix thoroughly. Place dough in warm place (80°). Allow to rise 2 hours or until double in bulk. Punch down, allow to rise 15 minutes more.

Ann Major, Capital Council,
Shreveport, La.

DROP DOUGHNUTS

1 3/4 c. flour
1 Tbsp. baking powder
1/2 tsp. nutmeg
1 egg

3/4 c. sugar
1 tsp. salt
3/4 c. milk

Mix all ingredients. Drop by teaspoonfuls into very hot oil. When brown, remove and roll in nutmeg and sugar. Very good for coffee or brunch.

Mrs. Sim (Sally) Davenport
Central Council
Alexandria, La.

RAISED DOUGHNUTS

Basic Sweet Dough   Deep hot fat

The recipe for Basic Sweet Dough is in this cookbook. Divide dough into 7 pieces. Allow to rise 15-20 minutes. Roll each piece into sheet 1/2-inch thick. Cut with floured doughnut cutter. Place in pan, cover pans and allow dough to rise about 30 minutes. Place doughnuts, a few at a time, into kettle of hot fat. Fry in hot deep fat (350°-360°) until golden brown on under side. Turn and fry on other side; drain on paper towels.

Ann Major, Capital Council,
Baton Rouge, La.

GOLDEN PUFFS

2 c. flour
1 Tbsp. baking powder
1 tsp. nutmeg or mace
3/4 c. milk
Cooking oil

1/4 c. sugar
1 tsp. salt
1/4 c. cooking oil
1 egg

Mix dry ingredients together. Add cooking oil, milk and egg. Mix well. Drop by small teaspoonfuls into hot oil. Fry about 3 minutes or until golden brown. Drain on absorbent paper. Roll warm puffs in mixture of 2 tablespoons each cinnamon and sugar or powdered sugar while warm, if desired. Batter may be kept in refrigerator several days before using.   Marie Pamplin, Shreveport

Works Council, Shreveport, La.

BEER DINNER ROLLS

2 c. Pioneer mix or Bisquick	2 Tbsp. sugar, or less
Butter	Beer

Combine biscuit mix and sugar. Pour beer into mix until dough is sticky and moist. Drink rest of beer. Grease muffin tin with butter plus small pat of butter in each. Allow 1 large spoon of dough for each muffin. Bake at 350° until light brown.
Mary C. Regan, Crescent
City Council, New Orleans, La.

CINNAMON ROLLS

Basic Sweet Dough	Melted shortening
1 lb. granulated sugar	1/4 oz. cinnamon

Basic Sweet Dough recipe found elsewhere in this cookbook. Divide Basic Sweet Dough into 7 pieces of equal size. Roll each into an oblong shape, 1/2-inch thick. Grease each piece with melted shortening. Mix sugar and cinnamon together. Sprinkle mixture over pieces of dough. Roll each piece tightly like jelly roll. Cut into pieces, 3/4-inch thick. Place close together in greased baking pan. Allow to rise until double in size. Bake in hot oven at 400°-450° about 20 minutes.
Ann Major, Capital Council,
Baton Rouge, La.

CINNAMON ROLLS

1/4 c. warm water (110°-115°)	1 pkg. active dry yeast
3/4 c. lukewarm milk, scalded and cooled to lukewarm	1/4 c. sugar
	1 tsp. salt
	1/4 c. shortening
	2 Tbsp. butter, softened
1 egg	2 tsp. cinnamon
3 1/2 - 3 3/4 c. flour	1/2 c. sugar

Dissolve yeast in warm water. Add milk, 1/4 cup sugar, salt, egg, shortening and half of flour to yeast. (Sift flour, then measure.) Mix with spoon until smooth. Add enough remaining flour to handle easily. Turn onto lightly floured board, knead about 5 minutes until smooth. Place in greased bowl in ball, leaving greased side up. Cover with cloth and let rise in warm place until doubled in bulk, about 1 1/2 hours. Punch down, let rise again until almost doubled, about 30 minutes. Roll dough into oblong, 15x9-inch shape. Spread with butter and sprinkle with sugar and cinnamon. Roll up tightly, beginning at wide side. Seal well by pinching edges of roll together. Cut rolls into 1-inch slices. Place in greased 13x9-inch pan or 18 greased muffin cups. Cover, let rise until double, about 35-40 minutes. Bake at 350° until brown. Frost while warm.

Frosting:

Powdered sugar   Milk
Flavoring

Sift desired amount of powdered sugar into bowl, mix with enough milk to achieve spreading consistency. Add flavoring. Yield: 1 1/2 dozen rolls.

Linda Teague, Caddo
Council, Shreveport, La.

RAISED CINNAMON ROLLS

1 pkg. dry yeast   1/4 c. warm water
3/4 c. warm milk   3 Tbsp. oleo or butter
1/2 c. sugar   1 tsp. cinnamon
1 tsp. salt   1 egg, well beaten
3 1/2 - 4 c. flour   Raisins (optional)
1/2 stick melted butter

Sprinkle yeast over warm water, set aside. Soften oleo in warm milk; add to egg and sugar. Mix with yeast in large mixing bowl. Sift flour, salt and cinnamon together. Add raisins. Stir into liquid mixture to make soft dough. Knead and shape into ball. Allow to rise until double in size. Roll out 1/2-inch thick. Spread with melted butter and sprinkle with mixture of 1/4 cup sugar and 1 tablespoon cinnamon. Roll into a long roll, cut in 3/4-inch slices. Place on greased baking sheet. Bake at 400° for 20-25 minutes.

Mary Armand, Central
Council, Cottonport, La.

EASY BREAKFAST ROLLS

1/2 c. brown sugar
1/2 pkg. butterscotch
   pudding mix

1/2 stick oleo
Frozen Parker House rolls
Chopped nuts (optional)

Combine sugar and oleo. Crumble together in bottom of bread pan. Sprinkle pudding mix and nuts over sugar mix. Place frozen rolls on top. Cover with paper towel and refrigerate overnight. Bake at 375° for 30 minutes or until brown. Take from oven and turn out immediately.

Mary Ahrens, Caddo Council,
Shreveport, La.

EASY SESAME ROLLS

1 can biscuits

1 stick butter (no oleo)
Sesame or poppy seed

Melt butter in pan. Cut each biscuit in half and make into roll in palms of hands. Lay the rolls of dough in butter. Sprinkle seed over top. Bake at 400°-425° for 10-12 minutes.

Carolyn Palmer, Capital
Council, Baton Rouge, La.

HONEY GLAZED SWEET ROLLS

3 3/4 c. all-purpose flour
1 c. milk
2 Tbsp. sugar
1 egg
1/2 c. packed brown sugar
1/2 c. honey
1/2 c. currants or raisins
1/2 c. chopped peanuts or
   pecans
1 tsp. salt

1 pkg. active dry yeast
1/4 c. butter or oleo
2 Tbsp. honey
2 Tbsp. butter or oleo,
   softened
2 tsp. cinnamon
1 Tbsp. butter or oleo, melted
1/2 c. maraschino cherries,
   halved
1/4 c. warm water

Combine flour and yeast in mixing bowl. Heat milk, water and 1/4 cup butter, sugar, 2 tablespoons honey and salt, stirring constantly until butter melts (115°-120°). Add to flour. Add egg. Stir until well blended; dough will be soft. Cover and let rise in warm place about 1 hour or until double. Stir dough down, divide in half. On well floured board, roll out half the dough to a 9x8 inch rectangle.

Brush with half the softened butter. Combine brown sugar and cinnamon, sprinkle half over the dough. Roll, jelly roll fashion, starting at long side; seal edges and cut in 1/2-inch to 5/8-inch slices. Repeat with remaining dough, butter and sugar mixture. Combine 1/2 cup honey and melted butter. Drizzle in bottom of 3 greased 9-inch round baking pans. Sprinkle currants or raisins in bottom of pan. Place rolls, cut side down, over fruit and nut mixture. Cover, let rise about 35-45 minutes or until nearly double. Bake at 350° for 25-30 minutes. Let stand in pans 5 minutes. Invert onto wire rack with waxed paper underneath.

Glaze:

2 1/2 c. sifted powdered sugar

3 Tbsp. water

Combine and mix until sugar is of drizzle consistency and drizzle over top of rolls. Makes 28 rolls.

Mrs. Iuka Goetz, Capital
Council, New Orleans, La.

HOT ROLLS

1 c. warm water
2 c. self-rising flour
2 Tbsp. sugar

1 pkg. yeast
1 stick oleo, melted

Dissolve yeast in warm water, mix in sugar, flour and 1/2 of oleo. Sprinkle more flour on waxed paper and knead. Let rise. Pinch off dough, make into rolls and place in pans greased with remaining oleo. Bake at 350° until done.

Vera J. Trosclair, Central
Council, Lecompte, La.

ICEBOX ROLLS

2 c. lukewarm water
1/2 c. sugar
1 yeast cake, or 1 pkg.
dry yeast

1 1/2 tsp. salt
1 beaten egg
1/2 c. cooking oil

Beat with electric mixer. Let rise; punch down. Refrigerate. Make into rolls and let rise 2-3 hours.

Calcasieu Council
Lake Charles, La.

MOTHER'S HOMEMADE ROLLS

5 lb. plain flour
1 c. Crisco
4 Tbsp. sugar
4 packs yeast
5 c. warm water
2 Tbsp. salt

Mix yeast, sugar, salt and Crisco in warm water. Add flour. Rub a little Crisco around dough and cover. Keep out of draft and in warm place. Let rise 1 hour, knead and let rise 30 minutes. Knead, cut in small pieces rubbed with a little Crisco. Place close together, let rise 1/2 hour. Cover and keep warm. Bake at 350° until brown.

Henrietta Victor, Magnolia
Council, New Orleans, La.

POTATO CHEESE ROLLS

4 servings instant
  mashed potatoes
2 c. shredded sharp
  process American cheese
1 1/2 tsp. salt
Melted butter
5 1/2 c. flour
2 pkg. dry yeast
1/2 c. milk
1/2 c. sugar
2 eggs

Prepare instant mashed potatoes according to package instructions for 4 servings; cool. Combine 2 cups flour and yeast; mix well. Stir in cheese. In saucepan, combine milk, sugar and salt. Cook over low heat until milk is warm, stir in potatoes. Add to flour-cheese mixture, stir in eggs. Beat at low speed for 1/2 minute, beat at high speed for 3 minutes. Stir in remaining flour; dough will be stiff. Place dough in large greased bowl, turn to bring greased side up. Cover. Chill until doubled or refrigerate overnight. Turn out on lightly floured board. Knead until smooth and elastic. Shape into favorite shapes, place in greased baking pan. Brush tops with melted butter. Cover, let rise at room temperature about 30 minutes or until doubled in bulk. Bake at 350° for 15-20 minutes until golden brown. Makes 3 dozen.

Lynn Babin, Westmoor
Council, Kenner, La.

QUICK CARAMEL ROLLS

1/3 c. butter
1/3 c. brown sugar
1/3 c. chopped nuts

1 Tbsp. syrup
1 pkg. canned biscuits

Melt butter, brown sugar and syrup over medium heat and bring to a boil. Pour mixture in 8-inch cake pan and sprinkle with chopped nuts. Arrange rolls on mixture and bake 15 minutes at 400°. Turn out on plate.

Calcasieu Council
Lake Charles, La.

QUICK ROLLS

2 c. self-rising flour
1 c. milk

1/4 c. mayonnaise
1 tsp. sugar

Mix all ingredients well. Spoon into lightly greased muffin tins. Bake at 450° for 10 minutes or until golden brown. Makes 1 dozen rolls. Una Mize, Caddo Council, Shreveport, La.

SIXTY MINUTE ROLLS

1 1/2 c. warm milk
1 pkg. dry yeast
2 Tbsp. shortening
1 beaten egg

2 Tbsp. sugar
1 tsp. salt
4 c. plain flour

Heat milk, sprinkle yeast over top. Allow time to dissolve. Add shortening, egg, sugar, salt and flour. Mix well, cover and let rise 15 minutes. Cover and let rise 15 minutes longer. Shape into rolls, cover, let rise 15 minutes. Bake at 400° for 15 minutes. Makes 3 dozen.

Calcasieu Council
Lake Charles, La.

TERRI'S EASY BATTERWAY ROLLS

1 1/2 c. warm water
4 c. sifted flour
1 1/2 tsp. salt
1 egg

2 pkg. dry yeast
1/4 c. sugar
1/3 c. shortening

1723-79

Pour warm water into large mixing bowl. Add yeast, let stand a few minutes to dissolve. Add 1/2 of the flour, sugar, salt, softened shortening and egg. Start mixer on medium speed, or beat by hand until smooth, about 2 minutes. Stop mixer. Stir in remainder of flour by hand. Scrape down batter on sides of bowl. Cover, let rise until doubled, about 30 minutes in warm place. Grease 1 large muffin and 1 small muffin tin. Stir batter 20-25 strokes. Spoon into muffin cups, filling about 1/2 full. Let rise another 30 minutes until double in bulk, about 30 minutes. Bake until browned, about 10-15 minutes in 425° oven. Remove and cool. Tin cans or loaf pans may also be used for any extra batter.

Adrienne Dezendorf, Central
Council, Alexandria, La.

BREAD STUFFING

8 c. soft bread crumbs
1/2 c. minced onion
2 tsp. salt
1/4 tsp. pepper
2 tsp. sage

2/3 c. butter
1 c. chopped celery, stalks
and leaves
Poultry seasoning and thyme
to taste

Saute onion and celery in melted butter. Mix with remaining ingredients. When used to stuff fowl, add chicken or turkey stock and giblets to moisten crumbs.

Ilene Arnold, Capital
Council, Waterbury, Ct.

ARNONE'S EGGPLANT STUFFING

4-5 medium eggplants
4 lb. peeled shrimp
Salt and pepper to taste
4 cloves garlic, chopped
2 c. water
12 bell peppers
Cooking oil

1 box seasoned croutons
2 medium onions, chopped
4 stalks celery, chopped
1 vegetable bouillon cube
1 onion bouillon cube
5 sprigs rosemary
Bread crumbs

Clean and cut up eggplants. Boil until tender, drain all water. Cut off tops of bell peppers, seed and parboil. Cool. Add vegetable and onion bouillon cubes to boiling water and dissolve. Remove from heat, add box of croutons to absorb liquid. Cover bottom of large skillet with cooking oil, fry chopped vegetables until tender. Add crouton mixture; stir.

Add eggplants, rosemary, salt and pepper. Fry for 10 minutes, add shrimp. Cook until done. Stuff mixture into bell peppers, top with bread crumbs. Place small amount of water in pan around peppers. Bake at 350° until peppers are done and tops are light brown. Peppers can be frozen before baked, or you can use eggplant mixture as a casserole. Mixture can also be used with ground meat, substituting meat for shrimp. Remainder of ingredients remain the same. Fry meat with chopped vegetables until done, add eggplant and continue with rest of recipe.

Evelyn Arnone, Westbank
Council, Gretna, La.

TURKEY STUFFING

1 c. bread crumbs
2 eggs
1 c. popcorn, unpopped
Salt and pepper to taste

4 onions, finely chopped
1 c. water
1 tsp. sage

Mix all ingredients and stuff into cavity of medium size turkey. Roast turkey in medium oven at 325°. It should be done when the popcorn blows the rear end off the turkey.

Rexford L. Coon, Caddo
Council, A.T.&T. - Long
Lines, Shreveport, La.

AMARETTO NUT PIE

1 unbaked pie shell
1 c. white Karo syrup
4 Tbsp. Amaretto
1/2 stick butter, melted

1 c. sugar
2 eggs
2 Tbsp. flour
1 c. chopped nuts

Combine all ingredients. Pour into pie shell. Bake at 350° for 35 minutes.

Carolyn Palmer, Capital
Council, Baton Rouge, La.

APPLELESS APPLE PIE

1 1/2 c. sugar
1 tsp. cream of tartar
2 c. water

21 Ritz crackers
1 unbaked pie shell
Cinnamon, butter

Mix sugar, cream of tartar and water. Bring to boil

and boil 1 minute. Drop in Ritz crackers, boil 2 minutes longer. Pour into pie shell, sprinkle with cinnamon and dot with a little butter. Bake until shell is done at 350°.

Marie Pamplin, Shreveport
Works Council, Shreveport, La.

APPLE PIE EN PAPILLOTE

2 1/2 lb. tart cooking
   apples, cored, peeled
   and cut into chunks
   (about 8 c.)
1 tsp. cinnamon
Dash of nutmeg

2 Tbsp. lemon juice
1/2 c. sugar
2 Tbsp. unsifted all-purpose
   flour
1 unbaked 9-inch pie shell

Topping:

1/2 c. unsifted all-
   purpose flour
1/2 c. oleo, softened

1/4 c. light brown sugar,
   firmly packed
1/4 c. sugar

In large bowl, toss apples with lemon juice. Combine sugar, flour, cinnamon and nutmeg. Sprinkle over apples and toss until well coated. Place in pastry shell. Combine Topping ingredients, stir until smooth paste. Gently dollop over apples, then spread topping to cover. Place pie in large brown paper bag, close opening with staples or paper clips. Place in preheated 400° oven on oven rack in center. Make sure bag does not touch sides or top of oven. Bake pie 1 hour and 10 minutes in metal pie plate, and 1 hour and 20 minutes in glass. Remove pie from oven; do not open bag. Let pie cool on wire rack 10 minutes. Cut bag open and carefully remove pie. Serve warm. Bag will smell like it is burning after about 5 minutes cooking time and until pie is done.

Joe Smythe, Caddo Council,
Shreveport, La.

CRUNCH TOP APPLE PIE

1 1/4 c. sugar
1 Tbsp. flour
3 1/2 c. peeled, chopped
   cooking apples
2 Tbsp. butter

1/2 tsp. cinnamon
Dash of salt
1 (16 oz.) can applesauce
1 Tbsp. lemon juice
Pastry for double crust
   9-inch pie

Roll half of pastry 1/8-inch thick, fit into 9-inch pie pan; trim. Combine sugar, flour, cinnamon and salt. Stir in apples, applesauce and lemon juice. Spoon into pie pan and dot with butter. Roll out remaining pastry to 1/8-inch thickness and cut into strips. Arrange in lattice design over apples. Sprinkle Crunch Topping over top crust. Bake at 425° for 10 minutes, reduce heat to 350° and bake about 45 minutes or until crust is golden brown.

Crunch Topping:

3 Tbsp. all-purpose flour	1 Tbsp. sugar
Dash of salt	1 Tbsp. butter

Combine flour, sugar and salt. Cut in butter until mixture resembles crumbs.　　Jeanette English, Caddo Council, Shreveport, La.

PEANUTTY APPLE PIE

1 c. sifted all-purpose flour	1/2 tsp. salt
	1/4 c. smooth peanut butter
1/4 c. shortening	2 Tbsp. ice water

Sift flour and salt together. Cut in shortening and peanut butter to resemble coarse corn meal. Sprinkle water over surface. Mix until dough holds together. Press into a ball. On lightly floured surface, roll out dough 1 inch larger than 9-inch pie pan. Fit dough into pan. Trim with scissors. Roll overhang up to rim to form tall edge. Flute edge; set aside.

Filling:

2/3 c. granulated sugar	1/3 c. light brown sugar
1/4 c. all-purpose flour	1/2 tsp. allspice
1/2 tsp. nutmeg	1/8 tsp. salt
1/4 c. butter or oleo	6 c. cored, pared, cooking apples
1 c. peanut butter flavored chips	3 Tbsp. lemon juice

Combine sugar, flour, spices and salt in large bowl. Cut in butter until resembles coarse corn meal. Add apples; stir well. Place 1/2 of apples in pie shell in even layer. Sprinkle with 1 1/2 tablespoons lemon juice and 1/2 cup of the peanut butter chips. Layer with remaining apples and

sugar mixture. Sprinkle with lemon juice. Bake in preheated 450° oven 10 minutes, reduce heat to 350° and bake
25 minutes or until apples are almost tender. Sprinkle with
remaining chips and bake 10 minutes longer. Serve warm.
Makes 6-8 servings.   Ann Orr, Evangeline
                                     Council, New Iberia, La.

AUNT LILLIE'S OLD-FASHIONED PIE

2 c. sugar   4 eggs, well beaten
2 Tbsp. flour   6 Tbsp. butter, melted
1 tsp. vanilla extract   1/4 tsp. salt
3/4 c. buttermilk   1 unbaked 9-inch pie shell

Blend sugar and eggs. Add flour, salt, butter, vanilla.
Mix well. Blend in buttermilk. Pour into pastry shell. Bake
in preheated 350° oven for 35-45 minutes until pie is very
brown. Try it! It's delicious! Louise Ward, Crescent City
                                Council, Shreveport, La.

BERRIED TREASURE PIE

1 (8 oz.) pkg. cream   2 Tbsp. sugar
  cheese, softened   1 graham cracker pie crust
2 Tbsp. milk   1 c. halved fresh straw-
1 env. Dream Whip   berries (can use frozen
1 (4 oz.) pkg. Jell-O   if necessary)
  lemon flavor instant   1 c. milk
  pudding

Beat cream cheese with sugar and 2 tablespoons milk
until smooth. Spread evenly in bottom of pie crust. Arrange
strawberries over cream cheese mixture. Prepare whipped
topping as directed. Prepare pudding mix with 1 cup milk
as directed on package for pie. Fold in 1 cup whipped
topping. Spoon over strawberries and chill until set, about
2 hours. Top with remaining whipped topping and additional
strawberries for garnish.   Eloise H. Stacy, Caddo
                               Council, Shreveport, La.

398

BLUEBERRY PIE

1 can blueberry pie
   filling
4 egg yolks, beaten

1 c. sour cream
1 c. sugar
1 unbaked pie shell

Spread pie filling in bottom of pie crust. Mix sugar and sour cream together. Add eggs, mix well. Spread evenly over blueberry pie filling. Bake for 10 minutes at 400°, reduce heat to 350° and continue baking for 30 or 35 minutes. Makes a delicious pie. Serve with cream or milk.

M. Coppola, Magnolia
Council, New Orleans, La

BLUEBERRY BANANA PIE

1 (8 oz.) pkg. cream
   cheese, softened
1 tsp. vanilla
1 can blueberry pie
   filling

2/3 c. powdered sugar
2 (8 oz.) bowls Cool Whip
3 bananas, sliced
2 baked pie shells

Cream together cheese and powdered sugar. Add vanilla, mix well. Stir in 1 bowl Cool Whip and fold in bananas. Divide evenly into pie shells. Top with blueberry pie filling and spread Cool Whip over all. Chill overnight.

Becky Sanders, Central
Council, St. Landry, La.

BLUEBERRY ICEBOX PIE

1 graham cracker crust
1 egg
1/3 c. sugar
1 can blueberry pie
   filling

1 (8 oz.) pkg. cream cheese,
   softened
1 tsp. vanilla
1/2 pt. whipping cream
1 unbaked pie shell

Whip together cream cheese, egg, sugar and vanilla. Pour into crust and bake 25 minutes at 325°. Cool. Top with pie filling and whipped cream.

Rebecca Scott, Caddo
Council, Shreveport La.

BUTTERMILK PIE

1/2 c. butter, softened
3 Tbsp. flour (rounded)
1 tsp. vanilla
Dash of nutmeg

2 c. sugar
3 eggs, beaten
1 c. buttermilk
1 unbaked 9-inch pie shell

Cream butter and sugar together. Add flour and eggs, beat well. Stir in nutmeg, buttermilk and vanilla. Pour into unbaked pie shell. Bake at 350° for 45-50 minutes. Place on wire rack to cool completely before serving.

Brenda Braxton   Faye Killen   Jeanette English
Ouachita Council   Central Council   Caddo Council
Monroe, La.   Pineville, La.   Shreveport, La.

BUTTERMILK PIE

3 eggs
1 c. sugar
2 Tbsp. flour
1/2 c. oleo, melted

1 c. buttermilk
1/2 tsp. vanilla extract
1/2 tsp. lemon extract
1 unbaked 9-inch pie shell

Beat eggs slightly, add sugar and flour, add oleo. Mix well. Add buttermilk and extracts. Pour into pie shell. Bake at 325° until custard is set and browned as desired.

Gretna Anderson, Central
Council, Alexandria, La.

BUTTERMILK PIE

3 3/4 c. sugar
1/2 tsp. salt
1 c. buttermilk
2 sticks oleo or butter,
   melted

1/2 c. flour
6 eggs
1 tsp. vanilla
2 unbaked pie shells

Blend sugar, flour, salt and eggs. Stir just enough to blend eggs and sugar mixture together. Add buttermilk and vanilla, stir only until blended. Add melted oleo and pour into pie shells. Bake at 350° for 40-60 minutes or until center is set.

Rose M. Malone, Central
Council, Alexandria, La.

BUTTERMILK PIE

1/2 c. butter or oleo
3 Tbsp. plain flour
  (rounded)
1 c. buttermilk
Dash of cinnamon

1 c. sugar (rounded)
3 eggs
1 tp. vanilla
1 unbaked 9-inch pie shell

Have butter soft. Add sugar, add eggs, beat well. Stir in buttermilk, vanilla and cinnamon. Pour into pie shell. Bake at 350° for 40-45 minutes. Place on wire rack to cool completely before serving.

Jerrie Cleveland, Caddo
Council, Shreveport, La.

BUTTERSCOTCH PIE

1 can condensed milk
3 bananas, sliced

Cool Whip (small)
Graham cracker crust

Place unopened can of condensed milk in pot and cover with water. Bring to boil, then turn down to simmer for 2 1/2 hours (making sure water always covers can). Set can aside to cool until lukewarm. Open and put into crust, lining bottom of crust with sliced bananas. Top with Cool Whip and refrigerate.

Calcasieu Council
Lake Charles, La.

GOLDEN CARROT PIE

2 c. sliced, cooked
  carrots, pureed
1/2 tsp. nutmeg
1 tsp. cinnamon
3/4 c. evaporated milk
1 unbaked 9-inch pie shell

3 eggs, slightly beaten
1/2 tsp. salt
1/2 tsp. ginger
1/8 tsp. ground cloves
1 c. honey

Combine carrots, eggs, salt and spices. Mix well. Add milk and honey, blending until smooth. Pour filling into pie shell. Bake at 400° for 40-45 minutes.

Mae Briley, Central Council,
Alexandria, La.

CHEESE PIE

1 vanilla wafer pie shell
Juice of 2 lemons
1 c. chopped peaches,
   drained

1 can Eagle Brand milk
1 (3 oz.) pkg. cream cheese
Cool Whip

Mix milk, lemon juice and cheese well. Fold in peaches lightly. Pour into pie shell and top with Cool Whip. Refrigerate. For a variety, let this same pie chill until well set and pour 1 can cherry pie filling over it before topping with Cool Whip.   Marie Pamplin, Shreveport
                              Works Council, Shreveport, La.

CHERRY-O CHEESE PIE

1 (8 oz.) pkg. cream
   cheese, softened
1 tsp. vanilla
1 (1 lb. 5 oz.) can cherry
   pie filling, or your
   choice

1 can sweetened condensed
   milk
1/2 c. reconstituted lemon
   juice
1 baked 9-inch pie shell
Cool Whip (optional)

In medium bowl, beat cheese until fluffy. Stir in milk until blended. Stir in lemon juice and vanilla. Pour into crust and chill 1 hour. Spread pie filling over top and cover with Cool Whip if desired. Chill until served.
                              Jada Rowland, Ouachita
                              Council, Monroe, La.

CHESS PIE

1 c. sugar
3 egg yolks, beaten
4 1/2 Tbsp. flour
1 tsp. vanilla
1 unbaked pie shell

1/2 c. butter
1 Tbsp. corn meal
1 tsp. nutmeg
1/2 c. milk

Cream sugar and butter together until light, add beaten egg yolks; beat mixture. Add sifted dry ingredients, vanilla and milk. Pour into unbaked pie shell. Bake at 375° until set. If desired, add meringue and let brown.
                              Frankie Meeks, Ouachita
                              Council, Monroe, La.

402

CHESS PIE

3 eggs, well beaten
2 c. sugar
1 tsp. vanilla
1 c. milk

1 stick oleo
2 Tbsp. flour
1 unbaked 10-inch pie shell

Combine eggs, oleo, sugar and flour; mix well. Stir in vanilla and milk. Pour into pie shell. Bake at 450° for 10 minutes, reduce heat to 350° and continue baking 25-30 minutes or until set.
Becky Flack, Central Council, Natchitoches, La.

CHOCOLATE CHESS PIE

1 1/2 c. sugar
2 beaten eggs
1 tsp. vanilla

3 1/2 Tbsp. cocoa
1/2 can Carnation milk
1 unbaked 9-inch pie shell

Combine all ingredients and pour into pie shell. Bake at 325° for 45 minutes.
Pat Brown, Ouachita Council, Monroe, La.

GRANDY'S CHESS PIE

1 c. sugar
2 Tbsp. flour
1 tsp. lemon juice
1/2 c. butter
1 unbaked pie shell

1 tsp. vanilla
1 tsp. corn meal
3 eggs
2 drops almond flavoring

Mix ingredients together. Pour into pie shell. Bake at 350° about 35 minutes or until knife inserted comes out dry. If oven is too hot, set pan of water beneath pie.
Marie Pamplin, Shreveport Works Council, Shreveport, La.

NEVER-FAIL CHESS PIE

4 eggs, beaten
2 tsp. corn meal
1/4 c. melted oleo
1 tsp. vanilla extract

1 1/2 c. sugar
Pinch of salt
4 Tbsp. cream
1 unbaked 10-inch pie shell

Combine ingredients and blend well. Pour into pie shell. Bake at 350° for 30 minutes. Yield: 1 pie.

Jean Coon, Caddo Council,
Shreveport, La.

CHOCOLATE PIE

1 c. sugar minus 3 Tbsp.
3 Tbsp. cornstarch
2 c. milk
1 tsp. vanilla

1/4 c. cocoa
3 egg yolks
3 Tbsp. oleo
1 baked pie shell

Stir in egg yolks to sugar, cocoa and cornstarch mixture. Add small amount of milk, stir until smooth, then stir in remaining milk gradually. Bring to boil over low heat, stir until thick. Remove from fire, blend in oleo and vanilla. Pour into pie shell. Top with meringue or Cool Whip when cool.

Jerrie Cleveland, Caddo
Council, Shreveport, La.

CHOCOLATE PIE

1 1/2 large chocolate
  almond candy bars
  (9 oz. needed)
1 c. whipping cream

1/2 c. milk
22 large marshmallows
1 graham cracker crust

Melt chocolate bars and marshmallows with milk in top of double boiler. Cool completely. Whip cream and fold into chocolate mixture. Pour into graham cracker shell. Chill 5 hours before serving.

Mary C. Regan, Crescent
City Council, New Orleans, La.

CHOCOLATE PIE

1 1/2 c. sugar
3 heaping Tbsp. cocoa
3 or 4 egg yolks
2 Tbsp. oleo or butter
1 1/2 tsp. vanilla extract

3 heaping Tbsp. flour
3 c. milk (I use 1 c. regular
  milk + 2 c. diluted evaporated milk)
1 baked 9 or 10-inch pie shell

Combine sugar, flour and cocoa in saucepan. Add milk, blend well and then add slightly beaten egg yolks. Cook over low heat until mixture thickens. Remove from heat,

404

add oleo and vanilla. Cool. Pour into pie shell. Cover with meringue from egg whites and bake at 400° for 15 minutes or until brown. This recipe was given to me years ago by Mrs. Virgie Henry, whose husband was a supervisor here in the 1950's (now deceased).

Mrs. Joe Nasello, Central
Council, Alexandria, La.

CHOCOLATE CHIFFON PIE

2 (3 oz.) sq. chocolate
1 c. sugar, divided
3 stiffly beaten egg whites
1/2 c. boiling water
1 tsp. vanilla

1 env. gelatin
1/4 tsp. salt
3 egg yolks
1/4 c. water
1 baked 10-inch pie shell

Melt chocolate in boiling water, add gelatin softened in 1/4 cup water. Stir until thickened. Add egg yolks, beaten with 1/2 cup sugar. Add salt and vanilla. Beat egg whites, add remainder of sugar, fold into chocolate mixture. Pour into pie shell. Chill until firm.

Mearl S. Byles, Central
Council, Natchitoches, La.

CHOCOLATE CREAM CHEESE PIE

1 1/2 c. finely crushed
chocolate wafers
1/2 c. sugar, divided
1 tsp. vanilla
1 (6 oz.) pkg. semi-sweet
chocolate morsels,
melted

1/3 c. melted oleo
1 (8 oz.) pkg. cream cheese,
softened
2 eggs, separated
1 c. heavy cream, whipped
3/4 c. chopped pecans
Whipped cream for topping

Combine chocolate wafers and melted oleo. Press firmly into 9-inch pie pan. Bake 10 minutes at 325°. Cool. Combine cream cheese, 1/4 cup sugar and vanilla. Blend well. Stir in beaten egg yolks and hot melted chocolate. Beat egg whites until soft peaks form. Gradually beat in remaining sugar. Fold in whipped cream and pecans. Pour into chocolate crust. Freeze overnight. Cover with additional whipped cream before serving. Makes 8-10 servings.

Ann Orr, Evangeline
Council, Lafayette, La.

CHOCOLATE CREAM PIE

3 1/2 c. milk
3/4 c. sugar
2 egg yolks, slightly
  beaten
1 tsp. vanilla

2 sq. (2 oz.) unsweetened
  chocolate
2/3 c. flour
3/4 tsp. salt
1 baked 9-inch pie shell

Heat milk and chocolate in heavy saucepan over low heat, stirring until blended. Combine dry ingredients, add milk mixture gradually, stirring until smooth. Return to sauce-pan and cook, stirring until thickened. Stir small amount of hot mixture into egg. Then stir quickly into remaining mix-ture in saucepan. Cook 2 minutes over low heat, stirring constantly. Remove from heat, add vanilla. Pour into pie shell. Chill. Top with Whipped Cream Topping.

Whipped Cream Topping:

1 small container whipping
  cream

4 Tbsp. sugar
1/4 tsp. vanilla

Beat whipping cream until cream peaks. Fold in sugar and vanilla. Spread over pie. Pat Mora, LeBayou Council, Franklin, La.

CREAMY CHOCOLATE PIE

1 (4 1/2 oz.) pkg. Jell-O
  chocolate instant pudding
1 c. milk

1 (9 oz.) Cool Whip
1 c. chopped nuts
1 baked 8-inch pie shell

Prepare pudding as directed on package, using only 1 cup milk. Blend in 1 1/2 cups Cool Whip and 1/2 of nuts. Spoon into baked pie shell, spread remainder of Cool Whip over top and sprinkle with remaining nuts. Chill 1 hour.
Beverly Lumm, Caddo Council, Shreveport, La.

FRENCH CHOCOLATE PIE

1/2 c. butter
2 sq. Baker's unsweet-
  ened chocolate
1 baked pie shell

3/4 c. sugar
2 eggs
4 1/2 oz. Cool Whip

Cream butter with sugar. Stir in cooled, melted chocolate. Add eggs, 1 at a time, beating 5 minutes after each addition at high speed. Fold in Cool Whip. Pour into pie shell. Chill about 2 hours before serving.

Jan Prestridge, Capital
Council, Baton Rouge, La.

FROZEN CHOCOLATE PIE

1 (4 oz.) pkg. German's
   sweet chocolate
1 (3 oz.) pkg. cream
   cheese, softened

1/3 c. milk
2 Tbsp. sugar
1 (8 oz.) container Cool Whip
1 graham cracker pie shell
   (8 inch)

Melt chocolate and 2 tablespoons milk over low heat, stirring until melted. Beat sugar into cream cheese, add remaining milk and chocolate mixture. Beat until smooth. Fold cooled chocolate mixture into whipped topping, blending until smooth. Spoon into crust. Freeze about 4 hours or until firm. Return any leftover pie to freezer.

Marilou Bridges, Caddo
Council, Shreveport, La.

GERMAN SWEET CHOCOLATE PIE

1 (4 oz.) pkg. Baker's
   German's sweet choco-
   late
1 1/2 c. sugar
3 Tbsp. cornstarch
2 eggs
1 1/3 c. Baker's Angel
   Flake coconut

1/4 c. butter
1 (13 oz.) can evaporated
   milk
1/8 tsp. salt
1 tsp. vanilla
1/2 c. chopped pecans
1 unbaked 9 5/8-inch pie
   shell

Melt chocolate with butter over low heat, stirring until blended. Remove from heat. Gradually blend in milk. Mix sugar, cornstarch and salt thoroughly, beat in eggs and vanilla. Gradually blend in chocolate mixture and pour into pie shell. Combine coconut and nuts, sprinkle over filling. Bake at 375° for 45-50 minutes. Filling will be soft, but will set while cooling. Cool at least 4 hours before cutting. If top browns too quickly, cover loosely with foil last 15 minutes of baking.

Joy Faught, Central Council,
Alexandria, La.

CHOCOLATE MERINGUE PIE

1 c. sugar
5 Tbsp. cornstarch
1/2 tsp. salt
3 egg yolks, slightly
  beaten
1/2 tsp. almond extract

5 sq. unsweetened chocolate,
  cut up
2 1/2 c. milk
1/2 tsp. vanilla extract
1 baked 9-inch pie shell

Combine sugar, cornstarch, chocolate and salt in saucepan; mix well. Gradually stir in milk. Cook over medium heat, bring to boil, stirring. Boil 1 minute, stirring constantly. Remove from heat. Stir half of the mixture into egg yolks, pour all back in pan. Bring back to boil, stirring. Boil 1 minute. Remove from heat and stir in extracts. Pour into pie shell. Make up Meringue, spread over warm pie and bake in preheated 400° oven for 7-10 minutes or top with whipped cream if preferred.

Meringue:

3 egg whites, room
  temperature

1/4 tsp. cream of tartar
6 Tbsp. sugar

Beat egg whites with cream of tartar until stiff peaks form. Gradually beat in sugar. Cover pie.

Rebecca Scott Bockmon, Caddo
Council, Shreveport, La.

CHOCOLATE SILK PIE

3/4 c. butter, softened
3 eggs
3 sq. unsweetened choco-
  late
1 baked pie shell

3/4 c. sugar
1 tsp. vanilla (Mexican
  preferred)
Whipped cream or Cool Whip

Cream butter and sugar together, add eggs, 1 at a time, then vanilla. Melt chocolate, cool. Add to mixture. Blend ingredients with electric mixer until thickened and pour into pie shell. Chill before topping with whipped cream. Pie is better if refrigerated overnight.

Katherine Slover, Caddo
Council, Phoenix, Az.

COCONUT PIE MURRELL

2 cans coconut
3 c. sugar
1 c. sweet milk
2 unbaked pie shells

6 eggs
2 tsp. vanilla
1/2 c. butter

Cream butter and sugar. Add eggs, vanilla and milk, add coconut. Pour into pie shells. Bake at 450° for 15 minutes, reduce heat to 350° and bake for 30 minutes. Makes 2 pies.

Mavis W. O'Rourke, Shreveport
Works Council, Shreveport, La.

EASY COCONUT PIE

1 1/2 c. sugar
1/2 c. flour
2 c. milk
1 tsp. vanilla

4 eggs
1/2 stick oleo, melted
1 (7 1/2 oz.) pkg. Angel
Flake coconut

Mix sugar and flour, add eggs, oleo, milk and vanilla. Pour into greased 9-10-inch pie pan. Sprinkle coconut on top and bake at 350° for 35-40 minutes. Makes own crust.

Betty Barron, Caddo
Council, Shreveport, La.

FRENCH COCONUT PIE

1 stick oleo, melted
1 1/2 c. sugar
1 can flake coconut
2 drops almond flavor

3 eggs, beaten
1 Tbsp. vinegar
1 tsp. vanilla
1 unbaked pie shell

Mix ingredients together. Pour in pie shell. Bake at 350° for 1 hour.

Marie Pamplin, Shreveport
Works Council, Shreveport, La.

IMPOSSIBLE PIE

1/2 c. very soft oleo
3/4 c. sugar
1 tsp. vanilla
1 c. coconut

2 c. milk
4 eggs
1/2 c. Bisquick

1723-79

Reserve 1/2 cup coconut. Put remaining ingredients in blender. Pour in greased 9-inch pie plate. Sprinkle coconut over top. Bake 45 minutes at 350°. Chill before serving.

Mary C. Regan, Crescent City
Council, New Orleans, La.

IMPOSSIBLE TO FAIL COCONUT PIE

4 eggs
2 c. milk
1 tsp. vanilla
1/4 c. melted oleo

1 3/4 c. sugar
1/2 c. self-rising flour
1 (7 oz.) pkg. flaked coconut

In large mixing bowl, beat together eggs, sugar, milk, vanilla, flour and oleo until all ingredients are well combined. Fold in coconut. Turn into 2 greased and floured 9-inch pie pans. Bake in preheated 350° oven for 40 minutes or until golden brown. Crust forms as pies bake.

Althea Brossett
Capital Council
Baton Rouge, La.

Rosalie T. Fitzmorris
Crescent City Council
New Orleans, La.

DERBY PIE

1 unbaked pie shell
2 eggs
1 c. chopped pecans or
  walnuts
1 stick melted oleo

1 c. sugar
1 c. chocolate chips
1/2 c. flour
1 tsp. vanilla

Mix ingredients together. Pour into pie shell. Bake at 350° for 40 minutes.

June E. Nickels, Shreveport
Works Council, Shreveport, La.

FRUIT PARTY PIE

1 can water packed cherries
  with liquid
1 1/2 c. sugar
1 small pkg. strawberry
  jello
Whipped cream

1 small can crushed pineapple
3 Tbsp. cornstarch
3 sliced bananas
1 c. chopped nuts
2 (9 inch) baked pie shells

Combine cherries, pineapple, sugar and cornstarch.

410

Cook until thick. Cool. Add bananas and nuts. Pour into pie shells and top with whipped cream. Refrigerate.

Retha Logans, Caddo
Council, Shreveport. La.

FUDGE PIE

1/2 c. butter	3 sq. unsweetened chocolate
4 eggs	1 1/2 c. sugar
3 Tbsp. white Karo syrup	1 tsp. vanilla
1/4 tsp. salt	1 unbaked 9-inch pie crust

Melt butter and chocolate in top of double boiler. Cool. Beat eggs until light. Beat in remaining ingredients. Add chocolate mixture. Mix thoroughly and pour into pie shell. Bake at 350° for 25-30 minutes. Top should be crusty and pie should shake like custard. Top with ice cream to serve.

Pat Brown, Ouachita
Council, Monroe, La.

HEAVENLY PIE

1 (8 oz.) pkg. cream cheese, softened	1 can sweetened condensed milk
1/2 c. chopped pecans	1/3 c. lemon juice
1 (9 oz.) bowl Cool Whip	1 c. drained canned fruit (pineapple, peaches, or fruit cocktail)
2 baked 9-inch graham cracker pie shells	

Combine cheese, milk and lemon juice. Beat until smooth. Fold in Cool Whip. Stir in pecans and fruit. Pour into pie shells and chill for several hours. Yield: 2 pies.

Mary McDow, Caddo
Council, Shreveport, La.

HOLIDAY CREAM PIE

2 env. whipped topping mix	1 (8 oz.) pkg. cream cheese, softened
1 (1 lb.) box powdered sugar	2 (8 inch) baked pie shells

Prepare whipped topping mix according to package

directions; blend in cream cheese and sugar. Spoon into pie shells and refrigerate overnight. Yield: 2 pies.

Mearl S. Byles, Central
Council, Natchitoches, La.

HOLIDAY PRALINE DELIGHT PIE

1/3 c. butter or oleo
1/2 c. chopped pecans
1 (5 oz.) pkg. Jell-O
   vanilla pudding and
   pie filling

1/3 c. firmly packed brown
   sugar
1 baked 9-inch pie shell
3 c. milk
1 env. Dream Whip topping mix

Heat butter and brown sugar with nuts in saucepan until melted. Spread in bottom of pie shell and bake at 450° for 5 minutes. Cool. Prepare pie filling with milk as directed for pie. Cool 5 minutes, stirring occasionally. Measure 1 cup, cover with waxed paper and chill thoroughly. Pour remaining into pie shell and chill. Prepare whipped topping. Fold 1 1/3 cups into 1 cup of chilled pie filling. Spread over filling in pie shell. Garnish with remaining whipped topping and additional pecans, if desired.

Sue Hosch, Metairie Council,
Metairie, La.

ICE CREAM PIE

2 c. cold milk
2 small pkg. instant
   pudding and pie filling

1 1/2 c. softened butter
   pecan ice cream
1 graham cracker pie crust

Mix milk and ice cream. Blend in pudding and pour into pie shell. Chill 1 hour or until firm. Any combination of ice cream and pudding mix can be used. Use your favorite.

Dianne Crocker, Central
Council, Alexandria, La.

JALAPENO PIE

1 (7 oz.) jar jalapeno
   peppers
4 eggs
Salt

1/2 lb. sharp grated cheese
Dash of red pepper
   (optional)

412

Drain and seed peppers, cut into thin lengthwise slices and lightly line bottom and sides of 9-inch pie plate. Leave spaces between pieces of pepper. Press grated cheese over peppers, making pie shell. Beat eggs, adding salt and red pepper. Pour over cheese and bake at 350° for 25-30 minutes.

Theda S. Thomas, Caddo
Council, Shreveport, La.

JALAPENO PIE

4 eggs, beaten
4-8 jalapeno peppers, chopped

Grated cheese
Cheese slices

Place grated cheese in bottom of Pyrex dish, pour eggs over cheese. Sprinkle chopped jalapeno peppers over eggs and top with cheese slices. Bake in preheated 350° oven until hot and bubbly.

Gail Cummings, Caddo
Council, Shreveport, La.

JAPANESE PIE

1 stick softened butter
  or oleo
1/2 c. coconut
3 eggs
1 tsp. vinegar

1 c. sugar
1/2 c. pecans, chopped
1/2 c. raisins
1 (9 inch) unbaked pie shell

Mix butter, sugar and eggs. Add remaining ingredients and pour into pie shell. Bake at 325° until brown, or about 50 minutes.

Mrs. Eddie (Vera) Howie
Ouachita Council, Monroe, La.

JAPANESE FRUIT PIE

1 stick oleo, melted
1 c. white sugar
1/2 c. chopped dates or
  raisins

2 eggs, beaten well
1 tsp. vanilla flavoring
1/2 c. flaked coconut
1/2 c. chopped pecans
1 unbaked pie shell

Add ingredients to beaten eggs, mix well. Pour into pie shell. Bake at 450° for 10 minutes, reduce heat to 325°, bake 30-35 minutes more.

Reete Keller, Central
Council, Tioga, La.

1723-79

413

JAPANESE FRUIT PIE

2 egg yolks
1 c. sugar
1/2 c. nuts
2 egg whites

1 stick melted oleo
1/2 c. coconut
1/2 c. raisins
1 unbaked pie shell

Beat egg yolks, sugar, oleo together. Add coconut, nuts, raisins. Beat egg whites, fold into mixture. Pour in pie shell and bake 1 hour at 300°.
Beverly Lumm, Caddo
Council, Shreveport, La.

JELLO PIE

1 pkg. black cherry jello
1 pkg. lime jello
1 pkg. strawberry jello
1 small can pineapple, or
  box of frozen straw-
  berries
1 Tbsp. lemon juice

3 c. boiling water
1 c. sugar
1/2 c. water
1 pkg. orange jello
1 large can evaporated milk
Graham cracker crumbs
Nuts (optional)

Prepare black cherry, lime and strawberry jello with 1 cup boiling water each. Place in 3 shallow pans to congeal in refrigerator. Combine sugar, water and pineapple or strawberries. Bring to a boil. Dissolve orange jello and put in refrigerator until thick and syrupy. Have canned milk in freezer. Add lemon juice and whip until stiff. Cut all congealed jello into small squares and fold into whipped milk. Stir in syrupy mixture. Line 3 pie pans with graham cracker crumbs. Pour jello mixture into pie pans. Sprinkle with nuts, if desired. Refrigerate 3 or 4 hours before serving. Makes 3 pies.
Rebecca Scott Bockmon, Caddo
Council, Shreveport, La.

LEMON PIE

1 c. sugar
1 c. boiling water
4 Tbsp. lemon juice
1 Tbsp. butter

2 egg yolks
3 Tbsp. cornstarch
1 lemon rind, grated
1 baked 8-inch pie shell

Mix sugar and cornstarch, add boiling water, stirring constantly. Cook for 2 minutes in double boiler. Add beaten egg yolks, butter, rind and lemon juice. Cook until

414

thick. Cool, fill pie shell and top with meringue. Brown
top in 300°-325° oven. Jerrie Cleveland, Caddo
Council, Shreveport, La.

HOPE'S LEMON PIE

1 1/3 c. sugar
Dash of salt
3 eggs, separated
2 Tbsp. oleo
1 baked (9 inch) pie
   shell

6 Tbsp. cornstarch
1 1/4 c. boiling water
1/3 c. lemon juice
2 tsp. lemon rind
1 (7 oz.) jar marshmallow
   creme

Combine sugar, cornstarch and salt in saucepan, gradually add water. Bring to boil, stirring constantly. Cook
1 minute or until mixture is clear and thickened. Stir
small amount of hot mixture into beaten egg yolks, return to
hot mixture. Cook over medium heat 3 minutes, stirring
constantly. Stir in lemon juice, oleo and lemon rind. Pour
into pastry shell. Beat egg whites with a dash of salt
until soft peaks form. Gradually add marshmallow creme,
beating until stiff peaks form. Spread over filling, sealing
to edge of crust. Bake at 350° for 12-15 minutes or until
lightly browned. Cool. Ann Orr, Evangeline
Council, New Iberia, La.

LEMON ICEBOX PIE

1 can Eagle Brand milk
1 large Cool Whip
1 graham cracker pie shell

1 can lemonade mix, or
   1 small can frozen lemonade
   concentrate

Mix ingredients together. Spoon into crust. Chill.
Maxine Fletcher, Ouachita
Council, Monroe, La.

LEMON ICEBOX PIE

1 can Eagle Brand milk
Juice of 2 lemons

2 egg yolks
1 graham cracker crust

Add milk and egg yolks together, stir. Add lemon juice,
blend well and pour into pie crust. Cover with Meringue.

Meringue:

8 tsp. sugar   2 egg whites
1 tsp. vanilla

Beat egg whites until fluffy. Add sugar very slowly. When stiff, add vanilla. Spread meringue over pie and place in 325° oven. When meringue is rich golden brown, remove very slowly from oven, not letting cold air hit pie all at once. Set on counter and let cool until pie is at room temperature. Refrigerate.   Maxine Fletcher, Ouachita
           Council, Monroe, La.

KENTUCKY LEMON PIE

5 eggs   1 1/2 c. white Karo syrup
1 c. sugar   Juice of 2 lemons
1/4 c. butter   Rind of 1 lemon
1 unbaked pie shell

Beat eggs well, add syrup. Add sugar, lemon juice and grated rind. Add butter and beat together until well mixed. Pour into pie shell and bake on lower shelf of oven for 10 minutes at 375°. Move to middle shelf and reduce heat to 350° for 30-40 minutes. LaVanira B. Spivey, Evangeline
           Council, New Iberia, La.

MOM'S LEMON PIE

1 1/2 c. sugar   2 heaping Tbsp. cornstarch
1/4 tsp. salt   2 c. milk
4 egg yolks, beaten 1/4 stick butter
Juice and rind of 2 1 baked pie shell
 lemons

Combine sugar, salt, cornstarch and milk; mix thoroughly. Place on fire, bring to boil, stirring constantly until thick. Add beaten egg yolks, pour in drop by drop, stirring constantly. Remove from heat, add butter, lemon juice and rinds. Place back on heat for few minutes, stirring. Cool. Pour into shell and cover with meringue. Place in 300° oven about 15 minutes or until meringue is golden brown.

Meringue:

4 egg whites
3 or 4 drops vanilla

3 Tbsp. sugar
Pinch of cream of tartar

Beat egg whites until peaks stand. Add vanilla. Beat in sugar and cream of tartar until stiff. Spread over Lemon Pie.
Sylvia S. Williams, Metairie Council, Kenner, La.

OLD FASHIONED LEMON PIE

1 1/4 c. sugar
1 Tbsp. lemon rind
3 eggs, separated
1/3 c. lemon juice
1 baked pie shell

4 Tbsp. cornstarch
1/2 c. cold water
2 Tbsp. oleo
1 c. boiling water
Meringue

Mix cornstarch, sugar and lemon rind. Add cold water; mix. Stir in beaten egg yolks, add boiling water. Stirring constantly, bring to a boil. Add butter and boil for 3 minutes. Remove from heat and stir in lemon juice. Cool. Pour into pie shell and cover with meringue made from egg whites.
Mrs. Drew Holloway, Central Council, Alexandria, La.

LEMONADE PIE

1 can Eagle Brand milk
1 (9 oz.) carton Cool Whip
Juice from 1 lemon

1 (6 oz.) can frozen lemonade
2 baked pie shells, or
   graham cracker crusts

Mix milk and lemonade. Slowly stir in whipped topping. Add lemon juice and spoon into pie shells. Refrigerate until ready to serve. Yield: 2 pies. Betty Barron, Caddo Council, Shreveport, La.

LEMONADE PIE

1 small can frozen pink
   lemonade
1 (9 oz.) bowl Cool Whip

1 can Eagle Brand milk
1 graham cracker pie shell

Mix lemonade, milk and Cool Whip. Pour into pie shell and chill.
Phylles Wilkerson, Central Council, Natchitoches, La.

KEY LIME PIE

1/4 c. lime juice
3 egg yolks
1 tsp. green food coloring
1 baked pie shell (9 inch)

1 can sweetened condensed
  milk
6 egg whites
1/4 c. sugar
Dash of salt

Mix lime juice, milk and egg yolks. Fold in 3 stiffly beaten egg whites, salt and food coloring. Pour into pie shell that has not been quite browned. Bake at 250° for 6 minutes. Beat remaining egg whites until soft peaks form, add sugar and beat until stiff. Cover pie with meringue after removing from oven. Return to oven until meringue is golden brown.
Rebecca Scott Bockmon, Caddo
Council, Shreveport, La.

MALT SHOPPE PIE

1 qt. vanilla ice cream
1 c. crushed malted milk
  balls
3 Tbsp. instant chocolate
  flavored malted milk
  powder
2 Tbsp. milk

1 Tbsp. milk
1 c. whipping cream (Cool
  Whip can be used instead)
1/2 c. crushed malted milk
  balls
1 (9 inch) graham cracker
  crumb crust
3 Tbsp. marshmallow topping

In a chilled medium bowl, stir ice cream to soften, blend in the cup of crushed malted milk balls and the first 2 tablespoons milk. Spread in prepared crust, freeze while preparing top layer. In medium bowl, blend malted milk powder, marshmallow topping and 1 tablespoon milk. Add whipping cream, whip until soft peaks form. Cool Whip may be substituted. Spread mixture over layer in crust. Freeze until firm, several hours or overnight. Sprinkle with crushed malted milk balls.
Betty Villarrubia
Crescent City Council
New Orleans, La.

418

MILE HIGH PIE

1 (10 oz.) pkg. frozen
   strawberries
1 Tbsp. lemon juice
1 pt. whipping cream,
   whipped

1 c. sugar
2 egg whites, unbeaten
1 tsp. vanilla extract
1 baked 10-inch pie shell

Combine strawberries, sugar, lemon juice and egg whites in large mixing bowl. Beat 15 minutes or until very stiff. Fold in whipped cream and vanilla. Spoon into pie shell. Refrigerate until firm. Serves 8.

Mae Briley, Central
Council, Alexandria, La.

MILLIONAIRES PIE

1 (8 oz.) pkg. cream
   cheese
1 small can crushed
   pineapple, drained

1 c. sugar
1 large Cool Whip
1/2 c. pecans
1 baked pie crust

Cream sugar and cream cheese together, add pineapple. Fold in Cool Whip and pecans. Place into pie crust and refrigerate.

Pie Crust:

1 stick butter or oleo,
   melted
1/2 c. chopped nuts

1 c. flour
4 Tbsp. sugar

Combine flour, sugar and nuts. Mix into melted oleo. Place in pan and bake at 325° until light brown. Cool before filling with the above ingredients.

Barbara Chauvin
Crescent City Council
New Orleans, La.

MIRLITON MERINGUE PIE

5 large, 7 medium or
   9 small mirlitons
2 tsp. vanilla extract
Egg whites

1 can condensed milk
4 egg yolks
1 partly baked pie shell

Peel, seed and boil mirlitons until tender. Place in colander and press through with masher. Mix egg yolks and milk together and add the mashed mirliton slowly. Mix well and place in top of double boiler, cook until mixture is thick and bubbly. Add vanilla extract and pour into pie shell. Whip up egg whites until stiff and spread over pie. Bake slowly until brown. Serve cool.

Floyd Shumann, Ozone
Council, Hammond, La.

ORANGE PIE

Crust:

1 1/4 c. flour
2 Tbsp. oleo
1 egg

1/2 c. Crisco
1 (3 1/4 oz.) pkg. coconut

Combine all ingredients at low speed with mixer until moistened. Press into pie plate. Bake at 350° for 15-18 minutes until light brown. Cool crust before adding filling.

Filling:

2 c. sour cream
1 (4 5/8 oz.) can Start
   breakfast drink mix

1 can Eagle Brand milk
Cool Whip

Combine sour cream, milk and Start breakfast mix in mixing bowl. Beat 1 minute and pour into cooled pie crust. Cover with Cool Whip and refrigerate.

Joyce Gonzales, Capital
Council, Baton Rouge, La.

PARFAIT PIE

6 oatmeal cookies (large)
1 pkg. instant vanilla
   pudding

1 pt. ice cream (your
   choice)

Grate cookies; cover bottom of 8-inch pie plate with half of the crumbs. Make up vanilla pudding following directions on package. Beat in the ice cream on low speed. Pour

carefully over the crumbs and place in freezer. When almost frozen, sprinkle top with remaining crumbs. Serves 8.   Henrietta Victor, Magnolia
Council, New Orleans, La.

PEACH PIE

1 can sliced peaches
1 stick butter or oleo
1 1/2 tsp. baking powder
1/2 c. milk

1 1/3 c. sugar, divided
1 c. flour
1/4 tsp. salt

Heat peaches and 1/3 cup sugar. Melt butter in bottom of 12 x 7 x 1 1/2-inch dish. Make batter of 1 cup sugar, flour, baking powder, salt and milk. Pour over melted butter. Place sliced peaches on top of batter. Do not stir. Bake at 350° for 45 minutes.   Ethel Courtney, Ozone
Council, Baton Rouge, La.

PEACHES AND CREAM PIE

1 unbaked pie shell
  (9 inch)
10 Tbsp. sugar
1/4 c. flour
1 tsp. cinnamon

6 fresh peaches, or frozen
  sliced peaches
1 (8 oz.) carton sour cream
1 small can evaporated milk

Peel, pit and cut peaches in half. Place cut side up in pie crust. Stir together 8 tablespoons sugar, flour and 1/2 teaspoon cinnamon. Mix in sour cream and milk. Pour over peaches. Combine remaining sugar and cinnamon. Sprinkle over top of pie. Bake at 450° for 10 minutes, lower heat to 350° and bake for 30 minutes until firm.
Ann Orr, Evangeline
Council, New Iberia, La.

PEANUT BUTTER PIE

1 pkg. vanilla pudding
1 tsp. vanilla
1/3 c. smooth peanut
  butter

2 Tbsp. oleo
3/4 c. powdered sugar
1 (9 inch) baked pie shell
Cool Whip

Make pudding according to directions on box. Add

oleo and vanilla. Mix peanut butter and powdered sugar in mixer. Place 1/2 of pudding in pie shell. Spread 3/4 of peanut mixture on top, layer remainder of pudding and peanut mixture. Top with Cool Whip. Chill.

Velma Carruth, Capital
Council, Baton Rouge, La.

PEANUT BUTTER PIE

1 c. light brown sugar	1 c. light corn syrup
1/8 tsp. salt	1/4 c. oleo
1 tsp. vanilla	3 eggs
1 unbaked pie shell	3/4 c. crunchy peanut butter

Combine sugar, corn syrup, oleo and salt in saucepan. Bring quickly to a boil, stirring until sugar dissolves. Remove from heat. Beat eggs until foamy. Add small amount of hot syrup mix to eggs, mixing well. Add remaining syrup to eggs. Stir in peanut butter and vanilla. Pour into pie shell and bake at 350° for 45-50 minutes.

Grace Bell, Ouachita Council,
Monroe, La.

PEANUT BUTTER CREAM PIE

3/4 c. powdered sugar	1/3 c. peanut butter
2/3 c. white sugar	3 Tbsp. cornstarch
1 Tbsp. plain flour	1/2 tsp. salt
3 egg yolks	3 c. milk
2 Tbsp. oleo	1 tsp. vanilla extract
1 baked 9-inch pie shell	

Cream powdered sugar and peanut butter together and set aside. Combine remaining ingredients. Cook over medium heat, stirring constantly until thick. Sprinkle 2/3 of peanut butter in bottom of baked pie shell, pour custard over top. Spread Meringue over custard. Sprinkle remaining peanut mixture over Meringue and bake at 350° about 20 minutes or until golden brown. Delicious!

Meringue:

3 egg whites	1/4 tsp. cream of tartar
1/4 c. sugar	

Beat egg whites with cream of tartar until stiff, gradually add sugar. Spread over custard.

Maxine Botzong, Central
Council, Tioga, La.

FLUFFY PEANUT BUTTER PIE

1/2 c. peanut butter,
   creamy or crunchy
1 (8 oz.) pkg. cream
   cheese, softened
1 c. finely chopped
   peanuts

1/2 c. milk
1 c. powdered sugar
1 (9 oz.) bowl Cool Whip
   thawed
1 graham cracker crumb
   crust (9 inch)

Whip cheese until soft and fluffy. Beat in peanut butter and sugar. Slowly add milk, blending thoroughly into mixture. Fold in Cool Whip. Pour into prepared crust. Sprinkle with chopped peanuts. Freeze until firm.

Thelma Slay, Caddo
Council, Shreveport, La.

PEAR PIE

6 c. sliced pears
1 tsp. nutmeg or
   cinnamon
1 1/2 Tbsp. oleo

3/4 c. sugar
2 Tbsp. flour
2 unbaked pie shells or
   pastry for 2 crust pie

Pare and slice firm pears; 1 pear, sliced, makes about 1 cup. Combine sugar, spice and flour. Mix lightly with pears and pour into pie shell. Dot with oleo. Cover with top crust. Cut slits for steam to escape. Seal and flute. Bake in preheated 350° oven for about 1 hour and 10 minutes. Bake on cookie sheet to prevent spills in oven.

Virginia Bryce, Central
Council, Pineville, La.

PEAR MINCEMEAT PIE

1 pt. mincemeat mix
1/2 c. sugar
1 tsp. vanilla
1 unbaked 9-inch pie shell

2 eggs, well beaten
1/2 c. chopped pecans
1 tsp. melted butter

Mincemeat recipe is in another section of this book. Mix

all ingredients together and pour into pie shell. Bake for 15 minutes at 425°, reduce oven to 375° and continue cooking for additional 35 or 40 minutes.

Twila "Pete" Dysart, Ouachita
Council, Monroe, La.

PECAN PIE

1 c. white corn syrup
1/3 tsp. salt
1 tsp. vanilla
1 c. pecans
Whipped cream or ice cream

1 c. dark brown sugar
1/3 c. melted butter or oleo
3 eggs
1 (9-inch) unbaked pie shell

Combine syrup, sugar, salt, butter, vanilla and mix well. Add slightly beaten eggs. Pour into pie shell. Sprinkle pecans over all. Bake in preheated oven for approximately 45 minutes. Serve topped with whipped or ice cream when cool.

Doris Reeves, Capital
Council, Baton Rouge, La.

PECAN PIE

1/2 c. brown Karo syrup
1 tsp. flour
2 tsp. milk
1/2 c. butter or oleo,
  melted

1 c. sugar
2 eggs
1 tsp. vanilla
1 c. pecans or other nuts
1 unbaked pie shell

Mix sugar and flour together. Beat in eggs, milk, vanilla and butter, fold in nuts. Pour in pie shell and bake 40-50 minutes at 350°.

Delores Bridges, Shreveport
Works Council, Shreveport, La.

PECAN PIE

1 3/4 c. sugar
1/4 c. butter or oleo
1 tsp. vanilla
1 c. pecans

1/2 c. Karo syrup
3 eggs
1/2 tsp. salt
1 (9-inch) unbaked pie shell

Mix sugar, syrup, butter; heat to boiling point. Beat eggs; add to mixture. Add nuts, salt, vanilla. Pour in pie shell. Bake at 325° for 35-40 minutes.

Marjorie B. Harris, Capital
Council, Baton Rouge, La.

424

PECAN PIE

1 c. pecans
1/2 c. sugar
1/8 tsp. salt
1/4 c. melted butter

3 eggs
1 c. light corn syrup
1 tsp. vanilla
1 unbaked pie shell

Beat eggs, add sugar and syrup. Mix in salt and vanilla, adding melted butter last. Place pecans in bottom of pie shell. Pour in filling. Bake at 350° for 50-60 minutes. The nuts will rise to top and form a crusted layer.

Cleo Taylor, Ouachita
Council, Monroe, La.

PECAN PIE

1 c. pecans
1 c. sugar
1/8 tsp. salt
1 unbaked pie shell

1 c. light Karo syrup
3 eggs
1 tsp. vanilla

Beat eggs, add sugar, Karo syrup, salt and pecans; mix well. Add vanilla and pour in pie shell. Bake at 350° for about 35-45 minutes.

Annie Hawkins, Caddo
Council, Shreveport, La.

PECAN PIE

3 eggs
3/4 c. brown sugar
1 c. corn syrup
1/4 c. butter or oleo
1 tsp. vanilla

1 c. pecans
1/4 tsp. salt
2 Tbsp. cornstarch
1 tsp. vinegar
1 pie shell

Cream butter, add brown sugar and mix well. Add eggs, corn syrup, salt, vanilla and cornstarch which has been mixed with the vinegar. Beat thoroughly. Add pecans and pour into pie shell which has been partially baked at 400° for 10 minutes. Bake pie at 350° for about 40-45 minutes or until knife inserted into pie comes out clean.

John E. Haygood, Caddo
Council, Shreveport, La.

PECAN PIE

1/2 c. butter
2 c. sugar
1 tsp. vanilla
3 eggs, slightly beaten

1 c. Karo syrup
1 c. pecans
1/2 tsp. salt
1 unbaked pie shell

Cream butter. Add sugar gradually and cream together until light and fluffy. Add rest of ingredients. Blend well and pour into pie shell. Bake at 375° until done.

Cecile Gallet, Evangeline
Council, Lafayette, La.

ANGEL PECAN PIE

3 egg whites
1/2 tsp. cream of tartar
1 c. sugar

16 (2-inch) Waverly Wafers
1 tsp. vanilla
1 c. chopped nuts

Beat egg whites until foamy, add cream of tartar and beat until stiff. Gradually add sugar, vanilla and nuts. Fold in coarsely broken cracker crumbs. Pour in buttered pie plate. Bake at 325° until brown. Cool and top with whipped cream or Cool Whip. Lorene Savage, Caddo Council, Shreveport, La.

CARAMEL PECAN PIE

36 Kraft caramels
1/4 c. oleo
3 eggs, beaten
1/4 tsp. salt
1 1/2 c. chopped pecans

1/4 c. water
3/4 c. sugar
1/2 tsp. vanilla
1 unbaked (9-inch) pie shell

Melt caramels with water and oleo in saucepan over very low heat, stir frequently until sauce is smooth. Combine sugar, eggs, vanilla and salt. Gradually add caramel sauce, mix well. Stir in nuts. Pour into pie shell. Bake at 350° for 45-50 minutes. Pie filling will appear to be very soft but becomes firm as it cools. Fae Wells, Central Council, Alexandria, La.

MINIATURE PECAN PIES

Crust:

1 (3 oz.) pkg. cream
  cheese
1 stick oleo

1 c. flour
1 Tbsp. sugar

Mix cream cheese, flour, oleo and sugar together, chill. Form small balls and place in miniature cupcake or muffin tins. Form crust in bottom and sides with fingers.

Filling:

3/4 c. brown sugar
1 c. chopped pecans
1 tsp. vanilla

1 egg
1 Tbsp. oleo

Cook brown sugar, egg, oleo and vanilla until dissolved, add pecans. Fill crust with about 1 teaspoon of filling. Bake at 350° for 25 minutes. Makes about 2 dozen.

L. Monnin, LeBayou
Council, Franklin, La.

MRS. CUTRER'S PECAN PIE

1/2 stick melted oleo
3 Tbsp. Pet milk
3 eggs
1 Tbsp. vanilla

1 1/2 c. sugar
2 Tbsp. vinegar (exactly)
1 c. chopped pecans
1 unbaked pie shell

Mix sugar, oleo, cream, vinegar and vanilla. Beat eggs and add to mixture. Add pecans. Pour into pie shell and bake in preheated 350° oven for 40-45 minutes.

Denise Burdette, Capital
Council, Zachary, La.

MOCK PECAN PIE

2 eggs, beaten
2/3 c. melted margarine
2/3 c. granulated sugar
2/3 c. light corn syrup

2/3 c. uncooked oatmeal
1/4 tsp. salt
1 tsp. vanilla

Mix all ingredients, leaving oatmeal last, and pour into 8-inch unbaked pie shell. Bake at 350° for 1 hour.

Calcasieu Council
Lake Charles, La.

PARTY PECAN PIES

Crust:

2 (3 oz.) pkg. cream
  cheese
2 c. sifted flour

1 stick oleo
Finely chopped pecans

Mix cream cheese, flour and oleo together; chill. Roll into small balls. Makes about 50 in small cupcake pans. Press into small muffin tins at bottom and sides. Sprinkle finely chopped pecans over bottom.

Custard Filling:

1 egg
3/4 c. brown sugar
Pecan pieces

Pinch of salt
1 Tbsp. soft oleo and vanilla

Combine egg, brown sugar, salt, oleo and vanilla. Add small amount of custard to pastry crust. Top with a few more pieces of pecans. Bake at 350° for about 25 minutes or until good and brown.

Anne Harrison's Recipe, by
Verle Oliphant, Caddo
Council, Shreveport, La.

TEA TIME TASSIES

1 (3 oz.) pkg. cream
  cheese, softened

1 c. sifted flour
1/2 c. oleo, softened

Mix softened cream cheese and oleo together until well blended. Stir in flour and chill for 1 hour. Shape into 2 dozen 1-inch balls. Place in small ungreased muffin tins, press dough on side and bottom of cups. Fill with Pecan Filling.

Filling:

1 egg	3/4 c. brown sugar
1 Tbsp. soft oleo	2/3 c. coarsely broken
1 tsp. vanilla	pecans

Beat egg, sugar, oleo and vanilla just until smooth. Add pecans. Fill pastry and bake at 325° for about 25 minutes.

Cecile Gallet, Evangeline
Council, Lafayette, La.

PINEAPPLE CHIFFON PIE

2 eggs	1 small can crushed pineapple
1 pkg. lemon jello	1 c. sugar
1 large can Pet milk	1 baked pie shell

Mix eggs, sugar, pineapple, then add jello; cook until thick. Cool, then fold in 1 can whipped Pet milk (that has been chilled). Pour into baked pie shell.

Mrs. Virginia McCullough
Central Council
Alexandria, La.

PINEAPPLE COCONUT PIE

3 eggs	1 c. white Karo syrup
1/2 c. sugar	1 small can pineapple
1 tsp. vanilla	2 Tbsp. melted butter
1 can Angel Flake coconut	1 unbaked pie shell
Small pinch of salt	

Mix ingredients, pour into pie shell. Bake at 450° for 10 minutes, reduce heat to 350° and bake until done.

Jeanette Williams, Caddo
Council, Shreveport, La.

FROZEN PINEAPPLE PIE

3 eggs	1 small can crushed pineapple
1 c. sugar	1 pkg. orange-pineapple
1 tall can evaporated milk	gelatin
1 c. nuts	2 graham cracker crusts
1/2 pt. whipped cream	

Cook eggs, sugar and pineapple in double boiler until thick. Cool until warm. Add gelatin and stir. Whip chilled evaporated milk and fold into mixture. Add nuts. Pour into graham cracker crust. Top with whipped cream. Wrap in foil and freeze until ready to serve. Makes two 9-inch pies.

Jean Coon, Caddo Council,
Shreveport, La.

PUMPKIN PIE

2 Tbsp. butter	2 eggs
3/4 c. sugar	1 tsp. salt
1/4 tsp. cinnamon	1/4 tsp. ginger
1/4 tsp. nutmeg	1 c. mashed pumpkin
1 1/4 c. Pet milk	4-5 Tbsp. ice water
1/2 c. shortening	1 1/2 c. flour

Combine shortening, flour, 1/2 teaspoon salt and ice water. Roll out pastry and place in pie pan. Cream butter, add sugar and eggs. Add remaining ingredients, mix well. Pour into pie shell and bake at 375° for about 1 hour.

Cecile Gallet, Evangeline
Council, Lafayette, La.

SHERRIED PUMPKIN CHIFFON PIE

1 env. gelatin	1/4 c. cold water
3 eggs, separated	1 c. pumpkin
1/2 c. sherry wine	1 c. sugar
1/4 tsp. salt	1/2 tsp. cinnamon
1/4 tsp. nutmeg	1/4 tsp. ginger
1 baked pie shell	Whipped cream

Soften gelatin in cold water. Beat egg yolks slightly in top of double boiler. Stir in pumpkin, sherry, 1/2 cup sugar, salt, cinnamon, nutmeg and ginger. Cook over water, stirring constantly for 5 minutes. Remove from heat, add softened gelatin, stir until dissolved. Chill. When it starts to thicken, fold in egg whites which have been beaten with remaining 1/2 cup sugar. Pour in pie shell and chill for several hours. Top with whipped cream flavored with sherry or ginger.

Connie Younker
Shreveport Works Council
Shreveport, La.

PUMPKIN CHIFFON PIE

1 pkg. Whip & Chill
   vanilla dessert mix
1/2 tsp. nutmeg
1/2 c. cold milk
2 egg whites
1 unbaked crumb crust
   (9-inch)

1 tsp. cinnamon
1/4 tsp. ginger
1 c. canned pumpkin, chilled
1/4 c. cold water
1/4 c. sugar
1 env. Dream Whip

Combine dessert mix, spices, pumpkin, milk and water. Whip 3 minutes with electric mixer, starting at low speed and increasing to high. Beat egg whites until foamy, gradually add sugar, beating after each addition until soft peaks form. Fold in pumpkin mixture. Spoon mixture into crust. Chill 3 hours or more. When ready to serve, mix Dream Whip according to directions on package and top pumpkin pie.

Viola Kehrer, Ozone
Council, Hammond, La.

RAISIN PIE

2 c. raisins
1/2 c. sugar
1/2 c. chopped pecans
3 Tbsp. lemon juice

1 1/2 c. water
2 Tbsp. all-purpose flour
1 tsp. grated lemon rind
Pastry for 2 crust pie

In saucepan, combine water and raisins. Cook covered 10 minutes or until raisins are plump. Combine sugar and flour, stir in raisins. Cook over low heat, stirring constantly until mixture thickens and bubbles. Cook 1 minute more. Remove from heat, stir in nuts, lemon peel and juice. Pour into pastry shell, adjust top crust and cut slits to allow steam to escape. Bake at 425° for 30-40 minutes.

Betty Elenburg, Caddo
Council, Shreveport, La.

RAISIN CREAM PIE

1/2 c. sugar
2 heaping Tbsp. flour
2 egg yolks
1 tsp. vanilla
1 baked pie shell

Dash of salt
1 3/4 c. sweet milk
1 Tbsp. butter
1/2 c. raisins

Soak raisins in boiling water 5 minutes, drain and set aside. Combine sugar, salt and flour. Add 1/2 cup milk and egg yolks, then remainder of milk. Cook over medium heat until thick and smooth, stirring constantly. Add butter, vanilla and raisins. Pour into baked pie shell and top with meringue. Put in oven and brown lightly.

Lela Bonner, Ouachita
Council, Bastrop, La.

SOUR CREAM RAISIN PIE

1 c. cooked raisins
2 Tbsp. flour
1 c. sour cream

1 c. sugar
2 egg yolks

Beat egg yolks slightly, add sugar and blend well. Add sour cream, mix well. Pour into baked pie shell. Use egg whites for meringue.

Calcasieu Council
Lake Charles, La.

RAISIN SOUR CREAM PIE

1 c. sour cream
3 egg yolks
1/2 tsp. salt
1 unbaked pie shell

1/2 c. sugar
1 c. raisins
1/2 tsp. nutmeg

Mix cream, sugar, raisins, egg yolks and salt together. Pour into pie shell, sprinkle nutmeg on top. Bake 1 hour at 350°. Beat egg whites, add 3 tablespoons sugar and vanilla. Spread meringue on pie and brown at 375° for 15 minutes or until brown.

Shirley Lumsden, Ouachita
Council, Monroe, La.

RITZ CRACKER PIE

3 egg whites
1 c. sugar
1 c. chopped pecans
1 tsp. baking powder

2 c. crushed Ritz crackers
1 tsp. vanilla
Whipping cream or Cool Whip

Beat egg whites until stiff, add sugar and vanilla. Fold egg whites into bowl with crackers, pecans and baking powder. Spread in greased pie pan. Bake at 325° for 30 minutes. Cool. Top with Cool Whip or whipped cream to serve. Store in refrigerator. Gertrude Juneau, Crescent City Council, New Orleans, La.

RHUBARB PIE

Rhubarb	3 Tbsp. flour
1 1/4 c. sugar	Pinch of salt
1 double crust pie shell	1 tsp. oleo, melted

Mix sugar, flour, salt and oleo. Sprinkle over rhubarb in pie shell. Top with another crust. Bake at 400° about 40-45 minutes. Anita Tempalski, Ouachita Council, Monroe, La.

STRAWBERRY PIE

1/2 c. cornstarch	2 c. sugar minus 2 Tbsp.
2 Tbsp. strawberry jello	2 c. water
Dash of salt	Few drops red food coloring
1 baked pie shell	Fresh strawberries
Whipped cream	

Combine sugar, jello and 1 1/2 cups water. Bring to rapid boil. Mix cornstarch and remainder of water, add slowly to boiling mixture. Add salt and food coloring. Cook until thickened. Wash strawberries and place in bottom of baked pie shell. Pour mixture over top. Store in refrigerator. Top with whipped cream when cool. Marjorie Rowell, Evangeline Council, Lafayette, La.

STRAWBERRY PIE

1 pt. fresh strawberries	1 c. sugar
1 c. water	2-3 Tbsp. cornstarch
3 Tbsp. strawberry jello	1 baked pie shell
Few drops red food coloring (optional)	1 c. Cool Whip

Slice berries, set aside. Mix sugar and cornstarch together. Add water. Cook until thickened, remove from

heat and stir in jello. Mix well and cool. Fold in berries.
Pour into pie shell. Refrigerate 1 hour. Spread Cool Whip
on pie. Serve.   Jan Prestridge, Capital
                                      Council, Baton Rouge, La.

STRAWBERRY ALASKA PIE

1 baked pie shell   1 qt. strawberry ice cream
4 egg whites   1/4 tsp. cream of tartar
6 Tbsp. sugar   1 c. strawberry preserves

Combine egg whites, cream of tartar in small mixer bowl.
Beat at high speed until frothy. Gradually beat in sugar,
beat until stiff, glossy peaks form. Set aside. Spoon half of
softened ice cream evenly into pie shell. Spread with strawberry preserves. Spoon remaining ice cream over top.
Swirl meringue over ice cream, sealing completely to edge of
pie shell. Bake at 450° for 3-5 minutes or until peaks are
light golden brown. Freeze until firm, at least 4 hours or
overnight. Remove from freezer 10 minutes before cutting.
Complete pie can be made ahead and frozen up to 2 weeks.
                                  Lynn Babin, Westmoor
                                  Council, Kenner, La.

STRAWBERRY CREAM PIE

1 c. sugar   1/2 c. cornstarch
1/2 tsp. salt   2 1/2 c. milk, scalded
2 eggs   3 Tbsp. butter
1/2 tsp. vanilla   1 pt. strawberries, sliced
1/2 pt. heavy cream,   1 baked 9-inch pie shell
   whipped

Mix sugar and cornstarch. Add milk, cook until thick.
Beat eggs slightly, add some of the hot mixture to eggs.
Add eggs to mixture, stirring. Cook until thick. Add
butter, chill and add vanilla. Place strawberries in pie
shell. Pour chilled custard over strawberries immediately.
Top with whipped cream.   Shirley Lumsden, Ouachita
                                 Council, Monroe, La.

434

FRESH STRAWBERRY PIE

1 c. water
4 Tbsp. flour
1 pt. fresh strawberries,
   cut into halves or
   fourths

1 c. sugar
4 Tbsp. strawberry jello
1 baked pie shell
1 small container Cool Whip

Cook sugar, water and flour until thick. Add jello, cool. Pour 1/2 of mixture in cooled pie shell. Spread strawberries over top and pour remaining mixture over them. Let set. Top with whipped cream or Cool Whip.

Jerrie Cleveland, Caddo
Council, Shreveport, La.

FRESH STRAWBERRY PIE

3/4 c. sugar
3 Tbsp. cold water
1 c. boiling water
Red food coloring
1 baked pie shell

3 Tbsp. cornstarch
Pinch of salt
3 Tbsp. lemon juice
1 1/2 pt. fresh sliced strawberries
Whipped cream

Combine sugar, cornstarch, salt and 3 tablespoons cold water and mix. Add boiling water. Cook over medium heat until stiff and thick. Remove from fire, add lemon juice and few drops of food coloring to mixture. Cool. Add strawberries and pour into pie shell. Let sit 1 hour. Top with whipped cream.

Cecile Gallet, Evangeline
Council, Lafayette, La.

FRESH STRAWBERRY PIE

1 c. sugar
3 Tbsp. strawberry jello
1 c. strawberries (may
   use more)

3 Tbsp. cornstarch
1 c. hot water
1 baked pie shell
Cool Whip or whipped cream

Mix sugar, cornstarch and jello. Add hot water and cook about 1 minute, cool. Put sliced berries in cool pie shell. Pour cooled syrup over berries and refrigerate. Top with Cool Whip or whipped cream.

Betty Wood, Ozone Council,
Bogalusa, La.

FRESH STRAWBERRY PIE

1 c. sugar
2 Tbsp. cornstarch
1 tsp. vanilla
2 pt. fresh strawberries,
  washed and hulled

3 Tbsp. strawberry jello
1/4 tsp. salt
1 c. boiling water
1 baked pie shell
Whipped cream

Mix sugar, jello, cornstarch and salt in saucepan, stir in boiling water. Bring mixture to boil, stirring constantly and boil for 3 minutes. Add vanilla. Cool completely. Arrange whole strawberries in pie shell. Pour glaze over berries. Chill several hours and top with whipped cream. For best results, make glaze day before and chill overnight. About 3 hours before serving, remove glaze, beat and add strawberries. Pour in shell, top with whipped cream and rechill.

Jeanette English, Caddo
Council, Shreveport, La.

GLAZED STRAWBERRY PIE

1 (8 oz.) pkg. cream
  cheese
1 can condensed milk

1/3 c. fresh lemon juice
1/2 tsp. lemon flavoring
1 baked pie shell

Whip softened cream cheese until fluffy. Gradually add milk, continue beating until well blended. Add lemon juice and flavoring. Pour into pie shell.

Glaze:

1 c. sugar
3 Tbsp. cornstarch
1/2 tsp. red food coloring
1/2 tsp. lemon flavoring

1 c. boiling water
3 Tbsp. water
1 1/2 pt. fresh or frozen
  strawberries, sliced

Mix sugar and cornstarch with 3 tablespoons water. Add this mixture to 1 cup boiling water. Cook until clear and thick. Add food coloring and lemon flavoring. Cool. Add sliced strawberries. Pour Glaze over cream cheese filling. Top with whipped cream.

Doris Reeves, Capital
Council, Baton Rouge, La.

STRAWBERRY ICE CREAM PIE

1 qt. vanilla ice cream
1 qt. fresh strawberries
1 Tbsp. cornstarch

1 baked (9-inch) pie shell
1/3 c. sugar
1/2 c. water

Stir ice cream until slightly softened, spread in bottom of pie shell. Freeze. Mash and sieve 1 cup of the strawberries. Combine sugar and cornstarch in saucepan, stir in water, then mashed berries. Cook and stir until thickened and bubbly. Cool to room temperature. About 20 minutes before serving time, arrange remaining whole berries, stem down, over ice cream. Spoon thickened glaze over berries. Freeze until serving time. Mrs. Jeannine Prattini
Capital Council
Chalmette, La.

STUPID PIE

3 egg whites, stiffly beaten
1 tsp. vanilla
Whipped cream or Cool
  Whip

3/4 c. sugar
20 round Ritz crackers (or
  soda crackers)
1 c. chopped nuts

Add vanilla and sugar to egg whites. Beat until smooth. Add crackers, coarsely broken, and nuts. Mix well. Pour into ungreased pie plate. Bake at 350° for 1/2 hour. Cool. Cover with whipped cream or Cool Whip and chill 2 or 3 hours. Rich and delicious. Katherine Slover, Caddo
Council, Phoenix, Az.

SWEET POTATO PIE

1 1/4 c. sugar
1 tsp. vanilla
2 eggs
1 1/2 c. cooked, mashed
  sweet potatoes

1 tsp. pumpkin pie spice
1/2 tsp. salt
1 large can Pet milk
1 unbaked 9-inch pie crust

Blend sugar, spice and salt together. Beat eggs, add milk and vanilla. Mix well and combine with sugar mixture and sweet potatoes. Beat until smooth. Pour in pie shell. Bake at 425° for 15 minutes, reduce heat to 350° and continue baking 30 minutes or until knife inserted in pie comes out clean. Cool before serving. Jeanette English, Caddo
Council, Shreveport, La.

SWEET POTATO PIE

1 1/2 c. hot mashed sweet
   potatoes
1/2 tsp. nutmeg
1/2 tsp. baking powder
1/2 tsp. soda
1 unbaked pie shell

1 Tbsp. butter
1 c. sugar
1/2 tsp. cinnamon
1/2 c. buttermilk
2 eggs, beaten until frothy

Mix spices and baking powder with sugar. Add soda to buttermilk. Mix butter with potatoes. Mix all of these ingredients together. Pour into pie shell and bake 10 minutes at 400°, reduce heat to 300° and bake for 45 minutes.

Mavis W. O'Rourke, Shreveport
Works Council, Shreveport, La.

SWEET POTATO PIE

3-4 large sweet potatoes
2 c. sugar
1/2 tsp. nutmeg
1 tall can evaporated milk
1/2 tsp. salt

1/2 c. butter, softened
4 eggs
3 pie shells (9-inch), or 2
   deep dish pie shells (9-inch)

Cook sweet potatoes, remove skins and mash until creamy (yield: 3 1/2 cups). Stir in butter, sugar and eggs, 1 at a time. Add nutmeg, salt and milk. Pour into unbaked pie shells. Place pans on cookie sheets, bake in preheated oven for 20 minutes, reduce heat to 325° and bake 30-45 minutes until knife inserted into center comes out clean. Cool before serving. Yield: 3 pies. Francis Kennedy, Caddo
Council, Shreveport, La.

AUDREY'S SWEET POTATO PIE

1 c. mashed, cooked
   sweet potatoes
3 eggs
1 tsp. vanilla flavor
1 small can evaporated milk
1 unbaked pie shell

2 c. sugar
3 Tbsp. flour
1 stick butter or oleo
1 1/2 tsp. lemon flavor
Speck of salt

Mix all ingredients and pour into pie shell. Bake at 375° until firm and brown. Audrey M. Lee, Capital
Council, Zachary, La.

438

ENGLISH WALNUT PIE

3 egg whites
1 c. chopped nuts,
   walnuts or pecans
1 tsp. vanilla

1 c. sugar
3/4 c. crushed saltine
   crackers

Mix crumbs, nuts and half of sugar. Beat egg whites until stiff. Add remaining sugar and vanilla. Fold into cracker crumb mixture. Pour into buttered pie pan. Bake at 350° for 20 minutes. Chill and serve with ice cream or whipped cream. Very easy and good.

Frances Lamb, Central
Council, Afton, Tn.

FROZEN YOGURT PIE

2 (8 oz.) cartons yogurt,
   any flavor

1 (8 oz.) bowl Cool Whip
1 graham cracker shell

Combine yogurt and whipped topping. Pour into pie shell and freeze until firm. Put pie in refrigerator section for an hour before serving to make slicing easier. For variations, add 1/4 - 1/2 cup crushed pineapple when using pineapple yogurt. Add chopped nuts or shredded coconut to any flavor, or add 1 ounce liqueur or flavored brandy to yogurt mixture.

Ann Orr, Evangeline
Council, New Iberia, La.

PASTRY SHELL

1 1/2 c. sifted all-
   purpose flour
4-5 Tbsp. cold milk

1 tsp. salt
1/3 c. Crisco

Mix flour and salt, add Crisco and cut into flour until smooth. Add cold milk and blend. Put some dry flour on waxed paper and roll out pie crust and place in pie pan. Bake in very hot oven at 400°-450° until brown. Makes one 9-inch pie shell.

Pat Mora, LeBayou
Council, Franklin, La.

HOT PASTRY PIE SHELL

1 1/2 c. flour
1/4 c. boiling water
1/2 tsp. salt
1/2 c. Crisco
1 pinch baking powder

Stir Crisco in boiling water until melted. Pour into dry ingredients and mix. Roll out to form pie shell.

Marjorie Rowell, Evangeline
Council, Lafayette, La.

PIE CRUST FOR 13x9x2-INCH PAN

1 stick oleo
1/2 c. chopped pecans
1 c. graham cracker
   crumbs
3 Tbsp. brown sugar
Vanilla to taste
1 c. vanilla wafer crumbs

Combine ingredients, press into pan and bake at 350° for about 15 minutes.

Lucille Smith, Ouachita
Council, Monroe, La.

SWEET DOUGH PIE CRUST

4 eggs
2 c. sugar
6 c. flour
3 tsp. vanilla flavoring
1/2 tsp. nutmeg
1 1/2 c. shortening
1 c. milk
5 tsp. baking powder
1/2 tsp. cinnamon

Cream shortening, eggs and sugar until mixture has turned very light yellow. Add milk and mix well. Add flour and baking powder along with vanilla and spices. Beat until mixture is light and fluffy. Cool in refrigerator; the colder the dough, the easier it is to roll. Roll or pat dough into 9-inch pie plates. Add your favorite fruit filling and either strip or cover completely with more dough. Bake at 350° until top is brown. This amount of dough makes 5 or 6 pies or make 2 pies and tea cakes with remainder of dough. Bake tea cakes only until light brown or they will be too dry.

Beverly Foret, Evangeline
Council, Opelousas, La.

CAKES, COOKIES, DESSERTS

HANDY CHART OF KITCHEN MATH
(Size of Pans and Baking Dishes)

Cooking need never become a crisis, when you use our handy charts. Need a 4 or 6-cup baking dish? Will your fancy mold be the right size for the recipe? See below for the answers.

COMMON KITCHEN PANS TO USE AS CASSEROLES WHEN THE RECIPE CALLS FOR:

4-cup baking dish:
- 9-inch pie plate
- 8x1¼-inch layer cake pan—**C**
- 7 3/8 x 3 5/8 x 2¼-inch loaf pan—**A**

6-cup baking dish:
- 8 or 9x1½-inch layer cake pan—**C**
- 10-inch pie plate
- 8½ x 3 5/8 x 2 5/8 inch loaf pan—**A**

8-cup baking dish:
- 8x8x2-inch square pan—**D**
- 11x7x1½-inch baking pan
- 9x5x3-inch loaf pan—**A**

10-cup baking dish:
- 9x9x2-inch square pan—**D**
- 11¾x7½x1¾-inch baking pan
- 15x10x1-inch jelly-roll pan

12-cup baking dish and over:
- 13½x8½x2-inch glass baking pan — 12 cups
- 13x9x2-inch metal baking pan — 15 cups
- 14x10½x2½-inch roasting pan — 19 cups

TOTAL VOLUME OF VARIOUS SPECIAL BAKING PANS

Tube Pans:
- 7½x3-inch "Bundt" tube pan—**K** — 6 cups
- 9x3½-inch fancy tube or "Bundt" pan **J** or **K** — 9 cups
- 9x3½-inch angel cake pan—**I** — 12 cups
- 10x3¾-inch "Bundt" or "Crownburst" pan—**K** — 12 cups
- 9x3½-inch fancy tube mold—**J** — 12 cups
- 10x4-inch fancy tube mold (Kugelhupf)—**J** — 16 cups
- 10x4-inch angel cake pan—**I** — 18 cups

Melon Mold:
- 7x5½x4-inch mold—**H** — 6 cups

Spring-Form Pans:
- 8x3-inch pan—**B** — 12 cups
- 9x3-inch pan—**B** — 16 cups

Ring Molds:
- 8½x2¼-inch mold—**E** — 4½ cups
- 9¼x2¾-inch mold—**E** — 8 cups

Charlotte Mold:
- 6x4¼-inch mold—**G** — 7½ cups

Brioche Pan:
- 9½x3¼-inch pan—**F** — 8 cups

AMBROSIA CAKE

1/2 c. butter	2 c. sugar
1 c. buttermilk	2 tsp. soda, dissolved in
2 eggs, beaten	buttermilk
1 tsp. cinnamon	3 c. all-purpose flour
1 tsp. ground cloves	1 cake of chocolate or 3 Tbsp.
1 tsp. nutmeg	cocoa dissolved in 1/2 c.
1 apple, chopped fine	boiling water

Combine and mix ingredients well. Bake in 3 greased and floured cake pans at 350° about 25 minutes.

Filling:

3 c. sugar	2 c. sweet milk
1/2 c. butter	1/4 tsp. soda
1 tsp. baking powder	1 orange, grated
1 c. coconut	1 c. nuts
1 c. raisins	

Mix sugar, butter, milk, soda and baking powder. Cook until soft ball forms in water. Add remaining ingredients.

Selman Kinaul, Ouachita
Council, Monroe, La.

AMBROSIA CAKE

2 c. flour	1 1/2 c. granulated sugar
1 tsp. salt	2 tsp. soda
2 eggs, beaten slightly	1 (No. 303) can fruit cocktail
1/2 c. nuts	1/2 c. brown sugar

Add white sugar and fruit cocktail to beaten eggs. Add flour, salt and soda. Pour into greased 13x9x2-inch pan. Combine nuts and brown sugar, sprinkle over cake batter. Bake at 325° for 35 or 45 minutes.

Topping:

3/4 c. sugar	1/2 c. Pet milk
1 stick oleo	1 can Angel Flake coconut
1 tsp. vanilla	

Mix sugar, oleo and milk together in saucepan, stir

until it comes to a boil. Cool for 2 minutes, stirring constantly. Remove from heat, add remaining ingredients. Stir well and spread evenly over hot cake.

Doris Reeves, Capital
Council, Baton Rouge, La.

ANGEL CAKE

1 angel food cake	1 1/2 env. Knox gelatine
1 c. cold water	1 c. boiling water
1 c. sugar	1 c. orange juice
Juice of 1 lemon	1/2 pt. whipped cream

Break cake into bite sized pieces and place in bottom of pan. Dissolve gelatine in cold water. Add boiling water, sugar, orange and lemon juice. Chill until partially congealed. Add whipped cream and pour over angel food pieces. Refrigerate for 24 hours. Slice to serve.

Linda Bagur, Caddo Council,
Shreveport, La.

APPLE CAKE

4 c. chopped apples	2 c. sugar
2 eggs	1 c. cooking oil
1 c. chopped pecans	2 1/2 c. flour
2 Tbsp. baking soda	1 tsp. cinnamon
1 tsp. salt	

Mix apples and sugar, let stand. Separate eggs. Beat whites, fold in egg yolks. Add oil to eggs, let stand. Mix together flour, soda, salt and cinnamon. Pour egg mixture over apples. Add dry ingredients. Pour into greased and floured tube pan. Bake at 350° for 1 hour.

Jean Turton, Calcasieu
Council, Lake Charles, La.

APPLE CAKE

1/2 tsp. salt	2 c. sugar
1 c. cooking oil	2 eggs
1 tsp. cinnamon	1/2 tsp. nutmeg
1 tsp. soda	3 c. flour
1/2 c. raisins	3 c. apples, cut up
1/2 c. nuts	1 tsp. vanilla

442

Mix oil, sugar and eggs. Add dry ingredients and beat. Add remaining ingredients and mix well. Pour in greased and floured tube or Bundt pan. Bake at 350° for 1 hour and 15 minutes or until done. Cecile Gallet, Evangeline Council, Lafayette, La.

APPLE BLOSSOM CAKE

4 medium size apples,
  grated fine
1/2 tsp. cinnamon
1 tsp. salt
1/4 tsp. allspice
1 c. chopped dates
1 1/2 c. cooking oil

2 c. sugar
2 c. flour
1/4 tsp. nutmeg
1 1/2 tsp. soda
1 c. chopped pecans
3 eggs

Blend sugar and oil, add eggs, 1 at a time, mix well. Add 1 3/4 cups flour. Mix remaining flour with pecans and dates. Set aside. Add remaining ingredients to sugar mixture. Mix well. Fold in pecans, dates and flour. Bake in 10x12-inch pan in preheated 350° oven for 35 minutes or until cake springs back when touched.

Cream Cheese Frosting:

1 (3 oz.) pkg. cream
  cheese

2 or 3 Tbsp. milk
Powdered sugar

Add milk to softened cream cheese. Stir in powdered sugar until it is smooth enough to spread. Gloria Fontenot, Evangeline Council, Lafayette, La.

DUTCH APPLE COFFEE CAKE

4 Tbsp. butter
1 egg, beaten
1 tsp. vanilla
2 tsp. baking powder
1 c. water

1 c. sugar
1/2 c. milk
1 c. flour
2 c. apples, thinly sliced

Cook apples in water about 5 minutes or until tender, drain. Combine egg and milk, add to remaining ingredients. Mix well and pour batter into pan. Arrange apples on top of batter. Spread Hard Sauce over apples and bake at 300° for 35-40 minutes.

1723-79

Hard Sauce:

1/3 c. butter   2 c. sugar
1 tsp. cinnamon

Mix together and spread over apples.

Mrs. Travis D. Guin, Sr.
(Rubye Morgan's Mom)
Campti, La., Central Council

FRESH APPLE CAKE

2 eggs, well beaten   2 c. sugar
1 1/2 c. cooking oil   3 c. peeled and chopped
3 c. sifted flour   Delicious apples
1 tsp. soda   1/2 tsp. salt
2 tsp. cinnamon   2 Tbsp. vanilla
1 c. chopped pecans   1 c. raisins (I use white)

Mix eggs and sugar, add remaining ingredients. Bake in greased and floured tube pan for about 1 1/2 hours at 325°. Test for doneness after 1 hour and 15 minutes. Do not overcook.

Gayle Cummings, Caddo
Council, Shreveport, La.

FRESH APPLE CAKE

1 1/2 c. cooking oil   2 c. sugar
3 c. fresh apples,   3 c. all-purpose flour
   chopped   1 tsp. vanilla
1 tsp. soda   1 c. chopped nuts
2 eggs   2 tsp. cinnamon
1/2 tsp. salt

Mix oil, sugar and apples together. Add flour, soda and vanilla. Stir in remaining ingredients. Pour batter into greased and floured Bundt pan. Bake at 350° for 1 hour or until done.

Jeanette B. Armand, Central
Council, Bunkie, La.

444

FRESH APPLE CAKE

2 c. sugar
2 eggs
1 1/2 tsp. soda
3 c. grated apples

1 1/2 c. salad oil
3 c. flour
1 tsp. salt
1 c. chopped nuts

Combine sugar, oil, eggs and mix well. Sift flour with soda and salt. Stir into sugar mixture. Add apples and nuts. Mix well. Makes 3 layers (9-inch pans). Bake at 350° for 30 or 40 minutes. Cool.

Icing:

1 (8 oz.) pkg. cream
  cheese
1 c. chopped nuts
1 stick oleo

1 tsp. vanilla
1 (1 lb.) box powdered
  sugar
3-4 Tbsp. milk

Soften cream cheese, add butter. Mix and add vanilla. Mix in powdered sugar and milk alternately. Stir in nuts. Ice cake.
Carlotta Thomas, Ouachita Council, Monroe, La.

FRESH APPLE CAKE

3 c. apples, peeled and
  cut in small pieces
3 c. plain flour
2 eggs, beaten
1 tsp. cinnamon
1 c. Wesson oil

1 c. chopped dates
1 c. chopped pecans
2 c. sugar
1 tsp. vanilla
1 tsp. soda
1 tsp. salt

Combine apples, dates and pecans, mix in 1 cup flour. Add sugar, eggs, vanilla, cinnamon, soda and remaining flour. Mix well. Add oil and salt. Pour into well greased and floured tube or Bundt pan and bake at 350° for 1 hour or until tests done.
Lydia M. Gremillion, Central Council, Pineville, La.

FRESH APPLE CAKE

1 1/2 c. oil
3 eggs
1 c. chopped dates
1 tsp. soda
1 tsp. cinnamon
1723-79

2 c. sugar
3 c. flour
1 tsp. salt
1 tsp. baking powder
1 tsp. nutmeg

| 3 c. fresh, chopped apples | 1 c. chopped nuts |
| | 2 tsp. vanilla |

Mix all ingredients and pour into greased and floured Bundt pan. Bake at 325° for approximately 1 - 1 1/2 hours.

Doris Reeves, Capital
Council, Baton Rouge, La.

FRESH APPLE CAKE

4 1/2 c. raw apples, pared and chopped	Lemon juice
2 c. sugar	1 c. Crisco oil
2 1/2 c. all-purpose flour	2 large eggs
1 tsp. baking soda	1 tsp. salt
2 tsp. vanilla	2 tsp. baking powder
	1 1/2 c. pecans, chopped

Prepare apples. Sprinkle a little lemon juice over apples and set aside. Add sugar and eggs to oil, mix well at low speed until creamy and smooth. Sift flour and measure. Sift again with salt, soda and baking powder. Add flour mixture to oil mixture, little at a time. Add vanilla. When batter is stiff, remove beaters and finish mixing by hand. Fold in apples and nuts. Bake in 9x13-inch greased pan for 55 minutes to 1 hour at 350°.

Frosting:

1 stick butter or oleo	1/8 tsp. salt
2 Tbsp. milk	1 c. dark brown sugar, firmly packed
1/2 c. powdered sugar	

Combine butter, salt, milk and brown sugar in saucepan. Heat and stir until smooth. Remove from fire, add powdered sugar and continue stirring until spreading consistency.

Elmer E. Harrison, Crescent
City Council, New Orleans, La.

FRESH APPLE CAKE

1 1/2 c. corn oil	2 c. sugar
3 eggs	2 tsp. vanilla
3 c. flour	1 tsp. cinnamon
1/2 tsp. nutmeg	2 c. finely chopped apples
1 c. chopped nuts	1/2 c. raisins

Beat oil, sugar, eggs and vanilla until well blended. Combine dry ingredients and add to sugar mixture. Mix well. Stir in apples, nuts and raisins. Spoon batter into greased and floured tube or Bundt pan. Bake at 325° for 1 hour and 15 minutes or until tests done. Cool 10 minutes before removing from pan. Jean Heppner, Shreveport
Works Council, Shreveport, La.

FRESH APPLE CAKE

2 eggs
1 c. cooking oil
3 c. flour
1/2 tsp. salt
1 tsp. cinnamon
1 c. pecans

2 c. sugar
1 tsp. vanilla
1 1/2 tsp. soda
1 tsp. nutmeg
3 c. finely chopped apples

Mix all ingredients together, except apples and pecans. Mix these in by hand. Pour into greased and floured tube or Bundt pan. Bake at 375° for 1 hour or until done.
Hazel McIntyre, Capital
Council, Baton Rouge, La.

SOUSED APPLE CAKE

4 c. baking apples,
    peeled, cored and
    chopped
2 tsp. cinnamon
1 tsp. nutmeg
1/4 tsp. ground cloves
1 c. raisins
2 c. sugar

6 Tbsp. brandy
2 c. flour
2 tsp. baking soda
1 tsp. salt
1 c. pecans or walnuts,
    coarsely chopped
1/2 c. salad oil
2 eggs

Pour brandy over apples. Sift together flour, soda, salt, cinnamon, nutmeg and cloves. Add to apples and toss to mix. Beat together sugar, eggs and oil. Add to apple mixture. Add nuts and raisins. Stir well. Pour into greased and floured 9x13-inch baking pan or tube pan. Tube pan bakes for 1 hour at 300°; baking pan at 350° for 1 hour or until done. Serve warm or cold topped with whipped cream.
Helen Patton, Shreveport
Works Council, Shreveport, La.

APPLE SWIRL

1/4 c. sugar
3 tsp. cinnamon
1 pkg. yellow cake mix

1 2/3 c. applesauce
3 eggs

Blend sugar and cinnamon. Grease 10-inch Bundt or tube pan and dust with 1 tablespoon sugar-cinnamon mixture. Blend cake mix, applesauce and eggs until moistened. Beat as directed on package. Reserve 1 1/2 cups batter. Pour remaining batter into pan, sprinkle with remaining cinnamon mixture and top with reserved batter. Bake at 350° for 35-45 minutes or until done. Cool cake, top side up, for 15 minutes and invert on serving plate.

Della Delposen, Ouachita
Council, Monroe, La.

APPLESAUCE CAKE

2 c. fresh cooked apples
2 c. sugar
2 tsp. cinnamon
1 pkg. raisins
3 tsp. soda

1 c. shortening
2 tsp. ground cloves
1 c. chopped nuts
4 c. all-purpose flour

Mix apples, lard and sugar while apples are still hot. Mix spices, soda and 3 1/2 cups flour together, add to apple mixture. Roll raisins in remaining 1/2 cup flour and add to mixture. Bake in greased and floured tube pan at 350° for about 1 hour or until done.   Adrienne Delery, Ouachita
Council, Monroe, La.

APPLESAUCE CAKE

1 c. shortening
2 1/4 c. sugar
2 1/2 c. sifted flour
2 tsp. cinnamon
1/2 c. chopped walnuts
2 c. applesauce

2 eggs
1 tsp. vanilla
2 tsp. baking soda
1 tsp. cloves
1 c. raisins
1/2 tsp. salt

Mix shortening, sugar, eggs and vanilla together. Add flour, soda, salt, cloves, walnuts and raisins. Blend well. Add 2 cups hot applesauce that has been made from fresh green or Winesap apples. Do not use canned or sweetened applesauce. Pour in greased sheet pan or 3 layer pans

448

(9-10 inch). Bake at 350° for 25 minutes or more. Recipe can be halved if desired. Cool and frost.

Icing:

1 (8 oz.) pkg. cream
  cheese
1 1/2 tsp. cinnamon
1 tsp. vanilla
1 lb. powdered sugar

1/2 stick oleo
Grated rind of 1 lemon
1 tsp. lemon flavoring
Raisins or nuts (optional)

Combine ingredients and ice cake.

Jeanette English, Caddo
Council, Shreveport, La.

APPLESAUCE DATE CAKE

2 c. applesauce
1 box chopped dates
3 c. chopped pecans
2 sticks melted oleo
2 tsp. soda
1 tsp. allspice

2 1/2 c. sugar (1/2 brown)
1 c. raisins
3 eggs
3 1/2 c. flour
1 tsp. cloves (ground)
1 tsp. cinnamon

Heat applesauce to boiling point, add soda and stir. Pour into mixing bowl. Add oleo, sugar and eggs. Beat. Add flour, spices and beat. Add nuts, dates and raisins and mix thoroughly. Bake in loaf pans or cylinder pan at 325°-350° until toothpick comes out clean.

Marilyn Hibbard, Caddo
Council, Shreveport, La.

BABY FOOD CAKE

2 c. self-rising flour
2 c. sugar
1 c. chopped pecans
1 tsp. cinnamon

3 eggs, slightly beaten
1 c. oil
2 jars plum baby food with
  tapioca
1 tsp. nutmeg

Mix ingredients, pour into greased and floured tube or Bundt pan. Bake at 350° until done.

Glaze:

1/2 stick butter, melted
1 c. powdered sugar

Juice and rind of 1 lemon

Mix ingredients for Glaze. Heat and pour over cake while it is still hot.

Sybil Callahan, Central
Council, Alexandria, La.

Hazel Blouin, Shreveport
Works Council, Shreveport, La.

BANANA CAKE

3 c. sifted cake flour
1 c. shortening
3/4 c. milk
2 eggs, slightly beaten

2 tsp. soda
2 c. sugar
1 1/2 c. mashed ripe bananas
(3-4 medium bananas)

Line bottom of three 9-inch cake pans with waxed paper. Sift together flour and soda. Cream shortening thoroughly. Add sugar gradually and cream until light and fluffy. Add 2 tablespoons milk, then eggs. Add dry ingredients and remaining milk alternately, beating thoroughly after each addition. Fold mashed bananas into batter and pour into cake pan. Bake at 350° for 25-30 minutes. Frost with Cream Cheese Frosting. Makes 16 servings.

Mary McDow, Caddo Council,
Shreveport, La.

BANANA CAKE

1 pkg. yellow cake mix
(Duncan Hines)
1/2 c. mashed bananas,
or 1 whole banana
1/4 c. oil

1 pkg. Jell-O instant banana
cream pudding
4 eggs
1 c. water

Combine all ingredients in large mixing bowl. Blend, then beat at medium speed for 2 minutes. Pour in greased and floured 10-inch tube or Bundt pan. Bake at 350° for 50-55 minutes.

Glaze:

1 c. powdered sugar

1 Tbsp. milk

Combine and mix well. Pour on cake while it is still hot.

Frankie Meeks, Ouachita
Council, Monroe, La.

450

HUNGARIAN BANANA CAKE

1 1/2 c. sugar
4 Tbsp. buttermilk
3 medium bananas, mashed
2 egg yolks, beaten

1/2 c. Crisco
1 1/2 c. flour
1 tsp. soda
2 egg whites, beaten

Cream sugar and shortening, add egg yolks, flour and bananas. Fold in beaten egg whites. Pour batter in 6x14-inch pan. Place Topping on unbaked dough mixture. Bake at 300° about 25-30 minutes.

Topping:

2/3 c. brown sugar
1 can Angel Flake coconut

1 stick oleo, softened
1/2 c. chopped pecans

Combine ingredients and mix with hands.

Edna S. Phillips, Capital
Council, Baton Rouge, La.

BANANA NUT CAKE

2 c. all-purpose flour
1/4 tsp. baking powder
2/3 c. shortening
2/3 c. buttermilk
1 1/4 c. mashed bananas

1 2/3 c. sugar
1 tsp. salt
1/4 tsp. baking soda
3 eggs
2/3 c. chopped nuts

Measure all ingredients into mixer bowl, blend 1/2 minute on low speed, scraping bowl constantly. Beat 3 minutes on high speed, scraping bowl occasionally. Pour into 3 greased and floured 8-inch round cake pans. Bake in pre-heated 350° oven for 25-30 minutes.

Cream Cheese Frosting:

1 box sifted powdered sugar
1/4 lb. butter or oleo,
  softened

1 (8 oz.) pkg. cream cheese,
  softened

Blend butter and cream cheese in mixer. Add sugar gradually until smooth. Frost cake.

Dorothy H. Daigle
Calcasieu Council
Lake Charles, La.

BANANA NUT CAKE

2 c. sugar
1 1/2 c. oil
3 c. flour
1 tsp. cinnamon
2 tsp. soda
1 c. chopped pecans

3 eggs (add separately)
4 bananas, broken up
1/2 tsp. salt
1 tsp. nutmeg
1 tsp. vanilla

Mix ingredients together and pour into greased and floured tube pan. Bake at 350° for 1 hour or until done. Cool and frost.

Icing:

1 stick oleo, softened
1 box powdered sugar

1 (8 oz.) pkg. cream cheese, softened

Combine ingredients and frost cake.

Becky Sanders, Central
Council, St. Landry, La.

BANANA SPLIT CAKE

Crust:

1 stick melted butter   2 c. crushed vanilla wafers

Mix together and pat in 9x11x2-inch pan.

Filling:

2 eggs
2 c. powdered sugar
2 (15 oz.) cans crushed
  unsweetened pineapple,
  drained

2 sticks butter
4 medium bananas
1 large Cool Whip
Pecans and cherries

Beat eggs, butter and powdered sugar together 15 minutes. Spread over crust. Cover with bananas, spread pineapple over bananas. Cover with Cool Whip. Sprinkle with pecans and cherries. Refrigerate overnight.

Clarabell J. Hosch, Metairie
Council, Metairie, La.

BANANA SPLIT CAKE

2 c. graham cracker
  crumbs
2 c. powdered sugar
4-5 bananas
1 carton Cool Whip
3/4 c. chopped cherries

1 stick melted oleo
2 sticks cold oleo
2 eggs
1 large can crushed pine-
  apple, drained
3/4 c. chopped pecans

Mix graham cracker crumbs and melted oleo together. Press into large, long baking dish. Combine cold oleo, powdered sugar and eggs. Beat 15 minutes and spread over graham cracker crust. Slice bananas over egg mixture. Cover with crushed pineapple. Spread Cool Whip over pineapple and top with cherries and pecans. Refrigerate until served.

Cindy Kendrick, Caddo
Council, Shreveport, La.

BANANA SPLIT CAKE

2 c. graham cracker
  crumbs
3 c. powdered sugar
1 can crushed pineapple,
  drained
Cherries and pecans
  (optional)

2 sticks melted butter or oleo
2 egg whites
4 large bananas
1 large bowl Cool Whip, or
  2 pkg. Dream Whip,
  whipped

Mix graham cracker crumbs, 1 stick butter and 1 cup powdered sugar together. Press mixture into 13x9-inch pan. Slice bananas over crumb crust. Combine egg whites, 1 stick butter and remaining 2 cups powdered sugar. Beat for 10 minutes and pour over bananas. Spread well drained pineapple over top. Spread Cool Whip topping over pineapple. Garnish with cherries and pecans if desired. Refrigerate. Best if it sets overnight.

Sharon Keating, Ozone
Council, Covington, La.

BANANA SPLIT CAKE

1 stick melted oleo
2 (8 oz.) pkg. cream
  cheese

2 c. graham cracker crumbs
1 tsp. vanilla
1 box sifted powdered sugar

4 or 5 bananas
1 tub Cool Whip
Cherries
Chocolate syrup

1 large can crushed pine-
  apple, drained
Nuts

Mix together cracker crumbs and melted oleo. Press in pan. Mix together cream cheese, powdered sugar and vanilla. Spread over crumbs. Slice bananas lengthwise and lay on cream cheese. Sprinkle with crushed pineapple. Spread with Cool Whip and sprinkle with cherries and nuts. Top with chocolate syrup.   Henrietta Victor, Magnolia
Council, New Orleans, La.

BANANA SPLIT CAKE

2 sticks oleo
1 box powdered sugar
2 eggs
Bananas
1 large bowl Cool Whip
Cherries

2 c. graham cracker crumbs
2 tsp. vanilla
1 (No. 303) can crushed
  canned pineapple, drained
Chopped pecans

Mix 1 stick melted oleo and graham cracker crumbs; mix well. Spread evenly in bottom of 9x13-inch pan. Combine sugar, eggs, vanilla and remaining stick of oleo. Beat for 20 minutes with electric mixer. Spread over crust. Slice bananas lengthwise and cover filling. Top bananas with crushed pineapple. Cover with layer of Cool Whip. Mark off into small squares. Place 1/2 of cherry on each square and sprinkle with chopped pecans.
Julia B. Ulmer, Caddo
Council, Shreveport, La.

BLACK WALNUT CAKE

1 c. butter or oleo
2 c. sugar
4 eggs, separated
3 c. flour

1/2 tsp. salt
2 tsp. baking powder
1 c. milk
2 tsp. vanilla
1 c. chopped black walnuts

Cream butter with 1 cup sugar until light and fluffy. Beat egg yolks, gradually adding remaining sugar until very thick. Add beaten egg yolks to the butter mixture. Sift flour, salt and baking powder together. Add to the

454

egg-butter mixture alternately with the milk. Add vanilla and fold in egg whites, beaten until soft peaks form. Add chopped nuts. Pour into greased, floured and lined with waxed paper 9-inch cake pans. Bake at 350° for 35-40 minutes. Remove from pans, pull off paper and cool on racks. Frost with Butter Frosting.

June Harllee, Caddo
Council, Shreveport, La.

BLACK WALNUT CAKE

2 c. plain flour, sifted	2 c. sugar
1/2 lb. oleo or butter	5 eggs
2 tsp. vanilla	Dash of salt
2 tsp. butter extract	2 tsp. black walnut extract
(if oleo is used)	1 tsp. baking soda
	1 1/2 c. black walnuts

Cream sugar and soft oleo. Add eggs alternately with flour. Mix well. Add salt, vanilla, walnut extract and black walnuts. Pour into greased and floured tube pan. Bake at 350° for about 1 hour or until tests done.

Virginia Lowrey, Ouachita
Council, Monroe, La.

BLUEBERRY ANGEL FOOD CAKE

1 box angel food cake mix	1 pkg. cream cheese
1/2 c. sugar	1 bowl Cool Whip
1/2 c. powdered sugar	1 can blueberry pie filling

Prepare angel food cake mix according to directions on box. Cool. Slice into 3 layers. Combine sugars, cream cheese and Cool Whip. Put filling between layers and over cake. Cover with can of pie filling.

Becky Flynn, Central
Council, Alexandria, La.

BUBBLE CAKE

2 pkg. yeast	1/2 c. shortening
1/4 c. lukewarm water	1 tsp. salt
3/4 c. scalded milk	2 eggs, well beaten
1/2 c. sugar	4 1/2 c. sifted flour
1 stick melted oleo	1 c. sugar + 1 tsp. cinnamon

Mix yeast in water, set aside. Combine milk, salt, sugar and shortening in large bowl. The hot milk will melt shortening. Cool until lukewarm. Add yeast mixture and eggs. Add flour and mix to form smooth but soft dough. Knead until elastic on floured surface. Let rise until double in size in a greased bowl, covered with damp cloth. Punch down, let rise 10 minutes more. Shape into small walnut size balls and roll in melted oleo, then in sugar-cinnamon mixture. Place balls into ungreased 10-inch Bundt pan. No special arrangement necessary. Bake at 350° for 45 minutes. Turn over on plate and pull off individual balls to eat.

Elaine Squyres, Central
Council, Alexandria, La.

BUTTER CRUMSHUS CAKE

3/4 c. butter or oleo, divided
1/2 c. firmly packed brown sugar
1 1/4 c. sugar
1 c. (8 oz.) cream cheese
1 tsp. vanilla
2 1/2 c. all-purpose flour
2 tsp. baking powder
1/2 tsp. soda
1/2 tsp. salt
2 eggs
1/2 c. chopped nuts (optional)
1/2 c. milk

Cream 1/2 cup butter or oleo with cream cheese. Gradually add 1 1/4 cups sugar; cream well. Blend in eggs and vanilla; beat well. Sift 2 cups flour, baking powder, soda and salt together. Add alternately with milk, beginning and ending with dry ingredients; blend well after each addition. Turn into greased and floured 13x9x2-inch pan. Combine remaining butter, remaining flour, brown sugar and nuts to make a crumb mixture. Sprinkle over batter. Bake at 350° for 30-40 minutes.

Cindy Fuller, Capital
Council, Baton Rouge, La.

BUTTERSCOTCH PUDDING CAKE

1 box yellow cake mix
1 box instant butterscotch pudding mix
3/4 c. Wesson oil
2 eggs
1 (6 oz.) pkg. butterscotch chips
3/4 c. chopped pecans or sliced almonds

Mix pudding as directed on box. Pour into dry cake mix and beat well. Add eggs and Wesson oil, beating well.

456

Pour mixture into greased and floured 9x12-inch pan.
Sprinkle chips and nuts on top. Bake at 325° for 1 hour
or until done.   Dorothy Trent, Caddo
                                  Council, Shreveport, La.

CARAMEL FLECKED CAKE

2 c. sifted self-rising   3/4 c. shortening
   flour   2 1/2 c. powdered sugar
3 eggs   1 c. water
1 tsp. vanilla   1 c. caramel chips
1 c. flaked coconut

Chill caramel chips and grind through fine blade of
food chopper. Cream shortening and powdered sugar until
light and fluffy. Add eggs, 1 at a time, beating well after
each addition. Beat flour into creamed mixture alternately
with the water and vanilla, beginning and ending with
flour. Stir in ground caramel chips. Pour into 2 (9-inch)
layer pans, prepared with waxed paper. Spread coconut
over top of each layer. Bake at 350° for 30-40 minutes.
Remove from pans and cool completely.

Frosting:

4 Tbsp. flour   1 c. milk
1 stick oleo   1/2 c. Crisco
1 c. sugar   2 tsp. vanilla

Cook flour and milk until thick, cool. Cream all other
ingredients together. Beat into cooled flour-milk mixture
about 1 tablespoon at a time, beating well after each addition. Frost cake.   Fae Wells, Central
                                 Council, Alexandria, La.

CARROT CAKE

4 eggs   1 1/4 c. salad oil
2 c. sugar   2 c. flour
1 tsp. salt   1 tsp. soda
1/2 tsp. baking powder   2 tsp. cinnamon
2 c. grated carrots

Beat eggs until fluffy, add sugar gradually. Mix in oil
slowly; beat well. Sift dry ingredients together and add to
batter in 3 additions; beat well. Fold in carrots. Pour into
3 greased and floured 9-inch layer pans. Bake at 350° for
about 35 minutes. Cool; frost with Cream Cheese Frosting.

Cream Cheese Frosting:

1 (8 oz.) pkg. cream
  cheese
2 tsp. vanilla
1 box powdered sugar

1/2 c. oleo
1/8 tsp. salt
1 c. chopped pecans

Blend cream cheese and oleo. Add vanilla and salt. Beat well. Add sugar. Stir in pecans. Spread over top and sides of cake layers.   Carol A. Bergen, Caddo Council, Shreveport, La.

CARROT CAKE

2 c. sugar
4 eggs
1 1/4 c. oil
3 small jars strained baby
  food carrots
1 c. nuts

2 c. flour
2 tsp. soda
2 tsp. cinnamon
1 tsp. salt
1 tsp. vanilla

Beat sugar, eggs and oil together. Mix flour, soda, cinnamon and salt together, add to sugar mixture. Fold in remaining ingredients. Pour batter into greased and floured 10x15-inch pan. Bake at 350° for 35-45 minutes.

Icing:

4 oz. soft cream cheese
1 3/4 c. powdered sugar

1/4 c. soft butter
1 tsp. vanilla

Blend cream cheese and butter together. Add powdered sugar and vanilla. Spread on cool cake.

Louise Malone, Caddo
Council, Shreveport, La.

CARROT CAKE

2 c. sugar
3 c. flour
1 tsp. baking soda
1 tsp. cinnamon
1 c. chopped walnuts

1 1/2 c. oil
3 eggs
1 tsp. baking powder
2 jars strained carrots
  (baby junior size)

Blend sugar, oil, carrots together, add dry ingredients. Add flour and eggs, mix well. Pour into greased and floured layer pans; bake at 350° until done. Frost cooled cake with icing of your choice.   Cher White, Capital Council, Waterbury, Ct.

458

CARROT RAISIN CAKE

3 c. all-purpose flour
2 tsp. cinnamon
4 c. grated raw carrots
1 tsp. salt
5 eggs
1 1/2 c. raisins

1 tsp. soda
3 c. sugar
3 tsp. baking powder
2 c. Wesson oil
1 1/2 c. finely chopped
  pecans

Sift together flour, soda, baking powder, salt and cinnamon; set aside. Combine oil and sugar; cream until light and fluffy. Add eggs, 1 at a time, creaming well after each addition. Add sifted dry ingredients. Fold in carrots, raisins and nuts. Bake in 3 layers or 2 large square greased and floured cake tins at 350° for 30-40 mintues.

Frosting:

1 lb. pkg. powdered sugar
1 small pkg. pecan meal
3 tsp. vanilla

1/2 stick butter or oleo
1 1/2 pkg. (8 oz.) cream
  cheese

Cream together butter, cheese, sugar and vanilla. Add pecan meal. Spread on cake and between layers.

Mary A. Watkins, Crescent
City Council, New Orleans, La.

CHEESE CAKE

40 graham crackers
1 1/2 c. white sugar
1/2 c. chopped cherries,
  drained
1/4 tsp. salt

1/2 c. melted butter
1 lb. cream cheese
1 c. pineapple, drained
1 tsp. vanilla
3 eggs

Crush graham crackers very fine and mix with butter. Reserve 1 cup of mixture and place remainder in bottom of pan. Cream sugar and cream cheese together. Add remaining ingredients. Pour into pan and top with reserved crumbs. Bake at 350° for 15-20 minutes.

Bettie Lalonde, Evangeline
Council, Opelousas, La.

CHEESE CAKE

20-25 crushed graham crackers
3 large pkg. cream cheese
1 c. sugar
1 tsp. vanilla

3/4 stick oleo
4 eggs, separated
Pinch of salt
1 pt. sour cream
Small amount of sugar (optional)

Combine crushed graham crackers and oleo, mix thoroughly and press into pan. Mix 1 cup sugar, cheese and egg yolks until creamy. Add salt and vanilla, whip well. Beat egg whites until stiff. Fold into mixture. Pour in crust. Bake at 375° for 40 minutes. Cool for 10 minutes. Add small amount of sugar to sour cream that is at room temperature. Spread over cake. Return to oven and bake at 375° for 10 minutes; chill. Can be frozen.

Cecile Gallet, Evangeline
Council, Lafayette, La.

CHEESE CAKE

Crust:

1/3 c. powdered sugar
1/4 lb. butter or oleo

1 1/2 c. graham cracker crumbs

Melt butter, add to graham crumbs and sugar. Line the bottom of spring form pan, packing firmly.

Filling:

1 c. granulated sugar
1 tsp. vanilla flavoring
1 pt. sour cream

3 (8 oz.) pkg. cream cheese
4 eggs
1 can pie filling of your choice

Combine sugar, vanilla, cream cheese and eggs. Pour over unbaked crust. Bake in preheated 350° oven about 50 minutes. Remove cheese cake and top with sour cream. Return to oven for another 5 minutes, cool cake. Top with prepared pie filling and chill overnight.

Doris Reeves, Capital
Council, Baton Rouge, La.

CHEESE CAKE

Crust:

1 stick butter	1 c. flour
1/2 c. powdered sugar	1 c. chopped pecans

Cream butter, flour and sugar. Add pecans. Press in 9x12-inch baking pan. Bake at 350° for 20 minutes. Cool.

Filling:

2 (8 oz.) pkg. cream cheese	2 c. powdered sugar
1 large Cool Whip	1 can cherries or blueberries

Cream sugar and cheese, add Cool Whip; mix well. Pour Filling into cooled Crust. Top with cherries or blueberries and refrigerate.

Agnes F. Rodrigue, LeBayou
Council, Houma, La.

CHEESE CAKE

20 graham crackers, crushed	1/3 c. butter or oleo
3 (8 oz.) pkg. cream cheese	1 Tbsp. flour
3 tsp. vanilla, divided	1 1/2 c. sugar + 2 Tbsp., divided
	5 eggs
	1 pt. sour cream

Combine crushed graham crackers, butter, 2 tablespoons sugar and flour. Press and line 9x13x2-inch pan with mixture. Combine cream cheese, 1 1/2 teaspoons vanilla and 1 cup sugar. Add eggs, beating thoroughly after each addition. Beat until well blended. Pour into crust and bake at 300° for 1 hour. Combine remaining sugar, 1 1/2 teaspoons vanilla and sour cream. Spread over cake and return to oven for 5 minutes.

Pauline Thompson, Capital
Council, Baton Rouge, La.

CHEEZE CAKE A LA SILVA

2 Tbsp. butter	3/4 c. graham cracker crumbs
1 1/2 lb. cream cheese	1 c. sugar
3 eggs	2 tsp. vanilla
2 c. sour cream	3 Tbsp. sugar
1/8 tsp. cinnamon	

Combine graham cracker crumbs and butter, line bottom of 9 or 10-inch spring form pan. Cream the cheese, add 1 cup sugar, eggs and 1 teaspoon vanilla. Pour over crust and bake at 350° until set. Remove from oven and reset to 400°. Mix sour cream, 3 tablespoons sugar, cinnamon and 1 teaspoon vanilla. Spread over cake and return to oven for 5 or 10 minutes.

Richard Silva, Crescent City
Council, New Orleans, La.

CHERRY CHEESE CAKE

1 pkg. lemon cake mix	1 c. water
4 eggs	1 (8 oz.) pkg. cream cheese,
1/3 c. evaporated milk	softened
1 can cherry pie filling	

Combine dry cake mix, water and eggs. Beat as directed on package. Pour half of batter into a greased and lightly floured 10-inch tube pan. Beat cream cheese and milk until smooth, spoon over batter without touching sides of pan. Spoon 1 cup cherry filling over cheese mixture. Spread with remaining batter. Bake at 350° for 50-55 minutes. Cool upright for 15 minutes. Do not invert while cooling. Remove from pan, top with remaining cherries. After serving, refrigerate any remaining cake.

Mrs. Johnnie Cole, Caddo
Council, Shreveport, La.

CHERRY TOPPED CHEESE CAKE

Crust:

3/4 stick butter	1 c. graham cracker crumbs
1 Tbsp. sugar	

Melt butter and combine with graham cracker crumbs. Add sugar and mix well. Pour into pie pan and shape into crust. Chill 1 hour.

Filling:

1 (8 oz.) pkg. cream	1/2 c. sugar
cheese	1 can cherry or blueberry
2 c. Cool Whip	pie filling

Cream sugar and cheese until very smooth. Sugar must be melted completely. Add Cool Whip and cream together.

Pour into chilled pie crust and surround edges with pie
filling.   Richard P. Mohr, Crescent
                                            City Council, New Orleans, La.

CHOCOLATE SWIRL CHEESE CAKE

1 (6 oz.) pkg. Nestle's   1/2 c. sugar
  semi-sweet real choco-   1 1/4 c. graham cracker
  late morsels   crumbs
2 measuring Tbsp. sugar   2 (8 oz.) pkg. cream cheese,
1/4 c. melted butter   softened
3/4 c. sugar   4 eggs
1/2 c. sour cream   1 tsp. vanilla

Combine over hot, not boiling, water, the chocolate
morsels and 1/2 cup sugar. Heat until morsels melt and
mixture is smooth. Remove from heat. In small bowl, combine graham crumbs, 2 tablespoons sugar and melted butter;
mix well. Pat firmly into 9-inch spring form pan, covering
bottom and 1 1/2 inches up sides. Beat cream cheese until
light and creamy. Gradually beat in 3/4 cup sugar. Mix in
sour cream and vanilla. Add eggs, 1 at a time, beating
well after each addition. Divide batter in half. Stir
melted chocolate in first half, pour into crumb lined pan.
Cover with plain batter with a knife. Swirl plain batter
with chocolate to marbleize. Bake in preheated 325° oven for
50 minutes or until a 2 or 3-inch circle in center will shake.
Cool at room temperature. Refrigerate until ready to serve.
                                            Dianne Crocker, Central
                                            Council, Alexandria, La.

INDIVIDUAL CHEESE CAKES

2 (8 oz.) pkg. cream   2/3 c. sugar
  cheese   2 eggs
1 tsp. vanilla   Cherry or blueberry pie
1 box Nabisco vanilla   filling
  wafers   1 box paper muffin cups

Allow cream cheese to soften. When soft, mix with
sugar, eggs and vanilla. Beat until creamy. Place a
vanilla wafer in each muffin cup. Fill with cream cheese
mixture to about half full. Bake at 350° for 10 minutes.
Let cool and top with pie filling of your choice. Refrigerate. You might also like to try Jell-O lemon pudding mix

(small size). Cook according to instructions on box and use as topping. Makes 24 cupcakes.

Joyce Silva, Capital
Council, Baton Rouge, La.

MILNOT CHEESE CAKE

1 pkg. lemon flavored
  gelatin
1 (8 oz.) pkg. cream
  cheese
1 tsp. vanilla

1 c. boiling water
1/2 c. sugar
1 tall can Milnot, whipped
3 c. graham cracker crumbs
1/2 c. butter or oleo, melted

Dissolve gelatin in boiling water. Chill until slightly thickened. Cream together cheese, sugar and vanilla, add thickened gelatin and blend well. Fold in stiffly whipped Milnot (chill Milnot before beating). Mix graham cracker crumbs and melted butter together; pack 2/3 of mixture on bottom and sides of 9x13x2-inch pan. Add filling and sprinkle with remaining crumbs. Chill several hours or overnight. Cut in squares to serve. Serves 12-16.

Vickie Daigle, Capital
Council, Baton Rouge, La.

MOLDED CHEESE CAKE

1 1/2 c. graham cracker
  crumbs
1 pkg. lemon jello
1 (8 oz.) pkg. cream
  cheese

1/2 stick oleo
1 c. sugar, divided
1 c. hot water
1 tsp. vanilla
1 c. whipping cream,
  whipped

Combine graham cracker crumbs, oleo and 1/2 cup sugar. Press in bottom of 12x8-inch pan, reserving about 1/2 cup of mixture. Dissolve jello in hot water, let cool until slightly thick. Cream sugar, vanilla and cream cheese together. Combine with gelatin mixture and fold in whipped cream. Pour on crust. Sprinkle with reserved crust mixture. Refrigerate overnight; the longer this dish refrigerates, the better it gets.

LaJuan Durand, Central
Council, Alexandria, La.

SOUR CREAM CHEESE CAKE

2 eggs
2 tsp. vanilla extract
2 (8 oz.) pkg. cream
  cheese, softened and
  cut up
1 baked Crumb Crust

1/2 c. sugar
1 1/2 c. sour cream
2 Tbsp. butter or oleo,
  melted
1 (21 oz.) can cherry pie
  filling, or filling of your
  choice (optional)

Blend eggs, sugar, vanilla and sour cream for 15 seconds in blender. Continue blending and gradually add cream cheese. Add butter and blend well. Pour cheese mixture into 9-inch Crumb Crust. Bake at 325° for 35 minutes or until set in center. Filling will be soft, but will firm as cake cools. Top with cherry pie filling if desired. Chill thoroughly before serving.

Crumb Crust:

15 graham crackers,
  crushed
1/2 tsp. cinnamon

1/2 c. sugar
1/4 c. butter or oleo,
  melted

Combine all ingredients. Press into buttered 9-inch pie pan. Bake at 400° for 6 minutes. Cool before filling.

Denise Barteet, Caddo
Council, Shreveport, La.

STRAWBERRY CHEESE CAKE

1 c. chopped pecans
30-35 graham crackers,
  crushed
1 c. sugar
1 c. water, boiling
1 pkg. strawberry jello

1 stick oleo or butter
1 (16 oz.) pkg. cream cheese
3 eggs
2 pt. sour cream
1 pkg. or more frozen strawberries

Mix until well blended the graham crackers, pecans and butter. Place in bottom of baking pan. Blend cream cheese, eggs and sugar. Place over graham cracker crust and bake for about 20 minutes. Spread sour cream over baked cream cheese mixture and bake for additional 20-30 minutes. Cool. Dissolve jello in boiling water, cool. Add frozen strawberries and spoon over top of cake. Refrigerate until jello is jelled. Cake is now ready to serve.

Lynn Babin, Westmoor
Council, Kenner, La.

STRAWBERRY CHEESE CAKE

1 baked pie crust	3/4 lb. cream cheese (12 oz.)
1/2 c. sugar	1/4 tsp. vanilla
1 egg	1/2 c. slivered almonds

Add sugar to softened cream cheese and cream. Gradually add egg, beat well. Add vanilla and almonds. Spoon into baked pie shell and place in 375° oven for 20 minutes. Spoon chilled Topping over cooled cheese cake. Chill until set.

Topping:

1 c. sugar	2 Tbsp. cornstarch
1 qt. strawberries	1 (3 oz.) pkg. strawberry
1 Tbsp. butter	jello
Water	1 Tbsp. lemon juice

Combine sugar and cornstarch in saucepan. Mash 1 cup strawberries, add 1 cup water to make 2 cups. Stir into sugar mixture. Cook and stir until comes to a boil, boil 2 minutes and remove from heat. Strain. Add jello, butter and lemon juice. Stir until jello dissolves. Chill until partially set. Spoon 1 1/2 cups of mixture over cheese cake, arrange remaining gelatin over berries. Chill until set.

Collette Bergeron, Capital
Council, Baton Rouge, La.

CHERRY CRUNCH

1/2 c. butter + 4 Tbsp.	1 pkg. cake mix (Duncan
2 Tbsp. lemon juice	Hines orange supreme)
2 cans cherry pie filling	3/4 c. walnuts

Cut 1/2 cup butter into cake mix. Remove 1 cup of mixture. Pat remaining cake mixture into 13x9-inch or 8x12-inch pan, building up around edge. Blend 4 tablespoons melted butter and lemon juice into pie filling and pour into shell. Add walnuts to reserved mixture and sprinkle over pie filling. Bake 45 minutes in preheated 350° oven.

Connie Younker
Shreveport Works Council
Shreveport, La.

CHERRY NUT CAKE

1 lb. cherries
1 c. sugar
1/2 tsp. salt
1 lb. dates, chopped
1 tsp. vanilla

4 eggs
2 c. flour, plain
1 tsp. baking powder
1 lb. pecans

Beat eggs slightly, add sugar, flour, salt and baking powder. Pour over fruit and nuts, mix thoroughly. Pour into greased and floured tube pan and bake 1 1/2 - 2 hours at 350°. Especially good for holidays; rich and festive looking.
Ruth Albin for Martha Starkey, Capital Council Baton Rouge, La.

CHERRY TORTE

1 c. crushed graham
 crackers
1 (8 oz.) pkg. cream
 cheese
3 Tbsp. milk
1 1/2 c. chopped pecans

1 stick oleo
1-2 Tbsp. sugar
1 c. powdered sugar
1 large container Cool Whip
1 (15 oz.) can cherry pie
 filling

Combine graham crackers, butter and 1 or 2 tablespoons sugar. Press into large baking dish and bake at 325° about 5 minutes. Cool. Combine cream cheese, milk and powdered sugar. Cream together until smooth and spread over crust. Sprinkle pecans over cheese filling. Spread Cool Whip over pecans. Spoon cherry pie filling over Cool Whip and refrigerate overnight.
Suzanne Dickerson, Central Council, Alexandria, La.

CHOCOLATE CAKE

2 sticks butter or oleo
1 c. water
1/2 tsp. soda
2 eggs
1 tsp. vanilla

4 Tbsp. cocoa
2 c. self-rising flour
2 c. sugar
1/2 c. buttermilk

Melt oleo with cocoa and water. Bring to a boil. Cool slightly. Sift flour, soda and sugar together. Add butter and cocoa mixture to flour and beat well. Add eggs, buttermilk and vanilla. Bake in large sheet pan, 9x13 inches, at 350° until done, about 30-40 minutes. Frost cake.

Note: Plain flour may be used with 1 teaspoons soda and 1/2 teaspoon salt.

Icing:

1 stick oleo	4 Tbsp. cocoa
4-6 Tbsp. buttermilk	1 box powdered sugar
1 tsp. vanilla	Pecans (optional)

Melt oleo with cocoa and buttermilk. Bring to a boil. Add powdered sugar and vanilla. Beat until smooth. After icing cake, top with pecans if desired.

Margain Tynes, Ozone
Council, Bogalusa, La.

CAPPUCCINO CHOCOLATE CAKE

1 pkg. Pillsbury Plus	1 c. orange juice
devils food cake mix	1/3 c. cold coffee
1/3 c. cooking oil	1 Tbsp. brandy
1 tsp. grated orange peel	3 eggs

Combine ingredients and blend. Beat 2 minutes at highest speed. Pour batter in 2 greased and floured 8 or 9-inch round cake pans. Bake in preheated oven for 30-40 minutes for 8-inch layers, and 25-35 minutes for 9-inch layers. Cool in pans 15 minutes, invert onto cooling racks to cool completely before frosting.

Frosting:

1 can chocolate ready-	1 tsp. grated orange peel
to-spread fudge frosting	12 pecan halves or chopped
1/2 tsp. brandy	pecans

Mix frosting ingredients, except nuts, by hand. Fill and frost cake using 1/4 cup frosting between layers. Garnish with pecan halves or sprinkle with chopped nuts. Serves 12.

Henrietta Victor, Magnolia
Council, New Orleans, La.

CINNAMON CHOCOLATE CAKE

1 c. Crisco	1 stick oleo
4 Tbsp. cocoa	1 c. water
2 c. sugar	1/2 c. buttermilk
2 c. flour	1 tsp. soda
1 tsp. cinnamon	1 tsp. vanilla
2 eggs	

Melt Crisco and oleo in saucepan. Add cocoa and water. Heat to boiling point; do not boil. Remove from heat, add remaining ingredients and beat until smooth. Pour into 9x13-inch pan and bake at 350° for 35-45 minutes. Ice while still hot.

Icing:

1 stick melted oleo	4 Tbsp. cocoa
6 tsp. milk or more	1 tsp. vanilla
1 box powdered sugar	3/4 c. pecans

Combine ingredients and mix well. Spread over hot cake. Leave cake in pan.   Jimmie Ruth Vance, Caddo
Council, Shreveport, La

ANNIE'S CHOCOLATE CAKE

2 c. flour	1 tsp. soda
1/2 tsp. salt	2 c. sugar
2 eggs	1/2 c. buttermilk
1 tsp. vanilla	1 stick oleo, room tempera-
1/2 c. cooking oil	ture
1 c. water	3 Tbsp. cocoa

Sift flour, salt, soda and sugar together. Add eggs. buttermilk, vanilla and oleo. Beat with mixer until well blended. Bring cooking oil, cocoa and water to a boil, slowly pour into other ingredients, mix well. Pour into greased and floured 9x13-inch pan. Bake at 350° for 30-40 minutes or until tests done. Cool, then frost.

Frosting:

1 stick oleo	3 Tbsp. cocoa
1 tsp. vanilla	1 box powdered sugar
4 or 5 Tbsp. milk	1/2 c. chopped pecans

Melt oleo and cocoa together, bring to boil. Add

powdered sugar and vanilla to cocoa mixture. While beating
with electric mixer, slowly add milk. Fold in pecans. Spread
over cooled cake.   Ann Orr, Evangeline
                                     Council, New Iberia, La.

BRAZILIAN CHOCOLATE CAKE

1 1/4 c. hot coffee
1 c. quick or old fashioned
  oats, uncooked
2 eggs
1 1/2 c. sifted all-purpose
  flour
1 tsp. soda
1/2 tsp. salt

1/2 c. butter or oleo
1 1/2 c. sugar
1 tsp. vanilla
2 sq. (2 oz.) unsweetened
  chocolate, melted and
  cooled
1 (6 oz.) pkg. semi-sweet
  chocolate pieces

Pour hot coffee over oats, stir, cover and let stand 20
minutes. Beat butter until creamy. Gradually add sugar,
beating until fluffy. Blend in vanilla, eggs and melted chocolate. Add oats, mix well. Sift flour, soda and salt together.
Add to creamed mixture, mixing well. Stir in chocolate
pieces. Pour batter into well greased and floured tube pan.
Bake in preheated 350° oven for 50-60 minutes. Cool 10 minutes before removing from pan, cool completely before frosting.

Frosting:

2 c. powdered sugar
Semi-sweet chocolate
  pieces (optional)

1/4 c. melted butter
Milk or cream to soften
1 tsp. vanilla

Combine sugar, butter, vanilla and cream; mix well and
ice cake. Sprinkle chocolate pieces on top if desired.
                                     Carlotta Thomas, Ouachita
                                     Council, Monroe, La.

CHOCOLATE COOKIE CAKE

2 c. sugar
1/2 tsp. salt
1/2 c. oil
3 Tbsp. cocoa
1 tsp. soda
1 tsp. vanilla

2 c. flour
1 stick oleo
3/4 c. water
2 eggs
1/2 c. buttermilk

470

Sift sugar, flour and salt together. Combine oleo, oil, water and cocoa in saucepan. Bring to a boil and pour over flour mixture. Blend well. Mix eggs, soda, buttermilk and vanilla together. Stir into other mixture. Beat until well mixed and pour into well greased pan, about 8 1/2 x 11 inches. Bake at 350° for 20-30 minutes.

Icing:

1 stick oleo	3 Tbsp. cocoa
1 box powdered sugar	1 tsp. vanilla
1 c. broken pecans	6 Tbsp. milk

Place oleo and cocoa in saucepan and melt. Add remaining ingredients. Stir well to mix. Spread hot icing over hot cake as you take it from oven. Cool and cut into squares.   Becky Sanders, Central
Council, St. Landry, La.

CHOCOLATE FUDGE NUT CAKE

2 c. flour	4 Tbsp. cocoa
2 c. sugar	1 tsp. soda
1 tsp. cinnamon	2 eggs
1 stick butter	1 c. water
1/2 c. shortening	1 tsp. vanilla
1/2 c. buttermilk	1 c. nuts

Melt butter, shortening and water. Mix flour, sugar, cocoa, soda and cinnamon. Mix in other ingredients. Pour into 13x9x2-inch pan and bake at 350° for 30-40 minutes.
Stella L. Thrash, Caddo
Council, Shreveport, La.

FROZEN CHOCOLATE CAKE

4 sq. semi-sweet chocolate	1/2 c. butter or oleo
2 tsp. vanilla	2 c. sugar
2 tsp. baking powder	1 tsp. salt
1 1/2 c. milk	2 c. flour
2 eggs	1 c. pecans

Melt chocolate. Cream butter and sugar, add eggs and chocolate. Add dry ingredients with milk. Beat. Add nuts. Bake in sheet pan at 325° for 35-40 minutes. Freeze.

Frosting:

1/2 c. butter	2 sq. semi-sweet chocolate
1/2 box powdered sugar	1 tsp. vanilla
1 egg, beaten	1 c. nuts

Melt butter and chocolate. Add egg. Add other ingredients. Beat. Frost frozen cake. Keep frozen.

Jean Coon, Caddo Council,
Shreveport, La.

GRANDMA KING'S CHOCOLATE CAKE

1/2 c. butter	1 1/2 c. sugar
3 eggs	1 c. water
2 c. flour	1 tsp. baking soda
3 sq. chocolate, melted	1/2 tsp. baking powder
	1 tsp. vanilla

Cream butter, add sugar. Add eggs, 1 at a time. Add water alternately with flour with soda and baking powder in last cup. Add vanilla and melted chocolate. Bake in greased and floured 9x13-inch pan. Start oven just before cake goes in at 325°-350°. Bake about 40 minutes. Turn oven up to full a minute or so before removing from oven.

Base for Frosting:

1 sq. melted chocolate	Butter, size of walnut
2 heaping Tbsp. flour	1/2 c. water
Nuts	1 c. brown sugar

Mix chocolate, sugar, butter and flour. Stir in water. Bring to a boil, cool. Spread on cake and sprinkle with nuts.

Fudge Frosting:

1 c. brown sugar	1/4 c. white syrup
1 c. granulated sugar	1/2 c. cream + 1 Tbsp.
2 sq. chocolate	Butter size of walnut

Combine sugars, chocolate, syrup, butter and 1/2 cup cream. Cook to a boil and time 6 minutes from start of boiling. Cool slightly and beat. When it starts to get creamy, beat in tablespoon of cream to keep it spreading consistency. Spread over nuts.

Connie Younker
Shreveport Works Council
Shreveport, La.

CHOCOLATE SHEATH CAKE

2 c. plain flour	2 c. sugar
1/2 tsp. salt	2 eggs
1/2 tsp. soda	1/2 c. Crisco
4 Tbsp. cocoa	1/2 c. buttermilk
1 tsp. vanilla	1 stick oleo
1 c. water	1 Tbsp. cinnamon

Mix flour, sugar and salt. Melt oleo, water, shortening and cocoa. Bring to a boil. Pour over flour mixture and blend. Beat eggs, add soda mixed with buttermilk and vanilla. Mix well. Stir and blend with flour mixture. Pour in greased pan and bake 20 minutes at 350° or until done. Ice while hot.

Icing:

1 stick oleo	4 Tbsp. cocoa
6 Tbsp. cream	1 box powdered sugar
1 tsp. vanilla	1 c. chopped pecans
2 c. mini marshmallows	

Melt oleo, cocoa and milk. Add powdered sugar, vanilla and pecans. Mix well. Spread marshmallows over cake 2 minutes before removing from oven. Pour Icing over cake as soon as it comes from oven. Delicious!

Sonia A. Hunt, Capital Council
Greenville Springs, La.

CHOCOLATE SHEET CAKE

2 c. sugar	2 c. flour
2 sticks oleo	1 c. water
3 Tbsp. cocoa	2 eggs, beaten
3/4 c. buttermilk	1 tsp. soda
1 tsp. vanilla	

Mix sugar and flour together. Combine oleo, water and cocoa in boiler and bring to a boil. Pour over sugar-flour mixture and mix. Combine remaining ingredients and add to mixture. Blend well. Pour in greased and floured cookie sheet with sides or square. Bake in preheated 350° oven until done. Prepare the following Icing.

Icing:

1/2 stick oleo
1/2 c. nuts (optional)
3 Tbsp. milk

1/2 box powdered sugar
3 Tbsp. cocoa

Mix over heat until smooth and creamy. Spread over cake while hot.

Christine Moras, Central
Council, Hessmer, La.

CHOCOLATE SHEET CAKE

2 c. flour
2 c. sugar
2 Tbsp. cocoa
1/2 c. buttermilk
1 tsp. vanilla

2 sticks oleo
1 c. water
2 eggs, slightly beaten
1 tsp. soda
Mini-marshmallows

Combine oleo, water and cocoa. Bring to hard boil in saucepan. Sift flour and sugar together. Combine eggs, buttermilk, soda and vanilla. Add all ingredients together. Mix well in electric mixer or by hand. Pour into greased and floured 13x15 inch pan. Bake at 400° for 20 minutes or until done. Remove from oven and cover completely with mini-marshmallows. Spread Frosting over marshmallows while hot.

Frosting:

1 stick oleo
6 Tbsp. milk
1 c. chopped nuts

2 Tbsp. cocoa
1 box powdered sugar
1 tsp. vanilla

Combine oleo, cocoa and milk. Bring to a boil. Remove from heat, add remaining ingredients and spread over hot cake. Cool cake and frosting before cutting. This cake freezes well.

Cecile Gallet, Evangeline
Council, Lafayette, La.

SUE'S UPSIDE DOWN CHOCOLATE CAKE

Icing:

1 stick oleo, melted
1 c. nuts
1 1/2 c. coconut

1/4 c. water
1 c. brown sugar
Maraschino cherries, well
    drained (optional)

474

Batter:

1 1/2 c. sugar
2 c. flour
1 c. milk

3 Tbsp. cocoa
1/2 c. cooking oil
2 eggs

Mix ingredients for Icing and pat down in 13x9x2-inch
pan. Mix ingredients for Batter and pour over Icing.
Bake at 350° for 35-40 minutes. Let stand 5 minutes. Invert on platter. Icing will be on top.

Marie Pamplin, Shreveport
Works Council, Shreveport, La.

WHITE CHOCOLATE CAKE

1/2 lb. white chocolate
2 c. sugar
2 1/2 c. flour
1/2 tsp. salt
1 c. chopped pecans
1 tsp. vanilla

1 c. butter
4 eggs, separated
1 tsp. baking powder
1 c. buttermilk
1 c. flaked coconut

Melt chocolate over hot water. Cream butter and
sugar. Add egg yolks, beat. Add chocolate to creamed
mixture. Sift flour, baking powder and salt together. Add
alternately with buttermilk to chocolate mixture. Add
pecans, coconut and vanilla. Beat egg whites until stiff
and fold into batter. Pour into ungreased tube pan.
Bake at 325° for 1 hour and 10 minutes. Cool for a few
minutes and turn out onto cake rack to cool.

Mrs. Ted Bounds, Caddo
Council, Shreveport, La.

WHITE CHOCOLATE CAKE

1/4 c. white chocolate
1/2 c. boiling water
4 egg yolks
4 egg whites, beaten stiff
2 1/2 c. cake flour
1 c. buttermilk
1 c. coconut

1 c. oleo
2 c. sugar
1 tsp. vanilla
1 tsp. chocolate flavoring
1 tsp. soda
1 c. pecans

Grate the chocolate and melt in the boiling water; cool.
Cream oleo and sugar until fluffy. Add egg yolks, 1 at a

time, and blend well. Add vanilla and chocolate flavoring.
Add flour and buttermilk alternately, starting wtih the flour.
Fold in beaten egg whites and stir in coconut and nuts
gently. Bake in 3 greased and floured 9-inch cake pans for
30-35 minutes at 350°. Frost when cool.

Frosting:

1 large can evaporated milk	1 c. sugar
1 tsp. vanilla	4 Tbsp. oleo
1 medium can coconut	3 egg yolks
	1 1/2 c. pecans

Blend milk, sugar and oleo in heavy pan and bring to
boil, stirring constantly. Let cool. Add a small amount of
milk mixture to the beaten egg yolks. Then blend all together with vanilla and cook until mixture thickens, cooking
over low heat. Remove from heat and add coconut and
pecans.   Mrs. Floyd (Barbara) Jessup
                                      Calcasieu Council
                                      Lake Charles, La.

COCONUT CAKE

1 pkg. Duncan Hines butter cake	1 tsp. butter flavoring

Bake according to directions. Add butter flavoring to
batter before baking. Let cool and split each layer.

Icing:

2 c. powdered sugar	1 (9 oz.) bowl Cool Whip
1 carton sour cream	2 pkg. frozen coconut

Mix sugar and sour cream. Add Cool Whip and coconut.
Refrigerate overnight.   Lela Bonner, Ouachita
                                      Council, Bastrop, La.

COCONUT CAKE

1 box Duncan Hines butter flavor cake mix	1 pt. (16 oz.) sour cream
	1 c. sugar
2 pkg. frozen or fresh coconut	1 (9 oz.) bowl Cool Whip

Bake cake as directed on box into 2 thick layers. Cool,

cut with a thread, making 4 thin layers. Combine sour cream, coconut and sugar. Stack cake, spreading sour cream mixture between layers; reserve 1 cup. Mix this cup with Cool Whip and frost sides and top. Refrigerate.

Betty Wood, Ozone Council,
Bogalusa, La.

COCONUT CAKE

1 box white cake mix
1 (8 oz.) carton sour
  cream

1/4 c. oil
1 (8 1/2 oz.) can cream
  of coconut

Mix all ingredients well. Bake in 350° oven for 40 minutes. Ice while warm.

Icing:

1 (8 oz.) pkg. cream
  cheese, softened
2 Tbp. milk

1 box powdered sugar
1 tsp. vanilla
1 can Angel Flake coconut

Mix sugar, cheese, milk and vanilla together and spread on cake. Sprinkle coconut on top.

Clarence Travers, Caddo
Council, Shreveport, La.

COCONUT CAKE

1 box yellow cake mix
1 c. sugar
1 (8 oz.) carton sour cream

1 large Cool Whip
2 pkg. (6 oz.) frozen coconut

Bake cake mix according to directions on box. Split the 2 layers to make 4. Mix remaining ingredients and fill and frost cake. Cover and place in refrigerator for 3 days. This is delicious and so easy to make.

Bertile Sanchez, Capital
Council, Baton Rouge, La.

MA BELL'S COCONUT CAKE

1 box white cake mix
1 tsp. coconut flavoring
1 (9 oz.) bowl Cool Whip

2 c. sugar
1 c. milk
1 (7 oz.) can flaked coconut

Bake white cake mix in 9x13-inch oblong pan as per cooking instructions. Cool. Mix sugar and milk, bring to boil. Let boil 1 minute. Remove from heat. Add coconut flavoring. Punch holes all over cooled cake. Pour filling over entire cake. Cool. Spread Cool Whip over top and sprinkle with coconut. Keep refrigerated. Ruby Santangelo, Ozone Council, Hammond, La.

RAVE REVIEWS COCONUT CAKE

1 pkg. yellow cake mix
1 1/3 c. water
4 eggs
2 c. coconut
1/4 c. oil

1 (4 serving size) pkg.
  instant French vanilla
  pudding mix
1 c. chopped walnuts or
  pecans

Blend cake mix, pudding mix, water, eggs and oil in large mixer bowl. Beat at medium speed 4 minutes. Stir in coconut and chopped nuts. Pour into 3 greased and floured 9-inch layer pans. Bake at 350° for 35 minutes. Cool in pans for 15 minutes. Remove and cool on racks. Frost with Coconut Cream Cheese Frosting.

Coconut Cream Cheese Frosting:

4 Tbsp. butter or oleo
1 (8 oz.) pkg. cream
  cheese
1/2 tsp. vanilla

2 c. coconut
2 tsp. milk
3 1/2 c. powdered sugar,
  sifted

Melt 2 tablespoons butter or oleo in skillet, add 1/4 cup coconut. Stir constantly over low heat until golden brown. Spread on paper towels to cool. Cream 2 tablespoons butter with cream cheese. Add milk, beat in sugar gradually. Blend in vanilla, stir in 1 3/4 cups coconut. Spread on tops of cake layers. Do not frost sides. Sprinkle top layer with browned coconut. (Note: A 14 ounce package of coconut will make both cake and icing.)

Denise Barteet   Ellen McDermott   Marie Louise Pizzitola
Caddo Council   Magnolia Council   Capital Council
Shreveport, La.   New Orleans, La.   Chalmette, La.

478

COCONUT SOUR CREAM CAKE

1 pkg. butter flavored
  cake mix
1 (12 oz.) pkg. frozen
  coconut, thawed

2 c. sugar
1 (16 oz.) carton sour cream
1 1/2 c. frozen whipped
  topping, thawed

Prepare cake mix according to package directions, making two 8-inch layers. When cool, split both layers. Combine sugar, sour cream and coconut. Blend well and chill. Reserve 1 cup sour cream mixture for frosting, spread remainder between layers. Combine the 1 cup reserved sour cream mixture with the whipped topping. Blend until smooth. Spread on top and sides of cake. Seal in airtight container and refrigerate for 3 days before serving.

                          Doris Reeves, Capital
                          Council, Baton Rouge, La.

COCONUT SOUR CREAM CAKE

1 box white cake mix
1/3 c. plain flour
1/3 c. powdered sugar

1 tsp. coconut flavoring
1/3 c. cooking oil

Mix cake according to directions on box and add remaining ingredients. Mix well and bake at 350° in greased and floured layer pans until done. Let cool.

Frosting:

1 pt. sour cream
1 1/2 c. granulated sugar

2 pkg. frozen coconut
1 (9 oz.) bowl Cool Whip

Reserve 1/2 package coconut; mix remaining coconut, sour cream and sugar together. Stir until sugar has dissolved. Reserve 1 1/2 cups of this mixture and spread remainder between cake layers. Add Cool Whip to the 1 1/2 cups of frosting and mix well. Spread on top and sides of cake. Sprinkle reserved coconut on top. This cake will keep in refrigerator indefinitely and also freezes well.

                          Marcia A. Horton, Capital
                          Council, Baton Rouge, La.

SOUR CREAM COCONUT CAKE

1 pkg. Duncan Hines yellow
  cake mix
1 box powdered sugar

1 (8 oz.) sour cream
1 (3 1/2 oz.) can flaked
  coconut

Prepare cake mix according to package directions and bake in two 9-inch cake pans. When layers are cool, slice each layer in half, making 4 layers in all. Mix sour cream and coconut and stir in powdered sugar. Spread between layers and on top of cake. Keep refrigerated.

Delores Bridges, Shreveport
Works Council, Shreveport, La.

COCONUT-SOUR CREAM LAYER CAKE

1 pkg. butter flavored
  cake mix
1 (12 oz.) pkg. frozen
  coconut, thawed

2 c. sugar
1 (16 oz.) carton sour cream
1 1/2 c. whipped topping

Prepare cake mix according to package directions, making two 8-inch layers. Split both layers when cool. Combine sugar, sour cream and coconut, blending well. Chill. Reserve 1 cup sour cream mixture for frosting, spread remainder between layers of cake. Combine reserved sour cream mixture with whipped topping. Blend until smooth. Spread on top and sides of cake. Seal cake in an airtight container and refrigerate for 3 days before serving.

Patricia R. Caraway, Capital
Council, Baton Rouge, La.

COCONUT SOUR CREAM CAKE

1 box white cake mix
1 (8 1/2 oz.) can cream
  of coconut

3 eggs
1/4 c. oil
1 (8 oz.) sour cream

Mix ingredients together with electric mixer. Bake in greased 9x12-inch pan at 350° for about 30 minutes.

Icing:

1 (8 oz.) pkg. cream
  cheese
1 can Angel Flake coconut

1 box powdered sugar
2 Tbsp. milk
1 tsp. vanilla

480

Blend sugar into softened cream cheese. Work in milk and vanilla. Spread on cooled cake. Sprinkle coconut over icing.   Dorothy Trent, Caddo
Council, Shreveport, La.

SOUTHERN COCONUT DELIGHT CAKE

1 pkg. Duncan Hines   1/2 c. chopped pecans
   butter batter cake mix

Prepare according to package directions. Fold in nuts. Bake in 3 layers.

Frosting:

1 pt. sour cream   2 pkg. frozen grated coconut
1 c. chopped pecans   1 c. sugar
1 (9 oz.) bowl Cool Whip

Mix sugar and sour cream, add nuts and coconut. Fold in Cool Whip. Frost cooled cake. Cover tightly and refrigerate 3 days before serving.   Margaret Aletha Kennan
Ozone Council, Bogalusa, La.

COFFEE CAKE

1 pkg. Duncan Hines   1/4 c. oil
   yellow cake mix   2 eggs
1/2 c. water   1 can peach pie filling, or
                          your choice

Mix all ingredients, except pie filling. Pour into greased 13x9x2-inch pan. Spread evenly, spoon pie filling over top of batter. Use a fork to fold into batter to create a marbled effect. Bake in preheated 350° oven for 35-45 minutes.

Frosting:

3 Tbsp. milk   Powdered sugar

Heat milk to boiling point, add enough sugar to make glaze. Pour over hot cake.   Fae Wells, Central Council,
Alexandria, La.

COFFEE CAKE

2 sticks oleo	2 c. sugar
2 c. all-purpose flour	2 eggs
1 c. sour cream	2 tsp. baking powder
	1/2 tsp. salt

Mix ingredients. Pour into greased and floured Bundt pan. Sprinkle on Topping and bake for about 55 minutes at 350°.

Topping:

1/2 c. chopped pecans	2 Tbsp. sugar
2 tsp. cinnamon	

Mix together.

Doris Reeves, Capital
Council, Baton Rouge, La.

COFFEE CAKE

1/2 c. oleo	3/4 c. sugar
2 eggs	1/2 c. milk
2 1/2 c. flour	2 tsp. baking powder
1 tsp. vanilla	Pecans, cinnamon and sugar

Cream oleo and sugar. Add flour, eggs, milk, baking powder and vanilla. Sprinkle with pecans, cinnamon and sugar. Dot with additional oleo. Bake at 350° until done.

Ann Orr, Evangeline
Council, New Iberia, La.

SOUR CREAM PECAN COFFEE CAKE

1/2 c. soft butter	1 c. sugar
3 eggs	2 c. sifted all-purpose flour
1 tsp. baking powder	1/2 tsp. soda
1 c. sour cream	1/2 c. white raisins

Cream butter and sugar until light. Add eggs, 1 at a time, beating after each addition. Add sifted dry ingredients alternately with sour cream, beating until smooth. Stir in raisins. Spread in greased 13x2-inch baking pan and sprinkle with Topping. Bake at 350° for 40-45 minutes. Serve warm or cold.

Pecan Topping:

3/4 c. packed brown sugar
1 tsp. cinnamon

1 Tbsp. flour
2 Tbsp. butter
1 c. chopped pecans

Mix brown sugar, flour and cinnamon. Cut in butter. Stir in nuts. Sprinkle over coffee cake before baking. This is a delightful, delicious coffee cake.

Sylvia Campbell, Caddo Council, Shreveport, La.

TREAT COFFEE CAKE

1 c. white sugar
1 stick butter or oleo
2 c. flour
1 c. brown sugar

1/4 tsp. salt
1 c. milk
2 tsp. baking powder
Cinnamon and flour to sprinkle

Mix 1 tablespoon of the butter with white granulated sugar. Add milk alternately with mixture of flour, baking powder and salt. Pour batter into greased pan. Sprinkle batter with flour lightly. Top with brown sugar, dot with remainder of butter and sprinkle cinnamon over all. Bake at 425° for 20 minutes.

Cecile Gallet, Evangeline Council, Lafayette, La.

COKE CAKE

2 sticks butter, melted
3 Tbsp. cocoa
2 c. flour
2 eggs, well beaten
1/2 c. buttermilk

1 c. Coke
1 1/2 c. small marshmallows
2 c. sugar
1 tsp. baking soda

Add Coke, cocoa and marshmallows to butter, pour over flour and sugar, mix well. Add eggs. Dissolve soda in buttermilk and add to batter. Pour into 9x13-inch greased pan and bake at 325° for 45 minutes.

Coke Cake Frosting:

1 stick butter, melted
3 Tbsp. cocoa
1 tsp. vanilla

6 Tbsp. Coke
1 lb. powdered sugar
1 c. nuts (optional)

Mix Coke and cocoa with butter. Add powdered sugar while mixture is still warm. Add vanilla and nuts. Mix well and ice cake. Linda Crawford, Shreveport
Works Council, Shreveport, La.

FRESH CRANBERRY CAKE

1 c. fresh cranberries, cut up	1 c. sugar
	2 1/2 c. flour
1 tsp. soda	1 c. buttermilk
3/4 c. Crisco oil	2 eggs
1 tsp. salt	1 c. chopped dates
1 c. chopped pecans	Rind of 2 oranges

Mix oil and sugar well, add eggs. Dissolve soda in buttermilk, add buttermilk and flour to mixture, beat well. Cut berries and add enough sugar to cover, set aside. Combine dates, nuts and grated orange rind. Add to mixture. Bake in greased and floured tube pan for 1 hour at 350°.

Glaze:

1 c. orange juice 1 c. sugar

Boil and pour over warm cake. This is very good and keeps moist for days. Jean Coon, Caddo Council,
Shreveport, La.

FRESH CRANBERRY CAKE

2 1/4 c. flour	1 c. sugar
1/4 tsp. salt	1 tsp. baking powder
1 tsp. soda	2 eggs
1 c. buttermilk	3/4 c. salad oil
1 c. black walnuts	1 c. fresh whole cranberries
1 c. chopped dates	1 grated orange rind

Sift dry ingredients and mix. Add eggs, buttermilk and salad oil. Beat well. Add cranberries, dates and rind. Mix and pour into well greased tube pan. Bake at 350° for 1 hour. Cool and glaze. Let stand 24 hours before serving.

Glaze:

1/2 c. orange juice 1/2 c. sugar

Mix ingredients for Glaze and boil until sugar melts. Cool and glaze cake.

Alva Reed, Ouachita
Council, Monroe, La.

CREAM SHERRY CAKE

1 pkg. yellow cake mix
  (Duncan Hines)
4 eggs
1/2 c. water
1/2 c. chopped walnuts

1 (3 3/4 oz.) pkg. instant
  vanilla pudding
1/2 c. salad oil
1/2 c. Gallo cream sherry

Sprinkle walnuts in bottom of greased Bundt pan. Mix eggs, sherry, vanilla pudding, cake mix, salad oil and water. Combine until well moistened on low, then 3 minutes on medium speed of mixer. Pour batter into Bundt pan. Bake at 325° for 1 hour. Remove from oven and pierce top of cake all over with a skewer or fork. Have hot Glaze ready and immediately pour Glaze over top of cake. Cake must remain in pan for 1 hour or until completely cool before removing from pan.

Glaze:

1 stick butter
1/4 c. water

1 c. sugar
2 oz. cream sherry

Combine butter, sugar and water, bring to a boil. Boil for 1 minute on medium heat. Remove from heat and add sherry. Pour immediately over hot cake.

Henrietta Victor, Magnolia
Council, New Orleans, La.

CREME DE MENTHE CAKE

1 pkg. white cake mix
4 large eggs
1/2 c. Crisco or Mazola oil
1/4 c. creme de menthe
1 (5 oz.) can chocolate
  syrup

1 pkg. instant vanilla
  pudding
1/2 c. orange juice
1/4 c. water
1/4 tsp. vanilla

Mix all ingredients, except chocolate syrup, for 2 minutes. Divide batter, add 1/3 chocolate syrup to 1/3 of batter; add creme de menthe to 2/3 of batter. Pour the green batter in Bundt pan, then add 1/3 chocolate batter.

Do not mix. Bake at 350° for 35-45 minutes in well oiled and floured Bundt pan. Sprinkle warm cake with powdered sugar if desired.
Lois Pullen Bonin, Central
Council, New Iberia, La.

CREOLE CAKE

1 c. sugar
2 eggs, beaten light
1/2 tsp. cinnamon
1 1/3 c. flour
1/4 tsp. salt

3 Tbsp. melted butter or oleo
2 oz. melted chocolate
1/2 c. milk
2 1/2 tsp. baking powder

Gradually beat the sugar into eggs, add melted butter and chocolate. Sift flour, baking powder, salt and cinnamon twice. Add alternately with milk. Bake in 7x11-inch pan about 25 minutes at 350°. Cool and cover with Creole Frosting.

Frosting:

2 Tbsp. strong black
  coffee
1/2 tsp. vanilla

2 Tbsp. cocoa
1 c. powdered sugar

Stir ingredients together. Alma B. Duvegneaud
Crescent City Council
New Orleans, La.

CREOLE CAKE

1/4 c. ground chocolate
1/2 c. butter or oleo
3 eggs, separated
3/4 tsp. soda

1/2 c. hot coffee
1 1/2 c. brown sugar
2 c. cake flour
1/3 c. sour cream

Blend chocolate with hot black coffee. Cool. Cream butter with sugar. Add egg yolks, 1 at a time, beating after each addition. Add coffee mixture. Add flour. Mix soda in sour cream, add to batter. Beat egg whites until stiff and fold into batter. Bake in 2 greased and floured layer pans at 350° for 30 minutes or 1 long pan about 45 minutes. Prepare the following Creole Frosting.

Creole Frosting:

1 tsp. instant coffee	1/4 c. hot water
1/3 c. soft butter or oleo	2 c. powdered sugar
1 egg yolk	

Dissolve instant coffee in hot water, add butter and beat thoroughly. Add sugar and egg yolk. Beat well. Allow to stand for awhile before putting on cake,

Marie Pamplin, Shreveport
Works Council, Shreveport, La.

CRUSADER'S CAKE

1 (18 1/4 oz.) pkg. yellow cake mix	1 (4 oz.) pkg. vanilla pudding mix
1 c. beer	4 eggs
1/2 c. salad oil	1/2 tsp. ground ginger
1 tsp. cinnamon	1/2 tsp. ground cardamon
1/2 tsp. ground cloves	1/4 tsp. ground allspice

In large mixing bowl, blend all ingredients. Beat at medium speed for 2 minutes. Pour into greased and floured 10-inch tube pan. Bake at 350° for about 50-60 minutes. Cake springs back in center when done. Cool right side up in pan about 25 minutes, remove to wire rack and cool completely. Cover with Lemon Glaze.

Lemon Glaze:

1 1/2 c. powdered sugar	2 Tbsp. soft butter
1-2 Tbsp. lemon juice	1/4 tsp. grated lemon peel

Blend all ingredients until smooth. Spread on top of cooled cake allowing Glaze to drip down sides of cake. Decorate with lemon slices.

Alva Reed, Ouachita
Council, Monroe, La.

DATE NUT LOAF CAKE

4 eggs, separated	1 c. sugar
1 c. flour	2 tsp. baking powder
1 tsp. vanilla	1/3 tsp. salt
2 c. pecans, broken	2 c. dates, quartered

Beat egg yolks and sugar together until light. Mix

flour, baking powder and salt, add to mixture. Add vanilla, dates and nuts, mix well. Beat egg whites until stiff, fold into mixture until well blended. Bake in loaf pan, lined with brown paper, greased and floured, about 1 hour at 300°. This recipe was given to me by my mother, Jody B. Corley, in 1928.

Mildred Lee, Central
Council, Pineville, La.

DATE AND PECAN CAKE

1 c. butter	2 c. sugar
4 eggs	4 c. sifted light crust flour
1 tsp. soda	1/2 tsp. salt
1 1/2 c. buttermilk	1 Tbsp. grated orange rind
1 c. chopped pecans	1 (3 oz.) pkg. dates, chopped

Cream together sugar and butter. Beat eggs and add to butter and sugar. Beat together. Sift flour, soda and salt together, add to creamed mixture alternating with buttermilk. Add rind, dates and pecans. Pour into greased and floured tube pan. Bake at 325° for 1 1/2 hours or until done. Before removing cake from pan, while still hot, punch many holes all the way to the bottom with ice pick or skewer. Pour hot Glaze over and down into holes in cake. If cake has not pulled away from sides of pan, loosen with knife so that some of the Glaze runs down sides and center of cake. Do not remove cake from pan for several hours or overnight. Decorate top with pecans after removing from pan if desired.

Glaze:

1 c. orange juice	2 c. sugar
2 Tbsp. grated orange rind	

Dissolve sugar and orange juice in small pan over fire. Do not boil. Add orange rind. Pour over cake.

R.H. Elliott, Ouachita
Council, Monroe, La.

DEVILS FOOD CAKE

1 3/4 c. sugar	2/3 c. shortening
1 1/2 tsp. salt	3 oz. unsweetened chocolate
3 eggs, beaten	1 1/2 tsp. vanilla
2 1/4 c. flour	1/2 tsp. baking powder
1 tsp. baking soda	1 1/3 c. buttermilk

Cream sugar, salt and shortening together. Add melted chocolate and vanilla. Add beaten eggs. Mix flour, baking powder and soda together. Add to mixture alternately with buttermilk, mix well. Pour into 2 greased and floured 8-inch layer pans. Bake at 350° for 35 minutes or until done. Remove layers from pans and cool. Frost with your favorite frosting.

Ann Orr, Evangeline
Council, New Iberia, La.

DEVILS FOOD CAKE

2 c. sugar	1/2 c. cocoa
2 1/4 c. flour	2/3 c. salad oil
2 tsp. soda	2 tsp. vinegar
2 tsp. vanilla	2 c. water

Combine sugar, cocoa and oil. Add vinegar and vanilla, stir well. Combine soda and flour and add alternately with water. Bake at 350° until done.

Chocolate Frosting:

1 1/4 c. sugar	3 Tbsp. cornstarch
Dash of salt	3 Tbsp. cocoa
2 Tbsp. oleo	1 1/2 c. milk

Combine sugar, cornstarch, cocoa and salt in saucepan. Add milk. Bring mixture to full boil, stirring constantly. Remove from heat, add oleo and stir until melted and frosting is smooth. Spread on cake while still warm.

Ethel Courtney, Ozone
Council, Baton Rouge, La.

IVY'S FILIGREE DEVILS FOOD CAKE

2/3 c. soft butter	1 1/2 c. sugar
2 eggs	1 1/2 c. sifted cake flour
1/2 c. cocoa	1 tsp. baking soda
1/4 tsp. cream of tartar	1/2 tsp. salt
1 c. buttermilk	1 tsp. vanilla

Cream butter and sugar, add eggs. Add soda to buttermilk. Add cocoa, cream of tartar and salt to flour. Alternate flour mixture and buttermilk mixture to butter mixture. Add vanilla. Pour into two 8-inch round layer cake pans that have been greased and dusted with flour. Bake at

350° for 30-35 minutes or until cake tests done. Cool, spread with Filling.

Filling:

2 c. sugar   3/4 c. cream
1/2 tsp. vanilla

Cook on low heat until soft ball stage is reached. Set in pan of cool water about 15 minutes. Pour between layers. Cool; spread the rest on top.   Estelle Banker, Capital
Council, Baton Rouge, La.

DREAM CAKE

1 box Jiffy cake mix   1 small box strawberry jello
1 small box instant vanilla   1 c. boiling water
   pudding and pie filling   1 large bowl Cool Whip
Fresh strawberries

Prepare cake mix as directed. Bake in 8x10-inch pan. Mix jello with hot water. When cake is removed from oven, pour jello mixture over cake slowly and refrigerate. Mix pudding according to package instructions. Spread over cooled cake. Spread Cool Whip over top. Decorate with fresh strawberries. Refrigerate until ready to serve.
Henrietta Victor, Magnolia
Council, New Orleans, La.

DREAM CAKE

1 pkg. yellow, white or   1 env. Dream Whip
   devils food cake mix   4 eggs
1 c. tap water

Combine cake mix, water, eggs and envelope of Dream Whip (do not whip; use right from envelope). Blend until all ingredients are moistened. Beat at medium speed 4 minutes. Pour into greased and floured layer pans. Bake at 350° until done. Cool. Frost cake if desired with favorite frosting.   Viola Kehrer, Ozone
Council, Hammond, La.

DOBERGE DREAM CAKE

1 pkg. yellow cake mix
1 pkg. chocolate pudding
  mix
2 Tbsp. sugar

1 pkg. vanilla pudding mix
1 pkg. Dream Whip (2 env.)
2 Tbsp. cocoa

Prepare cake mix as directed and pour into 4 greased and floured cake pans. This will make thin layers. Cook at 350° until done. Mix vanilla and chocolate pudding together (do not use instant); cook as directed on package. Cover and cool. When cake layers are cool, place pudding thickly between layers. Mix Dream Whip according to package directions. Add sugar and cocoa, blend well. Ice top and sides of cake with Dream Whip. Chill 1 or more hours before serving.　　　　　Joyce Hattier, Magnolia
Council, New Orleans, La.

DUMP CAKE

1 can apple pie filling
2 sticks butter, melted

1 box yellow cake mix

Spread pie filling evenly in 13x9-inch pan. Sprinkle dry cake mix over top of filling. Pour melted butter over top of cake mix. Let butter saturate cake mix while oven heats for 10 minutes. Bake at 350° for about 45 minutes until brown.　　　　　Jan Prestridge, Capital
Council, Baton Rouge, La.

EGGNOG CAKE

1 c. butter
5 Tbsp. bourbon
1 lb. powdered sugar
1 carton whipping cream

5 eggs, separated
2 tsp. white sugar
1 c. chopped pecans
3 (3 oz.) pkg. ladyfingers

Cream butter and powdered sugar. Add bourbon to egg yolks, beat well. Add egg mixture to butter and sugar. Add nuts. Beat egg whites with 2 teaspoons sugar and gently fold into mixture. Line bottom and sides of 9-inch spring form pan with ladyfinger halves (sugar side out). Pour in mixture. Top with halves of ladyfingers (sugar side up). Refrigerate 24 hours. Remove from pan and ice with whipped cream.　　　Joyce Silva, Capital
Council, Baton Rouge, La.

EGGLESS, MILKLESS AND BUTTERLESS CAKE

1 c. sugar
1 tsp. cinnamon
1/2 c. cooking oil
1 apple, cut up (optional)
1 tsp. soda

2 c. raisins
1 c. cold coffee
1/3 tsp. salt
2 c. plain flour
2 c. chopped nuts

Combine sugar, raisins, cinnamon, coffee, oil and apple. Boil about 5 minutes. Cool and add flour, soda and nuts. Bake at 350° in greased Bundt or tube pan for 35-40 minutes or until tests done. Dates, cherries and more nuts can be added to batter to taste more like fruit cake; more coffee can also be added if dough seems too dry.

Ozone Council, Hammond, La.

FATHER'S DAY CAKE

2/3 c. corn oil oleo
3 eggs
2/3 c. cocoa
1/4 tsp. salt
1 c. milk

1 2/3 c. sugar
2 c. cake flour
1 1/4 tsp. soda
1 tsp. baking powder
1/3 c. bourbon (Jack Daniels)

Cream oleo, sugar and eggs until fluffy, beat on high speed 3 minutes. Combine dry ingredients, add alternately with milk. Add bourbon. Bake in 3 greased and floured cake pans at 350° for 30 minutes.

Frosting:

3 c. powdered sugar
1/3 c. bourbon
Chopped nuts

1 stick oleo
Small amount hot water

Mix sugar, bourbon and oleo together. Add hot water for consistency desired. Frost cake and sprinkle top with nuts.

B.B. Wynne, Shreveport
Works Council, Shreveport, La.

FIG CAKE

1 large egg
1 tsp. vanilla
1/2 tsp. salt
1 c. + 3 Tbsp. flour

4 Tbsp. sugar
1/2 c. salad oil
1 Tbsp. baking powder or
   soda
1 pt. fig preserves

Combine sugar, salt, baking powder and flour. Add slightly beaten egg, mix and add remaining ingredients. Mix well. Pour into greased and floured tube or Bundt pan. Bake at 350° for 35 or 40 minutes.

Ethel Courtney, Ozone
Council, Hammond, La.

FIG CAKE

1 pt. figs, mashed	1/2 tsp. soda
2 eggs	1 tsp. baking powder
1 stick oleo	1 3/4 c. flour
3 heaping Tbsp. sugar	1 tsp. vanilla
1/2 c. pecans	1/4 c. coconut

Cream oleo and sugar, add unbeaten eggs. Sift in all dry ingredients. Add vanilla, coconut, pecans and figs. Beat well. Pour into greased and floured pan. Bake at 375° for 25-30 minutes. Test with toothpick.

Cecile Gallet, Evangeline
Council, Lafayette, La.

FIG CAKE

2 c. sugar	1 c. buttermilk
3 eggs	2 1/2 c. flour
3/4 c. Crisco oil	1 tsp. baking soda
1 c. fig preserves	1/2 tsp. cloves (ground)
1/2 tsp. allspice	1/2 tsp. cinnamon
Pinch of salt	1 c. pecans

Mix sugar and eggs. Add oil, beat well. Add spices and salt to sifted flour. Add buttermilk, figs and pecans to sugar mixture. Stir in flour. Pour batter into greased and floured Bundt pan. Bake at 325° about 1 hour.

Gretna S. Anderson, Central
Council, Alexandria, La.

FIG LOAF

1 block oleo	1 c. sugar
3 eggs	1 tsp. cinnamon
1 tsp. salt	1 tsp. soda
1 c. sour milk	2 c. flour
2 c. pulverized figs	

1723-79

If no sour milk is available, add 1 tablespoon vinegar to 1 cup sweet milk. Cream oleo, add sugar, then eggs. Alternate dry ingredients. Add milk. Add figs. Pour batter into greased loaf pan. Cook at 350° until done. Test with finger for doneness. If it springs back, it's done. Decorate top with sliced cherries and powdered sugar.

Mrs. Sim S. Davenport, Central
Council, Alexandria, La.

FIG PRESERVE SHEET CAKE

2 c. flour	1 tsp. salt
1 tsp. soda	1 1/2 c. sugar
1 c. cooking oil	3 eggs
1 c. buttermilk	1 c. fig preserves, mashed
1 c. chopped pecans	1 tsp. vanilla

Mix flour, salt, soda and sugar together. Add oil and beat well. Add eggs, 1 at a time. Add remaining ingredients, mix well and pour into greased 9x13x2-inch pan. Bake at 325° for 45 minutes. Spread Sauce on cake while still hot.

Sauce:

1 c. sugar	1 stick oleo
1 tsp. flour	1 tsp. vanilla
1/2 c. buttermilk	1/2 tsp. soda

Dissolve soda in buttermilk. Mix all ingredients together and cook about 3 minutes. Spread on cake.

Marie Pamplin, Shreveport
Works Council, Shreveport, La.

FRUIT CAKE

1 lb. cherries	1 c. sugar
1 lb. dates	2 c. flour
1 lb. pineapple	2 tsp. baking powder
2 lb. whole pecans	1/2 tsp. salt
4 eggs	

Chop cherries, dates and pineapple, add pecans. Dredge fruit and nuts with 1 cup flour. Mix remaining flour, baking powder and salt, add eggs to flour mixture. Add all ingredients together with hands or rubber spatula. Press firmly

into greased baking pans or dishes. Bake at 200° for
2 1/2 hours with pan of water in bottom of oven.

Bernice Wright, Caddo
Council, Shreveport, La.

FRUIT CAKE

2 lb. pecans, cut up
2 lb. dates, cut up
2 1/2 c. flour
2 tsp. baking powder
1 tsp. salt
8 eggs

2 lb. candied pineapple
    chopped
1 lb. candied cherries,
    whole (1/2 red and 1/2
    green)
1 1/2 c. sugar
3 tsp. vanilla

Stir flour and baking powder in all fruits. Mix sugar,
salt, vanilla and eggs. Mix all together. Pour in greased
and floured cake pan lined with paper and bake 5 hours at
300°.

Verle Oliphant, Caddo
Council, Shreveport, La.

ARKANSAS FRUIT CAKE

2 qt. broken nuts
1/2 lb. red cherries
1/2 lb. green cherries
2 cans Eagle Brand milk

2 cans coconut
2 boxes dates, chopped
1/2 lb. pineapple

Mix all ingredients thoroughly. Place in buttered tube
pan and press down well. Bake at 200° for 2 hours. Do not
remove cake from pan until it is barely warm. Very good.

B. B. Wynne, Shreveport
Works Council, Shreveport, La.

BETTIE'S FLOURLESS FRUIT CAKE

1 lb. coconut
1 lb. mixed nuts
1 lb. candied cherries,
    cut in half or quarters
1/2 tsp. allspice
1/2 tsp. nutmeg
1 Tbsp. vanilla

1 lb. pecans
1 lb. chopped dates
1 lb. mixed candied fruit
1/2 tsp. cinnamon
1/2 tsp. ginger
1 can sweetened condensed
    milk

Mix coconut, pecans, mixed nuts, dates, cherries and candied fruit. Add spices and vanilla to milk. Add milk to mixture. Bake in loaf pan lined with greased heavy brown paper at 300° for 1 hour; or make cupcakes using paper liners; or bake in Bundt-lette pan at same temperature for about 45 minutes.

Bettie Lalonde, Evangeline
Council, Opelousas, La.

CANDIED FRUIT CAKE

2 c. flour
1 - 1 1/2 c. chopped
  candied cherries
2 sticks butter
1 Tbsp. lemon juice
2 c. sugar

1 1/2 c. chopped candied
  pineapple
4 c. chopped pecans
2 Tbsp. vanilla flavoring
5 eggs

Sift flour into a bowl. Add cherries, pineapple and nuts and mix well. Melt butter in pot, add sugar, vanilla, lemon juice and eggs. Mix well. Add to fruit and nut mixture, mix well. Pour into 2 greased loaf pans. Cook at 200° for 2 hours.

Jan Prestridge, Capital
Council, Baton Rouge, La.

DIETETIC FRUIT CAKE

2 c. water
1 c. unsweetened apple-
  sauce
2 Tbsp. liquid sweetener
1/2 tsp. nutmeg
3/4 c. cooking oil

2 c. raisins
2 eggs
1 tsp. baking soda
1 1/4 tsp. cinnamon
2 c. flour
1 tsp. vanilla

Cook raisins in water until water is gone. Add apple-sauce, eggs, sweetener and oil and mix well. Sift dry ingredients together and add. Add vanilla. Pour into greased and floured loaf pan. Bake at 350° for 1 hour.

Patti Regep, Matairie
Council, River Ridge, La.

EASY FRUIT CAKE

1 c. chopped dates
1 c. dark raisins
1 1/2 c. brown sugar
1 1/2 c. hot water
2 tsp. cinnamon
1 tsp. soda
1 tsp. baking powder
1 lb. candied fruits and
  peels

1 c. white raisins
1 c. butter
1/4 c. dark molasses
3 c. flour
1/2 tsp. ground cloves
1 tsp. allspice
3 eggs, well beaten
1 lb. nuts

Combine dates, raisins, butter, brown sugar, molasses and water. Bring to boil and boil for 3 minutes over very low heat. Cool. Add eggs, candied fruits and peels and nuts to cooled mixture. Sift together remaining ingredients and blend into mixture. Pour into well lined pans and bake at 250° for 2 1/2 - 3 hours, depending on size of pans.

Ina Z. Gaspard, Central
Council, Cottonport, La.

ICEBOX FRUIT CAKE

1 (15 oz.) pkg. vanilla
  wafers
1 c. pecans

1 c. raisins
1 (14 oz.) can condensed
  milk

Crush cookies. Add remaining ingredients, mix well. Mold in tin foil in small bowl. Refrigerate until cold. Remove foil and slice in bite sized pieces.

Kathryn L. Jackson, Capital
Council, Baton Rouge, La.

ICEBOX FRUIT CAKE

1 lb. marshmallows
2 sticks butter
1 lb. raisins
1 lb. graham crackers,
  crushed

1 qt. nuts
1 lb. candied red and green
  cherries
3 Tbsp. whiskey

Melt butter and marshmallows in top of double boiler. Crush crackers to flour fine. Combine crackers and remaining ingredients, pour marshmallow mixture over all.

Mix thoroughly. Mold back into cracker box lined with waxed paper. Tie box in shape. Refrigerate until very cold.

Twila "Pete" Dysart, Ouachita Council, Monroe, La.

ITALIAN FRUIT CAKE

4 eggs
1 lb. sour cream
2 tsp. vanilla
1/2 lb. butter
2 c. sugar
1 c. sliced dates

3 3/4 c. flour, sifted
1 tsp. baking soda
1 c. walnuts, coarsely chopped
1 c. maraschino cherries, chopped
1/2 c. candied pineapple, cut up

Cream together eggs, sour cream, vanilla, butter and sugar. Add flour and baking soda, mix until blended. Fold in dates, cherries, pineapple and nuts. Fill greased and floured Bundt pan 2/3 full and pour remainder into a loaf pan. Bake about 40 minutes at 350° or until cake tester comes out clean. Cool 15 minutes before removing from pan.

Helen Bartram, Capital Council, Bethel, Ct.

JAPANESE FRUIT CAKE

1 c. butter
3 c. flour
1 c. sweet milk
Pinch of salt
1 tsp. vanilla
1 tsp. allspice
1 tsp. cinnamon

2 c. sugar
4 eggs
1 tsp. baking powder
1 c. chopped nuts
1 lb. seedless chopped raisins

Cream butter, sugar, eggs and milk together. Mix flour, salt and baking powder together and add to creamed mixture. Divide into 2 equal parts. To one part, add nuts and vanilla. To the other part, add raisins, cinnamon and allspice. Bake in floured and greased pans at 350° until done; each part in 3 thin layers (6 layers in all).

Icing:

2 lemon rinds, grated
2 c. sugar
5 Tbsp. flour

1 coconut, grated
1 c. hot water

Combine lemon rinds, sugar, coconut and water. Bring to boil and add flour. Cook until drops from spoon. When cold, place between layers, alternating the nut layer with the raisin layer. Cover with Icing and let stand 15 days.

Marie Pamplin, Shreveport
Works Council, Shreveport, La.

MRS. SCOTT'S FRUIT CAKE

4 eggs
1 1/2 c. sugar
4 or 5 c. flour
1/2 c. cocoa
Pinch of salt
1 c. butter or oleo
1 pkg. mincemeat, cut up
1 c. pear preserves, cut up
1 lb. English walnuts
1 c. raisins
1 small bottle red cherries
1 small bottle green
  cherries
1 pkg. candied cherries,
  cut up

1 tsp. allspice
1 tsp. cloves
1 tsp. vanilla
1/2 lb. orange candy, cut up
1 c. sweet milk
3 tsp. baking powder
1 c. fig preserves, cut up
1 lb. pecans
1 c. dates, cut up
1 (No. 2) can sliced, drained
  pineapple, cut up
1 small pkg. candied pineapple, green, red and
  white; cut up

Mix all ingredients well. Place batter in greased and floured large tube pan or 2 small tube pans. Bake at 250° for 2 1/2 - 3 hours.

Brenda Braxton, Ouachita
Council, Monroe, La.

NO BAKE FRUIT CAKE

1 (3 oz.) can coconut
1 can condensed milk
1 (8 oz.) pkg. dates,
  chopped
1 c. candied pineapple

1 c. candied cherries
3/4 - 1 c. toasted and
  almonds
1 (9 oz.) pkg. vanilla
  wafers, crushed

Mix ingredients together. Pack in pans and refrigerate. Slice when ready to serve. Very good.

Louise Malone, Caddo
Council, Shreveport, La.

UNBAKED FRUIT CAKE

1 tsp. vanilla flavoring
1 box white raisins
1 box graham crackers,
  crushed

3/4 lb. butter or oleo
1 qt. pecans
48 large marshmallows
1 lb. candied cherries

Heat butter and marshmallows together until melted. Pour over other ingredients. Mix and form into roll, similar to icebox cookies. Keep refrigerated. Slice into 1/4-inch rounds when ready to serve. Jeanette English, Caddo Council, Shreveport, La.

SUE'S FRUIT CAKE

1 box spice cake mix
1 c. raisins
1 c. nuts
1 pt. jar fig preserves

1/2 c. coconut
1 lb. bag of small gumdrops
  or orange candy slices,
  chopped

Make up cake mix according to directions on box and add remaining ingredients. Pour into floured and greased tube pan. Bake at 350° for about 1 1/2 hours. Cool 15 minutes before removing from pan. Marie Pamplin, Shreveport Works Council, Shreveport, La.

FRUIT COCKTAIL CAKE

1 (No. 2) can fruit
  cocktail, drained
Vanilla wafers

1 can Eagle Brand milk
1/3 c. lemon juice

Mix fruit cocktail, milk and lemon juice. Alternate layer of fruit cocktail mix and layer of vanilla wafers until used up. Refrigerate until set. Frankie Meeks, Ouachita Council, Monroe, La.

FRUIT COCKTAIL CAKE

1 1/2 c. sugar
2 c. flour
2 eggs
1 tsp. vanilla

2 tsp. soda
1/2 tsp. salt
1 (No. 303) can fruit cocktail, undrained

Sift sugar, flour, soda and salt together. Stir in eggs,

500

vanilla and juice from fruit cocktail, then gently fold in fruit cocktail. Pour into 13x9-inch greased pan. Bake at 350° for 40 minutes.

Icing:

1 stick butter or oleo	1 1/2 c. granulated sugar
1 c. canned milk	1/2 c. chopped nuts
1 c. coconut	1/2 c. brown sugar

Mix butter, milk and white sugar, bring to boil and pour over hot cake. Mix remaining ingredients, sprinkle over cake and brown lightly under broiler.

Connie Younker, Shreveport
Works Council, Shreveport, La.

FRUIT COCKTAIL CAKE

1 can fruit cocktail, undrained	1 1/2 c. granulated sugar
2 eggs, beaten	1/2 can coconut
2 Tbsp. soda	2 c. flour
1/2 c. brown sugar	1/2 tsp. salt

Mix fruit cocktail, eggs, granulated sugar together. Sift flour, soda and salt together and add to fruit cocktail. Mix and pour batter into greased pan. Sprinkle brown sugar and coconut over batter. Bake at 300° for 40-50 minutes. Leave in pan.

Icing:

3/4 c. sugar	1/2 stick butter
1/2 tsp. vanilla	1/2 c. coconut
1/2 c. pecans	1 c. evaporated milk

Mix ingredients together and boil 2 minutes. Spread on cake.

Sadie Foil, Ozone Council,
Bogalusa, La.

FUDGE CAKE

2 sticks butter	2 c. sugar
4 eggs	5 Tbsp. chocolate
1 Tbsp. vanilla	1 1/2 c. all-purpose flour
2 c. chopped pecans	

Cream butter and sugar, add chocolate. Beat eggs with vanilla. Add to butter mixture alternating with flour. Add pecans. Pour batter into two 9-inch layer pans, oiled and waxed paper lined. Bake at 350° for 30-35 minutes. Turn out of pans after 5 minutes from oven. Ice about 10 minutes after removing from oven.

Icing:

1 stick butter
1 box powdered sugar
4 Tbsp. chocolate
2 c. chopped pecans

1/2 small can evaporated milk
  or more
1 Tbsp. vanilla

Marjorie Rowell, Evangeline
Council, Lafayette, La.

GELATIN CAKE

1 box yellow cake mix
1 (3 oz.) pkg. lemon gelatin
3/4 c. oil

3/4 c. milk
4 eggs

Combine cake mix and gelatin, add remaining ingredients, mix at low speed. Beat at medium speed for 3 minutes. Bake at 350° for 35 minutes.

Glaze:

2 c. powdered sugar
4 Tbsp. melted oleo

4 Tbsp. lemon juice

Combine ingredients, mix well. Pour over hot cake, cool before serving.   Calcasieu Council
                                     Lake Charles, La.

GERMAN NUT CAKE

1 lb. butter (not oleo)
6 eggs
1 c. candied chopped
  cherries
Dash of salt
1 lb. ground pecans

2 c. sugar
3 c. flour
1/4 tsp. soda
1 (2 oz.) bottle lemon extract
1 c. chopped candied pineapple

Cream butter and sugar, add beaten eggs and extract.

Sift flour, soda and salt together, fold into cake mixture. Add fruit and pecan mix. Pour into greased and floured tube or Bundt pan. Bake for 3 hours at 275°. During final hour of cooking, place pan of water under cake and cover top with piece of brown paper. Delicious; and freezes well.   Catherine (Chadwick) McCraw
Caddo Council, Shreveport, La.

GRAHAM CRACKER CAKE

2 c. sugar
1/2 lb. butter
5 eggs
1 c. evaporated milk

2 tsp. vanilla
2 tsp. baking powder
4 c. graham cracker crumbs
1 1/2 c. coconut

Mix all ingredients. Pour into 3 greased and floured 8-inch pans. Bake at 350° for about 30 minutes.

Icing:

2 Tbsp. flour
1 stick butter
1 box powdered sugar

1 can coconut
1 small can crushed pineapple

Cook butter, pineapple and flour together until thickened, add sugar and coconut. Mearl S. Byles, Central
Council, Natchitoches, La.

NUTTY GRAHAM PICNIC CAKE

2 c. all-purpose flour
1 c. firmly packed brown
   sugar
1 tsp. salt
1 tsp. soda
1 c. butter or oleo, softened
1 Tbsp. grated orange peel

1 c. graham cracker crumbs
1/2 c. granulated sugar
1 tsp. baking powder
1/2 tsp. cinnamon
1 c. orange juice
3 eggs
1 c. chopped nuts

Combine all cake ingredients, except nuts, in large mixing bowl. Beat 3 minutes at medium speed. Stir in nuts. Pour into greased and floured 12-cup tube pan or 10-inch tube pan. Bake at 350° for 45-50 minutes or until tests done. Cool upright 15 minutes, invert onto serving plate and cool completely. Glaze when cool.

Glaze:

2 Tbsp. brown sugar	5 tsp. milk
1 Tbsp. oleo	3/4 c. powdered sugar
1/4 c. chopped nuts	

Heat brown sugar, milk and butter in small saucepan just until melted. Remove from heat, add powdered sugar and blend until smooth. Drizzle over cake and sprinkle with nuts. Makes 12-16 servings. Henrietta Victor, Magnolia Council, New Orleans, La.

HEAVENLY HASH CAKE

1 c. melted butter	2 c. sugar
4 eggs	1 1/2 c. self-rising flour
2 c. chopped pecans	1 1/2 c. miniature marsh-
1 Tbsp. vanilla extract	mallows

Combine butter, sugar and eggs. Beat slightly. Add flour and pecans, mix well. Stir in vanilla. Spread batter in greased 13x9x2-inch pan. Bake at 350° for 30-40 minutes. Remove from oven and sprinkle marshmallows over hot cake. Return to oven until marshmallows are melted. Pour Chocolate Topping over hot cake, let cool.

Chocolate Topping:

2 Tbsp. melted butter	1/2 c. evaporated milk
4 Tbsp. cocoa	1 lb. box powdered sugar

Combine ingredients and pour over hot cake.
Sybil Callahan, Central Council, Alexandria, La.

HEAVENLY HASH CAKE

4 eggs, well beaten	2 sticks melted oleo
2 c. sugar	4 Tbsp. cocoa
1 1/2 c. self-rising flour	2 c. pecans
2 tsp. vanilla	Marshmallows, cut in half

Mix all ingredients, except marshmallows. Pour into ungreased long pan. Bake at 325° for 30-40 minutes or until done. Remove from oven and cover top of cake with marshmallows. Return to oven for 5 minutes until marshmallows melt. Prepare the following Icing.

504

Icing:

1 box powdered sugar
1 tsp. vanilla
4 Tbsp. softened butter
   (optional)

4 Tbsp. cocoa
1/4 c. milk (add more milk
   if too thin)

Mix the icing and spread on cooled cake.

Mrs. Sim (Sally) Davenport
Central Council
Alexandria, La.

Jo Ann Everhardt
Gentilly Council
Meraux, La.

Pat Uhle
West Bank Council
Gretna, La.

Clarabell J. Hosch
Metairie Council
Metairie, La.

HEAVENLY HASH CAKE

1 stick butter or oleo
2 eggs
Pinch of salt
1 c. chopped nuts

2 Tbsp. cocoa
1 c. sugar
3/4 c. self-rising flour
1 jar marshmallow creme
   or marshmallows

Melt oleo in saucepan, add cocoa and stir well. Mix eggs, sugar and salt together. Alternately stir in melted ingredients and flour into sugar mixture. Add nuts. Pour batter into greased and floured 7x11-inch pan. Bake for 30 minutes at 375°. Remove and spoon on marshmallow creme or marshmallows. Spread with knife to make a layer on top of hot cake.

Icing:

1/4 c. milk
2 Tbsp. butter or oleo

2 Tbsp. cocoa
2 c. powdered sugar

Mix ingredients, heat and pour over cake. Serve hot, topping each slice with vanilla ice cream.

Doris Reeves, Capital
Council, Baton Rouge, La.

Lynda Fox, Caddo Council,
Shreveport, La.

HERSHEY BAR CAKE

2 1/2 c. flour
2 sticks oleo
1 c. buttermilk
2 Tbsp. vanilla
1/4 tsp. salt
1 c. nuts

2 c. sugar
4 eggs
8 small Hershey's bars
1/4 tsp. soda
1 large (16 oz.) can Hershey's
   chocolate syrup

Melt Hershey's bars in double boiler; cream sugar and oleo. Add syrup and melted candy. Add eggs, 1 at a time. Mix well. Sift dry ingredients together, mix with Hershey's batter alternately with buttermilk. Beat well. Stir in nuts and vanilla. Pour in greased and floured tube pan. Bake at 350° for 1 1/2 hours. Makes large cake.

Verle Oliphant, Caddo
Council, Shreveport, La.

HOT MILK CAKE

4 eggs
3 c. flour
1 c. milk
1 tsp. vanilla

2 c. sugar
1/2 c. oleo
2 tsp. baking powder

Beat eggs until foamy, add sugar, beat well. Add flour. Melt oleo in milk and heat to scalding. Add hot milk to batter, mixing well. Add baking powder and vanilla. Bake in greased and floured tube pan at 350° until cake shrinks from side of pan.

Evelyn Bledsoe, Ouachita
Council, Monroe, La.

HUMMINGBIRD CAKE

3 c. all-purpose flour
1 tsp. salt
1 tsp. ground cinnamon
1 1/2 c. salad oil
1 (8 oz.) can crushed
   pineapple, undrained
2 c. chopped bananas

2 c. sugar
1 tsp. soda
3 eggs, beaten
1 1/2 tsp. vanilla extract
2 c. chopped pecans, or
   1 c. pecans and 1 c. walnuts

Combine dry ingredients in large mixing bowl. Add eggs and oil, stirring until dry ingredients are moistened. Do not beat! Stir in vanilla, pineapple, bananas and 1 cup nuts. Spoon batter into 3 well greased and floured 9-inch cake pans. Bake at 350° for 25-30 minutes or until done. Cool in pans 10 minutes. Remove and cool completely. Spread frosting between layers, sides and top. Sprinkle with remaining nuts.

Cream Cheese Frosting:

2 (8 oz.) pkg. cream
   cheese, softened
2 tsp. vanilla

1 c. softened butter
2 lb. powdered sugar

Combine cheese and butter, cream until smooth. Add sugar, beating until light and fluffy. Stir in vanilla.

Mrs. Para Lee Nugent Cline (Billy and Harold Nugent's Mom), Dry Prong, La. Central Council

HUMMINGBIRD CAKE

3 c. plain flour
1 1/2 c. oil
1 1/2 tsp. vanilla
1 (8 oz.) can crushed
   pineapple, drained
2 bananas, mashed

2 c. sugar
1 tsp. soda
1 tsp. cinnamon
1 c. chopped nuts
3 eggs, beaten

Beat eggs, add remainder of ingredients and mix well. Bake in greased and floured tube pan for 45-50 minutes.

Dolly Daly, Crescent City Council, New Orleans, La.

ICEBOX MARSHMALLOW CAKE

32 large marshmallows
1 medium bottle maraschino
   cherries and juice
1 box seedless raisins

1 large box graham crackers,
   crushed
2 sticks oleo
1 qt. pecans or less

Melt oleo and marshmallows in cherry juice. Add to crushed graham crackers. Add remaining ingredients and mix thoroughly. Press into loaf pans and refrigerate.

Marie Pamplin
Shreveport Works Council
Shreveport, La.

ITALIAN CREAM CAKE

1 c. buttermilk
2 c. sugar
1/2 c. Crisco
2 c. flour
1 c. chopped pecans

1 tsp. soda
1 stick oleo
5 eggs, separated
1 tsp. vanilla
1 small can coconut (optional)

Combine soda and buttermilk and let stand a few minutes. Cream sugar, oleo and Crisco. Add egg yolks, 1 at a time. Beat well after each addition. Add buttermilk alternately with flour to creamed mixture. Stir in vanilla. Beat egg whites until stiff, but not dry. Fold into batter. Gently stir in pecans and coconut. Bake in 3 greased and floured 9-inch pans for 25-30 minutes.

Icing:

1 (8 oz.) pkg. cream
  cheese, softened
1 tsp. vanilla

1 stick oleo
1 lb. box powdered sugar

Cream the cheese, oleo and vanilla. Beat in sugar, a little at a time, until of spreading consistency. Jim's mother uses the same recipe, but only uses 1/2 cup pecans in the cake and the other half in the icing along with 1/2 cup coconut.

Dimple Whitehead, Crescent
City Council, New Orleans, La.

ITALIAN CREAM CAKE

1 stick butter
1 stick margarine
2 c. sugar
5 egg yolks
2 c. flour
1 tsp. soda

1 c. buttermilk
1 tsp. vanilla extract
1 small can Angel Flake coconut
1 c. chopped pecans
5 egg whites, stiffly beaten

Cream butter and margarine, add sugar and beat until smooth. Add egg yolks and beat well. Combine flour and soda and add to creamed mixture alternately with buttermilk. Stir in vanilla extract, add coconut and pecans, fold in egg whites. Pour batter into 3 greased and floured 8-inch cake pans. Bake at 350° for 25 minutes or until well done. Prepare the following Frosting.

Frosting:

1 (8 oz.) pkg. cream cheese	1 tsp. vanilla extract
1/2 stick margarine	1 box powdered sugar
	Chopped pecans

Beat cream cheese and margarine until smooth. Add sugar and mix well. Add vanilla extract and beat until smooth. Spread on cake, then sprinkle top with pecans.

Ann Suire, Capital
Council, Baton Rouge, La.

ITALIAN CREAM CAKE

1 stick butter	2 c. sugar
1/2 c. vegetable oil	5 egg yolks
2 c. flour	1 tsp. soda
1 c. buttermilk	1 tsp. vanilla extract
1 small can (3 1/2 oz.) flaked coconut	4 egg whites, stiffly beaten
	1 c. chopped pecans

Cream butter and shortening, add sugar. Beat until smooth. Add egg yolks, beat well. Combine flour and soda and add to creamed mixture alternately with buttermilk. Add vanilla. Beat in coconut and pecans. Fold in stiffly beaten egg whites. Pour batter into 4 greased and floured 8-inch cake pans. Bake at 350° for 25-30 minutes or until done. Cool and frost.

Cream Cheese Frosting:

1 (8 oz.) pkg. cream cheese	1 box powdered sugar
1/2 stick butter	1 tsp. vanilla extract
	Chopped pecans

Beat cream cheese. Add butter and sugar, add vanilla. Spread between layers and on top. Sprinkle top with chopped pecans.

Jeanette English, Caddo
Council, Shreveport, La.

AUNT JENNIE'S CHRISTMAS JAM CAKE

1 c. butter	2 c. sugar
4 eggs	3 c. flour
1 tsp. cinnamon	1 tsp. ground cloves
1 tsp. allspice	1 c. buttermilk
1 tsp. soda	1 c. jam
1 c. nuts	1 c. citron or figs

1723-79

Beat eggs, add butter and mix well. Stir in buttermilk. Add sifted flour, spices and soda. Mix well. Stir in all fruit and nuts. Bake in greased and floured tube or Bundt pan for about 1 1/2 hours in very slow oven.

Rubye G. Morgan, Central
Council, Alexandria, La.

JELLY ROLL

3 large or 4 small eggs	1 c. sugar
5 Tbsp. cold water	1 tsp. vanilla
1 tsp. baking powder	1 c. sifted flour
1/4 tsp. salt	1/2 c. jelly, jam or your favorite filling

Beat eggs until light and fluffy. Beat in sugar gradually. Blend in water and vanilla. Sift flour, salt and baking powder together. Stir into egg mixture. Pour into jelly roll pan which has been lightly greased and lined with greased waxed paper. Bake at 375° for 15-18 minutes. Do not overbake. Turn immediately on towel. Roll up while hot. Cool, unroll and spread favorite filling. Reroll.

Mary Armand, Central
Council, Cottonport, La.

JELLY ROLL

1 c. flour	1 tsp. baking powder
1/4 tsp. salt	4 eggs
1 c. sugar	1/3 c. water
1 tsp. vanilla	Jelly (your choice)
Powdered sugar	

Sift together flour, baking powder and salt. Beat eggs until very thick and lemon colored. Pour into large bowl. Gradually beat in sugar. Blend in water and vanilla on low speed. Slowly mix in dry ingredients on low speed until batter is smooth. Grease a 15 x 10 1/2 x 1-inch jelly roll pan and line bottom with waxed paper. Bake in preheated 375° oven for 12-15 minutes, until top springs back when lightly touched. Loosen edges and turn upside down on waxed paper. Remove paper from cake. Trim off stiff edges. Roll cake and waxed paper from narrow end while hot. Cool, unroll, remove waxed paper. Spread with jelly. Reroll; sprinkle with sugar. Lynn Babin, Westmoor
Council, Kenner, La.

JELLY ROLL

3 eggs, well beaten
1 c. flour
1 tsp. vanilla

3/4 c. sugar
1 1/2 tsp. baking powder
6 Tbsp. hot water
Jelly or lemon filling

Combine eggs, flour, vanilla, sugar, baking powder and hot water. Pour into jelly roll pan lined with waxed paper. Grease paper and sides of pan. Bake at 400° for only 12 minutes. Turn cake out onto damp cloth, remove paper and trim edges of cake. Spread with jelly or lemon filling and roll up. Dust with powdered sugar if desired.

Helen Bartram, Capital
Council, Bethel, Ct.

JIFFY CREAM CAKE

1 (No. 2) can crushed
   pineapple, drained
1 box Jiffy yellow cake
   mix
1 large pkg. cream cheese,
   softened

1 egg
1 1/2 c. milk
1 small pkg. vanilla instant
   pudding
2 pkg. Dream Whip, pre-
   pared

Prepare cake mix using pineapple juice instead of water. Add egg. Mix and bake in 9x13-inch pan for 15-20 minutes at 350°. Beat pudding with milk. Blend in cream cheese. Spread over cooled cake. Dribble pineapple over top. Spread Dream Whip over all.

Betty Jackson, Shreveport
Works Council, Shreveport, La.

KATYDID CAKE

1 tin or 14 Katydids
   (candy)
2 c. sugar
2 1/2 c. flour
1/4 tsp. salt

1/2 c. chopped nuts
2 sticks oleo, divided
5 eggs
1/2 tsp. soda
1 c. buttermilk

Melt Katydids and 1/4 stick oleo in double boiler. Cream sugar and remaining oleo. Add eggs, 1 at a time, beat after each addition. Sift dry ingredients together and add to creamed mix. Add buttermilk and fold in Katydids.

Add the nuts. Bake in greased and floured tube pan at 350° for 1 - 1 1/2 hours. Grace Bell, Ouachita
Council, Monroe, La.

LAZY DAISY CAKE

2 eggs, well beaten
1 tsp. baking powder
1 c. flour
1 Tbsp. butter

1 c. sugar
1 tsp. vanilla
1/2 c. milk

Mix all ingredients, except milk and butter. Heat milk and butter to boiling point and add at once to mixture. Bake in 8-inch cake pan 1/2 hour in 350° oven. Cover with Icing while cake is hot and return to oven until Icing bubbles up and browns slightly.

Icing:

6 Tbsp. melted butter
10 Tbsp. brown sugar

4 Tbsp. cream
1 c. shredded coconut

Mix ingredients and pour over hot cake.
Doris Reeves, Capital
Council, Baton Rouge, La.

LEMON LOAF

1 Tbsp. lemon peel
1 1/2 tsp. baking powder
1 1/2 c. sugar
3 eggs

2 1/4 c. all-purpose flour
3/4 tsp. salt
3/4 c. oleo
3/4 c. milk

Mix flour, baking powder, salt and sugar. Cut in oleo until mixture resembles coarse crumbs. Stir in lemon peel. Add slightly beaten eggs with milk to flour mixture just until flour is moistened. Spoon into greased 9x5-inch loaf pan. Bake at 350° for 1 hour and 15 minutes. Glaze loaf while still warm. Makes 1 loaf.

Glaze:

4 1/2 tsp. lemon juice

2 Tbsp. sugar

Cook until slightly thickened, about 5 minutes. Brush over top of bread. Barbara H. Harris, Central
Council, Bunkie, La.

CHRISTMAS LEMON CAKE

1 lb. butter
2 c. sugar
6 eggs, separated
1/2 lb. red candied
  cherries
Grated rind of 1 lemon

4 c. cake flour
1 1/2 oz. lemon extract
1 qt. pecans
1/2 lb. green candied
  cherries

Coarsely chop pecans and cherries. Dredge with 1/4 cup of the flour. Cream butter and sugar, add egg yolks, 1 at a time, beating well after each addition. Fold in remaining flour. Add lemon extract and grated rind. Fold in well beaten egg whites. Pour over fruit and nut mixture. Bake in greased and floured tube pan or long pan for 2 1/2 - 2 3/4 hours at 275°.   Virginia Ingram, Shreveport
                              Works Council, Shreveport, La.

LEMON JELLO CAKE

1 pkg. Duncan Hines
  yellow cake mix
2/3 c. orange juice
1 tsp. lemon extract
Juice of 1 lemon

1 pkg. lemon jello
1 stick butter, very soft
4 eggs
1 c. powdered sugar

Mix lemon jello with cake mix, add butter and orange juice. Blend well by hand. Add eggs, 1 at a time. Put in electric mixer for 4 minutes. Pour batter into floured and greased tube pan. Bake at 350° for 50-60 minutes. Turn pan upside down for 10 minutes. Remove cake while still warm. Combine lemon juice and powdered sugar. Drizzle over cake.   Mary Weekes, Metairie
                              Council, Metairie, La.

LEMON NUT CAKE

1 lb. butter or oleo,
  softened
4 c. plain flour
6 eggs
2 c. chopped pecans

2 c. sugar
1 tsp. baking powder
2 oz. pure lemon flavoring
1 box white raisins

Cream butter and sugar together. Add eggs, 1 at a time. Add flour and baking powder. Add flavoring. Add pecans and raisins. Pour into greased and floured angel food pan and bake for 3 hours at 250°. Cut a piece of foil to fit over top of pan while baking, if desired. Remove about 20 minutes before through baking for top to brown.

Odie Mae Reynolds, Ouachita Council, Tallulah, La.

DOUBLE LEMON STREUSEL CAKE

1 pkg. Pillsbury Plus lemon cake mix	1/2 c. oleo or butter
2 eggs	3/4 c. milk
1 (8 oz.) pkg. cream cheese, softened	1/4 c. sugar
	1 Tbsp. lemon juice
1/2 c. chopped nuts	1 tsp. grated lemon peel

Cut oleo into cake mix until crumbly. Reserve 1 cup crumbs for topping. Add milk and egg to remaining crumbs. Beat 2 minutes at highest speed. Pour batter into greased and floured 13x9-inch pan. Combine cream cheese, sugar, lemon juice and peel. Blend until smooth. Drop by teaspoonfuls onto cake batter. Spread to edges of cake pan. Add nuts to reserved crumbs. Sprinkle over cream cheese mixture. Bake in preheated 350° oven for 30-35 minutes or until golden brown. Store in refrigerator. Makes 15-18 servings.

Henrietta Victor, Magnolia Council, New Orleans, La.

GREEK LEMON CAKE

2 3/4 c. flour	6 eggs, separated
1 tsp. baking soda	1 c. lemon yogurt
1/4 tsp. salt	2 c. sugar, divided
2 tsp. grated lemon rind	2 Tbsp. lemon juice

Sift flour, soda and salt together; set aside. Beat egg whites in mixer bowl until soft peaks form, gradually add 1/2 cup sugar, beating until stiff and glossy peaks form; set aside. Beat butter, egg yolks, remaining 1 1/2 cups sugar, lemon rind and juice until fluffy. Stir flour mixture alternately with yogurt into creamed butter mixture. Fold in egg whites gently. Pour into greased 10-inch tube pan. Bake in preheated 325° oven for 50-60 minutes or until tests done with toothpick. Cool in pan 10 minutes, then turn out on rack to finish cooling. Cake is good served with ice cream

514

or fresh fruit marinated in a liqueur, or ice with Cream Cheese Icing.

Cream Cheese Frosting:

2 (3 oz.) pkg. cream   1 tsp. vanilla
  cheese   1/2 stick oleo
1 lb. sifted powdered   2 tsp. lemon rind, grated
  sugar   Lemon juice to taste

Cream butter and cream cheese. Add sugar, vanilla and lemon rind. Add strained lemon juice to taste. If lemon juice does not make icing thin enough to spread, add Pet milk; however, icing should be thick and cake should be completely cool before icing.

Jeanette English, Caddo
Council, Shreveport, La.

LEMON SUPREME CAKE

1 box lemon supreme   1 c. apricot nectar
  cake mix (Duncan   1/2 c. cooking oil
  Hines)   1/2 c. sugar
4 eggs

Mix sugar, cake mix, oil and nectar together. Add eggs, 1 at a time, beating after each addition. Bake in greased and floured tube pan for 1 hour at 325°. Cool right side up 15 minutes before removing from pan.

Glaze:

1 c. powdered sugar   Juice of 1 lemon
2 Tbsp. apricot nectar

Mix ingredients and pour over cake while it is still
warm.   Virginia Ingram, Shreveport
                             Works Council, Shreveport, La.

LIME REFRIGERATOR SHEET CAKE

1 small pkg. lime jello   1 pkg. lemon cake mix
3/4 c. boiling water   1 env. Dream Whip
1/2 c. cold water   1 small pkg. lemon instant
1 1/2 c. cold sweet milk   pudding mix

Dissolve jello in boiling water, add cold water. Set

aside at room temperature. Make up cake according to
directions. Bake in 13x9x2-inch pan. Cool cake in pan
20-25 minutes after removing from oven. Take fork and
punch holes all over cake. Pour jello over and into holes in
cake. Refrigerate cake while preparing topping. In chilled
deep bowl, blend and whip Dream Whip, instant pudding and
milk until stiff, 3-8 minutes. Immediately frost cake. Refrigerate cake and serve chilled. Cake may be frozen for
storage if desired.   Artie Tabor, LeBayou
                          Council, Morgan City, La.

LINCOLN LOG

4-5 c. unsifted flour	1 1/2 tsp. salt
1/2 c. milk	1/4 c. (1/2 stick) oleo
1 (8 oz.) pkg. cream	3/4 c. sugar
cheese, softened	2 pkg. dry yeast
1/2 c. water	2 eggs, room temperature
	1 egg yolk

In large bowl, thoroughly mix 1 1/4 cups flour, 1/2 cup
sugar, salt and undissolved yeast. Heat milk, water and
oleo in saucepan until warm. Oleo need not melt. Gradually
add to dry ingredients and beat 2 minutes at medium speed.
Add 2 eggs and 1/2 cup flour to mixer. Beat at high speed
2 minutes. Stir in 2 1/4 cups flour to make soft dough. Turn
out on lightly floured board and knead until smooth and
elastic, about 8-10 minutes. Place in a greased bowl, turning to grease top. Cover, let rise in warm place about 1
hour or until double in size. Prepare filling by combining
cream cheese and 1/4 cup sugar. Cream until light and
fluffy. Blend in egg yolk, mix well. Punch dough down,
turn onto lightly floured board. Roll 1/2 of the dough into
a 10x14-inch rectangle. Spread with half the cheese filling.
Roll up as a jelly roll to form 14-inch roll. Place on greased
baking sheet. Cut slits 3/4-inch through log at 1-inch intervals. Repeat with remaining dough and filling. Cover, let
rise in warm place about 1 hour. Bake at 275° for 30-45
minutes or until light brown. Remove and cool. Frost and
decorate with cherry halves, if desired.

Frosting:

2 c. powdered sugar	3 Tbsp. milk
1 Tbsp. butter	Cherry halves (optional)

Combine and mix ingredients. Frosting should be like icing. I add cherry halves to frosting when mixing.

Jeanette Armand, Central
Council, Bunkie, La.

LOAF CAKE

1 c. Crisco, softened	3 c. sugar
6 eggs	3 c. flour
1 c. buttermilk	1/2 tsp. salt
1/4 tsp. soda	2 1/2 tsp. lemon or vanilla extract

Add salt and soda to flour. Cream Crisco and sugar together. Add eggs, 1 at a time, beating after each addition. Stir in flour and buttermilk alternately. Beat well. Pour into greased and floured loaf pan or 2 small ones. Bake at 350° for 1 hour or until toothpick comes out clean.

Jerrie Cleveland, Caddo
Council, Shreveport, La.

LOVE CAKE

8 egg whites	1 c. sweet milk
1 c. butter or oleo	1 tsp. lemon extract
2 c. sugar	3 tsp. baking powder
3 c. flour	

Cream butter and sugar. Sift baking powder with flour and add alternately with milk. Beat egg whites stiff and add to mixture. Add lemon flavor. Mix well and bake in floured and greased cake pans at 350° until done.

Icing:

8 egg yolks	1 c. coconut
1 c. pecans, chopped	1 c. butter
1 c. sugar	1 c. raisins

Beat egg yolks very lightly. Put butter and sugar in top of double boiler and mix well when butter melts. Add egg yolks and cook until thick. Remove from fire, add pecans, coconut and raisins. Ice each layer and sprinkle top and sides with dry coconut.

Betty Harmon, Caddo
Council, Shreveport, La.

LOUISIANA NUT CAKE

1 c. butter	2 c. sugar
6 eggs	1 c. whiskey
4 c. flour	1 tsp. allspice
1 pkg. raisins	2 pkg. dates, chopped
2 qt. pecans	1 tsp. soda
1 tsp. cinnamon	1 tsp. cloves

Cream butter and sugar, add eggs, 1 at a time, beating after each addition. Dredge nuts, dates and raisins in 2 cups of the flour. Mix remaining flour with spices and soda. Add to butter mixture alternately with whiskey. Fold in nuts, dates and raisins, thoroughly coated with flour. Bake in greased and floured tube, angel or Bundt pan at 250° for about 2 hours. Mary H. Armand, Central Council, Cottonport, La.

PATTY'S MAYONNAISE CAKE

2 c. flour	1 c. sugar
1 c. mayonnaise or	4 Tbsp. cocoa
salad dressing	2 tsp. soda
1 c. water	1/2 tsp. vanilla

Mix dry ingredients. Add wet ingredients. Bake in 350° oven for 30 minutes. Adrienne Dezendorf, Central Council, Alexandria, La.

MEXICAN WEDDING CAKES

3/4 c. butter or oleo	4 Tbsp. powdered sugar
2 tsp. vanilla	1 tsp. cold water
2 c. sifted flour	1/8 tsp. salt
1 c. finely chopped nuts	Powdered sugar

Cream butter and sugar together. Add vanilla and cold water. Mix thoroughly and stir in flour, salt and nuts. Shape into roll 1/2-inch in diameter. Wrap in waxed paper and chill. Cut chilled roll into 1/4-inch slices and place on ungreased cookie sheet. Bake in 400° oven for 6-8 minutes. Remove from sheet, roll in powdered sugar while still hot, cool and roll again in powdered sugar. Yield: 3 1/2 - 4 dozen cookies. Katherine Slover, Caddo Council, Phoenix, Az.

518

MILKY WAY CAKE

8 large Milky Way candy
  bars
2 c. sugar
2 1/2 c. sifted all-purpose
  flour

2 c. butter or oleo
4 eggs
1/2 tsp. baking soda
1 1/4 c. buttermilk
2 c. chopped walnuts

Combine candy bars and 1 cup oleo in top of double boiler over hot, not boiling, water until melted. Cream sugar and remaining butter until light, add eggs, 1 at a time, beating after each addition. Dissolve soda in buttermilk and add to creamed mixture alternately with flour. Add melted candy and nuts, mix until well blended. Spoon into 2 greased 9-inch round cake pans. Bake in preheated 325° oven for 35-40 minutes or until tests done. Frost cooled cake with your favorite frosting.

Henrietta Victor, Magnolia
Council, New Orleans, La.

OATMEAL CAKE

1 c. cooked quick oats
1/2 stick butter or oleo
1 Tbsp. soda
1 1/2 c. flour
2 eggs, beaten
1/2 tsp. salt

1 1/2 c. boiling water
1 tsp. vanilla
1 c. brown sugar
1 c. white sugar
1 Tbsp. cinnamon

Combine water and oatmeal. Let set 15 minutes. Combine and mix ingredients and bake in layers at 370° for 30 minutes. Cool and frost.

Coconut Pecan Frosting:

2/3 c. sugar
1/4 c. oleo
1 1/2 c. coconut
1 tsp. vanilla

2/3 c. milk
1 egg, slightly beaten
2/3 c. pecans

In heavy 2-quart saucepan, mix sugar, milk, oleo and egg. Stir over medium heat until mixture thickens and begins to bubble. Remove from heat and stir in remaining ingredients. Cool thoroughly before frosting.

Becky Flack, Central
Council, Natchitoches, La.

OATMEAL CAKE

1 1/4 c. boiling water
1 stick oleo
1 c. brown sugar
1 1/3 c. flour
1/2 tsp. baking powder
1/2 tsp. salt

1 c. 3-minute oatmeal
1 c. white sugar
2 eggs
1 tsp. soda
1 tsp. cinnamon

Pour boiling water over oatmeal, add oleo, cover and let stand 20 minutes. Add remaining ingredients. Mix well. Pour batter into greased 13x9x2-inch pan and bake at 350° for 35 minutes.

Icing or Filling:

6 Tbsp. soft oleo
1 can coconut
Nuts (optional)

1/2 c. white sugar
1/3 c. Pet milk

Mix ingredients and spread on cake. Place under broiler until coconut browns.   Twila (Pete) Dysart
                                    Ouachita Council, Monroe, La.

$100.00 CAKE

2 c. Swans Down cake
   flour
4 Tbsp. cocoa
1 c. Kraft salad dressing

1 c. sugar
2 tsp. soda
1 c. cold water
1 tsp. vanilla

Mix dry ingredients together. Place salad dressing and water in quart jar. Shake until creamy. Add vanilla. Slowly add liquid mixture to dry ingredients. Bake in greased and floured cake pans at 350° until tests done. Makes 2 layers.

Icing:

8 egg yolks
1/2 c. butter
1 c. raisins
1 c. shredded coconut

1 1/4 c. sugar
3 Tbsp. evaporated milk,
   diluted
1 c. chopped pecans
1/4 c. maraschino cherries

Mix egg yolks, sugar, butter and cream. Slowly cook until barely thickened. Do not overcook. Take off and add fruit. Ice cake.   Hazel Blouin, Shreveport
                                    Works Council, Shreveport, La.

520

OOEE GOOEE CAKE

1 box yellow cake mix
1 egg

1 block butter
1 c. chopped pecans

Mix ingredients together. Spread into 13x9x2-inch pan. Mix will be crumbly.

Topping:

1 (8 oz.) pkg. cream
  cheese

1 box powdered sugar
1 egg

Mix all ingredients together. Spread on top of cake mixture. Bake at 350° for 35-40 minutes, until golden brown. Let cake cool completely before cutting.

Joyce Silva, Capital
Council, Baton Rouge, La.

ORANGE CANDY CAKE

1 c. butter
1 (8 oz.) pkg. dates,
  cut up
2 c. chopped pecans
1 tsp. salt
1 Tbsp. vanilla
1/2 tsp. soda

5 eggs
1 pkg. orange candy slices
  (1 lb.), cut up
2 c. sugar
1 (4 oz.) can coconut
3/4 c. buttermilk
4 c. sifted flour

Cream butter and sugar until light and fluffy. Beat in eggs, 1 at a time. Add vanilla. Mix dates, candy, nuts and coconut with 1/4 cup of the flour. Sift remaining flour with baking soda and salt. Alternately fold into creamed mixture with buttermilk. Fold in date mixture. Pour batter into greased and floured 10-inch tube pan. Bake at 300° for 2 1/2 hours. Remove cake and pour on Lemon Syrup immediately. Set pan on rack, cool. Remove cake from pan when cooled thoroughly. Wrap tightly in foil and refrigerate 1 day or longer before serving.

Lemon Syrup:

1 tsp. grated lemon peel
1/4 c. lemon juice
1/4 c. orange juice

1 tsp. grated orange peel
1/2 c. sifted powdered
  sugar

Mix ingredients together; pour over hot cake.

Mearl S. Byles, Central
Council, Natchitoches, La.

FRESH ORANGE CAKE

2 1/2 c. sifted cake flour
3/4 c. strained orange
  juice
1 tsp. salt
3 eggs
1 Tbsp. grated orange rind

1 2/3 c. sugar
2/3 c. Crisco
3 1/2 tsp. baking powder
1/3 c. water
1 tsp. vanilla

Measure flour, Crisco, sugar, salt and orange juice in mixing bowl. Beat for 2 minutes. Stir in baking powder. Add remaining ingredients and mix thoroughly for 2 minutes. Pour into 2 greased and floured 9-inch cake pans. Bake at 350° for 25-30 minutes. Allow cake to cool in pan on rack before removing. Ice with Cream Cheese Icing with orange juice and grated orange rind added.

Jeanette English, Caddo
Council, Shreveport, La.

MANDARIN ORANGE CAKE

1 box Duncan Hines butter
  cake mix
4 eggs

1 (11 oz.) can Mandarin
  oranges
3/4 c. Crisco oil

Mix ingredients together and bake 18-20 minutes at 350°. Save a few oranges as garnish for top of cake.

Icing:

1 large bowl Cool Whip
1 large can crushed
  pineapple

1 large box instant vanilla
  pudding

Mix ingredients together and spread on cake.

Sylvia Campbell, Caddo
Council, Shreveport, La.

ORANGE SLICE CAKE

1 c. butter or 2 sticks
3 1/2 c. flour
1 tsp. soda
2 Tbsp. grated orange rind
2 c. pecans, chopped
1 pkg. dates, chopped

2 c. sugar
1/2 c. buttermilk
4 eggs
2 c. candy orange slices,
  cut small, or candy gumdrops (no black)

Mix butter, sugar and eggs. Dissolve soda in buttermilk, add to mixture. Add orange rind, fruits, nuts and candy. Mix and bake in floured and greased tube pan at 250° (very slow) for 3 1/2 hours.

Glaze:

2 c. powdered sugar   1 c. fresh orange juice

Mix and pour over cake while it is still hot.

Marie Pamplin, Shreveport
Works Council, Shreveport, La.

ORANGE SLICE CAKE

1 c. butter
2 c. sugar
3 1/2 c. flour
1 pkg. chopped dates
2 c. nuts
1 can coconut

4 eggs
1 tsp. orange juice
1/2 c. buttermilk
3 c. orange slice candy,
    cut fine

Mix dates, orange slices, nuts and coconut with 1/2 cup of the flour. Combine and mix ingredients. Pour batter into greased and floured tube or Bundt pan and bake 2 hours at 250°.

Glaze:

1 c. powdered sugar   1/4 c. orange juice

Mix and pour over cake while hot.

Cream Icing:

2 c. sugar
1/2 c. butter
1 c. nuts
1 tsp. orange juice

1 Tbsp. flour
2/3 c. evaporated milk
1 c. coconut

Combine sugar, butter, flour and milk. Cook until soft ball stage is reached. Add remaining ingredients and frost cake.

Rebecca Scott, Caddo
Council, Shreveport, La.

PEA PICKIN CAKE

1 pkg. Duncan Hines butter cake mix
3 eggs

1 can Mandarin oranges with juice
1/4 c. Crisco oil

Blend well. Grease and flour 3 round pans. Bake at 350° for 30-40 minutes.

Frosting:

1 can crushed pineapple
1 container Cool Whip

1 large pkg. instant vanilla pudding mix

Make up instant pudding according to directions. Fold in pineapple and add Cool Whip. Frost cooled cake.

Mearl S. Byles, Central Council, Natchitoches, La.

DELL'S PEACH NUT CAKE

2 c. sugar
3 whole eggs
2 tsp. soda
1 c. chopped pecans

2 sticks oleo
1 c. buttermilk
2 c. flour
2 c. mashed, drained peaches

Mix sugar, oleo, eggs, buttermilk in which soda has been dissolved. Dredge nuts in small amount of flour, add remaining flour to mixture. Add peaches, well drained, and nuts. Pour into greased and floured cake pan or 9x13x2-inch pan.

Icing:

1 stick oleo
1 can Pet milk (large)
1 Tbsp. flour

3 egg yolks
1 c. sugar

Heat and bring to desired thickness for spreading. Ice cake and refrigerate any leftover Icing for use later.

Marie Pamplin, Shreveport Works Council, Shreveport, La.

PEACH PRESERVE CAKE

1 c. buttermilk
1 c. oleo (2 sticks)
4 eggs
1 tsp. cinnamon
1 c. chopped nuts

1 tsp. soda
2 c. sugar
3 c. self-rising flour
1/2 tsp. ground cloves
1 c. peach preserves

Mix soda with buttermilk. Add oleo, eggs and sugar. Combine flour, cinnamon, cloves and nuts, add to sugar mixture. Add preserves last. Do not use mixer after adding preserves. Pour into greased and floured tube or long pan. Bake at 300° for 1 hour or until done.

Judy Crosslin, Shreveport
Works Council, Shreveport, La.

FRESH PEAR CAKE

4 c. grated fresh pears
1 c. chopped nuts
1/2 tsp. salt
1/2 tsp. nutmeg or
   cinnamon
1 c. cooking oil

2 c. sugar
3 c. flour
2 tsp. soda
2 large eggs, beaten
1 tsp. vanilla

Mix pears, sugar and nuts together and set aside to accumulate juice for 1 hour. Add oil, vanilla and beaten eggs to pear mixture. Sift dry ingredients and add to pear mixture. Do not use mixer to mix ingredients. Pour into floured and greased tube pan and bake at 350° for 1 hour and 15 minutes.

Vivian Furlow, Caddo
Council, Shreveport, La.

PINA COLADA CAKE

1 pkg. white cake mix
4 eggs
1 c. flaked coconut
1/3 c. dark rum

1 small pkg. Jell-O instant
   vanilla or coconut pudding
   mix
1/2 c. water
1/4 c. Wesson oil

Blend all ingredients, except coconut, in large mixer bowl. Beat 4 minutes at medium speed. Pour into 2 greased and floured 9-inch layer pans. Bake at 350° for 25-30 minutes or until cake tests done. Cool in pan 15 minutes.

Remove and cool on racks. Fill and frost. Sprinkle with coconut. Chill. Refrigerate leftover cake.

Note: If vanilla flavor pudding mix is used, increase water to 3/4 cup; add 1 cup flaked coconut to batter.

Frosting:

1 (8 oz.) can crushed pineapple, undrained
1/3 c. dark rum

1 small pkg. Jell-O coconut or vanilla instant pudding mix
1 (9 oz.) bowl Cool Whip or frozen whipped topping

Combine all ingredients except Cool Whip in bowl. Beat until well blended. Fold in thawed whipped topping.

Betty Tujague, Crescent City Council, New Orleans, La.

PINEAPPLE CAKE

2 c. sugar
1 tsp. soda
2 c. self-rising flour
1/4 tsp. salt

1 tsp. vanilla
2 eggs, beaten
1 (No. 2) can crushed pineapple and juice

Mix sugar, soda, flour and salt together. Add remaining ingredients. Mix well and pour into greased and floured pan. Bake at 350° until done. Pour Icing over cake while it is still hot.

Icing:

1 c. sugar
1 stick oleo

1/2 c. evaporated milk
1/2 c. coconut

Combine sugar, milk and oleo. Cook until thick, about 10 minutes. Add coconut. Pour over hot cake.

Dell Watson, Shreveport Works Council, Shreveport, La.

PINEAPPLE CAKE

1 box yellow cake mix
1 small instant vanilla pudding
Nuts

1 large can crushed pineapple, undrained
1 medium bowl Cool Whip

Mix cake as directed on package. Bake in 13x9-inch pan. Cool. Make up instant pudding as directed. Jab holes in cake with fork and pour pineapple and juice all over cake. Spread instant pudding over cake. Top with Cool Whip and sprinkle with nuts. Refrigerate.

Della Delposen, Ouachita
Council, Monroe, La.

PINEAPPLE CAKE

1 pkg. Duncan Hines butter recipe yellow cake mix
1 stick oleo

1 medium can crushed pineapple
1 c. sugar

Mix cake according to package instructions. Save 1 cup batter for icing. Bake according to directions, cool. Combine crushed pineapple, oleo, sugar and batter in saucepan. Bring to boil. Cook until clear and thick. Frost cooled cake.

Bernice Wright, Caddo
Council, Shreveport, La.

CREAMY PINEAPPLE CAKE

1 box yellow cake mix
1 small can crushed pineapple
1 Tbsp. finely chopped pecans

1/2 stick butter
1 small pkg. cream cheese
1 Tbsp. pineapple preserves

Make up cake mix as directed on box, except use 1 tablespoon less liquid than called for. Combine crushed pineapple and butter, cream until smooth and add to cake mixture. Pour cake mix into greased and floured Bundt pan and bake at 350° until done. It may be necessary to bake slightly longer than box directions call for. Cream together cream cheese, pineapple preserves and pecans. Serve glob of cheese mixture with each slice of cake, or use cake decorator to garnish top of cake with this mixture. This is especially good served warm.

Enola Fee, Crescent City
Council, New Orleans, La.

PINEAPPLE SHEET CAKE

2 c. sugar
2 c. plain flour
1 tsp. soda
Pinch of salt

2 eggs
1/3 c. cooking oil
1 large (20 oz.) can crushed
  pineapple, undrained

Mix ingredients and pour into 13x9x2-inch pan. Bake at 300° for 45 minutes.

Icing:

2/3 c. milk
1 c. sugar
1 c. chopped pecans

1 stick oleo
1 tsp. vanilla
1 c. coconut

Combine milk, sugar, oleo and vanilla. Bring to boil, boil for 10 minutes. Add pecans and coconut and spread over top of cake while hot. Marie Pamplin, Shreveport Works Council, Shreveport, La.

PLUM CAKE

2 c. flour
1/2 tsp. salt
3 eggs
1/2 tsp. cloves
3/4 c. vegetable oil
2 jars plum baby food

1 3/4 c. sugar
1/2 tsp. baking powder
1/2 tsp. soda
1 tsp. cinnamon
1 c. chopped pecans

Mix all ingredients together until well blended. Pour into greased and floured Bundt pan. Bake at 300° for 1 hour - 1 hour and 15 minutes. Rebecca Thames, Caddo Council, Shreveport, La.

PLUM CAKE

2 c. self-rising flour
2 jars baby food (plums)
1 c. broken pecans
  (large pieces)
1 tsp. ground cloves

2 c. sugar
1 c. salad oil
1 tsp. cinnamon
3 eggs

Mix ingredients together. Pour into greased and floured Bundt pan or 2 loaf pans. Bake at 325° for 60-90 minutes. Cool in pan 25 minutes. Remove from pan and drizzle with Glaze.

Glaze:

1 c. sifted powdered
  sugar

2 Tbsp. lemon juice

Aline Well, Capital Council,
Baton Rouge, La.

CHRISTMAS PECAN CAKE

2 c. butter or oleo
6 eggs
1 tsp. grated lemon peel
4 c. chopped pecans
3 c. sifted all-purpose
  flour

2 c. sugar
1 Tbsp. lemon juice
1 Tbsp. vanilla
1 1/2 c. golden raisins
1/4 tsp. salt
1 tsp. baking powder

Cream butter and sugar until fluffy. Beat in eggs, 1 at a time. Add lemon juice, peel and vanilla. Mix nuts and raisins with 1/4 cup of the flour. Sift remaining dry ingredients and fold alternately with nuts and raisins into butter and sugar mixture. Pour into greased and floured tube or Bundt pan. Bake at 350° for about 1 hour.

Martha Starkey, Capital
Council, Baton Rouge, La.

BEN FRANKLIN PECAN CAKE

1 lb. butter or oleo
6 eggs
1 tsp. baking powder
1/2 lb. candied cherries
1 lb. chopped pecans

2 c. sugar
4 c. flour
1/4 tsp. salt
1/2 lb. candied pineapple
2 tsp. vanilla

Cream butter and sugar. Add beaten eggs all at once. Add 3 cups flour sifted with baking powder and salt. Dredge candied fruit and pecans with remaining flour and add to mixture. Add vanilla and mix thoroughly. Pour into greased and floured tube pan. Bake at 250° for 3 hours. Cool in pan completely before removing.

Julia B. Ulmer, Caddo
Council, Shreveport, La.

POPPY SEED CAKE

3 c. flour, unsifted	2 c. sugar
12 oz. cooking oil	4 eggs
1 tsp. vanilla	1/2 tsp. salt
1 1/2 tsp. baking soda	13 oz. canned milk
1 c. chopped nuts (optional)	1 can Solo poppy seed mix

Sift dry ingredients, add liquids and mix until smooth. Add poppy seed and nuts. Beat well on medium speed for 10 minutes. Pour into ungreased 10-inch angel food tube pan (2 piece). Bake in preheated 350° oven for 1 hour and 10 minutes or until tested done. Cool cake before removing from pan. Very good as is or with almond flavored glaze.

Mrs. Floyd (Barbara) Jessup
Calcasieu Council
Lake Charles, La.

POUND CAKE

2 sticks oleo	1/2 c. Crisco
5 eggs	3 c. sugar
3 c. flour	1 c. milk
1 tsp. baking powder	1 tsp. vanilla

Mix ingredients together thoroughly. Pour batter into greased and floured tube or Bundt pan. Bake at 350° for 1 hour.

Bettye Lee, Shreveport Works
Council, Shreveport, La.

POUND CAKE

2 c. flour	1 c. butter
2 c. sugar	4 eggs
1/2 tsp. cream of tartar	1 tsp. vanilla
1 c. chopped pecans	

Cream sugar and butter. Beat in eggs, 1 at a time. Add vanilla, cream of tartar and 1 1/2 cups of the flour. Mix well. Dredge pecans in remaining flour and fold all into batter. Pour into greased and floured tube pan. Bake at 350° for 1 hour or until toothpick comes out clean.

Gloria Fontenot, Evangeline
Council, Lafayette, La.

POUND CAKE
(Ulcer Diet)

6 eggs
1 3/4 c. sugar
2 c. plain flour

2 tsp. vanilla
2 1/4 c. butter or oleo

Cream sugar and butter. Add eggs, 1 at a time. Add flour and flavoring. Pour into greased and floured tube or Bundt pan. Bake at 350° for 1 hour or until tester comes out clean.

Mrs. Vernie McAlister
Crescent City Council
Chalmette, La.

BOURBON POUND CAKE

1 lb. oleo
3 c. sugar
8 eggs, separated
3 c. flour

1 tsp. vanilla
1 tsp. almond flavoring
4 Tbsp. bourbon
1 c. chopped nuts

Cream butter and sugar, add egg yolks. Beat well. Add flour, flavoring and bourbon. Add beaten egg whites gradually with mixer set on "fold." Sprinkle 1/2 of nuts in bottom of pan. Add batter and sprinkle remainder of nuts on top. Bake at 325° for 1 1/2 hours in greased and floured tube pan.

Verle Oliphant, Caddo
Council, Shreveport, La.

BUTTERMILK POUND CAKE

1 1/2 c. cooking oil
4 eggs
1/2 tsp. salt
1 c. buttermilk
1 Tbsp. vanilla

2 1/2 c. sugar
3 1/2 c. flour
1/2 tsp. soda
1 Tbsp. hot water

Dissolve soda in hot water. Mix all ingredients together. Bake in floured and greased tube pan at 325° for 1 1/2 hours. Ice with Lemon Glaze while hot.

Lemon Glaze:

1 c. powdered sugar   Juice of 1 lemon
1 tsp. lemon extract

Combine ingredients and ice cake.

Mary Quimby, Ouachita
Council, Monroe, La.

BUTTERMILK POUND CAKE

3 c. flour   3 c. sugar
1 c. shortening   1 c. buttermilk
6 eggs (beat separately)   1/2 tsp. salt
1/4 tsp. soda   1 tsp. lemon flavoring

Blend sugar and shortening. Add egg yolks, 1 at a time. Sift dry ingredients together. Mix alternately with buttermilk to sugar mixture. Fold in egg whites. Bake in greased and floured tube pan at 350° for 1 hour.

Jeanette Williams, Caddo
Council, Shreveport, La.

BUTTERMILK POUND CAKE

3 c. sugar   1 stick oleo
6 eggs   1/2 c. Crisco
2 tsp. vanilla   1 c. buttermilk
3 c. flour   1/4 tsp. baking soda

Cream butter and sugar together. Add remaining ingredients. Stir until well mixed. Bake in greased and floured Bundt pan at 350° for 1 hour and 20 minutes or until done.

Rebecca Thames, Caddo
Council, Shreveport, La.

BUTTERMILK POUND CAKE

1/4 lb. butter   2 1/2 c. sugar
4 eggs   3 c. cake flour
1/4 tsp. soda   1/2 tsp. salt
1 c. buttermilk   1 tsp. vanilla

Cream butter, add sugar and cream thoroughly. Add eggs, 1 at a time, beating constantly. Sift flour, soda and

532

salt 4 times. Add alternately to mixture with buttermilk. Add vanilla. Cut waxed paper for bottom of tube pan and grease well. Pour batter into pan and bake at 350° for 1 hour and 15 minutes. Remove from pan and dust with powdered sugar.

Mearl S. Byles, Central
Council, Natchitoches, La.

BUTTERNUT POUND CAKE

3 c. sugar
1 (8 oz.) pkg. cream
   cheese
6 eggs, separated
3 c. cake flour

1 1/2 c. butter
2 tsp. vanilla, butter and
   nut flavorings
Powdered sugar

Cream sugar, butter and cream cheese until light and fluffy, beat in flavorings. Add egg yolks, 1 at a time, beating well after each addition. Add cake flour, mixing well. Beat egg whites until stiff peaks form, fold into batter. Pour into greased 10-inch tube or Bundt pan. Bake at 325° for 1 hour and 15 minutes or until done. Cool thoroughly and sprinkle with sifted powdered sugar.

Jeanette English, Caddo
Council, Shreveport, La.

CHOCOLATE POUND CAKE

1 c. butter
3 c. sugar
3 c. flour
1/2 tsp. salt
1 c. milk

1/2 c. Crisco shortening
5 eggs
1 tsp. vanilla
1/2 tsp. baking powder
4 Tbsp. cocoa

Cream fats, add sugar and continue creaming. Add eggs, 1 at a time, beating well after each addition. Stir in vanilla, then the sifted dry ingredients alternately with milk. Bake in greased and floured angel food or Bundt pan for 1 hour and 20 minutes at 325°; if divided into loaf pans, bake shorter time.

Frosting:

2 sq. chocolate
Powdered sugar
Milk or cream

1/2 stick butter
1 tsp. vanilla

1723-79

Melt chocolate and butter. Add powdered sugar, vanilla and cream as needed for proper consistency.

Doris Reeves, Capital
Council, Baton Rouge, La.

CHOCOLATE POUND CAKE

3 c. all-purpose flour
1/2 c. cocoa
1 tsp. baking powder
1/2 c. Crisco
1 1/4 c. milk

3 c. sugar
1/4 tsp. salt
2 sticks oleo
6 large eggs
3 tsp. vanilla

Cream oleo, shortening and sugar together. Add eggs, 1 at a time, beating well after each addition. Sift all dry ingredients together and add alternately with milk. Add vanilla, blend thoroughly. Bake in greased and lightly floured tube pan at 325° for about 1 1/2 hours or until tests done.

Mrs. R.D. (Vermelle) Sylvest
Ozone Council, Hammond, La.

COCONUT POUND CAKE

3 sticks oleo
3 c. sugar
5 egg yolks
3 c. Swans Down cake flour

2 tsp. coconut flavoring
1 c. milk
1 can Angel Flake coconut
5 egg whites, beaten stiff

Cream oleo and sugar. Add egg yolks, 1 at a time, beating the flour and milk alternating about 3 times until all is added. Add remaining ingredients and fold in stiffly beaten egg whites. Pour batter into greased and floured angel food cake pan. Bake at 325° for 1 hour and 10 minutes. I place a small pan of water on rack under my cake while baking.

Mollie Haskins, Caddo
Council, Shreveport, La.

COCONUT POUND CAKE

3 sticks butter
6 eggs
1 tsp. baking powder
2 Tbsp. vanilla or lemon
    flavoring

3 c. sugar
3 c. plain flour
1 c. canned milk
3 drops almond flavor
1 pkg. coconut

Cream butter and sugar until light and fluffy. Add eggs, 1 at a time, beating after each addition. Mix flour and baking powder together. Add alternately with milk and flavoring. Fold in coconut. Pour in greased, lined (bottom only) 10-inch tube pan. Bake at 325° for 1 1/2 hours.

Dell Watson, Shreveport
Works Council, Shreveport, La.

COCONUT POUND CAKE

6 eggs	1 c. shortening
1/2 c. oleo	3 c. sugar
1/2 tsp. almond flavoring	3 c. sifted flour
1/2 tsp. coocnut flavoring	1 c. milk
2 c. fresh coconut	

Mix ingredients together. Pour into greased and floured tube or Bundt pan. Bake in preheated 300° oven for 2 hours.

Mrs. Lucille Smith, Ouachita
Council, Monroe, La.

COCONUT POUND CAKE

3 sticks oleo	1/4 tsp. soda
3 c. sugar	1 (8 oz.) carton sour cream
3 c. flour	1 tsp. coconut extract
6 eggs	1 tsp. rum extract
3/4 c. coconut	

Cream sugar and oleo, add eggs, 1 at a time. Add flour and soda. Add sour cream, coconut and flavorings. Pour into greased and floured tube pan. Bake at 325° for 1 1/2 hours. Remove from pan and glaze cake.

Glaze:

3/4 c. sugar	3/4 c. water
1 tsp. almond extract	

Cook over high heat for 5 minutes and pour over cake.

Sadie Foil, Ozone Council,
Bogalusa, La.

COLD OVEN POUND CAKE

3 c. sugar
1/2 c. Crisco
5 eggs
1/2 tsp. baking powder
1 c. milk
1/2 tsp. lemon extract

2 sticks oleo, or 1/2 lb. butter
3 c. flour
1/2 tsp. salt
1/8 tsp. vanilla
1 small container sour cream

Cream sugar, oleo and Crisco until light, add eggs; mix well. Add alternately flour, baking powder, salt, milk, vanilla and lemon extract. Beat 12 minutes total. Before beating is stopped, add sour cream and finish beating. Start cake in cold oven and bake about 75 minutes at 325°. This is my mother's recipe.   Marcia A. Horton, Capital
                                                Council, Baton Rouge, La.

CONFEDERATE POUND CAKE

2 c. all-purpose flour,
   sifted
1 tsp. vanilla

2 sticks butter or oleo
2 c. sugar
5 eggs

Cream butter and sugar until light and fluffy. Blend in vanilla. Add eggs, 1 at a time, alternately with flour, beating well after each addition. Bake in greased and floured tube pan for about 1 1/2 hours at 325°.
                                                Mrs. Richard D. (Vermelle)
                                                Sylvest, Ozone Council,
                                                Hammond, La.

CREAM CHEESE POUND CAKE

6 eggs
3 c. self-rising flour
3/4 lb. butter
1 tsp. lemon extract

3 c. sugar
1 (8 oz.) pkg. cream cheese
1 tsp. vanilla extract

Mix cream cheese, butter and sugar. Sift flour and add to other ingredients. Add 2 eggs at a time. Add extracts. Pour into 2 greased and floured loaf pans. Bake at 325° for 1 hour and 25 minutes.   Patti Regep, Metairie
                                                Council, River Ridge, La.

CREAM CHEESE POUND CAKE

3 sticks butter, softened
3 c. sugar
6 eggs
3 c. plain flour

1 (8 oz.) pkg. cream cheese, softened
1 Tbsp. lemon or vanilla flavoring

Whip cream cheese and butter together. Add sugar, blend well. Add eggs alternately with flour, beating well after each addition. Add flavoring. Pour batter into greased and floured Bundt pan. Bake at 350° for 1 1/2 hours.

Ann Flint, Caddo Council, Shreveport, La.

EASY POUND CAKE

2 c. sugar
2 sticks oleo, softened
1 tsp. lemon flavoring

5 eggs
1 tsp. vanilla flavoring

Cream sugar and oleo together. Add eggs, 1 at a time. Add remaining ingredients. Pour batter into greased and floured tube, loaf or Bundt pan. Bake at 350° for 1 hour.

Bernice Wright, Caddo Council, Shreveport, La.

GERMAN CHOCOLATE POUND CAKE

1 pkg. German's sweet chocolate
2 sticks oleo or butter
2 tsp. vanilla extract
3 c. sifted flour
1/2 tsp. soda
1 tsp. salt

2 c. sugar
4 eggs
2 tsp. imported butter flavoring
1 c. buttermilk, or 1 c. milk + 1 Tbsp. white vinegar may be substituted

Partially melt chocolate in double boiler over hot water; cool. Cream sugar and butter. Add eggs, 1 at a time, beating after each addition. Add flavorings and buttermilk. Sift flour, salt and soda together, add to mixture. Blend in melted or softened chocolate. Pour into well greased and floured tube pan. Bake at 300° about 1 hour and 10 minutes. Remove from pan in about 15 minutes, while still hot. Place under a tightly fitted cover until cool. This makes a moist cake. Glaze with German Sweet Chocolate Glaze. This cake is my family's favorite. Its best advantage is that it stays fresh to the last slice.

German Sweet Chocolate Glaze:

1 pkg. German's sweet chocolate	1 Tbsp. oleo or butter 1/4 c. water
1 c. or more sifted powdered sugar	1/2 tsp. vanilla extract Dash of salt

Melt chocolate, oleo and water in saucepan over low heat. Mix sugar and salt. Blend in chocolate mixture. Add vanilla. Pour over cake and let drip over sides of cake or add more sifted sugar and ice the cake completely.

Mrs. Joe Nasello, Central
Council, Alexandria, La.

FIVE MINUTE POUND CAKE

2 2/3 c. plain flour	2 c. sugar
1 tsp. baking powder	1 1/2 tsp. salt
1 c. shortening	5 eggs
3/4 c. milk	1 1/2 tsp. vanilla

Sift dry ingredients together. Add shortening and eggs. Mix for 3 minutes on medium speed, scraping bowl and beaters often. Add milk and vanilla. Mix on medium speed additional 2 minutes, scraping bowl and beaters often. Pour batter into greased and floured 10-inch tube pan, 4 inches deep. Bake at 325° for 1 1/4 hours or until done.

Grace Bell, Ouachita Council,
Monroe, La.

MILLION DOLLAR POUND CAKE

3 c. sugar	1 lb. butter or oleo, softened
6 eggs, room temperature	
3/4 c. milk	4 c. all-purpose flour
1 tsp. almond extract	1 tsp. vanilla extract

Cream sugar and butter together until light and fluffy. Add eggs, 1 at a time, beating well after each addition. Add flour alternately to creamed mixture with milk, beating well after each addition. Stir in flavorings. Pour batter into greased and floured 10-inch tube pan. Bake at 350°

for 1 hour and 40 minutes, or until cake tests done. This recipe makes a big beautiful pound cake.

Denise Barteet, Caddo
Council, Shreveport, La.

MISSISSIPPI POUND CAKE

1 c. butter	3 c. sugar
6 large eggs	3 c. cake flour
1 carton whipping cream	2 tsp. vanilla

Mix sugar, butter and 1 egg at a time. Beat well. Stir in flour, vanilla and whipping cream (do not whip). Pour in greased and floured tube pan and bake at 325° for 1 hour and 15 minutes. Do not preheat oven.

B.B. Wynne, Shreveport
Works Council, Shreveport, La.

MAHOGANY POUND CAKE

2 1/2 c. flour	1/2 c. cocoa
1 c. softened butter	2 c. white sugar
1 c. brown sugar	6 egg yolks
1 tsp. vanilla	1 c. sour cream
1/4 tsp. baking soda	6 egg whites

Sift flour and cocoa together, set aside. Combine butter and sugars, beat until light and fluffy. Add egg yolks, 1 at a time, beating after each addition. Stir in vanilla. Combine sour cream and baking soda. Add to creamed mixture, alternately with dry ingredients. Beat egg whites until stiff, fold into batter. Pour into well greased 10-inch tube pan. Bake in preheated 325° oven for 1 1/2 hours or until tests done. Cool slightly, remove from pan. Dust with powdered sugar.

Lynn Babin, Westmoor
Council, Kenner, La.

PINEAPPLE POUND CAKE

1/2 c. vegetable shortening	1/2 c. butter or oleo
2 1/2 c. sugar	6 large eggs
3 c. sifted all-purpose flour	1 tsp. baking powder
1/4 c. milk	3/4 c. crushed pineapple
1 tsp. vanilla extract	with juice

Cream shortening, butter and sugar. Add eggs, 1 at a time, beating after each addition. Add flour sifted with baking powder, a little at a time, alternately with milk. Add vanilla. Stir in crushed pineapple and juice. Pour batter into well greased 10-inch tube pan. Bake at 325° for 1 1/2 hours or until tests done. Let stand a few minutes in pan. Run knife around edge and remove to rack.

Topping:

1/4 c. butter or oleo
1/2 c. powdered sugar

1 c. crushed pineapple, drained

Combine butter, sugar and pineapple. Pour over cake while hot.

Ann Orr, Evangeline Council, New Iberia, La.

SHERRY POUND CAKE

1 pkg. Duncan Hines yellow cake mix
5 eggs

1 pkg. instant vanilla pudding
1 c. cream sherry
3/4 c. buttery Wesson oil

Mix ingredients and whip for 10 minutes. Bake in greased and floured Bundt cake pan at 350° for approximately 55 minutes.

Verle Oliphant, Caddo Council, Shreveport, La.

SOUR CREAM POUND CAKE

1 pkg. Duncan Hines yellow butter cake mix
1 c. sour cream
1/4 c. apricot nectar

4 eggs
1/4 c. sugar
1 stick butter or oleo, melted

Whip eggs, sugar and melted butter together. Add nectar, mix well. Add cake mix. Stir only until well mixed. Add sour cream. Pour into greased and floured tube pan and bake at 350° for 45 minutes. Glaze.

Glaze:

2 Tbsp. apricot nectar

1 c. sugar

Mix and drizzle over cake.

Lynn Elkins, Caddo Council, Shreveport, La.

SWEET CREAM POUND CAKE

6 eggs
3 c. plain flour
1/2 pt. whipping cream
  (do not whip)

3 c. sugar
1/2 lb. butter (2 sticks),
  room temperature
1 Tbsp. vanilla or almond
  flavoring

Cream butter and sugar. Add 2 eggs and 1 cup flour alternately until eggs and flour are all mixed in. Fold in whipping cream. Pour batter into greased and floured Bundt pan. Place in cold oven. Set at 300° and bake for 1 1/2 - 2 hours.
    Maxine Fletcher, Ouachita Council, Monroe, La.

PRALINE ICEBOX CAKE

2 sticks butter
5 egg yolks
7 Tbsp. praline liqueur
Large size Cool Whip
3 doz. ladyfingers

1 box powdered sugar
5 egg whites
1 c. nuts, chopped fine
1/4 c. broken pecan pieces
1/4 tsp. cream of tartar

Marinate the 1/4 cup pecan pieces in 1 tablespoon liqueur. Cream butter and sugar together. Beat egg yolks well and add the remaining 6 tablespoons liqueur to them. Mix well and add to oleo mixture. Beat egg whites with cream of tartar until stiff. Fold into mixture. Fold in chopped nuts. Line bottom of 9x13-inch glass dish with waxed paper. Open ladyfingers and cover bottom. Cover with layer of butter mixture. Repeat layers, finishing with ladyfingers. Top with Cool Whip. Sprinkle with marinated pecans. Cover with Saran Wrap and refrigerate at least 4 hours.
    Joyce Hattier, Magnolia Council, New Orleans, La.

QUICKIES

Day old bread
Eagle Brand milk

Coconut

Trim crusts, cut bread in half or fingers. Dip in milk, roll in coconut. Bake at 350° for 5-6 minutes, or can be placed under broiler until bubbly.
    Clara Westbrook, Shreveport Works Council, Shreveport, La.

PUMPKIN ROLL

3 eggs
1 c. sugar
1/2 tsp. cinnamon
Chopped nuts

2/3 c. canned pumpkin
1 tsp. baking soda
3/4 c. all-purpose flour
Powdered sugar

Mix eggs, sugar, cinnamon, pumpkin, soda and flour together. Pour batter into greased and waxed paper lined jelly roll pan. Sprinkle with nuts. Bake at 375° oven for 15 minutes. Sprinkle dish towel with powdered sugar, turn and roll up in dish towel until cool.

Filling:

2 Tbsp. butter
1 (8 oz.) pkg. cream
  cheese

3/4 tsp. vanilla
1 c. powdered sugar
1 c. chopped nuts

Mix together. Unwrap and spread Filling. Rewrap roll and sprinkle with powdered sugar if desired.

Beverly Krause, Ouachita
Council, Monroe, La.

RAINBOW ICE CREAM CAKE

1 (10-inch) angel food
  cake
1 (3 oz.) pkg. lime jello
1 (10 oz.) pkg. frozen
  strawberries, partially
  thawed, undrained
1 (11 oz.) can Mandarin
  oranges

1 (3 oz.) pkg. strawberry
  jello
1 (3 oz.) pkg. orange-pineapple jello
1/2 gal. vanilla ice cream,
  softened
1 (15 1/2 oz.) can crushed
  pineapple, drained

Cut cake into thirds. Tear each third into bite size pieces and place in separate mixing bowls. Sprinkle each portion with 1 flavor of dry jello; strawberry, lime and orange-pineapple. Toss cake pieces until all are evenly coated with dry jello. Place strawberry flavored cake pieces in 10-inch tube pan, spoon strawberries over cake pieces and spread evenly with 2 2/3 cups ice cream. Repeat layering in following order - lime flavored cake pieces topped with pineapple and 2 2/3 cups ice cream; orange-pineapple cake pieces topped with Mandarin oranges and remaining 2 2/3 cups ice cream. Cover pan tightly with foil. Freeze at least 2 days. Unmold onto chilled plate. Let stand at room temperature for 10-15 minutes. Slice and serve. Yield: About 15 servings.

Mae Briley, Central
Council, Alexandria, La.

RED CAKE

1/2 c. shortening	2 eggs
1 1/2 c. sugar	1 small bottle red food
2 Tbsp. cocoa	coloring
1 tsp. vanilla	2 1/4 c. sifted flour
1 c. buttermilk	1/2 tsp. salt
	1 tsp. vinegar

Cream shortening, sugar and eggs. Make paste of cocoa and food coloring, add to creamed mixture. Sift flour and salt together, add alternately with buttermilk. Add vanilla. Stir soda in vinegar and add to mixture. Stir, don't beat. Bake in 2 large greased and floured cake pans at 350° for 25-30 minutes. Cool on rack. Split the layers with string to have 4 thin layers and frost.

Frosting:

1 c. milk	1 c. oleo
3 Tbsp. flour	1 c. powdered sugar
1 tsp. vanilla	

Cook milk and flour until thick, cool; must be cool. Beat oleo and powdered sugar until light and fluffy. Add vanilla and cooked milk-flour mixture. Beat until it reaches consistency of whipped cream. Spread between the 4 layers and on top.

Johnnie Mae Cole, Caddo
Council, Shreveport, La.

RED VELVET CAKE

1/2 c. Crisco	1 1/2 c. sugar
2 eggs	2 c. Swans Down cake flour
1 Tbsp. cocoa	1 tsp. salt
1 c. buttermilk	2 oz. red food coloring
1/2 tsp. vanilla concentrate	1/2 tsp. almond flavoring
1 tsp. baking soda	1 Tbsp. vinegar

Cream Crisco, sugar and eggs. Sift cake flour,

cocoa and salt together 3 times. Add alternately with buttermilk to Crisco mixture. Add food coloring, flavorings and soda mixed with vinegar. Pour into greased and floured cake pans and bake at 350° for 25-30 minutes. Test for doneness. Cool.

Red Velvet Icing:

1 c. milk	1/2 c. Crisco
1/4 c. flour	1 stick oleo
Dash of salt	1 c. sugar
1 tsp. vanilla	1 tsp. almond flavoring
Desugared Oreo cookies	

Cook milk, flour and salt over low flame to pudding stage. Cool in refrigerator. Cream Crisco, oleo and sugar. Add flavorings. Add mixture to cooled pudding mix. Beat until smooth. Add desugared, crumbled Oreo cookies. Spread between layers and then ice thickly the top and sides of cake. Refrigerate until ready for special occasion. Yum! Delicious!   Sylvia S. Williams, Metairie
Council, Kenner, La.

R. C. COLA CAKE

2 c. flour	2 c. sugar
2 Tbsp. cocoa	1 tsp. salt
1 tsp. soda	2 sticks oleo
1 c. R.C. cola	1/2 c. buttermilk
2 eggs	1 1/2 c. miniature marsh- mallows

Combine flour, sugar, cocoa, salt and soda in large bowl. Bring oleo and R.C. cola to a boil and add to flour mixture. Add buttermilk and eggs. Stir in marshmallows. Bake in greased 13x9 inch pan at 350° about 45 minutes.

Icing:

1 stick oleo	1 Tbsp. R.C. cola
2 Tbsp. cocoa	1 box powdered sugar
1 tsp. vanilla	1 c. chopped pecans

Mix oleo, R.C. cola and cocoa together, bring to boil. Remove from heat, add remaining ingredients. Spread on cake while hot.   Becky Sanders, Central
Council, St. Landry, La.

RUM CAKE

2 sticks oleo	1/2 c. Crisco
3 c. sugar	5 eggs
1 tsp. butter flavoring	1 tsp. coconut flavoring
1 tsp. lemon flavoring	1/2 tsp. rum flavoring
3 c. Gold Medal plain flour	1 c. buttermilk

Cream oleo, Crisco and sugar. Add eggs, 1 at a time. Add flavorings. Sift flour 3 times and add to mixture. Add buttermilk. Mix well and pour batter into greased and floured Bundt or tube pan. Bake at 350° for 1 1/2 hours.

Rubye G. Morgan, Central
Council, Alexandria, La.

RUM CAKE

1 pkg. yellow cake mix	1 small box instant vanilla pudding
4 eggs	
1/2 c. salad oil	1/2 c. water
1/2 c. rum	3/4 c. pecans, crushed

Sprinkle pecans in bottom of greased Bundt or angel food pan. Mix remaining ingredients and pour batter over pecans. Bake at 325° for 30-35 minutes or until done. Remove from oven and pierce holes in cake with toothpick. Pour hot Glaze over top of cake. Do not remove from pan until completely cool.

Glaze:

1 stick butter or oleo	1 c. sugar
1/4 c. water	1 jigger rum

Boil butter, sugar and water 1 minute. Add rum after removing from heat. Pour over hot cake.

Mrs. Bob (Brenda) Doherty
Ozone Council, Hammond, La.

RUM CAKE

1 c. chopped pecans	1 pkg. yellow cake mix
1 (3 3/4 oz.) pkg. instant vanilla pudding mix	4 eggs
	1/2 c. cold water
1/2 c. rum	1/2 c. oil

Mix all ingredients, except nuts. Grease and flour 10-inch tube or 12-cup Bundt pan. Sprinkle nuts over bottom of pan. Pour cake batter over nuts. Bake in preheated 325° oven for 1 hour. Cool. Invert on serving plate. Prick top. Drizzle and smooth Glaze evenly over top and sides. Allow cake to absorb Glaze. Repeat until Glaze is used up.

Glaze:

1/4 lb. butter (1 stick)	1/4 c. water
1/2 c. rum	1 c. granulated sugar

Melt butter, stir in water and sugar. Boil 5 minutes, stirring constantly. Remove from heat. Stir in rum.

June Harllee, Caddo
Council, Shreveport, La.

SAD CAKE

1 box light brown sugar	1/3 c. corn oil
4 eggs	2 c. Pioneer biscuit mix
1 tsp. coconut oil flavor	1 c. chopped pecans
or vanilla	

Mix ingredients together and pour into lightly greased and floured 13x9x2-inch pan. Bake at 350° for 35 minutes.

Emerite L. Herbert
Evangeline Council, Scott, La.

SAD CAKE

1 biscuit mix	1 box brown sugar, or
4 eggs	3/4 liquid brown sugar
1/3 c. oil	1 tsp. vanilla flavor
1/2 c. pecans	

Mix ingredients together. Bake at 350° for 30 minutes.

Lillie C. Patin, Evangeline
Council, Lafayette, La.

SCOTCH CAKE

2 c. flour	2 c. sugar
1 stick oleo	1/2 c. vegetable shortening
4 Tbsp. cocoa	1 c. water
1/2 c. buttermilk	2 eggs
1 tsp. soda	1 tsp. vanilla

Combine flour and sugar in large mixing bowl. Combine oleo, shortening, cocoa and water. Bring to a boil. Pour into flour and sugar mixture, mix well. Add remaining ingredients. Pour into greased and floured 11x16-inch pan. Bake at 400° about 30 minutes. Make Icing 5 minutes before cake has finished baking.

Icing:

1 stick oleo	6 Tbsp. evaporated milk
4 Tbsp. cocoa	1 box powdered sugar
1 tsp. vanilla	1 c. chopped pecans
1 c. flaked coconut	

Combine oleo, cocoa and milk. Bring to boil, stirring constantly, to keep from burning. Remove from heat and add other ingredients. Spread on hot cake.

Theda S. Thomas, Caddo
Council, Shreveport, La.

SEC. CAKE

2 sticks oleo	2 c. sugar
4 eggs	3/4 c. buttermilk
1 tsp. soda	1/2 tsp. salt
3 c. all-purpose flour	Rum or vanilla flavoring
2 c. chopped dates	2 c. coconut
2 c. pecans	

Cream oleo and sugar together. Add eggs. Add buttermilk, soda and salt. Add remaining ingredients. Mix well. Bake at 350° for 1 hour and 25 minutes. Have Glaze ready when cake is removed from oven. Pour over hot cake. Let cake remain in pan until Glaze is all soaked up. This is my mother's recipe, Mrs. J. L. Adkins of Port Allen, La.

Glaze:

1 c. orange juice   2 or 3 c. powdered sugar

Marcia A. Horton, Capital
Council, Baton Rouge, La.

SAUSAGE CAKE

1 lb. sausage   1 pt. boiling water
1 lb. raisins   1 Tbsp. ground cloves
1 lb. dates   1 Tbsp. cinnamon
4 c. brown sugar   1 Tbsp. soda
4 1/2 c. flour   1 c. black walnuts

Dissolve soda in a little cold water. Break up sausage in mixing bowl. Add sugar, raisins or dates. Pour boiling water over all mixture. Stir in soda water. Sift other ingredients together. Add the contents of bowl. Stir in nuts. Bake in tube pan at 300° for 1 1/2 hours or until done.

Calcasieu Council
Lake Charles, La.

7-UP PINEAPPLE CAKE

1 box lemon supreme   1 box instant pineapple
  cake mix   pudding mix
1 c. cooking oil   1 1/4 c. 7-Up
4 eggs

Mix all ingredients and pour in 3 greased and floured layer pans. Bake at 350° until done.

Frosting:

1 large can crushed   2 Tbsp. flour
  pineapple   2 eggs
3/4 c. sugar   1/2 c. evaporated milk

Combine ingredients, cook until thick. Spread over cool cake layers.

Mrs. E. L. Hoskins, Caddo
Council, Shreveport, La.

548

7-UP CAKE

1 (10 oz.) bottle 7-Up
3/4 c. cooking oil
4 eggs

1 box pineapple cake mix
1 box pineapple instant
  pudding

Mix together and bake in layers at 350° until done. Cool and ice.

Icing:

1 1/2 c. sugar
2 eggs
1 small can crushed
  pineapple

1 stick oleo
2 Tbsp. flour
1 c. coconut
1 tsp. vanilla

Mix ingredients. Cook slowly until thick.

Horace M. O'Quin, Calcasieu
Council, Sulphur, La.

SHERRY CAKE

4 eggs
1 pkg. yellow cake mix
3/4 c. sherry
3/4 c. oil

1 tsp. nutmeg
1 pkg. instant lemon pudding
  or jello
1/3 c. poppy seed

Combine ingredients, beat well. Pour batter into oiled Bundt pan. Bake at 350° for 50 minutes. Sprinkle with powdered sugar if to be used as coffee cake or served with wine. If for dessert, make glaze of:

2 c. sugar

2/3 c. wine

Blend and spoon over cake until absorbed.

Mrs. Raymond Sparkman
Crescent City Council
New Orleans, La.

SOCK IT TO ME CAKE

1 pkg. butter recipe cake
  mix (Duncan Hines)
4 eggs

1/2 c. sugar
3/4 c. cooking oil
1/2 pt. sour cream

Mix ingredients together with beater.

Topping:

1/2 c. pecans   1/2 c. brown sugar
3 tsp. cinnamon

Mix ingredients for Topping in separate bowl. Pour 1/2 of cake batter into greased tube pan. Sprinkle Topping mix over batter. Add remainder of batter and bake at 325° for 1 1/2 hours. Can be iced with canned vanilla frosting or powdered sugar-butter frosting if desired.

Patricia R. Caraway, Capital
Council, Baton Rouge, La.

SOUR CREAM CAKE

1 box Duncan Hines white   1/2 c. sugar
  cake mix   3/4 c. Wesson oil
1 c. sour cream   4 eggs
1 tsp. vanilla flavoring   1 tsp. butter flavoring
2 tsp. cinnamon   3 Tbsp. light brown sugar

Mix sugar, cake mix, sour cream and oil together, beat until creamy. Add eggs, 1 at a time, beating after each addition. Stir in flavorings. Beat for 5 minutes. Pour 1/2 of batter into greased and floured tube or angel food pan. Combine brown sugar and cinnamon, sprinkle half of the mixture over batter. Pour remaining batter into pan and sprinkle with rest of cinnamon mixture. Bake at 350° until done.

Glaze:

1 c. powdered sugar   1 Tbsp. milk
1/2 tsp. vanilla flavoring

Combine ingredients and glaze cake.

Cynthia Haynes, Caddo
Council, Shreveport, La.

SPONGE CAKE

1 1/4 c. plain flour   1 1/2 c. sugar
1/2 tsp. salt   1/2 tsp. baking powder
6 eggs, separated   1/4 c. water
1 tsp. vanilla   1 tsp. almond

Sift flour, 1 cup sugar, salt and baking powder

together in bowl. Add water, vanilla and almond flavoring to egg yolks and mix well. Beat whites until stiff, add remaining 1/2 cup sugar. Beat to blend. Add flour mixture to eggs, mix well. Fold this mixture into egg whites. Do not stir or beat, but continue to fold until well mixed. Pour into ungreased 10-inch tube pan and bake at 325° for 50 minutes. Remove from oven, invert on Coke bottle to cool at least 1 hour. Run knife around sides of cake pan to loosen. Put on plate.　　　　Elaine Squyres, Central
Council, Alexandria, La.

STRAWBERRY CAKE

1 pkg. white cake mix
1 pkg. strawberry jello
1/2 c. oil

4 eggs
1/2 c. water
1 (14 oz.) pkg. frozen strawberries, well drained

Combine all ingredients, except strawberries, until mixed. Add strawberries. Pour into 3 greased and lightly floured 8-inch layer pans. Bake at 350° until done, about 30-40 minutes. Cool and frost.

Frosting:

1 stick oleo
1/2 c. frozen strawberries

1 box powdered sugar
Juice from strawberries

Combine all ingredients, adding just enough juice to make a spreading consistency. Spread on cake. Cake may be frosted with whipped cream if desired.
Ethel Arender, Central
Council, Alexandria, La.

STRAWBERRY CAKE

1 pkg. Duncan Hines white
　cake mix
3/4 c. cooking oil
1/2 c. strawberries,
　mashed

1 pkg. strawberry jello
4 eggs
3/4 c. sweet milk
1/2 c. pecans
1/2 c. coconut

Mix ingredients together and pour batter into 11x14-inch Pyrex pan. Bake at 325° for about 30 minutes. Prepare the following Icing.

Icing:

3/4 pkg. powdered sugar   1/2 c. strawberries
1/2 c. pecans   1/2 c. coconut

Ann Suire, Capital Council,
Baton Rouge, La.

STRAWBERRY CAKE

1 box white cake mix   1 small box strawberry jello
  (Betty Crocker with   1 c. Crisco oil
  pudding best)   1/2 c. milk
4 eggs   1 c. coconut
1 c. sliced strawberries   1 c. nuts (optional)

Combine cake mix and dry jello. Add oil, eggs and milk. Mix well. Stir in strawberries, coconut and nuts. Bake in greased and floured 13x9-inch pan or 3 layers at 350°; test for doneness.

Frosting:

1 stick oleo, softened   1 box powdered sugar
1/2 c. sliced strawberries   1/2 c. coconut
1/2 c. chopped nuts

Cream oleo and sugar until light. Stir in berries, coconut and nuts. If too thick for spreading consistency, add a tablespoon of milk.   Jean Coon, Caddo Council,
Shreveport, La.

STRAWBERRY DELIGHT

1 angel food cake   2 small pkg. strawberry jello
2 1/2 c. hot water   2 env. Dream Whip
1 pt. frozen strawberries

Dissolve jello in hot water, add berries and let stand. Mix Dream Whip according to package directions and fold into jello mixture. Break cake into bite sized pieces and place 1/2 of the cake in bottom of 13x9-inch pan. Pour 1/2 of the jello mixture over cake. Repeat layers. Chill until firm.   Della Delposen, Ouachita
Council, Monroe, La.

SUNDAY SPECIAL TORTE

1 c. butter
5 egg yolks
2 tsp. vanilla
3/4 tsp. salt
1/3 c. raspberry or
   strawberry preserves
1 carton whipping cream,
   whipped

1 1/2 c. sugar
2 Tbsp. milk
1/2 tsp. baking powder
2 c. sifted flour
5 egg whites
1 1/3 c. coconut
1 carton sour cream

Cream butter with mixer, add 1/2 cup sugar, creaming well. Blend in egg yolks, milk, 1 teaspoon vanilla, baking powder and 1/2 teaspoon salt. Beat well. Stir in flour; if using self-rising, omit baking powder and salt. Spread evenly on bottom of 3 greased 9-inch layer pans. Spread preserves on each layer to within 1 inch of edge. Beat egg whites with remaining salt until mounds slightly, gradually add remaining cup of sugar, beating well after each addition. Continue to beat until stiff peaks appear. Fold in coconut and remaining teaspoon of vanilla. Spread over preserves in pans to the edge. Bake at 350° for 35-40 minutes or until light golden brown. Remove from pans and cool completely after 15 minutes. Mix whipped cream and sour cream. Spread generous amounts between each layer and on top. Do not frost sides. Refrigerate. The longer kept in refrigerator, the better the taste.

Maxine Botzong, Central
Council, Alexandria, La.

TUNNEL OF FUDGE

1 1/2 c. butter
1 1/2 c. sugar
1 pkg. double Dutch
   fudge frosting mix

6 eggs
2 c. flour
2 c. nuts (walnuts or
   pecans)

Cream shortening at high speed. Add eggs, 1 at a time, beating well after each addition. Gradually add sugar. Continue creaming at high speed until light and fluffy. Stir in flour, frosting mix and nuts by hand until well blended. Pour batter into well greased and floured Bundt pan. Bake at 350° for 60-65 minutes. Cool 2 hours before removing.

Linda Crawford
Shreveport Works Council
Shreveport, La.

B. B. Wynne
Shreveport Works Council
Shreveport, La.

SWEET POTATO SURPRISE CAKE

1 1/2 c. cooking oil
4 eggs, separated
3 tsp. baking powder
1 tsp. ground cinnamon
1 1/2 c. grated raw sweet
  potatoes

2 c. sugar
2 1/2 c. sifted cake flour
1/4 tsp. salt
1 tsp. ground nutmeg
1 c. chopped nuts
1 tsp. vanilla

Combine cooking oil and sugar. Beat until smooth. Add egg yolks and beat well. Add dry ingredients which have been sifted together. Stir in potatoes, nuts and vanilla, beat well. Beat egg whites until stiff. Fold into mixture. Bake in 3 greased and floured 8-inch layer pans at 350° for 25-30 minutes. Cool and frost.

Frosting:

1 large can evaporated
  milk
3 egg yolks
1 1/3 c. flaked coconut

1 c. sugar
1 stick oleo
1 tsp. vanilla

Combine milk, sugar, oleo, egg yolks and vanilla in saucepan. Heat until boiling. Add coconut.

Mae Briley
Central Council
Alexandria, La.

Marjorie W. Rowell
Evangeline Council
Lafayette, La.

TOMATO SOUP CAKE

2 1/4 c. cake flour, or
  2 c. all-purpose flour
1 tsp. baking soda
1 tsp. cinnamon
1 can tomato soup
2 eggs

1 1/3 c. sugar
4 tsp. baking powder
1 1/2 tsp. allspice
1/2 tsp. ground cloves
1/2 c. Crisco shortening
1/4 c. water

Measure dry ingredients into large bowl. Add soup and shortening. Beat at low to medium speed 2 minutes, scraping sides and bottom of bowl constantly. Add eggs and water. Beat 2 minutes longer, scraping bowl frequently. Pour into greased and floured 8 or 9-inch round layer pans or an oblong 13x9x2-inch pan. Bake in preheated 350° oven for 35-40 minutes. Let stand 10 minutes before removing from pans. Cool on rack. Frost with Cream Cheese Frosting (recipe follows).

Frosting:

1 stick oleo
1 (8 oz.) pkg. cream
  cheese
1 tsp. vanilla

1 (1 lb.) box powdered
  sugar
1 c. chopped nuts, or
  1 c. raisins (optional)

Soften oleo and cream cheese, mix with sugar and add
vanilla. Add nuts or raisins if desired. Use as filling and
frosting. Denise Barteet, Caddo
Council, Shreveport, La.

UGLY DUCKLING CAKE

1 pkg. yellow cake mix
2 1/3 c. coconut
1/2 c. firmly packed
  brown sugar
1/2 c. evaporated milk

1 (16 oz.) can fruit cocktail
2 eggs
1/2 c. butter or oleo
1/2 c. granulated sugar

Combine cake mix, fruit cocktail with syrup, 1 cup
coconut and eggs in large mixer bowl. Blend, then beat at
medium speed for 2 minutes. Pour into greased 13x9-inch
pan. Sprinkle with brown sugar. Bake at 325° for 45
minutes or until cake springs back when lightly touched.
Bring butter, granulated sugar and milk to boil in saucepan. Boil 2 minutes. Remove from heat, stir in remaining
coconut. Spoon over hot cake in pan.
Sherri Wilson, Caddo
Council, Shreveport, La.

UGLY DUCKLING CAKE

1 pkg. yellow cake mix
2 1/2 c. coconut
2 eggs
1/2 c. butter or oleo
1/2 c. granulated sugar

1 (16 oz.) can fruit cocktail
1/2 c. firmly packed brown
  sugar
1/2 c. evaporated milk

Combine cake mix, fruit cocktail with syrup, 1 cup
coconut and eggs in large mixer bowl. Blend, then beat
at medium speed for 2 minutes. Pour into greased 13x9-
inch pan. Sprinkle with brown sugar. Beat at 325° for
45 minutes or until cake springs back when touched. Bring
butter, granulated sugar and milk to a boil in small

1723-79

saucepan. Broil for 2 minutes. Remove from heat, stir in remaining coconut and spoon over hot cake in pan.

Carole Smith, Caddo
Council, Shreveport, La.

UGLY DUCKLING PUDDING CAKE

1 pkg. yellow cake mix
1 can fruit cocktail,
  undrained
1 c. coconut
1/2 c. chopped nuts
  (optional)

1 pkg. Jell-O lemon instant
  pudding and pie mix
4 eggs
1/2 c. firmly packed brown
  sugar
1/4 c. oil

Blend all ingredients, except brown sugar and nuts, in large mixer bowl. Beat 4 minutes at medium speed. Pour into greased and floured 13x9-inch pan. Sprinkle with brown sugar and nuts. Bake at 325° for 45 minutes or until tests done. Cool in pan 15 minutes. Spoon hot Butter Glaze over warm cake. Serve warm or cool with Cool Whip or whipped cream, if desired.

Butter Glaze:

1/2 c. butter or oleo
1/2 c. evaporated milk

1/2 c. granulated sugar
1 1/3 c. flaked coconut

Combine butter, sugar and milk in saucepan, boil 2 minutes. Stir in coconut.

Edith Basco, Central Council,
Alexandria, La.

VANILLA WAFER CAKE

1 (12 oz.) box vanilla
  wafers, crushed
2 sticks oleo
1/2 c. sweet milk

2 c. sugar
6 eggs
1 c. coconut
1 c. pecans

Cream sugar and butter until fluffy, add eggs, 1 at a time, beating after each addition. Add milk and crushed wafers. Fold in coconut and pecans. Pour into greased and floured tube or Bundt pan and bake at 300° for 1 hour or until done.

Jeanette Williams, Caddo
Council, Shreveport, La.

WATERGATE CAKE

1 (18 1/2 oz.) pkg. white
  cake mix
1 c. salad oil
1/2 c. chopped pecans

1 (3 1/2 oz.) pkg. pistachio
  pudding mix
3 eggs
1 c. club soda

Combine ingredients, beat 4 minutes at medium speed of electric mixer. Pour batter into greased and floured 10-inch tube pan. Bake at 350° for 45-50 minutes. Turn out on wire rack to cool. Frost with Pistachio Frosting, garnish with pecans. Yield: One 10-inch cake.

Pistachio Frosting:

2 env. whipped topping
  mix
1 1/2 c. cold milk

1 (3 1/2 oz.) pkg. pistachio
  pudding mix

Combine whipped topping mix and milk, beat at high speed of electric mixer until peaks form. Add pudding mix and beat until fluffy. Frost cake.

Magnolia Council
New Orleans, La.

WHIPPED CREAM CAKE

1 1/2 c. whipping cream
1 1/2 tsp. vanilla
1 1/2 c. sugar

3 eggs, well beaten
2 1/4 c. flour
2 tsp. baking powder

Whip cream, fold in eggs and vanilla. Mix together separately all dry ingredients and fold with cream mixture. Pour into 2 greased and floured 8-inch cake pans. Bake at 350° for 30-35 minutes. Ice cooled cake with frosting of your choice.

Ann Orr, Evangeline
Council, New Iberia, La.

YUM YUM CAKE

2 eggs
2 c. sugar
2 1/2 tsp. baking powder

2 c. flour
2 c. crushed pineapple,
  undrained

Beat eggs and sugar until light and fluffy. Stir in pineapple. Sift flour and baking powder, mix well with egg mixture. Spread into greased and floured 13x9x2-inch pan. Bake at 350° for 30 minutes or until done.

Topping:

1 c. sugar
1 c. coconut
1 c. chopped nuts

1/2 lb. butter or oleo
1 small can evaporated milk
1/2 tsp. lemon and vanilla
    flavoring

Put sugar, milk and butter in boiler. Boil 2 minutes. Remove from heat, add coconut, nuts and extracts. Spread while hot.

Mrs. Delbert Henderson
Ouachita Council, Monroe, La.

FOUR LAYER DELIGHT, YUM-YUM CAKE, OR MISSISSIPPI MUD PIE

First Step:

1 c. all-purpose flour
1/2 c. pecans

1 stick oleo
2 Tbsp. sugar (optional)

Mix and spread in bottom of 9x13-inch pan and bake at 350° until lightly brown. Cool.

Second Step:

1 c. Cool Whip
1 (8 oz.) pkg. cream cheese

1 c. powdered sugar
1 tsp. vanilla (optional)

Mix ingredients together and spread over cool crust.

Third Step:

1 large or 2 small pkg.
    instant chocolate, butter-
    scotch, lemon, coconut
    pudding, or flavor of
    your choice

2 1/2 - 3 c. milk

Mix and beat well with electric mixer and spread over cream cheese mixture.

Fourth Step:

Cool Whip
Coconut (optional)

Chopped pecans (optional)
Grated chocolate (optional)

Top with Cool Whip and any or all of the other ingredients. Refrigerate overnight.

This recipe submitted by:

Mildred Pace
Caddo Council
Shreveport, La.

Sue Hosch
Metairie Council
Metairie, La.

Vada Jones (Mrs.
Dick), Caddo Council
Shreveport, La.

Audrey M. Lee
Capital Council
Zachary, La.

Bill Lang
Capital Council
Baton Rouge, La.

C. Pierce
LeBayou Council
Morgan City, La.

Loys Sterling
Caddo Council
Shreveport, La.

Doris Reeves
Capital Council
Baton Rouge, La.

Julia B. Ulmer
Caddo Council
Shreveport, La.

Jan Prestridge
Capital Council
Baton Rouge, La.

Mearl S. Byles
Central Council
Natchitoches, La.

Mavis W. O'Rourke
Shreveport Works
Council, Shreveport, La.

Edna B. Phillips
Capital Council
Baton Rouge, La.

Rebecca Thames
Caddo Council
Shreveport, La.

Debbie Thayer
Central Council
Bunkie, La.

Ilene Arnold
Capital Council
Waterbury, Ct.

Jeanette English
Caddo Council
Shreveport, La.

Linda Teague
Caddo Council
Shreveport, La.

Joyce Silva
Capital Council
Baton Rouge, La.

Mary Armand
Central Council
Cottonport, La.

Stanley McMahon
West Bank Council
Gretna, La.

WHITE CAKE

1 c. butter
3 1/2 c. sifted cake flour
1 tsp. vanilla
8 egg whites, beaten

2 c. sugar
2 tsp. baking powder
1 c. milk
1 tsp. salt

Cream butter and sugar together until light. Sift dry ingredients together 2 times, add to creamed mixture alternately with milk. Add vanilla. Fold in egg whites. Pour into greased and floured Bundt pan. Bake at 350° for 20 to 25 minutes or until done.   Rebecca Thames, Caddo
Council, Shreveport, La.

APRICOT CAKE FILLING

2 c. dried apricots
1 Tbsp. lemon juice

1 1/2 c. sugar
1/2 tsp. grated lemon rind

Cover apricots with water and cook until tender and very little juice remains; drain. Beat apricots 1 minute at medium speed. Add sugar, lemon juice and rind, continue beating 1/2 minute to dissolve. Return to fire and cook 1 minute. Cool and use as filling for cake. Makes enough for 2 layers.
Clara Westbrook, Shreveport
Works Council, Shreveport, La.

CHOCOLATE ICING

1 stick oleo
1 c. sugar
1 tsp. vanilla

1 Tbsp. chocolate
1 Tbsp. flour
5 Tbsp. milk

Bring to a rolling boil. Cook 2 minutes, remove from heat and spread on cake fast. Marie Pamplin, Shreveport
Works Council, Shreveport, La.

CHOCOLATE FROSTING

2 c. sugar
1/2 c. cocoa
1/2 lb. oleo

1 tsp. vanilla
1/2 c. cream or milk

Mix ingredients together and bring to a slow boil in saucepan. Boil about 2 minutes, set aside and cool thoroughly. Beat until creamy. Pour over cooled cake. Continue pouring back over cake as it runs down until icing begins to set. The cake is very rich and moist.
Mrs. Richard D. (Vermelle)
Sylvest, Ozone Council,
Hammond, La.

CHOCOLATE ICING

1 (6 oz.) pkg. semi-
    sweet chocolate
1/2 c. sour cream
1/4 tsp. salt

1/4 c. butter
1 tsp. vanilla
3 c. powdered sugar

Melt chocolate and butter in top of double boiler. Remove from heat, blend in sour cream, salt and vanilla. Gradually beat in sugar. Ann Orr, Evangeline Council, New Iberia, La.

COCONUT ICING

2 c. sour cream	1 box powdered sugar
1 (9 oz.) bowl Cool Whip	3 c. coconut

Mix ingredients together in large bowl. Do not use mixer. Spread on cool layered cake. Refrigerate until served. Marion Carter, Central Council, Bunkie, La.

COCONUT PECAN FROSTING

2/3 c. sugar	2/3 c. evaporated milk
2 egg yolks	1/3 c. Crisco shortening
1/2 tsp. vanilla	1 1/3 c. flaked coconut
2/3 c. chopped pecans	(3 1/2 oz. can)

Combine sugar, milk, egg yolks, Crisco and vanilla. Cook and stir over medium heat about 12 minutes or until mixture comes to a boil. Remove from heat, add coconut and pecans. Beat until frosting is thick. Cool 15 minutes. Only enough frosting to spread on top of layers. Marie Pamplin, Shreveport Works Council, Shreveport, La.

COCONUT PECAN FROSTING

1 c. sugar	1 c. evaporated milk
3 egg yolks, slightly beaten	1/2 c. butter
	1 1/3 c. coconut
1 tsp. vanilla	1 c. chopped pecans

Combine sugar, milk, egg yolks, butter and vanilla. Cook and stir over medium heat until thickened, about 12 minutes. Remove from heat, add coconut and pecans. Cool and beat occasionally. Frost your favorite cake. Frances Keller Lamb Central Council Alexandria, La.

CREAM CHEESE FROSTING

1 (3 oz.) pkg. cream 3 c. powdered sugar
 cheese 1/2 tsp. vanilla
1/4 c. sweet cream

 Cream the cheese, add powdered sugar. Thin with cream. Add vanilla. Beat until of consistency to spread.
       Mary McDow, Caddo
       Council, Shreveport, La.

CREAM CHEESE FROSTING

1 (8 oz.) pkg. cream 1/2 c. butter
 cheese 1 tsp. vanilla
1 lb. powdered sugar 3 Tbsp. evaporated milk

 Combine ingredients and blend well.
       Ann Orr, Evangeline
       Council, New Iberia, La.

PEANUT BRITTLE CREAM CHEESE FROSTING

2 Tbsp. butter or oleo 1 (8 oz.) pkg. cream cheese
2 Tbsp. milk 3 1/2 c. sifted powdered
1 (1 lb.) box peanut sugar
 brittle 1/2 tsp. vanilla

 Cream butter with cream cheese. Add milk, beat in sugar gradually. Blend in vanilla. Break or crush peanut brittle into small pieces, stir into cream cheese mixture. Spread or ice over all sides of cake. I buy 1 angel food cake about 10 or 12-inch size. Very good.
       Mrs. Marie Louise Pizzitola
       Capital Council, Chalmette, La.

FUDGE FROSTING

1 1/2 c. white sugar 1 1/2 sq. bitter chocolate
1/2 c. sour cream

 Boil slowly until very soft ball forms in cold water. Cool. Beat thoroughly until it becomes consistency of fudge.
       Helen Patton, Shreveport
       Works Council, Shreveport, La.

ICE CREAM ICING

4 Tbsp. flour
1 c. milk
1 c. sugar

1 c. butter or 1/2 c. Crisco
and 1/2 c. oleo
1 tsp. vanilla

Heat milk and flour until thick, cool. Combine butter, sugar and vanilla. Beat about 4 minutes until smooth and creamy. Add cooled milk mixture and beat until fluffy.

Cecile Gallet, Evangeline
Council, Lafayette, La.

LEMON CAKE FILLING

3/4 c. sugar
Pinch of salt
1/2 c. water
2 Tbsp. butter

3 Tbsp. flour
1/4 c. lemon juice
3 egg yolks, slightly beaten
1 lemon rind, grated

Mix sugar, flour and salt together, mix well, add lemon juice. Add rind, water, egg yolks and butter and mix well. Place over hot water in double boiler and cook until smooth and thick, stirring constantly about 15 minutes. Cool and spread on cake. Marie Pamplin, Shreveport
Works Council, Shreveport, La.

LEMON JELLY FILLING

2 eggs
1 Tbsp. butter

1 c. sugar
2 lemons (juice and grated
rind)

Beat eggs, add other ingredients. Cook over low heat until thick. Carolyn Palmer, Capital
Council, Baton Rouge, La.

ORANGE NUT FROSTING

3 c. powdered sugar
1/2 stick oleo or butter,
softened

1 Tbsp. grated orange
3 Tbsp. orange juice
1/2 c. chopped pecans

Cream butter and sugar, add grated orange. Mix in orange juice, little at a time, until it gets to spreading consistency, add pecans; mix well. Zella White, Shreveport
Works Council, Shreveport, La.

PERFECT ICING

5 Tbsp. flour
1 c. sugar
1/2 c. Crisco (no sub-
   stitutes)
Pinch of salt

1 c. milk
1/2 c. butter
2 tsp. vanilla or other
   flavoring

Cook flour and milk together until thick. Cream remaining ingredients and add cooled flour mixture. Mix together for 8-10 minutes. For variety, add any of the following: 1/3 cup chocolate chips; lime, strawberry or lemon jello; 1/3 cup thawed strawberries; 1 tablespoon cocoa, coconut and chopped pecans.

Marie Pamplin, Shreveport
Works Council, Shreveport, La.

PROFESSIONAL DECORATOR ICING

1 1/2 c. Crisco shortening
2 Tbsp. flour
2 lb. powdered sugar
1/2 c. water

1/2 tsp. salt
1/2 tsp. meringue (powdered)
2-3 tsp. flavoring

Mix shortening, salt, flour and meringue powder. Mix well. Add remaining ingredients.

Ann Orr, Evangeline
Council, New Iberia, La.

SEVEN MINUTE ICING

2 egg whites, room
   temperature
1/8 tsp. cream of tartar

1 c. sugar
1/4 c. water (7 Tbsp.)
1 tsp. vanilla

Place egg whites, sugar and water in top of double boiler, beat thoroughly. Place over hot water. Beat and cook until hot, add cream of tartar. Continue to cook until icing is thick and holds peaks. Remove, add vanilla and beat 1 minute. Spread on cake.

Maxine Fletcher, Ouachita
Council, Monroe, La.

STRAWBERRY ICING

1 c. crushed straw-
  berries or raspberries

1/2 c. egg whites
1 c. sugar

Whip ingredients in large bowl until stiff peaks are formed. Spread on cake and decorate with berries. Refrigerate.
Viola Kehrer, Ozone Council, Hammond, La.

AMISH COOKIES

1 c. oleo or butter
1 c. powdered sugar
2 eggs
1 tsp. soda

1 c. white sugar
1 c. oil
4 c. flour
1 tsp. salt

Mix ingredients, roll into balls and flatten. Bake on greased cookie sheet at 375° until done.
Viola Kehrer, Ozone Council, Hammond, La.

APPLE CHOCOLATE CHIP BARS

5 or 6 apples
2 tsp. vanilla
3 eggs
1 tsp. salt
2 tsp. baking soda
1 c. chocolate chips

1 1/2 c. Crisco oil
2 c. white sugar
3 c. flour
1 c. nuts
3 tsp. cinnamon

Peel, core and slice apples. Combine oil, vanilla, sugar and eggs together. Combine flour, salt, nuts, soda, cinnamon and chocolate chips together. Add oil-sugar mixture gradually. Fold in apple slices. Pour batter into floured and greased 13x9-inch pan. Bake at 350° for 1 hour.
Dorothy Beaudoin, Capital Council, Waterbury, Ct.

APPLE OATMEAL COOKIES (WHOLE WHEAT)

1/2 c. oleo	1 c. brown sugar
2 eggs	1 3/4 c. whole wheat flour
1/2 c. regular oatmeal	1/2 tsp. salt
(not instant)	2 tsp. baking powder
1/2 tsp. cinnamon	1 c. raisins
1 c. pecans or walnuts	1 1/2 c. grated apples

Cream oleo and sugar, beat in eggs. Stir in other ingredients. Drop by teaspoonfuls on oiled cookie sheet and bake 10-12 minutes. Makes 3-4 dozen.

Rebecca Scott, Caddo
Council, Shreveport, La.

BANANA OATMEAL COOKIES

1 1/2 c. quick oats	1 c. sugar
1 1/4 c. unsifted flour	1 egg
3/4 tsp. salt	1 tsp. vanilla
1/2 tsp. baking soda	1 (6 oz.) pkg. butterscotch
1/2 tsp. nutmeg	morsels
3/4 c. butter	1 c. mashed bananas (2)
1/2 c. chopped nuts	1 c. chopped dates

Combine oats, flour, salt, baking soda and nutmeg. Set aside. Cream butter and sugar, add egg and vanilla. Stir in flour mixture. Fold in butterscotch morsels, mashed bananas, dates and nuts. Drop by heaping teaspoonfuls onto greased cookie sheet. Bake at 350° for 10 minutes. Makes 5 dozen (2 1/2-inch) cookies.

Jeanette English, Caddo
Council, Shreveport, La.

BAPTIST COOKIES

1 small pkg. chopped dates	4 Tbsp. butter
3/4 c. sugar	1 large or 2 small eggs
1 Tbsp. vanilla	2 1/2 c. Rice Krispies
3/4 c. chopped pecans	Coconut

Melt butter and dates over low heat, add sugar and stir until melted; cool slightly. Beat eggs, add to mixture; add vanilla, Rice Krispies and pecans. Cool enough to shape into small balls and roll in coconut. Makes 48.

Ann Orr, Evangeline
Council, New Iberia, La.

BOILED COOKIES

2 c. sugar
1/2 c. milk
1/4 lb. oleo
2 1/2 c. quick oats
1/2 c. chopped nuts

2 Tbsp. cocoa
2 Tbsp. vanilla
1/2 c. peanut butter or
  wheat germ (optional)

Mix sugar, milk, oleo and cocoa. Bring to a boil; boil 1 1/2 minutes (time it). Pour over remaining ingredients. Mix well and drop on waxed paper. Cool.

Mollie Hoskins, Caddo
Council, Shreveport, La.

BOILED COOKIES

2 c. sugar
1 block butter or oleo
1/2 c. peanut butter

1 Tbsp. cocoa
1/2 c. milk
2 c. oatmeal

Combine sugar, butter, cocoa and milk. Bring to a rolling boil. Boil for 3 minutes, add peanut butter and oatmeal. Mix well and spoon onto waxed paper.

Gay Irwin, Capital
Council, Baton Rouge, La.

AUNT EMMA'S BROWN COOKIES

4 c. flour
1 tsp. allspice
2 tsp. cinnamon
Pinch of salt
1 tsp. vanilla
1/2 lb. Crisco, melted

4 tsp. baking powder
1/2 tsp. cloves
1 1/2 c. sugar
1 1/2 c. milk
1/2 lb. chopped walnuts
1/2 c. cocoa

Mix all dry ingredients. Add nuts, then milk, Crisco and vanilla. Shape into balls and bake on cookie sheet at 400° about 10 minutes. You may ice with chocolate on top or leave plain.

Carol Hufnagel, Ouachita
Council, Monroe, La.

BROWNIES

1 c. butter
4 eggs, well beaten
1/2 tsp. baking powder
1 c. nuts

2 c. sugar
1 1/2 c. flour
1/4 c. cocoa
1 tsp. vanilla

Cream butter and sugar, add eggs. Sift dry ingredients together and blend the entire mixture. Bake in greased pan at 400° until done.

Donna McPhearson, Central
Council, Natchitoches, La.

COCOA BROWNIES

3/4 c. flour
1/4 tsp. salt
1/2 c. soft butter
1 tsp. vanilla

1 c. sugar
1/4 c. cocoa
2 eggs
1/2 c. chopped nuts

Sift flour, sugar, salt and cocoa. Add butter, eggs and vanilla. Beat 2 minutes on medium speed or 300 strokes by hand. Stir in nuts just until evenly distributed. Pour batter into greased 8x8x2-inch pan and bake at 350° for 20-22 minutes or until barely done.

Mavis W. O'Rourke
Shreveport Works Council
Shreveport, La.

ROCKY ROAD BROWNIES

1 c. flour
1 c. sugar
2 eggs
1 c. chopped nuts

1/3 c. cocoa
1 c. melted butter or oleo
1 tsp. vanilla
1 (6 1/4 oz.) pkg. miniature
  marshmallows

Combine flour, sugar and cocoa. Stir in butter, add eggs, 1 at a time, beating well after each addition. Stir in vanilla and nuts. Pour into greased and floured 13x9x2-inch pan. Bake at 275° for 35-40 minutes. Sprinkle marshmallows evenly over top of hot brownies. Spread with Fudgy Frosting. Cool and cut into squares.

Fudgy Frosting:

1 lb. powdered sugar
1/2 c. melted butter
1 tsp. vanilla

1/3 c. cocoa
1/3 c. Pet milk

568

Combine sugar and cocoa, add remaining ingredients. Spread on marshmallow layer while brownies are hot.

Jeanette English, Caddo
Council, Shreveport, La.

VIENNESE BROWNIES

2 sq. (1 oz. each) un-
   sweetened chocolate
1 c. sugar
1/2 tsp. baking powder
Sliced almonds

1/2 c. butter
2 eggs
3/4 c. flour
1/2 tsp. salt

Melt chocolate and butter, cool. Beat eggs, add sugar and chocolate mixture. Sift flour, baking powder and salt together, add to chocolate mixture and blend well. Pour half of chocolate batter into greased 8-inch square pan. Spread with Cream Cheese Filling. Top with remaining batter and sprinkle with almonds. Bake at 350° for 45 minutes.

Filling:

1 (8 oz.) pkg. cream cheese
1 egg

1/3 c. sugar
1/4 tsp. almond extract

Combine ingredients and spread between batter.

Rebecca Scott Bockmon, Caddo
Council, Shreveport, La.

CHOCOLATE CHIP COOKIES

1/2 c. oleo
1/4 c. light brown sugar
1 tsp. vanilla
3/4 tsp. salt
1 (6 oz.) pkg. semi-
   sweet chocolate pieces

1/2 c. white sugar
1 egg
1 c. sifted flour
1/2 tsp. soda
1/2 c. nuts

Cream together sugar, oleo, egg and vanilla. Add flour, salt and soda. Blend well. Stir in chocolate pieces and nuts. Drop on ungreased cookie sheet, bake at 350° for 7 minutes without opening oven.

Ervis Broussard, Crescent
City Council, New Orleans, La.

CHOCOLATE CHIP COOKIES

2 eggs
1/4 c. softened butter
1 (12 oz.) pkg. choco-
   late chips

1/3 c. water
1 pkg. Betty Crocker yellow
   cake mix

Add liquid ingredients to 1/2 of cake mix. Stir in remainder of ingredients. Drop by rounded teaspoonfuls
2 inches apart on ungreased cookie sheet. Bake 10-12 minutes. Makes 6 dozen.   Adrienne Dezendorf, Central
                        Council, Alexandria, La.

NO BAKE CHOCOLATE COOKIES

2 c. sugar
1/4 - 1/2 c. cocoa
1 tsp. vanilla
1 c. graham cracker
   crumbs

1/4 tsp. salt
1 c. evaporated milk
4 Tbsp. butter
1 c. chopped nuts

Combine sugar, salt, cocoa and milk. Bring to a soft
boil. Add remaining ingredients, mix well and drop on
waxed paper. Place half of pecan on each cookie if desired.
Makes about 4 dozen.   Carlotta Thomas, Ouachita
                        Council, Monroe, La.

CHOCOLATE SQUARES

2 c. sugar
1/2 tsp. salt
1 stick oleo
3 Tbsp. cocoa
1 tsp. soda
1 Tbsp. vanilla

2 c. flour
1 c. water
1/2 c. cooking oil
2 eggs
1/2 c. buttermilk

Combine sugar, flour and salt in bowl. Combine water,
oleo, cooking oil and cocoa. Bring to a boil and pour over
sugar-flour mixture. Add eggs, beating after each. Mix
soda with buttermilk. If no buttermilk, add 1 teaspoon vinegar to whole milk. Add to mixture. Add vanilla. Pour
batter into greased oblong pan. Bake at 350° about 20 minutes. Pour Icing over cake when it is first removed from
oven.

Icing:

1 stick butter or oleo
6 Tbsp. milk
2 tsp. vanilla

1 box powdered sugar
3 Tbsp. cocoa

Melt oleo, add remaining ingredients. Warm until blended. Pour over cake. Jeanette B. Armand, Central Council, Bunkie, La.

CHOCOLATE BUTTER PECAN SQUARES

2 c. all-purpose flour
1 1/2 c. firmly packed
  brown sugar

1 c. chocolate chips
1 c. pecans, chopped
2 1/3 sticks butter, softened

Combine flour, 1 cup brown sugar and 1 stick butter in bowl. Mix 2-3 minutes and pat firmly into 13x9-inch pan. Sprinkle pecans over crust. Combine 1 1/3 sticks (2/3 cup) butter and remaining 1/2 cup brown sugar in saucepan. Cook over medium heat, stirring constantly until mixture begins to boil. Continue to boil about 1 minute, stirring constantly. Pour caramel mixture evenly over pecans and uncooked crust. Bake in preheated 350° oven for 18-22 minutes. Watch! This will brown quickly. Do not over-cook. Remove from oven and immediately sprinkle with chocolate chips. Slightly swirl chips. Cool completely and cut into squares. Jean Coon, Caddo Council, Shreveport, La.

BUTTER COUCHA

1 pkg. yellow cake mix
1 stick oleo, melted

1 egg

Mix ingredients and pat in bottom of 13x9-inch un-greased pan. Pour Filling over layer and bake at 350° for 40 minutes. Sprinkle with powdered sugar while warm. Cut into squares to serve.

Filling:

1 (8 oz.) pkg. cream
  cheese, softened

3 eggs
3/4 box powdered sugar

Combine ingredients; mix in electric mixer. Use remaining powdered sugar in box to sprinkle over Coucha. Jean Wilson, Metairie Council, Metairie, La.

BUTTERSCOTCH NUT SLICKS

1/2 c. butter	2 c. brown sugar
2 eggs	2 c. flour
2 tsp. baking powder	1/2 tsp. salt
1 c. chopped nuts	1 tsp. vanilla

Melt butter, add sugar and blend. Let cool. Add beaten eggs and vanilla. Add all dry ingredients. Spread on greased and floured cookie sheet and bake. When done, cut in bars, placing a pecan half on each bar and add Glaze.

Glaze:

Milk	Powdered sugar
Vanilla	

Mix and pour over bars. Verle Oliphant, Caddo Council, Shreveport, La.

CARROT 'N' RAISIN CHEWS

1 c. butter or oleo	1 c. firmly packed brown
2 eggs	sugar
1 tsp. vanilla	1 c. all-purpose flour
1 tsp. baking powder	1 tsp. cinnamon
1/2 tsp. salt	1/4 tsp. nutmeg
1/4 tsp. cloves	2 1/2 c. quick or old
2 c. shredded carrots	fashioned uncooked oats
3/4 c. raisins	3/4 c. chopped nuts

Beat together butter and sugar until light and fluffy. Blend in eggs and vanilla. Combine and add flour, baking powder, cinnamon, salt, nutmeg and cloves. Stir in oats, carrots, raisins and nuts. Drop by rounded teaspoonfuls onto greased cookie sheet. Bake in preheated 350° oven for 12-15 minutes. Cool. Store in loosely covered container. Makes about 5 dozen cookies. Shirley J. Peoples, Crescent City Council, New Orleans, La.

CHESS SQUARES

1 box butter cake mix	4 eggs, divided
1 stick butter	1 (8 oz.) pkg. cream cheese
1 box powdered sugar	2 tsp. vanilla

Mix cake mix, butter and 1 egg, press into 9x13-inch

pan. Mix remaining ingredients and pour over cake mix.
Bake at 350° for 30-40 minutes. Let cool and cut into
squares.   Gayle Palermo, Westmoor
                                        Council, Kenner, La.

CHINESE CHEWS

1 c. sugar
1 tsp. vanilla
1 c. flour
Dash of salt
1 c. chopped pecans

1 egg
3 tsp. water
1/2 tsp. baking powder
1 c. chopped dates
Powdered sugar

Beat egg, add sugar, vanilla and water. Add flour,
baking powder, salt and beat well. Add pecans and dates.
Grease 7 1/2 x 11-inch pan. Spread mixture and bake at
350° until brown. Cut in squares. Cool, drench in
powdered sugar. This is a rather sticky dough since no
shortening is used.   Doris Reeves, Capital
                                 Council, Baton Rouge, La.

CHRISTMAS COOKIES

2 lb. nuts
2 lb. candied cherries
2 lb. pineapple
1 lb. chopped dates
1/2 tsp. cloves
4 well beaten eggs
1 tsp. salt

3/4 c. oleo
1 c. brown sugar
1 small jar apple jelly
2 tsp. cinnamon
2 tsp. nutmeg
2 1/2 c. flour

Chop fruit and nuts. Make batter with remaining ingredients. Add fruit and nuts to batter. Drop by teaspoon on cookie sheets. Bake at 250° for 25 minutes. You
can place a lot of cookies on the sheets; they do not spread.
They also freeze well.   Sally Walker, Ouachita
                                 Council, Shreveport, La.

CHEWY CHRISTMAS COOKIES

2 c. brown sugar
1/4 c. honey
2 c. pecans
1 tsp. vanilla
1/2 tsp. salt
2 c. raisins

4 eggs
2 tsp. baking powder
3 c. chopped dates
2 1/2 c. sifted flour
2 c. candied cherries
1 can coconut

1723-79

Mix brown sugar, eggs and honey together. Mix remaining ingredients together and add to egg and honey mixture. Drop by teaspoon on greased cookie sheet. Bake at 375° for 15 minutes.

Mollie Hoskins, Caddo
Council, Shreveport, La.

CHEWY SQUARES

1 stick butter
1 c. flour
1 Tbsp. baking powder
2 eggs

1 1/2 c. brown sugar, firmly
  packed
1/2 tsp. salt
1/2 c. chopped nuts
Powdered sugar

Melt butter, add sugar and cool. Add remaining ingredients, except powdered sugar. Bake in 12-inch square pan at 350° until done. Cool in pan, sprinkle with powdered sugar and cut into squares to serve.

Gayle Cummings, Caddo
Council, Shreveport, La.

CHRISTMAS JEWELS

1/3 c. shortening
1 egg
1/2 c. molasses
1/2 tsp. soda
1/4 c. sugar
1 1/2 c. plain flour
1/4 tsp. salt

1 tsp. nutmeg
2 1/2 c. mixed candied fruit
1/4 tsp. ginger
2 c. nuts, chopped coarse
1/4 tsp. allspice
1 tsp. cinnamon

Mix shortening, sugar, molasses and egg. Add flour, stir in remaining ingredients. Drop by teaspoon about 1 inch apart on slightly greased baking sheet. Top each with candied cherry. Bake in preheated 325° oven until done. Half of this makes about 6 dozen cookies.

Mollie Hoskins, Caddo
Council, Shreveport,La.

CHRISTMAS WREATH COOKIES

1 c. butter or oleo
1/2 c. light corn syrup
2 1/2 c. flour
2 c. finely chopped nuts

1/2 c. sugar
2 egg yolks
Egg whites, slightly beaten
Candied red and green
    cherries, cut in halves

Cream butter and sugar. Stir in corn syrup, egg yolks and flour. Chill. Roll dough into 1-inch balls. Dip into egg whites, then into chopped nuts. Place on greased baking sheet. Press candied cherry halves in centers. Bake at 325° for 20 minutes. Yield: 4 dozen.

Patricia Spitz, Ouachita
Council, Monroe, La.

COCONUT-OATMEAL COOKIES

1 1/4 c. butter
2 eggs
1 c. oatmeal
2 c. coconut
1/2 tsp. soda
2 1/4 c. flour

1 c. white sugar
1 c. brown sugar
1 c. nuts
2 tsp. baking powder
1/2 tsp. salt

Cream butter, sugars and eggs together. Add remaining ingredients. Drop by teaspoonfuls onto ungreased cookie sheet. Bake at 325° for 10-12 minutes.

Sadie Foil, Ozone Council,
Bogalusa, La.

COCOONS

1/2 c. butter
1/2 tsp. vanilla
1/4 c. powdered sugar

1 c. flour
1 c. chopped pecans
1/2 tsp. water

Mix ingredients together. Shape into small crescents on ungreased pan. Chill. Bake at 250° for 45 minutes. Roll in powdered sugar.

Mary C. Regan, Crescent
City Council, New Orleans, La.

COCOON DELIGHTS

2 c. butter
3 c. self-rising flour
5 tsp. powdered sugar

1 tsp. vanilla
2 c. chopped nuts

Blend softened butter, flour and powdered sugar. Add vanilla and nuts, mix well. Pinch off in small pieces and shape. Bake at 325° for 8 minutes. Roll in additional powdered sugar when cool. Makes about 12 dozen.

Sonia A. Hunt, Capital
Council, Baton Rouge, La.

CREAM CHEESE KOLACKY COOKIES

2 (3 oz.) pkg. cream
   cheese
2 c. flour

1/2 lb. butter
1/2 tsp. baking powder
Prune or apricot jam

Cream together cheese and butter, add flour sifted with baking powder and mix thoroughly. Roll out thin and cut with small size glass. Place 1/2 teaspoon jam in center of each cookie. Bake at 375° until light brown.

June E. Nickels, Shreveport
Works Council, Shreveport, La.

CRUNCHY FUDGE SANDWICHES

1 (6 oz.) pkg. Nestle's
   butterscotch morsels
1 (6 oz.) pkg. semi-sweet
   chocolate morsels
1 Tbsp. water

1/2 c. peanut butter
4 c. Kellogg's Rice Krispies
1/2 c. sifted powdered
   sugar
2 Tbsp. butter or oleo

Melt butterscotch morsels and peanut butter over low heat, stirring until blended. Stir in Rice Krispies. Press half of mixture in buttered 8-inch square pan. Chill. Stir over hot water, remaining ingredients until chocolate melts. Spread over chilled mixture and top with balance of cereal mixture. Chill. Cut into 1 1/2-inch squares. Yield: 25 squares.

Katherine Slover, Caddo
Council, Shreveport, La.

DATE BARS

3 eggs, well beaten
1 c. flour
1 tsp. baking powder
1 tsp. vanilla
1 c. sugar
1/4 tsp. salt
1 1/2 c. pitted, sliced dates
1 c. pecans, chopped

Beat eggs with sugar until thick. Add sifted dry ingredients. Beat smooth. Add dates, vanilla and nuts. Bake in waxed paper lined 9x13-inch pan at 350° for 30 minutes. Cut into 1x4-inch bars and roll in powdered sugar while warm. Makes 2 dozen.   Juanita Ridings

DATE COOKIES

1 c. brown sugar
1 c. white sugar
4 c. flour
1/2 tsp. salt
1 c. butter or shortening
2 eggs, well beaten
1 tsp. soda
1 tsp. vanilla

Cream sugars and shortening. Add eggs and vanilla. Add soda, salt and flour. Roll out 1/2 inch or thinner and spread with Filling mixture that has been cooked and cooled overnight. Roll like cinnamon rolls. Place in refrigerator overnight. Slice thin and bake at 350° until done. Cool. Lift out of pan.

Filling:

1 lb. dates, cut up
1 c. nuts
1 c. sugar
1 1/2 c. water

Cook until thick, stirring to prevent scorching. Cool overnight before spreading on dough.

Mattie Lou Smith, Caddo
Council, Shreveport, La.

DATE COCONUT BALLS

1 (8 oz.) pkg. pitted
    dates, cut up
1/4 c. lightly salted
    butter
1 c. crisp rice cereal
1 egg
1/2 c. light brown sugar
1/2 c. finely chopped pecans
1/4 c. shredded coconut

Mix dates, butter, egg and sugar. Cook over moderate

heat for 5 minutes, stirring constantly until mixture is smooth and thickened. Remove from heat and stir about 5 minutes until cooled. Stir in cereal and nuts. With buttered hands, roll rounded teaspoonfuls of the mixture into balls and roll balls in coconut. These are simple to make; very tasty and can be made ahead of time and frozen.

Mrs. J. E. Rutledge, LeBayou
Council, Houma, La.

DATE AND NUT COOKIES

2 c. brown sugar
3 eggs
1 tsp. vanilla
3 c. flour
1 c. nuts

1 c. shortening
3 tsp. sweet milk
1/2 tsp. salt
1 c. chopped dates
1 tsp. soda

Dissolve soda in milk. Mix all ingredients together. Drop by teaspoons on cookie sheet and bake at 375° until done.

Sally Walker, Ouachita
Council, Monroe, La.

DATE FILLED ICEBOX COOKIES

1 box brown sugar
2 eggs, well beaten
1 tsp. soda
1 tsp. vanilla

1 c. shortening
4 c. sifted flour
1 tsp. cream of tartar

Mix together sugar, shortening and eggs. Work in flour with soda and cream of tartar. Add vanilla, mix well. Divide dough into 3 parts. Roll out and spread with Filling. Shape into rolls and chill. Slice into thin slices. Place on cookie sheet about 10 minutes at 375°.

Filling:

1/2 c. sugar
1 pkg. dates, chopped

1/2 c. water
1 c. chopped nuts

Combine and cook over heat the sugar, dates and water. Cook until dissolved. Beat and add nuts. Cool before spreading on cookie dough.

Jeanette English, Caddo
Council, Shreveport, La.

ARLINE'S DATE SQUARES

1 1/2 c. flour
1 c. brown sugar
1/2 c. oil

1 1/2 c. oatmeal
1 tsp. soda

Mix dry ingredients and add oil. Take half of mixture and pat into pan. Pour Filling over crust. Sprinkle other half of oatmeal mixture over Filling for top crust. Bake at 350° until brown.

Filling:

1 (8 oz.) pkg. pitted
  dates, cut up
1 tsp. vanilla

3 Tbsp. flour mixed with
  sugar
1 c. sugar
2 c. water

Mix sugar and flour with dates. Add water and vanilla. Cook until thick. Pour between crusts.

Marie Pamplin, Shreveport
Works Council, Shreveport, La.

DATE RAISIN NUT COOKIES

1 c. flour
1/4 tsp. salt
1 c. nuts, chopped fine
1/2 c. pitted dates, finely
  cut up and packed
2 tsp. brandy or bourbon

1 tsp. baking powder
1/2 c. butter or oleo,
  softened
1 c. flaked coconut
1/2 c. raisins
1 egg

Mix flour, baking powder and salt, cut in butter until particles are size of peas. Stir in coconut, nuts, dates, raisins, egg and brandy. Mix with wooden spoon or hands until dough forms. Chill 1 hour, shape in 1-inch balls. Place 1/2 inch apart on greased cookie sheet. Dip fork in flour and flatten balls to form 1 1/2-inch cookies with tines of fork. Bake in preheated 350° oven about 15 minutes or until golden brown. Makes about 48 cookies.

Verle Oliphant, Caddo
Council, Shreveport, La.

DELECABITES
(Cookies)

1/2 c. butter or oleo
1 tsp. vanilla
1 c. finely chopped walnuts

2 Tbsp. sugar
1 c. sifted all-purpose flour

Mix butter, sugar and vanilla. Gradually stir in flour and walnuts. Chill so dough can be easily handled. Shape in finger sized rolls. Bake on ungreased cookie sheet at 350° about 15-17 minutes. Turn if necessary; do not brown. Roll in powdered sugar, cool and roll in powdered sugar again.

Marjorie Harris, Capital
Council, Baton Rouge, La.

DROP COOKIES

1/2 c. soft butter
1 egg
1 tsp. vanilla
1 1/2 c. flour

1 c. sugar
4 Tbsp. milk
2 tsp. baking powder

Mix ingredients together. Drop on cookie sheet. Bake at 350° about 10-15 minutes.

Cher White, Capital Council,
Waterbury, Ct.

EAGLE BRAND COOKIE BARS

1/2 c. butter or oleo
1 can Eagle Brand milk
1 (6 oz.) pkg. semi-sweet
   chocolate morsels
1 c. chopped nuts

1 1/2 c. graham cracker
   crumbs
1 (3 1/2 oz.) can flaked
   coconut

Melt butter in 13x9-inch baking dish. Sprinkle crumbs over butter. Pour milk evenly over crumbs. Top evenly with remaining ingredients, press down gently. Bake in preheated 350° oven for 25-30 minutes or until lightly browned. Cool before cutting into bars. Store, loosely covered, at room temperature. Makes 24 bars.

Jeanette Williams, Caddo
Council, Shreveport, La.

FARFEL COOKIES
(Jewish)

2 c. farfel
1 1/2 c. sugar
4 eggs
1 c. white raisins

2 c. matzo meal
1 c. nuts, chopped fine
2/3 c. Crisco cooking oil

Mix all dry ingredients together by hand. Beat eggs separately and add to mixture until all ingredients are absorbed. Grease cookie sheet slightly. Drop by spoonfuls onto cookie sheet. Bake in preheated 350° oven for 20-25 minutes. Cinnamon may be dropped on each cookie before baking if desired. Let cookies get completely cold before removing from cookie sheet. If Teflon is used, grease that also.

Henrietta Victor, Magnolia
Council, New Orleans, La.

FIG CHEWIES

1 c. dried chopped figs
1 3/4 c. sifted flour
3/4 tsp. salt
1 egg
1/3 c. Angel Flake
   coconut

1/2 c. water
2 tsp. baking powder
1 c. packed brown sugar
1 tsp. vanilla
1 c. butter
Pecan halves

Combine figs and water in saucepan, bring to boil over medium heat. Cook and stir until tender, about 5 minutes, and cool. Sift flour with baking powder and salt. Cream butter, gradually add sugar, beating until light and fluffy. Add eggs and vanilla. Stir in figs. Add flour mixture, little at a time, beating well after each addition. Chill about 1 hour until firm enough to handle. Drop from teaspoon into coconut. Shape into balls. Place on greased, lightly floured baking sheet. Press a pecan half on each. Bake at 350° for 15 minutes or until lightly browned. Makes 4 dozen.

Jeanette English, Caddo
Council, Shreveport, La.

FIG NEWTONS

1 c. sugar
1/2 c. oleo
1/2 tsp. soda
1/4 tsp. salt

2 c. sifted flour
1 egg, beaten
1 tsp. vanilla

Blend sugar and butter. Sift dry ingredients together, add alternately with beaten egg to sugar mixture. Add vanilla. Pinch off dough about size of baseball. Roll to 1/8-inch thickness and about 5 inches wide by 12 inch long strip. In the center of 5x12-inch strip, spread the cooked fig mixture. Fold one side of dough over the fig mixture, fold the other side to where they lap. Flip the folded side down on a greased cookie sheet. Bake at 350° for 15-20 minutes. Cut into bars while still warm.

Fig Filling:

1 c. figs

3/4 c. sugar

Cook figs and sugar in saucepan for 30-40 minutes. Drain and mash up figs for filling or use drained canned fig preserves.   Jeanette English, Caddo
                                  Council, Shreveport, La.

FILLED LOGS

1 1/2 - 2 c. flour
1/2 c. salted butter
1/2 tsp. baking powder
Nuts or any jar filling

1 Tbsp. milk
1 large pkg. cream cheese
1 egg yolk

Combine flour, butter, milk, baking powder, egg yolk and cream cheese. Mix together and work dough. Roll 1/4-inch thick and cut with round cutter. Fill with nuts or any jar filling and roll into little logs. Bake on ungreased cookie sheet until light brown in 425° oven.

                                  Dee Delposen, Ouachita
                                  Council, Monroe, La.

FORGOTTEN COOKIES

2 egg whites
1 c. sugar
1 c. pecan pieces

Pinch of salt
1 (12 oz.) pkg. semi-sweet
    chocolate pieces

Preheat oven to 350°. Beat egg whites until foamy, add salt; beat again. Fold in 1 cup sugar; beat. Fold in chocolate chips and nuts. Drop on buttered cookie sheet. Place in oven and turn off oven. Leave overnight until oven is cool. Keep door closed.   Mrs. Claude J. Merrill
                                        Shreveport Works Council
                                        Shreveport, La.

FORGOTTEN COOKIES

2 egg whites
1 c. chopped pecans
1 tsp. vanilla

2/3 c. sugar
1/8 tsp. salt
1 c. chocolate or butter-
    scotch chips

Preheat oven to 350°. Beat egg whites and salt until stiff, gradually add sugar and beat until peaks form. Add vanilla. Stir in nuts and chocolate chips. Drop mixture by teaspoonfuls on greased cookie sheet. Place in oven and turn oven off. Leave overnight or all day until oven has completely cooled.   Billie Longkabel, Ouachita
                                Council, Monroe, La.

FORGOTTEN COOKIES

2 egg whites
1 c. chopped pecans

3/4 c. sugar
1 c. Rice Krispies

Preheat oven to 400°. Fold sugar into stiffly beaten egg whites. Add pecans and Rice Krispies. Drop on greased cookie sheet by teaspoonfuls. Turn oven out and place cookies in oven for 2 or 3 hours or overnight. Cookies can be moved easily off sheet when done.
                                Juanita Ridings, Ouachita
                                Council, Monroe, La.

FORGOTTEN COOKIES

2 egg whites
Pinch of salt
1 c. chopped pecans
1 c. coconut (optional)

2/3 c. sugar
1 tsp. vanilla extract
1 c. chocolate bits, or corn
   flakes or crisp rice cereal

Have eggs at room temperature. Beat egg whites until foamy. Gradually add sugar and continue beating until stiff. Add salt and vanilla, mix well. Add pecans and choice of other ingredients. Preheat oven to 350°. Drop cookies by teaspoonfuls onto ungreased foil covered cookie sheet. Place cookies in oven and immediately turn oven off. Leave cookies in closed oven overnight. Yield: 2 dozen cookies.

Jean Marzoni, Caddo
Council, Shreveport, La.

FROSTED CREAM
(Old Fashioned Molasses Cookie)

1/2 c. butter or oleo
1 egg
4 c. flour
1 tsp. salt
1 tsp. nutmeg
1 c. hot water

1 c. sugar
1 c. dark New Orleans
   molasses
1 tsp. cloves (ground)
2 tsp. ginger
2 tsp. soda

Cream butter and sugar well. Add eggs and beat. Add molasses. Sift flour, spices and soda. Add alternately with hot water. Chill dough several hours. Drop on cookie sheet by teaspoon. Bake at 400° for 14 minutes. Frost cookies.

Frosting:

2 c. powdered sugar
1 tsp. vanilla

3 or 4 Tbsp. cream

Sift sugar. Add cream and vanilla. Mix to consistency to spread easily. Frost cookies. Keeps well in a covered cookie jar.

Molly Hoskins, Caddo
Council, Shreveport, La.

584

FRUIT CAKE COOKIES

1/2 c. butter
4 eggs
3 scant tsp. soda
1 tsp. ground cloves
Dash of cinnamon
1 lb. chopped raisins
Small glass full of what-
ever "liquid" you use
in your fruit cake

1 c. brown sugar
3 Tbsp. sweet milk
3 c. flour
Dash of nutmeg
1 1/2 lb. chopped pecans
1/2 lb. chopped candied
cherries
1/2 lb. chopped candied
pineapple
1/2 lb. chopped citron

Mix as for fruit cake. Drop by teaspoonfuls. Cook for 30 minutes at 350°. Do not rush this baking period or you won't get a good cookie. It takes the full time. This is my favorite cookie recipe.   Molly Hoskins, Caddo
Council, Shreveport, La.

GINGERBREAD

2 c. syrup
1 c. sugar
3 eggs
2/3 c. shortening, melted
and cooled

3 1/4 c. flour
2 tsp. soda
2/3 c. buttermilk with soda
added to it
2 tsp. ginger

Stir syrup, sugar and shortening together. Add flour and ginger, which have been mixed together, alternately with buttermilk and soda. Add eggs, 1 at a time, beating until well mixed. Cook in greased and floured loaf pan at 325° until well done.   Calcasieu Council
Lake Charles, La.

GINGERSNAPS

2 c. flour
2 tsp. baking soda
1/2 tsp. salt
1 c. sugar
1 egg

1 Tbsp. ginger
1 tsp. cinnamon
3/4 c. oil
1/4 c. molasses, or 1/8 c.
brown sugar and 1/8 c.
corn syrup

Combine and mix flour, ginger, soda, cinnamon and salt. Sift and return to sifter. Beat oil and sugar together, beat in eggs and molasses. Sift 1/4 of flour mixture over molasses mixture. Stir to blend. Repeat until all flour is added. Form teaspoonful of dough into small balls, rolling lightly between palms. Roll balls in extra sugar and place 2 inches apart on ungreased cookie sheet. Bake at 350° about 12 minutes or until top is slightly rounded and crackly.

Faye Killen, Central Council, Pineville, La.

GINGERSNAPS

3/4 c. oleo	1 c. sugar
1/4 c. light molasses	1 egg
2 1/4 c. flour	2 tsp. soda
1/4 tsp. salt	1 tsp. cloves
1 tsp. ginger	1 tsp. cinnamon

Mix all ingredients. Roll into balls. Bake on ungreased cookie sheet at 375° for 12-15 minutes.

Karen Thompson, Ouachita Council, Monroe, La.

GOLDEN STICKS

1 (12 oz.) pkg. dried apricots	1 c. golden raisins
1 c. flaked coconut	1 c. condensed milk
1 c. finely chopped coconut	1/2 c. finely chopped nuts (optional)

Force apricots and raisins through food chopper twice, add flaked coconut and milk. Mix well. Wet hands and shape mixture into sticks or balls. Roll in chopped coconut. Let stand 20 minutes before placing in airtight container. Refrigerate or freeze. Makes about 60 pieces.

Barbara Clover, Central Council, Austin, Tx.

GREAT COOKIES

1 c. butter	1 c. white sugar
1 c. brown sugar	2 eggs, beaten
1 (6 oz.) pkg. chocolate chips	1/2 c. nuts
2 c. crushed potato chips	2 c. plain flour
	1 tsp. soda

Cream butter and sugars. Add eggs, flour and soda. Fold in chocolate chips, nuts and potato chips. Mix and drop on greased cookie sheet. Bake at 350° for 10 minutes or until done.
Sylvia Campbell, Caddo Council, Shreveport, La.

GUMDROP COOKIES

1 c. butter or margarine, softened
1 c. granulated sugar
1/2 c. firmly packed brown sugar
1 egg
1 tsp. vanilla

1 1/2 c. sifted all-purpose flour
1/2 tsp. baking powder
1/2 tsp. salt
3/4 c. quick or old fashioned oats, uncooked
1 c. chopped, assorted gumdrops

Beat together butter, sugars, egg and vanilla until creamy. Mix and sift flour, baking powder and salt. Add to creamed mixture, blending well. Stir in oats and gumdrops. Drop by teaspoonfuls onto ungreased cookie sheet. Bake at 375° for 10-12 minutes. Makes about 4 dozen.
Calcasieu Council
Lake Charles, La.

HONEY KRINCKLES
(Cookies)

2 c. flour
2 tsp. soda
1 c. sugar
1 egg

3/4 tsp. mace
2/3 c. salad or corn oil
1/4 c. honey
Granulated sugar for coating

Sift flour, mace and soda together. Beat oil and 1 cup sugar together with fork. Add egg, beat well. Add honey, add flour mixture. Drop by half teaspoonful into granulated sugar. Shape into balls, coated with sugar. Place 3 inches apart on ungreased cookie sheet. Bake 12-15 minutes at 350°. Let stand 1 minute before removing from pan. Makes 8 dozen.
Mrs. R.O. (Eloise) Beckham
Crescent City Council
New Orleans, La.

HOPSCOTCH COOKIES

1/2 c. peanut butter	1 (6 oz.) pkg. Nestle's
1 can chow mein noodles	butterscotch morsels
1 1/2 c. marshmallows	1/2 c. pecans

Combine peanut butter and morsels. Blend and melt. Remove from heat. Add noodles and marshmallows. Mix well, add pecans. Drop onto waxed paper by teaspoonfuls.

Beverly Lumm, Caddo Council, Shreveport, La.

ITALIAN FIG COOKIES

5 lb. Gold Medal plain flour	10 heaping Tbsp. baking
2 1/2 c. sugar	powder
1/2 lb. butter	1 lb. Crisco
6 eggs	1 c. milk
1 large can cream	1 tsp. cinnamon
1/2 tsp. nutmeg	1/2 small bottle vanilla
1/2 tsp. allspice	1 small bottle anise flavor-
1 small bottle almond	ing
flavoring	

Follow instructions for smaller batch of cookies (Italian Fig) in this book. This recipe makes 150 cookies.

Fig Mixture:

6 lb. dried figs	1 small bottle vanilla
2 lb. candied mixed fruit	2 1/2 c. syrup
4 c. sugar	1 or 2 pt. fig preserves,
	as needed

Prepare as for smaller batch.

Evelyn Arnone, West Bank Council, New Orleans, La.

ITALIAN FIG COOKIES

4 c. plain flour	4 tsp. baking powder
2 sticks butter	2 eggs
1/4 c. milk	1 tsp. anise flavoring
1 c. sugar	

Mix all dry ingredients in 1 bowl. Mix all liquids in separate bowl. Have butter at room temperature and mix

well with dry ingredients. Add liquid and knead thoroughly. Roll sections into 3-inch strips. Fill with fig mixture.
Fold dough and cut into pieces about 2-3 inches long. Place
on cookie sheet and bake at 350°. Place on bottom shelf of
oven and bake about 15 or 20 minutes to bake bottom.
Move to top shelf to bake tops for 15 or 20 minutes. Remove and cool. Decorate with Butter Icing and beads.
Makes 2 dozen cookies.

Fig Mixture:

2 lb. dried figs
1 lb. mixed candied fruit
1/2 lb. sugar

2 Tbsp. vanilla
1 c. maple syrup
1 pt. fig preserves

Grind fruit, except preserves, and place in container
which can be covered. Sprinkle sugar and vanilla on top of
fruit mixture. Leave covered at room temperature for 1
week. This will cause fermentation. To make cookie filling
soften, add fig preserves and work with hands until soft.

Evelyn Arnone, West Bank
Council, New Orleans, La.

LEMON BARS

Crust:

1 stick butter or oleo
1/4 c. sugar

1 1/2 c. all-purpose flour

Combine and mix at low speed until crumbly or in small
balls. Pat into ungreased 8-inch cookie pan (makes 2
batches). Bake in preheated 350° oven for 18-20 minutes
or until slightly brown.

Filling:

2 eggs
3/4 c. sugar
3 Tbsp. lemon juice

2 Tbsp. all-purpose flour
1/4 tsp. baking powder

Combine ingredients, heat and pour over crust. Bake
at 350° for 18-20 minutes. Pour over crust either hot or
warm. Let cool and sprinkle with powdered sugar.

Annie Uchello, West Bank
Council, Gretna, La.

LEMON BARS

2 sticks oleo
1/2 c. powdered sugar

2 c. plain flour

Combine ingredients for crust and cut until dough is spreadable. Press into 18x12x1-inch cookie pan. Press dough until complete bottom of pan is covered. Bake at 350° for 12 minutes. Do not brown.

Filling:

4 eggs, slightly beaten
1 tsp. baking powder
2 c. sugar

Juice and grated rind of
    1 lemon
4 Tbsp. flour

Mix ingredients for filling and pour over baked crust. Bake at 350° for 20-25 minutes. Sprinkle with powdered sugar and cut into squares. Ellen McDermott, Magnolia Council, New Orleans, La.

LEMON BUTTER SNOWBARS

Crust:

1/2 c. butter, soft
1 1/3 c. flour

1/4 c. sugar

Combine Crust ingredients. Mix on low speed about 1 minute. Pat into ungreased 8-inch square pan. Bake at 350° near center of oven for 15-20 minutes or until brown on edges. Pour Filling over partially baked crust. Return to oven for 18-20 minutes or until set. Sprinkle with powdered sugar and cool.

Filling:

2 eggs
3/4 c. sugar
3 Tbsp. bottled lemon juice

2 Tbsp. flour
1/4 tsp. baking powder

Combine all ingredients, blend well. Have Filling ready when Crust comes from oven and pour over immediately.
Jeanette English, Caddo Council, Shreveport, La.

LEMON SNOBARS

Crust:

1/2 c. butter, softened	1 1/3 c. flour
1/4 c. sugar	

Combine and mix on low speed 1 minute until blended and crumbly. Press into 8-inch square baking dish. Bake in center of oven at 350° for 15-20 minutes or until starting to brown.

Filling:

2 eggs	1/4 tsp. baking powder
3/4 c. granulated sugar	3 tsp. lemon juice
2 Tbsp. flour	Powdered sugar

Combine eggs, granulated sugar, flour, lemon juice and baking powder. Mix with spoon and pour over crust. Return to oven for 18 or 20 minutes until set. Pour powdered sugar over top. Cool and remove.

Debi Magalian, Central
Council, Silver Spring, Md.

MOTHER BAILEY'S LEMON SOURS

3/4 c. sifted all-purpose flour	1/3 c. butter
1 c. brown sugar	2 eggs
1/2 c. nuts, put through food chopper	3/4 c. flaked coconut
	1/8 tsp. baking powder
Juice and rind of 1 lemon	1/2 tsp. vanilla
	2/3 c. powdered sugar

Mix flour and butter to a fine crumb, sprinkle in pan, 9x13 inches. Bake at 350° for 10 minutes. Beat eggs, mix in brown sugar, coconut, nuts, baking powder and vanilla. Pour over crust. Return to oven and bake for 25 minutes at 350°. Make up mixture of lemon rind, juice and powdered sugar. Spread over cake as soon as it is taken from oven. Cool, cut into squares. If you like cookies with more of a lemon flavoring, add juice of 3 lemons and rind of 2. Yum! Yum!

In memory of my beloved mother, Missouri A. Bailey.

LaVanira B. Spivey
Evangeline Council
New Iberia, La.

LEMON SQUARES

Crust:

2 c. flour	1/2 c. powdered sugar
1 c. soft butter	

Mix ingredients. Beat well and press into 9x13-inch greased Pyrex dish. Bake at 350° for 25 minutes.

Topping:

4 eggs, beaten	2 c. sugar
1/3 c. lemon juice	1/4 c. flour
1/2 tsp. soda	Powdered sugar

Combine and pour over crust. Bake at 350° for 25-30 minutes. Sprinkle with powdered sugar and cut into squares when cool.
Jeannette Grice, Ozone
Council, Hammond, La.

LEMON SQUARES

Crust:

1 c. butter	2 c. flour
1/2 c. powdered sugar	1/4 tsp. salt

Mix and press in pan. Bake at 350° for 15 minutes.

Filling:

4 eggs	2 c. sugar
5 Tbsp. lemon juice	1 1/2 tsp. grated rind
4 Tbsp. flour	

Mix ingredients and pour on top of baked Crust. Bake 25 or 30 minutes at 350°. When cool, cut into squares.
Doris Reeves, Capital
Council, Baton Rouge, La.

LEMON SQUARES

Crust:

1/2 c. melted butter	2 c. flour, sifted
1/2 c. powdered sugar	1/4 tsp. salt

Mix ingredients and pat or press into bottom of 13x9-inch baking pan. Bake at 350° for 20 minutes.

Topping:

4 eggs, beaten
4 tsp. sifted flour
5 Tbsp. lemon juice

2 c. granulated sugar
1 1/2 Tbsp. grated lemon
rind

Mix ingredients and pour on top of baked crust. Place back in 350° oven for 25-30 minutes. Cool, sprinkle with powdered sugar and cut into squares. Makes about 24 small squares.
Cecile Gallet, Evangeline
Council, Lafayette, La

LIZZIES

1/2 c. butter
4 eggs
2 2/3 tsp. soda
2/3 c. whiskey
1 tsp. nutmeg
6 c. nuts
1 lb. red cherries

1 c. brown sugar
3 Tbsp. milk
3 c. flour
1 tsp. cloves
1 tsp. cinnamon
1 lb. white raisins
1/2 lb. green pineapple

Cream sugar and butter. Add eggs and beat. Add milk and whiskey, then dry ingredients. Add chopped fruit last. Bake on greased cookie sheet at 300° for 30 minutes.
Gay Irwin, Capital Council,
Baton Rouge, La.

PECAN MACAROONS

2 c. chopped pecans
2 c. brown sugar
1 tsp. vanilla

2 egg whites
2 Tbsp. flour
Pinch of salt

Mix flour with pecans. Whip egg whites and salt until stiff. Add vanilla. Fold in brown sugar and stir well. Add pecans, mix well. Dough will be stiff. Line cookie sheet with foil and butter well. Drop by teaspoonfuls onto cookie sheet. Bake at 275° for 20 minutes. Turn off oven. Let set to cool in oven for crispier cookies. If chewy cookie is wanted, remove from oven when done. Store in tight container. Makes 42 cookies.
Joyce Hattier, Magnolia
Council, New Orleans, La.

MARMALADE SQUARES

1 c. flour	1 tsp. baking powder
1/4 tsp. salt	1/2 c. butter
1 egg, beaten	1/2 c. orange marmalade
1 Tbsp. milk	

Combine flour, baking powder and salt. Cut in butter until mixture resembles coarse crumbs. Blend in egg and milk. Spread dough in greased 8x8x2-inch pan. Spread marmalade evenly over dough. Spoon Topping over marmalade. Bake at 375° for 30 minutes. Cool completely. Cut into squares.

Topping:

| 1/4 c. melted butter | 1 egg, beaten |
| 1/2 c. flaked coconut | 1 tsp. grated orange peel |

Combine all ingredients, mixing well.

Jeanette English, Caddo
Council, Shreveport, La.

MARSHMALLOW-CHOCOLATE SQUARES

1 c. oleo	1 1/2 c. sugar
4 eggs	1 1/2 c. flour
1/2 tsp. salt	5 Tbsp. cocoa
1/2 tsp. baking powder	1 c. chopped nuts
1 tsp. vanilla	1 large bag miniature marsh-mallows

Cream oleo and sugar together, add eggs. Add flour, salt, cocoa and baking powder to creamed mixture. Stir in vanilla and nuts, mix well. Pat into jelly roll pan, 15x10x1-inch. Bake at 350° for 15-20 minutes. Remove from oven, top with marshmallows and return to oven about 2 minutes for marshmallows to melt. When cool, spread with Chocolate Butter Icing and sprinkle with chopped nuts. Cut into squares.

Marie Feiertag, Ouachita
Council, Monroe, La.

MAPLE BARS

1/3 c. butter
1 egg
1/8 tsp. salt
3/4 c. sifted flour

1/3 c. powdered sugar
1/3 c. maple syrup
1/8 tsp. soda
1 c. broken nutmeats

Cream butter until soft. Beat in egg, syrup, salt and soda. Mix in sifted flour. Stir in nuts and pour into 8x8-inch greased pan. Bake at 375° for 15 minutes. Cut into bars while warm and roll in powdered sugar. Makes 36 bars.

June Harllee, Caddo
Council, Shreveport, La.

MERINGUE COOKIES

2 egg whites
2 c. powdered sugar
1 tsp. vinegar

1/4 tsp. salt
1 tsp. vanilla
1/2 c. pecans

Beat egg and salt together until stiff. Slowly add sugar and continue to beat. Add vanilla, vinegar and nuts. Drop on greased baking sheet with teaspoon. Bake in preheated oven at 350° for 12-15 minutes until light brown. Makes 2-3 dozen.

Billie Longkabel, Ouachita
Council, Monroe, La.

NO BAKE COOKIES

2 c. sugar
1/2 c. oleo
1 tsp. vanilla
3 c. oats

1/2 c. milk
1/8 tsp. salt
1 c. peanut butter

Combine sugar, milk, oleo and salt in pan. Place over heat and bring to a full boil for 1 minute. Remove from heat, add vanilla, peanut butter; stir until smooth. Add oats. Cool until mixture holds shape and drop by teaspoon onto waxed paper. Cookies harden as they cool.

Sally Walker, Ouachita
Council, Monroe, La.

OATMEAL COOKIES

1 c. Crisco
1 c. white sugar
1 c. brown sugar
1 1/2 c. flour
Vanilla flavoring

2 eggs
1 tsp. soda
1/2 tsp. salt
3 c. oatmeal

Mix eggs, sugars, soda, Crisco, salt and flour. Add oatmeal and flavoring. Drop by spoonfuls on greased cookie sheet. Bake at 350° until brown.

Twila "Pete" Dysart
Ouachita Council, Monroe, La.

OATMEAL COOKIES

2 c. shortening
2 1/2 c. brown sugar,
    firmly packed
1/2 c. water
5 1/2 c. quick cooking
    oatmeal
1 large bag chocolate
    chips (optional)

2 c. white sugar
4 eggs
5 tsp. soda
5 1/2 c. flour
1 tsp. salt
2 tsp. vanilla
3 c. raisins (optional)
2 c. chopped pecans (optional)

In large mixing bowl, cream sugar and shortening, add eggs, 1 at a time, while beating. Add water mixed with soda, salt and vanilla. Blend in the mixer about half the flour, stopping when mixer begins to feel overloaded. Transfer to largest bowl, mix in rest of flour and oatmeal, preferably by hand. If using raisins, chocolate chips or nuts, work them in last. Form into 5 or 6 rolls, 1 1/2 - 2 inches in diameter, depending how large you like your cookies. Store in refrigerator overnight or freeze for a couple of hours to make them easier to slice. Slice cookies 1/4-inch thick and bake at 375° for 10-12 minutes on un-greased cookie sheets. These cookies keep indefinitely in the freezer.

Betty Marshall, Shreveport
Works Council, Shreveport, La.

OATMEAL DATE BALLS

1 c. butter or oleo, softened
3 Tbsp. sugar
1 1/2 tsp. cinnamon

2 (8 oz.) pkg. whole, pitted dates, finely chopped
1 c. quick cooking oats
3/4 c. finely chopped nuts

In large bowl with mixer at medium speed, beat oleo, sugar and cinnamon until fluffy. Stir in dates and oats with spoon. Cover and refrigerate dough 2 or 3 hours until firm. When firm, shape into 1-inch balls with hands. Roll in nuts. Chill. Makes about 3 1/2 dozen.

Carlotta Thomas, Ouachita Council, Monroe, La.

OATMEAL DROP COOKIES

1 c. shortening
1 c. brown sugar
2 c. flour
1 tsp. baking powder
3/4 c. pecans
Pinch of salt

1 c. granulated sugar
2 eggs
1 tsp. soda
2 c. cooking oatmeal
1 (6 oz.) pkg. chocolate chips

Cream shortening and sugar together until fluffy, add eggs and beat well. Sift together flour, soda, baking powder and salt. Add to creamed mixture and stir well. Stir in remaining ingredients. Drop from teaspoon 2 inches apart on greased cookie sheet. Bake at 350° for 12-15 minutes.

Gertrude Juneau, Crescent City Council, New Orleans, La.

OATMEAL ICEBOX COOKIES

1 c. shortening
1 c. brown sugar
1 tsp. vanilla
1 tsp. salt
3 c. quick Quaker oats

1 c. sugar
2 eggs
1 1/2 c. flour
1 tsp. soda
1/2 c. nuts

Cream shortening, sugar and eggs together; add remaining ingredients. Mix well. Spoon drop on cookie sheet. Bake at 350° until golden brown.

Lorraine McNanemin
Calcasieu Council
Lake Charles, La.

OATMEAL-PECAN COOKIES

1 c. Crisco shortening
1 tsp. vanilla
1 c. brown sugar
2 beaten eggs
1 tsp. soda

1 c. white sugar
1 tsp. salt
2 c. quick oats
1 1/2 c. flour
1 c. pecans

Cream shortening and sugars. Add in remaining ingredients. Mix well. Shape into rolls and put in waxed paper. Chill until hard. Slice 1/4-inch thick and place on ungreased cookie sheet. Bake at 325° for 10 or 15 minutes.

Mary C. Regan, Crescent City
Council, New Orleans, La.

PEANUT BLOSSOMS

1 3/4 c. flour
1/2 tsp. salt
1/2 c. brown sugar
1/2 c. peanut butter
2 Tbsp. milk
48 milk chocolate kisses

1 tsp. soda
1/2 c. granulated sugar
1/2 c. shortening
1 egg
1 tsp. vanilla

Combine all ingredients, except candy kisses. Mix on lowest speed of mixer until dough forms. Shape dough into balls, using a rounded teaspoonful for each cookie. Roll balls in sugar, place on ungreased cookie sheet. Bake at 375° for 10-12 minutes. Top each cookie immediately with a candy kiss. Press down firmly so cookie cracks around edge.

Dorothy Weber, Ouachita
Council, Monroe, La.

PEANUT BUTTER COOKIES

1 c. sugar
3/4 tsp. baking powder
1/2 c. shortening
1 1/2 c. flour

1 egg
1/8 tsp. salt
1 c. peanut butter

Mix together thoroughly and drop on cookie sheet. Bake at 350° for 10-15 minutes until golden brown.

Cher White, Capital Council,
Waterbury, Ct.

PEANUT BUTTER COOKIES

2 1/2 c. plain flour
1 tsp. baking powder
1 c. white sugar
1 c. brown sugar, firmly
  packed
1 c. peanut butter

1/2 tsp. soda
1/4 tsp. salt
2 sticks oleo
2 eggs
1 tsp. vanilla

Mix dry ingredients and set aside. Cream remaining ingredients. Slowly mix all ingredients together. Drop on ungreased cookie sheets by teaspoon. Press lightly, crisscross over top with damp fork. Bake at 375° for 5-6 minutes. Makes 5 dozen.

Hazel Blouin, Shreveport
Works Council, Shreveport, La.

PEANUT BUTTER COOKIES

1 (12 oz.) jar peanut butter
1 c. white Karo syrup
1 tsp. vanilla

1 c. sugar
1/2 box Special K

Mix sugar and syrup. Bring to boil, stir in peanut butter and vanilla, mix well. Stir in Special K and drop by spoonfuls on waxed paper. Fast and easy.

Molly Hoskins, Caddo
Council, Shreveport, La.

CHOCOLATE PEANUT BUTTER CHEWIES

2 c. sugar
1/2 c. milk
1 tsp. vanilla
3 c. oatmeal

1/4 c. cocoa
1 stick oleo
1/2 c. peanut butter
Pinch of salt

Mix sugar, cocoa, milk and oleo. Heat until mixture boils. Cool 1 minute, add remaining ingredients. Spoon on waxed paper.

Becky Flack, Central
Council, Natchitoches, La.

EASY PEANUT BUTTER COOKIES

1 c. peanut butter   1 c. sugar
1 egg   1 tsp. vanilla

Mix all ingredients. Roll into 1-inch balls. Place on ungreased cookie sheet. Press down lightly with fork to make crisscross. Bake at 350° for 8-10 minutes.

Sharon Bell, Capital Council,
Waterbury, Ct.

PECAN HONEYS

2 sticks butter or oleo   Cinnamon graham crackers
1 c. brown sugar   1 c. broken pecans

Mix butter and sugar together and boil 2 minutes. Pour over single layer of graham crackers placed on cookie sheet. Sprinkle with pecans. Bake 12 minutes at 350°. Cool before removing from pan.   Annie Hawkins, Caddo
Council, Shreveport, La.

PECAN PIE SURPRISE BARS

1 pkg. yellow cake mix   1/3 c. butter or oleo, melted
4 eggs, divided   1 c. chopped pecans
1/2 c. brown sugar, firmly   1 1/2 c. dark corn syrup
  packed   1 tsp. vanilla

Reserve 2/3 cup dry cake mix; combine remaining cake mix, butter and 1 egg. Press into greased bottom and sides of 9x13-inch baking pan. Bake at 350° for 15-20 minutes until light golden brown. Combine brown sugar, corn syrup, vanilla, reserved cake mix and 3 eggs. Beat at medium speed 1-2 minutes. Pour filling over partially baked crust, sprinkle with pecans. Return to oven and bake 30-35 minutes until filling is set.   Gayle Palermo, Westmoor
Council, Kenner, La.

PECAN STICKS

2 c. light brown sugar
2 tsp. vanilla
2 tsp. baking powder
Chopped pecans

1 stick oleo
2 eggs
2 c. flour
Dash of salt

Mix sugar, oleo, eggs and vanilla until creamy. Add flour, baking powder and salt. Stir in 1 cup chopped pecans. Mix well and press dough into a greased 13x9x2-inch pan lined with waxed paper. Press dough evenly in pan and sprinkle generously with chopped pecans, pressing lightly into the dough. Bake for about 25 minutes at 350°. Do not overbake. Cut into bars or sticks to serve.

Theda S. Thomas, Caddo
Council, Shreveport, La.

PLANTATION CREAMS
(Soft Cookies)

3 3/4 c. flour
2 c. brown sugar
2 tsp. baking soda
1/2 tsp. salt
1 tsp. vanilla

1 c. butter
1 c. rich cream, or 1 c.
   milk and 1 tsp. vinegar
2 eggs

Sift, then measure flour. Cream butter until light and fluffy. Gradually add sugar, beating after each addition. Mix soda and salt with cream and immediately add to butter mixture. Add eggs, 1 at a time, beating after each. Add vanilla, then gradually add flour, blending thoroughly. Roll and cut. Bake on cookie sheet at 350° for 13 minutes.

Kathy Derdich, Ouachita
Council, Monroe, La.

POTATO CHIP COOKIES

1 c. shortening
1 c. brown sugar
1 c. white sugar
1 tsp. soda

2 c. flour
2 eggs
1 tsp. vanilla
1 c. crushed potato chips
3/4 c. nuts

Cream shortening, sugar and eggs until creamy, add remaining ingredients; mix well. Drop by teaspoonfuls onto cookie sheet, slightly flatten with fork. Bake at 350° for 10-15 minutes.

Jean Heppner, Shreveport
Works Council, Shreveport, La.

PUMPKIN COOKIES

Frosting (Make first.):

3 Tbsp. butter
1/2 c. brown sugar
3/4 tsp. vanilla

4 tsp. milk (if needed, add extra)
1 c. powdered sugar

Cook butter, milk and brown sugar until dissolved. Cool, add powdered sugar and vanilla.

Cookies:

1 c. shortening
1 c. pumpkin
2 c. flour
1 tsp. cinnamon

1 c. sugar
1 egg
1 tsp. soda
1 c. raisins

Cream together shortening, sugar and pumpkin. Add egg and mix well. Add sifted dry ingredients in 3 parts, mixing well after each addition. Stir in raisins. Drop by teaspoons onto ungreased cookie sheets. Bake at 375° for 10-12 minutes. Spread Frosting on hot cookies.

Kathy Derdich, Ouachita
Council, Monroe, La.

PUMPKIN COOKIES

2 1/2 c. sifted flour
1/2 tsp. soda
3/4 tsp. cinnamon
1 c. packed brown sugar
3/4 c. pumpkin puree

1/2 tsp. salt
1/4 tsp. cloves
3/4 c. vegetable shortening
1 egg
1 c. raisins

Sift flour, salt, baking soda, cloves and cinnamon on waxed paper. Beat shortening, sugar, egg and pumpkin in large bowl until well blended. Stir in flour mixture until thoroughly mixed. Stir in raisins. Drop by heaping teaspoonfuls onto greased cookie sheet. Bake at 375° for 15 minutes or until lightly browned. Remove to a wire rack to cool.

June Harllee, Caddo
Council, Shreveport, La.

PUMPKIN SQUARES

1 c. flour
1/2 tsp. salt
1/2 c. butter or oleo
1 egg
1/4 c. dry instant mashed
  potatoes

1 tsp. baking powder
1/2 tsp. cinnamon
1 1/2 c. sugar
3/4 c. pumpkin
1/2 c. chopped pecans
Powdered sugar

Sift flour, salt, baking powder, cloves and cinnamon onto waxed paper. Beat butter, sugar and egg in large bowl until light and fluffy. Stir in pumpkin and potato. Stir in flour mixture, little at a time, beating well after each addition. Fold in pecans. Turn batter into a greased 9x9x2-inch pan, spreading evenly. Bake at 350° for 40 minutes or until center springs back when lightly touched with fingertips. Cool in pan on wire rack. Sprinkle with powdered sugar and cut into squares.

June Harllee, Caddo
Council, Shreveport, La.

QUICK SUGAR COOKIES

2 c. biscuit mix
2 eggs
1/2 c. butter or oleo

1 c. sugar
1 tsp. vanilla
Milk

Cream butter, sugar and vanilla together. Add biscuit mix. Add enough milk to make stiff dough. Place by teaspoonfuls on greased cookie sheet. Bake at 350° until light golden brown.

Susan Lackney, Westmoor
Council, Kenner, La.

ROCKS

3 eggs
4 c. sugar
1 c. Crisco
4 3/4 c. flour

4 c. nuts
1 box raisins
2 Tbsp. soda
1 tsp. flavor
2 Tbsp. boiling water

Beat eggs well. Add sugar and Crisco. Mix well. Dissolve soda in boiling water and add to mixture. Add nuts, raisins and flavoring. Add flour and mix until dough is very thick. Use more flour if necessary. Shape and place

on floured cookie sheet. Bake in preheated 350° oven about
15 minutes or until browned.   Marjorie Rowell, Evangeline
Council, Lafayette, La.

ROCKS

1 c. butter or oleo
1 1/2 c. granulated sugar
3 eggs, beaten slightly
3 c. flour
1 tsp. cinnamon
1 tsp. nutmeg
1 tsp. soda

1 lb. dates, chopped
1 1/2 lb. pecans, broken
in large pieces
1 1/2 lb. walnuts, broken in
large pieces
1 tsp. allspice
2 Tbsp. hot water

Mix nuts and dates with flour. Cream butter and sugar
well, add spices. Blend eggs with nut mixture. Dissolve
soda in hot water. Combine all ingredients together. Drop
by teaspoonfuls on buttered baking sheet. Bake at 350°
until golden brown. Makes about 250 Rocks.
Theda S. Thomas, Caddo
Council, Shreveport, La.

ROCKY ROAD FUDGE BARS

1/2 c. butter or oleo
1 c. sugar
1 c. unsifted flour
1 tsp. baking powder
2 eggs

1 (1 oz.) sq. unsweetened
chocolate
1/2 c. chopped nuts
1 tsp. vanilla

Filling:

6 oz. cream cheese,
softened
2 Tbsp. flour
1 egg

1/2 c. sugar
1/4 c. butter, softened
1/4 c. chopped nuts

Frosting:

2 c. miniature marsh-
mallows
1 sq. unsweetened choco-
late
1/4 c. milk

1/4 c. butter
2 oz. cream cheese
1 lb. (3 c.) powdered sugar
1 tsp. vanilla

In large saucepan, melt butter and chocolate over low
heat, remove from heat. Add sugar, flour, nuts, baking
powder, vanilla and eggs. Mix well. Spread in greased and
604

floured 13x9-inch pan. In bowl, combine Filling. Spread over chocolate mixture in pan. Bake 25-35 minutes or until done. Sprinkle with marshmallows and bake 2 minutes longer. Combine butter, chocolate, cream cheese and milk in saucepan for Frosting. Heat over low fire until chocolate melts. Stir in powdered sugar and vanilla until smooth. Pour over marshmallows and swirl together. Cool and cut into bars. Makes about 36 bars. Tracey Delposen, Ouachita Council, Monroe, La.

ROLLED WHEAT RAISIN CRISPIES

1 c. shortening	2 c. brown sugar, packed
2 eggs	2 c. flour
1 tsp. baking soda	1 tsp. salt
2 c. uncooked quick oatmeal	1 c. raisins

Mix fat, sugar and eggs. Beat well. Add flour, baking soda and salt. Mix in raisins and oatmeal. Drop dough from teaspoon on baking sheet. Bake at 375° for 10-12 minutes or until light brown. Makes 4 dozen.
Cecile Gallet, Evangeline Council, Lafayette, La.

SAND TARTS

1/4 lb. butter	8 Tbsp. powdered sugar
1 1/2 c. sifted flour	1 tsp. almond extract
1 c. finely chopped nuts	Powdered sugar for rolling and sprinkling

Cream butter and 8 tablespoons powdered sugar. Add flour gradually. Add extract and nuts. Shape into cocoons and roll in powdered sugar. Bake at 340° for 30-40 minutes. Sprinkle with powdered sugar.
Cecile Gallet, Evangeline Council, Lafayette, La.

SELF-FILLED CUPCAKES
(Kids will love them!)

1 (2 layer) pkg. chocolate
  cake mix
1 (8 oz.) pkg. cream
  cheese, softened

1/3 c. sugar
1 egg
1 dash of salt
1 (6 oz.) pkg. semi-sweet
  chocolate pieces (1 c.)

Mix cake according to package directions. Fill paper baking cups in muffin pans 2/3 full. Cream the cheese with sugar. Beat egg and salt, stir in chocolate pieces. Drop 1 rounded teaspoon cheese mixture into each cupcake. Bake as package directs. Makes about 30 cupcakes.

Calcasieu Council
Lake Charles, La.

SKILLET COOKIES

1 c. chopped nuts
1 stick butter
2 egg yolks
Flaked coconut

1 (8 oz.) pkg. chopped dates
1/2 c. sugar
2 c. Rice Krispies

Melt butter in heavy skillet. Add sugar and egg yolks. Add dates and nuts. Cook 5 minutes. Remove from fire, add Rice Krispies. Shape into balls and roll in coconut.

Marguerite Oliver, Shreveport
Works Council, Shreveport, La.

SNOWBALL COOKIES

1 stick butter + 2 Tbsp.
  oleo
1 tsp. vanilla
2 c. chopped nuts

1/2 c. powdered sugar
2 c. flour
2 drops almond flavor
  (optional)

Cream butter and sugar. Add flour, flavoring and nuts. Roll into small balls. Bake 15 minutes at 350°. While still hot, shake in bag of powdered sugar.

Marie Pamplin
Shreveport Works Council
Shreveport, La.

Ann Kaplan
Shreveport Works Council
Shreveport, La.

606

SOFT SUGAR COOKIES

1 c. Crisco
3 eggs
1 3/4 c. sugar
1 tsp. salt
1 tsp. vanilla

1 tsp. soda
2 tsp. baking powder
1 c. milk
2 Tbsp. vinegar
4 c. flour

Have eggs and milk at room temperature. Cream sugar, eggs, salt and shortening together. Add baking powder and vanilla. Add vinegar to milk, dissolve soda in milk, add alternately with flour to creamed mixture. Drop by teaspoonfuls onto greased cookie sheet. Sprinkle top with sugar. Bake at 350° for 8-10 minutes. Yield: 4 dozen. One teaspoon nutmeg or 1 teaspoon lemon flavoring can be added sometimes for a different taste, if desired.

Karen Thompson, Ouachita
Council, Monroe, La.

SWEDISH NUT ROLLS

1 stick oleo
1/2 lb. dates, chopped
1 tsp. vanilla
3 c. Rice Krispies

1 c. sugar
2 eggs
1 c. chopped nuts
Coconut

Mix oleo, sugar, dates and eggs. Cook 10 minutes until smooth. Remove from heat, add vanilla, nuts and Rice Krispies. Mix together with hands and form into balls. Roll in coconut.

Sally Walker, Ouachita
Council, Monroe, La.

TEA CAKES

2 c. plain flour
1/2 tsp. salt
1 c. sugar
1 egg, beaten
1 tsp. vanilla

1/2 tsp. baking powder
1/2 tsp. soda
2/3 c. shortening, creamed
2 Tbsp. milk

Cream sugar and shortening together. Add egg, milk and vanilla. Sift dry ingredients together, gradually add to creamed mixture and blend thoroughly. Roll out on cloth or board. Cut with cutter 1/16-inch thick. Place cookies on ungreased cookie sheet. Bake at 400° for 5-7 minutes. Sprinkle with sugar if desired.

Maxine Fletcher, Ouachita
Council, Monroe, La.

ARKANSAS TEA CAKES

1 3/4 c. sugar
2 eggs
1 tsp. soda
3 tsp. Pet milk

1 c. butter or corn oil oleo
1/2 tsp. salt
1/2 tsp. vanilla
3 c. flour

Mix ingredients together. Can be chilled in rolls and sliced, or made into small balls. Bake at 350° until lightly brown.

B.B. Wynne, Shreveport
Works Council, Shreveport, La.

AUNT DOLLIE'S TEA CAKES

1/2 c. shortening
2 eggs
1/2 c. buttermilk

1 c. sugar
1 tsp. vanilla
3 c. flour

Mix ingredients until stiff enough to roll out thin. Cut and bake on cookie sheet until brown at 350°.

Brenda Braxton, Ouachita
Council, Monroe, La.

GRANDMA'S TEA CAKES

1 egg
1 c. sugar
1/4 c. buttermilk
1 tsp. vanilla

2 c. flour
3 Tbsp. butter
1 tsp. soda

Cream sugar and butter, add vanilla and egg; beat well. Sift dry ingredients and add alternately with buttermilk. Roll in small amount of flour and pinch off about 1 teaspoonful of dough at a time. Flatten with your hands. Place on lightly greased cookie sheet and bake for 10 minutes at 350°. For added flavor, use 1/2 teaspoon vanilla and 1/2 teaspoon lemon flavoring.

Jeanette English, Caddo
Council, Shreveport, La.

GRANDMOTHER'S TEA CAKES

2 c. sugar
1/2 c. sweet milk
2 tsp. baking powder
1 tsp. vanilla

3 eggs
3/4 c. Crisco shortening
3 c. flour

Mix all ingredients together and drop on greased cookie sheet. Bake at 350° until done. These are plain cookies for kids.
Winnie Holden, Crescent
City Council, New Orleans, La.

MOM'S OLD FASHIONED TEA CAKES

1 stick butter or oleo
1 c. sugar
2 eggs
1 tsp. vanilla

2 c. flour
1 tsp. baking powder
Pinch of salt

Cream butter and sugar, add beaten eggs, vanilla and flour. Makes a soft dough. Best to chill in refrigerator. Sprinkle some sugar in flour you roll dough out on and sprinkle sugar on top of cookies. Bake at 300° until brown.
Thelma Slay, Caddo
Council, Shreveport, La.

OLD FASHIONED TEA CAKES

2 c. sugar
2 or 3 drops yellow
   food coloring (optional)

2 sticks butter or oleo
2 eggs
4 c. flour

Mix and drop on cookie sheet. Bake at 350° until done.
Johnnie Sampson, Shreveport
Works Council, Shreveport, La.

OLD FASHIONED SOUTHERN TEA CAKES

1/2 c. oleo or butter
1 tsp. vanilla
2 eggs, well beaten
2 tsp. baking powder

1 c. sugar
1 Tbsp. milk
2 1/2 c. plain flour
1/4 tsp. salt

Cream oleo with sugar. Mix vanilla and milk, add to

1723-79

oleo mixture. Add eggs. Sift and mix in flour, baking powder and salt. Mix well. Grease cookie sheet with sides, spread dough on sheet with hands which have been dipped in flour. Pat and smooth in pan. Bake at 400° until light brown, 10-12 minutes. Cut in squares in pan. Cool on rack. Remove to cool.

Grace Bell, Ouachita Council, Monroe, La.

OLD   TIME   TEA   CAKES

1 c. butter, softened	1 1/3 c. sugar
2 eggs	1/4 c. buttermilk
1 tsp. soda	1 tsp. vanilla
	4 c. flour

Cream butter and sugar, add 3 cups flour and remaining ingredients, mix well. Use remaining cup of flour in rolling out dough. Place cookies on greased cookie sheet and bake at 350° until done. Sprinkle with sugar if desired.

Becky Sanders, Central Council, St. Landry, La.

TOLL   HOUSE   PAN   COOKIES

2 1/4 c. unsifted flour	1 tsp. baking soda
1 tsp. salt	1 c. butter, softened
3/4 c. white sugar	3/4 c. brown sugar, firmly
1 tsp. vanilla	packed
2 eggs	1 (12 oz.) pkg. chocolate
1 c. chopped nuts	chips

Combine flour, soda and salt; set aside. Combine butter, sugars, vanilla; beat until creamy. Beat in eggs. Gradually add flour mixture; mix well. Stir in chocolate chips and nuts. Spread into greased 15x10x1-inch pan. Bake 20 minutes in preheated 375° oven. Makes 35 squares.

Note: Halve recipe if using only 6 ounce package chocolate chips and use 13x9x2-inch pan. Bake 12-15 minutes. Yield: 24 squares.

Carole Smith	Sylvia Campbell	Patricia Edmonson
Caddo Council	Caddo Council	Caddo Council
Shreveport, La.	Shreveport, La.	Shreveport, La.

TURTLE BARS

1 3/4 c. all-purpose flour
3/4 c. firmly packed
  brown sugar
1/2 tsp. salt
1 (6 oz.) pkg. semi-
  sweet chocolate pieces

1 1/2 c. uncooked oatmeal,
  quick or old fashioned
3/4 c. oleo, melted
1/2 c. coarsely chopped
  pecans
1 (12 1/4 oz.) can caramel
  ice cream topping

Combine 1 1/2 cups flour, oats, sugar and salt. Add
butter, mixing until crumbly; reserve 3/4 cup of mixture.
Press remaining mixture into bottom of greased 13x9-inch
pan. Bake at 375° for 10 minutes. Remove from oven,
sprinkle chocolate and nuts over crust. Combine topping
and remaining flour, drizzle over chocolate and nuts.
Sprinkle reserved crumb mixture over caramel topping.
Return to oven, bake additional 20 minutes at 375°. Chill
until chocolate is set. Cut into bars.

Shirley J. Peoples, Crescent
City Council, New Orleans, La.

VANILLA WAFER LOG

1 large bag vanilla
  wafers, crushed fine
1 c. raisins

1 can Eagle Brand milk
1 c. pecans or other nuts

Mix all ingredients thoroughly. Wet hands and shape
into a log on sheet of waxed paper. Mixture will be rather
stiff. Refrigerate overnight. Cut into slices when ready
to serve.

Jerry O. Stafford, Ozone
Council, Hammond, La.

VIENNESE CRESCENTS

1 c. ground walnuts or
  pecans
2 1/2 c. sifted flour

1 c. butter (no substitute)
3/4 c. sugar
1 1/2 tsp. vanilla extract

Knead to a smooth dough and shape about 1 teaspoon
of dough at a time into small crescents, about 1 1/2 inches
long. Bake on ungreased cookie sheets at 350° until slightly
browned, about 15-17 minutes. Cool 1 minute. While still

warm, roll cookies in Vanilla Sugar. Cool completely, roll again in Vanilla Sugar. Makes about 70.

Vanilla Sugar:

1 lb. powdered sugar   2 or 3 vanilla beans

Cut beans into inch long pieces. Place in jar with sifted powdered sugar. Let stand at least 3 days. The longer sugar stands, the more fragrant.

Betty Marshall, Shreveport
Works Council, Shreveport, La.

CHRISTINE'S WALNUT CLUSTERS

1/2 c. flour   1/4 tsp. baking powder
1/2 tsp. salt   1/2 c. soft butter
1/2 c. sugar   1 egg
1 1/2 tsp. vanilla   1 1/2 sq. chocolate, melted
2 c. nutmeats

Sift flour, baking powder and salt. Mix butter and sugar until creamy. Add eggs and vanilla; mix well. Mix in chocolate; mix in flour mixture. Fold in nuts. Drop by teaspoon 1 inch apart on greased cookie sheet. Bake at 350° for 10 minutes.

Mollie Hoskins, Caddo
Council, Shreveport, La.

WALNUT SANDIES

1/3 c. sugar   2 sticks oleo
2 tsp. vanilla flavoring   2 tsp. water
2 c. plain flour, presifted   1 c. finely chopped walnuts
1 box powdered sugar   or pecans

Cream sugar and oleo for 8 minutes at high speed until light and fluffy. Add vanilla and water, mix well. Add flour at low speed until well blended. Remove from mixer and stir in nuts. Chill dough for 1/2 hour, roll into round balls and place on ungreased cookie sheet. Bake at 325° for 20 minutes on lowest rack, place on middle rack for 5 more minutes. Remove and cool for 10 minutes. Place in plastic bag with powdered sugar and shake bag to cover cookies.

Henrietta Victor, Magnolia
Council, New Orleans, La.

WHISKEY BALLS

1 pkg. vanilla wafers
2 Tbsp. white Karo syrup
2 jiggers whiskey or rum

3/4 c. powdered sugar
1 c. nuts, chopped

Break vanilla wafers, then crush with rolling pin. Combine all ingredients. Put more powdered sugar on waxed paper and roll into balls.
Barbara E. Wellman, Metairie Council, New Orleans, La.

YUM-YUM BARS

1 c. sugar
1 c. oleo
1 c. coconut
1 c. chopped nuts

1/2 c. milk
1 egg
1 c. graham cracker crumbs
Whole graham crackers

Line 13 1/2 x 8 1/2-inch pan with whole graham crackers. Combine sugar, milk, oleo and egg and bring to boil 2 minutes. Remove from heat, stir in coconut, chopped nuts and graham cracker crumbs. Spread this mixture evenly on layer of graham crackers. Cover with another layer of graham crackers, pressing down firmly.

Icing:

1/2 c. oleo, melted
1 tsp. vanilla

2 c. powdered sugar
Enough lemon juice for
  spreading

Mix ingredients together and ice graham crackers. Cover and refrigerate. Cut in small bars when ready to serve. Rich.
Molly Hoskins, Caddo Council, Shreveport, La.

ALMOND FLOAT

1 Tbsp. plain gelatin
1/4 c. cold water
2/3 c. sweet milk
1 1/2 tsp. almond extract
2 1/2 Tbsp. sugar
1 c. water

2/3 c. boiling water
1/4 c. sugar
1/3 c. cream
1 can lichee nuts or Mandarin orange segments
1 1/4 tsp. almond extract

Soften gelatin in 1/4 cup water, then add 2/3 cup

boiling water and 1/4 cup sugar. Stir until thoroughly dissolved. Add milk, cream and extract. Mix well and pour into shallow oblong dish; refrigerate until set. Cut gel into squares about 1-inch square and place in crystal or glass bowl. Pour canned fruit with liquid on gel squares. There should be considerable amount of liquid; if not enough, make a syrup of the remaining sugar, water and almond extract and pour into bowl. Stir well and serve in individual dessert dishes when a light finish to a meal is desired.

Ann Orr, Evangeline
Council, New Iberia, La.

AMBROSIA

4 pt. whipping cream
1 medium can pineapple
  chunks
1 large jar maraschino
  cherries

2 large cans fruit cocktail
3 cans (medium) Mandarin
  oranges
1 large can walnuts
1/4 c. sugar

Whip 3 pints of cream, add sugar. Drain fruit. Chop cherries and nuts. Fold into whipped cream. Place in large punch bowl and top with remaining pint of cream, whipped.

Terri DiFusco, Capital
Council, Naugatuck, Ct.

APPLE DELIGHT

1 can apple pie filling
1 c. sugar
Dash of cinnamon
2/3 c. oil
2/3 c. chopped nuts

2 c. flour
1 1/2 tsp. soda
2 eggs
1 tsp. vanilla
Raisins (optional)

Mix ingredients together until well blended. Add raisins, if desired. Bake at 350° for 45-50 minutes until toothpick is clean. Sprinkle with powdered sugar and nuts.

Tracey Delposen, Ouachita
Council, Monroe, La.

614

APPLE FRITTERS

1 1/2 c. sifted flour
1/2 tsp. salt
Powdered sugar
2 tsp. baking powder
1 tsp. cinnamon (optional)

1/4 c. sugar
1/2 c. milk
2 apples, cored and quartered
2 eggs

Sift flour, sugar, salt and baking powder together in bowl. Put milk, eggs and apples in blender until slightly blended. Stir into dry ingredients until smooth. Drop by spoonfuls into hot deep fat. Sprinkle with powdered sugar and cinnamon if desired. Delicious with coffee for a late morning snack or with fresh coffee in the early afternoon.
Sonia A. Hunt, Capital
Council, Baton Rouge, La.

APPLE PAN DOWDY

5 or 6 tart apples
1/2 c. molasses
3 Tbsp. butter
1/2 tsp. mace
2 c. all-purpose flour
1/3 c. shortening

1/2 c. hot water
3/4 c. sugar
3 Tbsp. cornstarch
1 tsp. salt
4 tsp. baking powder
2/3 c. milk

Pare, core and slice apples in wedges in buttered baking dish, 8x13x2-inches. Add water and cook in oven a few minutes until soft. In saucepan, mix molasses, sugar, butter, cornstarch, mace and 1/2 teaspoon salt. Boil together until thoroughly blended. Pour this mixture over apples. Mix and sift flour, baking powder and remaining 1/2 teaspoon salt. Cut in shortening as for biscuits, add milk and mix. Roll this dough to 1/4-inch thickness and cut with 2 1/2-inch biscuit cutter. Place biscuits over the apples and molasses mixture. Bake at 425° until biscuits are brown.
Sonny Foreman, Ouachita
Council, Monroe, La.

APPLE SLUMP

3 pt. apples, pared,
  cored and quartered
2 tsp. cinnamon
1/2 c. water

1 c. sugar
1 recipe baking powder
  biscuit dough

Roll out and cut biscuit dough into 2-inch rounds. Combine apples, sugar, water and cinnamon in saucepan. Cover, heat slowly to boiling. When boiling, cover with unbaked biscuits. Place tight fitting cover on pan and continue to cook over low heat about 25 minutes. Remove biscuits, pour cooked apple mixture over biscuits and serve with cream. Serves 8.
Sonny Foreman, Ouachita
Council, Monroe, La.

APRICOT DELIGHT

2 small pkg. apricot
  jello
1 c. small marshmallows
1/2 c. chopped pecans

2 c. hot water
1 (No. 2) can crushed pineapple, undrained

Dissolve jello in hot water, add remaining ingredients. Pour into mold or pan. Let jell. Cover with Topping.

Topping:

1/2 c. sugar
1 egg, beaten
1 (3 oz.) pkg. cream cheese

1/2 c. pineapple juice
2 Tbsp. butter
1 pkg. Dream Whip

Combine sugar, pineapple juice, egg and butter. Cook until thick. While still warm, beat in cream cheese and Dream Whip, whipped as directed. This Topping is ready to be used on congealed salad.
Mrs. Virginia McCullough
Central Council
Alexandria, La.

BAKED CARAMEL CUSTARD

12 vanilla caramels
2 1/4 c. milk, divided
1/4 tsp. salt

4 eggs
1/3 c. sugar

Heat caramels and 1/4 cup milk together until caramels melt, stirring occasionally. Spoon this mixture in bottom of round baking dish, flan pan or 6 small custard cups. Combine remaining milk, eggs, sugar and salt. Carefully pour sauce in cups or pans. Set dish or cups in shallow baking pan. Place pan on oven rack. Pour hot water into pan to depth of 1 inch. Bake at 350° for 30 or 40 minutes, or until center is nearly set. Serve cool or chilled. Just before serving, invert onto dessert platter or plates.

Marilou Bridges, Caddo
Council, Shreveport, La.

BANANAS FOSTER

1 c. rum
1/2 c. banana liqueur
8 bananas, peeled and
quartered

1 stick oleo
1 c. brown sugar
Dash of cinnamon

Heat rum and banana liqueur in saucepan. Melt oleo and brown sugar in large skillet. Add bananas and cinnamon and cook lightly. Pour rum and liqueur over bananas. Do not stir. Ignite; serve immediately over vanilla ice cream. Serves 8.

Robert Carnahan, LeBayou
Council, Houma, La.

BANANAS FOSTER

6 Tbsp. butter
1/2 tsp. ground cinnamon
4 bananas, halved
lengthwise
3/4 c. rum

1/2 c. firmly packed brown
sugar
1/2 c. banana flavored
liqueur
1 pt. vanilla ice cream

Melt butter in frying pan or chafing dish. Add sugar and cinnamon, cook over medium heat until syrup is bubbly. Add bananas, heat 3 or 4 minutes, basting constantly with syrup. Combine liqueur and rum in small pan, heat until just warm. Ignite with long match and pour over bananas. Baste bananas with sauce until flames die down. Serve immediately over ice cream. Makes 4 servings.

Marilou Bridges, Caddo
Council, Shreveport, La.

BLACKBERRY GRUNT

1 qt. fresh blackberries or
blueberries
Pinch of salt
1 tsp. baking powder
3 Tbsp. milk

1 1/2 c. sugar
1/2 c. water
1 c. flour
1 egg, slightly beaten
2 Tbsp. butter or oleo,
melted

In saucepan, bring to boil the blackberries, sugar, water and salt, stirring to dissolve sugar. Simmer 10 or 15 minutes, skimming off any scum that rises to top. Mix flour with baking powder and salt. Mix egg, milk and butter. Add to flour mixture. Mix thoroughly. Drop batter by tablespoon on top of berry mixture. Cover and simmer for 10-12 minutes or until dumplings are fluffy and pick inserted in center comes out clean. Place dumplings in serving dish. Spoon on berry mixture. Serve warm with heavy cream, whipped cream or ice cream. Serves 6.

Sonny Foreman, Ouachita
Council, Monroe, La.

BLUEBERRY BUCKLE

3/4 c. sugar
2 eggs
1 1/2 c. all-purpose flour
1/2 tsp. salt
1/4 tsp. cloves

1/4 c. vegetable shortening
1/2 c. milk
2 tsp. baking powder
1/2 tsp. nutmeg
2 c. fresh or frozen blueberries

Cream sugar with shortening, add eggs and mix thoroughly. Stir in milk, baking powder, salt, nutmeg, cloves and flour. Fold in blueberries. Spread batter in 9-inch square pan. Top with Crumb Crust. Bake at 375° for 45 minutes or until top springs back when lightly touched. Cut in squares and serve warm with Lemon Sauce.

Crumb Crust:

1/2 c. sugar
1/3 c. flour

1/2 tsp. cinnamon
1/4 c. soft butter or oleo

Combine ingredients and mix until crumbly. Sprinkle crumbs over batter.

Lemon Sauce:

2 egg yolks
1/3 c. melted oleo
2 Tbsp. lemon juice

1/3 c. sugar
1 Tbsp. grated lemon rind
1/3 c. cream, whipped

Beat egg yolks until thick, beat in sugar gradually. Add butter, lemon rind and juice. Fold in whipped cream. Serves 8.

Sonny Foreman, Ouachita
Council, Monroe, La.

BLUEBERRY DELIGHT

1 1/2 sticks oleo, melted
1/2 c. chopped pecans
1 (8 oz.) pkg. cream
   cheese
1 c. powdered sugar

1 1/2 c. flour
2 bananas
2 c. Cool Whip
1 can blueberry pie filling

Combine oleo, flour and pecans. Press into 9x13-inch pan. Bake at 375° about 15 minutes. Cool. Slice bananas and cover cooled crust. Cream powdered sugar, cheese, 1 cup Cool Whip together. Spread over bananas. Pour blueberry filling over cheese mixture and top with 1 cup Cool Whip. Refrigerate.   Linda Teague, Caddo
Council, Shreveport, La.

LAYERED BLUEBERRY DELIGHT

Whole graham crackers
1 c. Cool Whip

1 pkg. (6 servings) instant
   vanilla pudding mix
1 can blueberry pie filling

Line 9-inch pan with graham crackers. Prepare pudding as directed, let stand 5 minutes. Blend with Cool Whip. Spread half of this mixture over crackers. Repeat layers. Cover with graham crackers. Top with pie filling. Chill in refrigerator 3 hours.   Lela Bonner, Ouachita
Council, Bastrop, La.

FIVE LAYER BLUEBERRY TART

2 1/2 c. graham cracker
   crumbs
1 1/2 c. powdered sugar
1 can blueberry pie mix
   or pie filling of your
   choice

1/2 c. melted butter
1/2 c. soft oleo
2 eggs
1 large can crushed pine-
   apple, drained
1 c. Cool Whip

Combine melted butter and 2 cups graham cracker crumbs. Blend together and press into 9x13-inch pan. Bake at 300° for 15 minutes, cool. Cream oleo, add powdered sugar. Beat in eggs until light. Spread over cooled crust. Spread blueberry pie mix over creamed oleo layer. Fold pineapple and Cool Whip together. Cover pie mix.

Sprinkle with remaining 1/2 cup crumbs and refrigerate for 2 hours or overnight.   LaJuan Durand, Central
                                               Council, Alexandria, La.

CHERRY DELIGHT

1 (20 oz.) can cherry   1 (20 oz.) can crushed pine-
  pie filling   apple, drained
1 (9 oz.) bowl Cool Whip   1 can Eagle Brand milk
1 c. chopped pecans

Mix well, let stand a few minutes, then refrigerate. Do not freeze.   Emerite L. Hebert, Evangeline
                                               Council, Scott, La.

EASY CHERRY DESSERT

1 can cherry pie filling   2 Tbsp. melted butter or oleo
6 slices pound cake,   1/2 tsp. almond extract
  brushed with butter   Vanilla ice cream

Pour pie filling into 10x6x2-inch baking dish. Add melted butter and flavoring. Heat for 5 minutes in 375° oven. Remove from oven, top with slices of buttered pound cake and bake for 10-12 minutes at 375° or until lightly browned. Serve topped with vanilla ice cream.
                                               Gretna Anderson, Central
                                               Council, Alexandria, La.

CHERRY DELIGHT DESSERT

6 egg whites   3/4 tsp. cream of tartar
2 c. sugar   2 c. soda crackers
1 container Cool Whip   1 large can cherry pie filling

Beat egg whites until stiff. Add tartar and sugar. Break crackers into 1-inch pieces. Fold into egg white mixture. Spread in 9x12-inch cake pan and bake at 350° until brown. Cool. Spread Cool Whip over egg crust and spoon cherry pie filling over Cool Whip. Chill.
                                               Pat Pryor, West Bank
                                               Council, Gretna, La.

620

QUICK CHERRY DELIGHT

1 can cherry pie filling
1/2 box white cake mix, or
  1 box Jiffy mix

1/2 c. chopped nuts
1 stick oleo, melted

Grease long shallow pan with oleo. Spread cherry pie filling over bottom, add layer of nuts. Sprinkle dry cake mix over layers. Pour oleo over mix. Bake at 350° for 45 minutes. Serve warm, if desired; or equally delicious when cold. Other pie fillings may be substituted for cherry.

Marilyn Woolley, Central
Council, Alexandria, La.

CHOCOLATE ALMOND SOUFFLE

4 oz. baking chocolate
3 egg yolks
3 egg whites
4 cup souffle dish

2 tsp. almond extract
1/2 c. sugar
Pinch of salt
1/8 tsp. cream of tartar

Preheat oven to 400°. Melt chocolate on a plate over simmering water. Beat egg yolks and add sugar. Continue to beat until light in color. Add almond extract. Fold in melted chocolate, cool slightly. Beat egg whites with cream of tartar and pinch of salt. Fold chocolate mixture into egg whites. Fill a prepared souffle dish. Place in oven and immediately reduce heat to 375°. Bake 15-20 minutes. Dust surface with sifted powdered sugar. Serve with whipped cream or Chocolate Sauce.

Chocolate Sauce:

6 oz. semi-sweet choco-
  late pieces
1 Tbsp. butter

3 Tbsp. cold water
1/3 c. cream
1 Tbsp. dark rum

Melt chocolate in water and add remaining ingredients. Serve hot or cold. The sauce will thicken as it cools and will require reheating and thinning out with a little more cream or water if taken directly from refrigerator.

Peggy Childers, Crescent
City Council, New Orleans, La.

CHOCOLATE PEPPERMINT DESSERT

1 (6 oz.) pkg. semi-
   sweet chocolate bits
2 Tbsp. sugar
Pinch of salt
Whipped cream

1 egg
1 tsp. vanilla
3/4 c. scalded milk
Crushed peppermint stick
   candy

Combine chocolate bits, sugar, egg, salt and vanilla and blend ingredients. After blending, add milk and blend for 1 minute at slow speed. Pour into individual cups. Top with whipped cream and sprinkle with crushed candy.

Ruth Smolenski
Evangeline Council

COBBLER

1 c. all-purpose flour
3/4 c. milk
1 pinch salt
3/4 block butter or oleo

1 c. sugar
1 tsp. baking powder
Peaches, apples, berries,
   etc.

Melt butter in large baking dish. Mix flour, sugar, milk, salt and baking powder; pour batter over melted butter. Place fruit of your choice in center of flour mixture. Bake at 350° until brown.

Betty Winston, Caddo
Council, Shreveport, La.

CAKE COBBLER

2 cans blueberry pie filling, or filling of choice

1 box white cake mix
1 stick butter or oleo

Pour cans of pie filling in bottom of long cake pan. Sprinkle white cake mix over filling. Do not stir. Slice stick of butter over top. Bake at 350° about 20-25 minutes or until knife inserted comes out clean.

Marie Pamplin
Shreveport Works Council
Shreveport, La.

APRICOT COBBLE-UP

1 c. buttermilk baking mix
1 Tbsp. brown sugar
1/4 tsp. nutmeg

1/3 c. milk
1 Tbsp. soft oleo
1 (1 lb. 1 oz.) can apricot
halves

Mix all ingredients, except apricot halves, with fork to a soft dough. Spread in ungreased 8x8x2-inch square pan. Pour apricots, including syrup, over batter. Bake at 400° for 25-30 minutes.

Jesse Jackson, Shreveport
Works Council, Shreveport, La.

CHERRY CAKE COBBLER

1 pkg. white cake mix

1 can cherry pie filling

Prepare cake mix as directed on box. Pour batter into a greased and floured 13 x 9 1/2 x 2-inch oblong pan. Spread cherry filling over batter. Bake at 350° about 25 minutes.

Mary Armand, Central
Council, Cottonport, La.

CHERRY COBBLER

4 cans cherry pie filling
2 Tbsp. quick cooking
tapioca

1 c. sugar
2 tsp. red food coloring
1/2 c. butter

Combine all ingredients, except butter, in saucepan. Let stand 5 minutes. Cook and stir until slightly thickened and bubbly. Stir in butter and cook 5 minutes. Pour into pan, 12 3/4 x 10 1/2 x 2 1/2 inches. Sprinkle with Crust. Bake at 400° for 20-25 minutes. Makes 10 servings.

Cobbler Crust:

3 c. flour
1 1/2 c. butter or oleo
1 1/2 tsp. nutmeg

1 1/2 c. dry milk
1 c. sugar
1 1/2 tsp. cinnamon

Mix all ingredients together with hands until mixture makes crumbs.

Antoinette Uchello, West
Bank Council, Gretna, La.

EASY COBBLER

1/2 c. butter or oleo
1/2 c. sugar
1/2 c. milk
Cinnamon or nutmeg
  (optional)

1/2 c. flour
1/4 tsp. salt
1 (No. 2) can favorite pie
  filling
1 tsp. baking powder

Melt butter in 1 1/2-quart casserole. Mix flour, sugar, baking powder, salt and milk together. Pour over melted butter. Do not mix. Pour pie filling over mixture. Do not mix. Bake at 350° for 45–50 minutes. Sprinkle with cinnamon or nutmeg, if desired.   Audrey M. Lee, Capital Council, Zachary, La.

PEACH COBBLER

1 stick butter or oleo
3/4 c. milk
1 large can sliced peaches

1 c. sugar
1 c. self-rising flour

Make batter of milk, sugar and flour. Melt butter in large pan, pour batter over melted butter. Place peach slices on top of batter. Do not stir. Bake at 350° about 40 minutes.   Una Mize, Caddo Council, Shreveport, La.

GEORGIA PEACH COBBLER

3/4 c. milk
3/4 c. flour
1 1/2 c. sugar, divided

3/4 stick oleo
3 c. fresh peaches, peeled
  and sliced

Mix flour, milk and 3/4 cup sugar. Melt oleo in pan. Pour flour mixture into melted oleo. Mix peaches with remaining sugar and pour over batter. Bake at 350° about 40 minutes.   Louise Ward, Crescent City Council, New Orleans, La.

IONA'S PEACH COBBLER

Filling:

3 c. fresh peaches, sliced thin	1 stick oleo 1 c. sugar

Pie Crust:

1/4 tsp. salt	1/2 tsp. baking powder
1/2 tsp. soda	3/4 c. buttermilk
3 Tbsp. shortening	

Mix ingredients for pie crust. Divide dough into 3 parts. Roll out one crust and place in deep baking dish. Divide ingredients for filling in half; place half of peaches, oleo and sugar on top of crust. Roll out second crust and place over the layer of fruit. On top of this crust, place remainder of peaches, oleo and sugar. Roll out third crust and place over fruit mixture. Bake at 400° for about 35 or 40 minutes or until golden brown.

Iona Krouse Botzong, Central Council, Tioga, La.

CRANBERRY DELIGHT

2 c. whole cranberries	1/2 c. chopped walnuts
1 1/2 c. sugar	2 eggs
1 c. flour	2/3 stick oleo, melted

Coat 10-inch pan with vegetable spray. Place in bottom of the tin in layers - cranberries, walnuts and 1/2 cup sugar. Combine eggs, flour, 1/3 oleo and remaining sugar. Beat mixture; pour and spread evenly over cranberry mixture. Pour remaining oleo over top. Bake at 325° for 1 hour. This pie freezes well. Sonny Foreman, Ouachita Council, Monroe, La.

CRANBERRY MARSHMALLOW YAM BAKE

1/2 c. flour	1/2 c. packed brown sugar
1/2 c. oats	2 (17 oz.) cans yams, drained
1 tsp. cinnamon	
1/3 c. butter or oleo	1 1/2 c. miniature marsh-
2 c. cranberries	mallows

Combine flour, sugar, oats and cinnamon; cut in butter

until mixture resembles coarse crumbs. Toss 1 cup of crumbs with yams and cranberries. Place in 1 1/2-quart casserole. Top with remaining crumbs. Bake at 350° for 35 minutes. Sprinkle with marshmallows and place under broiler until slightly browned. Serves 6.

Rebecca Scott, Caddo Council,
Shreveport, La.

CRANBERRY ROLY POLY

1 recipe shortcake biscuits
2 Tbsp. melted butter

2 c. whole cranberry sauce, drained

Roll biscuit dough on lightly floured board to 1/4-inch thickness. Brush with melted butter and cover with cranberry sauce. Roll up like a jelly roll. Place seam down in buttered pan. Cover tightly and steam for 1 1/4 - 1 1/2 hours. Serve with Hard Sauce. Serves 8. Two cups canned cherries, drained, may be substituted for cranberries. Serve with Cherry Sauce made from the juice.

Sonny Foreman, Ouachita
Council, Monroe, La.

CREAM CHEESE TARTS

Crust:

1 (8 oz.) pkg. cream cheese

2 sticks oleo or butter
2 c. flour

Let cream cheese and oleo soften at room temperature, blend together; stir in flour. Refrigerate overnight. Shape into 1-inch balls. Place in ungreased 1 3/4-inch muffin pans, pressing dough in bottom and sides of tins.

Filling:

2 Tbsp. butter or oleo
1 1/2 c. brown sugar
1 Tbsp. vanilla

2 eggs
1 c. coarse pecans or walnuts

Beat together eggs, sugar, oleo and vanilla. Add nuts, making sure Filling is smooth. Place Filling mixture in muffin pans. Bake at 350° for 15 minutes, reduce heat to 300° and cook another 15 minutes.

Roberta Nemeth, Capital
Council, Waterbury, Ct.

CREAM PUFFS

1 c. water   1 c. flour
1/2 c. butter   4 eggs

Bring water and butter to boil over moderate fire in saucepan. Sift in flour; beat vigorously with spoon while it is still cooking. Keep mixture over heat until forms a ball of dough and pulls away from sides of pan, about 2 minutes. Turn into bowl and cool until lukewarm. Add eggs, 1 at a time, beating after each addition. Should make rather stiff dough. Do not beat beyond this point. Drop by spoon onto buttered baking sheet. Set pan on bottom rack of 375° oven. When they have puffed, reduce heat to about 325°. Cook until done, about 35 minutes. Pick one up; if it feels hollow, they're done and won't fall. Fill with Filling when cool.

Filling:

7/8 c. sugar   Pinch of salt
1/3 c. flour   2 c. scalded milk
2 eggs, slightly beaten   1 tsp. vanilla

Mix sugar and flour. Stir in scalded milk in top of double boiler. Cook about 15 minutes, stirring constantly. Add eggs; cook 2 minutes more. Remove from fire and add vanilla. Cut cap or make slit in Cream Puff and fill and fill. Oh, wow!   Sylvia S. Williams, Metairie
Council, Kenner, La.

CREAM PUFFS

1 c. water   1 c. flour
1 stick butter or oleo   1/2 tsp. baking powder
4 eggs   Pinch of salt

Combine water, salt and oleo in saucepan. Allow to come to rapid boil. Reduce heat to low. Combine baking powder and flour; stir into oleo mixture. Blend until a ball is formed. Remove from heat. Beat in eggs, 1 at a time. Drop by tablespoons on ungreased or Teflon baking sheet. Bake 15-20 minutes in preheated 425° oven. Reduce heat to 375° and bake 30-40 minutes longer until well browned. Cool; split and remove wet portions. Fill with your favorite custard. Jell-O pie filling or pudding is good when pressed for time.   Ina Z. Gaspard, Central
Council, Cottonport, La.

CREAM PUFFS

1 c. water
1/2 c. Crisco
1/4 tsp. salt

1 c. air sifted flour
4 eggs, unbeaten

Bring water, Crisco and salt to a boil. Stir in flour and cook until dough forms a smooth ball and leaves sides of pan clean. Remove from heat; cool slightly. Add eggs, 1 at a time, beating well after each addition. Drop by spoonfuls on a greased cookie sheet. Bake at 450° for 10 minutes, reduce heat to 400° for 25 minutes more; cool. Slit with knife and fill with Filling. Makes 12 Cream Puffs.

Cream Puff Filling:

1/2 c. sugar
5 Tbsp. flour
1/4 tsp. salt
2 c. milk

2 egg yolks, unbeaten
1 Tbsp. butter
1 tsp. vanilla
1/4 tsp. almond extract

Mix sugar, flour and salt together in saucepan. Add small amount of milk and mix to form smooth paste. Add unbeaten egg yolks and beat thoroughly. Add remaining milk and blend. Cook 5-7 minutes over medium heat, stirring constantly until smooth and thick. Add butter and blend; cool. Add flavorings. Fill Cream Puffs.

Pat Mora, LeBayou Council,
Franklin, La.

CREAM PUFFS

1/2 c. butter or oleo
Pinch of salt
4 eggs

1 c. water
1 c. flour

Combine butter and water in heavy saucepan. Cook, stirring with wooden spoon, until butter is melted. Add salt. Add flour at once, stirring hard. Cook and stir over medium heat until mixture leaves sides of pan and collects in ball around spoon. Remove from heat. Using either wooden spoon or electric mixer, beat in eggs, 1 at a time, beating hard after each addition. Continue to beat until mixture holds peak when spoon is lifted. Recipe makes 12 large puffs or 2-3 dozen party puffs, depending on size of spoon you use. Pick up portion of dough and deposit on greased cookie sheet. Leave 2 inches between large puffs,

1 inch between small ones. To make puffs crustier, sprinkle them lightly with water just before baking (I use a mist sprayer). Bake large puffs at 400° for 10 minutes, reduce heat to 350° and bake about 25 minutes longer or until firm outside and lightly browned. Bake small puffs 10 minutes at 400°, reduce heat to 350° and bake about 10 minutes longer. Remove from oven and cool on racks. When cool, split crosswise; not quite through. Pull out filaments of soft dough and fill as desired.

Denise Barteet, Caddo
Council, Shreveport, La.

CURRIED BAKED FRUIT

1 (29 oz.) can pear halves
2 (16 oz.) cans apricot halves
1 (26 oz.) can sliced pineapple
1 (3 1/2 oz.) pkg. sliced almonds, toasted
1 1/2 c. firmly packed light brown sugar

1 (29 oz.) can peach halves
1 (20 oz.) can pineapple chunks
1 (14 oz.) jar maraschino cherries
1/2 c. butter or oleo, melted
2 Tbsp. curry powder

Drain all fruits. Alternate drained fruit halves, pineapple chunks and almonds in layers in a 3-quart casserole. Arrange sliced pineapple on top of fruits and place a cherry in center of each slice. Combine sugar, curry powder and butter. Sprinkle mixture over fruit. Bake at 325° for 1 hour. Makes 16 servings.   Mearl S. Byles, Central
Council, Natchitoches, La.

EGG CUSTARD

4 eggs
2/3 c. sugar
1 large can cream
Nutmeg

Pinch of salt
1 tsp. vanilla
1/2 can water

Combine eggs, sugar, salt and vanilla. Beat well. Add cream and water; beat. Pour in dish. Sprinkle nutmeg on top. Bake in pan of hot water at 350° about 45 minutes. Test with knife. When knife comes out clean, the custard is done. Cool.   Rose Broderick, West Bank
Council, Gretna, La.

CARAMEL CUSTARD

6 Tbsp. brown sugar
1 small can evaporated
  milk
1/3 c. sugar

4 eggs
1 c. milk
2 tsp. vanilla

Preheat oven to 350°. Press 1 tablespoon brown sugar in each custard cup. Combine and mix in blender or electric mixer the remaining ingredients and pour over brown sugar in custard cups. Set cups in shallow pan holding 1 inch hot water. Bake 50 minutes or until knife blade comes out clean when inserted in custard. Serves 6.

Bonnie Williams, LeBayou
Council, Thibodaux, La.

FUDGICLES

1 box chocolate pie filling
1/2 c. sugar

2 3/4 c. milk

Mix all ingredients over low heat until comes to a boil. Cool and pour into ice cups and freeze.

Genevieve Whitehead, Capital
Council, Baton Rouge, La.

GRAND MARNIER SOUFFLE

4 eggs
1 Tbsp. brandy
1/2 c. whipped cream
Pinch of salt

2 Tbsp. sugar
1 Tbsp. Grand Marnier
1/2 c. prepared Melba Sauce

Separate eggs. Beat egg yolks and sugar. Add brandy and Grand Marnier. The mixture should be thin. Beat egg whites with a small pinch of salt until they stand in soft peaks. Turn mixer to lowest speed and add egg yolk mixture to egg whites. Stop mixer when egg yolks are only partially combined with egg whites. Do not attempt to fold in egg yolks completely or your mixture will deflate. Butter and sugar 2 individual souffle dishes. Divide mixture between prepared dishes and bake in preheated 375° oven for 15 minutes. Serve immediately with whipped cream and Melba

Sauce. The souffle will double in size as it bakes. It's a sensational dessert and tastes of orange air.

Peggy Childers, Crescent
City Council, New Orleans, La.

HAWAII DESSERT

1 box yellow cake mix
1 can pie filling (apricot,
cherry or peach)
2 1/2 c. cold milk
Nuts

1 (8 oz.) pkg. cream cheese
1 large vanilla instant
pudding
1 large Cool Whip

Mix cake as directed on box. Bake on cookie sheet with sides, 15 1/4 x 10 1/4 x 3/4 inch, at 350° about 15 minutes. Mix cream cheese, milk and instant pudding. Put on cooled cake. Spread pie filling on next, then Cool Whip and top with nuts.

Tracey Delposen, Ouachita
Council, Monroe, La.

HOLIDAY DESSERT

1 c. sherry
1 c. heavy cream,
whipped
Dash of almond flavoring

10-12 large marshmallows
2 c. canned fruit cocktail,
drained
Maraschino cherries

Pour sherry over marshmallows. Chill several hours or overnight. Whip marshmallow mixture until blended and gently fold in whipped cream, canned fruit cocktail and almond flavoring. Spoon into sherbet glasses and decorate with whipped cream topped with a maraschino cherry.

Katherine Slover, Caddo
Council, Phoenix, Az.

EASY TIME HOLIDAY SQUARES

1 1/2 c. sugar
1 Tbsp. lemon extract
1 c. butter or oleo
2 c. all-purpose flour

4 eggs
1 can lemon or cherry pie
filling
Powdered sugar

Add sugar to butter gradually. Beat until light and fluffy in mixer bowl. Add eggs, 1 at a time, beating well after each addition. At low speed, add flour and lemon extract. Pour in well greased 13x9x2-inch pan. Mark off into squares. Place 1 teaspoon of pie filling in center of each square. Bake at 350° for 45 minutes. Sprinkle with powdered sugar while warm. Jell-O lemon pie and pudding mix may be substituted for pie filling if desired.

Joyce Silva, Capital Council,
Baton Rouge, La.

TASTY HOLIDAY DESSERT

1 c. sherry
1 c. whipped cream
Dash of almond flavoring

10-12 large marshmallows
2 c. fruit cocktail, well
    drained

Pour sherry over marshmallows. Chill several hours or overnight. About 1 hour before serving, whip marshmallow mixture until blended; gently fold in whipped cream. Add fruit cocktail and flavoring. Spoon into sherbet glasses. Decorate with additional fruit cocktail and chill until serving time.

Katherine Slover, Caddo
Council, Phoenix, Az.

ICE CREAM

2 cans condensed milk
1 large can evaporated milk
1 c. sugar
Whole milk

4 eggs, beaten
1/2 pt. whipping cream
Vanilla to taste
Fruit (optional)

Combine condensed milk, evaporated milk, sugar, eggs, whipping cream, vanilla and fruit. Pour into ice cream freezer. Pour in whole milk to fill container 3/4 full. Makes a very rich, creamy ice cream. Any of ingredients can be reduced, but not omitted to produce the strength and texture your family favors. This also freezes well if not all used at time of making.

Elaine Squyres, Central
Council, Alexandria, La.

BROOKSHIRE'S ORANGE-PINEAPPLE ICE CREAM

6 Barq's orange drinks
1 flat can crushed pine-
   apple

2 cans Eagle Brand milk
Pinch of salt

Combine ingredients. Pour into the gallon container of an electric or hand-type ice cream freezer. Freeze according to manufacturer's directions.

> Gayle Wilkening, Shreveport
> Works Council, Longview, Tx.

BUTTER PECAN ICE CREAM

6 eggs, separated
1 can Eagle Brand milk
2 Tbsp. brown sugar
Milk

2 c. sugar
1 c. chopped pecans
1 Tbsp. butter

Beat egg whites until foamy; gradually add 1 cup sugar and beat until thick. Beat egg yolks and add remaining cup of sugar, beating until creamy. Add Eagle Brand milk to egg yolk mixture. Brown pecans in butter, stirring constantly. Add brown sugar. Combine all mixtures; stir well or beat to mix thoroughly. Pour into freezer can and fill with regular milk. Freeze. Makes 1 gallon.

> Dona Stephens, Central
> Council, Houston, Tx.

CHOCOLATE MINT ICE CREAM

2 eggs
1 c. milk
1/4 c. light corn syrup
1/4 tsp. salt
Few drops green food
   coloring

3 c. whipping cream
1/2 c. sugar
1 tsp. vanilla
1/3 c. green creme de menthe
2 sq. (2 oz.) semi-sweet
   chocolate, shaved

Beat eggs about 4 minutes on high speed in mixer. Add cream, milk, sugar, syrup, vanilla and salt. Stir until sugar dissolves. Add creme de menthe and food coloring. Pour into 4-quart ice cream freezer container. Freeze according to manufacturer's directions. Remove dasher, stir in chocolate. Cover. Pack with additional salt and

ice, using 1 part rock salt to 4 parts ice. Let ripen 3 hours. Makes about 5 cups.   Floyd N. Moody, Crescent
City Council, Covington, La.

COUNTRY VANILLA ICE CREAM

4 eggs	2 1/4 c. sugar
5 c. milk	4 c. heavy cream
4 1/2 tsp. vanilla	1/2 tsp. salt

Add sugar gradually to beaten eggs. Continue to beat until mixture is very stiff. Add remaining ingredients and mix thoroughly. Pour into gallon freezer and freeze as directed.   Betty Elenburg, Caddo
Council, Shreveport, La.

EASY ICE CREAM

2 cans Eagle Brand milk	1 qt. homogenized milk
2 c. ice water	2 Tbsp. vanilla

Mix together. Pour in ice cream freezer and freeze.
Maxine Fletcher, Ouachita
Council, Monroe, La.

HOMEMADE ICE CREAM

3 eggs	2 c. sugar
1 tsp. salt	1 can evaporated milk
1/2 gal. homogenized milk	1 can Eagle Brand milk
1/2 pt. whipping cream	2 tsp. vanilla

Beat eggs until light and frothy. Beat in sugar and salt. Add milks, whipping cream and vanilla. Mix and pour into ice cream freezer.   Mary Anne Andrews
Ouachita Council, Monroe, La.

JEAN'S HOMEMADE ICE CREAM

1 1/4 c sugar	5 eggs
1 can condensed milk	2 1/4 qt. milk
Vanilla to taste	Fresh fruit (optional)

Combine eggs and sugar; mix with electric mixer. Add remaining ingredients. Mix well and pour into 1-gallon freezer. Freeze until firm. Fresh fruit, such as pineapple, peaches, etc., may be added. Omit vanilla when fruit is added.
Jean Coon, Caddo Council, Shreveport, La.

PEACH ICE CREAM

4 c. sliced fresh ripe peaches
1/2 tsp. almond extract

1 1/2 c. sugar
2 tall cans evaporated milk

Place peaches and sugar in blender; puree until smooth. Combine puree with milk and almond extract. Pour into 2-quart freezer container. Churn and freeze according to manufacturer's directions. Makes 2 quarts of ice cream.
Ann Orr, Evangeline Council, New Iberia, La.

STRAWBERRY ICE CREAM

1 can Eagle Brand milk
6 eggs, well beaten
2 qt. milk

3 c. sugar, divided
4 Tbsp. flour
2 tsp. vanilla flavoring
2 pt. strawberries

Mix 2 cups sugar and flour. Add mixture to beaten eggs. Add milk, stirring as added. Cook in double boiler 20-30 minutes, or until it begins to thicken. Cool. Crush strawberries with remaining cup of sugar and add to mixture. Freeze and serve.
John E. Haygood, Caddo Council, Shreveport, La.

ICE CREAM SOUFFLE

1 pt. ice cream, any flavor
3 Tbsp. Kirsch
1/2 c. sugar
1 tsp. vanilla
2 Tbsp. whipping cream
Powdered sugar

1 c. fresh fruit
3 egg yolks
4 egg whites
1/8 tsp. cream of tartar
Pinch of salt
Ice

Prepare a 4-cup souffle dish with a collar. Pack the ice cream in bottom of dish. Cover with fresh fruit and sprinkle fruit with Kirsch or any other fruit based liqueur. Return dish to freezer while preparing remainder of ingredients. Beat egg yolks and sugar together, add whipping cream and vanilla. Beat egg whites with cream of tartar and pinch of salt. Fold egg whites into egg yolk mixture. Pile this mixture over fresh fruit. Sprinkle surface with sifted powdered sugar. Place the souffle dish in ovenproof dish of salted ice. Bake for 5-7 minutes at 400° until lightly browned. Transfer to a fresh bowl of ice to serve. Serve with Melba Sauce, if desired.

Melba Sauce:

1 pkg. frozen strawberries	Juice of 1 lemon
3 Tbsp. sugar	1 Tbsp. Framboise, cognac or Kirsch (optional)

Defrost berries and place in blender with ingredients for 10 seconds. Pass the liquid through fine sieve to remove tiny seeds. This and all fruit sauces can be thickened, if desired, with 1-2 teaspoons arrowroot or cornstarch dissolved in 1 tablespoon cold water. Bring the sauce to a boil and add the thickening. It will thicken immediately, leaving no taste.　　Peggy Childers, Crescent City Council, New Orleans, La.

VANILLA ICE CREAM

4-5 eggs	2 cans Pet milk
2 1/2 c. sugar	2 Tbsp. cornstarch
1 Tbsp. vanilla	Whole milk
1 tsp. salt	

Combine eggs, sugar, vanilla, salt, Pet milk and cornstarch. Pour into gallon freezer. Fill remainder of freezer with whole milk. Freeze according to manufacturer's instructions. Makes 1 gallon.　　Mavis W. O'Rourke Shreveport Works Council Shreveport, La.

MINCEMEAT ICE CREAM BALLS

1 qt. vanilla ice cream,
  softened
Cherry halves

1/2 jar mincemeat
Flaked coconut

Combine softened ice cream and mincemeat; mix well.
Freeze until firm. Scoop into balls; coat balls with coconut.
Place on flat pan and return to freezer. Serve in sherbet
dishes. Garnish with cherry halves.

Lynn Babin, Westmoor
Council Kenner, La.

CARAMEL ICE CREAM TOPPING

1 1/2 c. brown sugar,
  firmly packed
1 (5 1/2 oz.) can evap-
  orated milk

2/3 c. light corn syrup
1/8 tsp. salt
1/4 c. butter or oleo

Combine sugar, corn syrup and butter in small saucepan; cook over medium heat until soft ball stage is
reached, stirring constantly. Remove from heat, stir in
salt and milk. Serve hot over vanilla ice cream. Yield:
2 1/4 cups.

Marilou Bridges, Caddo
Council, Shreveport, La.

BLACK CHERRY JELLO MOLD

2 (3 oz.) pkg. black
  cherry jello
2 c. hot water
Chopped nuts (optional)

1 (8 oz.) pkg. cream cheese
1 (16 1/2 oz.) can pitted
  black cherries, undrained
Ice water

Make cream cheese into balls about 3/4 inch in diameter.
Drain cherries and cut into halves or quarters as desired;
reserve juice. Dissolve jello in hot water, add cherry juice
plus enough ice water to make additional 1 3/4 cups. Cool
in refrigerator. Pour 1/3 of jello into pan or mold, add
1/3 of cherries and 1/3 of cream cheese balls. Put in
freezer until firm. Repeat layers until all ingredients are
used. Chopped nuts may be added, if desired.

Jeanette English, Caddo
Council, Shreveport, La

SPICED PEACH JELLO DELIGHT

1 large pkg. lemon jello
2 c. spiced pickled
   peach juice
2 c. boiling water

2 pkg. Dream Whip
1/4 c. sugar
1 pkg. Knox gelatine
Small amount of ice water

Prepare 1 large or 2 small jello molds by oiling lightly and placing in refrigerator. Dissolve jello and sugar in boiling water. Melt gelatine in small amount of ice water. Stir into jello mixture until completely dissolved. Add spiced peach juice and refrigerate until it begins to thicken and get rather syrupy. Prepare Dream Whip as directed and fold into the thickened jello. Pour into molds and refrigerate overnight. Slice and serve. It is very good with meat, casseroles, etc. You may add cake coloring for a desired color scheme and garnish with fresh parsley.

Johnye Roberts, Caddo
Council, Shreveport, La.

STRAWBERRY BANANA JELLO

1 large pkg. strawberry-
   banana jello
1 can Mandarin oranges
1 egg, beaten
1 c. juice from drained
   pineapple and Mandarin
   oranges
Dash of salt

1 medium can crushed pineapple
3 sliced bananas
1/2 c. sugar
3 Tbsp. flour
2 pkg. Dream Whip
Coconut and nuts (optional)

Dissolve jello as directed on package. Add oranges, bananas and pineapple. Mix together and pour into 13x9-inch pan or dish. Refrigerate for 3 hours. Combine juice, egg, flour and salt in saucepan. Cook until thick; cool. Mix Dream Whip packages according to directions. Fold in cooled sauce and spread on top of jello. Sprinkle with coconut and crushed nuts, if desired.

Marie Leo, Capital Council,
Waterbury, Ct.

LEMON FREEZ

7 c. Wheat Chex, crushed
1/3 c. Wheat Chex (for
   garnish)
1 can lemon pie filling
1/2 c. real lemon juice

2/3 c. butter or oleo
1/3 c. sugar
1 can fruit cocktail, drained
1 can condensed milk
Whipped cream or Cool Whip

Melt butter, mix with sugar and crushed Wheat Chex. Press into bottom of 9x13-inch pan. Bake for 12 minutes at 350° or 2 minutes in microwave oven. Cool. Mix lemon pie filling, fruit cocktail, lemon juice and milk together. Pour into cooled crust. Top with whipped cream or Cool Whip. Sprinkle with 1/3 cup Wheat Chex for garnish.

Virginia Jenkins, West
Bank Council, Gretna, La.

1942 REFRIGERATOR ROLL

1 can Eagle Brand milk
Crushed vanilla wafers
1 1/2 c. chopped pecans
1/2 c. chopped mara-
   schino cherries

Juice of 2 lemons
1 pkg. chopped dates
1/2 c. green seedless
   raisins (black will do)
Sugar

Mix milk, lemon juice and enough vanilla wafers to make a dough resembling biscuit dough. Pat mixture down on waxed paper which has been sprinkled with sugar. Pat down on top of dough in layers, the dates, pecans, raisins and red cherries which have been well blotted with paper towels. Roll up jelly roll style and refrigerate 2 or 3 hours. Slice to serve.

Marie Pamplin, Shreveport
Works Council, Shreveport, La.

ORANGE DELIGHT

1 pkg. orange jello, dry
1 can Mandarin oranges
1 (9 oz.) bowl Cool Whip

1 small can crushed pineapple
1 carton cottage cheese

Mix all ingredients together and chill.

Joan Russell, Caddo
Council, Shreveport, La.

PEACH CRISP

2 c. sliced fresh or
  canned peaches
1 3/4 c. sugar, divided
1/2 c. milk
1/4 tsp. ground nutmeg
  or cinnamon

1/4 c. butter or oleo,
  softened
1 c. self-rising flour
1 Tbsp. cornstarch
1 c. boiling water

Place peach slices in an 8-inch square baking dish. Cream butter and 3/4 cup sugar. Add flour to creamed mixture alternately with milk. Spoon mixture over fruit. Sift together sugar, cornstarch and whichever spice you prefer. Sprinkle over batter. Pour boiling water over top. Bake at 300° for 1 hour or until brown and cooked through. Serve with Cool Whip or ice cream.

Martha Simmons, Shreveport
Works Council, Shreveport, La.

PEACH CRUNCH

1 c. oatmeal
1/3 c. flour
1 tsp. cinnamon
1 stick melted oleo

1/2 c. sugar
1/2 c. brown sugar
1 large can peaches, or
  5-6 fresh peaches

Arrange peaches in bottom of cake pan. Mix remaining ingredients together and pour over top of fruit. Bake at 350° for 30-35 minutes. Apples or pears may be substituted for peaches.

Donna McPhearson, Central
Council, Natchitoches, La.

PEACH POTATO PUFFS

3 c. mashed sweet potatoes
1/4 tsp. salt
2 Tbsp. butter
8 peach halves

1 1/2 tsp. lemon juice
3 Tbsp. brown sugar
1 1/2 tsp. vanilla flavoring
1/2 c. flaked coconut

Combine sweet potatoes, lemon juice, brown sugar, salt, coconut and butter; whip until fluffy. Arrange peaches in greased baking dish. Pile with potato mixture; dot with additional butter. Bake at 400° for 20 minutes.

Mrs. Ella V. Payton, Caddo
Council, Shreveport, La.

OLD FASHIONED LEMON PEAR HONEY

6 large ripe pears, grated   1 lemon, thinly sliced
5 c. sugar

Pears should equal 4 cups. Combine pears, lemon and sugar in large saucepan. Bring to a boil, stirring constantly. Reduce heat, simmer, stirring occasionally until thickened and clear, about 45 minutes. Spoon into sterilized jars and seal. Makes 3 pints or 6 half-pints.

Jeanette English, Caddo
Council, Shreveport, La.

PEAR MINCEMEAT

1 gal. pears (measure
   after grinding)
2 lemons
6 c. sugar
1 Tbsp. cinnamon
1 Tbsp. cloves

6 large apples
2 large oranges
1 box seedless raisins
3 c. dark Karo syrup
1 Tbsp. nutmeg

Remove seeds from fruit, but do not peel. Grind all ingredients together. Cook slowly at least 1 hour. Put in sterilized jars and seal.

Twila "Pete" Dysart
Ouachita Council, Monroe, La.

PEAR BETTY

1 qt. cooking pears, stewed
   in light syrup; drained
1/4 tsp. salt
1/4 c. orange juice
2 Tbsp. lemon juice
1 tsp. nutmeg
1 tsp. vanilla
4 c. soft bread crumbs

1 1/2 c. drained pear juice
1 c. sugar
1/4 c. flour
1 Tbsp. orange rind
1 Tbsp. lemon rind
1 tsp. cinnamon
1 lb. butter or oleo, divided,
   + 2 Tbsp.

Add water to pear juice and measure 1 1/2 cups liquid. Mix 1 stick butter and remaining ingredients, except bread crumbs and butter. Cook over low heat until thick and clear. Set aside. Melt remaining 3/4 pound butter, add bread crumbs. Mix well. In 9x9-inch pan, spread layer of crumb mixture, then pear mixture. Alternate layers, ending

with crumbs on top. Dot with 2 tablespoons butter or oleo.
Bake at 350° for 1 hour. Serve warm or freezes well.

Lou Teixeira, LeBayou
Council, Thibodaux, La.

PECAN TARTS

1/4 lb. oleo   1 (3 oz.) pkg. cream cheese
1 c. flour

Mix ingredients well with hands. Line tart pans with
mixture.

Filling:

2 eggs   1 1/2 c. brown sugar
2 Tbsp. butter   1 tsp. vanilla
Crushed nuts

Put crushed nuts in bottom of each tart shell. Combine
remaining ingredients and pour into tart shells. Sprinkle
nuts on top. Bake at 350° for 30 minutes.

Karen Thompson, Ouachita
Council, Monroe, La.

ALICIA'S PINEAPPLE SHERBET

4 oz. pineapple juice 12 oz. water
 (1/2 small can)   3 Tbsp. sugar, or to taste
1 beaten egg white

Mix all ingredients, except egg white. Freeze to semi-
hard stage in ice tray or other container. Add egg white.
Place back in freezer until hard.

Christy Miller, Metairie
Council, New Orleans, La.

BANANA PUDDING

3/4 c. sugar   2 Tbsp. flour
3 egg yolks   2 c. milk
1 tsp. vanilla   Sliced bananas
Vanilla wafers

Combine sugar, flour and egg yolks; mix well and add

milk. Cook over medium heat until thick; mixture will begin to bubble, but don't boil. Remove from heat, add vanilla and pour over bananas and vanilla wafers. Top with meringue if desired. Betty Barron, Caddo Council, Shreveport, La.

BANANA PUDDING

2 c. milk
5 Tbsp. flour
2 Tbsp. oleo
4-6 bananas

1 c. sugar
3 eggs, separated
1 tsp. vanilla
Vanilla wafers

Scald milk in top of double boiler. Mix flour and sugar together, add to milk. Stir constantly until mixture thickens. Turn off fire. Beat egg yolks; add small amount of hot mixture to egg yolks, stirring constantly. Add to hot mixture and return to fire. Cook until it becomes as thick as desired. Remove from heat; add oleo and vanilla. Pour over wafers and sliced bananas. Top with Meringue.

Meringue:

3 egg whites
1/4 tsp. cream of tartar

6 Tbsp. sugar
1/2 tsp. vanilla

Beat egg whites with cream of tartar until frothy. Gradually beat in sugar, little at a time; continue to beat until stiff and glossy. Beat in flavoring. Put on top of pudding and bake at 400° about 8-10 minutes.

Dorothy Trent, Caddo Council, Shreveport, La.

BANANA PUDDING

2 eggs, separated
3/4 c. sugar
1/4 tsp. salt
Vanilla wafers

2 c. milk
1/3 c. flour
1 tsp. vanilla
Sliced bananas

Mix 1/2 cup sugar, flour and salt in double boiler. Add 1/2 cup milk. Stir until smooth. Add remaining milk and cook until thick; cover and cook 15 minutes. Beat egg yolks slightly; add custard slowly to egg yolks. Put back in double boiler and cook 2 minutes. Make up meringue with egg whites and remaining sugar and vanilla. Alternate

layers of vanilla wafers, sliced bananas and custard. Top
with meringue. Substitute 1 cup pineapple juice from
crushed pineapple for 1 cup milk and use crushed pineapple
for sliced bananas for Pineapple Pudding.

Betty Elenburg, Caddo
Council, Shreveport, La.

BANANA PUDDING

2 eggs, beaten
6 Tbsp. flour
4 c. milk
1 tsp. vanilla
9 oz. whipped topping

8 Tbsp. sugar
Pinch of salt
4 or 5 bananas (medium size)
Vanilla wafers

Add flour, sugar and salt to eggs. Add milk, a little at
a time, and stir until smooth. Cook until thickened. Cool
thoroughly; mixture thickens as it cools. Line bottom of
baking dish with vanilla wafers and then alternate with a
layer of sliced bananas. Continue until dish is approximately
2/3 full. Add the cooled pudding. Top with whipped
topping before serving.

Vickie Daigle, Capital
Council, Baton Rouge, La.

BANANA PUDDING

1 c. sugar
Dash of salt
1 pat oleo
3 eggs, beaten
Vanilla wafers

3 c. milk
2 serving spoons plain flour
1 tsp. vanilla
2 bananas, sliced

Mix sugar, salt, flour, eggs and milk in top of double
boiler; cook over boiling water until pudding thickens.
Remove from heat, add vanilla and oleo. Line bottom and
sides of a bowl with wafers; add layer of bananas. Pour
pudding over bananas. Top with whole wafers or wafer
crumbs. Needs no baking. Ready to serve when cool.
Refrigerate.

Elaine Squyres, Central
Council, Alexandria, La.

COLD BANANA PUDDING

1 small box instant
  vanilla pudding
7 or 8 bananas, sliced

1 can Eagle Brand milk
1 (9 oz.) container Cool Whip
1 box vanilla wafers

Make up pudding by directions on box. Mix with condensed milk. Fold in Cool Whip. Layer cookies, bananas and pudding in 9x13-inch pan in order given.

Francene Johnson, Ouachita
Council, Monroe, La.

DOT'S BANANA PUDDING

1 small box vanilla
  instant pudding
4 oz. sour cream
3 or 4 bananas, sliced

1 1/3 c. sweet milk
1 (9 oz.) bowl Cool Whip
Vanilla wafers

Mix pudding and milk, stir until thick. Add sour cream and Cool Whip, reserving some for the topping. Mix well. Layer pudding mixture, bananas and vanilla wafers. Cover top with thin layer of Cool Whip.

Marie Pamplin, Shreveport
Works Council, Shreveport, La.

BREAD PUDDING

3 c. bread crumbs
2 eggs
1/4 tsp. salt
1 tsp. vanilla

4 c. scalded milk
1/2 c. sugar
3/4 tsp. nutmeg
1/2 c. raisins (optional)

Soak bread crumbs in milk. Beat eggs until light, add sugar, salt, nutmeg and vanilla. Mix thoroughly with bread crumbs. Pour into baking dish and cook in 350° oven for 1 hour. Serve hot or cold.

Cher White, Capital Council,
Waterbury, Ct.

BREAD PUDDING

1 stick butter or oleo	1/2 c. sugar
4 egg yolks	1 can condensed milk
1 can evaporated milk	1 condensed milk can of water
1 can homogenized milk	Stale French bread
(fill evaporated milk can)	1 or 2 tsp. vanilla
Raisins	

Cream butter and sugar until smooth and creamy. Add egg yolks, 1 at a time, beating after each addition. Add condensed milk and water; mix well. Add evaporated and homogenized milk; mix well. Add vanilla. Fill deep 3 or 4-quart baking dish with sliced bread. Pour mixture over bread and dunk bread into mixture until well soaked and softened. Add more bread if needed, until of right consistency. Should be very moist and soft, but not liquid. Add raisins and mix thoroughly. Bake at 350° about 1 hour. Test for doneness. Top with Whiskey Sauce before serving.

Whiskey Sauce:

1 stick butter or oleo	1 c. whiskey
1 1/2 c. sugar	

Cream butter and sugar until creamy. Add whiskey, few drops at a time, beating after each addition. Place ingredients in blender, cover and blend until reaches right consistency. Keep refrigerated. This will keep indefinitely.

Suzanne Spitzfaden, Crescent
City Council, New Orleans, La.

BREAD PUDDING

1 c. raisins	1 1/2 c. sugar
1 medium apple, peeled	3 eggs
and cut into small pieces	1/2 tsp. cinnamon
1/2 tsp. ground cloves	2 c. evaporated milk
1 stick butter or oleo	2 French bread juniors

Break bread in small pieces. Pour milk over and mix until bread is completely moistened. In another bowl, combine sugar, butter, eggs, cinnamon, cloves together. Add apples, raisins and bread. Pour mixture in baking dish or pan and bake at 350° for 1 hour.

Lorine S. Foster, Crescent
City Council, New Orleans, La.

BREAD PUDDING

1 loaf French bread
  (Po Boy)
3 eggs, beaten
3 Tbsp. vanilla
1 c. raisins

1 qt. milk
2 c. sugar
1 c. chopped pecans
1/2 tsp. nutmeg
Butter or oleo

Soak bread in milk and work until well mixed. Add eggs, sugar, nutmeg, vanilla, pecans and raisins; mix well. Grease 9x13-inch pan with oleo. Pour in ingredients and bake at 350° for 1 1/2 hours or until firm. Cool, slice and top with Sauce.

Sauce:

1/2 c. butter
1 egg

1 c. sugar
3 Tbsp. real lemon juice

Cream butter and sugar; heat in double boiler until sugar dissolves. Pour in mixer or blender. Add egg at top speed in hot mixture so egg doesn't scramble. Add real lemon and spoon over pudding.

Judy North, Crescent City
Council, New Orleans, La.

BREAD PUDDING

6 slices bread
1/2 c. raisins, soaked
1 tsp. cinnamon
1/2 c. sugar
2 c. milk

2 Tbsp. butter, melted
2 Tbsp. sugar
4 eggs, slightly beaten
1 tsp. vanilla

Mix 2 tablespoons sugar and cinnamon with butter. Brush on trimmed bread; cut bread into quarter squares and arrange in bottom of casserole. Mix remaining ingredients and pour over bread. Bake at 350° for 55-60 minutes with casserole set in water.

Leigh Hargis, LeBayou
Council, Lockport, La.

BREAD PUDDING

1 1/2 c. milk
3 Tbsp. sugar
1/2 tsp. vanilla extract
Ground nutmeg

2 eggs, beaten
Pinch of salt
1/3 c. raisins
3 slices day old bread, cubed

Beat together milk, eggs, sugar, salt, vanilla and raisins. Stir in cubed bread. Pour mixture in greased 1-quart baking dish. Sprinkle top with nutmeg. Put 1 inch hot water in larger pan and set filled baking dish in it. Place in 375° oven. Bake 35 minutes. Using fork, stir gently to mix raisins. Try not to break up the top. Continue baking about 25 minutes longer or until knife inserted in center comes out clean. Serve hot or cold.

Mrs. J. B. Coker, Central
Council, Alexandria, La.

BREAD PUDDING CUSTARD

6 eggs
2 Tbsp. vanilla
1 can Carnation evaporated
   milk (low fat)

1 1/3 c. sugar
1 can water
1 apple, peeled and sliced
French bread (approx.
   10 inches)

Soak French bread in water 1/2 hour; squeeze in colander slightly to remove excess water. Beat eggs well, add sugar, continue to beat, add cream and water. Add bread, apple and vanilla. Pour into buttered 2-quart baking dish. Place dish in pan of water and bake at 400° for 1 1/2 hours or until brown. Note: Mix custard by hand.

Mary D. Tonglet, Crescent
City Council, New Orleans, La.

BREAD PUDDING WITH RUM SAUCE

1 loaf stale French bread
2 c. sugar
3 Tbsp. oleo, melted
1 c. fresh apples, chopped

1 qt. milk
3 eggs
2 Tbsp. vanilla
1 c. raisins

Soak bread in milk; crush with hands until well mixed. Add eggs, sugar, vanilla and fruit. Pour oleo in bottom of pan, then spoon in bread mixture. Bake at 350° until firm. Let cool, cut into squares; serve with Rum Sauce.

Rum Sauce:

8 Tbsp. butter or oleo
1 egg, well beaten

1 c. sugar
Rum or whiskey to taste

Cream butter and sugar. Cook in double boiler until sugar is well dissolved. Add egg and whip quickly so that egg does not curdle. Add rum to taste.

Doris Reeves, Capital
Council, Baton Rouge, La.

BRENDA'S BREAD PUDDING

1 medium size loaf stale
  French bread
2 c. raisins
1 large apple, peeled
  and chopped
1 tsp. vanilla
2 Tbsp. sugar

1 can evaporated milk
1 can fruit cocktail
1 c. coconut
2 eggs, beaten
1 can condensed milk
Dash of cinnamon
1 banana, sliced (optional)

Break bread in small pieces and soak in evaporated milk until milk is absorbed. If moister consistency is desired, add more milk. Mix in remaining ingredients and pour mixture in large casserole dish. Bake at 350°-375° until edges are brown.

Brenda Bazile, Crescent
City Council, New Orleans, La.

CREOLE BREAD PUDDING

2 1/2 c. cubed stale
  French bread
2 egg yolks
1 1/4 c. milk
Water

1/4 c. raisins
2 Tbsp. butter
6 Tbsp. sugar
1 tsp. vanilla

Moisten bread cubes with water; squeeze dry. Mix bread cubes with raisins and butter in 1-quart baking dish. Beat egg yolks with sugar; stir in milk until smooth. Add vanilla and pour over bread mixture. Bake at 350° for 45 minutes. Serve with Whiskey Sauce. Makes 4 servings.

Whiskey Sauce:

1 pkg. vanilla pudding
  mix (not instant)
1 jigger whiskey

2 2/3 c. milk
1 tsp. grated nutmeg

1723-79

Put pudding mix in saucepan and add nutmeg. Add milk slowly and stir. Cook over medium heat about 15 minutes. Remove from heat and add whiskey. Stir to blend. Sauce may be served on bread pudding, pound cake, cupcakes, rice pudding, etc. John E. Haygood, Caddo Council, Shreveport, La.

DUTCH CRACKER PUDDING

24 double thin saltine
  crackers
4 eggs, separated
1 1/2 tsp. vanilla extract
1/2 c. sugar

4 c. milk, scalded
1 (3 1/2 oz.) pkg. flaked
  coconut
6 Tbsp. sugar

Break crackers into coarse crumbs (2 cups); set aside. Beat egg yolks until light; add heated milk to yolks, stirring well. Return to heat, stir in 1/2 cup sugar. Stir constantly about 2 minutes. Add cracker crumbs and coconut; cook until crumbs are soft and pudding has thickened. Stir in vanilla. Pour gently into buttered baking dish, 7x11 inches. Beat egg whites until soft peaks are formed, gradually beat in 6 tablespoons sugar until mixture holds firm peaks. Spread over pudding and swirl. Bake at 350° until meringue is golden brown, about 15 minutes. Cool on rack and serve at room temperature. Makes 8 servings.
Henrietta Victor, Magnolia Council, New Orleans, La.

DATE PUDDING

1 c. dates
1 c. English walnuts
1 c. bread crumbs
1 c. milk

1 c. sugar
1 egg
1 tsp. baking powder
Butter (size of walnut)

Blend sugar and butter. Add beaten egg, bread crumbs, dates, nuts, baking powder and milk. Turn into greased baking dish, 8x8x2 inches. Bake for about 40-45 minutes at 375°. Betty Jackson, Shreveport Works Council, Shreveport, La.

KISS PUDDING

6 eggs
1 c. sugar
2 doz. ladyfingers or
   round sponge cakes

1 qt. milk
1/4 c. cornstarch
3 tsp. vanilla
Peach slices and juice

Mix egg yolks, sugar, milk and cornstarch. Cook on slow fire until mixture thickens. Add vanilla. Dip ladyfingers or cakes in peach juice and line casserole. Pour layer of custard, then layer of peach slices; repeat layers and top with Meringue.

Meringue:

6 egg whites   Powdered sugar

Beat egg whites, add enough powdered sugar until it thickens, stands and forms peaks. Spread Meringue on pudding, making peaks and swirls with fork. Place under broiler for a few seconds or until light brown.

Lynn Babin, Westmoor
Council, Kenner, La.

LEMONADE PUDDING

2 egg yolks, slightly
   beaten
1 (3 1/4 oz.) pkg. vanilla
   pudding
1 (6 oz.) can frozen lemonade concentrate, thawed
1/2 c. vanilla wafer
   crumbs

1 1/2 c. milk
1 (3 oz.) pkg. cream cheese,
   softened
2 egg whites
1/4 c. sugar
2 Tbsp. chopped walnuts
2 Tbsp. butter or oleo,
   melted

Combine egg yolks and milk. Prepare pudding mix according to package directions, using egg-milk mixture as the liquid. Add cream cheese and beat smooth with beater; stir in lemonade concentrate. Cover and cool 10 minutes; beat smooth again. Beat egg whites to soft peaks; gradually add sugar and beat until stiff. Fold egg whites into pudding. Combine crumbs, nuts and butter. Sprinkle half the crumb mixture into 6 sherbet glasses. Spoon in pudding and top with remaining crumbs; chill. Just before serving, stand a vanilla wafer in each, if desired. Makes 6 servings.

Stanley McMahon, West Bank
Council, Gretna, La.

LEMON PUDDING

4 eggs, separated
2 cans condensed milk
4 lemons (juice)
Vanilla wafers

Beat egg yolks, add condensed milk and mix well; add lemon juice and mix. Pour into casserole dish, then drop vanilla wafers in pudding to desired amount. Beat egg whites until stiff and spread over pudding mixture. Bake at 325°–350° until meringue is brown.

Fayrene Brown, Shreveport
Works Council, Shreveport, La.

ORANGE PUDDING

2 Tbsp. butter or oleo
1 c. sugar
4 egg yolks
1/2 c. frozen orange concentrate
1/4 tsp. salt
2 Tbsp. flour
1 c. milk
4 egg whites, beaten

Cream butter and sugar until light and fluffy. Add egg yolks and beat well. Add orange concentrate and salt. Stir to blend. Add flour, milk and egg whites. Mix well. Pour into 8 greased custard cups. Place in pan of water and bake at 375° for 25 minutes.

Molly Hoskins, Caddo
Council, Shreveport, La.

PEACH PUDDING

1 can peaches
1 1/2 c. sugar
1 tsp. vanilla flavoring
1 1/2 c. milk
Vanilla wafers
3 egg yolks
4 Tbsp. flour
Large lump of butter

Layer peaches (reserving juice) and vanilla wafers in baking dish. Combine remaining ingredients, including peach juice. Cook in top of double boiler until thick. Pour over peaches and vanilla wafers. Make up meringue from egg whites; spread on top and brown in oven.

Sadie Foil, Ozone Council,
Bogalusa, La.

PEANUT CHIP BREAD PUDDING

2 c. milk
2 eggs, beaten slightly
1/4 tsp. salt
3 c. soft bread cubes
1/2 c. seedless raisins

1/4 c. butter or oleo
1/2 c. sugar
1 tsp. ground cinnamon
1 c. peanut butter flavored
  chips

Heat milk in small saucepan until small bubbles appear around edge; remove from heat. Add butter or oleo; stir until melted. Stir milk mixture, sugar, salt and cinnamon into beaten eggs. Place half of bread cubes in 1/2-quart baking dish; sprinkle with half the raisins and half of the chips. Repeat layers. Pour milk-egg mixture over layers; stir gently. Place baking dish in pan of hot water. Bake in preheated 350° oven for 40-45 minutes or until knife inserted 1 inch from edge comes out clean. Serve warm or cold. Makes 6 servings.   Ann Orr, Evangeline
Council, New Iberia, La.

PURPLE PUDDING

6 egg whites
2 c. saltine cracker
  crumbs
1 large Cool Whip
1/2 c. nuts

2 c. sugar
1 can blueberry pie filling,
  or cherry pie filling if
  preferred

Beat egg whites until stiff, add sugar and beat. Fold in coarse crumbled crackers and nuts. Put in large oblong cake pan and bake at 350° until slightly brown and firm. Allow to cool completely and spread with entire container of Cool Whip and top with pie filling.
W. C. Hahn, Capital Council,
Baton Rouge, La.

QUEEN OF PUDDINGS

2 c. bread crumbs
1 c. sugar
1 lemon, juice and grated
  rind

1 qt. milk
4 egg yolks
Salt and nutmeg to taste

Mix together and pour into 1 1/2-quart casserole. Place in pan of cold water in 325°-350° oven for 1 hour or until knife comes out clean. Spread with Meringue and return to oven for about 15-20 minutes or until golden brown.

Meringue:

4 egg whites	3 Tbsp. sugar
Pinch of baking powder	

Helen Bartram, Capital
Council, Bethel, Ct.

RICE PUDDING

Rice	3-4 eggs
Sugar	1 tsp. vanilla
Milk	1/4 stick butter or oleo

Cook rice for amount of pudding you desire; rinse. Mix ingredients. Heat over low fire and stir. Add sugar to sweeten to taste. Pour into baking dish and bake at 350° until brown.

Stella L. Thrash, Caddo
Council, Shreveport, La.

MY FAVORITE RICE PUDDING

2 Tbsp. rice (heaping; not long grain)	1 c. sugar
	1 1/2 qt. milk
1/3 c. raisins	Nutmeg and salt to taste

Soak raisins in hot water 1 hour; drain and add to pudding 1/2 hour before removing from oven. Mix other ingredients and bake at 300°-325° for 2-3 hours.

Helen Bartram, Capital
Council, Bethel, Ct.

SQUASH PUDDING

4 yellow squash	4 eggs
1 1/2 c. flour	1 tsp. baking powder
1/4 c. brown sugar	1 1/2 c. granulated sugar
1/4 tsp. salt	1 tsp. vanilla
1/2 c. evaporated milk	1/2 stick oleo

Dice and boil squash until tender; drain. Liquefy in

blender or mixer. Beat eggs, add squash and remaining ingredients. Place in casserole. Bake at 325° for 45 minutes or until light brown. Makes 16 servings.

Ann Orr, Evangeline
Council, New Iberia, La.

SWEET POTATO PUDDING

4 large raw sweet potatoes
1 c. molasses
1/2 c. butter
Dash of salt

2 eggs
1/2 c. milk
Nutmeg, cinnamon or all-
spice (optional)

Peel and grate sweet potatoes. Beat eggs, add molasses, milk, butter and salt. Stir in grated potatoes and add spices, if desired. Pour into a buttered pan (I always used a black cast iron skillet to cook in). Bake at 350° for about 2 hours or until pudding is almost caramelized.

Virginia Bryce, Central
Council, Pineville, La.

THANKSGIVING PUDDING

1 box Duncan Hines
yellow cake mix
3 Tbsp. whiskey
1 c. dark raisins

3 eggs, divided
1 c. sugar
1/2 c. milk or more
1 c. nuts

Bake cake as directed and crumble. Combine egg yolks, sugar, whiskey, raisins, nuts and milk. Use more milk if needed to make mixture fairly thin. Add crumbled cake pieces and bake until thick. Beat egg whites to make a meringue, spread on pudding and brown.

Sauce:

1 c. sugar
1 Tbsp. flour

2 c. milk
3 Tbsp. whiskey

Combine sugar, flour and milk; cook until thickened; add whiskey. Serve with or on pudding.

Mary Ahrens, Caddo
Council, Shreveport, La.

TIPSY PUDDING

3 egg yolks
1/8 tsp. salt
1 Tbsp. sherry
Whipped cream
Chopped nuts (optional)

1/4 c. sugar
2 c. milk, scalded
6 slices sponge cake or any
    plain dry cake

Beat egg yolks and add sugar and salt. Add scalded milk gradually, stirring constantly. Cook in top of double boiler until mixture thickens, stirring constantly. Remove from heat; add sherry; cool. When custard is cool, pour over cake and top with whipped cream. Garnish with nuts, if desired. Serves 6.   Sonny Foreman, Ouachita Council, Monroe, La.

TIPSY PUDDING

4 eggs, divided
2 c. chopped pecans
1 large bottle maraschino
    cherries
1 pkg. gelatin

1 c. whiskey
1 qt. milk
1 1/2 doz. macaroons
1 c. sugar
Whipped cream

Mix egg yolks with sugar, gradually add milk. Boil until mixture begins to thicken. Add gelatin dissolved in cherry juice to hot custard; cool. Add stiffly beaten egg whites and whiskey. Line 9x13-inch pan with macaroons, cherries and pecans. Pour custard over. Make day or two before serving. Cut into squares and top with whipped cream to serve.   Zelda Anderson, Calcasieu Council, Lake Charles, La.

PUMPKIN DESSERT

1 box yellow cake mix
3 eggs
2/3 c. evaporated milk
1/4 c. sugar

1 stick oleo
1 large can (1 lb. 14 oz.)
    pumpkin pie mix

Reserve 1 cup of cake mix. Combine remaining cake mix, 1/2 stick oleo and 1 egg; mix together and press in bottom of greased 9x13-inch pan. Mix pumpkin pie filling, 2 eggs and milk. Spread over crust. Combine reserved

656

cup of yellow cake mix, sugar and 1/2 stick oleo. Sprinkle on top of pumpkin mixture. Bake at 350° for 45-50 minutes.

Mollie Hoskins, Caddo
Council, Shreveport, La.

SAILOR'S DUFF

2 Tbsp. butter	2 Tbsp. brown sugar
1 egg	1/2 c. molasses
1 1/2 c. sifted flour	1/2 tsp. baking soda
1/8 tsp. salt	1 tsp. baking powder
1/2 c. boiling water	

Cream butter and sugar together until fluffy. Add beaten egg and molasses. Sift flour, soda, salt and baking powder together and add alternately with boiling water in small amounts. Mix thoroughly. Turn into greased mold and steam 1 1/2 - 2 hours. Serves 6.

Sauce:

2 egg yolks	1 c. powdered sugar
1 c. cream, whipped	1 Tbsp. sherry

Beat egg yolks and, while still beating, gradually add powdered sugar. Fold in whipped cream and flavor with the sherry.

Sonny Foreman, Ouachita
Council, Monroe, La.

SOME OF THIS AND THAT DESSERT

1 can apple pie filling	1 (1 lb. 4 oz.) can crushed
1/2 c. brown sugar	pineapple
1 can Angel Flake coconut	1 box yellow cake mix
2 sticks oleo	1 c. chopped nuts

Spray 9x14-inch pan with Pam. In layers in order given, put apple pie filling, crushed pineapple, brown sugar, box of cake mix, coconut and nuts. Slice oleo thin on top of nuts. Bake at 350° about 50 minutes. Cut in small squares. Can be eaten hot or cold. Makes 24 servings. Very rich.

Eloise H. Stacy, Caddo
Council, Shreveport, La.

SPICE CAKE AND APPLE CASSEROLE

1 (1 lb. 6 oz.) can sliced
   apples
Oleo

1 box spice cake mix
1/2 c. brown sugar
2 c. chopped pecans

Arrange apple slices in bottom of ungreased 9-inch square pan. Sprinkle brown sugar over apples. Spread dry cake mix over sugar. Sprinkle pecans over cake mix. Cover entire top with thin pats of oleo. Bake at 350° for 45 minutes. Cool before serving.

Elaine Squyres, Central
Countil, Alexandria, La.

ANNA'S STRAWBERRY DESSERT

Bananas
Coconut macaroons
Toasted coconut

Frozen strawberries
Cool Whip

Layer bananas, strawberries, macaroons and Cool Whip in order given; twice. Top with toasted coconut and chill.

Anna Oliver, Capital
Council, Baton Rouge, La.

STRAWBERRY DELIGHT

1 large angel food cake
1 c. milk

1 large Cool Whip
1 (8 oz.) pkg. cream cheese

Break cake into pieces and line 9x13-inch dish. Mix remaining ingredients and pour over cake.

Topping:

1 c. sugar
1/2 c. water
3 Tbsp. cornstarch

1/2 tsp. lemon juice
Red food coloring
1-2 pt. fresh strawberries

Mix sugar, water, cornstarch, lemon juice and food coloring. Cook until thick. Fold in fresh strawberries. Cool and top cake. Chill.

Doris Reeves, Capital
Council, Baton Rouge, La.

STRAWBERRY DELIGHT

1 can strawberries in
  syrup, or 1 pkg.
  frozen strawberries

1 pkg. strawberry jello
1 pt. whipping cream
1 qt. vanilla ice cream

Drain strawberries; reserve syrup. Prepare jello as directed on box, using syrup as part of water. Add strawberries to jello. When jello is almost firm, add ice cream, a little at a time, mixing with electric mixer. Whip cream and fold into mixture. Place in freezer and serve when frozen.
Isabelle Stenger, Capital
Council, Shreveport, La.

STRAWBERRY DELIGHTS

1 large container Cool Whip
1 large can crushed pine-
  apple

1 can strawberry pie filling
1 c. chopped pecans
1 can Eagle Brand milk

Mix all ingredients together, including 1/2 of juice from pineapple. Use large bowl and chill until firm.
Rose M. Malone, Central
Council, Alexandria, La.

STRAWBERRY DESSERT

1 pkg. strawberry jello
2 pkg. Dream Whip
1 angel food cake
1 c. hot water

1 (16 oz.) pkg. frozen strawberries
1 c. cold water

Dissolve jello in hot water; add cold water and stir in strawberries. Mix 1 package Dream Whip according to directions and fold into jello mixture. Crumble angel food cake into large pan, pour jello mixture over cake. Top with other package of Dream Whip. Refrigerate.
Cleo Taylor, Ouachita
Council, Monroe, La.

STRAWBERRY LUSCIOUS

2 small pkg. strawberry
   jello
1 large pkg. frozen strawberries, thawed (with
   juice)
1/2 c. chopped nuts
   (optional)

2 c. boiling water
1 (No. 2) can crushed pineapple, undrained
1/2 large carton sour cream
2 large ripe bananas, mashed
   whipped

Dissolve jello in boiling water. Add strawberries, pineapple and bananas. Pour half of mixture into 8x12-inch pan.
Chill until set; spread sour cream over top of congealed
layer. Cover with remaining gelatin. Chill until firm.

Dorothy Trent, Caddo
Council, Shreveport, La.

STRAWBERRY SUSAN

Sliced bananas
Coconut macaroon cookies
Toasted coconut

Frozen sweetened strawberries
Cool Whip

In bottom of deep casserole dish, place layer of sliced
bananas, layer of thawed strawberries; crumble cookies
over strawberries. Top with Cool Whip. Repeat layers and
sprinkle with toasted coconut. Chill.

Jan Prestridge, Capital
Council, Baton Rouge, La.

SWISS WHIPPED CREAM NUT LOAF

1 c. heavy whipping cream
1 c. sugar
1 c. chopped pecans
1 3/4 c. flour
1/4 tsp. salt

1 egg
2 tsp. grated lemon peel
1 c. golden raisins
1 1/2 tsp. baking powder

Beat cream until soft peaks form. Soak raisins in warm
water until plump. Beat egg and sugar into whipped cream,
add lemon peel, pecans and raisins. Fold in dry ingredients. Grease bottom of loaf pan and pour in batter. Bake
at 325° about 1 hour and 10 minutes. Cool in pan 15 minutes.
Turn out of pan and cool. This is especially good with cream
cheese for party sandwiches. Faye Killen, Central Council,
Pineville, La.

TARTE TATIN

Butter
Sugar
1 tsp. grated lemon rind
1 egg white, slightly beaten

8 cooking apples, peeled,
cored and cut in thin
wedges
1 pie pastry crust

Use round pan about 2 or 3 inches deep; butter pan heavily and sprinkle bottom of pan heavily with sugar. Layer apple wedges over entire bottom, overlapping them in a circular pattern. Sprinkle apples with 1/2 cup sugar, grated lemon rind and dot generously with butter. Cover apples with pastry, tucking edges inside of pan. Brush top with egg white and prick with fork. Bake at 400° for 30-45 minutes. Loosen edge all around with knife and allow to set about 5 minutes. Invert onto serving plate so that apples are on top. Serve warm with plain or whipped cream.   Ann Orr, Evangeline
Council, New Iberia, La.

ENGLISH TRIFLE

1 medium size angel food
  cake
1 large box strawberry
  jello
2 (10 oz.) pkg. frozen,
  sliced strawberries

1/2 pt. Cool Whip
2 c. boiling water
1 small can crushed pineapple
2 pkg. vanilla pudding
3 c. milk
1 can regular Royal Anne
  cherries, drained and pitted

Dissolve jello in boiling water. Add strawberries; stir well. Refrigerate until partially congealed. When jello mixture becomes syrupy, add pineapple and cherries. Prepare vanilla pudding with 3 cups milk. Break cake in about 1-inch pieces and place in bottom of rectangular dish. Spoon jello mixture over cake. Spread cooled pudding over jello. Cover with Cool Whip; mix by pushing Cool Whip down into mixture at intervals with back of spoon. Refrigerate overnight.   Fae Wells, Central Council,
Alexandria, La.

WINE GELATIN

2 env. plain gelatin
1 c. sherry wine
1 c. sugar

1 c. cold water
2 c. boiling water
Juice of 1/2 lemon

Dissolve gelatin in cold water; add boiling water, sugar

and lemon juice. Stir well and add wine; congeal. Very good when one is feeling puny and has no appetite. Good light dessert.
Catherine (Chadwick) McCraw
Caddo Council, Shreveport, La.

WOOPIE PIES

1 c. oil
2 eggs
3 c. flour
1/2 tsp. salt
1 c. milk

2 c. brown sugar
8 Tbsp. cocoa (level)
1 tsp. baking soda
1/2 tsp. vanilla

Cream oil and sugar together. Beat in eggs. Add remaining ingredients, beat until smooth. Let sit 1/2 hour. Drop by teaspoonfuls onto greased cookie sheet. Bake at 375° for 8 minutes. Remove from sheet and cool.

Filling:

1/2 c. milk
1/4 c. butter or oleo
1/2 c. granulated sugar

3 Tbsp. flour
1/4 c. Crisco shortening
1 tsp. vanilla

Blend milk and flour together in pan until smooth. Cook until mixture thickens; cool. Cream remaining ingredients and combine the two mixtures. Beat until fluffy.
Pauline Thompson, Capital
Council, Baton Rouge, La.

YUMMY DESSERT SQUARES

1 pkg. yellow cake mix
3 eggs
1/2 c. brown sugar
2/3 c. milk
1 tsp. cinnamon
1 c. pecans

1/2 c. oleo, melted
3 c. mashed, cooked sweet
 potatoes
1/4 c. granulated sugar (white)
1/2 c. oleo
1 Tbsp. pumpkin spice

Reserve 1 cup cake mix. Combine remaining cake mix, 1/2 cup melted oleo and 1 egg. Spread in bottom of greased 13x9-inch pan. Combine mashed yams, pumpkin spice mix, brown sugar, 2 eggs and milk until smooth and pour over crust. Combine 1 cup reserved cake mix, sugar, cinnamon, 1/2 cup oleo and pecans. Spread over filling. Bake at 350° for 55 minutes to 1 hour, or until knife inserted in center comes out clean. Cool and cut into squares. Serve with whipped cream, if desired.
Sharon Ivie Smith, Central
Council, Alexandria, La.

CANDY, JELLY, PRESERVES

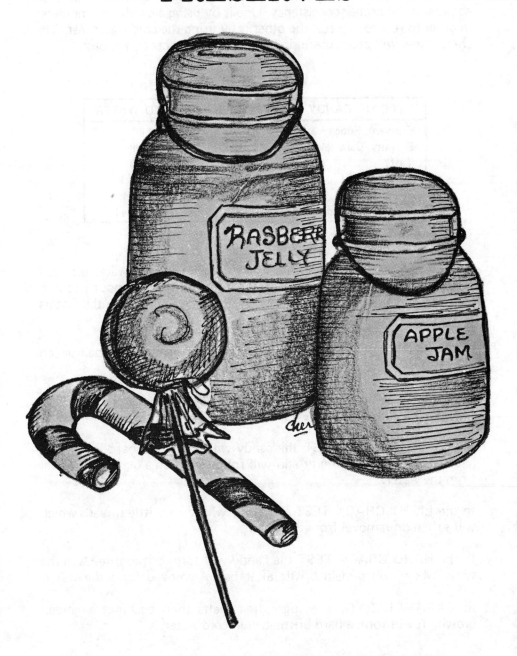

TEMPERATURE TESTS
FOR CANDY MAKING

There are two different methods of determining when candy has been cooked to the proper consistency. One is by using a candy thermometer in order to record degrees, the other is by using the cold water test. The chart below will prove useful in helping to follow candy recipes:

TYPE OF CANDY	DEGREES	COLD WATER
Fondant, Fudge	234 - 238°	Soft Ball
Divinity, Caramels	245 - 248°	Firm Ball
Taffy	265 - 270°	Hard Ball
Butterscotch	275 - 280°	Light Crack
Peanut Brittle	285 - 290°	Hard Crack
Caramelized Sugar	310 - 321°	Caramelized

In using the cold water test, use a fresh cupful of cold water for each test. When testing, remove the candy from the fire and pour about ½ teaspoon of candy into the cold water. Pick the candy up in the fingers and roll into a ball if possible.

In the SOFT BALL TEST the candy will roll into a soft ball which quickly loses its shape when removed from the water.

In the FIRM BALL TEST the candy will roll into a firm but not hard ball. It will flatten out a few minutes after being removed from water.

In the HARD BALL TEST the candy will roll into a hard ball which has lost almost all plasticity and will roll around on a plate on removal from the water.

In the LIGHT CRACK TEST the candy will form brittle threads which will soften on removal from the water.

In the HARD CRACK TEST the candy will form brittle threads in the water which will remain brittle after being removed from the water.

In CARAMELIZING, the sugar first melts then becomes a golden brown. It will form a hard brittle ball in cold water.

BURNT SUGAR CANDY

5 1/2 c. white sugar
1 stick butter
2 tsp. vanilla

1 large can evaporated milk
1 1/2 c. chopped pecans

Mix 4 cups sugar and milk together. Melt 1 1/2 cups white sugar in heavy skillet. When melted, pour in sugar and milk mixture. Cook until soft ball stage is reached. Remove from fire, add butter and beat with electric beater until creamy. Add pecans and vanilla. Drop on waxed paper by spoonfuls. Theda S. Thomas, Caddo Council, Shreveport, La.

BUTTERSCOTCH CANDY

2 (6 oz.) pkg. Nestle's
 butterscotch tidbits
1 (6 1/2 oz.) can cocktail
 peanuts

1 can chow mein noodles,
 broken in pieces

Melt butterscotch tidbits over hot water, not boiling. Add remaining ingredients and mix well. Drop by teaspoonfuls onto waxed paper; cool. Phyllis Henderson, Central Council, Alexandria, La.

CHOCOLATE COVERED CANDY

2 boxes powdered sugar
1 stick oleo
1 Tbsp. vanilla
1 tsp. salt

1 can heavy sweetened condensed milk
1 box Angel Flake coconut
2 c. nuts, chopped extra fine

Mix above and chill 1/2 hour. Roll into small balls. Melt over double boiler:

2 (6 oz.) pkg. chocolate
 chips

3/4 block paraffin

With balls on toothpicks, dip into chocolate mixture.
Calcasieu Council
Lake Charles, La.

MARTHA WASHINGTON CHOCOLATE CANDY

1 c. flaked coconut
1 c. chopped pecans
1 c. condensed milk
1/4 lb. paraffin

1/4 lb. oleo
2 boxes powdered sugar
1 (12 oz.) pkg. chocolate
  chips

Combine coconut, pecans, milk, oleo and powdered sugar. Roll by hand into small balls; chill about 1 hour. Melt paraffin and chocolate chips together over low heat, preferably in double boiler. Insert toothpick into each ball and dip into paraffin mixture. Place on waxed paper to harden.
Sonia A. Hunt, Capital Council, Baton Rouge, La.

CHOCOLATE SCOTCHEROOS

1 c. sugar
1 c. peanut butter
1 (6 oz.) pkg. Nestle's
  semi-sweet chocolate
  morsels

1 c. light corn syrup
6 c. Kellogg's Rice Krispies
1 (6 oz.) pkg. butterscotch
  morsels

Cook sugar and syrup in 3-quart saucepan over moderate heat until mixture boils. Remove and stir in peanut butter and Rice Krispies. Press into buttered 13x9-inch pan. Let harden. Melt chocolate and butterscotch morsels over hot water and stir to blend. Spread over Krispies mixture. Chill about 5 minutes. Yield: 42 bars; 2x1 inch.
Jesse O. Jackson, Shreveport Works Council, Shreveport, La.

CHOW MEIN NOODLE CANDY

3 (6 oz.) pkg. butterscotch
  morsels

1 large can Spanish peanuts
1 large can chow mein noodles

Melt butterscotch morsels in top of double boiler over low heat. When melted, remove from heat, add remaining ingredients. Mix well and drop by spoonfuls onto waxed paper.
Cecile Gallet, Evangeline Council, Lafayette, La.

COCONUT CANDY

2 c. sugar
1 c. milk
1 grated coconut

2 Tbsp. butter
1 tsp. vanilla

Cook sugar, milk and butter to 238°. Add coconut; let come to boil again. Remove from heat. Beat and cool. Add vanilla; beat until creamy. Drop by spoonfuls on buttered foil.
Gloria Fontenot, Evangeline Council, Lafayette, La.

ORANGE COCONUT BALLS

1 (12 oz.) box vanilla
   wafers, crushed
1 (6 oz.) can frozen
   orange juice, thawed

1 box powdered sugar
1 stick oleo, melted
1 c. pecans, chopped fine
Angel Flake coconut

Combine all ingredients, except coconut. Mix well; form into balls. Roll in coconut.
Jean Coon, Caddo Council, Shreveport, La.

PHILIPPINE COCONUT CANDY

2 bags coconut flakes
1 evaporated milk can
   of sugar
1 1/2 evaporated milk
   cans of sweet milk

2 large cans evaporated milk
1 can condensed milk
1 stick oleo or butter
1 tsp. vanilla

Mix all ingredients together and place on slow fire, stirring constantly until mixture gets stiff. Shape into small balls. Place on cookie sheet and brown in oven.
Edith Smith, Shreveport Works Council, Shreveport, La.

COOLEY'S WHITE DELIGHTS

1 lb. white chocolate
2 c. salted peanuts

4 c. golden graham
   crackers, crushed

Melt chocolate in top of double boiler. Add graham

crackers and peanuts, mixing well. Drop by tablespoon onto waxed paper. Let harden and enjoy. <u>Guaranteed no leftovers!</u>
West Bank Council
Gretna, La.

BRETT'S CREOLE CANDY

3 c. sugar
3 c. pecan pieces
2 Tbsp. butter

2 egg whites
3 Tbsp. honey

Mix all ingredients well. Pour into buttered pan. Bake at 350° until dark brown. Easy and good!
Louise Ward, Crescent City
Council, New Orleans, La.

CRISPY CRITTERS

5/8 c. white sugar
1 c. peanut butter

5/8 c. white Karo syrup
1 large box Special K cereal

Cook sugar and Karo syrup over low heat until soft ball stage is reached; stir frequently. Remove from heat, add peanut butter and mix well. Stir in cereal. Pour into buttered cookie sheet or pan. Cut into squares or pull apart. Will be chewy.
Elaine Squyres, Central
Council, Alexandria, La.

DATE LOAF CANDY

3 c. sugar
Pinch of salt
1 1/2 c. milk
1 tsp. vanilla

4 Tbsp. syrup
1/2 stick butter
1 (8 oz.) pkg. pitted dates,
  chopped
1 1/2 c. pecans, broken

Mix sugar, syrup, salt, butter and milk in medium size heavy pan. Cook to 234° or until soft ball stage is reached over medium heat, stirring constantly. Add dates and re-cook to soft ball stage. Remove from heat and cool 10 minutes. Add vanilla and pecans. Beat until candy loses gloss and thickens. Place on damp dish towel and form with buttered hands several rolls, about 1 1/2 inches in diameter. Roll up in towel and refrigerate. Keep chilled until ready to slice and serve.
Fae Wells, Central Council
Alexandria, La.

DATE LOAF CANDY

1/2 small pkg. chopped
　　dates
1 tsp. butter

2 1/2 c. sugar
1 c. chopped pecans
1 c. milk

Mix milk and sugar, boil until soft ball stage. Add dates, stir, add pecans and butter. Remove from heat and beat until creamy. Pour onto damp cloth and roll. Chill and slice when served.　　　Doris Reeves, Capital
　　　　　　　　　　　　　Council, Baton Rouge, La.

DATE LOAF CANDY

3 c. sugar
3 Tbsp. oleo
1 c. pecans

1 c. milk
1 c. chopped dates

Combine sugar, oleo and milk. Boil, stirring occasionally, until hard boil stage is reached. Remove from heat; add dates and pecans. Beat until creamy. Form into roll on a damp cloth. Roll and let cool. Slice to serve.
　　　　　　　　　　　　　Dona Stephens, Central
　　　　　　　　　　　　　Council, Houston, Tx.

DATE LOAF
(Candy)

2 c. sugar
1 c. evaporated milk
2 c. chopped nuts

1/4 c. butter
1 (8 oz.) pkg. dates

Combine sugar, milk and butter in heavy saucepan. Cook until soft ball stage is reached, stirring frequently until candy becomes very thick. Bubbles will make hissing sound and mixture will follow spoon around pan. Add nuts and stir until mixture has consistency of soft cookie dough. Wrap in wet cloth. Slice when cool and store in Tupperware or airtight container.　　　Jeanette English, Caddo
　　　　　　　　　　　　　Council, Shreveport, La.

DIVINITY

3 c. pecans, chopped
1 c. white Karo syrup
4 egg whites

4 c. sugar
2/3 c. boiling water
1 tsp. vanilla

Combine 3 1/2 cups sugar, syrup and boiling water. Cook until mixture will spin a thread 6-8 inches long. Beat egg whites until stiff; add remaining sugar; beat again until stiff. Pour syrup over egg whites, beating constantly. Add pecans and vanilla. Beat until it can be dropped from spoon onto waxed paper and hold its shape.

Anniece Rutledge, Ouachita
Council, Monroe, La.

DIVINITY

3 c. sugar
1/2 c. white Karo syrup
1 Tbsp. vanilla

1/2 c. water
3 egg whites
Pecans, as desired

Bring sugar, water and Karo syrup to boil in 2-quart saucepan over high heat until it threads, about 10 minutes. Beat egg whites stiff, but not dry, in mixer. When syrup threads, add half of it to egg whites gradually while mixing on high speed. Scrape sides of bowl often. Return remaining syrup to stove and cook for 1-2 minutes or until bubbly. Add to egg whites and continue beating until it will stay on a spoon; mixture will be thick. Add vanilla; mix well. Remove from mixer; add pecans. Drop onto waxed paper, using 2 teaspoons; one to dip candy from bowl and the other to push onto the paper. Work rapidly as it will harden fast. Makes about 50 medium size patties.

Elaine Squyres, Central
Council, Alexandria, La.

DIVINITY CANDY

4 c. sugar
1/2 c. warm water
1 c. chopped nuts

3/4 c. white Karo syrup
3 egg whites, stiffly beaten

Cook syrup, sugar and water to cracked stage. Pour gradually into beaten egg whites; continue beating. Add nuts and drop by spoonfuls on greased sheet or waxed paper.

Verle Oliphant, Caddo
Council, Shreveport, La.

DIVINITY CANDY

2 c. sugar
1/2 c. water
1 tsp. vanilla

1/2 c. Karo syrup
2 egg whites, beaten stiff
2 c. chopped pecans

Mix sugar, Karo syrup and water. Cook until drop in water forms hard ball. Pour hot mixture <u>very slowly</u> into eggs, beating constantly. Add vanilla and chopped pecans and beat until mixture thickens. Drop by spoonfuls on waxed paper.

Pat (Ramsey) Caraway
Capital Council
Baton Rouge, La.

DIXIE DIVINITY

4 c. granulated sugar
1/4 tsp. salt
3 egg whites, stiffly
   beaten

1 c. white corn syrup
1 c. water
2 tsp. vanilla
1 c. pecans

Combine sugar, corn syrup, water and salt in large heavy saucepan. Cook, stirring constantly over low heat until sugar is dissolved and mixture comes to boil. Cook quickly to hard ball stage (250°) without stirring. Remove from heat. Pour hot syrup in thin stream over beaten egg whites, beating constantly. When all syrup has been added, continue beating until soft peaks form and candy loses gloss. Stir in vanilla and nuts. Drop by spoonfuls on waxed paper, giving each candy a swirl as you peak. If it becomes too stiff, add a few drops of hot water. Makes a very large batch of candy.

Mrs. Sim S. Davenport
Central Council
Alexandria, La.

FROZEN PEANUT BUTTER DIVINITY

2 1/2 c. sugar
1/2 c. water
2 large egg whites
1/2 c. chunky peanut butter

1/2 c. light corn syrup
1/4 tsp. salt
1 tsp. vanilla

Cook sugar, corn syrup, water and salt, stirring constantly over medium heat until sugar dissolves and mixture boils. Reduce heat, continue boiling without stirring until

reaches 265° on candy thermometer or hard ball stage is
reached. Beat egg whites with vanilla at high speed until
stiff. With mixer still at high speed, gradually beat syrup
mixture into egg whites and continue beating until mixture
begins to lose gloss. Quickly swirl in peanut butter. Drop
by teaspoonfuls onto waxed paper. Let stand until cold.
Arrange in layers, between sheets of waxed paper, in
freezer container and cover tightly. Freeze. Serve while
still frozen so the divinity fudge will be ice cold, chewy
and good. Makes about 1 1/4 pounds.

Ann Orr, Evangeline
Council, New Iberia, La.

MICROWAVE OVEN DIVINITY

4 c. sugar
3/4 c. water
3 egg whites
1 tsp. vanilla

1 c. light corn syrup
1/4 tsp. salt
1/2 c. chopped nuts
(optional)

Mix together sugar, corn syrup, water and salt in a
1 1/2-quart casserole. Cook in Radarange oven on full
power for 20-22 minutes. Stir once or twice during cooking.
While syrup cooks, beat egg whites until stiff peaks form in
large mixing bowl. Gradually pour hot syrup over egg
whites while beating at high speed until mixture is thickened
and candy starts to lose its gloss. Beating may require
about 12 minutes. Add vanilla and nuts. Drop by teaspoonful onto waxed paper. Candy may be tinted with food coloring, if desired. Makes 6-7 dozen pieces.

Verna Blankenship, Ouachita
Council, Monroe, La.

NO COOK DIVINITY

1 pkg. fluffy white
   frosting mix
1 (16 oz.) pkg. powdered
   sugar
1 tsp. vanilla

1/3 c. light corn syrup
1/2 c. boiling water
1 c. chopped nuts (your
   choice)

In small mixer bowl, combine frosting mix, corn syrup,
vanilla and boiling water. Beat on highest speed until stiff
peaks form, about 5 minutes. Transfer to large mixer bowl.
On low speed, gradually blend in sugar. Stir in nuts. Drop

by teaspoonfuls onto waxed paper. When outside candy feels firm, turn over and dry at least 12 hours. Store candy in airtight container. Makes 5-6 dozen candies.

Mrs. Claude J. Merrill
Shreveport Works Council
Shreveport, La.

NON FAIL DIVINITY

1 1/2 c. sugar
Dash of salt
1 tsp. vanilla

1 1/3 c. water
1 1/2 c. chopped nuts
1 pt. marshmallow cream

Dissolve sugar and salt in water over low heat, cook without stirring or scraping down sides of boiler until hard ball stage is reached. Place marshmallow cream in mixer bowl and pour hot syrup over. Beat until mixture begins to string from beaters. Add nuts and vanilla, stir to mix and drop on waxed paper by teaspoonfuls. Let set until candy looks dry.

Fae Wells, Central Council,
Shreveport, La.

FUDGE

2 c. sugar
12 regular marshmallows
1/2 c. oleo
1 (6 oz.) pkg. semi-
  sweet chocolate pieces

2/3 c. Pet evaporated
  skimmed milk
Few grains of salt
1 c. chopped nuts
1 tsp. vanilla

Mix sugar, milk, marshmallows, oleo and salt together and cook over medium heat to a boil; mixture will be bubbling over top. Boil and stir 5 minutes. Remove from heat and stir in chocolate pieces until melted. Stir in nuts and vanilla. Spread in a buttered 8-inch square pan. Cool. Cut into 30 pieces.

Mary Anne Andrews, Ouachita
Council, Monroe, La.

FUDGE

2 c. sugar
1 1/2 Tbsp. vanilla
1/2 c. milk
1 c. chopped pecans

4 Tbsp. cocoa
2 Tbsp. butter or oleo
1/3 c. white Karo syrup

Cook sugar, cocoa, milk and Karo syrup until soft ball stage is reached. Remove from heat; add vanilla, butter and pecans. Beat until creamy and pour onto buttered plate. Cool and cut into squares.

Lynda Vercher, Central
Council, Natchitoches, La.

FUDGE

1 1/4 c. milk
3 c. sugar
5 Tbsp. butter
1 tsp. vanilla

1/4 c. chocolate
1/4 c. Karo syrup
1 c. nuts

Combine milk, chocolate, sugar and Karo syrup in saucepan. Bring to a slow boil, but do not stir. Remove from heat when soft ball stage is reached. Add butter, nuts and vanilla. Beat until it has cooled and pour into a square pan.

Marjorie Rowell, Evangeline
Council, Lafayette, La.

ALBINO FUDGE

2 lb. white chocolate
1 stick oleo

3 pt. pecans
Salt

Toast pecans with salt and oleo for 1 hour and 20 minutes at 300°. Stir every 20 minutes. Drain on paper towels. About 20 minutes before pecans are done, melt chocolate over water on low heat. Add pecans to chocolate and drop on waxed paper.

Evelyn Arnone, West Bank
Council, Gretna, La.

BEST FUDGE

3 plain (4 1/4 oz.)
 Hershey's bars
1 (7 oz.) jar marshmallow
 creme
1 Tbsp. oleo
1 tsp. vanilla

1 (12 oz.) pkg. semi-sweet
 chocolate chips
12 oz. or more chopped
 pecans
1 tall can Pet milk
4 1/2 c. sugar

Mix Hershey's bars, broken into pieces, chocolate chips, vanilla, marshmallow creme and oleo in 6-8-quart container.

672

Mix sugar and milk in 4-6-quart saucepan. Bring to a full rolling boil, stirring constantly. Continue to cook, stirring constantly to prevent scorching for 6 minutes. Pour mixture of sugar and milk over Hershey's bar mixture and blend until smooth and creamy. After blending completely, add pecans. Drop by tablespoon onto waxed paper. Let stand 4-6 hours or until completely chilled before removing from waxed paper. Makes over 6 pounds.

Gladys Domingues, Caddo
Council, Shreveport, La.

BETTIE'S VANILLA FUDGE

1 lb. light brown sugar
Pinch of salt
2 sticks butter or oleo
1 qt. pecans

2 c. white sugar
1 large can evaporated milk
1 Tbsp. vanilla

Mix sugars, salt, milk and 1 stick butter. Cook until soft ball stage is reached. Remove from heat, add vanilla and remaining stick of butter. Do not stir in. Let cool until you can hold palm of hand on bottom of pot. Beat until creamy and it loses its gloss. Add pecans and spread in greased platters. Makes a large batch.

Bettie Lalonde, Evangeline
Council, Opelousas, La.

CAN'T FAIL FUDGE

16 marshmallows, cut up
2 Tbsp. butter
1/4 tsp. salt
1/2 c. nuts

2/3 c. evaporated milk
1 c. sugar
1 c. (6 oz.) chocolate chips
1/2 tsp. vanilla

Combine marshmallows, milk, butter, sugar and salt in saucepan. Stir over medium heat until mixture comes to a full boil. Boil for exactly 5 minutes, stirring constantly to prevent sticking; remove from heat. Add chips and beat until chips melt. Add nuts and vanilla; beat to blend. Pour into greased 8x8-inch pan. Chill and cut into squares. Makes 1 1/4 pounds candy.   Patricia Edmonson, Caddo
Council, Shreveport, La.

CAN'T FAIL FUDGE

4 c. sugar
1 stick oleo
2 c. pecans

1 large can Carnation milk
1 jar marshmallow cream
3 (6 oz.) pkg. chocolate chips

Combine sugar, milk and oleo. Bring to a boil over heat and boil exactly 9 minutes. Remove from heat, add remaining ingredients. Stir and pour into large greased pan. Makes 5 pounds of candy. Butterscotch chips may be substituted for chocolate chips, if desired. Mrs. J.E. Rutledge, LeBayou Council, Houma, La.

CHOCOLATE FUDGE

3 1/2 c. sugar
1 stick butter
4 Tbsp. cocoa
1 tsp. vanilla

1 small can Pet milk, rinsed
  with little water
1/2 jar marshmallow creme

Melt butter, add sugar, milk and cocoa. Let cook until soft ball stage is reached. Remove from heat, stir in marshmallow creme and vanilla. Beat until creamy; pour into buttered pan. Lydia M. Gremillion, Central Council, Pineville, La.

CHOCOLATE FUDGE

4 1/2 c. sugar
1 lb. oleo
3 pkg. Hershey's choco-
  late chips
6 Hershey's bars

1 large can evaporated milk
2 c. pecans
1 pt. Hip-O-Lite marshmallow
  creme

Boil sugar, milk and oleo together for 5 minutes. Remove from heat and mix well with remaining ingredients. Makes 5 pounds. Pat (Ramsey) Caraway Capital Council Baton Rouge, La.

CREAM CHEESE FUDGE

1 (3 oz.) pkg. cream
  cheese
1 lb. powdered sugar
3 Tbsp. water

1 tsp. vanilla
3 sq. chocolate, unsweet-
  ened, melted
3/4 c. chopped nuts

Cream the cheese and sugar; add water and vanilla. Melt chocolate and add with nuts. Shape into a roll on waxed paper. Chill in refrigerator. This fudge never fails.
Calcasieu Council
Lake Charles, La.

CREAMY FUDGE

3 c. sugar
1/2 c. Karo syrup
1 small can evaporated
  milk

1/4 c. cocoa
1 stick oleo
1 c. nuts
1 Tbsp. vanilla

Cook over medium heat about 45 minutes until soft ball stage is reached. Stir frequently to prevent burning to bottom of pot. Remove from heat; add nuts and vanilla. Mix well and pour into buttered dish to cool. Cut into squares while still warm. It's easier to cut before fudge is completely cool. Store in tightly closed container. Can be frozen. Yield: About forty 1 1/2-inch squares.
Elaine Squyres, Central
Council, Alexandria, La.

COCONUT FUDGE DROPS

2 Tbsp. butter
1 2/3 c. sugar
2 c. miniature marsh-
  mallows
1 tsp. grated orange peel
1 tsp. vanilla

2/3 c. evaporated milk
1/2 tsp. salt
1 1/2 c. semi-sweet
  chocolate pieces
1 c. flaked coconut
1/2 c. dark raisins

Combine butter, milk, sugar and salt in saucepan. Bring to a boil over medium heat. Cook 5 minutes, stirring constantly; start timing when bubbles appear around edge of pan. Remove from heat; stir in marshmallows, chocolate pieces, orange peel and vanilla. Stir vigorously for 1 minute, allowing marshmallows to melt and blend. Stir in coconut and raisins. Drop by teaspoonfuls onto buttered cookie sheet. Makes about 2 pounds.

Mary R. Quimby, Ouachita
Council, Monroe, La.

DROP FUDGE

1 (6-7 oz.) jar marsh-
  mallow creme
1 stick butter or oleo
1/2 tsp. salt
2 lb. chopped pecans

4 1/2 c. sugar
1 tall can evaporated milk
1 (12 oz.) pkg. Nestle's
  chocolate chips, or Baker's
  brick chocolate, chopped

Combine milk, sugar, salt and butter. Bring to a boil. Cook 7 minutes after it starts to boil. Sprinkle pecans in bottom of pan, add chocolate chips and marshmallow creme; pour hot mixture over all. Mix until gloss disappears. Drop from teaspoon on foil or waxed paper. Important to follow directions.

Jeanette English, Caddo
Council, Shreveport, La.

LOUISE'S "NEVER FAILS" PECAN FUDGE

2/3 c. Hershey's cocoa
1 c. sweet milk
1 tsp. pure vanilla extract
2 c. pecan pieces

3 c. sugar
1/2 c. evaporated milk
1/2 stick butter
1/4 tsp. salt

Be sure cocoa is fresh! Mix cocoa and sugar thoroughly. Add milks slowly. Add salt. Cook on medium heat, stirring constantly until mixture boils. Reduce heat, stir often. Cook until hard ball stage is reached. Remove from heat, add vanilla and butter. Stir until butter is melted; add pecans. Mix quickly and pour into buttered platters. Cool at room temperature. When hard, cut into squares and serve to your sweet-toothed family and friends.

Louise Ward, Crescent City
Council, New Orleans, La.

MARSHMALLOW CREAM FUDGE

1 (5-10 oz.) jar marsh-
   mallow creme
1/4 c. butter or oleo
1/2 c. chopped nuts
1 tsp. vanilla

1 1/2 c. sugar
2/3 c. evaporated milk
1/2 tsp. salt
2 (6 oz.) pkg. Nestle's semi-
   sweet chocolate morsels

Combine marshmallow creme, sugar, milk, butter and salt. Bring to full boil, stirring constantly over moderate heat. Boil for 5 minutes, stirring constantly, before removing from fire. Add remaining ingredients; stir until morsels are melted. Pour into greased 8-inch square pan. Chill until firm. Makes 2 1/4 pounds.

Dorothy Beaudoin, Capital
Council, Waterbury, Ct.

MILLION DOLLAR FUDGE

3 plain Hershey's bars
1 (12 oz.) pkg. chocolate
   chips
2 (7 oz.) jars marsh-
   mallow creme
1 Tbsp. butter

4 1/2 c. sugar
1 large Pet milk
1 Tbsp. vanilla
1 tsp. salt
3 c. chopped pecans

Mix sugar, milk and salt. Cook and let come to boil. Boil for 6 minutes, stirring often. Remove from heat, mix in remaining ingredients. Stir well and beat until smooth. Pour into buttered pan or drop by spoonfuls on buttered foil.

Gloria Fontenot, Evangeline
Council, Lafayette, La.

OLD FASHIONED CREAMY FUDGE

1/2 cube butter or oleo
7/8 c. milk (just under
   a cup)

2 sq. chocolate
2 c. sugar
1/2 c. chopped nuts

Melt butter with chocolate, add milk and cook until thick. It will look almost like pudding. Add sugar, stir well but stop stirring when mixture begins to boil. Cook until soft ball stage is reached. Cool to lukewarm; beat until creamy and it starts to thicken. Add nuts and pour onto buttered plate.

Molly Hoskins, Caddo
Council, Shreveport, La.

PEANUT BUTTER FUDGE

2 c. sugar
1 c. milk

1 c. marshmallow creme
1 c. peanut butter

Cook sugar and milk together until soft ball stage is reached. Remove from heat, add marshmallow creme and peanut butter. Beat until creamy. Pour into greased platter.
Maxine Fletcher, Ouachita Council, Monroe, La.

PEANUT BUTTER FUDGE

3 c. sugar
3/4 c. margarine
2/3 c. Pet milk

1 c. peanut butter
1 (7 oz.) jar marshmallow creme
1 tsp. vanilla

Combine sugar, margarine and milk in heavy 2 1/2-quart saucepan; bring to a full rolling boil, stirring constantly. Continue boiling 5 minutes over medium heat, stirring constantly to prevent scorching. Remove from heat, stir in peanut butter until melted. Add marshmallow creme and vanilla; beat until blended. Pour into greased 13x9-inch pan. Cool at room temperature; cut into squares. Makes approximately 3 pounds.
Gladys Domingues, Caddo Council, Shreveport, La.

CREAMY PEANUT BUTTER FUDGE

5 c. sugar
1 large jar marshmallow creme
1/4 tsp. salt

1 (16 oz.) jar peanut butter
1 stick butter
1 (13 oz.) can Pet milk
1 tsp. vanilla

Combine sugar, butter, milk and salt. Bring to a boil and cook for 15 minutes. Remove from heat, add other ingredients. Mix and stir well. Pour into 9x13-inch pan. Cool until firm.
Verna Blankenship, Ouachita Council, Monroe, La.

PEANUT BUTTER CREAM FUDGE

2 c. sugar
2/3 c. milk
1 tsp. vanilla

1 c. marshmallow cream
1 c. peanut butter

Cook sugar and milk until it reaches soft ball stage. Mix marshmallow cream and peanut butter until smooth; add to sugar mixture. Add vanilla and mix well. Pour into buttered pan. Cut in squares.

Evelyn Patton, Shreveport
Works Council, Shreveport, La.

WHITE FUDGE

2 1/4 c. sugar
1/4 c. milk
1 Tbsp. light corn syrup
1/3 c. quartered candied
   cherries

1/2 c. sour cream
2 Tbsp. butter
1/4 tsp. salt
2 Tbsp. vanilla
1 c. coarsely chopped pecans

Combine sugar, sour cream, milk, butter, corn syrup and salt in heavy 2-quart saucepan. Stir over moderate heat until sugar is dissolved and mixture reaches a boil. Boil 9-10 minutes to 238°; if damp weather, to 240°. Remove from heat, allow to stand until lukewarm (110°), about 1 hour. Add vanilla and beat until mixture just begins to lose its gloss and hold shape. Requires very little beating. Quickly stir in pecans and cherries and turn into oiled pan. Let stand until firm before cutting.

Jeanette Armand, Central
Council, Bunkie, La.

GOLD BRICK CANDY

2 sticks oleo
1 pt. marshmallow cream
4 c. pecans
4 1/2 c. sugar

1 1/2 pkg. semi-sweet
   chocolate chips
1 can Carnation milk

Mix butter, chocolate chips and marshmallow cream in electric mixer. In saucepan, put sugar and milk to boil. Stir constantly until mixture comes to a complete boil for 9 minutes. Pour boiling mixture into mixer, blend until all chocolate bits are melted. Add pecans and pour into a

1723-79

greased pan. Chill in refrigerator for 3 hours. Cut into squares. Keep refrigerated. Mollie Porrovecchio, Metairie Council, New Orleans, La.

HAY STACKS

1 (6 oz.) pkg. butterscotch chips
1 (6 oz.) pkg. chocolate chips

1/2 c. peanut butter
1 (3 oz.) can chow mein noodles

Mix chips and peanut butter in double boiler until melted and smooth. Add noodles and mix until well coated. Drop by teaspoon on waxed paper and let set until firm.
Mary Bonner, Caddo
Council, Shreveport, La.

HOPSCOTCH CANDY

1 (6 oz.) pkg. butterscotch morsels
1 (3 oz.) can chow mein noodles

2 c. miniature marshmallows
1/2 c. crunchy peanut butter

Mix marshmallows and noodles in large bowl. Melt butterscotch morsels in double boiler over water. Add peanut butter when melted. Combine mixture with noodles. Mix and drop by spoon on waxed paper. Cool.
Virginia Lowrey, Ouachita
Council, Monroe, La.

HORNED TOADS

1 c. white Karo syrup
1 small can coconut
5 or 6 c. corn flakes

1 c. sugar
1 (12 oz.) jar crunchy peanut butter

Bring Karo syrup and sugar to a boil. Remove from heat and add peanut butter. Pour mixture over corn flakes and coconut. Mix well and drop on waxed paper. Do not crush corn flakes. Molly Hoskins, Caddo
Council, Shreveport, La.

JELLO BALLS

2 pkg. jello (same
   flavor)
1 c. coconut

1 c. chopped pecans
2/3 c. condensed milk

Mix all ingredients together and chill. Roll in small balls and refrigerate overnight. Roll in powdered sugar.
Suzanne Dickerson, Central
Council, Alexandria, La.

MILLIONAIRES

1 lb. caramels
2 c. pecans
1/4 - 1/2 bar paraffin

2 lb. water
1 (8 oz.) Hershey's bar

Melt caramels in double boiler with water. Stir in pecans. Spoon onto waxed paper and chill. Melt Hershey's bar and paraffin in double boiler. Dip chilled pecan mound in chocolate mixture; cool.
Donna McPhearson, Central
Council, Natchitoches, La.

CHOCOLATE MILLIONAIRES

1 (14 oz.) pkg. caramels
2 c. pecan pieces
1/4 bar paraffin

3-4 tsp. milk
Butter or oleo
1 (12 oz.) pkg. semi-sweet
   chocolate morsels

Melt caramels in milk over low heat; add pecans. Drop by teaspoonfuls onto buttered waxed paper. Chill. Melt paraffin and chocolate morsels in heavy saucepan over very low heat. Dip candy into chocolate mixture and return to waxed paper. Chill. Yield: 3 1/2 dozen.
Sonia A. Hunt, Capital
Council, Baton Rouge, La.

TEXAS MILLIONAIRE CANDY

1 c. brown sugar
1 c. white Karo syrup
1 tsp. vanilla
2 large Hershey's bars

1 c. white sugar
2 c. Pet milk
1/4 lb. paraffin
1 lb. pecan halves

Mix sugar, Karo syrup, vanilla and 1 cup milk. Stir well and let come to a full boil. Stir; add other cup of milk slowly, so slowly that candy does not stop boiling. Cook until soft ball stage is reached. Add pecan halves and pour into a buttered 13x15-inch pan. Refrigerate overnight. Melt Hershey's bars and paraffin together in top of double boiler. Dip candy into mixture when cool.

Marie Pamplin, Shreveport
Works Council, Shreveport, La.

TING-A-LINGS

2 (6 oz.) pkg. semi-sweet chocolate bits

4 c. Cheerios

Melt chocolate over hot water. Cool at room temperature. Gently fold in Cheerios. Drop by tablespoon onto waxed paper. Refrigerate about 2 hours to set. Yield: 42 clusters.

Mearl S. Byles, Central
Council, Natchitoches, La.

PEANUT BRITTLE

1 1/2 c. sugar
1/4 c. water
1/4 tsp. salt

1 - 1 1/2 tsp. soda
1/2 c. white Karo syrup
2 c. shelled raw peanuts

Combine sugar, Karo syrup and water. Bring to boil. Stir in peanuts gradually, keeping at a rolling boil until peanuts pop and turn brown. Remove from heat; add soda, stirring well. Add salt. Pour on well greased platter, allowing room for candy to spread. When cool, break into pieces.

Emma G. McCoy, Central
Council, Bunkie, La.

PEANUT BRITTLE

1 1/2 c. sugar
1/2 c. hot water
1 1/2 tsp. baking soda

1/2 c. white Karo syrup
1 pt. raw peanuts

Combine and mix sugar, Karo syrup, water, peanuts. Cook over medium heat 30 or 35 minutes. Remove from heat; stir in soda. Pour on cookie sheet.

Mary R. Jones, Ouachita
Council, Monroe, La.

PEANUT BRITTLE

2 c. sugar
1/4 c. hot water
1 tsp. soda

1/2 c. white Karo syrup
2 c. raw peanuts

Cook sugar, Karo syrup and water in large iron skillet. Stir to moisten sugar. Add peanuts and cook over medium heat until peanuts make popping sounds and little brown streaks appear in syrup. Remove from heat, add soda and whip. Pour onto buttered cookie sheet. Break into pieces when cool.
Elaine Squyres, Central
Council, Alexandria, La.

PEANUT BRITTLE

1 c. sugar
1 tsp. soda
Pinch of salt

2 c. peanuts
1 c. white Karo syrup

Combine sugar, Karo syrup, peanuts and salt. Cook in a heavy skillet until syrup turns golden brown and peanuts begin to pop. Take off heat and add soda; stir in well. Pour out on buttered platter and let cool. Break into pieces.
Mearl S. Byles, Central
Council, Natchitoches, La

NUT BRITTLE

2 c. sugar
1/4 tsp. soda
2 c. peanuts

1/4 tsp. salt
1 tsp. vanilla

Heat sugar gradually in clean, smooth fry pan. Stir constantly until golden syrup is formed. Remove from heat and quickly stir in salt, soda and vanilla. Pour mixture over layer of peanuts in a greased pan. When cold, crack into small pieces.
Mrs. Claude J. Merrill
Shreveport Works Council
Shreveport, La.

PULLED PEANUT BRITTLE

1 1/2 c. sugar
2/3 c. cold water
2 c. fresh peanuts
1/2 tsp. salt

2/3 c. white Karo syrup
Hunk of butter
1 tsp. vanilla
1 Tbsp. soda

Combine sugar, Karo syrup and water. Bring to boil about 3 minutes. Add butter and peanuts. Using candy thermometer, cook to hard crack. If thermometer is not available, cook to hard ball stage. Remove from heat and quickly stir in remaining ingredients. Pour on buttered counter top. Cool slightly. Pull, beginning around the edges. Gloves may be worn. Jean Coon, Caddo Council, Shreveport, La.

PEANUT BUTTER BALLS

1 c. dark Karo syrup
6 c. Special K cereal

1 c. white sugar
1 1/2 c. crunchy peanut
butter

Mix Karo syrup and sugar and bring to slow boil; remove from heat, stir in peanut butter. Add Special K, 1 cup at a time. Use teaspoon to make marble size balls and roll in palm of hands. Make about 50 balls.
Marjorie Stearns, Caddo Council, Shreveport, La.

CHOCOLATE COVERED PEANUT BALLS

1 c. peanut butter
2 sticks oleo
1 c. coconut (optional)
1 (4 oz.) stick paraffin
wax

1 lb. box powdered sugar
2 c. graham cracker crumbs
1 c. chopped nuts
1 (6 oz.) pkg. chocolate chips

Melt butter and add peanut butter and powdered sugar. Mix well. Add cracker crumbs, coconut and nuts. Roll in small balls. Refrigerate 5-6 hours or overnight. When well chilled, melt the chocolate pieces and paraffin wax together in a double boiler. Dip peanut balls in hot melted chocolate, using toothpicks to dip with. Refrigerate.
Marie Pamplin
Shreveport Works Council
Shreveport, La.

684

PEANUT BUTTER CRUNCH

1 c. Karo syrup
1 c. chunky peanut butter

1 c. sugar
1 c. corn flakes

Melt sugar in Karo syrup. Add peanut butter and corn flakes. Stir to mix. Drop by spoonfuls on waxed paper.

Maxine Fletcher, Ouachita
Council, Monroe, La.

PEANUT BUTTER PANOCHA

3 c. brown sugar, firmly
  packed (1 lb.)
1 c. crunchy peanut
  butter
2 tsp. vanilla

1/4 tsp. salt
1/2 c. milk
1/4 c. salted peanuts,
  chopped

Combine brown sugar, salt and milk in large saucepan; cook until boiling, without stirring, until soft ball stage is reached or 238°. Remove from heat and stir in peanut butter and vanilla; mix well. Pour mixture into buttered 8-inch square pan. Sprinkle top with peanuts. Let stand at room temperature until hard. Cut in squares.

Carole Smith, Caddo
Council, Shreveport, La.

PEANUT BUTTER POTATO CANDY

1 medium white potato
Creamy peanut butter

1 box powdered sugar

Boil potato in peel until tender. Mash 1/2 of peeled potato in bowl with fork and add sugar, a little at a time. Use all of sugar but 1 tablespoon that is used to roll candy in. If more of the potato is needed, mash and add. Candy should be very stiff. Remove from bowl, turn over once and roll with rolling pin on waxed paper until very thin. Spread with peanut butter and shape into long roll. Roll in remaining sugar. Slice and put on plate in refrigerator until chilled, then place in covered container in refrigerator. This candy is delicious.

Aline Albin (Martha
Starkey's sister-in-law)
Capital Council
Baton Rouge, La.

POTATO-PEANUT BUTTER CANDY

3 medium potatoes, boiled
 and mashed
1 lb. powdered sugar

1 1/4 c. creamy peanut butter
Dash of salt

Mix all ingredients until smooth. Spread powdered sugar on waxed paper and shape candy as desired into rolls, circles, squares, etc. This is especially good when children want to help with the Holiday fixings.

Katherine Slover, Caddo
Council, Phoenix, Az.

POTATO CANDY

1/2 c. cooked and mashed
 Irish potatoes
1 tsp. vanilla

1 box powdered sugar
Few drops lemon juice
Peanut butter

After mashing potatoes and while still slightly warm, add lemon juice, vanilla and begin stirring in sugar. Continue to stir in sugar until mixture is consistency to roll out to about 1/4-inch thickness. Spread with peanut butter and roll up jelly roll fashion. Chill. Cut in thin slices to serve.

Molly Hoskins, Caddo
Council, Shreveport, La.

PEANUT PATTIES

3 c. sugar
1 c. white Karo syrup
1/2 tsp. vanilla
1 stick butter

1/2 c. water
3 c. raw peanuts
5-6 drops red food coloring

Mix sugar, water, Karo syrup and peanuts together. Heat to boiling and boil exactly 7 minutes. Remove from heat, add food coloring, vanilla and butter. Beat until color changes. Drop onto aluminum foil.

Mary Anne Andrews, Ouachita
Council, Monroe, La.

686

PECAN LOGS

1 jar marshmallow creme
1 tsp. vanilla
1 lb. caramel candy
  squares

1 lb. powdered sugar
1/4 tsp. almond flavor
5 c. chopped pecans
1 Tbsp. water

Mix marshmallow creme, vanilla and almond flavoring together. Add powdered sugar and mix well. Shape into 8 small rolls about 1-inch in diameter. Wrap in waxed paper and freeze overnight; do not let rolls touch each other. Melt caramels and water in top of double boiler; dip logs in caramel mixture and roll in chopped nuts.

Evelyn Patton, Shreveport
Works Council, Keithville, La.

JENNY'S PECAN PATTIES

2 c. white sugar
1/4 tsp. baking soda
1 qt. chopped pecans

1/2 c. canned milk
1/2 c. white Karo syrup
1 Tbsp. oleo

Mix sugar, soda, milk and Karo syrup. Cook until soft ball stage is reached. Remove from heat. Add oleo. Cool and whip. Drop by spoon on waxed paper.

Marie Pamplin, Shreveport
Works Council, Shreveport, La.

PECAN ROLLS

1 (7 1/2 oz.) jar marshmallow
  creme
1 tsp. vanilla
2 bags Kraft caramels
6 or 7 c. chopped pecans

1/4 - 1/2 tsp. almond flavoring
1 lb. sifted powdered sugar
2 Tbsp. water

Combine marshmallow creme, vanilla, almond flavoring and sugar; mix and knead. Form in balls or rolls 3/4-inch in diameter. Lay on cookie sheet on waxed paper and freeze. Then bag until ready to use. When ready to use, melt caramels with water in double boiler until smooth. Dip center in caramel mixture, using tongs. Roll in pecans. Press pecans into roll and lay on waxed paper. Refrigerate rolls while making in order to keep molded. After shape is held, remove from refrigerator and store in tight containers. Makes 16-18 medium rolls.

Jeanette English, Caddo
Council, Shreveport, La.

CATHEDRAL ROLL

1 (14 oz.) bag Hershey's
   kisses
1 c. chopped pecans

1 stick oleo
1 bag small colored marshmallows

Melt chocolate and butter. Do not boil. Remove from heat; mix in pecans. Cool until pot is not hot. Stir in marshmallows. Dump mixture on 2 1/2 - 3-foot piece of foil. Shape into long roll with hands; wrap foil around roll. Refrigerate for 12 hours before serving. Remove foil, slice in 1/2-inch slices to serve.   Jan Prestridge, Capital
Council, Baton Rouge, La.

POPCORN BALLS

1 c. sugar
1/2 c. water
1/2 c. butter
3 qt. popped corn

1/2 c. corn syrup
1/2 tsp. salt
1 tsp. vanilla

Mix sugar, syrup, water, salt and butter until butter is dissolved. Cook without stirring until a drop of the mixture forms a brittle ball in cold water. Remove from heat and add vanilla. Pour over hot popped corn and stir thoroughly until every kernel is coated. Press together lightly with wet hands.   Patricia R. Caraway, Capital
Council, Baton Rouge, La.

PEANUT BUTTER POPCORN BALLS

8 c. popped corn
1/4 c. light brown sugar
1/2 c. peanut butter

1/2 c. white corn syrup
1 tsp. vanilla

Place popped corn in large bowl; set aside. Mix syrup, brown sugar and oleo. Bring to a boil and stir in peanut butter. Cook until mixture reaches hard ball stage. Pour over popped corn and mix until corn is coated. Roll into balls when cool enough to handle. Makes 24 small balls.

Mavis W. O'Rourke
Shreveport Works Council
Shreveport, La.

BAKED CARAMEL CORN

1 c. oleo	2 c. firmly packed light
1/2 c. light corn syrup	brown sugar
1/2 tsp. soda	1 tsp. salt
6 qt. popped corn	1 tsp. vanilla

Melt butter; stir in sugar, syrup and salt. Boil, stirring constantly until sugar is dissolved. Boil without stirring 15 minutes. Remove from heat; add soda and vanilla. Mix well. Gradually pour over popped corn and mix well. Turn corn mixture into large roasting pan. Bake at 250° for 1 hour, stirring every 15 minutes. Remove from oven. Stir until cool. Will not be sticky. If you like caramel corn, this is the best!

Theda S. Thomas, Caddo
Council, Shreveport, La.

POPCORN CRACKLE

3/8 c. popcorn	1 stick butter or oleo
1 1/3 c. sugar	1/2 c. Karo syrup
Nuts (optional)	

Pop the uncooked popcorn and add nuts, if desired. Combine remaining ingredients and bring to a boil; boil 15 minutes or until changes color. Pour syrup mixture over corn. Stir quickly to coat popcorn and spread on waxed paper.

Donna McPhearson, Central
Council, Natchitoches, La.

PRALINES

3 c. sugar	1 1/2 c. milk
1 lb. shelled pecans	

Cook milk and sugar until soft ball forms; add pecans and continue to cook until firm ball forms in cup of cold water. Pour onto buttered dish in small amounts. Cool.

Marjorie B. Harris, Capital
Council, Baton Rouge, La.

PRALINES

1 c. sugar
1/2 c. milk
1 c. pecans

1/2 c. brown sugar
Lump of butter size of walnut
1 tsp. vanilla

Mix ingredients and place in pot. Let boil until forms soft ball in cold water. Takes about 5 minutes. Drop on waxed paper.   Verle Oliphant

PRALINES

1 c. brown sugar
1/2 c. evaporated milk
1 c. pecans

1 c. white sugar
2 Tbsp. butter

Mix ingredients. Cook to 228°, then to 238°. Remove from fire and beat 1 minute. Pour on waxed paper fast. Makes about 24 pralines.   Lee Campos, Crescent City
Council, New Orleans, La.

EASY PRALINES

1 small pkg. butterscotch
  pudding mix (not instant)
1/2 c. evaporated milk
1 1/2 c. pecan halves

1 c. white sugar
1/2 c. packed brown sugar
1 Tbsp. butter

Combine pudding mix, milk, sugars and butter in heavy saucepan; mix until smooth. Add pecans and bring to a boil. Boil slowly, stirring often until candy reaches soft ball stage. Remove from heat and beat until candy just begins to thicken. Drop quickly by spoon onto waxed paper. Flavors can be varied by using either coconut cream or chocolate; do not use instant mix.
Mrs. Tony Corcoran, Crescent
City Council, New Orleans, La.

ESMA'S SHERRY CREAM PRALINES

1 c. firmly packed brown
  sugar
2 c. pecans, halves or
  pieces

1 c. granulated sugar (white)
1/2 c. evaporated milk
1 Tbsp. sherry wine

Thoroughly mix all ingredients, except the sherry wine, in a heavy saucepan. Cook over medium heat (236°) until soft ball stage is reached, stirring constantly. Remove from heat and when mixture stops bubbling, stir in sherry. Cool slightly, then beat well until mixture begins to thicken, drop candy rapidly from tablespoon onto newspaper covered by waxed paper. If candy becomes too stiff to drop into smooth patties, stir in small amount of hot water, a few drops at a time.

Verle Oliphant, Caddo
Council, Shreveport, La.

Gayle Palermo, Westmoor
Council, Kenner, La.

MEXICAN PRALINES

3 c. sugar
1/2 stick butter

1 c. milk
3 c. pecans

Use 2 boilers. In one boiler, use 2 cups sugar and 1 cup milk. Heat to boiling point. In other boiler, place remaining cup of sugar to be caramelized. Be careful not to let burn. Add milk and sugar mixture to caramelized sugar, stir well. Let cook until soft ball stage is reached. Remove from fire, add butter and pecans. Cool to lukewarm. Beat, pour or spoon in desired sizes when mixture starts losing gloss.

Doris Reeves, Capital
Council, Baton Rouge, La.

MARSHMALLOW PRALINES

2 c. sugar
2 Tbsp. oleo
1/2 tsp. vanilla

8 large marshmallows
1 c. milk
Pecans (optional)

Combine sugar, marshmallows and milk in heavy 4-quart pot. Cook over medium heat, stirring constantly until soft ball stage is reached, about 30-40 minutes. Remove from heat, stir in oleo and vanilla. Beat about 1 minute with spoon until creamy. Add pecans and beat with spoon until mixture begins to thicken. Working rapidly, drop onto waxed paper or buttered cookie sheet. Cool. Store in airtight container. Yield: About 18 medium size pralines.

Elaine Squyres, Central
Council, Alexandria, La.

PECAN PRALINES

2 c. white sugar
1 c. evaporated milk

2 c. pecans
1 tsp. vanilla flavoring

Mix sugar, milk and vanilla. Cook very slowly for about 1 1/2 - 2 hours until soft ball stage is reached. Beat well and add pecans. Drop by tablespoonfuls onto waxed paper.

Jeanette English, Caddo
Council, Shreveport, La.

PLANTATION PRALINES

1 box light brown sugar
1/4 tsp. cream of tartar
2 Tbsp. butter
2 c. chopped pecans

1/8 tsp. salt
1 tsp. vanilla
1 c. milk

Combine sugar, salt, milk and cream of tartar. Cook on medium heat, stirring often. Cook to 236° on candy thermometer. Beat and cool to 220°; add butter, pecans and vanilla. Beat well and drop by spoonfuls on buttered foil.

Gloria Fontenot, Evangeline
Council, Lafayette, La.

TEXAS PRALINES

2 c. sugar
1/2 tsp. soda
1 tsp. vanilla

1/4 c. milk
1 1/2 c. pecans
1 Tbsp. oleo

Cook sugar, milk and soda together until soft ball stage is reached. Remove from heat and stir in pecans. Add vanilla and oleo. Beat until mixture begins to hold shape. Drop by spoon on waxed paper that has been sprinkled with salt.

Bill Picard, Calcasieu
Council, Westlake, La.

SHORTCUT CANDY

1 3/4 c. brown sugar
1/4 tsp. salt
6 Tbsp. butter
1/2 tsp. vanilla

1/4 c. milk
2 1/2 c. powdered sugar
1 c. chopped pecans or
  walnuts

Place in double boiler the brown sugar, milk and salt. Stir over medium heat until brown sugar dissolves. Place over simmering water; add powdered sugar and butter to mixture. Stir until candy is thoroughly blended. Remove from heat; add nuts and vanilla. Pour into buttered 8-inch square pan. Cool and cut into 25 squares. Makes 1 1/2 pounds.   Clara Westbrook, Shreveport
Works Council, Shreveport, La.

TURTLES
(Candy)

2 bags caramels
2 c. pecans, chopped
1/4 stick paraffin

3 Tbsp. water
2 (6 oz.) pkg. semi-sweet
chocolate pieces, or large
bag

Melt caramels and water in top of double boiler. Stir in pecans and spoon out on buttered cookie sheet or buttered waxed paper 6-8 hours or overnight. Melt chocolate pieces and paraffin in top of double boiler. Using 2 toothpicks, dip well chilled Turtles in mixture of chocolate while it is hot.   Marie Pamplin, Shreveport
Works Council, Shreveport, La.

HOT PEPPER JELLY

6 1/2 c. sugar
1 c. finely chopped green
peppers
1 bottle Certo

1 1/2 c. apple cider vinegar
1/4 - 1/2 c. finely chopped
hot Christmas peppers
1 (25¢) bag red hots

Put sugar and vinegar in large pot. Bring to a boil. Add red hots, green and red pepper. Let boil 15 minutes. Cool for 10 minutes. Add Certo and mix well. Pour directly into 8-ounce jars. Makes 8 or 9 jars. If clear jelly is desired, let sugar, vinegar and peppers cool for 15 minutes and strain the peppers. This jelly is highly recommended by Robert Carnahan.
From the last of the Red Hot Mamas.
Karen Odom, LeBayou
Council, Houma, La.

HOT PEPPER JELLY

6 or 6 1/2 c. sugar
1 1/2 c. cider vinegar
1 (6 oz.) bottle Certo
1 1/2 c. chopped green pepper
1 1/2 c. jalapeno peppers
Green food coloring

Place green peppers, jalapeno peppers and vinegar in blender. Blend well. Place in pot the sugar, pepper mixture and food coloring. Cook 10-12 minutes. Add Certo and cook additional 2 or 3 minutes. Put in jars and seal. Can be strained if desired before pouring into jars.

Richard Silva, Crescent City
Council, New Orleans, La.

HOT PEPPER JELLY

3/4 c. sweet bell peppers, ground
1/4 c. Louisiana hot peppers, ground (red or green, preferably both)
5 1/2 c. sugar
1 1/2 c. apple cider vinegar
1 small bottle Certo

Remove seeds and grind peppers in food chopper. Save juice and mix with vinegar and sugar. Bring to a full boil, about 5 minutes. Add ground peppers, cook 2 minutes. Cool for 5 minutes, then add Certo. Bring to a full rolling boil for about 1 or 2 minutes, then cool about 5 minutes. Skim and pour into glasses and seal with paraffin. Important: Wear rubber gloves or plastic ones when handling hot peppers and watch out for your eyes.

Calcasieu Council
Lake Charles, La.

HOT PEPPER JELLY

1 1/2 c. apple cider vinegar
1 (2 oz.) bottle Tabasco sauce, or 1/4 c. red hot peppers
6 1/2 c. sugar
1 1/2 c. chopped bell peppers
1/2 tsp. salt
1 bottle Certo fruit pectin

Measure sugar and salt into pot. Place vinegar, peppers and Tabasco sauce in blender and liquefy. Add this to sugar and salt. Bring to rapid boil and continue to boil heavily; stir until mixture rises to top and stirring does

not bring it down. Remove from heat, set 10 minutes. Skim film from top and discard. Add Certo to mixture, stirring well. Pour into clean, hot jars and seal. Turn jars upside down to vacuum seal.   Mrs. Stafford (Vickie) Juneau
Crescent City Council
Metairie, La.

PEPPER JELLY

6 1/2 c. sugar
3/4 c. ground bell pepper
1 bottle Certo

1 1/2 c. apple cider vinegar
1/4 c. hot peppers

Put vinegar and peppers through blender. Add to sugar and bring to a full rolling boil. Set off fire for 5 minutes. Add Certo; stir well and pour into glasses or jars. Delicious with meats and vegetables.

Maxine Fletcher, Ouachita
Council, Monroe, La.

DAMSON PLUM CONSERVE

3 lb. Damson plums,
  chopped
1 orange, peeled and sliced
1 lemon, peeled and sliced

3 c. sugar
1 lb. seedless raisins
1 c. coarsely chopped
  pecans (about 1/4 lb.
  shelled)

Combine plums, orange and lemon slices and 1/2 cup water in large kettle. Bring slowly to a boil. Reduce heat and simmer, covered, 20 minutes. Add sugar and raisins. Stir over moderate heat until sugar dissolves. Boil rapidly, uncovered, until gel stage is reached. Stir in pecans. Remove from heat and skim off foam. Ladle into hot sterilized glasses and seal immediately. Makes about eight 8-ounce glasses.   Calcasieu Council
Lake Charles, La.

FIG CONSERVE

2 lb. figs, mashed and
  unpeeled
1 orange, unpeeled and
  chopped fine

1/2 lb. raisins, chopped
1/2 c. pecans
1 1/2 lb. sugar

Mix all ingredients and cook in Dutch oven about 1 1/4 hours, over medium heat, stirring often to prevent sticking. Can in pint jars as you would any other fruit preserves.

Marie Reeves, Calcasieu
Council, Lake Charles, La.

GRAPE CONSERVE

4 c. halvea, seeded purple grapes (about 1 3/4 lb.)
4 c. halved, seedless green grapes (about 1 3/4 lb.)

1 large lemon, thinly sliced and seeded
6 c. sugar
1 c. coarsely chopped walnuts (about 1/4 lb. shelled)

Combine grapes, lemon and 1/2 cup water in large kettle. Bring slowly to a boil, reduce heat and simmer, covered, 20 minutes. Add sugar and stir over moderate heat until dissolved. Boil rapidly until gel stage is reached. Stir in walnuts. Remove from heat and skim off foam. Ladle hot mixture into hot sterilized glasses and seal immediately. Makes about seven 8-ounce glasses. Calcasieu Council
Lake Charles, La.

PUMPKIN CONSERVE

3 c. cooked pumpkin
1 1/2 c. dried apricots, coarsely chopped
2 Tbsp. finely chopped candied ginger
1 Tbsp. lemon juice

2 1/2 c. brown sugar, packed
1 1/2 c. raisins, coarsely chopped
1 Tbsp. freshly grated lemon peel

Combine all ingredients in 3-quart pan. Cook on low heat, stirring constantly for about 45 minutes or until thick. Pour into hot sterilized jars and seal. Store in cool dark place. Makes about 5 half-pints.

June Harllee, Caddo
Council, Shreveport, La.

STRAWBERRY CONSERVE

3 pt. strawberries
2 c. chopped fresh pine-
   apple (1 small to
   medium pineapple)

1 c. seedless raisins
1 orange
8 c. sugar
2 Tbsp. lemon juice

Sort, wash and hull berries. Crush slightly. Peel, core and remove eyes from pineapple. Put through food chopper, using fine blade. Add lemon juice to pineapple. Put raisins through food chopper. Cut orange in sections, remove seeds and put through food chopper. Combine all fruit and measure 8 cups crushed fruit. Add sugar and place in large kettle. Cook mixture, uncovered, over moderate heat, until very thick, stirring very frequently. Pour hot mixture into hot sterilized glasses and seal immediately. Makes about eight 8-ounce glasses.

Calcasieu Council
Lake Charles, La.

STRAWBERRY CONSERVE

4 1/2 c. prepared fruit
   (about 2 qt. fully ripe
   strawberries)
2 tsp. grated lemon rind
1/2 c. seedless raisins

1 c. chopped walnuts
1/4 c. sauterne wine
6 c. (2 lb. 10 oz.) sugar
1 (1 3/4 oz.) box powdered
   fruit pectin

First, prepare the fruit. Thoroughly crush, one layer at a time, about 2 quarts of strawberries. Measure 4 1/2 cups into a saucepan. Add lemon rind, raisins, walnuts and wine to fruit in saucepan. Then make the conserve. Measure sugar and set aside. Mix fruit pectin into mixture in saucepan. Place over high heat and stir until mixture comes to a hard boil. Immediately add all sugar and stir. Bring to a full rolling boil and boil hard for 1 minute, stirring constantly. Remove from heat and skim off foam with metal spoon. Then stir and skim for 5 minutes to cool slightly and prevent floating fruit. Ladle quickly into glasses. Cover at once with 1/8 inch hot paraffin. Makes about 9 cups.

Calcasieu Council
Lake Charles, La.

FIG MIXTURE

3 lb. dry figs
1 lb. raisins
1 jar mixed candied fruit
1 c. sugar

1 lb. dates
2 c. pecans
1 small jar orange rind
8 oz. Brier Rabbit syrup

Grind figs, raisins, dates, pecans, candied fruit and rinds together. Place in container. Pour sugar and syrup over and cover. Let ferment 3-7 days; will not go bad. When ready to use for cakes, work mixture with hot water or fig preserves. Can be frozen if any left.

Evelyn Arnone, West Bank
Council, Gretna, La.

BERRY JAM

4 c. crushed berries
(about 2 qt.)

4 c. sugar

Sort, wash, stem or hull, and drain berries. Crush and measure. Place in kettle, mix thoroughly with sugar. Bring to boil and boil, stirring constantly, until sugar dissolves and gel stage is reached. Remove from heat and skim off foam. Pour hot mixture into hot sterilized glasses and seal immediately. Makes about four 8-ounce glasses.

Note: This recipe can be used for blackberries, blueberries, boysenberries, gooseberries, loganberries, raspberries and strawberries. Calcasieu Council
Lake Charles, La.

FRUIT JAM

2 c. figs or other fruit

2 c. sugar

Blend fruit in blender. Add sugar, mix well. Place in shallow baking dish. Bake at 400° for about 1/2 hour or until transparent. Place in hot jars. Seal with wax or rubber lids.

Emerite L. Hebert, Evangeline
Council, Scott, La.

MOCK STRAWBERRY JAM

6 c. figs, peeled
3 c. sugar

2 small pkg. strawberry
jello

Combine all ingredients in large saucepan. Cook, stirring constantly until thick, about 40 minutes. Pour into sterilized jars and seal immediately. Makes 4-5 pints.

Evelyn Arnone, West Bank
Council, Gretna, La.

MAW MAW'S FIG PRESERVES

1 large colander over-
loaded with figs
6 c. sugar

1 c. water
Few slices of lemon
(optional)

Melt sugar in water. Add figs. Cook 3 hours.

Betty Winston, Caddo
Council, Shreveport, La.

STRAWBERRY-FIG PRESERVES

3 c. chopped figs
2 c. sugar

2 small boxes strawberry
jello

Chop figs fine and place in deep pot with other ingredients. Mix well. Cook on medium fire. When mixture comes to a boil, cook for about 25 minutes, stirring about every 5 minutes. Pour into sterilized jars and seal immediately.

Pat Uhle, West Bank
Council, Gretna, La.

PEAR HONEY PRESERVES

1 c. crushed pineapple
3 c. shredded or grated
pears

2 c. sugar
1/2 c. honey

Combine ingredients and mix thoroughly in saucepan. Cook until pears are transparent and juice has become a thick syrup. Pour into 1/2 or 1-pint jars and seal while boiling hot.

Jeanette English, Caddo
Council, Shreveport, La.

ROSIE'S TOMATO-CANTALOUPE PRESERVES

3 lb. tomatoes, peeled
  and quartered
2 1/2 lb. sugar
2 sticks cinnamon

2 small cantaloupes, peeled
  and cubed
1 lemon, sliced
5 or 6 cloves

Stir all together. Cook slowly 3-4 hours. Pack in sterilized jars. Seal. Makes about 3 pints.

Sonny Foreman, Ouachita
Council, Monroe, La.

FROZEN STRAWBERRY PRESERVES

3 c. strawberries
1 pkg. Sure-Jell

5 c. sugar
1 c. water

Crush strawberries; stir in sugar well and let set 25 minutes. Boil water and Sure-Jell 1 minute. Pour over berries and stir 2 minutes. Pour into jars fast. Do not seal jars too tightly.

Dorothy Trent, Caddo
Council, Shreveport, La.

CASSEROLES, BEVERAGES
MISCELLANEOUS

FOOD QUANTITIES
FOR SERVING 25, 50 and 100 PERSONS AT PICNIC

Do you have trouble deciding how much of various foods to take to a picnic? Here are some suggested figures on 25, 50 and 100 servings, taken from "Planning Food For Institutions," a USDA handbook.

FOOD	25 SERVINGS	50 SERVINGS	100 SERVINGS
Sandwiches:			
Bread	50 slices or 3 1-lb. loaves	100 slices or 6 1-lb. loaves	200 slices or 12 1-lb. loaves
Butter	½ pound	¾ to 1 pound	1½ pounds
Mayonnaise	1 cup	2 to 3 cups	4 to 6 cups
Mixed Filling (meat, eggs, fish)	1½ quarts	2½ to 3 quarts	5 to 6 quarts
Mixed Filling (sweet-fruit)	1 quart	1¾ to 2 quarts	2½ to 4 quarts
Lettuce	1½ heads	2½ to 3 heads	5 to 6 heads
Meat, Poultry or Fish:			
Wieners (beef)	6½ pounds	13 pounds	25 pounds
Hamburger	9 pounds	18 pounds	35 pounds
Turkey or chicken	13 pounds	25 to 35 pounds	50 to 75 pounds
Fish, large whole (round)	13 pounds	25 pounds	50 pounds
Fish, fillets or steaks	7½ pounds	15 pounds	30 pounds
Salads, Casseroles:			
Potato Salad	4¼ quarts	2¼ gallons	4½ gallons
Scalloped Potatoes	4½ quarts or 1 12x20" pan	8½ quarts	17 quarts
Spaghetti	1¼ gallons	2½ gallons	5 gallons
Baked Beans	¾ gallon	1¼ gallons	2½ gallons
Jello Salad	¾ gallon	1¼ gallons	2½ gallons
Ice Cream:			
Brick	3¼ quarts	6½ quarts	12½ quarts
Bulk	2¼ quarts	4½ quarts or 1¼ gallons	9 quarts or 2½ gallons
Beverages:			
Coffee	½ pound and 1½ gal. water	1 pound and 3 gal. water	2 pounds and 6 gal. water
Tea	1/12 pound and 1½ gal. water	1/6 pound and 3 gal. water	1/3 pound and 6 gal. water
Lemonade	10 to 15 lemons, 1½ gal. water	20 to 30 lemons, 3 gal. water	40 to 60 lemons, 6 gal. water
Desserts:			
Watermelon	37½ pounds	75 pounds	150 pounds
Cake	1 10x12" sheet cake 1½ 10" layer cakes	1 12x20" sheet cake 3 10" layer cakes	2 12x20" sheet cakes 6 10" layer cakes
Whipping Cream	¾ pint	1½ to 2 pints	3 pints

BAKED ARTICHOKE HEARTS, OYSTERS AND CHICKEN

1/2 stick butter
1 can artichoke hearts,
   chopped in 1/4
1 small chicken
1 tsp. lemon juice
1/8 tsp. thyme
3 Tbsp. fresh parsley,
   chopped
1/2 tsp. Tabasco sauce
Salt and pepper to taste

1/2 c. olive oil
1 1/2 doz. oysters and water
   (cut oysters in half)
1/2 c. chicken broth
1/2 tsp. oregano
1/2 tsp. garlic powder
2 Tbsp. green onion,
   chopped
1 c. Italian style bread
   crumbs

Boil chicken; skin, debone and cut into small pieces. Saute onion and parsley in butter and olive oil for about 10 minutes. Combine all ingredients and mix well. Place mixture in casserole dish sprayed with Pam. Bake at 350° for 25 minutes or until top is brown.

Floyd Shumann, Ozone
Council, Hammond, La.

ARTICHOKE OYSTER CASSEROLE

2 cans artichoke hearts,
   cut in fourths
1 stick butter or oleo
1 tsp. garlic puree
1 (4 oz.) can chopped
   mushrooms

1 pt. oysters, chopped
2 bunches chopped shallots
1 c. bread crumbs
1/2 c. Parmesan cheese
Salt and pepper

Reserve oyster juice. Saute shallots and mushrooms in butter; add hearts and oysters. Add garlic puree, cheese, bread crumbs, salt and pepper; oyster and mushroom juice may be used if needed. Mix well and put in casserole. Cover and bake at 350° for 30 minutes.

Mary Kay Dehring, Crescent
City Council, New Orleans, La.

ASPARAGUS AND ENGLISH PEA CASSEROLE

1 can English peas
1 can sliced water chestnuts
1 can mushroom soup
5 slices cubed, dried bread

1 can asparagus
1 can mushroom stems and
  pieces
2 c. grated Cheddar cheese
1 stick oleo, melted

Drain vegetables; layer in casserole. Add chestnuts, mushrooms and soup. Add grated cheese. Toast bread cubes in butter; sprinkle on top of cheese. Bake at 350° for 35-40 minutes.

Mavis W. O'Rourke
Shreveport Works Council
Shreveport, La.

BAKED BEEF AND RICE

1 lb. cubed boneless stew
  meat
2 soup cans water
1/2 stick oleo
Meat tenderizer

1 can mushroom soup
1 env. Lipton's onion soup
  mix
2 c. raw rice (not minute)
Salt and pepper to taste

Melt oleo in large deep dish or pan. Add soup, soup mix and water. Simmer until smooth. Add rice. Season meat with tenderizer, salt and pepper and add to mixture. Cover dish with foil. Bake at 325° for 1 1/2 - 2 hours. Remove foil and cook additional 10 minutes. This and a green salad is a complete meal.

Maxine Fletcher, Ouachita
Council, Monroe, La.

BEAN 'N BEEF CASSEROLE

2 lb. ground beef
2 cans mushroom soup
2 large pkg. frozen tater
  tots

2 (16 oz.) cans French style
  beans, drained
Salt and pepper to taste

Season beef and spread in bottom of pan. Layer beans over beef. Spread tater tots on top. Cover all with cream of mushroom soup. Do not add water. Bake at 350° for 1 hour, uncovered. Try it, you will like it.

Mary Weekes, Metairie
Council, Metairie, La.

BEEF CASSEROLE

3 green peppers, chopped
3 large chopped onions
2 c. cream style corn
1 Tbsp. salt
1 (8 oz.) pkg. noodles,
   cooked

1 1/2 lb. ground beef
1 1/2 c. canned tomatoes
2 Tbsp. shortening
2 Tbsp. chili powder
1 lb. shredded sharp
   Cheddar cheese

Cook beef in shortening until meat turns white. Add onions and peppers and cook until slightly browned. Add tomatoes, corn, salt and chili powder. Cover and simmer 45 minutes. Combine drained, cooked noodles with meat mixture. Place in two 2-quart baking dishes. Top with cheese. Cover and bake at 350° for 45 minutes. Freeze one.

      Dorothy Trent, Caddo
      Council, Shreveport, La.

MEAL IN ONE BEEF CASSEROLE

2 lb. beef round or chuck
   steak, cut 1/4-inch
   thick
2 Tbsp. flour
2 c. cooked or stewed
   tomatoes

2 tsp. salt
2 tsp. paprika
3 large potatoes, sliced
1 Tbsp. catsup
2 onions, sliced
Hot fat

Cut steak into 8 pieces; beat to tenderize. Season and dip into flour; cover thoroughly. Brown in hot fat in heavy skillet. Cover meat with onions and potatoes. Mix tomatoes, salt and catsup and pour over potatoes. Cover and bake at 350° until meat is tender, about 1 1/2 hours. Add water if needed, but do not make a stew of this. Makes 6-8 servings.

      Lois Leger, Evangeline
      Council, Lafayette, La.

BEEF NOODLE CASSEROLE

1 c. cottage cheese
1 (8 oz.) carton sour
   cream
1 lb. lean ground beef
3/4 c. Cheddar cheese,
   grated

1 (8 oz.) pkg. egg noodles
1/2 c. onion, minced
1 (8 oz.) can tomato sauce
1/2 tsp. garlic salt
1 tsp. salt

1723-79

Cook noodles in boiling salted water until done; drain. Add cottage cheese, sour cream and onion. Cook meat until done; drain. Add tomato sauce, salt and garlic salt; simmer 10 minutes. Spoon half of noodle mixture into a greased casserole; top with half the meat mixture. Repeat layers. Bake at 350° for 30 minutes. Remove from oven, sprinkle with cheese and bake few minutes longer until cheese melts. Makes 8 servings.

Marilou Bridges, Caddo
Council, Shreveport, La.

BEEF PIE

In a 1-quart casserole, combine:

1 c. cubed, cooked beef	3 Tbsp. chopped onion
1 can beef gravy	2 Tbsp. flour
1/2 c. cubed, cooked potatoes	1 tsp. Worcestershire sauce
1/2 c. cooked peas	1/2 tsp. salt

Top with pastry (enough for single crust pie). Prick with fork. Bake in a hot oven at 400° about 45 minutes, or until crust is brown. Serves 4.

Calcasieu Council
Lake Charles, La.

BEEF RICE CASSEROLE

2 lb. chuck	1/4 tsp. pepper
1 Tbsp. cooking oil	1/2 c. flour
1 c. raw rice	1 clove garlic, minced
1 can beef consomme	1 onion, sliced thin
1/2 tsp. salt	1 (4 oz.) can mushroom stems and pieces

Cut beef into strips, season with salt and pepper and coat with flour. Add beef to heated oil in skillet and brown. Place rice in buttered 1-quart casserole. Add salt, pepper, garlic and mushrooms. Arrange browned beef on top. Add beef consomme. Cover with onion slices. Cover and bake at 325° for 1 hour or until tender. Garnish with peaches and parsley.

Lois Leger, Evangeline
Council, Lafayette, La.

BEEF AND RICE CASSEROLE

1 lb. hamburger meat
1 can chicken noodle soup
1 soup can water

2 small onions, chopped
1 can mushroom soup
1/2 c. raw rice

Brown meat and onions. Add soup, water and rice. Mix well. Pour in greased casserole. Bake 1 1/2 hours at 350°.

Betty Elenburg, Caddo Council, Shreveport, La.

BEEF TACO CASSEROLE

1 lb. ground beef
1 1/2 oz. pkg. taco sea-
  soning mix
1 (6 oz.) can tomato
  paste

1 1/4 c. water
2 c. elbow macaroni
1 c. whole kernel corn
2 c. grated cheese

Cook beef until slightly browned. Stir in taco mix, tomato paste and water. Bring to boil; reduce heat and simmer 10 minutes. Stir occasionally. Cook macaroni. Stir in meat mixture, corn and 1 cup cheese. Pour into 2-quart buttered casserole. Sprinkle top with cheese. Bake 30-45 minutes at 350°.

Gayle Wilkening, Shreveport Works Council, Longview, Tx.

GROUND BEEF CASSEROLE

1/2 c. chopped green
  onion
1 (5 oz.) pkg. medium
  egg noodles
2 cans (8 oz.) tomato
  sauce
1/8 tsp. pepper

1 1/2 lb. ground meat
2 Tbsp. butter or oleo
1 tsp. salt
1 c. cottage cheese
3/4 c. shredded sharp
  process American cheese
1 c. sour cream

Cook noodles in boiling salted water; drain and set aside. Saute 1/4 cup onion in butter until tender. Add beef and cook until lightly browned; drain. Add tomato sauce, salt and pepper. Simmer 20 minutes, stirring occasionally. Combine cottage cheese, sour cream and remaining green onion. Place noodles in greased casserole dish; spoon cottage cheese mixture over noodles. Spoon meat mixture over cottage cheese and top with shredded cheese. Bake at 350° for about 25 minutes. Makes 6 servings.

Marilou Bridges, Caddo
Council, Shreveport, La.

CABBAGE ROLLS

1 medium cabbage
1 lb. hamburger
1 small onion
1/4 c. green pepper

1 can tomatoes
1/4 c. dry rice
1 tsp. salt
1/4 tsp. pepper

Wilt cabbage in boiling water for 5 minutes. Combine remaining ingredients. Place rounded tablespoonfuls of meat mixture in each loaf; roll up, tucking edges in as you roll. Place in heavy container with tight lid. Pour 1 cup tomatoes over rolls. Sprinkle with extra salt and pepper. Let steam for 1 hour at 350°.

Calcasieu Council
Lake Charles, La.

LOOSE CABBAGE ROLL

1 1/2 lb. ground beef
1/2 bell pepper, chopped
1/2 c. raw rice
Salt and pepper to taste

1 large onion, chopped
2 ribs celery, chopped
1 cabbage head, sliced
1 (12 oz.) can V-8 juice

Saute meat, onion, bell pepper and celery until meat is browned. Remove from heat, add rice, salt and pepper. In casserole, place layers of meat and cabbage. Pour juice over. Cover and cook 1 1/2 hours at 350°.

Lydia M. Gremillion, Central
Council, Pineville, La.

CARROT CASSEROLE

3 c. cooked, sliced
    carrots, drained
1 tsp. onion flakes
3 Tbsp. brown sugar

4 slices cooked crisp bacon,
    crumbled
1/2 tsp. salt
3 Tbsp. butter, melted

Combine and mix ingredients; pour into greased baking dish. Cover and bake at 375° for 25 minutes.

Mrs. J. B. Coker, Central
Council, Alexandria, La.

CHEESE BURGER PIE

1 lb. ground meat
1/2 tsp. oregano
1 tsp. salt
1/4 tsp. pepper
1 pie shell

1/4 c. chopped onions
1/4 c. chopped bell pepper
1/4 c. fine dry bread crumbs
1/2 can (8 oz. size) tomato
    sauce

Bake pie shell at 425° until just set and partially baked. Remove and set aside. Brown beef in small amount of fat or oil. Mix beef with remaining ingredients and spoon into pie shell. Cover with Cheese Topping.

Cheese Topping:

1 (8 oz,) pkg. Cheddar
    cheese, grated
1/2 tsp. Worcestershire
    sauce

1 egg
1/4 c. milk
1/2 tsp. salt
1/2 tsp. dry mustard

Mix and spread over top of hamburger pie. Bake 30 minutes.
Clara Westbrook, Shreveport
Works Council, Shreveport, La.

CHEESE AND CRACKER CASSEROLE

15 saltine crackers,
    crushed
1 1/2 c. milk
3 eggs, beaten
2 Tbsp. oleo

1 1/2 c. shredded Cheddar
    cheese
1 (2 1/2 oz.) jar sliced
    mushrooms, drained

Combine cracker crumbs, cheese, milk, eggs and mushrooms; mix well. Melt oleo in 1 1/2-quart casserole; pour in cheese mixture. Bake at 350° for 45-50 minutes or until puffy and set. Makes 4 servings.
Marilou Bridges, Caddo
Council, Shreveport, La.

CHICKEN ASPARAGUS CASSEROLE

1 chicken
1/4 c. raw rice
3/4 c. chicken broth
2 Tbsp. flour
Salt and pepper to taste

1/2 can cream of mushroom
    soup
1 can cut asparagus
1 Tbsp. oleo
Pimento

Cook chicken in water until tender; remove from bones and cut up. Cook rice in separate pan and set aside. Melt oleo in skillet; add flour and stir until smooth. Add chicken broth, mushroom soup and chicken. Cook slowly until thickened. Add asparagus, pimento, salt and pepper and simmer a few minutes. Place cooked rice in bottom of a casserole dish and pour chicken mixture on top. Bake at 350° until it bubbles. Can double recipe and freeze half for later.

Betty Croswell, Capital
Council, Baton Rouge, La.

BAKED CHICKEN AND RICE

1 large fryer, cut in pieces, salted and peppered
1 pkg. Lipton's onion soup mix
1 can cream of chicken soup
2 soup cans water
1/2 stick oleo
2 c. regular raw rice

Melt oleo in large deep dish or pan. Add chicken soup, onion soup mix and water. Simmer until smooth. Add rice. Place cut up chicken on top of mixture; cover with foil. Bake at 350° about 1 1/2 hours. Remove foil and cook 10 additional minutes.

Maxine Fletcher, Ouachita
Council, Monroe, La.

CHICKEN AND BROCCOLI CASSEROLE

1 bunch broccoli, or
2 boxes frozen broccoli
1/2 c. celery
1 tsp. curry powder
1 (3 lb.) chicken
1 can cream of mushroom soup
1 small onion, chopped
1/2 stick oleo
1 c. grated cheese

Boil chicken and debone. Cook broccoli in chicken broth and drain. Melt oleo and saute onions and celery in oleo until tender. Add soup and curry powder. Put chicken in 2-quart Pyrex dish. Layer with broccoli and cover with soup mixture. Top with grated cheese. Bake at 350° for 20 minutes.

Ava Burnett, Caddo Council,
Shreveport, La.

CHICKEN BROCCOLI CASSEROLE

5 whole chicken breasts,
   cooked and torn into
   large pieces
2 pkg. broccoli spears,
   cooked, drained
1 tsp. curry powder

2 cans cream of celery soup
1 Tbsp. lemon juice
1 c. mayonnaise
Salt and pepper to taste
1 c. sharp cheese, grated
1 c. Ritz crackers, crushed

Place cooked broccoli in bottom of casserole. Layer chicken pieces over broccoli. Mix soup, lemon juice, salt and pepper, mayonnaise and curry powder and pour over chicken. Sprinkle with cheese and top with cracker crumbs. Bake at 350° for 30 minutes.

Mildred Henderson, Ouachita
Council, Monroe, La.

BROCCOLI AND CHICKEN CASSEROLE

1 chicken
1/2 stick oleo
1 c. chicken broth
1 can cream of mushroom
   soup

2 pkg. broccoli, frozen and
   chopped
3/4 c. cracker crumbs
1 c. grated cheese

Boil chicken until tender, remove and debone. Reserve 1 cup broth. Cook broccoli per package directions. Mix oleo, chicken broth, soup and cheese. Heat until cheese melts. Line a greased casserole dish with cracker crumbs. Layer chicken, broccoli and cheese mixture over cracker crumbs. Bake 20-30 minutes at 400°. Top with grated cheese before baking, if desired.

Ozone Council, Hammond, La.

BROCCOLI CASSEROLE

1 fryer or 4 chicken
   breasts
2 pkg. broccoli
Bread crumbs

1 pkg. Stove Top dressing
1 can chicken broth
2 cans cheese soup

Cook chicken and chop into bite size pieces. Place in bottom of casserole. Prepare package of dressing according to directions. Place on top of chicken. Cook broccoli and drain; layer over dressing. Mix soup and broth together and pour over broccoli. Sprinkle with bread crumbs. Bake at 350° for 30 minutes. Velma Carruth, Capital Council, Baton Rouge, La.

CHICKEN CASSEROLE

3 lb. choice chicken pieces
3/4 c. chopped onion
1/2 c. chopped parsley
1 c. uncooked rice
1 1/2 c. canned tomatoes
1/2 tsp. pepper

1 Tbsp. butter or oleo, melted
3/4 c. chopped bell pepper, (optional)
1 1/2 c. chicken broth
2 tsp. salt

Place chicken pieces, skin side up, in a shallow greased 2 1/2-quart casserole. Brush lightly with butter. Bake uncovered at 450° for 30 minutes or until browned. Sprinkle with onion, green pepper, parsley and rice. Bring remaining ingredients to a boil. Pour over chicken-vegetable mixture. Stir. Cover and bake 30 minutes more or until chicken is tender and rice is done. Serves 6.

Joy Faught, Central Council, Alexandria, La.

CHICKEN CASSEROLE

2 pkg. frozen broccoli spears
1 large can evaporated milk

2 c. cubed, diced chicken
6 slices American cheese
1 can mushroom soup
1 c. fried onion rings

Cook broccoli in small amount of water and bring to a boil; drain. Arrange chicken in greased casserole dish. Layer broccoli over chicken; place cheese slices over broccoli. Combine milk and soup, pour over cheese. Bake at 350° for 25 minutes; remove from oven and sprinkle onion rings over casserole. Return to oven for 5-6 minutes. Makes 8 servings. Marilou Bridges, Caddo Council, Shreveport, La.

CHICKEN CASSEROLE

8 chicken breasts
1 large sour cream

2 cans cream of chicken soup
2 pkg. Ritz crackers (sticks)
1 stick butter

Cook and debone chicken, place in buttered casserole dish. Mix soup and sour cream, spread over chicken. Crumble crackers over melted butter on top. Bake for 30 minutes at 350°.

Margaret Aletha Keenan
Ozone Council, Bogalusa, La.

CHICKEN CASSEROLE

1 1/2 lb. cooked, cubed
chicken
1/2 c. melted fat
4 Tbsp. flour
Salt to taste

2 qt. uncooked poultry
stuffing
1 qt. chicken broth
3 eggs, divided
Bread crumbs

Combine flour with hot fat, chicken broth and salt. Stir until smooth. Add beaten egg yolks as you do for pudding. Beat egg whites until stiff and fold into mixture. Place a layer of dressing in bottom of baking dish. (The recipe for my stuffing is also in this cookbook.) Then put a layer of chicken and a layer of sauce. Repeat layers. Sprinkle with bread crumbs. Bake at 350° for 30 minutes.

Ilene Arnold, Capital
Council, Waterbury, Ct.

CHICKEN CASSEROLE

1 chicken
1 medium chopped onion
1/2 can diced green
chili peppers
Grated cheese

3 Tbsp. oleo
1/2 c. chicken broth
1 can cream of mushroom
soup
1 can cream of chicken soup
Tortillas

Boil chicken until tender, debone and dice. Saute onion in oleo, add chicken broth and chili peppers. Cook together until onion is done. Add soups. Grease casserole dish. Line with tortillas, broken in pieces. Add layer of diced chicken, layer of soup mixture. Repeat layers. Bake at 350° until hot and bubbly all the way through. Add cheese and let melt.

Betty Wood, Ozone Council, Bogalusa, La.

CHICKEN AND CHEESE CASSEROLE

1 pkg. chicken legs
1 pkg. chicken thighs
1 pkg. chicken breasts
2 medium chopped onions
3 Tbsp. butter or oleo
Doritos

1 can Ro-Tel tomatoes
1 can mushroom soup
1 can celery soup
1/2 can Cheddar cheese soup
1 lb. box (blue box) Blue Velveeta cheese, cut in chunks

Boil chicken until tender with no salt; debone and slice. Saute onions in butter, add soups, Velveeta cheese and tomatoes. Do not dilute soups. Add chicken to mixture and allow cheese to melt. In buttered casserole, place layer of Doritos, then layer of chicken mixture. Repeat layers until casserole is full. Make sure Doritos are covered by mixture to keep from burning. Bake at 350° for 30 minutes until hot and bubbly. Serves 12. This freezes beautifully. Do not bake before freezing.

Patricia R. Caraway, Capital Council, Baton Rouge, La.

CHICKEN CHINESE CASSEROLE

2 c. leftover or canned chicken
1 can cream of mushroom soup

1 can chicken noodle soup
1 c. milk
1 c. diced celery
1 can chow mein noodles

Mix chicken, soups, milk and celery together. Gently fold in chow mein noodles. Place in large casserole and bake 30-35 minutes at 350°. Serves 5 or 6.

June E. Nickels, Shreveport Works Council, Shreveport, La.

CHICKEN ENCHILADA CASSEROLE

1 chicken, stewed and boned
1 can green chilies, chopped
1 can cream of mushroom soup

1 can cream of chicken soup
1 small to medium onion
1 - 1 1/2 c. grated cheese
1 pkg. frozen tortillas

712

Heat together first 4 ingredients; dilute with water if too thick. Separate frozen tortillas under running water. Heat each a few seconds in hot skillet. Roll each tortilla with chicken, cheese, onions and place in baking dish, layering if necessary. Cover with soup and chicken mixture. Top with grated cheese. Bake at 375° until bubbly. Serve with green salad and bread.

Gayle Wilkening, Shreveport
Works Council, Longview, Tx.

CHICKEN ENCHILADAS

1 chicken
1 can broth
1 onion and jalapeno pepper

1 can mushroom soup
1 can Cheddar cheese soup
1 box taco shells

Boil chicken and take off bone. Mix mushroom soup, broth, Cheddar cheese soup, onion and jalapeno pepper. Boil until onions are tender. Layer shells with chicken and soup mixture. Bake about 30 minutes.

Calcasieu Council
Lake Charles, La.

CHICKEN ENCHILADA PIE

1 chicken
1 can cream of chicken
  soup
1 can cream of mushroom
  soup
1 (4 oz.) can chopped
  green chilies
1 tsp. chili powder

4 tsp. minced onions
1/8 tsp. garlic powder
1/4 tsp. black pepper
1/4 tsp. Tabasco sauce
1 c. chicken broth
4 c. corn chips
8 oz. Cheddar cheese, grated

Cook and debone chicken. Reserve 1 cup chicken broth. Combine soups, green chilies, spices, Tabasco sauce and chicken broth. Blend well. Preheat oven to 350°. Cover bottom of 3-quart casserole with 2 cups corn chips. Spread half the chicken over this layer, then half the sauce, then half the grated cheese. Repeat, ending with cheese. Bake at 350° for 25-30 minutes.   Calcasieu Council
Lake Charles, La.

OVERNIGHT CHICKEN CASSEROLE

8 slices bread, crusts removed
1/4 c. diced celery
1/4 c. mayonnaise
2 eggs, beaten
Salt and pepper to taste

3 c. diced, cooked chicken
1/4 c. diced onion
1/4 c. diced green pepper
2 c. milk, divided
1 can cream of mushroom soup

Place half of the bread in large greased casserole. Mix chicken, green pepper, celery, onion, mayonnaise, salt and pepper together and spread over bread. Top with remaining bread slices. Mix eggs and 1 1/2 cups milk together and pour evenly over bread. Cover and refrigerate overnight. When ready to bake, combine remainder of milk and soup and pour over top of casserole. Bake at 350° for 1 - 1 1/2 hours.

Marilou Bridges, Caddo
Council, Shreveport, La.

CHICKEN AND RICE

6 chicken breasts
1 pkg. dry onion soup mix
1 1/2 c. water

1 c. raw rice
1 can mushroom soup

Pour rice into greased casserole dish. Skin breasts and place over rice. Mix dry onion soup with can of mushroom soup and water. Pour over chicken. Cover and bake at 350° for about 1 hour, or until done.

Marilou Bridges, Caddo
Council, Shreveport, La.

CHICKEN AND RICE CASSEROLE

1/2 stick oleo
1 can cream of chicken or mushroom soup
1 1/2 c. water

1 can onion soup
1 1/2 c. raw rice
1 chicken (fryer), cut up and seasoned to taste

Melt oleo in loaf pan. Mix soups, rice and water together. Pour in melted oleo. Place chicken on top of rice mixture. Bake 45 minutes at 350° with skin side of chicken down. Turn chicken over and bake 15 minutes longer.

Patricia R. Caraway
Capital Council
Baton Rouge, La.

CHICKEN AND RICE CASSEROLE

1 frying-size chicken,
  cut, salted and peppered
1 stick oleo
1 can mushroom soup
1 soup can chicken stock
  or broth
2 green onions, chopped
Fresh parsley or parsley
  flakes (optional)

1 1/2 c. long grain rice,
  washed and drained
1 env. onion soup mix
1 can cream of chicken soup
2 ribs celery, chopped
1 small yellow onion, chopped
Black pepper to taste
1 can sliced mushrooms

Boil bony pieces of chicken and giblets in enough water to cover. Add some celery and onion for flavoring. When tender, cool and debone. Save broth. Melt 3/4 stick oleo in oblong baking pan. Spread rice around in melted butter. Saute celery and onions in remaining butter until tender. Add soups, 1 can of the chicken broth; blend until smooth. Sprinkle in about half of the onion soup mix, black pepper and parsley. Stir in deboned chicken and mushrooms. Pour half the mixture around and over the rice. Place the chicken pieces over the rice. Sprinkle remainder of soup mix over chicken and pour remaining liquid mixture over this. Bake in preheated 350° oven for 15 minutes uncovered. Cover and bake for about 30 minutes longer. Remove from oven, lift off chicken and stir the rice mixture well to separate. If too dry, add more chicken broth, if needed. Place chicken back on rice and return to oven until rice is tender and chicken is done. Remove cover last 10 minutes of baking.

Mrs. Richard D. (Vermelle)
Sylvest, Ozone Council,
Hammond, La.

CHICKEN AND RICE CASSEROLE

1 boiler chicken, cut up,
  or your choice of
  chicken pieces
1 pkg. dry onion soup mix

1 can celery soup
1 can mushroom soup
1 soup can milk
1 c. uncooked rice

Spread rice over bottom of greased 9x13-inch pan. Mix celery and mushroom soups with milk and pour over rice. Sprinkle dry soup mix on top. Place chicken pieces on top; cover with foil. Bake at 350° for 1 1/2 hours. Remove foil last 15 minutes for chicken to brown.

Marilou Bridges, Caddo
Council, Shreveport, La.

RICE AND CHICKEN CASSEROLE

2 - 2 1/2 lb. frying
  chicken, cut up
1 1/2 oz. dry onion
  soup mix or 1 packet

1 1/4 c. raw rice
2 c. milk
2 cans cream of mushroom
  soup

In a bowl, mix soups, milk, rice and dried onion soup mix. Place chicken on buttered deep baking casserole with skin side up. Pour soup mixture over chicken. Cover and bake at 350° for 1 hour until tender.

Betty Elenburg, Caddo
Council, Shreveport, La.

CHICKEN SOUFFLE

9 or 10 slices bread
4 c. boiled chicken
1 large can mushrooms
1 can water chestnuts
9 or 10 slices American
  cheese

Mayonnaise (approx. 1/2 c.)
2 c. milk
4 eggs
1 can mushroom soup
1 can celery soup
1 small jar pimiento

Line greased 9x13-inch baking pan with bread (with crusts trimmed). Brown mushrooms in margarine. Place chicken (cooked) over bread, then mushrooms and sliced water chestnuts. Dab mayonnaise and cover this with layers of cheese slices. Beat together eggs and milk and pour over all. Mix soups and pimiento and spread over top. Cover with foil and refrigerate 1 night. This is a must! Heat oven to 325°. Sprinkle corn flake crumbs, buttered, over the top. Bake for 1 1/2 hours.

Calcasieu Council
Lake Charles, La.

SPECIAL CHICKEN CASSEROLE

4 chicken breasts
Salt and pepper to taste
1 (5 oz.) can water chestnuts, sliced
1 tsp. thyme
2 Tbsp. chopped bell
  pepper

1 stick oleo
1 can cream of chicken soup
1 (3 oz.) can mushrooms,
  cut up
1 tsp. poultry seasoning
3/4 c. white wine

Cook chicken in oleo until brown. Remove from skillet.

Add chicken soup to drippings. Add wine and stir until smooth. Add remaining ingredients to sauce and heat. Do not boil. Place chicken pieces in baking dish and pour sauce over chicken. Cover with foil and bake at 350° for 30 minutes. Reduce heat to 325°, uncover chicken and cook additional 30 minutes or until done. Serve over hot cooked rice or mashed potatoes. Marilou Bridges, Caddo Council, Shreveport, La.

CHICKEN SPECTACULAR

3 c. cooked chicken, cut up
1 can cream of celery soup
1 medium jar pimentos
1 medium onion, chopped
1 c. mayonnaise
1 c. water chestnuts, sliced
1 pkg. Uncle Ben's combination wild and white rice, rice, cooked
2 c. drained French style beans
Salt and pepper to taste

Combine and mix all ingredients. Pour into 2 1/2 or 3-quart casserole. Bake at 350° for 25-30 minutes. To freeze part of mixture, do not cook prior to freezing.
Catherine (Chadwick) McCraw, Caddo Council Shreveport, La.

CHICKEN STRATA

1/2 c. chopped onion
8 slices white bread, cut in 1-inch cubes
1 c. shredded Swiss cheese (4 oz.)
1/2 tsp. salt
1/2 tsp. marjoram
1 Tbsp. butter or oleo
1 1/2 c. diced, cooked chicken
3 eggs
2 c. milk
1/2 tsp. thyme
1/4 tsp. black pepper

Saute onion in butter until tender. Spread half of bread cubes over bottom of lightly greased 9x9x2-inch pan. Top with chicken, cheese, onion, then remaining bread cubes. Mix eggs, milk and seasonings well. Pour over bread. Bake in preheated 325° oven for 40 minutes or until top is crusty and brown. Makes 4-6 servings.
Marilou Bridges, Caddo Council, Shreveport, La.

STUFFED CHICKEN CASSEROLE

1 (3 lb.) chicken
2 Tbsp. chopped pimiento
1 (7 oz.) box seasoned
  stuffing mix
1/4 c. finely chopped
  parsley

1 can mushroom soup
1 tall (13 oz.) can evaporated
  milk
1/2 c. shredded Swiss
  cheese

Cook chicken in water until tender; debone. Arrange chicken meat in shallow 2-quart casserole dish. Combine soup, pimiento and 2/3 cup evaporated milk. Pour over chicken. Toss stuffing mix with 1 cup evaporated milk until milk is absorbed by stuffing. Spread stuffing over chicken. Sprinkle cheese and parsley over top. Bake at 350° for 30 minutes or until bubbly. Serve hot. Makes 6 servings.

Ann Orr, Evangeline
Council, Lafayette, La.

CHICKEN AND TORTILLA CASSEROLE

1 large hen
1 bell pepper, chopped
1 can cream of chicken
  soup
1/2 - 1 can Ro-Tel toma-
  toes, drained
1 pkg. Dorito chips
  (nachos)

1 stalk celery, chopped
1 large onion, chopped
1 can cream of mushroom
  soup
1 can tomatoes, drained and
  chopped
1/2 - 1 lb. grated Cheddar
  cheese

Boil hen with celery, bell pepper and onion. Cook down until you have about 1 cup of broth. Let cool. Debone chicken and chop into small pieces. Combine broth and soups. Mix chicken and tomatoes in soup. Cover bottom of a greased 13x9-inch pan with layer of Doritos; sprinkle cheese over chips; reheat chicken mixture and pour half over chips and cheese. Repeat layers. Top with more chips and grated cheese. Bake at 350° for 45 minutes. This dish is good also when reheated as leftovers and freezes well.

Jean Coon, Caddo Council,
Shreveport, La.

SUPER EASY CHICKEN-SPAGHETTI CASSEROLE

1 small pkg. cut spaghetti
1/2 can mushroom soup
2 cans Swanson's boned
   chicken, or tender-
   chunk chicken
1 tsp. lemon pepper

1 can cream of chicken soup
1 can chicken broth
1 tsp. poultry seasoning
1 soup can water
Bread crumbs

Combine all ingredients in large covered casserole dish; stir and mix thoroughly. Bake at 350° until spaghetti is tender. Remove lid and sprinkle with bread crumbs and brown lightly.
     Marilyn Hibbard, Caddo
     Council, Shreveport, La.

CHICKEN AND WILD RICE CASSEROLE

1 large hen
2 Tbsp. Worcestershire
   sauce
1 1/2 tsp. Tabasco sauce
3 Tbsp. butter
1 tsp. milk
1/2 c. butter or oleo
1/2 c. chopped bell pepper

2 boxes Uncle Ben's wild and
   white rice
Cracked pepper
3 Tbsp. flour
3 c. chicken broth
1/2 c. chopped onion
1 small can sliced mush-
   rooms

Combine butter, flour, milk and chicken broth. Make about 3 cups of thin white sauce. Cook hen, debone and cut into bite size pieces. Cook rice according to directions on box. Saute onion, bell pepper and mushrooms in butter until soft. Combine all ingredients and add more seasoning if you like it hot. Place in buttered casserole and bake at 300° until hot and bubbly. Serves 6-8 people.
     Mavis W. O'Rourke
     Shreveport Works Council
     Shreveport, La.

CHILI BAKE

1 pkg. yellow corn
   bread mix
1 1/2 c. Cheddar cheese,
   shredded

1 can all meat chili, no
   beans, no juice

Mix corn bread according to directions on package. Pour into buttered and floured casserole dish. Spoon chili over.

Do not stir. Sprinkle cheese over and bake approximately 20 minutes or until corn bread is done, in hot oven.

Marie Pamplin, Shreveport
Works Council, Shreveport, La.

FRITO CHILI PIE

1 can chili   1 pkg. Fritos
2 c. shredded cheese

Layer Fritos, chili and cheese in casserole. Bake at 350° until hot and bubbly and cheese is melted.

Clara Westbrook, Shreveport
Works Council, Shreveport, La.

CHILES RELLENOS CASSEROLE

6 slices bread   Butter or oleo, softened
2 c. shredded Cheddar   2 c. shredded Jack cheese
  cheese   1 (4 oz.) can green chiles,
6 eggs   chopped
2 tsp. salt   2 c. milk
1 tsp. whole oregano   2 tsp. paprika
1/4 tsp. garlic powder   1/2 tsp. pepper
                                  1/4 tsp. dry mustard

Trim crusts from bread; spread each bread sliced with butter. Place bread in 11x7x2-inch baking dish, buttered side down. Top with Cheddar and Jack cheese; sprinkle with chiles. Beat eggs until frothy, add remaining ingredients, mixing well. Pour egg mixture over chiles. Cover; chill overnight or for at least 4 hours. Uncover; bake at 325° for 50-55 minutes or until lightly browned. Let stand 10 minutes before serving. Yield: 6 servings.   Ann Orr, Evangeline
Council, New Iberia, La.

CHILI-RICE CASSEROLE

1 c. chopped onion   2 Tbsp. melted butter or oleo
3 c. hot cooked rice   3/4 c. sour cream
Salt and pepper to taste   15 oz. can chili without beans

Saute onion in butter; combine onion, rice, sour cream. Spoon into casserole dish; mix well. Add salt and pepper. Spread chili over mixture. Bake at 350° for 15 minutes or until heated thoroughly. Makes 4 servings.

Rebecca Scott, Caddo
Council, Shreveport, La.

720

CORN CREOLE

1 lb. hamburger meat
1/2 c. chopped bell
  pepper
1 egg
1/2 c. corn meal

1/2 c. chopped onion
1 can cream style corn
1/2 c. milk
Crumbs
Butter

Cook meat, onion and bell pepper until meat is brown; drain. Add corn. Beat together egg and milk; add corn meal and mix well. Add to meat mixture. Pour in casserole dish; cover with crumbs and dot with butter. Bake until brown at 350° for 25 minutes. Bettye Lee, Shreveport Works Council, Shreveport, La.

CRABMEAT ARTICHOKE CASSEROLE

1 (No. 2) can whole
  artichoke hearts
4 1/2 Tbsp. butter,
  divided
1/2 lb. sliced mushrooms
1/2 tsp. salt
1/4 tsp. pepper
1/4 c. dry sherry

1 lb. fresh cooked crabmeat
2 1/2 Tbsp. flour
Dash of cayenne pepper
1 1/4 c. cream
1 Tbsp. Lea & Perrins sauce
Paprika
1/4 c. Parmesan cheese

Drain artichoke hearts and arrange in a buttered shallow baking dish. Spread crabmeat over hearts. Saute mushrooms in 2 tablespoons butter for 6-7 minutes and add to baking dish. Make up cream sauce of 2 1/2 tablespoons butter, flour, salt, pepper, cayenne pepper, cream, Lea & Perrins sauce and sherry. Pour over contents of baking dish. Sprinkle with cheese and paprika. Bake 20 minutes at 375°. Mary C. Regan, Crescent City Council, New Orleans, La.

CURRY BAKE

1 (6 oz.) pkg. Uncle Ben's
  seasoned long grain or
  wild rice
1 (10 oz.) pkg. chopped
  broccoli
1 c. cubed sharp Cheddar
  cheese

1/4 c. grated Parmesan
  cheese
1 c. mayonnaise
1 can celery soup
2 c. cooked and cubed
  ham, turkey or
  chicken

1723-79

2 tsp. prepared mustard
1 tsp. curry powder

1 (4 1/2 oz.) can mushrooms, bits and pieces

Cook rice and broccoli according to directions on package. Drain broccoli. Spread rice in bottom of buttered 13x9-inch pan or baking dish. In layers, top with broccoli, meat, mushrooms and Cheddar cheese. Blend soup, mayonnaise, mustard and curry together; pour over all. Sprinkle Parmesan cheese on top. Bake at 350° for 45 minutes. May be assembled day before and refrigerated.

Linda Bagur, Caddo
Council, Shreveport, La.

DEVILED OYSTERS

1 pt. oysters
1/4 lb. butter or oleo
1 small diced onion
1/2 c. chopped celery

1 c. cracker crumbs
1 beaten egg
1/2 lemon, squeezed

Heat oysters until they curl; chop. Cook celery and onion in melted butter until tender; combine with chopped oysters, cracker crumbs, beaten egg and seasonings (salt and cayenne pepper). Put in casserole. Cover with buttered crumbs, bake until brown.

Calcasieu Council
Lake Charles, La.

SOUR CREAM ENCHILADAS

1 pt. sour cream
1 can chopped green
  chiles, drained
1 small can sliced black
  olives
1 1/2 doz. corn tortillas

2 cans cream of chicken soup
1 1/2 bunches chopped green
  onions, including tops
1 - 1 1/2 lb. grated Cheddar
  cheese
Cooking oil

Mix sour cream, chiles, soup, olives and onions together and heat. Heat tortillas in oil until soft; cool. Put 1 - 1 1/2 tablespoons soup mixture on tortillas, sprinkle with grated cheese and roll up. Place in greased oblong pan. Repeat procedure until all tortillas are used, placing side by side, close together in pan. Spread remaining sauce and cheese on

top. Bake at 375° for 20 minutes. Let set for 10 minutes before serving.
Louise Malone, Caddo
Council, Shreveport, La.

SOUR CREAM ENCHILADAS

2 cans cream of mush-
   room soup
1/4 tsp. salt
1/2 tsp. garlic powder
1 c. chopped green onion
1 doz. corn tortillas

1 (8 oz.) carton sour cream
1 (4 oz.) can chopped green
   chiles
1/4 tsp. pepper
2 c. grated Cheddar cheese
Hot salad oil

Combine soup, sour cream, green chiles, salt, pepper and garlic powder; mix well. Cook over medium heat, stirring often until hot. Combine cheese and onion, mixing well. Cook each tortilla in hot oil for a few seconds until softened; drain. Spoon about 1 1/2 tablespoons cheese mixture and 2 tablespoons soup mixture into center of each tortilla. Roll up tightly and place in a greased 13x9-inch pan. Spoon remaining soup mixture over top of enchiladas and sprinkle with remaining cheese mixture. Bake at 350° for 20-30 minutes. Makes 6 servings.
Marilou Bridges, Caddo
Council, Shreveport, La.

EGGPLANT CASSEROLE

2 large eggplants
1 1/2 c. chopped celery
1 lb. ground meat
1 c. Italian style bread
   crumbs
1 stick oleo

1 large onion, chopped
1 bell pepper, chopped
1 lb. grated mild Cheddar
   cheese
3 c. water
2 eggs

Peel and cut eggplant in bite size pieces. Boil eggplant, onion, celery and bell pepper in water until tender; drain. Brown meat; drain. Combine all ingredients, except 1/2 of grated cheese. Place in casserole dish and sprinkle with the remaining cheese. Bake at 350° for 30-40 minutes.
Verlie McCoy, Central
Council, Bunkie, La.

AUNTIE'S EGGPLANT-CRABMEAT CASSEROLE

1 medium eggplant
1 Tbsp. butter or oleo
1/4 c. minced onion
Paprika, salt and pepper
   to taste

1/4 c. chopped celery
1 egg, beaten
2 c. milk
1 c. cracker crumbs
1 can white crabmeat

Peel, slice or cube eggplant and cook in boiling salted water until tender; drain and mash. Add half of cracker crumbs, butter, onion, celery and crabmeat. Place in greased casserole dish. Sprinkle with remaining cracker crumbs. Combine egg and milk, pour over contents of casserole. Sprinkle with paprika. Bake at 350° for 30 minutes or until golden brown on top. Serves 4-6.

Roxanna Bankston, Ozone
Council, Hammond, La.

EGGPLANT PARMIGIANA

2 Tbsp. salad or olive oil
1 clove garlic, crushed
1 (2 lb. 3 oz.) can Italian
   tomatoes, undrained
1 tsp. dried basil leaves
1/4 tsp. pepper
1 large (1 1/2 lb.) eggplant
1/2 c. Italian-flavored
   packaged dry bread
   crumbs
1 (8 oz.) pkg. Mozzarella
   cheese, sliced

1/2 c. chopped onion
1/2 lb. ground chuck
1 (6 oz.) can tomato paste
2 tsp. dried oregano leaves
1 1/2 tsp. salt
1 Tbsp. brown sugar
2 eggs, slightly beaten
1 1/4 c. grated Parmesan
   cheese
1/3 c. salad or olive oil
1 Tbsp. water

Saute onion, garlic and chuck in 2 tablespoons hot oil, stirring occasionally, until meat is no longer red, about 5 minutes. Add tomatoes, tomato paste, oregano, basil, salt, pepper and sugar; bring to boiling, stirring with wooden spoon. Reduce heat; simmer, covered and stirring occasionally, 45 minutes. Wash eggplant; do not peel. Cut crosswise into slices 1/4-inch thick. In pie plate, combine eggs and 1 tablespoon water; mix well with fork. On waxed paper, combine bread crumbs with 1/2 cup Parmesan cheese. Dip eggplant slices into egg mixture, coating well. Then dip into crumb mixture, coating evenly. Saute eggplant slices, a few at a time, in remaining oil until golden brown and crisp on both sides; drain. Arrange half of eggplant slices in bottom of greased 13x9x2-inch pan. Sprinkle with half of remaining Parmesan cheese. Top with half of Mozzarella cheese slices. Cover with half of tomato sauce. Repeat layers. Sprinkle with rest of Parmesan cheese. Bake uncovered in preheated 350° oven for 25 minutes or until cheese melts and top is browned. Serves 8. Can be made ahead and frozen. Bake frozen at 350°, covered, for 45 minutes; then bake uncovered for 15 minutes longer.

Carolyn Botzong, Central
Council, Melbourne, Fl.

SEAFOOD EGGPLANT CASSEROLE

4 large eggplants
1 large bell pepper, chopped
1 lb. prepared shrimp
4 slices bread
Salt, garlic salt, black pepper and Chef's seasoning to taste

3 large onions, chopped
1 large bunch chopped shallots
1 can crabmeat
2 eggs
1/4 c. milk
1 stick oleo
Bread crumbs

Boil eggplants; remove pulp and chop. Saute onions and bell pepper in melted oleo. Add shrimp and crabmeat. Pour milk and eggs over bread to make mushy. Add eggplant and seasonings. Put in pot to cook with soaked bread and cook 30 minutes, stirring often. Place in casserole dish and top with bread crumbs. Bake at 350° for 30 minutes.

Laura Baptist, Ozone
Council, Hammond, La.

STUFFED EGGPLANT CASSEROLE

2 large eggplants
3 stalks celery, chopped fine
Few pats of butter
1 large bell pepper, chopped fine

2 medium onions, chopped fine
Salt and pepper to taste
2 lb. ground beef
6 pieces bread, toasted dark on both sides

Boil eggplants in water until skin is wrinkled. When done, scoop out insides and mash thoroughly. Brown ground beef until about half done; drain. Add onions, celery, bell pepper, salt, pepper and eggplant to meat. Cook until done over medium heat. Crumble about half of

bread into mixture and pour into casserole. Crumble remaining bread and sprinkle over top. Dot with few pats of butter. Heat at 400° until butter is melted and casserole is heated through. Mixture can be made several days in advance or even frozen. Do not add bread until ready to cook if you freeze.
Betty Harman, Caddo
Council, Shreveport, La.

FRANKFURTER CASSEROLE

1 1/2 c. hot cooked rice
1/8 tsp. salt
1/2 c. chopped green
  pepper
1/2 c. chopped onion
1/2 c. barbecue sauce

1 can Cheddar cheese soup
Dash of pepper
1 c. Cheddar cheese,
  grated
1/2 pkg. frankfurters,
  sliced in 1/2-inch pieces

Stir salt and pepper into soup. Layer rice, onion, green pepper, soup and cheese into a greased casserole dish. Arrange slices of frankfurters evenly over cheese layer. Pour barbecue sauce on top. Bake casserole at 350° for 35-40 minutes or until browned. Makes 4 servings.
Marjorie B. Harris, Capital
Council, Baton Rouge, La.

GRITS CASSEROLE

2 c. regular grits (not
  quick)
3 c. hot milk
2 tsp. Worcestershire
  sauce
3/4 lb. grated cheese
  (medium or sharp)

1/2 stick oleo
3 Tbsp. flour
1/2 tsp. salt
1/2 tsp. Tabasco sauce
1 large can chopped pimentos,
  drained
Grated cheese for topping

Cook regular grits. Pour on cookie sheet; refrigerate overnight. Cut in 1-inch squares and place grits squares in large casserole sprayed with Pam. Make sauce of oleo, flour, hot milk, salt, Worcestershire sauce and Tabasco sauce. Add 3/4 pound grated cheese. When melted, add pimentos. Pour sauce over grits. Top with grated cheese. Cover with foil; bake at 350° for 1 1/2 hours. Tastes like potatoes. Serve at brunch or bar-b-que. May also freeze casserole and reheat to serve. Althea Rome Brossett, Capital
Council, Baton Rouge, La.

GRITS AU GRATIN CASSEROLE

6 c. water
1 stick oleo
1 tsp. salt
3 Tbsp. chopped green
  chili peppers

1 1/2 c. grits
1 Tbsp. cheese, grated
1 tsp. seasoned salt
3 eggs, beaten

Cook grits in water until done. Mix in other ingredients. Bake in large sheet pan for 1 hour at 250°.

Betty Wood, Ozone Council,
Bogalusa, La.

GARLIC CHEESE GRITS

1/2 lb. shredded sharp
  Cheddar cheese
1 stick butter, sliced
1/4 c. milk
Paprika (optional)

1 roll garlic cheese,
  shredded
1 c. uncooked grits
2 eggs
1 tsp. parsley flakes
Salt to taste

Cook grits until done; stir in butter, cheese and parsley. Lightly beat eggs and milk together and add to grits. Add salt as desired. Place in casserole which has been greased with butter. Sprinkle paprika on top, if desired. Bake at 300° for 30 minutes.

Mrs. J.B. Coker, Central
Council, Alexandria, La.

GROUND MEAT DISH

1 lb. ground meat
Salt and pepper to taste
1 can water
1 pkg. egg noodles,
  cooked

1 bell pepper, chopped
1 can mushroom soup
1 can whole kernel corn
Grated cheese
Sliced olives (optional)

Brown beef and bell pepper. Add salt, pepper, soup, water and corn. Add egg noodles and mix thoroughly. Sprinkle grated cheese over top; also sliced olives, if desired. Bake at 350° until brown.

Betty Elenburg, Caddo
Council, Shreveport, La.

HAMBURGER CASSEROLE

2 large onions, minced
1 medium carrot, grated
1 can mushroom soup
Oil

2 large potatoes, grated
1 lb. ground meat
Flour

Combine onion, potatoes, carrot and beef. Form into large patties. Coat with flour, brushing off surplus. Brown on both sides in small amount of oil over medium heat; drain. Add soup. Place in baking dish and bake at 300° for 1 hour. Makes 6 servings.

Mrs. Leona Smith, Central
Council, Corpus Christi, Tx.

HAMBURGER PIE CASSEROLE

1 lb. ground beef
1 can tomatoes, chopped
1/2 c. chopped bell pepper
Salt and pepper
1 Tbsp. Worcestershire sauce

1 can drained kidney beans
1 chopped onion
1 Tbsp. chili powder
1 pkg. corn bread mix

Add bell pepper and onions to ground beef; brown and drain. Add chili powder, salt, Worcestershire sauce and pepper. Stir and add tomatoes and kidney beans. Simmer about 15 minutes. Pour into casserole dish. Make up corn bread according to directions and spread over meat mixture. Bake at 400° about 20 or 25 minutes or until corn bread is brown.

Marilou Bridges, Caddo
Council, Shreveport, La.

HAM CASSEROLE

2 Tbsp. chopped onion
2 Tbsp. margarine
2 Tbsp. green pepper
1 can cream of chicken
  soup

1 1/2 c. chopped, cooked ham
Approx. 2 c. cooked noodles
  or spaghetti
1/2 c. grated cheese

Cook onion and green pepper in margarine until tender. Combine with all ingredients, except cheese. Place in a buttered casserole dish. Bake at 350° for 30 minutes. Remove and sprinkle top with cheese. Return to oven for

5 minutes or until cheese melts. If mixture is stiff, add milk until it is rather soupy. Calcasieu Council
Lake Charles, La.

MACARONI WITH HAM

1/4 c. bread crumbs
1 c. hot milk
3 Tbsp. melted butter
1 c. chopped, cooked
   ham

2 eggs, beaten
2 c. cooked macaroni
1 tsp. minced onion
1 Tbsp. chopped green
   pepper
Salt

Mix crumbs and hot milk. Add all of the remaining ingredients. Place in baking dish and bake in moderate oven at 375° for 45 minutes. Serve with 1 1/2 cups hot tomato sauce. Serves 4. Calcasieu Council
Lake Charles, La

JOHNNY MAZETTA

1 lb. ground beef
1 lb. noodles
2 c. grated American
   cheese (1/2 lb.)
1 can tomato sauce with
   mushrooms (small)
1/2 c. chopped stuffed
   olives
2 c. chopped green
   pepper
1 c. chopped celery

1 lb. ground pork or pork
   sausage
1 can Hunt's tomato herb
   sauce (small)
1 can tomato soup
1 (4 oz.) can sliced mushrooms, undrained
1 c. chopped onion
2 tsp. garlic salt
1 c. butter or oleo

In large skillet, fry pepper, celery, onion and ground meat in very hot butter. Add salt, reduce heat and cook 5 minutes. Stir in mushrooms, olives, soup and canned sauces; cook 5 minutes. Cook noodles in boiling salted water until done; drain. Turn noodles into a 14 x 10 x 2 1/2-inch roasting pan. Add sauce mixture; stir gently until well mixed. Sprinkle cheese over top. Bake at 350° for 35 minutes. Yield: 12 generous portions.
Louise Malone, Caddo
Council, Shreveport, La.

JUDY'S CASSEROLE

2 lb. lean ground beef
1 large chopped onion
1 green pepper, chopped
1 stick oleo
1 large can tomato paste

1 medium can white kernel
  corn, undrained
3/4 lb. grated sharp cheese
1 (8 oz.) pkg. cooked egg
  noodles

Saute onions and pepper in oleo, add meat and cook until brown. Add tomatoes, drained noodles and corn. Pour into 2 greased casserole dishes, 1 3/4-quart size. Top with grated cheese. Cover. Place one in freezer for future use. Bake the other in preheated 350° oven for 1 hour. Serves 4 generously.

Louise Ward, Crescent City
Council, New Orleans, La.

MACARONI AND CHEESE

1/4 c. chopped onion
1 Tbsp. butter
3 c. cooked macaroni

1 (11 oz.) can condensed
  Cheddar cheese soup
1/2 c. homogenized milk

Cook onion in butter until tender. Blend in soup, gradually add milk. Heat, stirring often. Mix in macaroni. Stir again until thoroughly heated.

Calcasieu Council
Lake Charles, La.

SHELL MACARONI SUPREME

1 lb. ground beef
3 c. medium shell maca-
  roni, uncooked
1 can Italian style
  tomatoes, undrained
1 1/2 Tbsp. Season-All
1 1/2 tsp. oregano
1/3 c. grated Parmesan
  cheese

1 env. Lipton's mushroom
  soup mix
1 can Hunt's herb sauce
1 large can mushroom stems
  and pieces, drained
1 Tbsp. Nature's Seasoning
2 1/4 c. water
Grated Mozzarella cheese
Salt to taste

Brown beef in large skillet. Add soup mix, herb sauce, oregano, seasonings and water. Mash Italian tomatoes and and add to mixture. Bring to a boil, stir in macaroni and simmer covered for 20 minutes, stirring occasionally. Remove from heat, stir in Parmesan cheese and top with grated

Mozzarella cheese. Cover for 2 or 3 minutes until cheese melts. Serve with garlic bread. Makes 6 servings.

L. Monnin, LeBayou
Council, Franklin, La.

MEAT CASSEROLE

2 cloves garlic, minced	1/2 c. oil
2 lb. ground meat	1 large onion, diced
1 bell pepper, diced	1/2 lb. spaghetti, broken
1 large can whole corn	in 3 pieces
1 large can English peas	1 large can tomatoes
1 or 2 cans black olives	1 lb. Old English grated
	cheese

Brown meat in oil with garlic, peppers and onions. Drain off grease. Cook spaghetti; drain. Mix all ingredients, except half of grated cheese. Put in large greased baking dish. Top with remaining cheese. Bake at 350° for about 30-45 minutes. This can be made ahead of time and frozen.

Gail Cummings, Caddo
Council, Shreveport, La.

MEAT AND POTATO PIE

1 can cream of mushroom	1/4 c. finely chopped onion
soup	1/4 c. shredded mild cheese
1/4 c. fine dry bread	1 egg, slightly beaten
crumbs	Dash of pepper
2 c. mashed potatoes	1/4 tsp. salt
1 lb. ground beef	

Combine beef, onion, egg, bread crumbs, seasonings and 1/2 of soup. Press firmly into a 9-inch pie plate. Bake at 350° for 25 minutes; spoon off fat. Cover with mashed potatoes and top with remaining soup and cheese. Bake additional 10 minutes or until done.

Dorothy Trent, Caddo
Council, Shreveport, La.

MEXICALE MEDLEY

1 large can tamales
  (1 lb. 14 oz.)
1 can cream of mushroom
  soup
1/2 c. milk

1 medium can whole kernel
  corn (12 oz.)
Medium size bag of potato
  chips

Drain tamales and cut into bite size pieces. Drain corn. Mix soup with milk. Break about 2 large handfuls of potato chips into large pieces; don't crush. Mix all together carefully. Place in casserole dish. Sprinke top generously with broken potato chips. Bake at 350° for 30-45 minutes or until bubbly.   Zelda Anderson, Calcasieu
                                          Council, Lake Charles, La.

MEXICAN CASSEROLE

1 c. grated cheese
12 tortillas
1 can Ro-Tel tomatoes
1 1/2 lb. ground beef
Salt and pepper to taste

1 c. chopped onion
1 can cream of chicken soup
1 large can Ranch Style
  beans

Brown ground meat; season with salt and pepper. Drain and place in bottom of casserole. Sprinkle 1/2 of onion and cheese over meat. Cover with 6 tortillas. Add beans and remainder of tortillas. Mix soup and tomatoes; pour over casserole. Sprinkle with remaining onion and cheese. Bake at 350° for 1 hour, covered.   Mavis W. O'Rourke
                                          Shreveport Works Council
                                          Shreveport, La.

MEXICAN CASSEROLE

1 (6 oz.) pkg. Fritos
1 can enchilada sauce
1 small can tomato paste
1 c. grated cheese

1 (15 oz.) can chili or chili
  with beans
1/4 c. chopped onion
1 c. sour cream (optional)

Mix all ingredients together, reserving 1/4 cup of cheese and sour cream. Place in a casserole. Bake at 350° for 30 minutes. Remove from oven, spread sour cream on top and sprinkle with remaining cheese. Return to oven until cheese melts.   Louise Malone, Caddo
                                          Council, Shreveport, La.

MEXICAN CASSEROLE

1 chopped onion
Salt and pepper to taste
1 can cream of chicken
  soup
1 Tbsp. chili powder

1 lb. ground meat
1 small can Pet milk
1 can Ro-Tel tomatoes
1 bag Doritos chips
Grated cheese

Brown meat, add onion, add chili powder and stir in well. Add soup, tomatoes and milk. Place Doritos in bottom of casserole dish; pour meat mixture over Doritos and top with grated cheese. Bake at 375° for 15-20 minutes or until cheese melts. Rebecca Thames, Caddo Council, Shreveport, La.

20 MINUTE MEXICAN CASSEROLE

1 can cream of mushroom
  soup
1 can tomato soup
1 1/2 lb. ground meat
1 small onion, chopped
Salt and pepper to taste
1 pkg. Doritos corn chips

1 can Cheddar cheese soup
1 can Ro-Tel tomatoes with
  chilies
1/2 lb. grated Cheddar
  cheese
1/2 bell pepper, chopped
1 tsp. chili powder

Mix soups and Ro-Tel tomatoes in saucepan and heat over low flame. In skillet, brown meat, onion, bell pepper, salt, pepper and chili powder. When done, add to the soup mixture. In large casserole dish, place layer of Doritos, layer of hot meat mixture and cover with grated cheese. Repeat layering in same order, ending with cheese. Cover with foil and let sit 5-10 minutes so the hot mixture will melt cheese. Serve immediately. Dorothy Slay, Shreveport Works Council, Shreveport, La.

MIRLITON A LA CECILE

1/4 c. oil
1 lb. ground pork
2 stalks celery, chopped
1 onion, chopped

8 medium mirlitons (vegetable
  pears)
1 medium bell pepper,
  chopped

Peel and dice mirlitons. Place in pot with oil and cook down until all water has evaporated. Cook pork, celery, bell pepper and onion in separate pot until tender. Mix all ingredients together. Serves 7 people as main dish.

Cecile Gallet, Evangeline
Council, Lafayette, La.

BAKED MIRLITON

6 medium mirlitons
1 large onion, finely
  chopped
1 clove garlic, minced
1 c. diced smoked sausage
Tomato juice, if needed
Salt and pepper to taste

1/2 c. olive oil
1 large green pepper, finely
  chopped
1 c. diced raw shrimp
3 c. seasoned bread crumbs
Lemon slivers or slices
  (garnish)

Peel, deseed and boil mirlitons until tender. Place in colander and press through with masher. Save water; cool. Combine olive oil, green pepper, onion and garlic in saucepan. Cook until soft and tender, but not browned. Add shrimp and sausage. Continue to cook for about 5 minutes. Add mirliton pulp and continue cooking until most of liquid from pulp has boiled off. Add bread crumbs and tomato juice if too dry and needed. Mix all ingredients thoroughly, adding salt and pepper to taste. Place in baking dish. Garnish with slivers of lemon and bake about 30 minutes at 400°. Serves 6 or more.

Floyd Shumann, Ozone
Council, Hammond, La.

STUFFED MIRLITON

6 mirlitons
3 or 4 Tbsp. oleo
4 or 5 cloves garlic, minced
1/2 chopped green pepper
1 lb. shrimp, cut in small
  pieces
Salt and pepper to taste

1/2 loaf stale French bread
1 large onion, finely chopped,
  1 bunch shallots
1 Tbsp. chopped parsley
1 egg
Bread crumbs

Cover mirlitons with cold water; boil until tender; cut in half. Scoop out pulp, being sure to discard seed and fibrous pulp around seed. Place tender pulp in colander over bowl. Chop pulp, reserving excess water; save shell. Soak stale bread in mirliton water and squeeze out water. Cook onion, garlic and green pepper in oleo 5 minutes. Add mirliton pulp and stale bread. Cook about 15 minutes over low fire, stirring often. Salt and pepper to taste. Add shrimp which have been slightly fried. Cool; add egg and parsley. Refill mirliton shells with mixture. Cover with bread crumbs and dot each shell with butter. Bake at 350° for 1/2 hour or until golden brown. Serves 12.

Barbara Wellman, Metairie
Council, Metairie, La.

NAME UNKNOWN MEAL

2 lb. stew meat
1 can onion soup

1 can cream of mushroom
soup (preferably with
mushrooms)

Mix ingredients and place in casserole dish. Bake at 325° for 4 hours, or cook in crock-pot or slow cooker overnight. Serve over cooked rice or noodles for a main dish.

Betty Elenburg, Caddo
Council, Shreveport, La.

NEPTUNE'S DELIGHT CASSEROLE

1/2 c. oleo
1 qt. milk
1/2 tsp. dry mustard
2 tsp. Worcestershire
    sauce
1/2 lb. crabmeat
1/2 c. Parmesan cheese

1/2 c. flour
1/2 tsp. salt
1/2 c. sherry
1/2 lb. cooked lobster
1/2 lb. cooked shrimp
1/2 tsp. paprika
1/2 c. cracker meal

Make sauce of all ingredients, except seafood, cracker meal, cheese and paprika. Place seafood in 2-quart casserole, cover with sauce. Sprinkle with cheese mixed with cracker meal and paprika. Brown in 400° oven for 15 minutes. Any combination of seafood may be used.

Mearl S. Byles, Central
Council, Natchitoches, La.

NEVER FAIL MEN'S CASSEROLE

1 head cabbage
1 small can pimento strips
1 Tbsp. sherry

1/2 can cheese soup
1 can biscuits
1/2 lb. corned beef, sliced
    thin

Boil cabbage leaves until tender; drain. Add pimento and cheese soup. Place in casserole dish. Cover with corned beef and biscuits. Heat at 350° until biscuits are brown.

Zelda Anderson, Calcasieu
Council, Lake Charles, La.

NOODLE CASSEROLE

6 Tbsp. butter or oleo	1 1/2 c. soft bread crumbs
1 c. finely chopped onion	1 Tbsp. poppy seed
1 c. grated Parmesan cheese	1 tsp. Worcestershire sauce
	1/2 tsp. salt
1 (8 oz.) pkg. wide noodles, cooked and drained	1/8 tsp. pepper
	6 hard boiled eggs, chopped
	2 c. small curd cottage cheese

Melt 3 tablespoons butter in small skillet. Toss bread crumbs in butter. Remove and reserve crumbs. Melt remaining 3 tablespoons butter in skillet; saute onions in butter over medium heat, about 5 minutes. Combine onions, noodles and eggs in large bowl. Stir in remaining ingredients. Pour mixture into buttered 2-quart casserole. Sprinkle crumbs on top. Bake at 350° until crumbs are golden, about 30 minutes.

June Harllee, Caddo
Council, Shreveport, La.

NOODLE CASSEROLE DISH

1 can cream of chicken soup	1/2 c. sour cream
2 tsp. parsley flakes	1/2 c. milk or cream
1 tsp. salt	Dash of pepper
2 Tbsp. pimento	2 c. wide noodles, cooked

Mix all ingredients, except noodles. Mix well, add noodles. Place mixture in casserole and bake at 325° for 25 minutes.

Mrs. Drew Holloway, Central
Council, Alexandria, La.

GREEN NOODLE CASSEROLE

1 large pkg. cream cheese
1 (7 oz.) can tuna
1 Tbsp. horseradish
1/4 tsp. salt
1/2 c. toasted almonds

1 c. sour cream
2 Tbsp. onion
2 Tbsp. pimento
1 (8 oz.) pkg. wide noodles, cooked and drained

Blend cheese and sour cream. Add remainder of ingredients. Fold in noodles. Bake in 1 1/4-quart dish for 20-30 minutes at 375° until brown. If doubling recipe, 1 can of shrimp or crabmeat is good with tuna.

Ruth Smolenski
Evangeline Council

OLE CASSEROLE

2 1/2 c. water, divided
1 tsp. salt
1 onion, chopped
1 pkg. taco seasoning
1 (8 oz.) can tomato sauce

1 lb. ground beef
1 tsp. black pepper
1 tsp. garlic
1 c. raw rice, uncooked

Brown ground beef, onion, garlic, salt and pepper; add 1/2 cup water. Add taco seasoning, rice, tomato sauce and remainder of water. Mix well. Cook covered over very low heat until rice is done, about 1 hour, stirring occasionally. Serves 4-6.

Betty Barron, Caddo
Council, Shreveport, La.

ONE TO ONE CASSEROLE

1 lb. lean ground beef
1 env. dry onion soup mix
1 can mushroom soup
Salt and pepper to taste

1 c. raw rice
1 c. water
1 c. green onion tops, sliced

Season meat and crumble in buttered 2 1/2-quart casserole. Sprinkle with rice and soup mix. Blend mushroom soup and water; pour over contents of casserole. Spread onion tops over mixture. Cover and bake at 350° for 1 hour or until rice is cooked.

Vera Trosclair, Central
Council, Lecompte, La.

OYSTER CASSEROLE

1 qt. oysters
4 Tbsp. flour
6 Tbsp. oleo
1/2 c. chopped parsley
6 slices dry toast
Salt and pepper to taste

1 c. chopped onion
1 clove garlic, minced
1 c. chopped celery
1/2 c. chopped bell pepper
1 Tbsp. hot sauce, or as
much as you like

Make fine crumbs from toast either with blender, food processor, rolling pin or what have you. Melt oleo, add flour and make rich dark roux. Add celery, onions and parsley; cook on low heat until vegetables are wilted. Add oysters, hot sauce, salt and pepper. Add 1 1/2 cups of crumbs to mixture and turn out into greased casserole dish. Top with remainder of crumbs. Bake at 350° for 25-30 minutes.

Theda S. Thomas, Caddo
Council, Shreveport, La.

PORK CASSEROLE

1 lb. elbow macaroni
2 cans mushroom soup
2 Tbsp. instant minced
onion
1 tsp. dried marjoram
leaves, crumbled
1/4 tsp. pepper

3 c. cooked, diced, leftover
pork
1 c. milk or chicken broth
2 tsp. salt
1 tsp. dried basil
1/2 tsp. garlic powder
Buttered bread crumbs

Cook macaroni until tender in boiling, salted water; drain. Combine with other ingredients, except bread crumbs and place in casserole dish. Top with crumbs; cover and bake at 350° until hot, bubbly and golden brown.

Helen Bartram, Capital
Council, Bethel, Ct.

PORK CHOP CASSEROLE

6 pork chops
1 pkg. onion soup mix
1 c. raw rice
1 Tbsp. Worcestershire
sauce

2 Tbsp. oleo
1 bell pepper, chopped
1/2 c. catsup
2 c. boiling water

Melt butter in baking dish. Place pork chops, salt and pepper in pan. Spread soup mix, bell pepper, rice, catsup and Worcestershire sauce over chops. Pour boiling water over contents, cover and bake at 350° for 1 hour.

Ann Aslinger, Gentilly
Council, Meraux, La.

PORK CHOP CASSEROLE

6-8 pork chops
2 cans cream of mushroom
  soup

6-8 potatoes, sliced round
3 onions, sliced round
Salt and pepper to taste

Brown chops in pan. Remove; add soup with small amount of water in pan until soup melts. In deep casserole dish, arrange alternately in layers, beginning with chops, potatoes, onions and soup until all ingredients are used. Add salt and pepper. Cover and bake at 350° for 1 hour or until potatoes are soft.

Pat Uhle, West Bank
Council, Gretna, La.

PORK CHOP AND POTATO CASSEROLE

4 pork chops
1 can cream of celery soup
1 c. evaporated milk
Salt and pepper to taste

5 c. thinly sliced potatoes
3 Tbsp. chopped onion
3 Tbsp. chopped bell pepper
Grated American cheese

Season chops and brown in oil. Arrange potatoes in 2-quart dish. Mix remainder of ingredients, except cheese, and pour over potatoes. Place chops over potatoes. Sprinkle with cheese. Bake 1 hour and 15 minutes at 350°.

Jan Prestridge, Capital
Council, Baton Rouge, La.

P&P CASSEROLE

4 medium raw potatoes
1 can beef gravy
1 small can mushrooms
12-15 stuffed, sliced
  olives (optional)

4 pork chops
1 medium onion, sliced in
  rings
Salt and pepper to taste

Peel and slice potatoes; place in casserole. In layers, add mushrooms, onions, olives. Top with pork chops. Pour gravy over; bake at 375° for approximately 1 1/4 hours. Salt and pepper to taste.

Rose Romano, Crescent City
Council, New Orleans, La.

RABBIT SUPREME CASSEROLE

1 medium rabbit
1 rib celery, chopped
3/4 stick oleo
1 can consomme
Salt and pepper to taste

1 large onion, chopped
1/4 c. chopped parsley
1 can mushroom soup
1 c. raw rice

Boil rabbit for 1 hour; debone and cut. Brown cubed rabbit in oleo. Remove; saute onion and celery in drippings for 10 minutes. Add soups, rabbit, parsley and rice. Mix and pour into 2-quart greased casserole. Cover with foil. Bake at 350° for 45 minutes. Serves 6.

Mona Reis, Metairie
Council, Metairie, La.

RICE CASSEROLE

1 box Uncle Ben's chicken
   flavored rice
1 jar marinated artichokes,
   drained and chopped

10 stuffed olives, chopped
12 green fresh onions,
   chopped
1/2 c. mayonnaise
1/2 bell pepper, chopped

Cook rice according to directions, omitting butter. Stir in other ingredients. Mix well and refrigerate overnight.

Joy Faught, Central
Council, Alexandria, La.

CAJUN RICE

1 c. raw rice
1/4 tsp. Tabasco sauce
1 can Cheddar cheese
   soup or mushroom soup
1/4 c. chopped bell pepper

1 tsp. salt
1 soup can water
1 small onion, chopped
1/4 c. chopped celery
1 can drained crabmeat, or
   drained shrimp

Mix and bake, covered, at 350° for 1 hour or until done. Stir once during baking.

Compliments of Calcasieu
Council, Lake Charles, La.

RO-TEL RICE CASSEROLE

1 lb. ground meat
1 bell pepper, chopped
1 can Ro-Tel tomatoes
1 c. dry Minute Rice
Sliced olives
Grated cheese

1 onion, chopped
2 cloves garlic, minced
1 small can tomato sauce
1 can mushroom soup
Salt and pepper to taste

Brown meat and drain. Add onion, bell pepper, garlic. Add tomatoes and tomato sauce; cook about 10 minutes. Add Minute Rice; add soup, olives, salt and pepper. Pour in casserole dish. Bake at 350° for 30 minutes. Remove from oven at 20 minutes, sprinkle cheese on top and return to oven for 10 additional minutes. Jan Prestridge, Capital
Council, Baton Rouge, La.

SPANISH RICE

1 onion, chopped
1 small green pepper,
  chopped
1 lb. ground beef
1 c. rice, uncooked
5 Tbsp. oil

2 (8 oz.) cans tomato sauce
2 c. hot water
1 tsp. prepared mustard
1 1/2 tsp. salt
1/4 tsp. pepper
Sugar to taste

Saute onion, green pepper, beef and rice in oil; brown well. Add remaining ingredients. Mix well; bring to a boil; cover tightly and simmer 25-30 minutes. Serves 6. Use instant rice. Calcasieu Council
Lake Charles, La.

SAUSAGE CASSEROLE

1 lb. pork sausage
1 chopped bell pepper
1/4 c. chopped celery
1 c. mushroom soup
2-3 c. water

1 lb. ground beef
1 c. raw rice
1/2 c. chopped onion
2 c. cream of chicken soup

Brown sausage and ground beef; drain. Saute bell pepper, celery and onion; drain. Combine ingredients and pour in casserole dish. Bake 1 hour at 350°, stirring occasionally. Serves 10-12. Peggy Childers, Crescent
City Council, New Orleans, La.

SAUSAGE CASSEROLE

1 lb. hot bulk pork sausage
2 c. macaroni
1 (8 oz.) carton sour cream
1 Tbsp. chili powder
1/2 c. Cheddar cheese,
  shredded

1 c. chopped onion
1 c. chopped bell pepper
1/2 c. milk
1 can tomatoes, drained and
  chopped
1 tsp. salt

Fry sausage, onion and pepper in skillet over low heat until done; drain. Cook macaroni and drain. Mix all ingredients together, except cheese, and spoon into greased casserole dish. Top with cheese. Bake at 350° for 20-25 minutes or until bubbly. Makes 6 servings.

Jeanette Williams, Caddo
Council, Shreveport, La.

SAUSAGE CASSEROLE

1 1/2 lb. fresh sausage
1 can celery soup
3/4 c. cabbage, grated fine
1/2 large onion, chopped
1/4 tsp. red pepper

1 c. uncooked rice
1 can beef consomme
1 clove garlic, minced
1/2 bell pepper, chopped
1 Tbsp. parsley

Remove sausage from casing; brown and drain. Mix all ingredients together and place in greased 2-quart casserole dish or Dutch oven. Cover and bake in preheated 350° oven for 1 1/2 hours.

Gloria Fontenot, Evangeline
Council, Lafayette, La.

SAUSAGE PILAF

1 lb. hot pork sausage
1/2 c. chopped bell pepper
1 c. raw rice (cooked
  separately)

1 c. chopped celery
1/2 c. chopped onion
1 can mushroom soup
1/2 c. cashews or peanuts
  (optional)

Brown sausage in skillet until brown; add celery, onion, pepper and cook 3-5 minutes. Stir in soup and rice. Bake at 250° for 30 minutes in quart casserole. Cover for first 20 minutes. Add nuts and bake uncovered for 10 minutes.

Gayle Wilkening
Shreveport Works Council
Longview, Tx.

SAUSAGE AND RICE CASSEROLE

1 lb. bulk sausage
1 c. chopped celery
2-3 c. cooked rice
2 cans cream of chicken
  soup

1 c. chopped onion
1 chopped green pepper
1 can cream of mushroom
  soup

Brown sausage in pan; drain. Add vegetables; fry until tender. Add soups and rice. Pour into casserole and bake at 350° for 45 minutes. LaJuan Durand, Central
Council, Alexandria, La.

RICE AND SAUSAGE CASSEROLE

3 c. cooked rice
1 lb. sausage
2 Tbsp. cheese, grated

1 medium onion, chopped
1 can condensed cream of
  tomato soup

Brown sausage in fry pan and drain the fat. Arrange rice and sausage in alternate layers in a greased casserole. Sprinkle each layer with chopped onion. Pour on tomato soup, undiluted; top with grated cheese. Cover and bake in moderate oven at 350° for 30 minutes. Serves 4-6.
Calcasieu Council
Lake Charles, La.

SAUSAGE AND RICE CASSEROLE

1 lb. hot bulk sausage
1 clove chopped garlic
1 c. chopped celery
1 can cream of mushroom
  soup

1 c. chopped onion
1 bell pepper, chopped
1 c. raw rice
2 cans cream of chicken soup
Salt and pepper to taste

In a frying pan, brown sausage; drain. Add vegetables and simmer until tender. Wash rice and add to this mixture. Add soups and seasonings. Pour in casserole dish. Bake in preheated 350° oven for 1 - 1 1/2 hours. Stir occasionally.
Evelyn Sinnigson, Capital
Council, Baton Rouge, La.

SHRIMP CASSEROLE

2 lb. shrimp, peeled and
  cleaned
3 green onions and tops,
  chopped
4-6 stale hamburger buns,
  slightly toasted
Garlic powder
Italian bread crumbs
2 medium white onions,
  chopped
1 medium green bell pepper,
  chopped
2 eggs
1 can mushroom soup
Salt, black and red pepper
  to taste
2-3 Tbsp. oil

Saute chopped vegetables in oil. Crumble buns; add eggs, soup, shrimp and seasonings to taste. Mix well. Add sauteed vegetables and mix. Pour into square casserole dish and top with bread crumbs and few of the shrimp. Bake at 350° about 20-30 minutes.   Evelyn Sinnigson, Capital
Council, Baton Rouge, La.

SHRIMP AND CAULIFLOWER CASSEROLE

1 large pkg. frozen, cut up
  cauliflower
1 can cream of shrimp soup
1 can sweet peas, drained
1/2 - 3/4 c. milk
1 (10 oz.) pkg. frozen tiny
  shrimp

Cook cauliflower according to directions; drain. Heat soup and milk. Add shrimp and peas. Place cauliflower in casserole. Pour soup and shrimp mixture over and mix well. Bake at 350° about 25 minutes.
    Mildred Hale, Ouachita
Council, Monroe, La.

SHRIMP MUSHROOM CASSEROLE

1/2 onion, finely chopped
4 shallots, finely chopped
4 Tbsp. flour
1/2 tsp. celery salt
1/2 tsp. paprika
Slight pinch of cayenne
  pepper
1/4 lb. mushrooms, sliced
Seasoned bread crumbs
1/2 bell pepper, finely
  chopped
1 1/2 c. light cream
4 Tbsp. butter
1/2 tsp. white pepper
1/2 tsp. salt
1 c. grated Cheddar cheese
2 lb. peeled and deveined
  shrimp, cooked in salted
  water

Saute onion, bell pepper and shallots in butter over low heat until tender; do not brown. Add flour; mix and cook 3 or 4 minutes. Add remainder of ingredients, except bread crumbs. Stir together and pour into well buttered baking dish. Top with bread crumbs. Bake in preheated 350° oven for 20 minutes. Makes 6-8 servings.

Mrs. Iuka Goetz, Capital
Council, New Orleans, La.

SHRIMP AND RICE CASSEROLE

1 lb. shrimp, cleaned
1/2 c. celery
1 can cream of mushroom
    soup
Small amount grease or oil

1/2 of a bell pepper, cut up
1 small onion, cut up
1 c. raw rice
Salt, black and red pepper
    to taste

Saute shrimp, bell pepper, celery and onion in small amount of oil; add soup and rice. Pour in casserole dish; season as desired; with plenty of red pepper. Bake at 350° for 35-40 minutes.

Mrs. Sim (Sally) Davenport
Central Council
Alexandria, La.

SHRIMP AND RO-TEL CASSEROLE

1 stick oleo
1 chopped bell pepper
2 ribs chopped celery
1/4 c. chopped pimentos
1/2 c. water
1 can mushroom soup
Buttered bread crumbs
    (optional)

1 1/4 c. chopped onions
3 cloves chopped garlic
1/4 c. chopped parsley
4 slices bread
1 can Ro-Tel tomatoes
3 c. boiled, cleaned shrimp,
    cut in half
3 c. cooked rice

Saute onions, pepper, garlic and celery in oil. Add shrimp and tomatoes. Cook 5 minutes. Add soup, water and pimentos. Cook 5 minutes more. Soak bread in water, squeeze out excess and add bread to mixture. Add rice and parsley. Pour into greased casserole dish and bake in preheated oven for 30 minutes. Serves 6-8. Casserole may be topped with buttered bread crumbs before baking, if desired.

Frances Bergeron
Crescent City Council
New Orleans, La.

SHRIMP THERMIDOR EN CASSEROLE

1 lb. frozen, shelled and
   deveined shrimp
1 c. thinly sliced celery
1 c. half & half
Dash of seasoned pepper

1 c. regular long grain rice
6 Tbsp. butter or oleo
1/4 c. all-purpose flour
1 tsp. seasoned salt
1/2 c. shredded Cheddar
   cheese

In skillet, over medium-high heat, melt butter. Add shrimp and celery; stir occasionally for about 10 minutes or until shrimp have turned pink. Remove about 6 for garnish. Reduce heat to medium, stir flour into remaining shrimp mixture until well blended. Gradually stir in half & half, salt and pepper. Cook, stirring constantly, until mixture thickens and shrimp are tender. Cook rice. Place hot rice into a 2 1/2-quart casserole. Top with shrimp mixture, sprinkle with cheese and garnish with reserved shrimp. Bake 5 minutes or until cheese is melted and hot. Makes 4-5 servings.

Vera Trosclaw, Central
Council, Lecompte, La.

SHORT RIB CASSEROLE

3 lb. beef short ribs, cut
   in 3-inch lengths (flour,
   salt and pepper)
2 Tbsp. pure vegetable oil
2 c. water
3 carrots, pared and sliced

1 (8 oz.) can tomato sauce
   with onions
4 small potatoes, pared and
   halved
1 (10 oz.) pkg. frozen cut
   green beans

Coat meat with flour, salt and pepper. Brown short ribs in oil in Dutch oven over medium heat. Add water and tomato sauce. Bake covered at 325° for 1 hour. Skim off fat. Arrange potatoes and green beans around ribs, sprinkle lightly with additional salt and pepper. Bake covered for 1 more hour. Makes 4 generous servings.

Calcasieu Council
Lake Charles, La.

SIX LAYER CASSEROLE

2 c. sliced raw potatoes
1 lb. lean ground beef
1 c. minced bell pepper
2 tsp. salt
Green pepper slices

2 c. chopped celery
1/2 c. sliced onions
2 c. cooked tomatoes
1/4 tsp. pepper

Grease a 2-quart casserole dish. Place potatoes, celery, ground beef, onions and green pepper in layers in casserole dish. Combine tomatoes, salt and pepper. Spoon over top. Cover and bake at 350° about 2 hours or until vegetables are tender. Garnish with green pepper slices. Serves 6-8. Casserole will be flavored better if made up day before and refrigerated. Betty Harman, Caddo
Council, Shreveport, La.

SIX LAYER DINNER

Sliced raw potatoes
1 1/2 lb. ground beef
Sliced carrots
2 tsp. salt
1 qt. tomatoes or juice

1/3 c. rice
Sliced onions
Chopped green peppers
1 Tbsp. sugar

Place layer of potatoes and sliced onions in buttered baking dish. Cover with layer of sliced carrots. Sprinkle rice over potatoes. Sprinkle with chopped peppers and cover with ground meat and salt. Add layers of onions and carrots with sugar and green peppers. Pour canned tomatoes over vegetables. Bake at 350° for 2 1/2 - 3 hours.
Della Delposen, Ouachita
Council, Monroe, La.

SQUASH CASSEROLE

3 or 4 lb. white squash,
  boiled and slightly
  mashed
1 clove garlic, minced
1 lb. boiled, chopped
  shrimp
1/4 tsp. thyme
Dash of liquid crab boil
  (optional)

1 c. chopped onions
1 c. chopped green pepper
1/2 stick butter
1 bay leaf
1/2 tsp. parsley
1 c. seasoned bread crumbs
Salt and cayenne pepper
1 egg, slightly beaten
Small amount of water

Saute onions, pepper and garlic in butter until tender. Add bay leaf, thyme, parsley, crab boil (if desired) and small amount of water. Cook over low heat for about 15-20 minutes. Add squash and shrimp. Add bread crumbs and egg. Mix well. Season to taste with salt and cayenne pepper. Place in baking dish; pat with additional butter; bake at 350° for 10-15 minutes or until heated through.

Pam Marchese, Metairie
Council, Metairie, La.

STUFFING FOR NOODLES

2 lb. ground meat
4 cloves garlic, chopped
 fine
2 Tbsp. oleo
Romano or Parmesan cheese

2 tsp. parsley, chopped fine
Pepper and salt
2 eggs
1 pkg. Mozzarella cheese,
 shredded

Mix meat with garlic, parsley, salt and pepper. Saute in butter over medium heat until it is a grey-brown color. Remove from heat. Cool. When cooled, add eggs and 3 or 4 ounces of Romano or Parmesan cheese. Mix well and stuff into cooked noodles. Stuffs about 37. In long baking dish or pan, pour a little sauce on bottom. Place stuffed noodles, side by side, in one layer. Pour sauce over top and sprinkle Romano or Parmesan cheese evenly over top. Add Mozzarella cheese. Cover with foil and bake at 350° for about 40 minutes. Allow to cool 10 or 15 minutes before serving. Noodles can be bought at Joe D's on Jefferson Highway in Baton Rouge.

Harriet E. Barton, Capital
Council, Baton Rouge, La.

SWEET POTATO CASSEROLE

2 medium size sweet
 potatoes
1/2 c. pecan bits
Large navel orange

1 (8 oz.) pkg. cream cheese
2 Tbsp. brown sugar or
 cinnamon, if preferred

Bake sweet potatoes; scoop out insides. Mix with room temperature cream cheese. Scoop out inside of large navel orange. Add pecan bits to mixture and place inside orange rind. Add brown sugar for topping. Just before serving, put in oven a few minutes to bake at 350°. Mixture should be light and fluffy; if not, add more cream cheese until fluffy. Sweet potatoes are large and vary inside, so sometimes it is hard to judge. Serves 10-12.

Peggy Childers, Crescent
City Council, New Orleans, La.

SWEET POTATO CASSEROLE

3 c. sweet potatoes   1/2 c. sugar
  (about 4 large size ones)   1/2 c. butter or oleo
2 eggs, beaten   1 tsp. vanilla
1/3 c. milk

Boil and mash potatoes. Mix in remaining ingredients and spoon in 13x9-inch dish. Sprinkle Topping over casserole. Bake 25 minutes at 350°. Serves 10-12.

Topping:

1/3 c. butter, melted   1 c. light brown sugar
1/2 c. flour   1 c. chopped pecans

Mix ingredients together and sprinkle on top of potato mixture.

Mavis W. O'Rourke
Shreveport Works Council
Shreveport, La.

TALLARENI

1 lb. ground beef   1 onion, chopped
1 clove garlic, minced   1 can kernel corn, drained
1 small jar pimentos,   1 medium size pkg. egg
  chopped   noodles, cooked and
1 Tbsp. chili powder   drained
1 can tomato soup   1 c. water
1/2 - 1 c. grated cheese   8-10 ripe olives

Saute onion, garlic and meat. Add remaining ingredients, except cheese. Spoon into greased casserole and cover top with grated cheese. Bake at 350° for 35-40 minutes.

Marilou Bridges, Caddo
Council, Shreveport, La.

TAMALE CASSEROLE

1 large can tamales
1 can cream of chicken soup

1 large onion, chopped
1/2 c. grated cheese

Unwrap tamales and arrange in single layer in bottom of casserole. Scrape sauce from can and tamale wrappings and spread on tamales. Sprinkle onion over tamales. Spread half of grated cheese over onions. Pour soup over top and sprinkle with remainder of cheese. Place in 400° oven until heated through.

Marjorie B. Harris, Capital
Council, Baton Rouge, La.

TEXAS HASH

1 c. chopped onions
2 Tbsp. shortening
1 lb. ground beef
1 c. chopped green pepper
2 tsp. salt

1/4 tsp. pepper
1 1/2 tsp. chili powder
1/2 c. uncooked rice
1 (No. 2 1/2) can tomatoes

Saute onions in shortening in 10-inch skillet until brown. Stir in ground beef, green pepper, salt, pepper, chili powder and rice. Pour tomatoes over mixture. Cover and bake at 350° for about 30 minutes.

Gayle Wilkening, Shreveport
Works Council, Longview, Tx.

TEXAS HASH

1 lb. ground beef
1 large bell pepper,
  chopped
2 tsp. salt
1/8 tsp. black pepper

2 or 3 onions, sliced
1 (16 oz.) can tomatoes
1/2 c. regular rice, uncooked,
  or 1/2 c. elbow macaroni
1-2 tsp. chili powder

Cook meat, onions and green pepper in skillet until meat is browned and vegetables are tender; drain. Stir in remaining ingredients; heat through. Pour into ungreased casserole dish, cover and bake in preheated 350° oven for 1 hour. Makes 6 servings.

Marilou Bridges, Caddo
Council, Shreveport, La.

TROY'S FAVORITE CASSEROLE

Finely sliced potatoes
Browned ground meat
1 can cream of mushroom
  soup

Thin sliced onions
Salt
Water

In a greased casserole, layer potatoes, onions and ground meat. Repeat these 3 layers, salting each layer a little. Heat soup with water and pour over layers. Bake at 400° about 45 minutes. Betty Elenburg, Caddo Council, Shreveport, La.

TUNA BROCCOLI CASSEROLE

1 (10 oz.) pkg. frozen
  broccoli
1 can cream of mushroom
  soup

1 (7 oz.) can tuna, flaked
1/2 soup can of milk
1/2 c. crushed potato chips
  (optional)

Split broccoli stalks into halves. Cook for 3 minutes; drain. Place broccoli in 1 1/2-quart casserole. Cover with tuna. Combine soup and milk, pour over tuna. Sprinkle potato chips over top. Bake at 450° for 15 minutes. Serves 4. Rebecca Scott, Caddo Council, Shreveport, La.

TUNA CASSEROLE

1 can tuna
1 can cream of mushroom
  soup
Jalapeno pepper to taste,
  chopped

1 small chopped onion
3/4 soup can water
1 (8 oz.) pkg. egg noodles
Shredded cheese
Bread crumbs

In oblong baking dish, mix tuna, onions and pepper. Pour in soup and water. Cook noodles until tender; drain and add to tuna mixture. Top with crumbled bread and shredded cheese. Bake at 350° for 30 minutes. Rebecca Thames, Caddo Council, Shreveport, La.

TUNA CASSEROLE

1/2 stick oleo
1 can celery soup
1 pkg. noodles
1/2 c. bell pepper, minced
1 small can pimento, finely
    cut

1 tsp. grated onion
1 (7 oz.) can tuna fish
1/2 c. minced celery
1/2 c. minced parsley
Salt, pepper, Tabasco sauce
    and Worcestershire sauce
    to taste

Cook and drain noodles. Cook onion in oleo until wilted. Add soup, bell pepper, pimento, noodles, celery, parsley and tuna fish. Taste and add seasonings if needed or desired. Bake in casserole dish at 350° for 1/2 hour.

Ann Orr, Evangeline
Council, New Iberia, La.

TUNA CASSEROLE

2 c. crushed potato chips
1/2 tsp. salt
1 c. diced celery

1 can tuna
4 boiled eggs, sliced or diced
1 can cream of mushroom or
    chicken soup

Place 1 cup crushed potato chips in bottom of 1 quart casserole. Then in layers, place half of tuna, layer of eggs, layer of celery. Pour 1/2 of soup over mixture. Repeat layers; sprinkle with salt if necessary and top with remaining potato chips. Bake at 300° for about 25-30 minutes.

Mrs. Walter (Ella V.) Payton
Caddo Council, Shreveport, La.

TUNA CASSEROLE

1 c. macaroni
1 can cream of mushroom
    soup
1 Tbsp. chopped pimento
1 tsp. mustard
1/2 c. bread crumbs

1 (3 oz.) pkg. cream cheese
1 (6 1/2 oz.) can tuna
1 Tbsp. chopped onion
1/3 c. milk
2 Tbsp. butter or oleo

Cook macaroni; drain. Blend cream cheese and soup until smooth in mixer. Stir in tuna, pimento, onion, mustard, milk and macaroni. Place in casserole dish. Sprinkle bread

crumbs on top and dot with butter. Bake at 375° for 20-25 minutes.
Dorothy Trent, Caddo
Council, Shreveport, La.

CHEESY TUNA NOODLE CASSEROLE

1/3 c. chopped onion
2 Tbsp. flour
3/4 c. water
1 1/4 c. grated American
cheese
3 c. cooked noodles,
drained

2 Tbsp. butter
1 2/3 c. evaporated milk
1 c. cooked, drained peas
1 1/2 tsp. Worcestershire
sauce
3/4 tsp. seasoned salt
1 (10 oz.) can drained tuna

Saute onion in butter in medium saucepan. Stir in flour. Gradually add milk and water; cook over medium heat until mixture boils; stir constantly. Remove from heat. Add 1 cup cheese, Worcestershire sauce and seasoned salt. Stir until cheese is melted. Combine cheese sauce, tuna, peas and cooked noodles. Pour into 1 1/2-quart casserole. Top with remaining cheese. Bake at 350° for 25 minutes.
Jeanette English, Caddo
Council, Shreveport, La.

DAMOND'S TUNA CASSEROLE

1 large can tuna
1 can cream of mushroom
soup
1 Tbsp. butter

4 slices American cheese
1 pkg. cooked egg noodles
1 can mixed vegetables
(optional)

Grease casserole dish with butter. Combine cooked noodles, tuna, cheese (broken into small pieces), and mushroom soup in mixing bowl. Mix well and pour into casserole dish. Bake at 375° for 1 hour. Serve hot. Serves 4
Mary Ann J. Francois
Metairie Council
New Orleans, La.

TUNA NOODLE CRISP

4 oz. uncooked noodles
1/3 c. chopped onion
1 can cheese soup
1/2 c. milk
1 tsp. salt
1 can tuna
1/4 c. Crisco
2 Tbsp. chopped green pepper
1 Tbsp. chopped pimento (optional)
1/8 tsp. pepper
1/2 c. bread crumbs

Cook noodles in boiling salted water until done; drain. Melt Crisco in large skillet, add onion and green pepper. Cook until tender. Stir in soup, milk, pimento, salt and pepper; add noodles and tuna. Place mixture in 1 1/2 or 2-quart casserole. Sprinkle with bread crumbs. Bake in preheated 350° oven for 25-30 minutes. Makes 4-6 servings.

Jo Ann Everhardt, Gentilly
Council, Meraux, La.

WESTERN BEAN CASSEROLE

1/2 lb. ground beef
1/2 c. chopped onion
Dash of cayenne pepper
1/3 c. ketchup
1 Tbsp. vinegar
1 egg
1/3 c. milk
1/2 c. sliced celery
Dash or 2 of garlic powder
2 (1 lb.) cans pork and beans with tomato sauce
1/2 pkg. (10 or 12 oz. size) corn muffin mix

Brown beef; cook celery, onion with garlic and pepper until tender in skillet; drain. Add beans, ketchup and vinegar. Heat; stir occasionally. Pour mixture in 1 1/2-quart shallow baking dish. Combine corn bread mix, egg and milk. Spread over bean mixture. Bake at 400° for 25 minutes or until golden brown. Makes 6 servings.

Andy Gubancsik, Capital
Council, Baton Rouge, La.

BOLO

1 large fresh pineapple, or or 2 cans drained pineapple chunks
1 block of ice (use 1/2 gal. milk carton and freeze)
1 fifth bourbon
1 fifth champagne

Put fresh pineapple cubes or drained canned pineapple chunks into container; cover with bourbon and chill for at least 24 hours. Pour bourbon, pineapple and chilled champagne over block of ice in punch bowl. Serve 2 cubes of pineapple in each punch cup of Bolo. Watch out for the pineapple. This will serve more than you think. Substantial amounts of hearty food (grillades and grits or a sauce piquante) should be on tap immediately after the last piece of pineapple is eaten.

Barbara M. Berry, LeBayou
Council, Houma, La.

BLOODY MARY

Step 1: Fill glass mug or tall glass with stem full of ice.

Step 2: Add 1 1/2 ounces vodka.

Step 3: Add 1 large piece of lime, squeezed well.

Step 4: Fill glass with Beef-A-Mato or V-8 juice.

Step 5: Add 3 drops Tabasco sauce and dash of Worcestershire sauce.

Step 6: Add "Janes Krazed" mixed up salt (found on gourmet shelf) or lots of celery salt.

Step 7: Put celery stalk in glass for stirring or nibbling.

Mary Weekes, Metairie
Council, Metairie, La.

PARTY BLOODY MARYS

3 qt. tomato juice
1/3 c. steak sauce
2 1/2 Tbsp. salt
1/4 tsp. hot sauce
Lime slices (optional)

3 c. vodka
1/4 c. Worcestershire sauce
3 tsp. sugar
Juice of 12 limes
Celery sticks

Combine all ingredients, except lime slices and celery. Pour into punch bowl. Float lime slices on top. To serve, pour Bloody Marys into ice filled glasses; garnish with celery sticks. Yield: 4 quarts.

Marilou Bridges, Caddo
Council, Shreveport, La.

"CALIFORNIA COFFEE"

1 oz. (2 Tbsp.) brandy   1 scoop chocolate ice cream
1/2 c. strong coffee

    Combine brandy and coffee in coffee mug. Add scoop
of chocolate ice cream and top with whipped cream. This is
an after dinner coffee and dessert also! Serves 1.

Calcasieu Council
Lake Charles, La.

CREOLE EGGNOG

12 eggs   1 qt. whipping cream
2 c. sugar   2 tsp. grated nutmeg
1 c. bourbon whiskey

    Whip cream until stiff, adding 1/2 cup sugar, 1 table-
spoon at a time. Break eggs and separate. Beat egg yolks,
slowly adding 1 cup sugar. Beat until sugar is dissolved
and the mixture smooth. Whip egg whites to frothy peaks by
adding 1/2 cup sugar, 1 tablespoon at a time. Mix yolks
with bourbon, add whipped cream. Fold in egg whites,
sprinkle with nutmeg and serve.

Calcasieu Council
Lake Charles, La.

FANCY EGGNOG

10 egg yolks   3/4 c. sugar
1 pt. rye whiskey   1 qt. heavy cream
10 egg whites, stiffly   Ground nutmeg
   beaten

    Beat egg yolks and sugar. Add whiskey slowly, stirring
constantly. Continue stirring and add cream. Add stiffly
beaten egg whites. Chill and top each serving with nutmeg.
Makes 20-25 servings.

Mrs. Ella V. Payton
Caddo Council
Shreveport, La.

MAMA'S HOT EGGNOG

6 eggs, separated
1 c. sugar
1 tsp. vanilla

1 tsp. nutmeg
1/2 gal. milk

Heat milk to a simmer over low heat. Mix egg yolks and sugar; beat until turns a light yellow. Beat egg whites until very stiff. Add egg yolk mixture to milk very slowly, stirring constantly on low heat. It's ready when you finish pouring mixture in. Just before serving, fold in egg whites, add nutmeg and serve. Serve in mugs. You may serve as is, or let each person add bourbon to their liking. Very good as a cold weather beverage.

Mrs. Sim (Sally) Davenport
Central Council
Alexandria, La.

DUMONT'S TWILIGHT DELIGHT

1/2 pt. whiskey
1/4 pt. heavy rum
12 eggs
1 qt. cream

1 pt. brandy
1/4 pt. sherry
12 Tbsp. sugar
1 qt. milk

Mix spirits together. Add slowly to beaten egg yolks with sugar, beating slowly. Add cream and milk to yolk mixture, beating slowly. Fold the stiffly beaten egg whites into mixture and put aside for a few days. Taste frequently.

West Bank Council
Gretna, La.

FROZEN STRAWBERRY DAIQUIRI

1 pkg. frozen sweetened
  strawberries

1/2 small can limeade
6 oz. white rum

Place ingredients in blender. Add crushed ice until blender is full. Serve.

Maxine Fletcher, Ouachita
Council, Monroe, La.

HOT CHOCOLATE

1 (8 qt.) box powdered
  milk
1 c. powdered sugar

1 lb. box Nestle's Quik
1 (6 oz.) jar Coffee-mate

Mix well. Keep in closed container. Use 1/3 cup mixture to 1 cup hot water.
  Margie Perkins, Ouachita
  Council, Monroe, La.

HOT CHOCOLATE MIX

8 qt. powdered milk
1 small jar non-dairy
  coffee creamer

1 (16 oz.) can chocolate flavor
  Nestle's Quik
1 c. powdered sugar

Mix all ingredients and store in large covered container. When ready to serve, mix 1/3 cup of chocolate mix with 1 cup hot water. Stir and serve hot.
  Mrs. Larry D. Chambers
  Metairie Council, Slidell, La.

HOT CHOCOLATE MIX

1 (25.6 oz.) box instant
  nonfat milk powder
1 (6 oz.) jar non-dairy
  creamer
6 Tbsp. cocoa

1 (16 oz.) box instant
  chocolate flavored mix
1 (16 oz.) box powdered
  sugar, sifted

Combine all ingredients and store in covered container. To serve, combine 1/3 cup of mix with 2/3 cup boiling water and stir well. Yield: 36 servings.
  Sylvia Campbell, Caddo
  Council, Shreveport, La.

INSTANT HOT COCOA

1 (8 qt.) box powdered
  milk
1/2 lb. powdered sugar

1 (8 oz.) jar Cremora
1 (1 lb.) box Nestle's Quik

Mix ingredients well. Store in closed container. Use desired amount to each cup of hot water.
  Maxine Fletcher, Ouachita
  Council, Monroe, La.

KAHLUA

4 c. sugar
2 c. water
1 fifth unflavored brandy
  or vodka

2 heaping Tbsp. instant
  coffee
1 vanilla bean, split open

    Mix sugar, water, coffee and vanilla bean. Boil 5 minutes. Cool. Add fifth of brandy or vodka. Bottle; age 30 days.
    Black Russian: Use 2 parts vodka and 1 part Kahlua. Serve on ice.

Connie Younker, Shreveport
Works Council, Shreveport, La.

LEMON MEAD

2 large lemons
1/2 c. brown sugar
1/8 tsp. yeast
15 raisins

1/2 c. granulated sugar
5 qt. boiling water
5 tsp. sugar

    Carefully peel off the yellow skins of the lemons with a rotary peeler and set aside. Remove white membranes and discard. Slice lemons very thinly. In a 6-8-quart stainless steel or enameled bowl, combine lemon slices, lemon peels and both sugars. Reserve the 5 teaspoons sugar. Pour boiling water over lemon mixture, stir and allow to cool to tepid. Stir in yeast. Allow the mead to ferment uncovered at room temperature about 12 hours. To bottle, use five 1-quart bottles with very tight covers or corks. Place 1 teaspoon sugar and 3 raisins in bottom of each bottle. Strain mead and pour liquid in the bottles. Cap bottles tightly and let them stand at room temperature for 1-2 days or until raisins have risen to surface. Chill the sealed bottle until ready to serve, as this sparkling mead has a tendency to explode if left at room temperature after 5 or 6 days.

Harry Lever, Caddo
Council, Shreveport, La.

MILK SHAKE

1 frozen banana
1 c. milk

1 tsp. vanilla and nut
  extract

    Combine in blender; beat until thick. One cup of any type frozen fruit may be substituted.

Mary Ahrens, Caddo Council
Shreveport, La.

BANANA SUPERSHAKE

2 bananas, cut up
2 c. crushed ice
1 c. water
1/3 c. reconstituted lemon juice
1 (14 oz.) can Eagle Brand milk

In blender, combine bananas, lemon juice, water and condensed milk; blend well. Add ice, blending until smooth. Serve in frosted soda glasses. Makes 5 cups.

Debi Magalian, Central
Council, Silver Springs, Md.

NECTAR SYRUP
(For Ice Cream Sodas)

1 c. sugar
1 c. evaporated milk
2 Tbsp. almond extract
1 c. water
1 Tbsp. vanilla extract
1 Tbsp. red food coloring

Let sugar and water come to full boil. Remove and cool slightly. Add milk, extracts and coloring. Store in jar in refrigerator. To use, place 3 tablespoons nectar in glass, add scoop of vanilla ice cream, fill glass with 7-Up or sparkling water. Place whipped cream with cherry on top, if desired.

Mrs. Jim (Verline) Bernard
Evangeline Council
Lafayette, La.

PINEAPPLE SURPRISE

1 fresh pineapple (Dole's preferred)
2 oz. white creme de menthe

Peel and slice pineapple; not necessary to core. Pour creme de menthe over pineapple and place in airtight container in refrigerator to marinate overnight. Serve with juices. Delicious and refreshing after a heavy dinner.

Jean Stanley, Crescent City
Council, New Orleans, La.

PUNCH

1/2 gal. lime and pine-
   apple sherbet
48 oz. 7-Up
1 (No. 2) can crushed
   pineapple

1 box lemon jello
1 box lime jello
3 large bottles ginger ale
1 (No. 2) can chunk pine-
   apple

Mix 7-Up, ginger ale and jello together. Put sherbet in ring before you serve. Put in pineapple last.

Henrietta Victor, Magnolia
Council, New Orleans, La.

PUNCH

1 gal. pineapple juice
1 doz. oranges
Cherries and peaches

1 doz. lemons
5 lb. sugar
Water

Take juice out of lemons and boil rinds for about 15 or 20 minutes. Blend lemons, oranges, cherries and peaches. Mix lemon juice and rest of ingredients. Add water to taste.

Cecile Gallet, Evangeline
Council, Lafayette, La.

BANANA PUNCH

3 c. water
1 (46 oz.) can pineapple
   juice
3 c. mashed bananas

2 c. sugar
2 c. orange juice
1/4 c. lemon juice
3 bottles ginger ale

Combine sugar and water; bring to a boil. Remove from heat, add fruit and juices. Pour into two 13x9-inch pans and freeze. When ready to serve, cut or break slush into punch bowl and add ginger ale.

Betty Barron, Caddo
Council, Shreveport, La.

BANANA PUNCH

Juice of 2 lemons
1 small can crushed pineapple
6 bananas
4 c. sugar

Juice of 5 oranges
1 (No. 2) can pineapple juice
6 c. water
Ginger ale

Place pineapple, juices and bananas in blender. Combine water and sugar; heat until dissolved. Cool and add ingredients from blender; freeze. Take out of freezer about 30 or 40 minutes before serving and add equal parts of ginger ale. I usually divide and freeze in 2 separate containers, using 2 bottles of ginger ale to each.

Verle Oliphant, Caddo
Council, Shreveport, La.

JIFFY CHAMPAGNE PUNCH

2 bottles white wine, chilled
2 bottles champagne, chilled

2 qt. sparkling water, chilled
1 fifth brandy, chilled

Place large cake of ice in punch bowl. Pour in wine, sparkling water, champagne and brandy. Float mint leaves on surface. Makes about 70 servings. Recipe can be cut in half.

Gladys Domingues, Caddo
Council, Shreveport, La.

GOOD PINK PUNCH

2 (46 oz.) cans apple juice, unsweetened
1 (48 oz.) bottle cranberry juice
4 c. sugar

1 (46 oz.) can pineapple juice, unsweetened
4 pkg. lemonade Kool-Aid
6 drops red food color

Blend together. Makes 3 gallons. When serving, add crushed ice and one 32-ounce bottle sugar free 7-Up.

Grace Bell, Ouachita
Council, Monroe, La.

QUICK PUNCH

2 pkg. cherry Kool-Aid
1/2 c. Tang or Borden's
  breakfast drink

2 c. sugar
4 qt. water

  Mix ingredients together. Stir and freeze half of mixture. Pour remaining liquid over top of frozen mixture. Delicious.

Mary La Combe, Central
Council, Alexandria, La.

SPICED GRAPE PUNCH

5 c. water
1 qt. grape juice
1 (6 oz.) can frozen
  orange juice

4 cinnamon sticks
10 whole cloves
3/4 c. sugar
1 (6 oz.) can frozen pink
  lemonade

  Do not dilute orange juice or lemonade. Place spices in small bag and simmer in water 15 minutes. Remove from heat and add juices to water. Serve hot. Makes 20 cups.

Mae Briley, Central
Council, Alexandria, La.

SPICED PARTY PUNCH

2 1/2 c. pineapple juice
2 c. cranberry juice
1/2 Tbsp. whole allspice
1/4 tsp. salt

1 1/4 c. water
1 Tbsp. whole cloves
3 sticks cinnamon
1/2 c. brown sugar, firmly
  packed

  Pour pineapple juice, water and cranberry juice in bottom of automatic coffee maker. Place remaining ingredients in basket. Set heat control on "strong" and complete perking cycle. Hold on "mild" setting. Serve hot in mugs or heatproof punch cups. Makes 8-10 servings.

Annie Hawkins, Caddo
Council, Shreveport, La.

SUSAN'S WEDDING PUNCH

6 pkg. unsweetened A&P
  Cheeriade lemonade
1 (46 oz.) can pineapple
  juice
5 c. sugar
1 (12 oz.) can apricot
  nectar

2 pkg. sweet apricot
  Cheeriade (1 qt.)
8 qt. water
1 large (12 oz.) can diluted
  frozen orange juice
1 Tbsp. almond extract
1 (6 oz.) can frozen lemon
  juice

Mix well. Serve with finely crushed (pea gravel) ice.

Grace Bell, Ouachita
Council, Monroe, La.

VOLCANO PUNCH

1 pt. dark rum
1 pt. vodka
Grenadine syrup to taste

1 large can frozen orange
  juice + 2 cans water
1 small can frozen lemon
  juice + 1 can water

Mix ingredients and pour over dry ice. Will give smoking, erupting volcano look.

Carolyn Palmer, Capital
Council, Baton Rouge, La.

RED ROOSTERS

1 (32 oz.) jar cranberry
  juice cocktail
12 3/4 oz. vodka (1/2 of
  a fifth)

1 (6 oz.) can orange juice
  concentrate (do not add
  water)

Mix cranberry juice, orange juice and vodka; stir well until orange juice dissolves. Pour into 1/2 gallon plastic container; cover with lid and freeze for 12-24 hours. Drink will be like an ice. Spoon into cocktail glasses and serve with a party straw. Makes 8-10 servings (5 ounces).

Ann Orr, Evangeline
Council, New Iberia, La.

HOT BUTTERED RUM

1 pat butter
1 jigger rum
1 tsp. sugar

1 tsp. lemon juice
Dash of powdered cinnamon
1 c. boiling hot water

Place butter in a mug. Add rum, sugar and lemon juice. Pour in the hot water and sprinkle with cinnamon.

Calcasieu Council
Lake Charles, La.

SANGRIA

1/2 sliced orange
1/4 c. sugar
1 fifth red wine (burgundy
  or other non-sweet wine)

1/2 sliced lemon
1/4 c. brandy
1 (10 oz) bottle sparkling
  water
Ice cubes

Place orange, lemon, sugar, brandy and wine in glass pitcher. Chill for several hours. Add sparkling water and ice cubes when ready to serve. This is Spanish wine punch that is good anytime with anything.

Barbara M. Berry, LeBayou
Council, Houma, La.

SANGRIA

1/2 c. lemon juice
1/2 c. orange juice
1/2 c. sugar
4/5 q⁴ dry red wine

7 oz. bottle club soda
1/2 c. mixed fruit (oranges,
  pineapple cubes)
Ice cubes

Mix ingredients together.

Willie Owen, Calcasieu
Council, Lake Charles, La.

SCREWDRIVERS

3 qt. orange juice
1/4 c. lime juice

3 c. vodka
Lime slices (optional)

Combine orange juice, vodka and lime juice; mix well and pour into punch bowl. Float lime slices on top, if

desired. Pour into ice filled glasses to serve. Yield: About
4 quarts.   Marjorie B. Harris, Capital
                                             Council, Baton Rouge, La.

SLUSH

1 large box strawberry   4 c. hot water
  gelatin   1 small can frozen lemonade
2 c. sugar   concentrate
1 (42 oz.) can pineapple   1 qt. ginger ale
  juice

Dissolve gelatin and sugar in hot water. Add pineapple
juice and lemonade; mix well. Pour in container and freeze.
Remove from freezer a few minutes before serving time.
Spoon into punch bowl and pour ginger ale over it. Makes
about 26 cups.   Mae Briley, Central Council,
                                             Alexandria, La.

SPICE TEA

2 c. Tang   2 c. sugar
1 tsp. cloves   1 tsp. cinnamon
3/4 c. lemon tea

Combine ingredients and store in container. To use, mix
2 teaspoons of the mix to each cup of hot water. One teaspoon brandy or bourbon may also be added per cup for a
cold weather warm-up, or in case of snake bite.
                                             Lois S. Leger, Evangeline
                                             Council, Lafayette, La.

SPICED TEA

2 c. Tang   2 c. sugar
3/4 c. Wyler's lemonade   1/2 c. Lipton tea with
  mix   lemon, unsweetened
1 tsp. cinnamon   1 tsp. cloves
3 dashes allspice

Mix well; store in jar. Use 3 teaspoonfuls per large cup
of hot water for each person. Twila "Pete" Dysart
                                             Ouachita Council
                                             Monroe, La.

766

SPICED TEA

3/4 c. instant tea with
  lemon
1 tsp. ground cloves

2 c. Tang
2 c. sugar
1 tsp. cinnamon

Mix well and store in tightly covered container. Use 2 teaspoons mix per cup of hot water.

Maxine Fletcher, Ouachita
Council, Monroe, La.

SPICE TEA MIX

1 c. instant low calorie
  lemon flavored tea
1 tsp. ground cloves
1/2 c. sugar

1 c. Tang
1 large pkg. lemonade mix
1 tsp. ground cinnamon

Mix all ingredients together. Can store mixture in covered jar indefinitely. Use 1 teaspoon of mixture per cup of hot water.

Joy Faught, Central
Council, Alexandria, La.

DIETETIC SPICE TEA MIX

2 c. Lipton low calorie
  lemon flavored instant
  tea mix
2 tsp. cinnamon

2 c. Tang
4 pkg. Sweet 'N Low
3/4 tsp. cloves
1 tsp. allspice

Mix ingredients together. Place in airtight jar. To serve, add 2 tablespoons of mixture per 1 cup (8 ounces) of hot water.

Grace Bell, Ouachita
Council, Monroe, La.

INSTANT RUSSIAN TEA

2 c. Tang
1/2 c. instant tea
2/3 c. sugar

1/2 pkg. Wyler's lemonade
1 tsp. cinnamon
1/2 tsp. ground cloves

Combine all ingredients; blend well. Store in covered container. Use 2 heaping teaspoonfuls per cup. Pour boiling water over; stir.

Mearl S. Byles, Central
Council, Natchitoches, La

WASSAIL

1 gal. apple cider
1 qt. orange juice
1 c. sugar

1 qt. pineapple juice
1 c. lemon juice
24 cloves
4 sticks cinnamon

Place cloves and cinnamon in small cloth and tie. Mix all ingredients; drop in cloth bag of spices. Heat to boiling and boil 10 minutes; simmer 20 minutes. Heat before serving.
Mildred Henderson, Ouachita Council, Monroe, La.

WASSAIL

6 c. apple cider or juice
1/4 tsp. nutmeg
3 Tbsp. lemon iuice

1 cinnamon stick
1'4 c. honey
1 (18 oz.) can unsweetened pineapple juice

In large saucepan, heat cider and cinnamon stick to boiling; reduce heat. Cover and simmer 5 minutes. Uncover; stir in remaining ingredients and simmer 5 minutes longer. Serve hot in punch bowl; float orange slices for garnish.
Evelyn Bledsoe, Ouachita Council, Monroe, La.

BLACKBERRY WINE

4 qt. blackberries
3 1/2 lb. brown sugar

Boiling water to cover

Cover blackberries with boiling water and let stand for 2 hours. Then squeeze through a cheesecloth and add sugar to the liquid. Pour liquid in an open jar, cover with cheesecloth and let stand until fermenting ceases. Then bottle. Simple!
Calcasieu Council
Lake Charles, La.

MISSISSIPPI BLACKBERRY WINE

1 qt. blackberry juice,
   squeezed from fresh
   berries
1 Campden tablet
3 1/2 lb. sugar
1 tsp. yeast nutrient

5 qt. water
3 tsp. acid blend
1/3 lb. raisins
1/2 tsp. pectic enzyme
1 pkg. wine yeast

Place all ingredients in crock or large plastic container. Stir twice daily. Drain off after 7 days. Wash raisins and place in refrigerator. Eat a few each day for your iron supplement; this will save on vitamin cost. After 3 weeks, siphon wine into gallon jugs. Let stand in cool dark place for 4-6 months. Serve chilled. Better than <u>moonshine</u>!!

John and Yvonne Lutenbacher
Chapter Vice President and
Pioneer Partner
New Orleans, La.

RECIPE FOR OLD FASHIONED BLACKBERRY WINE

6 lb. blackberries
3 3/4 lb. sugar
1 1/2 gal. water
1 1/2 tsp. yeast nutrient

1 1/2 tsp. acid blend
2 Campden tablets
1 tsp. peptic enzyme
1 pack yeast

1. Place all ingredients in a plastic or glass container.
2. Crush all blackberries (be sure feet have been washed during the past 2 days!!). 3. Combine all ingredients.
4. Stir well until sugar is completely dissolved. 5. Check specific gravity. Be sure it's above 1.092. If it's not, add sugar until specific gravity is brought up to 1.092.
6. Cover "must" with plastic to protect from flies. 7. Stir daily for 5-7 days. Start checking specific gravity on fifth day. When specific gravity is 1.020, drain off wine by racking into gallon jugs. 8. Allow wine to settle for 1 month. Putting a vapor lock as a cork in the gallon jug to allow fermentation gases to escape. 9. Rack wine again, leaving sediment in bottom of jugs and allow wine to age for 3 months. 10. Sweeten to taste with simple syrup (dissolve 2 cup sugar in 1 cup boiling water). 11. Stabilize wine to prevent refermentation and bottle. 12. Drink to your heart's content. Note: <u>Remember, a little wine is good for all that may ail you!</u>

John and Yvonne Lutenbacher
Chapter Vice President and
Pioneer Partner
New Orleans, La.

1723-79

769

CHOWNING'S TAVERN WINE COOLER

3/4 glass lemonade
1/4 glass claret

Sprig of mint
Maraschino cherry

Do not mix liquids together. Pour lemonade over crushed ice, then claret. Garnish with mint and a cherry. This makes a colorful as well as refreshing drink. Good for hot days.
Mearl S. Byles, Central
Council, Natchitoches, La.

CORN WINE RECIPE

2 doz. ears of fresh
    yellow corn
14 lb. sugar

3 gal. water
1 gal. grape juice
1 cake of yeast

1. Cut and scrape corn from cob in 5-7 gallon crock jar. Add cold water. Place crock in warm place (sun, if possible), and cover crock with cloth. Let mixture sit for about 5 days or until corn comes to the top. 2. Strain liquid through cheesecloth and put back in crock. Add Welch's grape juice and stir in sugar. Add 1 cake of yeast dissolved in a little warm water. Cover crock and sit in warm area. 3. Let mixture ferment for about 3 weeks or until it quits bubbling to the top. Strain mixture and put in bottles or jugs, but do not seal tight for a few days.
John and Yvonne Lutenbacher
Chapter Vice President and
Pioneer Partner
New Orleans, La.

ELDERBERRY WINE

3 lb. elderberries
1 Tbsp. citric acid (acid
    blend)
1 Campden tablet
3 lb. sugar

1 box seedless raisins
1/2 tsp. yeast nutrient
1 gal. water
1 pack wine yeast

Crush fruit, add all ingredients and dissolve in water. Stir twice each day and cover ingredients with cheesecloth to prevent fruit flies, insects and 2-legged varmints from getting into the mixture. After about 10 days, when active fermentation has stopped, remove fruit; strain wine through cheesecloth. Place in a 5-gallon bottle with a vapor lock and allow to mellow for 3 weeks. Siphon wine into another bottle, leaving residue. Allow wine to age additional 2-3 months. Serve chilled.

Ralph Herrmann
Gentilly Council
Mereaux, La.

John and Yvonne Lutenbacher
Chapter Vice President and
Pioneer Partner
New Orleans, La.

"ROSE-BUDS" ELDERBERRY WINE

3 pt. ripe elderberries
9 lb. white sugar
2 lb. raisins

3 gal. water
1 pkg. dry yeast, or
1 yeast cake

Mix elderberries, sugar and water together; let come to a slow boil for 3 minutes. Cool to lukewarm and add yeast. Cover and let stand 9 days. Strain and add raisins. Let stand 5 days; strain and bottle. Seal tightly and store in a dark place. Use stone, steel, enamel, glass or hard plastic to make wine in.

John and Yvonne Lutenbacher
Chapter Vice President and
Pioneer Partner
New Orleans, La.

CAJUN GRAPE OR MUSCADINE WINE

22 lb. grapes or
   muscadines
4 1/2 gal. water
5 tsp. yeast nutrient

6 Campden tablets
2 1/2 tsp. peptic enzyme
1 pack wine yeast
Sugar

1. Place all ingredients in a plastic or glass container or crock. 2. Crush all fruit and combine all ingredients. 3. Stir well until sugar is completely dissolved. 4. Check specific gravity. Be sure it's above 1.085. If it's not, add sugar until specific gravity is brought up to 1.085. 5. Cover "must" with plastic or cheesecloth to protect from fruit flies. 6. Stir twice a day for 5-7 days. Start checking specific gravity on fifth day. When specific gravity is 1.010, drain off wine by racking into gallon jugs. 7. Allow wine to settle for 3 weeks. Putting a vapor lock as a cork in the gallon jug to allow fermentation gases to escape. 8. Rack wine again leaving sediment in bottom of jugs and allow wine to age for 3 months. 9. Sweeten to taste with

simple syrup (dissolve 2 cups sugar in 1 cup boiling water).
10. Stabilize wine to prevent refermentation and bottle.
11. Drink as needed for medicinal use, or just for pleasure.
Bon Jour Mon Amis.

John and Yvonne Lutenbacher
Chapter Vice President and
Pioneer Partner
New Orleans, La.

CONCORD GRAPE WINE

5 lb. grapes (black
   Concord)
2 1/2 lb. sugar
1/2 tsp. yeast nutrient
1/2 tsp. peptic enzyme

1 gal. water
1 Campden tablet
1 pkg. wine yeast (use 1 pkg.
   yeast for from 1-5 gal.
   must)

Crush grapes. Add water and crushed Campden tablet.
Cover with plastic. Allow to rest for 1 day. Add yeast
nutrient, yeast, peptic enzyme and sugar. Stir once daily
for 5-7 days. Siphon off to secondary fermenter. Attach
fermentation lock and allow to work for 14 days. Siphon
into bottles.

John and Yvonne Lutenbacher
(VonJon), Chapter Vice
President and Pioneer Partner
New Orleans, La.

GRAPE WINE A LA WELSH GRAPE JUICE

6 qt. water
6 lb. sugar
3 Campden tablets
1/4 tsp. grape tannin

6 bottles (24 oz.) Welsh grape
   juice, or 2 frozen (12 oz.)
   cans
3 tsp. yeast nutrient
1 oz acid blend

Mix all ingredients, except wine yeast, in primary fermenter. When must is about 75°, add yeast. Cover fermenter with plastic sheet. Ferment 4-5 days or until specific
gravity is 1.030. Siphon into secondary fermenter and attach
fermentation lock. Rack in 2-3 weeks when specific gravity
is 1.000. Rack again in 3 months. When wine is clear and
stable, it may be bottled. If sweeter wine is desired,
sweeten to taste at time of bottling with instant wine con-
ditioner.

John and Yvonne Lutenbacher
(VonJon), Chapter Vice
President and Pioneer Partner
New Orleans, La.

LOUISIANA ORANGE WINE

2 doz. small oranges	2 cans frozen orange juice
(La. sweets)	1 tsp. yeast nutrient
1/4 tsp. peptic enzyme	2 Campden tablets
2 boxes raisins	2 gal. water
5 lb. sugar	1 wine yeast

Boil skin of oranges in water 30 minutes; discard peel and save water. Squeeze juice, add pulp of 3 oranges. To the juice and pulp, add frozen juice, the water saved, peptic enzyme, yeast nutrient, Campden tablets, raisins and sugar. Dissolve sugar and Campden tablets. Let stand overnight. Add yeast, sprinkle on top of must. Stir daily for 5-7 days. Start checking specific gravity on fifth day. When gravity is 1.000, drain off wine by racking into gallon jugs. Allow wine to settle for 1 month. Putting a vapor lock as a cork in the gallon jug to allow fermentation gases to escape. Rack wine again, leaving sediment in bottom of jugs and allow wine to age for 3 months. Sweeten to taste with simple syrup (dissolve 2 cups sugar in 1 cup boiling water). Stabilize wine to prevent refermentation and bottle.

John and Yvonne Lutenbacher
Chapter Vice President and
Pioneer Partner
New Orleans, La.

SAKI OR JAPANESE RICE WINE

1 lb. rice	2/3 lb. raisins, chopped or
1 orange, lemon or lime	ground
2 qt. water	4 c. sugar
1 pack wine yeast	

Place all ingredients in plastic or glass container. Stir daily for 21 days. Drain off all wine in gallon jug, leaving dregs of ingredients. Let wine stand for 3 weeks. Bottle, rack and let stand for 3 months. Keep in cool room (65° to 75°). Wine is ready to drink. A second batch of wine can be made by just adding sugar to original ingredients as soon as the first wine is drained off. No additional yeast is required   Follow instructions as for initial batch.

John and Yvonne Lutenbacher
Chapter Vice President and
Pioneer Partner
New Orleans, La.

LOUISIANA STRAWBERRY WINE

7 lb. strawberries	4 lb. sugar
2 gal. water	1 tsp. acid blend
1 tsp. peptic enzyme	2 tsp. yeast nutrient
1 pkg. wine yeast	

Place all ingredients in a plastic, glass container or crock. Crush berries and combine all ingredients, stirring well to dissolve sugar. Cover with plastic to keep fruit flies out. These small flies will contaminate and turn into vinegar. Stir daily for 3 days. This mixture will foam up on second or third day. Be sure to allow for this foaming when filling container at start of this process. Siphon off at end of fourth day into 5-gallon jugs. Cork with fermentation lock. Rack or siphon off again in 3 weeks, allowing the sediment to remain in old jug. Allow wine to age for 3-6 months. Sweeten to taste with simple syrup. Serve with any good cajun food.

John and Yvonne Lutenbacher
Chapter Vice President and
Pioneer Partner
New Orleans, La.

BAR-B-Q SAUCE

1 grated onion	1 c. tomato catsup
1 tsp. celery salt	1 tsp. dry mustard
2 Tbsp. brown sugar	Juice of 1 lemon
2 tsp. hickory salt	Salt, red and black pepper
1/2 can beer	to taste

Add beer after mixing other ingredients together.

Alonzo Jackson, Caddo
Council, Shreveport, La.

BARBECUE SAUCE

1 lb. chopped onions	4 lb. fat, bacon or ham,
2 qt. vinegar	melted
1 qt. water	1 pt. prepared mustard
1 1/2 qt. catsup	4 oz. brown sugar
4 oz. salt	4 oz. red pepper
4 oz. chili powder	2 oz. Worcestershire sauce
(optional)	(optional)

774

Fry onions in melted fat until tender and slightly brown. Add remaining ingredients; mix thoroughly. Refrigerate until ready for use. Makes 2 gallons.

Ann Major, Capital
Council, Baton Rouge, La.

BARBECUE SAUCE

1/2 c. vinegar	1 c. water
4 Tbsp. sugar	1 tsp. pepper
3 tsp. salt	2 Tbsp. prepared mustard
1 thick sliced lemon	1 sliced onion
1/2 c. butter	2 Tbsp. Worcestershire
1 c. catsup	sauce

Mix vinegar, water, sugar, pepper, mustard, onion and butter in saucepan; bring to a boil, simmer 20 minutes, uncovered. Add catsup and Worcestershire sauce. Heat to boiling. Keeps 2 weeks in refrigerator if made in advance. Yield: 2 1/2 cups.

Bertile Sanchez, Capital
Council, Baton Rouge, La.

FRANK'S BARBECUE SAUCE

2 sticks oleo or butter	1 c. catsup
1 c. Worcestershire sauce	1 c. white vinegar
1 tsp. powdered yellow mustard	2 Tbsp lemon juice
	3 Tbsp. brown sugar
3 cloves garlic, crushed or diced	1 large diced onion

Mix all ingredients in 2-quart saucepan. Bring to a good boil. Cover and simmer for 30 minutes.

Frank M. Richardson
Crescent City Council
New Orleans, La.

JIFFY BARBECUE SAUCE

1/2 c. Wesson oil	3 Tbsp. sugar
3/4 c. chopped onion	3 Tbsp. Worcestershire sauce
3/4 c. ketchup	2 Tbsp. mustard
3/4 c. water	2 tsp. salt
1/3 c. lemon juice	1/2 tsp black pepper

Cook onions in hot Wesson oil until soft. Add remaining ingredients. Simmer 15 minutes.

Calcasieu Council
Lake Charles, La.

JO LALA'S BAR-B-Q SPECIAL SAUCE

1 1/2 c. chopped green onions
1 c. chopped celery
5 garlic cloves, chopped
1 1/2 qt. corn oil
1/2 bottle A.1. sauce
1/2 tsp. liquid smoke
1 regular chopped onion
1/2 c. chopped parsley leaves
1 c. chopped bell pepper
2 bottles (32 oz.) catsup
1 Tbsp. Worcestershire sauce
Juice of 1/2 lemon

Put a small amount of oil in heavy deep pot. Saute vegetables and then put in remaining oil. Simmer for 45 minutes on low heat. Add remaining ingredients, salt and pepper to taste and simmer for 4 hours. Heat sauce when ready to use; only coat food with the oil on top of the sauce. A few minutes before removing food from fire, coat with residue from bottom of saucepan.

Elton A. Lala, Crescent City
Council, New Orleans, La.

QUICK 'N EASY BARBECUE SAUCE

3/4 c. catsup
1/2 c. brown sugar
2 Tbsp. yellow mustard
1 Tbsp. olive oil
1/3 c. chili sauce
2 Tbsp. A.1. steak sauce
1/2 c. cider vinegar
Dash of Tabasco sauce

Mix together and simmer for a few minutes. Can be used to brush on spareribs, etc. Also excellent thinned with water and used for cocktail meat balls or sausage slices.

Mrs. Jim (Verline) Bernard
Evangeline Council
Lafayette, La.

BASIC SOUFFLE DISH

6-Cup Souffle - 1 1/2 quart

2 Tbsp. butter
3 Tbsp. flour
1 c. liquid (milk, chicken
  broth, beer, wine, etc.)
3/4 c. flavoring (meat,
  cheese, vegetables,
  fish, fruit, etc.)
4 egg yolks
6 egg whites
Pinch of cream of tartar
2 Tbsp. liqueur (if dessert)
1/4 c. sugar (if dessert)

8-Cup Souffle - 2 quarts

3 Tbsp. butter
4 Tbsp. flour
1 1/2 c. liquid
1 1/2 c. flavoring
6 egg yolks
8 egg whites
Pinch of cream of tartar
3 Tbsp. liqueur (if dessert)
1/2 c. sugar (if dessert)

Any type or kind of souffle may be made by following this formula for ingredients. Use basic steps in preparing souffles.
Peggy Childers, Crescent
City Council, New Orleans, La.

COUNTRY BUTTER #2

1 lb. soft corn oil oleo   3/4 c. evaporated milk
1 tsp. butter extract

Mix ingredients and mold. Clara Westbrook, Shreveport
Works Council, Shreveport, La.

MATTIE'S COUNTRY BUTTER

1 lb. corn oil oleo   1 c. Mazola corn oil
1 c. buttermilk

Mix ingredients together and place in mold. Refrigerate.
Marie Pamplin, Shreveport
Works Council, Shreveport, La.

ORANGE BUTTER

1/2 c. oleo or butter,
   softened
1/2 c. white Karo syrup

2 Tbsp. powdered sugar
2 tsp. grated orange peel

Beat butter and powdered sugar in small bowl until light and fluffy. Beat in corn syrup gradually. Stir in orange peel.

Marie Pamplin, Shreveport
Works Council, Shreveport, La.

CHEESY MEXICAN OMELET

4 eggs, well beaten
1/2 c. picante sauce,
   divided
1 Tbsp. butter

2 Tbsp. milk
1/8 tsp. salt and pepper
1 or 1 1/2 c. shredded
   sharp cheese

Combine eggs, milk, 2 tablespoons picante sauce, salt and pepper; mix well. Melt butter in an 8 or 10-inch omelet pan. Heat until just hot enough to sizzle a drop of water. Pour in egg mixture all at once. As mix starts to cook, gently lift edges of omelet with a fork and tilt pan to allow uncooked egg mix to run underneath cooked part. When mix is set and no longer runs, sprinkle cheese on half of omelet; cover pan and remove from heat. Let stand 1-2 minutes or until cheese melts and eggs are firm on top. Fold omelet in half and place on warm platter. Top with remaining picante sauce. Serves 2-3.

Betty Harman, Caddo
Council, Shreveport, La.

EGGS IN SPANISH SAUCE

3 Tbsp. butter
1/2 c. chopped onion
3 Tbsp. flour
2 tsp. sugar
3/4 tsp. salt
Dash of pepper
1 lb. 12 oz. can tomatoes

1 small bay leaf
6 hard boiled eggs
1/4 c. mayonnaise
1 tsp. prepared mustard
1/8 tsp. salt
Dash of pepper
3/4 c. fine dry bread crumbs
2 Tbsp. melted butter

In a saucepan, melt butter, add onion and cook until tender, but not brown. Blend in flour, sugar, 3/4 teaspoon salt, pepper. Add tomato, bay leaf. Cook, stirring constantly, until thickened and bubbly. Remove bay leaf. Pour into 10 x 6 x 1/2-inch baking dish. Halve eggs; remove yolks and mash with mayonnaise, prepared mustard, 1/8 teaspoon salt, dash of pepper. Refill whites and arrange in baking dish. Combine bread crumbs and butter and sprinkle atop eggs. Bake at 425° for 10 minutes or until hot. Serve over buttered noodles or toast. This is an excellent way to use leftover Easter eggs.

Calcasieu Council
Lake Charles, La.

CREAM GRAVY

1/4 c. meat drippings
1 pt. half and half
Salt and pepper to taste

1/4 c. flour
1 Tbsp. chicken flavor
    instant bouillon

Pour drippings into roasting pan or skillet. Blend in flour until smooth. Cook over low heat, stirring constantly, until bubbly. Remove from heat, add pint of half & half slowly with bouillon. Return pan to heat, stirring and scraping all brown bits from pan. Continue stirring until mixture thickens. Season to taste with salt and pepper   Makes 2 1/2 cups.   Lynn Babin, Westmoor
Council, Kenner, La

EGG GRAVY

1 Tbsp. shortening
2 eggs
1 tsp. salt

2 Tbsp. self-rising flour
1 1/2 c. hot water
1/4 tsp. pepper

In large skillet, brown flour in shortening. Fold in eggs and scramble. Gradually stirring, add water, salt and pepper. Simmer until gravy is of desired thickness. Serve over hot homemade biscuits.

Ina B. Atkins, Ozone
Council, Covington, La.

DEAR ABBY'S TIPS FOR HUSBANDS

1. Don't ever forget her birthday, anniversary, Christmas or Valentine's day.

2. Don't keep talking about the beautiful young chicks at work.

3. Don't ever bring a friend home for dinner without asking her first.

4. Don't use her car and return it with an empty gas tank.

5. Don't pick up something to read when she's trying to talk to you.

6. If you know you're going to be late getting home, call and tell her.

7. Don't try to make her jealous.

8. Don't look like a slob all weekend.

9. If you know you're wrong, don't be too stubborn to admit it.

10. Don't ever go to sleep without telling her that you love her.

Marilou Bridges, Caddo
Council, Shreveport, La.

GRANOLA

3 c. regular oats, un- cooked	1 c. sunflower seed
1 (1 1/2 oz.) pkg. sesame seed	1 c. wheat germ
	1/2 c. honey
1/2 c. vegetable oil	1 c. dried apricots, diced
1 c. golden seedless raisins	1 c. flaked coconut
1 c. dates, chopped	1 c. sliced almonds

Combine oats, sesame seed, sunflower seed and wheat germ. Mix oil and honey together; pour over oat mixture, stirring well. Spread mixture on a greased cookie sheet. Bake at 250° for 45-50 minutes. Cool. Break into large pieces. Combine pieces with remaining ingredients and store in airtight container. Yield: 12 cups.

Betty Harmon, Caddo
Council, Shreveport, La.

GRANOLA

6 c. regular oats, un-
    cooked
1 1/2 c. coconut
3/4 c. honey
1/2 c. vegetable oil
1 tsp. ground cinnamon

1 1/2 c. chopped pecans
1 c. wheat germ
1/4 c. water
1 Tbsp. vanilla extract
1 tsp. ground nutmeg
1/2 tsp. salt

Combine oats, pecans, coconut and wheat germ. Combine honey and water in small saucepan; heat, stirring frequently until mixture thins and is thoroughly heated. Stir in oil and vanilla; pour over oat mixture and mix well. Stir in spices and salt. Pour into 2 greased 13x9x2-inch pans. Bake at 250° for 1 hour, stirring about every 15 minutes. Store in airtight container. Yield: 10 cups.

Rebecca Scott, Caddo
Council, Shreveport, La.

HELPFUL HINTS

1. Cut up chunks of fish fillets (bass and red fish are especially good) to use in casseroles, gumbos or any type of dish that calls for seafood.

2. Boil water to make clear ice; this is great when festive ice is needed. Just add fruit and freeze.

3. Cooked green vegetables stay bright green if cooked uncovered.

4. Sear meat before salting it as the salt draws out the juices.

5. When making an omelet, add salt just before cooking to prevent eggs from becoming watery.

6. If a soup or gravy is too salty, add a diced potato to absorb some of the saltiness.

7. To intensify the sweetness of any dish, add a pinch of salt.

8. Make your own homemade bread crumbs; it is the secret to tastier bread dishes.

9. When cooking with shrimp, add raw to a casserole before baking as they will stay plump and juicy.

10. Chop parsley, bell pepper and green onions and freeze. Use when needed.

11. Meringue -- be sure to have it touch pie crust at all points to prevent shrinking.

12. To lessen the size of the "crack" typical of any loaf cake, let the batter stand in pan 20 minutes before baking.

13. In using waxed paper for rolling pie crusts, dampen countertop and waxed paper will not slip.

14. Egg yolk added to chocolate fudge or chocolate fudge icing gives extra smoothness.

15. Be Prepared -- Careful forethought is the key to a successful party. Plan ahead.

16. Bread that has been frozen tends to dry out very quickly, so take precautions to keep fresh.

17. Allow 6-8 hors d'oeuvres per person.

18. Add salt and salad dressing to salads just before serving to prevent wilting.

19. To keep spaghetti from sticking after it is cooked, add a little margarine; blend well.

20. Save lemon and orange rinds. Store in the freezer and grate as needed.

21. Freshen wilted vegetables by letting them stand in cold water to which a few drops of lemon juice have been added (10 minutes).

22. To prevent fruits and vegetables from darkening, add a few drops of lemon juice.

23. Cook vegetables with the least amount of water; vitamins and flavor will be preserved.

Sonia A. Hunt
Capital Council
Greenwell Springs, La.

HINTS

Soak sliced onions in sugar water overnight for the sweetest, tenderest flavor ever.

Try using a pinch of sugar, in addition to salt, when cooking vegetables. Especially good when cooking tomatoes.

A pinch of baking powder added to potatoes when mashing them will make for more fluffier and whiter potatoes.

Lemon juice added to water for cooking rice will keep the grains separate and white.

Improve on canned cream style corn! Add 1 can drained whole kernel corn plus lots of black pepper and a dash of salt.

Add vinegar to chili while it simmers. Does something special. Start with small amount and add to taste.

Mrs. Johnnie B Cole, Caddo
Council, Snreveport. La.

HOT SAUCE

1 can whole tomatoes
1 Tbsp. garlic salt or
  powder
1 Tbsp. cooking oil
1/4 Tbsp. sugar

1 Tbsp. minced onion
1 crushed red pepper
1 Tbsp. vinegar
Salt and pepper to taste

Place ingredients in blender and blend for 10 seconds.

Mrs. Claude J. Merrill
Shreveport Works Council
Shreveport, La.

HOT SAUCE

1 tsp. bacon grease
2 cans tomatoes
Black pepper to taste
1 tsp. oregano

2 finely chopped onions
6 jalapena peppers, seeded
1 tsp. comino seed
Salt to taste

Saute onions in grease. Add tomatoes and jalapena peppers. Add all ingredients in blender and blend. Pour into saucepan and cook on low heat for 45 minutes.

Cindy Kendrick, Caddo
Council, Shreveport, La

JEZEBEL'S SAUCE

1 jar pineapple preserves
1 jar apple jelly
1 bottle fresh horseradish

1 jar Coleman's mustard or
  any other dry mustard
Salt and pepper to taste

Mix all ingredients in electric mixer. This is particularly good with ham and it keeps indefinitely in refrigerator. Serve also over cream cheese with crackers.

Aline Well, Capital Council,
Baton Rouge, La.

JEZEBEL SAUCE

1 (18 oz.) jar pineapple
  preserves
1 small jar horseradish
1 Tbsp. cracked pepper

1 (18 oz.) jar apple jelly
1 small can dry mustard
Red or green food coloring
  (optional)

Combine all ingredients by heating until well mixed. Put in jelly jars and refrigerate. This will keep indefinitely. A delicious condiment with pork or roast beef, or serve over block of cream cheese with crackers as hors d'oeuvres.

Sonia A. Hunt, Capital Council, Baton Rouge, La.

Noonie Wilkinson, Capital Council, Baton Rouge, La.

MUSHROOM SAUCE FOR STEAKS

1 can mushrooms, un-
   drained
1 c. water, divided

1/2 env. onion soup mix
2 Tbsp. cornstarch

Combine mushrooms with juice, onion soup mix and 3/4 cup water. Bring to a boil. Mix cornstarch and remaining water; add to mushroom mixture and thicken.

Mary Ahrens, Caddo
Council, Shreveport, La.

ORANGE SAUCE FOR RIBS

1/3 c. orange marmalade
1/4 c. soy sauce
2 tsp. cornstarch

1/4 c. lemon juice
1 clove garlic, minced
2 Tbsp. water

Combine marmalade, lemon juice, soy sauce and garlic in saucepan. Mix cornstarch and water until smooth. Stir into marmalade mixture. Cook, stirring constantly until mixture thickens and boils. Parboil good supply of ribs about 20 minutes in boiling water. Can be frozen in foil until ready for use. Grill ribs and brush with Orange Sauce. Turn and brush again until all of Orange Sauce is used up.

Mrs. Claude J. Merrill
Shreveport Works Council
Shreveport, La.

ORIENTAL SPICE
(Saltless Seasoning)

1/2 tsp. thyme
1/4 tsp. onion powder
1/2 tsp. garlic powder
1/2 tsp. celery seed

1/2 tsp. marjoram
1/4 tsp. dill weed
1/2 tsp. curry powder
3 tsp. Hungarian paprika

Crush all ingredients to a smooth consistency; blending

well. Keep in tightly sealed containers and make only in small amounts. Good for baked potatoes, hamburger patties, etc.

Althea Rome Brossett
Capital Council
Baton Rouge, La.

SEASONED SALT

26 oz. salt
4 oz. red pepper
2 oz. chili powder

4 oz. black pepper
2 oz. garlic powder
1 oz. Accent

Mix ingredients. Place in shaker.

Ed Kimble, Crescent City Council, New Orleans, La.

Floyd N. Moody, Crescent City Council, New Orleans, La.

SEASONING SALT

1 box salt
2 oz. red pepper
1 oz. chili powder

1 1/2 oz. black pepper
1 oz. garlic powder
1 oz. MSG

Mix ingredients together and store in airtight container This salt is great on barbeque or any food needing salt.

Marjorie Harris, Capital
Council, Baton Rouge, La.

SEASONED SALT

6 Tbsp. salt
1/2 tsp. marjoram
2 1/4 tsp. paprika
1 tsp. dry mustard
1/8 tsp. dill seed

1/2 tsp. thyme
1/2 tsp. garlic powder
1/2 tsp. curry
1/4 tsp. onion powder
1/2 tsp. celery salt

Put in mini-blend container. Process at Lo until blended.

Connie Younker
Shreveport Works Council
Shreveport, La.

CREOLE SEASONING

1 (26 oz.) box salt
1 (1 oz.) bottle garlic
  powder
1 (1 oz.) box Accent
1 (1 oz.) bottle chili pepper

1 (1 1/2 oz.) box ground
  black pepper
1 (2 oz.) bottle ground red
  pepper

Mix ingredients together and use like salt to properly season the meat as required in many recipes. This seasoning will keep, so make plenty. Eugene Cottrell, Caddo
Council, Shreveport, La.

SHAKE AND BAKE MIX

1 c. flour
1 tsp. pepper
1/2 c. cracker crumbs

2 tsp. salt
1 tsp. herbs (thyme, oregano,
  basil or a mixture)

Combine ingredients and stir to mix; store in tightly covered container. When ready to use, moisten chicken with milk or water. Shake chicken pieces with mix, a few at a time, in paper bag. Bake in greased shallow pan at 350° for 45 minutes to 1 hour. This mix makes enough for 6 pounds of chicken. Jeanette Williams, Caddo
Council, Shreveport, La.

TARTAR SAUCE

2 parts green leaves of
  cabbage
1/4 part bell pepper

1 part onion
1 part dill pickle
Mayonnaise

Grind cabbage, bell pepper, onion and dill pickle in food grinder. Double portion with mayonnaise. Will keep about 1 week in refrigerator. Mrs. Tony Corcoran, Crescent
City Council, New Orleans, La.

TARTAR SAUCE

1 qt. mayonnaise, thick
1/4 lb. pickles, dill,
   finely chopped

3 eggs, hard boiled and
   chopped
1/4 lb. onions, finely chopped
1 oz. parsley, finely chopped

Mix all ingredients together thoroughly.

Ann Major, Capital Council,
Baton Rouge, La.

VEGETABLE SAUCE

1 large bell pepper
2 stalks celery
1/4 c. cooking oil

2 onions
4 medium tomatoes
Salt and pepper to taste

Cut onions, celery and pepper into 1/2-inch pieces.
Saute in oil over low heat until tender, stirring often.
Add tomatoes and simmer 10 minutes. Add salt and pepper;
mix, cover and refrigerate. This keeps in refrigerator up
to 2 weeks. Good used to accompany meat or vegetables.
Also good in scrambled eggs, salad or on meat or fried egg
sandwiches.

Katherine Slover, Caddo
Council, Phoenix, Az.

WORLD WAR II PIMENTO CHEESE

1 c. Pet milk
1 large pimento, or
   3-4 pieces
3 or 4 Tbsp. mayonnaise

1 lb. medium or Cheddar
   cheese, grated
Salt and pepper to taste

Heat milk in double boiler. Fold in cheese; let cool.
Add remaining ingredients. Should be nice and creamy.

Frankie Meeks, Ouachita
Council, Monroe, La

INDEX OF RECIPES

SOUPS; SALADS, VEGETABLES

MEAT, SEAFOOD, POULTRY

BREAD, ROLLS, PASTRY

1723-79

CAKES, COOKIES, DESSERTS

CANDY, JELLY, PRESERVES

806